Becoming a Multicultural Educator

Developing Awareness, Gaining Skills, and Taking Action

Third Edition

William A. Howe

Quinnipiac University

Penelope L. Lisi

Central Connecticut State University

Los Angeles | London | New Delhi
Singapore | Washington DC | Melbourne

FOR INFORMATION:

SAGE Publications, Inc.
2455 Teller Road
Thousand Oaks, CA 91320
E-mail: order@sagepub.com

SAGE Publications Ltd.
1 Oliver's Yard
55 City Road
London, EC1Y 1SP
United Kingdom

SAGE Publications India Pvt. Ltd.
B 1/I 1 Mohan Cooperative Industrial Area
Mathura Road, New Delhi 110 044
India

SAGE Publications Asia-Pacific Pte. Ltd.
18 Cross Street #10-10/11/12
China Square Central
Singapore 048423

Printed in the United States of America

Library of Congress Cataloging-in-Publication Data

Names: Howe, William A., author.

Title: Becoming a multicultural educator/William A Howe, Penelope L Lisi.

Description: Third Edition. | Thousand Oaks, California: SAGE, [2019] | Includes bibliographical references and index.

Identifiers: LCCN 2018042829 | ISBN 9781506393834 (Paperback: acid-free paper)

Subjects: LCSH: Multicultural education–Study and teaching–United States. | Teaching–United States.

Classification: LCC LC1099.3 .H68 2019 | DDC 370.117–dc23
LC record available at https://lccn.loc.gov/2018042829

Acquisitions Editor: Steve Scoble
Editorial Assistant: Elizabeth You
Content Development Editor: Jennifer Jovin
Production Editor: Karen Wiley
Copy Editor: QuADs
Typesetter: Hurix Digital
Proofreader: Annette Van Deusen
Indexer: Amy Murphy
Cover Designer: Scott Van Atta
Marketing Manager: Jillian Ragusa

This book is printed on acid-free paper.

19 20 21 22 23 10 9 8 7 6 5 4 3 2 1

Becoming a
Multicultural Educator

Third Edition

I am fortunate to be teaching at Quinnipiac University and Albertus Magnus College where a study of multicultural education is seen as essential in teacher preparation. I am grateful for the steady support of administrators, staff, and fellow faculty.

Family, colleagues, and friends continue to provide reassurance that educational equity and social justice are even more relevant in this trying political climate. Dianne, my wife of 40 years now, has been patient, understanding, and encouraging throughout the writing process. Her training as a psychotherapist has benefitted me greatly in this regard. This third edition of our textbook is dedicated to her and our son Christopher, a successful publisher/journalist, and our daughter Katy, a magnificent licensed social worker. Both make their parents proud every day in every way.

—WAH

This book is dedicated to family, friends, and colleagues who have inspired, motivated, encouraged, and supported me over a 45-year career in education. In particular, I am blessed to have my husband Peter, a dedicated educational leader himself, as my partner in life. Together, we are so proud of our beautiful and talented daughter, Isabelle, who inspires us to be the best we can be as parents and as educators. Much of my motivation in life to do the things I do in the way I hope to do them is inspired by my late parents, Gordon and Jessie Leitner. I am truly privileged to continue my work as a faculty member at Central Connecticut State University and The College of New Jersey, where I join colleagues in teaching about leadership for social justice and equity in the United States and abroad. I extend my deepest appreciation to all of you.

—PLL

Brief Contents

SECTION IV: SKILLS 181

SECTION V: ACTION 311

Detailed Contents

2   Becoming a Multicultural Educator: A Four-Step Model   36

SECTION II: KNOWLEDGE   61

3   Historical Perspectives on a Multicultural America   62

SECTION III: AWARENESS   121

5   Understanding Cultural Identities and Their Influence on Teaching and Learning   122

8   Instructional Approaches Needed by Multicultural Educators   216

9   Developing Skills in Teaching Language and Understanding Linguistic Diversity   246

10   Assessment That Is Culturally Responsive   278

11   Creating the Multicultural Classroom   312

12   Creating the Multicultural School   342

Preface

Changes in the New Edition

Development of the third edition of this book has allowed us the opportunity to reconsider what we worked so hard to include in the first and second editions and the ways in which we addressed the content. Based on reviewer and reader comments and suggestions, plus the authors' own teaching of courses using this textbook, we have retained many of the same features from the other editions that appear to be serving our audience so well. At the same time, we have refined the presentation of the material in ways that we believe will add even greater depth to discussions of and engagement in becoming an effective multicultural educator. As with the first two editions, our approach to working on the third edition meant that both of us reviewed and rewrote, individually and collaboratively, all 12 chapters. The revision process is informed by the fact that our own work in multicultural education continues to evolve. We hope you, our readers, find the result even more useful than before!

New to the Third Edition

Learning objectives: Significant effort was given to refining the Learning Objectives in each chapter to focus the reader on acquisition of higher order thinking skills. In the third edition, the Learning Objectives are presented as statements, rather than questions. The Learning Objectives were then used as a framework throughout the chapter for the construction of each chapter's content, and were revisited in each chapter's presentations of the Introduction, Thinking Ahead, Chapter Summary, Reflecting Back, and Individual and Group Assessments. Each of these sections and features is clearly connected to the chapter's Learning Objectives.

Special features: Based on feedback from the reviewers, we have worked in the third edition to reduce the number of Special Features in each chapter so that readers may focus more intensively on the content. Special Features include chapter Exercises and Extended Explorations, as well as sections on Thinking Ahead, Reflecting Back, and Expert Profiles. We recognize that users of this textbook appreciate the applied nature of the book, and thus, we have worked to include the most powerful, in our own experiences, exercises and explorations in each chapter. The Extended Explorations feature is particularly powerful as a means of engaging students in graduate education programs. It certainly can be used with other audiences, including undergraduates and in-service educators. The feature is included multiple times in each chapter and asks students to engage in individual and group problem-based learning or reflections in response to higher order thinking questions that are posed.

New trends: For each chapter, consideration has been given to new trends related to that chapter's content. Third edition chapter additions reflect current activity in a variety of areas, such as curriculum and teaching standards, curriculum development, language diversity, gender diversity, class diversity, social skills and language diversity, professional development, and school cultures of collaboration.

Thinking ahead and reflecting back: In previous editions, each chapter included multiple Thinking Ahead and Reflecting Back sections that served as advanced organizers for each Learning Objective in that chapter. For the third edition, each chapter now includes only one Thinking Ahead section (reflecting the chapter's Learning Objectives) at the beginning of the chapter and one Reflecting Back section at the end of the chapter. This change will hopefully provide greater clarity and coherence in each chapter. For each chapter's Thinking Ahead section and Reflecting Back section, the questions have been revised to engage readers in higher order thinking about the whole chapter's topics and concepts. Readers are asked to respond to the questions through application, analysis, evaluation, or synthesis. Readers may also be asked to compare, classify, summarize, develop, predict, critique, or design.

Case studies and anecdotes: New introductory anecdotes were added to each chapter in the third edition. Also, more than one quarter of the 24 case studies in the textbook were revised or completely swapped out for new cases that address more directly the issues and ideas in those chapters.

Profiles in multicultural education: In the first two editions, one leading scholar/practitioner in the field of multicultural education was featured in each chapter. The profiles have been updated again in the third edition, and several have been replaced with profiles of other scholars. Also, in place of one follow-up question for the reader at the end of each profile in the second edition, for each scholar in the third edition, material has been added that describes that scholar's particular and special contributions to the field of multicultural education.

References, annotated resources, relevant organizations, and associations: All references and annotated resources have been reviewed and updated. New references and resources have been added to each chapter.

The appendix: This feature has been updated to reflect current resources.

Why This Text?

Too many educators struggle to find a good textbook on multicultural education that provides a balance of theory and practice. The authors of this text have worked together collaboratively in the field of multicultural education for more than 25 years in both the preK–12 school system and higher education teacher education. Their experience has produced a text that both teachers-in-training and veteran educators will find highly readable and practical. *Becoming a Multicultural Educator: Developing Awareness, Gaining Skills, and Taking Action* includes an important grounding of information, theories, and research, as well as exercises, case studies, and reflective experiences that will enhance your capacity in multicultural education.

There were two primary reasons the authors felt this work was necessary. First, many teacher preparation programs offer either a course or unit on the topic of multicultural education. For many years, the National Council for the Accreditation of Teacher Education (NCATE) served as the primary accreditation body for teacher preparation programs, specifically requiring that preservice teachers have training in this area. In July 2013, the Council for the Accreditation of Educator Preparation (CAEP) became fully operational as the sole accrediting body for educator preparation providers, and CAEP accreditation standards were fully implemented in 2016. CAEP standards also include requirements that address educator capacity in serving diverse populations. And yet, a review of the syllabi for courses taught under the name of multicultural education or intergroup relations found a wide variance in the content. In addition, our experiences indicate that many of these courses are quite theoretical and lack sufficient content that could be immediately applied in a classroom setting. Students leave without adequate preparation to teach in culturally responsive ways. Very specifically, all teachers need a firm understanding about culture and its influence on teaching and learning.

This text is very timely in that recent studies about levels of student achievement in the United States raise critical questions about whether or not teachers have been effectively prepared in how to teach. Other recent reports on the efficacy of teacher training indicate that some colleges are adjusting their curriculum to better prepare teachers by placing a greater emphasis on pedagogy, focusing on multicultural education in preparation for more diverse classrooms. On a national level, new calls for raising levels of student performance raise concurrent calls to hold teachers and schools more accountable. State legislatures are passing regulations that call for dismissing principals and wholesale firing of teachers in failing schools. This text will address the need to train teachers in how to work with diverse populations, offering solid theory and research, but with a very user-friendly component that shows teachers how to apply that theory and research effectively in the classroom.

One author is Professor Emerita, previously who worked in a university school of education for 24 years and is now consulting with educational institutions, and the other is recently retired from a state education agency and is currently teaching courses in multicultural education at the university level and in professional development workshops for preK–12 schools. In the course of working together on publications and teacher in-service programs, grant projects, and implementation of multicultural conferences, the authors searched extensively for a text that explained in practical terms approaches to supporting teachers and administrators in becoming multicultural educators. It became apparent that a more user-friendly text than the ones currently available was needed.

This text is grounded in a solid research base as well as more than 25 years of intensive work in multicultural education by the authors in urban, suburban, and rural schools. The experience of the authors is that teachers need a text that starts with essential questions and theoretical concepts about multicultural education. The text should then lead them through experiences to heighten their own awareness, knowledge base, and skill set and then describe for teachers how to apply those concepts in classroom and school settings. A common question asked by teachers is, "I understand the need to be more knowledgeable about other cultures, but how do I incorporate that knowledge in my classroom?"

Recent events, political and otherwise, on national and international levels have pointed out dramatically the need for teachers to be able to confront and address issues such as the rise of the alt-right/ neo-Nazi movement, anti-immigration sentiments, the #MeToo movement, increased reports of anti-Muslim and anti-Semitic hate crimes, the roll-back of civil rights protections, court battles over the rights of transgender students and the rights of gay people, and almost daily reports in the news on "calling police on Black people." Acknowledging personal biases, unconscious biases, micro-aggressions, and explicit bias should now be part of a comprehensive education for all. This text attempts to emphasize the need to prepare students to be culturally competent in a global society. Educators at all levels have become even more important in the front lines of social justice efforts.

Becoming a Multicultural Educator: Developing Awareness, Gaining Skills, and Taking Action specifically focuses on the development and application of research-based curriculum, instruction, and assessment strategies for multicultural education in the preK–12 classroom. The major conceptual framework supporting this approach is a four-step model for personal development in multicultural education developed by the authors in 1994 in an article on how to train adults. This model was conceptualized early on in the authors' collaboration to serve as the basis for teaching about multicultural education. The four steps are awareness, skills, knowledge, and action.

Although the first three are not original in and of themselves, it is the placement of action within a circular model of steps that flow from one to another that makes the model unique. The action step is a critical one since it appears that the issue concerning educators the most is not whether or not to engage in multicultural education or even to learn multicultural concepts and knowledge, but once teachers have learned critical knowledge and skills, how they should integrate culture into their daily practice. For school leaders (and this includes teacher-leaders), a significant challenge becomes how to establish a learning community in which educators are learning strategies for multicultural education from and with one another. An additional challenge for teacher-leaders is how to institutionalize multicultural education and secure the full support of teacher colleagues, parents, community, and school board members. In the section on action, this book will provide practical strategies and model personal and institutional action plans.

Audience

This text should be a primary text in the training of all teachers and in professional development for practicing educators at all levels. This text was created to meet the needs of each teacher preparation program. Since many teacher preparation programs in the United States work toward CAEP accreditation, they understand the need to address CAEP standards that specifically focus on preparing teachers for becoming multicultural educators. In fact, for the new CAEP standards, diversity and technology are themes that cut across all standards! This means that educator preparation programs need to include courses that specifically support multicultural education. From the CAEP website comes the following statement:

> No single candidate preparing for an education position can reflect, from his or her own location and personal experience, all facets of diversity. Regardless of their residence, personal circumstances and preparation experiences, candidates need opportunities to develop professional capabilities that will enable them to adjust and adapt instruction in appropriate ways for the diversity they are likely to encounter in their professional lives.

In terms of a primary audience, this text is designed to be a primary text in the preparation of preservice teachers at the undergraduate level who are majoring in teacher education. It would also be useful in graduate programs in teacher education. In different university settings, similar courses are offered but under slightly varied names. Therefore, rather than citing one example of a primary course for which this text is designed, examples of specific courses for which this text could be used include the following:

- Curriculum Development in Multicultural Education
- Education and Teacher Leadership in Diverse Settings
- Methods and Curriculum for Diverse Settings
- Assessment, Instruction, and Curricular Adaptations
- Developing Instructional Materials
- Effective Elementary Teaching
- Applied Learning Theories

- Multicultural Education in preK–12 Schools

- Teaching Culturally Diverse Students

- Multicultural Diversity in Education

- Diversity in the Classroom and School Community

- Culture and Intergroup Relations

These courses are taken by preservice teachers once they are accepted into the teacher preparation program, following their successful completion of a variety of general education courses and requirements. As part of the general education requirements, students take coursework in arts and humanities, social sciences, behavioral sciences, and natural sciences. They are often required to demonstrate skill in communication, mathematics, and foreign language proficiency. Thus, they have a solid knowledge base prior to entering the teacher preparation program. Participation in the teacher preparation program engages them in developing the knowledge and skill necessary for teaching, as well as provides reflection on critical dispositions for teachers.

Interestingly, these courses have changed in recent years in significant ways from courses that offered preservice teachers some strategies for "tinkering around the edges" in changing teaching and learning, to a solid commitment to preparing teachers to become multicultural educators. Current courses engage students in considering critical issues, developing a deeper understanding of themselves as cultural beings, and acquiring a deep knowledge base and skills in multicultural education. These changes are the result of teacher preparation program accreditation requirements, as well as recognition by educators at all levels that this is the right thing to do. What is needed are instructional materials in preservice courses that engage students in meaningful learning experiences and prepare them to address the needs of culturally diverse students on a daily basis in all courses and disciplines.

The vast majority of working educators would benefit from this text since it provides key information and strategies on how culture affects learning. The veteran teacher working in this high-stakes testing era will find that the text has very useful illustrations, examples, and exercises that can be applied immediately in the classroom. The authors believe strongly that closing the achievement gap is not possible without knowledge of how to incorporate the culture and experiences of students into teaching and learning. And in the ever-growing global economy where all workers must develop cultural competence, this text will help teachers prepare all students for successful careers and lives working with diversity.

Secondary Markets/Courses

The authors have found that educators in early childhood, social work, and nursing have been attracted to their work. There has been a very encouraging trend among professional groups to include requirements for diversity training or cultural competence both in initial training and in ongoing coursework to maintain licensure or certification.

Students in educational leadership would also merit from use of the textbook, particularly the sections on action planning. The increasingly diverse school population has demanded more knowledge and skills from its administrators in working with diverse students and preparing all students for a diverse workplace.

The authors have experience in overseas educational environments. Multicultural education is an increasingly popular topic in Australia, China, South Korea, South Africa, Iceland, Azerbaijan, New Zealand, England, and many other countries. Educators in international and American schools abroad would merit from use of the teachings in the textbook as they grapple with increasingly diverse student populations and a global economy.

Organization of the Text

Section I: Background

The text is organized under five primary sections. The first section, Background, includes two chapters that focus the reader on exploring what multicultural education is and on what a multicultural educator is.

Chapter 1: Multicultural Education: History, Theory, and Evolution introduces the reader to the concept of multicultural education and presents the rationale for multicultural education. It raises important issues in the argument for multicultural education. These include classroom issues (teaching in a culturally responsive and responsible manner, assessing student learning in a variety of ways, expanding the curriculum to be culturally inclusive), school issues (closing the achievement gap, prejudice and discrimination issues, the digital divide, climate), community and society issues, and teacher preparation issues (recruitment, teacher workforce issues, role of parents, teacher shortages, and credentialing and recruitment).

Major conceptual models of multicultural education, including those of Carl Grant and Christine Sleeter and of James Banks, are explained. Definitions of key terms in multicultural education are presented. In particular, multicultural education is defined as a process; it is basic education important for all students and is critical for the achievement of equity and social justice. Beyond definitions, educators must also understand the goals of multicultural education. A review of common myths or misconceptions is presented. While most people who have been accepted into a teacher preparation program may believe they have received a fairly adequate education to that point, instruction about the wide variety of cultural groups who constitute the United States of America is generally limited. Chapter 1 describes the Eurocentric nature of the American school curriculum and the negative effects on children because of a lack of multiple perspectives in the curriculum.

In Chapter 2: Becoming a Multicultural Educator: A Four-Step Model, the reader explores the notion that most teachers lack knowledge and understanding of other cultures and learning styles—a fact that affects negatively on classroom teaching and learning. In this chapter, the authors introduce their own model for the personal development of multicultural educators. This model is the result of the authors' engagement over several years in in-service workshops and research on teacher growth as multicultural educators. The model leads educators through four stages of development. These stages reflect critical knowledge, skills, and dispositions as defined by various standards-setting organizations. Descriptions are offered of educators prepared in a more traditional program as well as educators who are prepared to be multiculturalists.

Section II: Knowledge

When confronted with questions about their knowledge of cultures or groups of people other than those with which they identify, educators are often amazed to realize the limited exposure they have had to learning such information. To become resources for our students, we need to commit to expanding our knowledge base about people who are different from us. This includes knowledge of beliefs and values, communication and interaction patterns, histories, attitudes, and behaviors. This is a lifelong effort. Two chapters are included in this section.

Chapter 3: Historical Perspectives on a Multicultural America reviews the history of activities and movements of different societies and cultures in America. Through a study of immigration and transmigration patterns, teachers can develop a better understanding of the experiences and influences of different peoples, the common experiences of immigrants, early beginnings, and discrimination.

In Chapter 4: Foundational Knowledge for Culturally Responsive Teaching, the reader explores the fundamental knowledge about others that is required of educators. This fundamental knowledge is now encapsulated in multiple sets of standards and knowledge bases—expectations of what teachers should know and be able to do. While the knowledge base as described may seem daunting, educators must remember that becoming a multicultural educator, or an effective educator for that matter, is a lifelong process.

Also in this chapter, educators are engaged in exploring the connections between culture and teaching and learning. In addition to extensive descriptions of learning styles, readers will explore ways to understand and apply their knowledge of learning styles in the classroom.

Section III: Awareness

This section includes two chapters that help the reader to understand that education is value laden. Often as educators we are not aware that we operate under a given set of beliefs and values. To be able to work with diverse students, we must first examine our own beliefs, biases, and prejudices and become aware of our own cultural essence. Then we can begin becoming more aware of the value of the various dimensions of diversity in ourselves and others. Sensitivity, understanding, tolerance, and compassion about differences are key constructs. In Chapter 5: Understanding Cultural Identities and Their Influence on Teaching and Learning, the reader is engaged in exploring his or her own cultural identities. To be effective in helping students understand their own and others' cultural identities, educators must be well aware of their own cultural backgrounds. This process of self-exploration can be particularly challenging for White educators.

Cultural identities (race, ethnicity, gender, age, physical size, sexual orientation, class, religion, persons with disabilities, speakers of different languages) in the United States are described, along with an exploration of the common beliefs and assumptions and biases associated with that cultural identity.

In Chapter 6: Developing Awareness of All Humans as Cultural Beings, the readers explore their perceptions of and interactions with others as people who also have unique cultural identities. In this chapter, we discuss how individuals relate to people who have cultural backgrounds different from their own. Frequently teachers have said that they want to focus on the similarities among people because a focus on the differences seems to exacerbate the conflicts. Our contention is that teachers must focus on the differences, understand and appreciate the differences themselves, and then be adept at leading students to understand and value differences if we are to achieve equity in our society.

A critical component of exploring cultural differences is to explore personal biases, prejudices, assumptions, and perceptions around race, ethnicity, gender, sexual orientation, and other common cultural groups. While educators may believe that they are well intentioned and need to focus their teaching practice on the content, assumptions grounded in faulty information about what people are "supposed to be like" strongly influence our interactions with learners. Multicultural educators must learn the lifelong skills of challenging assumptions and uncovering biases. These are needed to learn about other peoples—their cultures, perspectives, and experiences. We must examine and understand the roots of hate and bias in our society and the effects they have had and continue to have on the lives of others.

Section IV: Skills

Working effectively with those who are different means learning new skills, including communication, lesson planning, integration of knowledge about motivation and diversity and multiple intelligences, and so forth. We need to learn gender-neutral language that is inclusive and to intercept statements and actions that are prejudicial. Teachers must also learn the various ways of infusing multiculturalism into the curriculum and pedagogical strategies. Four chapters are included in this section.

Chapter 7: Curriculum Development and Lesson Planning explains those aspects needed to create a multicultural curriculum. Steps are outlined on how to write multicultural lesson plans, including procedures for examining texts for bias. This chapter presents some of the most distinctive contents of this text. A key step in the authors' four-step model is skill development. In this stage, teachers are engaged in developing multicultural lesson plans in light of the standards, models, instructional strategies, and knowledge previously covered. In this chapter, teachers are engaged in practicing and developing skill in constructivist teaching and curriculum development and analyzing texts and materials for bias. A rubric for writing multicultural lesson plans is introduced, and several samples of multicultural lessons are provided.

In Chapter 8: Instructional Approaches Needed by Multicultural Educators, the readers investigate approaches to teaching that are relevant to diverse student populations. The negative characteristics of a reliance on a more traditional behavioral approach to teaching are explained. The authors then explore constructivism as a more promising approach—an approach that supports culturally responsive teaching and learning—to engage students in deep learning. Constructivism supports the teacher in beginning with the students, engaging in themes and problem solving with key concepts, as opposed to teaching content and process determined by the teacher alone. The importance of multiple teaching strategies is reviewed. Traditional versus nontraditional or more current teaching methods are discussed with a strong emphasis on constructivism.

In Chapter 9: Developing Skills in Language and Understanding Linguistic Diversity, the readers explore the topic of linguistic differences. Any discussion on best practices in education must include coverage of second-language acquisition. The topic of how to best educate English language learners is hotly contested, and even a full chapter will seem inadequate in light of all that needs to be known. Chapter 9 explains the circumstances facing students learning English and reviews key strategies and methods used in a multicultural context.

In Chapter 10: Assessment That Is Culturally Responsive, the focus on constructivism in Chapter 8 as a promising instructional practice is followed by a discussion in this chapter of the need to alter assessment practices so that the needs and learning styles of diverse learners are addressed. How does a teacher know if a student is learning? What are the traditional methods of determining this? What are more reliable and authentic means for doing so? This chapter will address issues of bias in testing and review the debates on standardized tests.

Section V: Action

Two chapters are included in this section. In order to make sure action happens, teachers must learn how to develop individual and organizational action plans in order to implement education that is multicultural. They must also learn how to develop support networks and collaborations with other teachers. Strategies are offered to encourage institutional supports for change efforts.

In Chapter 11: Creating the Multicultural Classroom, teachers consider ways to continue their own growth and development when entering their profession. Steps and strategies are outlined to make this transition easier. Pitfalls, barriers, and obstacles are raised. The importance of developing a lifelong self-improvement plan is stressed. This process will require a close examination of skills, attitudes, and experiences. Exercises help the readers identify and address potential barriers and obstacles to the implementation of their action plans. Checklists are offered to help the readers assess progress in integrating multicultural education into teaching and learning in the classroom as well as in the school.

Finally, in Chapter 12: Creating the Multicultural School, the readers consider the need on a schoolwide basis for an action plan. The readers are engaged in developing not only an individual action plan for a multicultural classroom but also a school action plan. Chapter 11 provides critical information on how to analyze an institution and how to develop and change a plan. Too often, teachers are left to develop innovations on their own in virtual isolation. Multicultural education will truly affect teaching and learning when accomplished within the context of a learning community. In this chapter, teachers plan how to analyze school readiness for change, how to build a multicultural workforce, how to develop a multicultural resource library, and how to ensure ongoing and focused staff development in achieving multicultural education.

Change to becoming a multicultural institution is an intentional act. Understanding school institutional culture is a key step toward making this change happen. Teachers must be knowledgeable about school culture as they participate in the school transformation process as teacher-leaders. There are both supports and obstacles, and teachers must be able to know where and how allies can be found, how change is made, and who holds power.

Key Features of the Book

To make this text as accessible, useful, and highly readable as possible for all readers, several distinctive features are included.

Opening quote: These were carefully selected to begin guiding the reader into thinking about the purpose of the chapter. A relevant photo follows to further illustrate the theme of the chapter.

Learning objectives: The content of each chapter is developed under the heading of Learning Objectives. Individual chapters begin with the listing of three to five objectives. The reader will know immediately what the chapter will cover and what specific issues will be addressed.

Chapter opening summary: This is a brief overview provided for the reader to create a foundation of understanding and to encourage critical thinking.

Opening case study: A case study is offered at the beginning of each chapter to engage the reader in an initial consideration of key concepts that will be addressed in that chapter. Following each case study, questions are posed to the reader in a component titled Your Perspectives on the Case.

Body of the chapter: Each chapter begins with a feature called Thinking Ahead, which is a statement about the Learning Objectives followed by questions for the reader to consider prior to reading about those objectives.

At the end of the presentation of material for each chapter, another feature—Reflecting Back—is shared. This feature is a statement about what was discussed accompanied by questions designed to guide personal clarifications. These features serve to prompt higher order thinking.

Profiles in multicultural education: Highlighted in each chapter is a profile of a leading scholar/ practitioner in multicultural education. Each scholar's specific contributions to the field are described.

Closing case study: A culminating case study is offered to illustrate key themes raised in the chapter. Key issues are outlined at the beginning. Discussion questions follow at the end.

Chapter summary: A brief review of the contents of the chapter is offered for important information presented according to the Learning Objectives. This is designed to help the reader solidify the awareness, knowledge, skills, and important actions.

Application: Activities and exercises: Activities are provided at the end of each chapter as extensions of learning.

Glossary: Key terms are highlighted in bold the first time they are raised in each chapter. Explanations are provided in the Glossary at the end of the book.

Annotated resources: Links to organizations and websites relevant to the content of the chapter are listed to provide the reader with more in-depth and current information.

Additional Key Features

A major feature of this book that should make it very attractive to both teachers in training as well as experienced educators is the numerous activities, exercises, and lesson plans that help bring the theory of multicultural education to life. These elements help bridge theory and practice. They provide opportunities to solidify understanding and resources to apply immediately to the classroom. Teacher educators, professional development staff in the preK–12 system, curriculum directors, and school administrators will find the text an invaluable guide in training and education.

Assessment list: There are several other distinctive features in the text. An assessment list created by the authors for developing multicultural lesson plans is incorporated into the text in the chapter on multicultural curriculum development. This assessment list was developed in collaboration with teachers and has been refined to meet the needs of both novice and experienced educators. It has been adopted for use in teacher preparation programs to show students how to develop multicultural lesson plans.

Analyzing school progress: Another major feature is an evaluation instrument to be used to analyze a school's progress toward a multicultural curriculum and environment. This instrument was developed in response to requests from teachers for an instrument designed to ascertain school progress in achieving equity and multicultural education and what additional steps need to be taken. As schools move more and more in the direction of developing collaborative approaches to their work, particularly through the development of professional learning communities, they are looking for assessment instruments to help them collect data that they can discuss collaboratively and in public forums about their progress in key areas related to teaching and learning and school improvement. Teachers are being empowered and trained to engage in action research, self-evaluation, and data-based decision making.

Major assessments: Major assessments have also been developed for each of the five primary sections. These assessments can be found at the end of each major section and engage students in multilayered, multi-issue problem solving.

Appendix: The vital multicultural classroom: Resources, organizations, and associations: The appendix offers a wealth of information on where to seek help. It lists extensive references to books, journals, videos, professional organizations, cultural associations, and Internet sources.

Digital Resources

The vast resources on the Internet are illustrated. These resources focus on the areas in which teachers most often ask for help, including definitions, applications, and lesson plans. Major multicultural education organizations and Listservs (Internet email discussion groups) will be of great help to teachers in learning about and applying the principles. For ethnic content infusion, various Internet sites will be listed that provide knowledge and skills as they relate to specific cultures. A website with additional material and teaching instructions and PowerPoints is offered.

SAGE edge offers a robust online environment featuring an impressive array of free tools and resources for review, study, and further exploration, keeping both instructors and students on the cutting edge of teaching and learning. Visit edge.sagepub.com/howe3e.

SAGE edge for Students provides a personalized approach to help you accomplish your coursework goals in an easy-to-use learning environment.

- Mobile-friendly Flashcards and quizzes that strengthen your understanding of key terms and concepts

- Learning objectives that reinforce the most important material

- EXCLUSIVE! Access to full-text SAGE journal articles that have been carefully chosen to support and expand on the concepts presented in each chapter

- Video and multimedia links that appeal to students with different learning styles.

SAGE edge for Instructors supports your teaching by making it easy to integrate quality content and create a rich learning environment for students. It includes the following:

- Test-banks with a diverse range of prewritten and editable options, helping you assess students' progress and understanding

- Sample course syllabi for semester and quarter courses assist in structuring your course

- Editable, chapter-specific PowerPoint® slides offering you flexibility in creating multimedia presentations

- EXCLUSIVE! Access to carefully selected SAGE journal articles that support and expand concepts presented in each chapter

- Video and multimedia links that appeal to students with different learning styles

- Lecture notes summarizing key concepts by chapter to aid in preparing lectures

- Discussion questions that spark conversation in class or serve as writing prompts outside of class

- Class activities that give instructors ideas for how to engage students in the topics and concepts from the text

Acknowledgments

We are indeed standing on the shoulders of giants. We wish to thank the 12 educators and scholars profiled in the third edition of this text for their invaluable contributions to the field of multicultural education. Their life work was a great influence in formulating *Becoming a Multicultural Educator: Developing Awareness, Gaining Skills, and Taking Action*. We would also like to thank them for their assistance in the writing of this text and their collaborations with us over the years. A profound thank you goes to James A. Banks, Carl A. Grant, the late Ronald Takaki, Linda Darling-Hammond, Sonia Nieto, Gloria Ladson–Billings, Christine E. Sleeter, Geneva Gay, Philip C. Chinn, Jacqueline Jordan Irvine, Jeannie Oakes, and Donna Gollnick. They are among the "giants" in the field. We are honored to call them colleagues and friends.

We wish to express our appreciation to the staff at SAGE Publications for guiding us through the revision process. There are many individuals at SAGE who have provided support along the way and over the years, each with an impressive set of skills. We are especially grateful to the editors and staff who guided us through the development of the first edition and who believed in the power and potential of our message. Thank you to all the people at SAGE who have helped us over the years in creating a work that we hope will change the lives of students and teachers everywhere.

A special thanks to the reviewers who have provided insightful feedback and helped develop a text that effectively meets the needs of students and instructors:

Reviewers of the Third Edition

Maria Balderrama, *California State University, San Bernardino*

Maryann Dudzinski, *Valparaiso University*

Raphael Heaggans, *Niagara University*

Lynne Kirst, *University of Rochester*

Reviewers of the Second Edition

Bret D. Cormier, *Kentucky State University*

Gisela Ernst-Slavit, *Washington State University*

Susan Foley, *Coastal Carolina University*

Bradley E. Wiggins, *University of Arkansas, Fort Smith*

Reviewers of the First Edition

Juan Carlos Arauz, *Dominican University of California, San Rafael*

Jamie Berry, *Armstrong Atlantic State University, Savannah*

Nancy Cardenuto, *Kutztown University*

Jose Cintron, *California State University, Sacramento*

Delayne Conner, *Bridgewater State College*

Constance Goodman, *University of Central Florida, Orlando*

Patsy Goodwin, *Texas Wesleyan University, Fort Worth*

Sherry Green, *Georgia Highlands College, Rome*

Sagini (Jared) Keengwe, *University of North Dakota, Grand Forks*

Greg Krueger, *Augsburg College*

James Lane, *Columbia College*

Mark Malaby, *Ball State University*

Angela Pack, *Hudson County Community College, Jersey City*

Jody Piro, *Texas Woman's University, Denton*

Jamia Thomas Richmond, *Coastal Carolina University, Conway*

Carmen Sanjurjo, *Metropolitan State University of Denver*

Schrika Shell, *University of Texas, El Paso*

Jose Villavicencio, *Columbus State University*

Alaric Williams, *Angelo State University, San Angelo*

Eboni Zamani-Gallahger, *Eastern Michigan University, Ypsilanti*

List of Exercises

About the Authors

William A. Howe has over 40 years of experience as an educator and professional staff developer from elementary grades to higher education in Canada and the United States. He is past president of the National Association for Multicultural Education (NAME). Dr. Howe has conducted more than 600 workshops and speaking engagements for over 22,000 participants on multicultural education, cultural competence, and diversity. He has chaired 9 national conferences and 18 regional conferences on multicultural education. He is a regular presenter at state and national conferences and has appeared on both radio and television on diversity issues. As an avid traveler he has made 7 trips to China to study multicultural education. In addition, he has also made educational visits to South Africa, Cuba, Mexico, Vietnam, Cambodia, Indonesia, and Greece. In 2007 he made his first trip to Israel to study the Holocaust at Yad Vashem. In 2006 he was named Multicultural Educator of the Year by NAME. In 2015 he has recognized by Teachers College/Columbia University as a Distinguished Alumni. He is a founding member of the Asian Pacific American Coalition of CT (APAC) and past-chair of the Connecticut Asian Pacific American Commission. He was an Honoree at the 11th-annual "Immigrant Day" at the Connecticut State Capitol in 2008, a day to honor immigrants from throughout Connecticut who have made valuable contributions to their communities and/or professions. On May 2, 2015 Dr. Howe received an Official Citation from the Connecticut General Assembly in recognition of a Commitment and Leadership to the Connecticut Asian Pacific American Community in Higher Education and Public Service. He is on the editorial boards of *Multicultural Perspectives,* the official journal of the National Association for Multicultural Education (NAME) and the *Journal of Family Diversity in Education.* His textbook on multicultural education, coauthored with Dr. Penelope Lisi, *Becoming a Multicultural Educator: Developing Awareness, Gaining Skills, and Taking Action* (2019, SAGE) won the 2013 Philip C. Chinn Multicultural Book Award from NAME. In addition, he is a coauthor of the *Handbook for Achieving Gender Equity through Education, 2nd Edition* (2007, Routledge). He was the former program manager for multicultural education, bullying, and civil rights at the Connecticut State Department of Education. From 1998 to 2015 he was the Connecticut State Title IX Coordinator. In addition to conducting workshops on Title IX he has served as an expert witness on sexual harassment in schools. Currently he is an adjunct professor of education at Albertus Magnus College and Quinnipiac University where he teaches courses in multicultural education.

Dr. Penelope L. Lisi is Professor Emerita at Central Connecticut State University (CCSU). Between 1994 and 2018, she taught in CCSU's graduate level programs in educational leadership, served as director of the doctoral program between 2014 and 2018, and taught in CCSU's master's degree program in Montego Bay, Jamaica, for 20 years. She continues to serve as an adjunct instructor for CCSU. In her faculty position at CCSU, Dr. Lisi served for 20 years as director of the Center for Multicultural Research and Education. As director, she implemented professional development projects to support faculty in addressing equity issues in the university classroom. She directed the Diversity in Teaching Network (DITN), a federally funded three-year project to recruit diverse students into CCSU's teacher preparation program. The Center for Multicultural Research and Education was a primary sponsor of and collaborator for the annual New England Conference for Multicultural Education (NECME) for 18 years.

Dr. Lisi's scholarly work focuses on leadership for social justice, leadership for teaching and learning, and leadership in international school settings. In 2000, Dr. Lisi received a Fulbright Scholar Award to the University of Iceland. Over the next 16 years, she received 12 research grants and made more than 25 trips to Iceland to investigate educational leadership in a changing environment. Dr. Lisi has delivered more than 50 peer-reviewed papers in the United States, Ireland, Cuba, England, Finland, Portugal, Hungary, Switzerland, Jamaica, Iceland, and Ukraine. Since 2005, she has been an adjunct professor for The College of New Jersey's Global Studies Program in Palma de Mallorca.

Prior to her work at CCSU, Dr. Lisi taught at the elementary, middle, and high school levels in the United States and for 3 years in international schools in Norway and Denmark. For 5 years, she served as executive director of the Connecticut State University Center for Educational Excellence, a system-wide faculty development resource. A primary outcome was the initiation, development, and implementation of Project IMPACT, a professional development project to support faculty on the four state university campuses in transforming university-level courses to include diverse perspectives and content. Dr. Lisi received her bachelor's degree in education and French at DePauw University, her master's degree at the University of Wisconsin– Milwaukee, and her doctoral degree at the University of Wisconsin–Madison.

Between 1998 and 2018, Dr. Lisi served as senior editor of *Multicultural Perspectives* for the National Association for Multicultural Education, and currently serves serve on the editorial board. Her textbook, coauthored with Dr. William A. Howe, *Becoming a Multicultural Educator: Developing Awareness, Gaining Skills, and Taking Action* (2014, SAGE) won the 2013 Philip C. Chinn Multicultural Book Award from NAME. Dr. Lisi serves on a variety of boards, including as a trustee for the Watkinson School.

SECTION I

BACKGROUND

1 Multicultural Education

HISTORY, THEORY, AND EVOLUTION

iStock/FatCamera

Learning Objectives

This first chapter is an introduction to the field of multicultural education and includes definitions, history, theories, and models. Readers will receive an overview of the field and its objectives. Subsequent chapters will expand on various aspects of the discipline, giving more detail and practical applications.

Through your study of and work on Chapter 1, you will be able to do the following:

1.1 Identify the rationale for implementing multicultural education

1.2 Explain the history of multicultural education

1.3 Define multicultural education

1.4 Discuss conceptual models of multicultural education

1.5 Identify the misconceptions and misunderstandings about multicultural education

Welcome! This first chapter will give you an overview of the field of multicultural education. It will give you a historical context. You will learn how multicultural education developed as a theory and a model of practice. The chapter will cover definitions and describe various conceptual models. It includes activities that you can do yourself and with others to gain a more in-depth understanding. By the end of the chapter, you should feel much more confident about how to become a multicultural educator.

LEARNING OBJECTIVE 1.1 Identify the Rationale for Implementing Multicultural Education

Changing Demographics

This text will contain frequent discussions of race and ethnicity. Therefore, an explanation of terms used is important. The English language is a living language that evolves, matures, and changes with the times to reflect current culture. Selection and use of words is important since words convey beliefs and values. Words, for example, such as *stewardess* and *spinster* convey negative messages about women and are now rarely used as a direct result of the recognition of women's rights and roles in society. Similarly, terms such as *oriental* and *colored* are dated and rarely used to describe people due to the negative history associated with the words.

Defining and categorizing *race* and *ethnicity* has always been fraught with problems. As each U.S. Census is taken, the controversy renews. In the 2000 Census, the standards for federal data on race and ethnicity included six categories: (1) American Indian or Alaska Native, (2) Asian, (3) Black or African American, (4) Native Hawaiian or Other Pacific Islander, (5) White, and (6) "Some Other Race." There were also two categories for ethnicity: Hispanic or Latino and Not Hispanic or Latino. Hispanics and Latinos may be of any race (U.S. Census Bureau, 2010).

> Real education should consist of drawing the goodness and the best out of our own students. What better books can there be than the book of humanity?
>
> —Cesar E. Chavez, Mexican American labor activist and leader of the United Farm Workers, he was awarded the Medal of Freedom posthumously by President Clinton.

CASE STUDY
THE ART TEACHER

My visit to the small alternative program of 20 students was routine. In my position as a school monitor, I regularly scheduled site visits to urban schools to assess progress. Located in a community center in a poor section of the city, the school was a last resort for high school students on the verge of dropping out. Classes were taught by a male and a female team that included Jamal, an African American teacher, and María, not Marfa, a Latina. Both seemed eager to show off the accomplishments of their students but were modest about their own hard work at making the program a success.

Touring through the school, I noticed the abundance of beautiful needlepoint, macramé, and other craftwork done by the students. When questioned about this, Jamal and María replied that they felt it important to give students creative experiences to balance the strict regimen of academics. Knowing that the school system was in a perpetual budget crisis, I asked how they managed to get time for an arts teacher in the budget. The reply that I got was, "We have been fortunate." My suspicious nature caused me to ask several more times about how they found funds in the budget and approval to bring in someone to teach the students. I got the same somewhat sheepish reply from both of them. Fearing budget improprieties or invalid teacher certification, I decided to investigate further. It was shortly after my visit to the school that I found out the truth.

(Continued)

(Continued)

Each payday, the two teachers met in their tiny office and put money from their own paychecks into an envelope. This they used to secretly pay an elderly retiree to come in twice each week to give classes to the students so that they would be able to use their creative energies and talents. The students called her "Grandma" and showered her with affection each time she came. Everyone in the community knew what was going on, and they approved.

Your Perspectives on the Case

1. What do you think of the actions of these two teachers?

2. What impact will their actions and those of the elderly woman have on the education of the students?

3. What does this story tell you about the state of education in this country?

THINKING AHEAD

Misconceptions and misunderstandings about multicultural education abound. Many critics do not grasp how a culturally responsive curriculum serves to increase academic achievement. It must be acknowledged, too, that multicultural education's social justice focus is not palatable to those less tolerant of differences.

1. How does culture influence teaching and learning?

2. What is your understanding of the theory of multicultural education and how and why it came about?

3. What is your knowledge of the major criticisms of multicultural education? What do you think is the root of these criticisms?

Schools have evolved in response to the needs of the workplace as well as a rapidly changing economy and society. The knowledge, awareness, and skills taught in schools must change to keep current with progress.

Jupiter images/Comstock/Thinkstock

The 2010 Census form listed 15 categories for race:

1. White

2. Black, African American, or Negro

3. American Indian or Alaska Native

4. Asian Indian

5. Japanese

6. Native Hawaiian

7. Chinese

8. Korean

9. Guamanian or Chamorro

10. Filipino

11. Vietnamese

12. Samoan

13. Other Asian

14. Other Pacific Islander

15. Some other race (U.S. Census Bureau, 2010)

The 2010 Census racial and ethnic categories reflect an ever-evolving society in which people do not clearly fit into a box. Increasing numbers of interracial marriages and biracial children and heightened interest in knowing and understanding one's race and ethnicity present both opportunities and challenges to the classroom teacher.

Understanding Why Race and Ethnicity Matter

One of the greatest challenges facing teachers today is the rapidly changing student population. Teaching does not take place in a vacuum. The participants in the teaching and learning process—including students, teachers, administrators, family members, community members—are cultural beings. They bring to the educational process differing cultural backgrounds, including a diversity of experiences, values, beliefs, histories, languages, communication patterns, and needs (Exercise 1.1). Naturally, when teachers and students enter the classroom, they enter and participate in the teaching and learning experience from the perspective of their own cultural background. Prior to the civil rights era of the 1960s, the majority of educators didn't give much thought to diverse cultural backgrounds and their impact on learning. Student populations at that time were seen as being, more or less, homogeneous, and educators used a "one-size-fits-all" approach to education. Culture was seen as neither relevant nor important.

Students come to school speaking a variety of native languages, with diverse cultural backgrounds, and with distinctly different experiences, values, and beliefs that clearly influence the learning process. Despite the **melting pot** theory of past years, America flourishes in a **persistence of ethnicity** (Banks, 2009). This country is more likened to a **salad bowl** in which individual members (ingredients of a salad) retain their unique culture while assuming common customs and habits (thereby creating a more desirable salad).

EXERCISE 1.1
WHERE DO YOU FIT?

Review the information above about racial categories as defined by the U.S. Census:

1. Which racial or ethnic category or categories are you in?

2. Consider your 10 closest friends. Make a table that shows the 15 ethnic or racial categories along one axis and the names of your friends along the other axis. Complete the table for the racial or ethnic category for each friend.

3. Now, consider 10 past or current classmates. Create a table similar to the one in Question 2 above about this information.

4. Reflecting on your responses to Questions 2 and 3 above, write a paragraph that summarizes your key conclusions about your connections to diverse peoples.

The school curriculum has evolved from teaching basic academics to the need to instill higher order thinking, teaching advanced technical knowledge and much more sophisticated subjects, unheard of in past generations. Educators must ensure that all students receive an equitable education and opportunities to succeed.

© iStockphoto.com/Catherine Yeulet

With a persistent **achievement gap**, an increasingly diverse population, and a global economy comes a need for the field of education to maintain its relevance to students' education needs. In addition, the world of work demands more **cultural competence** from its employees. Schools must take into consideration whether what is being taught is adequate for the workplace students will enter. Classrooms must change with the times.

The Need to Close the Achievement Gap

Fundamental to teachers' understanding of their role is that they are not just teachers of reading or teachers of mathematics—they are teachers of students. A teacher's function is not a narrow one of teaching a subject area. Teachers are influential in the many parts of a student's life. In their role in the classroom, teachers can serve in the capacity of social worker, psychologist, mentor, confessor, surrogate parent, and friend. One cannot teach with blinders on. Students face daily obstacles, barriers, and crises, such as **racism**, **sexism**, **classism**, and **homophobia**, that hinder and threaten their learning and their lives. Multicultural education is more than taking a traditional approach to **pedagogy**. Good pedagogy in today's schools includes the desire and ability to deal with issues of equity and **social justice**. This desire and ability are the essence of what a teacher is and what a teacher does. As the great Brazilian educator Paulo Freire once said, "Besides being an act of knowing, education is also a political act. That is why no pedagogy is neutral" (Shor & Freire, 1987, p. 13).

Several factors have influenced the development of multicultural education as a field of study and as an educational process. The U.S. student population is one of rapidly changing demographics, and a variety of achievement indicators show that teaching practices and procedures that seemed to work in the past with a predominantly White student population are not working with a more diverse student population (Howard, 2010). As evidenced by standardized test scores, graduation rates, dropout rates, and other academic indicators, minority students, particularly those who are poor, tend to have lower academic achievement. They have on average lower grades and more failing grades. Poor minority students tend to graduate in lower numbers and drop out of school in higher numbers. The gap or disparity in achievement has been a cause for alarm (Darling-Hammond & Bransford, 2005).

The widening achievement gap between White students and African American and Latino students, statistics about achievement test results and dropout rates, and the growing violence in schools lead us to believe that we must approach the process of teaching and learning in significantly different ways to benefit all students, not just students of color. Findings from the research of the Harvard Civil Rights Project (Frankenberg, Lee, & Orfield, 2003) provide interesting insights into the impact of the achievement gap:

- Minority children are overrepresented in special education.

- African American students, and to some degree Native American students, in affluent school districts tend to be labeled mentally retarded more frequently than are White students.

- African American children with emotional disturbances receive services of inferior quality and are diagnosed much later than their White counterparts.

- There is a higher incidence of suspensions and expulsions among African American students than among other students.

- Dropout rates are distinctly higher among urban students of color.

- High school graduation rates are distinctly lower among urban students of color.

- African American, Latino, and Native American students consistently score much lower on standardized tests.

- The percentage of African American, Latino, and Native American students who go to college and graduate is much lower than that of European American and Asian students.

- The incidence of poverty, drug and alcohol abuse, incarceration, and teen pregnancies is much higher for African American, Latino, and Native American students than for other students.

- Schools are becoming more segregated.

- The incidence of hate crimes, bias, prejudice, and discrimination against students of color, girls, and gay and lesbian students is still disconcertingly high.

It is clear that more needs to be done to address these problems. Improving what and how educators teach is a key strategy.

The **No Child Left Behind Act of 2001** created ambitious goals for closing the achievement gap—some say too ambitious. Despite much legislation, the allocation of resources in American schools continues to be inequitable. Not all schools are meeting the educational needs of all students. Many are not structured to assist each learner achieve at an optimal level. Linked to this is the fact that education as a system has yet to develop effective approaches for preparing students to be socially responsible citizens who are cognizant of critical social issues and committed to addressing them in a positive manner. We must ensure that all students receive an equitable education that leads to high levels of achievement. How we accomplish this may not be as daunting as one might imagine. We must start with a fundamental commitment to all our students to excel.

What does it take to increase student achievement? Ken Zeichner (1995) outlined key elements to enable students to achieve at high levels.

1. High expectations from teachers

   Teachers must see students as individuals, each with the potential to reach his or her highest level of competence. Stereotypes, preconceived notions, and prejudgments of a student's abilities set unfair limitations. Most teachers will automatically state that they do expect all students to achieve. However, when faced with an honest inner examination, teachers must consider whether their high expectations extend to special education students, students with **developmental disabilities**, vocational–technical students, and those students who belong to alternative school cultures, such as the **straight-edge** or **goth** cultures. In their groundbreaking research, Sadker and Sadker (1987, 1994) cited numerous examples and illustrations of how teachers treat children representing various races differently and even treat boys and girls differently to the benefit of the boys. Their research revealed, for example, that

   - teachers direct more questions to male students than to female students but are likely to direct more questions to White females than to African American and Native American males and

   - White teachers demonstrate more concern for White female students' academic work than African American females' academic work and demonstrate more concern for African American females' behavior (Sadker & Sadker, 1987, 1994).

2. Cultural congruence in instruction

   Students must see personal meaning in the teaching strategies and content offered to them. They can then make connections between past learning experiences and new learning. When teachers use language, examples, and illustrations that students recognize from their culture, students are more motivated to learn. While applying instructional strategies that are grounded in behaviorism, cognitive science, and constructivism, described by scholars such as Jeannie Oakes, Martin Lipton, Lauren Anderson, and Jamy Stillman (2012), teachers can make learning relevant and effective by using knowledge of students' cultural backgrounds. This is a good practice for all students.

3. Teacher knowledge of and respect for cultural traditions

    Embedded in and connected to education are deeply rooted beliefs, values, customs, and traditions. Knowledge of these will allow teachers to engage students more effectively, as teachers will show consideration for such traditions and use them as an asset to the curriculum. For example, examining horoscopes is forbidden by the religion of some students. The same applies to the celebration of birthdays. The creative teacher, instead of looking at these prohibitions as a hindrance, will build on this knowledge to create understanding of cultural differences.

    Knowledge of how students have experienced education in other cultures will enable teachers to approach students with better understanding. In the traditional American educational system, we place high value on parent involvement in all aspects of a student's education, from assisting in homework to attending parent–teacher conferences. This concept is not as familiar to families from other cultures where there is a sharper divide between teachers, who do the teaching, and parents, who do the parenting. Parents from some cultures are not accustomed to being deeply involved in their children's education. This does not reflect a lack of caring or support but merely the fact that in some societies the formal education of children lies with professional educators.

4. Teaching strategies that promote meaningful participation

    Generations of students, at all levels, have experienced lecture as their primary method of instruction. It is the most common teaching strategy, despite the fact that much research has shown that some students can learn more effectively in many other ways. There is certainly a time and place for direct instruction. Howard Gardner's (1985) work on **multiple intelligences** is one example of research that supports the importance of using a number of teaching strategies that can reach students on a variety of levels. Teachers can devise lesson plans and curricula that do not rely primarily on lecture but on extensive student active involvement.

Prejudice and Discrimination Issues

While many, if not most, educators believe that the ways in which they teach are nondiscriminatory, the fact is that bias, prejudice, and discrimination are still deeply embedded in our educational system. Instructional strategies that favor one particular learning style over another, curriculum materials that portray the experiences and cultures of a limited number of ethnicities and races, and policies and procedures that favor certain groups of students all contribute to an educational system that is discriminatory. At the core of each model of multicultural education (discussed later in this chapter) is the need to support teachers in becoming culturally competent and to instill in students the desire to become civic minded and to fight for social justice as well as educational equity.

Multicultural education requires individuals—both educators and students—to look beyond their own situation or worldview to understand the obstacles that diverse groups of people face. Here are some facts to consider:

- Every 2 minutes, someone is sexually assaulted in the United States (U.S. Department of Justice, 2010).

- Between 1995 and 1996, more than 670,000 women were victims of rape, attempted rape, or sexual assault (Ringel, as cited in Richie, 2000, p. 3).

- One out of every eight children under the age of 12 in America goes to bed hungry every night (Millions of Mouths, n.d.).

- About 1.6 million people were homeless in emergency shelters or transitional housing at some point during the year between October 1, 2007, and September 30, 2008 (U.S. Department of Housing and Urban Development, 2009).

- Hate crimes based on sexual orientation now constitute the third highest category reported in the United States, making up 16.6% of all reported hate crimes (Lewellen, 2009).

- In 2009, 28% of students of ages 12 to 18 reported having been bullied at school, and 6% reported being cyberbullied during the school year (National Center for Education Statistics, 2012).

- The Anti-Defamation League's 2009 *Audit of Anti-Semitic Incidents* "counted a total of 1,211 incidents of vandalism, harassment, and physical assaults against Jewish individuals, property, and community institutions across the U.S." (Anti-Defamation League, 2010).

Bias in many forms exists in our schools and society. Prejudice and discrimination hinder education and thereby impact society as a whole. In a global economy, it is critically important that we prepare a culturally competent workforce that works to right the wrongs inflicted due to bias.

Poverty and Class Issues

In addition to the critical issues of bias, prejudice, and discrimination that we must address, another critical issue that calls for the implementation of multicultural education is that of poverty and socioeconomic status. A great shame on our American society, arguably the richest and most powerful nation on earth, is the prevalence of poverty that crosses all racial and ethnic boundaries. In recent years, talk of the "1 percent" wealthiest Americans who live in great privilege while others suffer from hunger and homelessness usually ascribed to "third-world" nations has been in our national dialogue. The Occupy Wall Street and other similar movements have made clear the struggles of the middle class and the continuing injustices and inequities in our education system. There is a common statement that many have heard that has much validity: "How well a student does in school depends on the zip code in which he or she lives."

The National Center for Children in Poverty (Jiang, Ekono, & Skinner, 2014) reports,

Children under 18 years represent 23 percent of the population, but they comprise 34 percent of all people in poverty. Among all children, 45 percent live in low-income families and approximately one in every five (22 percent) live in poor families. Similarly, among children age 6 through 11 years in middle childhood, 45 percent live in low-income families and 22 percent live in poor families. Being a child in a low-income or poor family does not happen by chance. Parental education and employment, race/ethnicity, and other factors are associated with children's experience of economic insecurity.

In *The Matrix of Race*, Coates, Ferber, and Brunsma (2018) describe poverty as one of the most significant problems facing African American families, with single-female-headed families having "significantly higher poverty rates than other family types" (p. 91). They continue by citing research indicating that growing up poor is closely tied to low academic achievement.

Any discussion of multicultural education must include specific strategies and plans for how best to educate children of poverty. The U.S. Census Bureau defines poverty by the number of people in a household and their combined household income. For example, a family of four with a household income of $23,624 is considered to be living in poverty (U.S. Census Bureau, 2013). Gorski (2013) translates this, for educational purposes, as poverty resulting in an "opportunity gap" versus an "achievement gap." Poor or low-income students do not have access to the resources needed for an equitable education. Neuman (2009) illustrates this in *Changing the Odds for Children at Risk* by giving the example that in relatively large classes (20 or more) teachers incorporate concepts they assume children already know. When low-income children, who are behind in language development due to lack of reading resources, fail to connect to nursery rhymes and fairy tales, they fall behind. Teaching is affected as educators need to focus on how to provide additional supports. Learning does not occur. This results in some students developing feelings of hopelessness, while those who are advantaged financially and possess stronger language experiences become restless.

In *Reaching and Teaching Students in Poverty: Strategies for Erasing the Opportunity Gap*, Gorski (2013) describes what he calls "The Most Popular *Ineffective* Strategies for Teaching Students in Poverty" (pp. 113–116). He provides three examples:

1. "Foregoing engaging pedagogical approaches for lower-order pedagogies." Specifically, he mentions *direct instruction* or *teaching to the test* as being particularly devoid of any engaging qualities, and inducing mind-numbing rote memorization drills.

2. "Tracking or ability grouping." Gorski cites several examples from the research describing how this practice actually lowers achievement.

3. "Opening charter schools." Gorski is particularly harsh on criticisms of charter schools citing data that show how they draw valuable resources from state and district funding to create highly segregated schools depriving needy students of equal and adequate resources.

In contrast, Gorski (2013) outlines what he sees as eight "instructional strategies that work" (p. 119).

1. Music, art and theater need to be heavily embedded in all subjects.

2. Have high expectations for all students and let students know you support them.

3. Create student-centered instruction with high-order strategies.

4. Get students out of their seats and engage in classroom activities that involve movement.

5. Make corrections to the actual lives and experiences of students.

6. Talk about the effects of poverty and inherent bias.

7. Examine both content and process of teaching for indicators of bias.

8. Teach the joy of becoming literate.

These recommendations mirror basic tenets of multicultural education.

Issues on Working With Immigrants and Refugees

Understanding the difference between these two groups is essential. Immigrants are people who generally move from one country to another pursuing better economic opportunities. Refugees travel because of fear of persecution and to escape war and other conflicts. Immigrants must go through an application and vetting process to move to a new country legally. Those who enter a country without going through a formal process or who extend their stay beyond the limits of a visa are considered "illegal" or undocumented.

Although it is popular belief that undocumented immigrants are mostly Mexican Americans entering the country illegally, the facts say otherwise. Nearly half of undocumented immigrants are people who overstayed their visa according to the Pew Research Center (Ruiz, Passel, & Cohn, 2017). Of the 628,799 people who overstayed their visa in 2016, the overwhelming number were Canadians (119,448), followed by people from Mexico (46,658), and then Brazil (39,053).

Immigrants coming to the country often require second-language instruction, along with support to adapt to a new culture. Refugees often arrive with no possessions or financial resources and most frequently have experienced trauma in their homeland. In 2016, the United States admitted 86,994 refugees with the majority coming from the Democratic Republic of Congo, Iraq, Syria, Somalia, Burma, Ukraine, Bhutan, Iran, Eritrea, and Afghanistan (Zong & Batalova, 2017).

Gurwitch, Silovsky, Schultz, Kees, and Burlingame (2002) offer suggestions for working with students who have undergone severe stress. These include the following:

- Students need constant assurance that they are safe. Physical and emotional safety is a top concern.

- Students should be encouraged to talk about their feeling after a stress event, and they should be reassured that such reactions are normal.

- On the other hand, teachers should be cautious about exposing these children to frightening situations that might remind them of their traumatic experiences.

- Students need guidance on understanding what happened and also need help coming to terms as to their role during the event, stressing but not blaming themselves.

In addition to these concerns, Coates et al. (2018) point out the historical problem of racial profiling as a result of immigration. The authors cite The Act to Protect Free White Labor against Competition with Chinese Coolie Labor and to Discourage the Immigration of the Chinese into the State of California, or the Anti-Coolie Act, which was a law passed in 1862 as a result of racial animosity toward imported Chinese laborers. Chinese immigrants were heavily taxed, and immigration was restrictive. Chinese, as well as other ethnic groups including Middle Easterners, Hindus, East Indians, and Japanese were portrayed as criminals. At the turn of the 20th century, another large wave of immigrants arrived in the United States, causing yet another backlash from the White population. Soon the Irish, Italians, Jews, Blacks, Native Americans, and Asians were being portrayed as criminals.

Coates et al. (2018) point out that this legacy of racial profiling or targeting of people by law enforcement based on race and ethnicity continues to this day. Schools are not immune to this racism, so they not only work diligently to educate students and faculty about new arrivals but also prepare newcomers for resistance.

Curriculum, Instruction, and Assessment Issues

Books and other forms of written literature have helped shape our society's beliefs and values (Exercise 1.2). Imagine standing in the well of the Library of Congress looking up at the thousands of volumes of books. Who wrote most of those books? Historically, European males have written the majority of books. Early in our country's development, women and people of color were not supported in writing careers and/or were not permitted to publish. Thus, their voices are missing from much of our early history. Educators are coming to realize that they've been using a fairly narrow "content lens" through which to teach. Important content is missing from the curriculum that is critically important to all of today's learners.

Curriculum

Educators are recognizing that both the curriculum and the instructional practices in the majority of American schools are heavily influenced by a White, Eurocentric tradition. A saying heard in progressive educational circles is, "The problem with schools today is not that they're not what they used to be. The problem with schools today is that they are exactly what they used to be." The implication is that, in many aspects, we have not fundamentally changed the curriculum or the methods of teaching. For the longest time, teachers were, for the most part, trained as though all students were White and middle class. The curriculum is often **Eurocentric**, meaning the content and perspectives offered are dominated by Anglo, male, middle-class, Protestant thinking. The voices and perspectives of women and people of color and other ethnicities are missing.

EXERCISE 1.2

WHERE DO YOU READ ABOUT DIFFERENT PEOPLE?

1. Name 10 literary works written by women that you have read.

2. Name 10 literary works written by people of color that you have read.

3. Name 10 literary works written by people of color that could be used in high school. Explain your reasons behind these selections.

4. Name 10 literary works written by women that could be used in high school. Explain your reasons for these selections.

5. If you were standing in the Library of Congress and saw that most of the books had been written by European females, in what ways do you believe our society's beliefs and values would be different? Explain your rationale.

6. Imagine that the majority of people in the U.S. Congress were women instead of men. Describe at least five specific ways that our country might be governed differently as a result. Do you believe that it would it be managed better, the same, or worse? Explain your rationale.

Today, a Eurocentric approach to instruction does not reflect the racial makeup of the country. All of us are influenced by our culture and may view and perceive the world through our own narrow cultural lenses. By not realizing and accepting the fact that history as well as current reality can be judged differently by others with different perspectives, we can assume that only our own viewpoint is valid. A Eurocentric curriculum therefore offers only one perspective and invalidates the views of other cultures (Gollnick & Chinn, 2013).

An example of a Eurocentric approach to teaching is the concept of "westward expansion" or "manifest destiny" taught to so many grade-schoolers. Students were (and maybe still are) taught that in the early years of our country, it was the God-given right of settlers to move west, claim land for their own, and then bring "civilization" and Christianity to the savages. That is a Eurocentric perspective. It fails to recognize that Native Americans, who had lived on the land for hundreds of years, did not think they were uncivilized and believed that their faith traditions suited them quite well.

Slowly but surely, this Eurocentric approach to teaching is being recognized and replaced by a more balanced curriculum that integrates the histories, experiences, and work of diverse peoples. However, the curriculum in many schools continues to be biased. Often, when diverse groups of people are included in curriculum materials, they appear in the "margins" of the chapters. Or educators share information about diverse groups of people during specific times of the year (e.g., a focus on African American history during February, or Black History month). There is still much work to be done to develop a culturally responsive curriculum.

An important development throughout the United States is the use of common standards or expectations of what all students should know and be able to do. The **Common Core State Standards** in the major subject areas have been adopted by the overwhelming majority of states and are pushing school districts nationwide to revitalize their preK–12 curricula in keeping with national standards. Many state departments of education are publishing curriculum frameworks in major subject areas as a guide for local school districts. The ways in which the standards are written, while not fully supportive of diverse students, are moving schools in the direction of attending to diversity. That said, the ways in which schools and districts choose to implement the standards will determine the extent to which diverse students will be served.

Instruction

Teachers are becoming aware of the need to learn a wide variety of instructional strategies and find ways to integrate diverse perspectives in all content areas. Educators realize that, in fact, a "one-size-fits-all" approach does not support high levels of student achievement for all learners. The variety of differences that are represented in today's classrooms calls for an equally diverse repertoire of instructional strategies (Banks, 2009).

A growing body of research encourages educators to abandon a **deficit model of education**, which focuses on students' deficits or lack of skills and abilities. Reyes, Scribner, and Scribner (1999), in *Lessons From High-Performance Hispanic Schools: Creating Learning Communities*, describe the key considerations in successfully educating Hispanic students. Their focus is on the environment in which students are educated and how it relates to the home, community, and the organizational culture of the school. Instead of emphasizing what students *cannot* do, educators focus on what they *can* do—their strengths.

Fortunately, among the elements of teaching highlighted by these materials are cooperative learning, interdisciplinary learning, experiential learning, problem-solving and projects-based learning, and critical thinking. These instructional strategies are a sound basis for working with diverse student audiences. When linked with opportunities for exploration of self and others, engagement with multicultural curricular materials, and taking on multiple perspectives, the overall teaching and learning approaches of schools will, in fact, improve.

Assessment

If teachers are changing curriculum and instruction to be more responsive and responsible, then they must also assess student learning in new and different ways. Tests, quizzes, and other short-answer forms of assessment will not provide a true picture of what each student knows and is able to do. Assessment practices are often designed to favor particular groups of students. As a reminder of why this is problematic, refer to the key elements to enable students to achieve at high levels (Zeichner, 1995) discussed earlier in this chapter.

Furthermore, teachers are increasingly aware of the need to support the affective development of students so that they value themselves and their unique diversity and can communicate and interact effectively with a wide variety of people. Teachers need to prepare students to be socially responsible and contributing members of society.

Teacher Preparation and Professional Development Issues

Classroom teaching and learning issues are confounded by other factors, such as our mediocre capacity thus far to prepare educators to understand and value cultural differences. Lack of significant preparation in multicultural education may contribute to teachers not recognizing or understanding the educational needs of diverse students. As educators, we must analyze critically the practice of teaching and uncover those areas in which we lack the knowledge, awareness, and skill to educate all who enter our classrooms.

Teachers are often not prepared to work with diversity and, in fact, tend to rely on five to seven primary instructional approaches. Most of these strategies are traditional, didactic, content-driven, and teacher-centered. What is needed instead is a student-centered classroom where the focus is on the needs of the students' best learning modalities instead of the teacher's preferences for instruction. The culturally proficient educator is skilled in approximately 15 to 30 instructional strategies. Many of these additional strategies, which facilitate student-centered learning, emphasize a connection to cognitions, or to students' beliefs about themselves (Nuri-Robins, Lindsey, Lindsey, & Terrell, 2012).

Teachers must be the principal developers and initiators of multicultural education in their districts. Leadership by teachers is crucial for their long-term ownership of multicultural education. Providing teachers with educational handouts and a brief orientation session will produce negative, not positive, results. Substituting "quick fixes" in race relations and issues of diversity for deeper understanding flies in the face of a wealth of research noting the complexity of these problems. Students who have not been exposed to other cultures, races, and peoples may have many more questions about diversity and multicultural knowledge than can be explained by a videotape or an afternoon conversation or lecture. The nature of multicultural education requires teachers themselves to possess a sound knowledge base and personal understanding. Given the sensitive nature of some of the classroom activities, teachers should have the opportunity to test the materials firsthand and should have ample time to ask questions. Equally important, teachers should have time to experiment

---

Extended Explorations 1.1: Preparing Educators for Multicultural Education

Conduct an Internet search for the syllabi for undergraduate and graduate courses in multicultural education. Sometimes they are referred to as Diversity in Education or Intergroup Relations courses. Find at least two syllabi for undergraduates and two for graduate-level students.

Compare the four syllabi and include your findings in a chart or other **graphic organizer**. Specifically, address the following:

1. What are the primary topics in each course? Are these critical topics in your view? Why or why not?
2. What are the primary resources and readings for each course? Are these, in your view, essential and important resources?
3. Are courses taught from a theoretical or practical perspective?
4. Is each course focused on second-language acquisition, **oppression**, or what this text considers to be multicultural education?
5. Which syllabus do you feel best prepares an educator to teach? Justify your stance.
6. Provide three specific recommendations for enhancing each syllabus.

with multicultural education with the assistance of expert advisers. Only after these intensive learning experiences have been offered will teachers be ready to introduce multicultural education in their classrooms and serve as instructional leaders to their colleagues.

Available Teacher Workforce Issues

Another confounding factor is that while we seem to understand that all students need to receive instruction from diverse educators as a means of learning about diversity firsthand, the majority of classroom teachers continue to be White and, more often than not, female. Efforts at recruiting and preparing a diverse teaching population have met with significant challenges. It is difficult to encourage people of color to enter the teaching profession. Reasons abound, including better pay in other professions, a lack of encouragement to take up teaching, poor schooling experiences in childhood, and rigid (possibly biased) teacher-testing requirements. Teachers of color, when placed in suburban, virtually all-White school districts are more prone to leave the field or transfer to more diverse settings where they feel more accepted and comfortable. As a result, students lack diverse role models, and schools suffer from a dearth of diverse teachers who can offer perspectives and teaching approaches that enrich the school for all students.

Community and the Role of Parents

The schools of today, to be fully effective, must be structured to encompass the community. Not all that needs to be learned can be taught within the confines of the school day and school building. Not all that needs to be learned can be taught by teachers alone. Parents and other responsible adults and the community in general enrich and complete the teaching of students. A model in which parents and guardians are seen as partners with teachers ensures more follow-through, reinforcement of learning, and support at home.

Moral Obligations and Responsibilities

At a very basic level, the school, more so than any other public institution in this country, should be a safe haven for children. Students should expect to be able to enter their school and focus on the process of learning. Yet this optimal state is challenged by unhealthy school and classroom climates. Prejudice and discrimination, despite laws that have been enacted to protect our citizens, still have a dampening effect on how we teach our children, as well as on how teachers are trained.

Students benefit from multicultural education for many reasons apart from demographic-, economic-, and achievement-related reasons. When course content and curriculum are expanded, students learn more, not less. Multicultural education does not mean eliminating particular content but rather means opening up the possibilities and expanding what is presented to students. In addition, a primary goal of education is the preparation of students to be socially and culturally competent. If we focus in a very conscious way on skill building and development of attitudes for valuing differences, we will help students prepare to participate effectively in our global society.

In Summary

These are the challenges that teachers must contend with in schools everywhere. One of the key roles of education is to prepare students for life in a global society. A multicultural education therefore is a priority for all school districts: urban, suburban, and rural. Actually, *education that is multicultural* is a more precise term than *multicultural education*. The important distinction lies in that all education should be culturally relevant and responsive. It should be the context for the schooling of all students, regardless of color, ethnicity, or income. Preparation in multicultural education provides teachers with the knowledge and skills to meet these and other challenges in a direct and effective way.

LEARNING OBJECTIVE 1.2 Explain the History of Multicultural Education

Initial Focus on Ethnic Studies

Multicultural education is not a new phenomenon. It has evolved over several decades from an initial focus on intercultural education and ethnic studies in the 1920s (Gollnick & Chinn, 2013) to the current focus on achievement of educational equity and meeting the needs of diverse students. The initial rationale for a focus on *ethnic studies* in education was that members of the dominant culture, once they entered the world of work, would need to understand members of minority groups in America. This focus on ethnic studies as the primary approach to multicultural education lasted several decades and, stimulated by the civil rights movement of the 1960s, influenced the creation of ethnic studies programs in colleges and universities in that decade. In schools, educators were now called on to include content that focused on the contributions of members of ethnic groups who experienced discrimination (Gollnick & Chinn, 2013). This effort resulted in the creation of *multiethnic studies.*

Landmark legislation also influenced the evolution of multicultural education as a field of study. Beginning in 1954, with the landmark ***Brown v. Board of Education*** (347 U.S. 483, 1954) to the passage of the **Civil Rights Act of 1964**, the **Voting Rights Act of 1965**, and *Lau v. Nichols* (414 U.S. 563, 1974), significant changes in civil rights laws have encouraged and demanded that the educational community confront the plight and perspectives of people of color.

Federal troops were needed to escort nine brave Black students into previously all-White Central High school in Little Rock, Arkansas, in September 1957. Integration did not come easily.

Library of Congress

The civil rights movement of the 1960s and 1970s led not only to an interest in knowing more about ethnic groups but also to an interest in *intergroup and human relations studies*. In light of the apparent significant cultural differences among ethnic groups, educators were now interested in what needed to be done to promote understanding, conflict resolution, and the development of positive attitudes. The primary focus of this effort was on helping members of the dominant culture be accepting of differences. At about the same time, members of groups that experienced discrimination—women, people with physical challenges, people with low socioeconomic status—became more vocal in wanting their forms of discrimination recognized and addressed. At this point, the term *multicultural education* began to emerge. According to Gollnick and Chinn (1998),

> This broader concept focused on the different **microcultures** [emphasis added] to which individuals belong, with an emphasis on the interaction of membership in the microcultures, especially race, ethnicity, class, and gender. It also called for the elimination of discrimination against individuals because of their group membership. (p. 27)

Influential Publications and Organizational Forces

In the 1920s, W. E. B. DuBois, Carter G. Woodson, and other famed authors wrote some of the earliest publications that related to multicultural education and examined the history of slavery and the lives of African Americans (Banks & Banks, 2004). With an increased interest in ethnic studies in the 1960s came publications focused on ethnicity by James A. Banks, considered by many to be the father of multicultural education. These include seminal works such as *Teaching the Black Experience: Methods and Materials* (Banks, 1970) and perhaps his most popular work, *Teaching Strategies for Ethnic Studies* (Banks, 2009), whose first edition was published in 1975.

Publications aimed at helping educators and others to understand and value cultural differences are an important piece of the history of multicultural education. In a direct reaction to the increased focus on ethnic pride, scholars such as Ronald Takaki wrote books to provide insights into specific cultural groups. Takaki's *Strangers From a Different Shore: A History of Asian Americans* (1998) is considered a classic, groundbreaking text that shed light on the many untold stories of immigrants.

Multicultural Education in a Pluralistic Society by Gollnick and Chinn (2013), *Affirming Diversity* by Sonia Nieto and Patty Bode (2018), *Making Choices for Multicultural Education* by Christine Sleeter and Carl Grant (2009), and other texts on multicultural education offer solid theoretical and practical foundations for the field. In 1995, the first edition of *Handbook of Research on Multicultural Education* (Banks & Banks, 2004) was published; an extensive compilation of knowledge, it contained chapters by more than 60 of the top scholars in multicultural education and was a testament to the legitimacy of the field.

Textbook publishers, in reaction to the civil rights era and the demand for more ethnic content in education, began amending texts to reflect a more diverse perspective. Initial attempts were generally fairly superficial, as evidenced by shading in the faces of people in illustrations to be darker or changing Eurocentric names such as John to Juan. Social studies texts became a primary target for conversion, leading to a long-standing and faulty belief that multicultural education was a subject, not a core foundational philosophy. In later years, it became more evident that multicultural education should and could be infused across all disciplines. Books such as *Turning on Learning* (Grant & Sleeter, 2008) showed teachers how to write multicultural lesson plans across all disciplines.

Influential Agencies and Organizations in the Development of Multicultural Education

A wide variety of agencies and organizations are influencing the direction and development of multicultural education. These are found at the national and state levels and are involved in decision making related to areas such as accreditation, teacher preparation, curriculum, instruction, assessment, policy development and funding, and professional development.

The dominance of the **high-stakes testing** movement has pointed out more urgently the need to increase student achievement among students of color. Educators realize today that attempts to raise test scores must address how students are taught, students' learning styles and cultural backgrounds, and how the curriculum is used to support high levels of student learning. An understanding that culture affects learning, combined with the knowledge that much of our curriculum is Eurocentric, has pointed out the need for a more culturally responsive curriculum. Federal and state initiatives, accrediting bodies, and professional groups are increasingly addressing the importance of understanding the role of culture in teaching and learning.

In 1990, the National Association for Multicultural Education (NAME) was created; NAME was the first professional organization devoted to the promotion of multicultural education as the foundational philosophy of the nation's educational system, from preschool through higher education.

State education agencies have also been instrumental in enforcing an emphasis on multicultural education. In the preparation of a chapter for the first edition of the *Handbook of Research on Multicultural Education* (Banks & Banks, 2004), Gollnick found that 40 states required teacher education programs to include the study of ethnic groups, human relations, cultural diversity, or other standards or policies addressing multicultural education. While agency supports and mandates differ across states, one means of influencing the integration of multicultural education has been through the development of curriculum frameworks or guidelines.

Professional organizations established to support the ongoing professional development of teachers, such as Learning Forward (formerly the National Staff Development Council), also include key content standards on diversity.

The High-Stakes Testing Movement

The practice of establishing critical, standards-based tests is not a recent phenomenon. It has evolved in this country over decades. In recent years, it has escalated due, in part, to numerous studies that show American students performing much worse in academic subjects than students in other countries. That comparison and the recognition that the academic performance of American students was going down hastened the passing of the federal No Child Left Behind Act of 2001 legislation. The current controversy over standardized testing focuses on tight timelines that provide punitive sanctions ("high stakes") for failure to meet high standards and a common belief that standardized testing leads teachers to "teach to the test" and not support learning for deep meaning.

Similarities and Differences With Other Studies of Culture

A common mistake made by teachers is confusing multicultural education with global or intercultural education. A teacher might teach a unit studying the country of Kenya or the continent of Africa. The class studies the demographics, culture, customs, religion, form of government, and so on. This is considered to be multicultural education in that it is assumed that an extrapolation can be made to African Americans. While studying Africa can give some insight into the culture of African Americans, not all African Americans are from Africa. To understand African Americans, one must study Black people living in the United States whose experiences, values, and mores are different from those of, say, Kenyans. One would not assume that studying Italians in Italy would by itself foster an understanding of Italian Americans.

LEARNING OBJECTIVE 1.3 Define Multicultural Education

There is often confusion regarding definitions and terminology. Here is a brief review of some of the most commonly used terms. Please note that a discussion of definitions and differences can often lead to intense debate.

A Quick Comparison of Terms

Culturally relevant teaching, culturally relevant pedagogy, culturally responsive teaching, culturally responsive pedagogy, and culturally responsive education all refer to an approach in education where the cultural backgrounds and experiences of students play a prominent role in choosing curriculum content. Teachers subsequently adapt multiple methods of instruction and assessment to support this student-centered approach.

Global education: Global education focuses on teaching students to be citizens of the world, knowledgeable and skilled in working with different international cultures. The curriculum would include studying customs, perspectives, language, and social behavior of people in other countries.

Intercultural education: Intercultural education teaches the understanding of different people and cultures stressing the importance of celebrating diversity.

Cultural competence: It is the ability to think, act, and feel in ways that are respectful of diversity.

Social justice education: Often cited as one of the ultimate goals of education, this refers to educating students to become activists in changing things that need to be changed to better the lives of individuals. This can be actualized in varied actions such as efforts to eliminate racism to bringing about clean air and water.

Multicultural education: This concept will be explained in detail but one key factor is that it is a study of American ethnicities, acknowledging that studying about people in other countries is important, but we must learn about various cultures living in this country. The experiences of Irish people in Ireland in not the same as studying the experiences and perspectives of Irish Americans living in the United States.

There are many ways to define multicultural education, its characteristics, and its goals. Let's first explore multicultural education as defined by some of the noted researchers, authors, and educators in the field.

Sonia Nieto and Patty Bode: Nieto and Bode (2018) have provided what is described as one of the most inclusive and eclectic definitions. Their definition describes a process of comprehensive school reform and basic education for all students, a rejection of discrimination, and an infusion of multicultural education throughout the curriculum and instructional strategies, including interactions among teachers, students, and parents.

Nieto and Bode (2018) further outline seven basic characteristics of multicultural education:

1. It is *antiracist education* in that the fundamental purpose of multicultural education is to fight against racism.

2. It is *basic education*—education that is not an add-on subject but provides context to all subject areas.

3. Multicultural education *benefits all students*, not just students of color.

4. It is *pervasive*—fully infused into all aspects of school life.

5. It is *education for social justice* in that a main goal of education is to enable students to understand social inequities and to learn how to fight in order to improve society.

Library of Congress

A shameful era in history was the forcible relocation of more than 110,000 innocent people of Japanese ancestry from the Pacific coast of the United States into internment camps during World War II. One of multicultural education's key tenets is antiracist education.

6. Multicultural education is not a subject but a *process*—a comprehensive approach.

7. Finally, it is *critical pedagogy*, the essence of what equitable teaching and learning should be.

James A. Banks: According to James A. Banks (Banks & Banks, 2010), multicultural education is at least three things: (1) an idea or concept, (2) an educational reform movement, and (3) a process.

- It incorporates the idea that all students, regardless of their gender or social, ethnic, racial, or cultural characteristics, should have an equal opportunity to learn in school.

- It is a reform movement designed to make major changes in schools and other educational institutions so that students from all social classes, genders, and racial and cultural groups will have an equal opportunity to learn.

- It is an ongoing process whose goals, which include educational equality and improving academic achievement, will never be realized because they are ideals toward which human beings work but never attain.

Banks (1999) described six goals of multicultural education:

1. To help individuals gain greater self-understanding by viewing themselves from the perspectives of other cultures

2. To provide students with cultural and ethnic alternatives

3. To provide all students with the skills, attitudes, and knowledge needed to function within their ethnic culture, the mainstream culture, and within and across other ethnic cultures

4. To reduce the pain and discrimination that members of some ethnic and racial groups experience because of their unique racial, physical, and cultural characteristics

5. To help students master essential reading, writing, and computational skills

6. To help students acquire the knowledge, attitudes, and skills needed to participate in civic action to make society more equitable and just

Christine Bennett: According to Bennett (2014), multicultural education in the United States is

an approach to teaching and learning that is based upon democratic values and beliefs, and affirms cultural pluralism within culturally diverse societies and an interdependent world. It is based on the assumption that the primary goal of public education is to foster the intellectual, social, and personal development of virtually all students to their highest potential. (p. 9)

Bennett (2014) also outlines six goals of multicultural education:

1. To develop multiple historical perspectives

2. To strengthen cultural consciousness

3. To strengthen intercultural competence

4. To combat racism, sexism, and other forms of prejudice and discrimination

5. To increase awareness of the state of the planet and global dynamics

6. To build social action skills

National Association for Multicultural Education: NAME (n.d.), in its definition of multicultural education, talks about "social justice, equality, equity, and human dignity"; helping students develop "the attitudes and values necessary to live in a democratic society"; and creating an education that leads to "the highest levels of academic achievement for all students." Helping students develop a positive self-image by teaching about the history and culture of diverse people is a cornerstone of NAME's mission.

A New Definition of Multicultural Education

The theory and practice of multicultural education acknowledges that historically education has been biased toward a single point of view. Both the content (curriculum) and process (teaching strategies) of our education system have been influenced by a Eurocentric, upper-class, male-dominated perspective. Although there is great strength and worth in this perspective, missing are the voices of women, people of color, those who are underprivileged financially, and others. By creating a curriculum that encompasses the proportionate contribution of these individuals, the modern education system will better mirror the needs of today's students.

Gay Pride was not born of a need to celebrate being gay, but our right to exist without persecution. So instead of wondering why there isn't a Straight Pride movement, be thankful you don't need one.

—Anonymous

The theory and practice of education that is multicultural further seeks to meet the reality of the increasing numbers of diverse students in the education system. To be current, teachers must be prepared to teach a diversity of students. Furthermore, in an increasingly global economy, it is both an economic and political imperative that all students regardless of race, ethnicity, religion, sex, sexual orientation, **gender identity or expression**, class, or other differences be prepared to live and work in a multicultural world. All education should be multicultural.

To accomplish this, several goals are inherent in a multicultural curriculum:

1. Teach to eliminate racism, sexism, homophobia, and other forms of intolerance.
2. Create an equitable education system in which all students can achieve to high standards.
3. Use content and processes that meet the needs of diverse students.
4. Recognize bias and the importance of teaching from multiple perspectives.
5. Prepare all students to live and work in a global, multicultural world.
6. Instill in students a sense of civic responsibility and social consciousness.

These ideas can be summed up in this definition of multicultural education:

> Multicultural education is a model of education that recognizes the significant influence of culture on teaching, learning, and student achievement and the critical need to address issues of social justice and equity as part of a complete education.

The goals of multicultural education are to ensure that all students receive an equitable education and to prepare students to live a life promoting a just society. In this model, students are engaged and motivated to learn and succeed through the infusion of aspects of their culture, experiences, and perspectives into the development of curriculum and into numerous, varied, culturally responsive teaching strategies. Multicultural education stresses the importance of learning and developing pride in one's culture and understanding how culture influences personal beliefs, values, and actions. At the same time, students learn and understand the cultures and multiple perspectives of others and how to best reach harmony with differences.

One of the roots of multicultural education is an understanding of the harmful effects of the prejudice and discrimination that exist in society and of how education is a key to eliminating racism, sexism, homophobia, religious animosity, and all other forms of bias. Multicultural education further recognizes that we live in a global society in which cultural competence is essential to success in life and work.

Becoming a Multicultural Educator

The preparation of educators who are multicultural requires four steps. First, educators must develop an *awareness* of the reality of bias, prejudice, and discrimination faced by others and an acknowledgment of their own biases. Second, educators must have a sound *knowledge* of other cultures and perspectives. Third is the need to develop the *skills* required to teach to diverse learning styles and cultures. And fourth is the need to develop a lifelong personal *action plan* to increase one's knowledge, skills, and dispositions around diversity and to develop an institutional action plan to support education that is multicultural.

So What Is Multicultural Education?

The various definitions of multicultural education are consistent overall. In general, they address issues of content and process. Four prominent themes arise from these definitions.

1. A commitment to being culturally responsive and culturally responsible

   A multicultural educator acknowledges the fact that culture affects learning. Students come to the classroom with varying degrees and depths of life and cultural experiences. They bring with them unique values and beliefs. To engage students in the enterprise of learning, a skilled teacher makes efforts to understand the backgrounds and perspectives of students. The teacher then incorporates this information into teaching strategies and use of content. This approach results in students finding education more relevant and meaningful.

   The multicultural educator is highly conscious of diversity in many forms and seeks to celebrate it through the content and process of education. Students are taught to see differences as assets, not deficits. Diversity is regarded as a strength, not a distraction. Assumptions about race, ethnicity, religion, class, and other areas of diversity are challenged, and bigotry is exposed. Teachers are required to examine the very essence of teaching—philosophy, orientation, beliefs, and values—and then come to a clearer realization that a totally Eurocentric curriculum is a disservice to all students.

2. A process of changing pedagogical approaches

   The diversity of students and learning styles, coupled with research that shows that students excel given varied teaching and learning modalities, requires the teacher of today to use a broad array of teaching strategies. Assessment strategies must be varied also to capture true learning versus successful test-taking strategies.

3. A process of expanding the curriculum

   In an increasingly multicultural society, we must seek ways to expand the curriculum. The content must have meaning and relevance for students, or else it remains an academic exercise, devoid of purpose. This addresses one of the major controversies of multicultural education: "Whose history are we teaching, and are we elevating some cultural aspects to a higher level of significance than they deserve just to experience diversity?" As with any argument, there must be a balance of perspectives. The aim is not to rewrite history but to tell the untold stories of women and people of color. By including this lost history, we reflect the role all of our ancestors had in developing this nation so that all of us become a part of its history, not just observers.

   Since a key purpose of education is to help raise civic-minded and socially conscious citizens, it is also necessary to address critical social issues. The incorporation of ethnic studies and studies on power, oppression, class, racism, and gender inequality becomes an important component of a full curriculum.

4. Systemic change

   Schools are a microcosm of society. Thus, they must keep up with the ever-changing aspects of society. Not to do so would be to forsake school's relevance to preparing students to be citizens of the world. The curriculum, the nature of teaching and learning, and the role of the community in education become key adaptable elements of the school system. Educational policy and practice must take into consideration the needs of all students and their families.

LEARNING OBJECTIVE 1.4 Discuss Conceptual Models of Multicultural Education

While the field of multicultural education is relatively new, there is a significant body of research about multicultural education and numerous, well-developed theories. From an examination of the literature, students of multicultural education would find that there is a high level of agreement about how to achieve multicultural education. The research and theories about multicultural education have resulted in the development of several very useful models for its implementation. While the models may have different names and use different terms for each stage, all are in congruence with the idea that multicultural education is, ultimately, an approach to preparing students to be socially responsible and responsive, to be skilled in addressing social issues, and to live successfully in a multicultural society.

James Banks (1993) developed a four-stage model to describe "levels of integration of ethnic content." The first level in this model is what Banks called the "contributions approach." At this stage, educators make an effort to be multicultural by focusing on the more obvious elements of a cultural group. This can include a focus on famous people, foods, the arts, and other discrete elements. An example of this approach is a school that hosts a multicultural festival at some point during the school year. While such an event may appear just to skim the surface of what comprises a culture, teachers who use this approach are, at least, doing something.

However, as teachers expand their knowledge base and commitment to being culturally responsible and responsive, they may move to Level 2, the "additive approach." At this level, teachers begin to add concepts, content, and themes to the curriculum but without changing its essential structure. This level is evident when teachers focus on a particular ethnic group (e.g., African Americans, Hispanics) at a particular time (Black History Month, Cinco de Mayo) but not necessarily at other points during the year.

Attempts to desegregate schools were often met by ugly protests. *Brown v. Board of Education* challenged the legality of American public school segregation. In 1954, the U.S. Supreme Court ruled that segregated schools were unconstitutional. This decision helped pave the way for the creation of ethnic studies programs.

Photo by Marion S. Trikosko. Library of Congress, U.S. News & World Report Magazine Photograph Collection

Level 3 encompasses the "transformation approach," in which educators work to change the structure of the curriculum to allow students to see events, issues, and concepts from several perspectives. An example of this level is when a teacher engages students in considering how Native Americans would view Western expansion or Columbus's arrival in the Americas. Finally, Level 4, the "social action approach," occurs when students are engaged in decision making about key social issues.

Schools can easily accomplish Levels 1 and 2 of the Banks model because these levels do not require major revisions to the overall curriculum. It is at Level 3 that the entire curriculum becomes transformed.

Five Approaches to Multicultural Education

Carl Grant and Christine Sleeter (2008) have proposed a model for multicultural education that includes five approaches.

1. *Teaching the culturally different:* The teacher conducts the class in the usual manner, but with the presence of a student from another culture, the teacher makes adaptations to teaching approaches to help the student assimilate. For example, the teacher might work individually with the student using multiple methods of culturally relevant instruction to provide further instruction and to help include the student. The curriculum is not modified; the new student is helped to adjust to the standard curriculum as well as the school culture.

2. *Human relations approach:* The focus of education is on developing positive relationships among different cultures. Objectives include developing empathy, understanding, and tolerance. Students are taught about other cultures, particularly those within the classroom and school to increase understanding and to facilitate improved communication.

3. *Single-group studies:* Unit studies are conducted on discrete cultural groups, such as Native Americans or the Japanese. The goal is to educate all students on that culture and to help develop ethnic pride among those in the chosen group.

4. *Multicultural education:* Each subject area is taught infusing ethnic content and perspectives. Teaching strategies are varied to accommodate various learning styles. Multiple teaching strategies and assessment methods are used. The goal is to teach the values of different cultural groups, specifically promoting respect for diversity, human rights, and equity through social justice.

5. *Education that is multicultural and social reconstructionist:* A common teaching objective is the development of a social conscience and a sense of civic responsibility. Included in this are discussions of class and privilege and encouraging students to lead a life where they give back to the community and help seek social justice.

All five approaches are valid. Teachers should not be overly focused on one strategy but rather vary them to meet the needs of a variety of learning styles.

It is helpful to discuss the myths or misunderstandings about multicultural education. These are not the differences among theories of what multicultural education is, which are various philosophical interpretations of the term. Following are some of the misconceptions and misunderstandings that surround multicultural education:

LEARNING OBJECTIVE 1.5 Identify the Misconceptions and Misunderstandings About Multicultural Education

- *Multicultural education is only for students of color in the inner cities:* A common remark heard in suburban and rural districts is that there are no minority students in the schools, so multicultural education is not needed. This fallacy assumes that multicultural education benefits only minority students. Multicultural education requires teaching strategies and content that is culturally relevant to all students. It also demands preparation for living and working in a diverse world. It addresses issues of racism, sexism, classism, and other forms of discrimination and oppression. These dicta apply to all students regardless of color, income, or geographical location.

- *Multicultural education creates Balkanization:* The term *Balkanization* comes from the breakup of the Balkans in the early 21st century. The Balkans include southeastern European countries such as Albania, Bosnia, and Croatia. An outgrowth of ethnic studies programs and the teaching of ethnic pride has been the formation of organizations, clubs, and social agencies that service distinct cultural groups. On college campuses, these often take form as African American Centers, Chinese Student Associations, or Hispanic Cultural Clubs. Such clubs are formed for the same reason that many clubs are formed—to help needy members of the community, to teach about a language and culture, and to promote social and political agendas. They also serve as a safe haven where one's culture can be celebrated openly, without fear of ridicule. The formation of ethnic neighborhoods, such as China Town or Little Italy, are larger examples of this phenomenon.

  Naysayers claim that such organizations serve only to further segregate society and that they instill fear and hatred of other cultures. What this argument ignores is that exclusive clubs and organizations for White males existed long before current ethnic organizations. Many still exist today in the form of overt exclusionary entities such as certain golf clubs as well as in the form of businesses and corporations whose owners and managers are exclusively White, male, and often Protestant.

  Multicultural education encourages students of all races and ethnicities to explore, learn, and celebrate their culture. It also emphasizes the need to be multicultural by doing the same with other cultures. The process starts within one's own culture and broadens to include adopting and assimilating the richness of other cultures.

- *Multicultural education lowers standards:* The opposite is actually true. Multicultural education attempts to close the achievement gap by providing a culturally responsive education. In this way, all students are given an equal opportunity to learn and succeed. Culturally biased teaching methods, content, and assessment are minimized.

- *Multicultural education is done only in social studies, language arts, music, and art:* When multicultural education was first introduced, it was in these subjects,

Chiricahua Apaches Four Months After Arriving at Carlisle

Hugh Chee.   Fred'k. Eskelsejah.   Clement Seanilzay. Samson Noran.
Ernest Hogee.   Margaret Y.Nadasthilah.
     Humphrey Escharzay.   Beatrice Kiahtel. Janetta Pahgostatum.   Bishop Eatennah.   Basil Ekarden.

Wikimedia Commons

The infamous Carlisle (PA) Indian Industrial School housed Apache children, torn from their families and forced to give up their culture in order to become more "White." A multicultural education teaches that children should learn pride in their culture.

where it seemed the easiest to infuse. Unfortunately, it became associated with the "softer" subjects and not the "hard" subjects such as science, math, physics, chemistry, and so on. The mistake was in placing a heavy focus on content and less on diverse teaching strategies. There was also an overly strong focus on race and racism, which made infusion into other subjects seemingly more problematic. In practice, math is one of the easiest subjects to infuse with multicultural perspectives in that word problems, which are the basis for math texts, can be readily phrased to have cultural content. The same applies to other subject areas. In addition, through varied teaching methods, issues of multiple perspectives can be brought forth.

- *Multicultural education stresses the study of minority cultures at the expense of mainstream culture:* Up until the era of the civil rights movement, the American education system was steeped almost exclusively in a Eurocentric perspective. The advent of ethnic studies programs emphasized the need for a curriculum that included the perspectives of all the peoples of the country. The previously missing voices of African Americans, Hispanic Americans, Native Americans, Asian Americans, women, and other groups were now being heard in texts and other teaching materials. Where there once existed a single, biased perspective, there now was an invigorating blend of stories told from opposing views. These were included to complete the picture of America, not to eliminate the European viewpoint.

- *Multicultural education is necessary only when there are racial problems in schools:* Teaching awareness, understanding, and appreciation for other cultures helps prevent attitudes, feelings, and acts of prejudice and discrimination. Since school is preparation for life in a global economy and in an increasingly diverse community, multicultural education prepares students well. A school that exhibits racial tensions will most likely harbor intolerance for other forms of diversity, such as gender, sexual orientation, disabilities, class, and income. It is essential, therefore, that all schools incorporate a curriculum that expands the awareness and understanding of students beyond their singular viewpoint.

- *Multicultural education is only about race:* Multicultural education arose out of the civil rights era, when Africans Americans were finally able to achieve some degree of equality in constitutional rights. From this point onward, aided by ethnic studies programs, greater awareness was achieved not only of the injustices suffered by African Americans but also of the great contributions made. Takaki's work began exploring the hardships of and contributions made by immigrant groups, as well as by Native Americans and by African Americans brought to this continent as slaves. Thanks to landmark legislation such as *Lau v. Nichols* in 1974, which supported the rights of non-English-speaking students, and the Americans with Disabilities Act and events such as the Stonewall Riots in New York, other "minority" groups began asserting their rights to be heard. Multicultural education, to be true to its philosophy of including the "unheard" voices, must also now include the perspectives of women, gays and lesbians, persons with learning and physical disabilities, and other previously underrepresented groups. The fear that multicultural education will be diluted by straying from race is unfounded. Intolerance is intolerance. Prejudice and discrimination against one group breeds the same toward others.

- *Multicultural educators are unpatriotic:* Multicultural education advocates for both educational equity and social justice. It acknowledges that all students are not achieving equally, as documented by the dramatic achievement gaps that exist between students of color and White students and between low-income and economically privileged students. It also seeks to point out that, despite great strides in equity legislation, the achievement of women and minorities in government and business is still below that of their White, male counterparts.

REFLECTING BACK

Now that you have a better understanding of multicultural education, it is time to consider its application.

Questions

1. What do you think are the greatest strengths you bring to being a multicultural educator?

2. How would you explain your position on multicultural education during an employment interview?

3. How do you respond to the most common critiques of multicultural education?

PROFILES IN MULTICULTURAL EDUCATION

JAMES A. BANKS

© James A. Banks

James A. Banks is the retired Kerry and Linda Killinger Professor of Diversity Studies and Director of the Center for Multicultural Education at the University of Washington–Seattle. He is a specialist in multicultural education and in social studies education and has written widely in these fields. His books include *Teaching Strategies for Ethnic Studies*, 8th edition (2009); *Multicultural Education: Issues and Perspectives*, 7th edition (with Cherry A. McGee Banks, 2010); *Cultural Diversity and Education: Foundations, Curriculum, and Teaching*, 5th edition (2005); *An Introduction to Multicultural Education*, 5th edition (2014); *Multicultural Education, Transformative Knowledge, and Action* (1996); *Educating Citizens in a Multicultural Society*, 2nd edition (2007); *Diversity and Citizenship Education: Global Perspectives* (2004); and *Race, Culture, and Education: The Selected Works of James A. Banks* (2006). Professor Banks has written more than 100 articles, contributions to books, and book reviews for professional publications.

Professor Banks is the editor, with Cherry A. M. Banks, of the *Handbook of Research on Multicultural Education*, 2nd edition (2004). This landmark publication was the first research handbook on multicultural education to be published. In 1997, the first edition received the Book Award from NAME. Banks is an author of the Macmillan–McGraw-Hill social studies program for Grades K through 7. He edited the four-volume *Encyclopedia of Diversity in Education* (2012).

A former elementary school teacher, Professor Banks received his bachelor's degree in elementary education and social science from Chicago State University and his master's and doctorate degrees in these fields from Michigan State University. Renowned worldwide, James Banks has been one of the most significant contributors to the field of multicultural education. His writings range from the scholarly and theoretical to the very practical works, such as *Teaching Strategies for Ethnic Studies*, 8th edition (2009). When asked what was his most significant contribution to the field of multicultural education, he wrote,

> One of the most important contributions I have made to the field of multicultural education is the development of a series of conceptual and theoretical frameworks that researchers and practitioners are using to guide research, policy, and practice. One of the most widely used is the "Dimensions of Multicultural Education." (Howe & Lisi, 2013, p. 28)

The dimensions make it clear that *content integration* is only one of the five dimensions of multicultural education. The other dimensions are *the knowledge construction process, an equity pedagogy, prejudice reduction,* and *an empowering school culture and social structure.* Content integration is less important to most science and math teachers than creating an equity pedagogy, which consists of teaching strategies that will enable students from diverse groups to experience academic success.

James A. Banks has influenced generations of teachers and teacher educators and added greatly to the validity and legitimacy of multicultural education as an essential theory of education.

CASE STUDY
THE TIMES WE LIVE IN

Key Issues to Be Explored in the Case

1. Uncover personal biases.

2. Become aware of the obstacles sometimes faced by newcomers and people of color.

3. Describe teaching strategies and school policies to combat harassment and bias incidents.

Starsville was a typical, sleepy New England town comprising almost exclusively White, middle-class citizens whose families had lived there for generations. As is the case in many small towns, the residents seemed to appreciate the idea that they knew one another and shared similar pastimes, values, beliefs, and ways of living. What little diversity they had within the schools created little controversy.

Then one of the churches in town decided to sponsor a family of refugees from Syria. In another development, due to the close proximity of Starsville to a large metropolitan area, African American and Hispanic families from the city—upwardly mobile professionals—began buying homes in town. Starsville was quickly becoming a diverse community. Town leaders and school officials prided themselves that they had what they considered a very accepting and harmonious school climate.

Things began to change. A gay student was chased home by bullies throwing stones. A group of Mexican American girls were taunted by other girls as they walked through the high school hallways. Racist and homophobic graffiti began appearing around town. Fights were becoming more frequent in school. Derogatory comments about minority students became more common in the teachers' lounge. Chants of "build the wall" and drawings of swastikas on walls became more frequent. School officials were alarmed and puzzled by this change in student behavior. Previously kind and supportive students became intolerant in both behavior and words, fueled by what was appearing in the news. Normally supportive parents became divisive on the causes and solutions.

Discussion Questions

1. What problems exist in Starsville and how did this come about?

2. What needs to occur in the school and the community to make things right?

3. Compare and contrast the events in this case with a school setting with which you are familiar. How are the issues the same and different? What are school leaders doing to address the needs of all learners?

CHAPTER SUMMARY

1.1 Identify the rationale for implementing multicultural education

What are the demographic characteristics of our country and school population? How well are all students doing in school? What is the justification or rationale for implementing multicultural education?

- Our nation's classrooms are increasingly diverse, yet at the same time, there exists a gap in educational achievement between White, middle-class students and students of color and of lower socioeconomic status. We must address the negative impact of an education system that uses a Eurocentric curriculum and teaching methods that do not address different cultural learning styles. We must furthermore focus on reforming schools and the nature of education so that they address a concern for educational equity for all. Finally, we must provide an impetus for creating opportunities for social justice.

1.2 Explain the history of multicultural education

What is the foundation for the growth and evolution of multicultural education? When did it start as a field of study?

- The history of multicultural education in this country has gone through stages, starting with a classical education model with a limited perspective. Education now increasingly includes multiple perspectives. More attention is being paid to ethnic studies, bias, and alternative minority viewpoints commensurate with the changing demographics of the United States.

1.3 Define multicultural education

What is multicultural education? How is it different from traditional education as it is commonly known? Who are the key scholars who have defined multicultural education?

- Multicultural education is a philosophy of education that addresses educational equity and social justice. It recognizes that there has been bias inherent in what and how students have been educated. It attempts to increase the academic achievement of all students while at the same time creating a more just and equitable society.

1.4 Discuss conceptual models of multicultural education

What does multicultural education look like? What are the key models of multicultural education? What are the critical elements of multicultural education?

- There are many conceptual models of multicultural education. They all have common themes—reforming content and process to increase cultural knowledge and broaden perspectives while ensuring equitable academic achievement.

1.5 Identify the misconceptions and misunderstandings about multicultural education

What are some of the challenges to multicultural education? What are the facts that address these challenges? How has multicultural education been misunderstood?

- There are many misconceptions and misunderstandings of what multicultural education is and is not. Instruction in the philosophy of multicultural education is critical to the preparation of teachers. Multicultural education is about both the *content* and the *process* of education. "What" we teach—the content—must more accurately portray and illustrate the stories and perspectives of all the peoples of this country. "How" we teach speaks to the need to use multiple teaching methods that encompass and support the cultures of students. Multicultural education is about social justice as well as educational equity. The loftiest goal of education is to inspire students to work toward bettering the lives of all.

KEY TERMS

achievement gap 6
Brown v. Board of Education 17
Civil Rights Act of 1964 17
classism 7
Common Core State Standards 14
cultural competence 6
deficit model of education 14
developmental disabilities 8
Eurocentric 13
gender identity or expression 23

goth 8
graphic organizer 15
high-stakes testing 19
homophobia 7
Lau v. Nichols 17
melting pot 5
microcultures 18
multiple intelligences 9
No Child Left Behind Act of 2001 8
oppression 15

pedagogy 7
persistence of ethnicity 5
racism 7
salad bowl 5
sexism 7
social justice 7
straight-edge 8
Voting Rights Act of 1965 17

APPLICATION: ACTIVITIES AND EXERCISES

Individual

1. Immerse yourself in another culture. Attend a religious service not of your own faith tradition. Attend a meeting of a club organized by people of another culture. Attend a cultural fair or event. Attend a gay/lesbian/bisexual/transgender club meeting. Shop in a store where the employees or other customers do not speak your language. Go somewhere where no one is of your race or religion. Write about these experiences in a journal. Discuss how you think students feel in schools where they are in the minority.

2. Write an op-ed piece for the local newspaper highlighting social injustices in your community.

3. Participate in a demonstration. Interview other attendees. Journal about your experience.

Group

1. In pairs, divide a paper into two sections. On the left, write the heading "Model School" and brainstorm and list the characteristics of a model school. On the right, write the heading "Multicultural School." Brainstorm and list the characteristics of a multicultural school. Compare lists with other pairs. What are the similarities and differences, if any?

2. Each person should list three reasons a school should not adopt a multicultural curriculum. Line up two equal rows of chairs and have everyone take a seat facing each other, about a foot apart. Each person on one side will cite one of the reasons against a multicultural curriculum to the person sitting across from her or him. Set a timer to go off in 60 seconds. The other person will have 60 seconds to respond. Stop again when the timer goes off. Each person then gets up, as in musical chairs, and moves one person to the right. Debrief the discussions, charting the responses to reasons a school should not adopt a multicultural curriculum.

3. Do a think/pair/share. Individually, develop an original definition of *multicultural education* that is based on your readings and class discussions. In pairs, come to a consensus on a definition. Share and discuss your new definition with the class and come to a class consensus. Use this definition as the basis for future discussions throughout your study of multicultural education. Return to it regularly to see if you want to make any changes to the definition.

Self-Assessment

1. Indicate *yes* or *no* in response to the following questions, and then compare responses with another student.

1. I grew up in a very diverse community.	Yes	No
2. I am comfortable around people of other races and ethnicities.	Yes	No
3. I am knowledgeable about the experiences of diverse people.	Yes	No
4. I have had firsthand experience with discrimination.	Yes	No
5. I have a diverse group of friends outside of school and work.	Yes	No
6. I am willing to learn how to teach in an urban setting.	Yes	No
7. If confronted with a racially motivated incident in my classroom, I am prepared to deal with it.	Yes	No
8. I am comfortable talking about race, ethnicity, sexual orientation, and other ways in which people are diverse.	Yes	No
9. I can recall negative messages from my childhood about my race, ethnicity, or gender.	Yes	No
10. I am confident that I could defend multicultural education against the myths and misconceptions that exist about it.	Yes	No

ANNOTATED RESOURCES

The Civil Rights Project/Proyecto Derechos Civiles

http://civilrightsproject.ucla.edu

The Civil Rights Project (CRP) is a leading organization devoted to civil rights research. It has found eager collaborators among researchers nationwide and wide-open doors among advocacy organizations, policymakers, and journalists. Focusing initially on education reform, it has convened dozens of national conferences and roundtables; commissioned more than 300 new research and policy studies; produced major reports on desegregation, student diversity, school discipline, special education, dropout rates, and Title I programs; and published six books, with four more in the editing stage.

National Association for Multicultural Education

http://www.nameorg.org

NAME was founded in 1990 to bring together individuals from all academic levels and disciplines and from diverse educational institutions and other organizations, occupations, and communities who had an interest in multicultural education. NAME is the fastest growing professional organization in the United States that has as its sole objective the advocacy of multicultural education as the foundational philosophy of the nation's educational system from preschool through higher education.

Interstate New Teacher Assessment and Support Consortium

http://www.ccsso.org/projects/Interstate_New_Teacher_Assessment_and_Support_Consortium

The Interstate New Teacher Assessment and Support Consortium is a network of state education agencies and national educational organizations dedicated to the reform of the preparation, licensing, and ongoing professional development of teachers. Created in 1987, the consortium has as its primary constituency state education agencies responsible for teacher licensing, program approval, and professional development. Its work is guided by one basic premise: An effective teacher must be able to integrate content knowledge with the specific strengths and needs of students to ensure that all students learn and perform at high levels.

Get the tools you need to sharpen your study skills. SAGE edge offers a robust online environment featuring an impressive array of free tools and resources. Access practice quizzes, eFlashcards, video, and multimedia at **edge.sagepub.com/howe3e**

2

Becoming a Multicultural Educator
A FOUR-STEP MODEL

Learning Objectives

According to the U.S. Bureau of Labor Statistics (2014), in 2012, there were 3.5 million K–12 teachers, including high school teachers, middle school teachers, elementary teachers, and special education teachers. The largest occupation category was elementary teachers, accounting for approximately 37% of those employed in the entire group. This means that there were more educators than doctors, nurses, and lawyers combined. About 12.5 million people work in the field of education. Every year, U.S. schools hire more than 200,000 new teachers (Graziano, 2005). According to the U.S. Bureau of Labor Statistics, between 2014 and 2024, there will be nearly 1.9 million job openings for educators in preschool through postsecondary education (Vilorio, 2016). What kind of teacher will you be? With the critical challenges facing our students, teachers, and schools, it will take significant knowledge about what makes an effective teacher for us to provide a high-quality education for every individual student in our country.

Through your study of and work on Chapter 2, you will be able to do the following:

2.1 Define the characteristics of an effective multicultural educator

2.2 Identify professional teaching standards that will guide you in becoming a multicultural educator

2.3 Describe culture as the core element of becoming a multicultural educator

2.4 Outline a four-step model for the professional development of multicultural educators

In this chapter, we will investigate what characterizes an effective educator and how these characteristics are applied to becoming a multicultural educator. We will explore the characteristics through several lenses: (1) the research and literature on effective teaching, (2) professional standards that describe the expectations of what teachers should know and be able to do, and (3) the particular lens of culture. Finally, we will describe a four-component model for the development of a multicultural educator that has been developed by the authors. This model serves as the organizing framework for the remaining chapters in this book. In this process, we will discuss the knowledge, skills, and dispositions or attitudes that contribute to the effectiveness of a multicultural educator.

Specifically, through engagement in the learning and work of this chapter, students will learn about the research on effective teaching, as well as the research on the characteristics of effective multicultural educators. Students will also become familiar with standards or expectations for what effective teachers and multicultural educators should know and be able to do, and they will be able to analyze their own emerging capacity in relation to professional teaching standards. Finally, they will reflect on the influence and importance of culture in teaching and learning practices and come to understand a four-step process for the professional development of multicultural educators.

> The . . . advice I have to give you is, do not live your life safely. . . . I hope you will take some risks, exert some real leadership on issues, and if you will, dance along the edge of the roof as you continue your life.
>
> —Wilma P. Mankiller
> (2001, p. 52)

CASE STUDY
A TEACHER'S USE OF CULTURE

Bethany was ecstatic about her impending first teaching assignment. In her teacher preparation program in the Midwest, she had worked hard to learn about curriculum, instruction, and assessment. She had immersed herself in coursework that included practice in developing curriculum based on the Common Core State Standards (CCCS). She had dreamed of becoming a teacher for several years, and now that dream was about to become a reality. She had been offered a position as a first-grade teacher in a public school and was moving to Phoenix, Arizona.

Bethany had looked forward to moving away from the Midwest so she could experience the beauty of the mountains and deserts in Arizona. She was looking forward to exploring and learning about her new state. Admittedly, she didn't know much about the cultures of the peoples of Arizona, who included Native Americans and Mexican Americans, in addition to Caucasians. But she looked forward to learning about the cultures of the west in her spare time.

At the end of the first semester, however, Bethany found teaching her first-grade students to be more challenging than she anticipated. She really enjoyed teaching all of them, but for some reason, several of her students—many of whom were Mexican American—were not making the expected progress in reading and language arts. While it would have been easy to blame the students—after all, English was not their native language—Bethany knew that she needed some assistance. She had come to know her colleague across the hall, Marilyn, and asked to meet with her.

Marilyn was an experienced teacher who had participated in professional development toward starting multicultural education in school. She had spent considerable time in revising her curriculum, starting with a vision of how to support diverse learners. Marilyn saw great potential in Bethany and knew that she could have an impact on her diverse learners, but she also knew that Bethany needed some special support. She took Bethany under her wing and committed to mentoring and coaching her through a process for becoming a multicultural educator.

In her initial meetings with Bethany, Marilyn talked with her about a variety of topics. For example, she asked Bethany about what she knew about diverse cultural groups, particularly those who lived in the surrounding area and whose children attended the school. Bethany shared with Marilyn that she had tried to read about Native Americans and Mexican Americans before she arrived at the school. Marilyn responded that this was a good start. Marilyn next asked Bethany to think

(Continued)

(Continued)

about what her views and beliefs were about the use of standards in teaching and learning. Bethany said that she had learned a great deal about standards in her teacher preparation program. Marilyn concluded that Bethany possessed some good basic knowledge in this area. When Marilyn asked Bethany how she used her students' culture to create culturally relevant teaching, Bethany was hesitant. She knew that teacher–student relationships were critical, and that she needed to develop units and lesson plans based on standards, but she was not at all sure about how to use students' culture effectively, particularly the cultures of the students in her current classroom. They agreed to meet twice per week starting at the beginning of the spring semester, so that Marilyn could mentor and coach Bethany in enhancing her own practice of working effectively with diverse students.

Your Perspectives on the Case

1. In light of your current understanding of the importance of culture, what is contributing to Marilyn's effectiveness and Bethany's lack of effectiveness in their respective classrooms?

2. Imagine that you are also a grade-level colleague of Bethany and Marilyn. Marilyn has asked that you all work together as a team to support the development of multicultural education in the entire grade. What short-term and long-term strategies might you suggest to support improvement of teaching not only by Bethany but also by the grade-level team?

3. Compare this scenario with your teaching experiences so far. How much of it is similar to experiences you have had? What did you do to correct it? If you have not yet worked in a classroom, compare this scenario with a particular classroom situation in which you had found yourself as a student, a student teacher, or an observer.

THINKING AHEAD

Everyone encounters different kinds of teachers throughout the years of being a student. If you reflect on your own experiences as a student, you probably can recall teachers who really had a positive impact on your life and, unfortunately, teachers who were not effective. What makes a teacher effective at teaching individual students? This important question leads us into a discussion of what characterizes a multicultural educator. An effective teacher and a multicultural educator are close to being one and the same. If someone is effective at teaching all students in a variety of settings, that person is probably a multicultural educator.

1. What kind of teacher do you want to be? Describe yourself as that teacher using 10 different words or phrases.

2. What is your understanding of the role of standards in education? What is the role of standards in achieving equity in education?

3. Why do you think the development of standards has become so important over the past several years?

4. What do you know about teaching diverse students? Where did that knowledge come from?

5. Imagine that it is the beginning of the school year. You have received your class list and know that several of your students are newly arrived immigrants. Describe your plan for how you will make use of their cultural backgrounds as well as the backgrounds of all of your other students during the first month of school.

6. What do you think are the stages that educators go through as they work to become multicultural educators? As you think of the development of a multicultural educator in stages, what stage do you think you are in at this point in time? What evidence is there that you are at this stage? What do you think you need to do to become an effective multicultural educator?

LEARNING OBJECTIVE 2.1 Define the Characteristics of an Effective Multicultural Educator

What Is Effective Teaching?

Many scholars have conducted research on the characteristics of effective teachers. For many years in American schools, when the student population was fairly homogeneous, the concept of effective teaching was influenced by theories and research about behaviorism. Classrooms were designed so that students listened passively to the teacher and were assessed about the extent of their learning, particularly their capacity for memorization. It was believed that effective teachers set learning goals and taught from textbooks that were clearly biased in favor of a distinctly Eurocentric curriculum. For some students, this approach worked quite effectively. However, for a number of students, for a variety of reasons, this approach was not effective.

An investigation into more recent research about learning and about teaching indicates that this earlier, more limited approach does not support every student in learning at high levels. We now know that students learn in different ways and instruction needs to be differentiated to address diverse learning styles and needs. We know that education must be relevant to students' previous experiences and cultural backgrounds. We know that learning is essentially problem solving and that most learning takes place in a social context in which students collaborate and work together. We also know that one of the most important contributors to high levels of learning is the relationship established between the teacher and the student. The traditional "one-size-fits-all" approach to teaching that seemed to work in earlier centuries and decades is not effective in addressing the learning needs of the rapidly changing student populations in our schools today. We will need to attend to a more current, research-based definition of effective teaching.

Jeannie Oakes, Martin Lipton, Lauren Anderson, and Jamy Stillman (2012) described key findings from research about critical components of effective teaching. Based on the research (Gregg, 1995; Noddings, 2005; Ward, 2017), it appears that effective teachers convey a personal interest in and liking for students, use an "ethic of caring" to shape classroom conditions, believe that relationships are crucial to all learning, and make lessons and learning interesting. Many researchers believed that effective teachers work to make schooling child centered rather than subject centered. Oakes et al. (2012) wrote of the importance of effective teachers empowering students by giving them choices and engaging them in making important decisions.

Some common themes emerge from an examination of research on effective teaching. These themes are particularly relevant in preparing to teach today's learners. Richard Arends (2015) has written extensively and elegantly about four essential characteristics or qualities of effective teachers that mirror the research on effective teaching.

First, effective teachers have *personal qualities* that allow them to make important connections to students, parents, other teachers, and the community. It is critical that teachers firmly and deeply believe that every single child can achieve at high levels and can learn. If the teacher doesn't believe this, and believe it passionately, then the students will certainly not believe it either. One important personal quality, according to Arends (2015), that effective teachers possess is a commitment to social justice for children. What this means is that effective teachers are committed to providing what every individual student needs to achieve at high levels.

Second, effective teachers have developed a *knowledge base* in three primary areas: subject matter, human development, and pedagogy. More specifically, effective teachers have a wide knowledge of, and continue to study and learn, the content of their particular subject areas, such as a world language, science, or mathematics. Effective teachers also know how

Comstock Images/Comstock/Thinkstock

Most of us have our favorite teachers, the ones who have made lasting impression on our lives, who taught with passion, as well as the love of teaching. Few careers offer such amazing power to change lives for the better.

people learn. Finally, effective teachers know how to develop learning experiences, using a wide variety of research-based instructional strategies to teach the content while considering how learning occurs.

Third, according to Arends (2015), effective teachers have a significant *repertoire of instructional strategies* that can support student motivation, develop the learning environment such that every student wants to engage in learning, and produce learners who take responsibility for their own learning. Effective teachers are knowledgeable about and skilled in important models of instruction, including those that are more teacher centered (e.g., lecture and direct instruction) and those that are more student centered (e.g., cooperative learning and problem-based learning).

Fourth, effective teachers are knowledgeable about and committed to regular *reflection* on their own practice. They see themselves as lifelong learners, working to improve themselves and thereby improve the education they provide for their students. They reflect individually and in collaboration with colleagues about what they teach, why they teach in particular ways, and how they can improve their teaching.

What Is a Multicultural Educator?

In light of our previous discussion of the research and literature that reveal some important characteristics of effective teachers, we can now apply some of those themes common to current definitions of effective teaching to answering the question "What is a multicultural educator?"

Carl Grant and Maureen Gillette (2006) synthesized the ideas of expert multiculturalists, including Geneva Gay, Gloria Ladson-Billings, and Jacqueline Jordan Irvine, in a list of characteristics of multicultural educators. Among those ideas are important aspects of knowledge, skills, and dispositions. In particular, according to Grant and Gillette, the research about effective teaching with diverse student populations supports the four characteristics mentioned above. For example, research by Rosa Sheets (1995) indicates that

TABLE 2.1   What Is a Multicultural Educator?

Traditional Teacher	Effective Teacher Who Is a Multicultural Educator
Knowledge base	
Understanding of the content being taught is grounded primarily in a Eurocentric perspective	Understanding of the content is grounded in multiple perspectives; teacher works to learn about the contributions of people of diverse cultural backgrounds to that particular content area/discipline; appreciates the diversity of cultural identities and continually works to learn more about many diverse cultures
Has a limited approach to the design of teaching and learning experiences; is not knowledgeable about diverse learning styles and how to meet those learner needs	Knows that diverse students learn in many different ways and knows how to design instruction to reach learners according to their preferred learning styles
Personal awareness of own cultural identities and knowledge of other cultural groups is fairly limited	Has explored his or her own personal ethnic, racial, gender, and other identities; knows how own culture compares with those of the students; understands the strengths and struggles of various identities
Has limited or no understanding of issues of racism, sexism, classism, and other means of oppression and their effects on education	Has deep and personal insight into social injustices and inequities in society and incorporates this knowledge into the educational process
Is apolitical with respect to the practice of teaching	Understands the implications of and connections between public policies and laws and their effects on education and people at all levels; is current on the actions of government at the local, state, and federal levels
Repertoire of skills	
Operates from a **behaviorist** orientation to teaching and utilizes didactic and direct instruction as the primary teaching strategy; assessment strategies are limited to paper-and-pencil tests	Utilizes numerous and varied teaching strategies to accommodate diverse learning styles; is able to differentiate instruction and assessment to meet diverse learner needs
Classroom experience is teaching and teacher centered	Classroom experience is learning and student centered
Lesson plans tend to be Eurocentric and lack multiple perspectives	Creates lesson plans that incorporate a variety of cultural perspectives
Believes that the content is the most important component of classroom teaching, and communicating that content generally happens in the form most comfortable to the teacher	Communicates effectively with a variety of students; establishes deep and meaningful relationships with each student
Personal qualities and dispositions	
Believes that, while discrimination is a major concern in society, a focus on equity is not relevant to the teaching and learning process	Believes that racism, sexism, and other forms of discrimination are too prevalent and a deterrent to an equitable education
Believes that teaching in the subject areas is culture free	Believes that the infusion of ethnic content into the curriculum is critical to the learning process
Believes that students need to learn the "basic skills"	Is committed to preparing students to contribute to improving society; values student experience, student voices, and student perspectives

students of color who may have been low performing but then were placed in higher level classes in which the teachers maintained high standards and had high expectations for all students, provided complex and challenging tasks, and created warm and positive classroom environments, in fact, excelled. Gloria Ladson-Billings (2009) found that diverse students also perform at higher levels when working with teachers who

- engage them in challenging, cooperative, and hands-on learning experiences levels;

- expect that all students can achieve at high levels;

- believe that a critically important process for learning in the classroom is through collaboration and learning communities;

- make explicit and meaningful connections to families and the community, knowing that they are important contributors to the success of every student;

- know and use a variety of instructional strategies that meet the needs of diverse learners;

- use the experiences, cultural backgrounds, and knowledge that each student brings to the teaching and learning process to enhance the experience for all; and

- reflect deeply and regularly about how they can improve their practice and eliminate bias and prejudice from the classroom.

Cummins (2000) stressed the power and importance of an instructional approach known as transformative pedagogy, in which effective teachers of diverse students design learning experiences such that students can relate the curriculum to their own lives and consider broader social issues. Research by Bryk and Schneider (2002) and Demmert and Towner (2003) indicates that when teachers work to build trust and partnerships with families, especially with families marginalized by schools in the past, and are committed to involving family members in decision making about their children, then those students achieve at higher levels.

With these descriptions of effective teaching and effective multicultural educators in mind, a comparison can be made with a more traditional approach that is grounded in earlier research and thinking. Using several of the key themes of effective teaching, Table 2.1 compares teachers who are more traditional in their knowledge base, repertoire of skills, and personal qualities or dispositions with multicultural educators according to the same categories.

Essential Knowledge for Multicultural Educators

Being a multicultural educator means that one has a solid knowledge of the content area in which one is teaching and that one's knowledge is grounded in **multiple perspectives**. A grounding in multiple perspectives is a key concept. This means that the educator has come to know a particular topic by looking at the literature, histories, and experiences of diverse people who may perceive the same topic differently. A classic example of multiple perspectives is how the early settlers in America viewed their movement as a "westward expansion" while Native Americans viewed this activity as "westward invasion." Just this idea necessitates a deep and ongoing study of the literature in one's field or content area.

The perspectives that we as educators hold, and how we use those perspectives in teaching and learning situations, is critically important. For example, picture in your mind two different scenarios. In the first, schoolchildren were taught from the perspective that the early settlers were brave men and women who loaded their belongings, along with their hopes for a better future, onto Conestoga wagons and headed west to claim land, which they believed was their God-given right. They also felt, in many cases, that they needed to tame the "savages" and bring them Christianity and civilization. In the second scenario or perspective, imagine the Native Americans, whose ancestors had lived on that land for hundreds of years, observing the clouds of dust raised by wagon trains of settlers heading toward them. In their minds, did they see this as a welcoming sign? The Native Americans were perfectly happy with their faith and their culture. They were puzzled as to the concept of owning land—how could one own land? For Native Americans, no one owns the land. It would be like claiming that someone owns the air. Property was communal. In a multicultural approach, students must be taught both perspectives.

A multicultural educator also has a deep knowledge base about students, how they learn, and how their cultural identities affect the learning process. Multicultural educators know about learning styles and that different students learn in different ways and have different preferences for how they can best demonstrate their learning.

Multicultural educators know that students do not learn in a vacuum. Students' education is affected by economic, social, and political pressures. A child living in poverty will not flourish in school if the teachers do not take that predicament into account. While middle-class students may have access to parents with the time and resources to enrich their lives, poor students often lack help with homework and encouragement to study. Those students' parents are often working two or more jobs to make ends meet. The newspapers, books, magazines, and computers common in middle-class homes are not there to help in the education of a poor student. Students who come from a long line of poverty often lack a culture of the good study habits that are needed to succeed. Teachers who do not understand the culture of the poor will not know how to supplement and support the education of poor students.

Similar obstacles face those students who live and study in environments where racism, sexism, and homophobia as well as other psychologically, emotionally, and physically damaging evils afflict them and interfere with their right to learn. It becomes critical that our classrooms foster the valuing of diversity and that educators understand the lives that others lead and work toward social justice (Schneidewind & Davidson, 2014).

At different times, researchers and writers have worked to define the knowledge bases needed by multicultural educators. One of the richest and most comprehensive sources for educators is *Common Sense About Uncommon Knowledge: The Knowledge Bases for Diversity* by G. Pritchy Smith (1998). In this book, Smith provides an extensive review of the literature on critical aspects of culture and delineates 13 distinct bodies of knowledge that are now considered essential to becoming a multicultural educator. These knowledge bases are as follows:

1. Foundations of multicultural education

2. Sociocultural contexts of human growth and psychological development in marginalized **ethnic** and racial cultures

3. Cultural and cognitive learning–style theory and research

4. Language, communication, and interactional styles of marginalized cultures

5. Essential elements of culture

6. Principles of culturally responsive teaching and culturally responsive curriculum development

7. Effective strategies for teaching minority students

8. Foundations of racism

9. Effects of policy and practice on culture, race, gender, and other categories of diversity

10. Culturally responsive diagnosis, measurement, and assessment

11. Sociocultural influences on subject-specific learning

12. Gender and sexual orientation

13. Experiential knowledge

In his book, Smith (1998) discusses each of the knowledge bases in depth and provides suggestions for how to make use of them in teaching and learning. For example, Smith believes strongly that educators need a deep understanding of the ways in which human growth is affected by culture, definitions of and models for multicultural education, learning style as influenced by culture, strategies for becoming culturally responsive educators, and the impact of racism and other forms of discrimination, as well as policies, on the achievement of all students. Smith's book is a powerful resource for educators in their growth as multicultural educators.

Smith added two more knowledge bases in 2001: (1) identifying and working with special needs students and (2) understanding international and global education (Huber-Warring, 2008). The additions illustrate the challenges of defining a specific set of knowledge bases, the changing nature of what constitutes important knowledge for educators to have, and the critical need to keep defining it.

Other educators have also worked to develop recommendations for knowledge bases that are essential to multicultural educators (Arends, 2015; Gay, 2010; Sleeter & Cornbleth, 2011). Moule (2011) writes eloquently about essential knowledge bases that include a deep understanding of racism and prejudice, privilege, culture and cultural differences, bias in the curriculum and classroom, child development, and racial identity issues. Another useful resource for considering knowledge bases important to educators is *Growing a Soul for Social Change: Building the Knowledge Base for Social Justice* (2008), edited by Tonya Huber-Warring. In a rich variety of chapters, the authors address the knowledge needed by educators to develop culturally responsive teaching and curriculum, international and global education, cultural identities and cultural contexts for human growth and development, and the kind of knowledge that can be gained through experience. The way in which Huber-Warring has organized the chapters into sections is grounded in Smith's (1998) 13 knowledge bases, again showing that key themes have emerged in defining important knowledge.

Gollnick and Chinn (2016) describe in great detail the foundational knowledge for multicultural educators. Their book is grounded in the firm belief that an understanding of and use of students' culture is the basis for multicultural education. They describe groups of cultural identities that affect student and teacher identity, including ethnicity and race, class and socioeconomic status, gender and sexual orientation, exceptionality, language, religion, geography, and age. For example, in discussing gender and sexual orientation, Gollnick and Chinn provide background knowledge on male and female differences, gender identity, sexual orientation, the women's movement, and sexism and gender discrimination. They then provide extensive opportunities for teacher reflection through guided experiences.

A Repertoire of Skills for Multicultural Educators

A multicultural educator possesses skills in a wide variety of instructional strategies, communicates effectively with students, makes the content meaningful for students, and establishes a rich classroom learning environment. A primary responsibility of all educators is to

---

Extended Explorations 2.1: Knowledge Bases for Multicultural Educators

Often, when confronted with having to consider the knowledge bases required of multicultural educators, these educators respond that their capacity in each area is somewhat limited because they weren't taught these areas. They state that they weren't prepared to move beyond a traditional, fairly limited perspective about knowledge. Reflect on Smith's (1998) list of 13 essential knowledge bases. Assess your own capacity in each of these areas. Develop a plan with specific actions for how you will enhance your capacity in the 13 knowledge bases.

provide equitable educational opportunities for all students to achieve at high levels. This means that new teachers need to be skilled in the use of research-based instructional strategies that will help them support all students in achieving at high levels. One way of addressing this is to make use of the work of Howard Gardner (2000, 2006, 2011) on multiple intelligences. His research showed that people are intelligent in different ways and that different kinds of intelligences beg different instructional strategies. More specifically, teachers need to use a wide variety of explicit instructional strategies and curriculum development approaches that make use of culture in order to be culturally proficient teachers. And they need to be provided time to work on multicultural curriculum development (Howe & Lisi, 1995; Lisi & Howe, 1999). To achieve **educational equity** and social justice, we must prepare culturally proficient teachers to work in culturally proficient schools (Robins, Lindsey, Lindsey, & Terrell, 2012).

Several models have been developed to support teachers in their development of a curriculum that is multicultural. Banks (2009) developed a model with four stages: (1) the contributions approach, (2) the ethnic additive approach, (3) the transformation approach, and (4) the decision-making and social action approach. Schools at the contributions level focus minimally on token representations of culture in the curriculum that are not connected to the curriculum. An example is celebrating Martin Luther King Day in February and ignoring Black history the rest of the year. In the additive approach, units of ethnic studies, such as a week on the Nazi Holocaust, are tacked onto an otherwise unchanged curriculum. Most schools are at these two levels since they require no restructuring of the curriculum.

At the third level—transformative—each subject is infused with ethnic content, and teaching strategies are increased to accommodate different cultural learning styles. The fourth stage of decision making and social action is similar in most models of multicultural education in that it focuses on infusing social change into the curriculum. Students are taught to be civic minded. A desire to improve society and work toward social justice is instilled.

Grant and Sleeter (2009) developed a model for multicultural education that includes five levels: (1) teaching the exceptional or culturally different, (2) human relations, (3) single-group studies, (4) education that is directed at reducing prejudice, and (5) education that is both multicultural and social reconstructionist. Both the Banks model and the Grant and Sleeter model were introduced in Chapter 1. It appears that the ultimate goal for most experts in the field is developing education models that prepare students to be socially responsible in a global and diverse society.

> **Extended Explorations 2.2: Dispositions**
>
> A particularly useful experience for educators, novice and experienced alike, is to reflect on their own attitudes, values, and beliefs about children, learning, teaching, diversity, equity, and so forth. This can be a daunting exercise. Fortunately, dispositions inventories have been developed in the field of multicultural education that can support educators in reflecting on their own capacity and perspectives. For example, you may try to locate Franklin Thompson's (2009) Multicultural Dispositions Index. Find an inventory of dispositions for educators, and take the inventory. Assess your own stance in terms of important dispositions for multicultural educators. Then develop a plan for enhancing your dispositions in specific areas.

Personal Qualities or Dispositions for Multicultural Educators

In terms of social justice, a multicultural educator values the diverse backgrounds of students and is deeply committed to helping them make a difference in society. The multicultural educator invests time and energy in getting to know each individual student, including his or her cultural background, and uses that information to establish a meaningful and sincere relationship with each student. Related to a deep knowledge base about culture is the fact that educators must be committed to eliminating bias, discrimination, and prejudice. Teachers need to examine their own attitudes so they can project positive attitudes toward and higher expectations for all students. When teachers have equal expectations for all students, there is more interracial friendship and interaction among students. A classroom climate of acceptance among students is related to increased student achievement, especially among minority students (Bennett, 2011). Teachers must be aware of their own prejudices and how those prejudices may contribute to lowering expectations for some students. Teachers must accommodate the differences among students and help all students achieve mastery without compromising the instructional content and standards.

A multicultural educator understands and appreciates the critical importance of social justice and educational equity and believes that understanding issues such as race, class, gender, and socioeconomic status is essential for teachers since it will inform what and how they teach (Adams & Bell, 2016).

LEARNING OBJECTIVE 2.2 Identify Professional Teaching Standards That Will Guide You in Becoming a Multicultural Educator

As you may have learned by this time in your preparation for becoming a teacher, standards are a very important part of the process. Standards are often a means of encapsulating the important knowledge, skills, and dispositions discussed in the previous section. Standards can be viewed as expectations of what a person—for example, a preK–12 student, a teacher, a school leader—needs to know and be able to do.

Sets of standards have been established by a variety of entities to guide the development of curriculum in schools, colleges, and universities. The Council for Accreditation of Educator Preparation has been one of the primary authors of standards to guide the preparation of teachers and school leaders, as well as for the examination and accreditation of education programs at the university level. An understanding of standards is important for educators, especially as they work to become multicultural educators.

Teaching demands rigorous training and ongoing education. The educator of today is highly skilled and held to demanding professional standards.

Comstock Images/Comstock/Thinkstock

Curriculum Standards as a Guide for Multicultural Education in Schools

Curriculum standards have been established for students in public preK–12 school settings for most, if not all, subject areas, and they are used to support the development of curriculum. While standards have been established by state-level offices, professional organizations, and independent collaborative bodies, at the national level, the CCSS have been established to provide a consistent and clear understanding of what students need to know and be able to do across educational settings and across states in the areas of mathematics and English/language arts. As of 2018, 42 states, the District of Columbia, four territories, and the Department of Defense Education Activity have adopted the CCSS as the standards to be used by public schools in mathematics and English/language arts.

Proponents of the CCSS believe that the standards will help close the nation's achievement gap. A major focus in the use of the standards is on persistence, or on supporting students in working through mistakes and coming to deeper understandings of important concepts. The standards are designed to promote equity by ensuring that all students are supported in achieving success. While experts in multicultural education (e.g., Sleeter, 2011) do believe in the value of standards, such as the CCSS, they caution that the starting point for the development of curriculum is a vision of a culturally relevant unit. Once the unit is developed, it is important to connect the unit directly to the relevant standards.

In addition to the CCSS for math and English/language arts, curriculum standards have been developed in other content areas. The Next Generation Science Standards (NGSS) is a state-led effort to develop standards to improve science education for all students. The work, initially completed in April 2013, was undertaken by the National Research Council and Achieve and has been supported by the Carnegie Corporation of New York. Individual states decide whether or not to use the NGSS. If a state decides to use the NGSS, it also determines whether or not to develop assessments that align with the standards. Believing in the critical importance of equitable learning opportunities, the National Research Council worked to develop research- and standards-based classroom strategies that teachers can use to ensure that the NGSS are applicable to all students.

Professional organizations have also developed sets of standards for what preK–12 students should know and be able to do. The National Council for the Social Studies (NCSS) is a professional association whose members include educators at the preK–12 levels as well as faculty in higher education in the fields of, among others, history, anthropology, political science, sociology, and psychology. In 1994, the NCSS developed a set of performance expectations for students in preK–12 grades. In 2010, the NCSS standards were revised. The result was the *National Curriculum Standards for Social Studies: A Framework for Teaching, Learning, and Assessment*. Included in that document is the chapter "Ten Themes of the National Curriculum Standards for the Social Studies: A Framework for Teaching, Learning, and Assessment." First among the 10 themes is culture and the expectation that social studies programs include opportunities for students to learn about culture and cultural diversity. In *Using the NCSS National Curriculum Standards for Social Studies: A Framework for Teaching, Learning, and Assessment to Meet State Social Studies Standards*, Michelle Herzog (2010) linked the use of the standards to effective teaching. Interestingly, Herzog believed that, with the newest set of social studies standards, the NCSS standards promote the teaching of essential principles of social studies, as opposed to the content addressed in most sets of standards. The 10 themes provide ways to organize knowledge important to social studies into meaningful and relevant learning experiences for students. The result is that students will acquire not only essential knowledge but also important higher order thinking skills and the disposition to be responsible members of society.

> **Extended Explorations 2.3: Learning Standards and Equity in Education**
>
> Locate the website for the CCSS. Select a content area of interest (e.g., literacy) and a grade level of interest. Look carefully at the standards for that particular area and grade level. Critique the standards in terms of how they address diverse learner needs, interests, cultural backgrounds, and so on. What conclusions can you draw from this critique about the potential for the CCSS to address diverse learner needs? In what ways do the standards hold promise for achieving equity in education and supporting all diverse learners in achieving at high levels? If they do not, suggest a new way to address the need for expectations about what learners should know and be able to do.

Professional Teaching Standards as a Guide for Multicultural Educators

Since the use of standards had proven to be very useful in directing the design of teaching and learning at the preK–12 levels, it was believed that the same approach would be useful for directing the learning experiences of preservice and in-service educators. Once again, different entities have developed standards or expectations for what teachers should know and be able to do.

Perhaps of most relevance to candidates who are preparing to become teachers are the standards developed by the Interstate New Teacher Assessment and Support Consortium

(InTASC, 2017), a program of the Council of Chief State School Officers. The InTASC is a consortium of state education agencies and national educational organizations dedicated to the reform of the preparation, licensing, and on-going professional development of teachers. The InTASC project created a set of 10 principles, or standards, as well as key indicators under each principle that reflect the knowledge, skills, and dispositions critical for new teachers. While each of the 10 principles is important for all multicultural educators, Principle or Standard 2 specifically speaks to the critical need for a teacher who "communicates verbally and nonverbally in ways that demonstrate respect for and responsiveness to the cultural backgrounds and differing perspectives learners bring to the learning environment" (InTASC, 2011, p. 12). In reading the standards, you will notice that each one contributes in its own way to an understanding of how teachers should be prepared to work effectively with diverse learners. The InTASC standards define what teachers need to know and be able to do regarding the learner and learning, content, instructional practice, and professional responsibility (Exercise 2.1). Teacher preparation institutions that commit to the pursuit of accreditation must use the InTASC standards as a basis for curriculum development in their programs.

EXERCISE 2.1

LOCATE THE SET OF INTASC STANDARDS ON THE INTERNET

Review the document at https://ccsso.org/resource-library/intasc-model-core-teaching-standards-and-learning-progressions-teachers-10. For each InTASC standard, reflect on what that standard means for you as a multicultural educator. What will you need to learn and be able to do specific to being an effective teacher with diverse student populations? Complete the matrix for this exercise about important knowledge, skills, and dispositions or qualities that you believe you will need to be competent in that particular standard.

Matrix to Use in Reflection on Important Knowledge, Skills, and Dispositions

InTASC Standard	Knowledge	Skills	Dispositions
1. Learner development			
2. Learner differences			
3. Learning environments			
4. Content knowledge			
5. Application of content			
6. Assessment			
7. Planning for instruction			
8. Instructional strategies			
9. Professional learning and ethical practices			
10. Leadership and collaboration			

The National Council for the Teaching of Mathematics (NCTM) has developed standards for the teaching of mathematics. *Principles and Standards for School Mathematics*, published by the NCTM in 2000, outlines the essential components of a high-quality school mathematics program. The NCTM standards are grounded in six principles. The first principle focuses on equity, stressing that excellence in mathematics education requires high expectations and strong support for all students. Furthermore, equity does not mean that every student receives the same type of instruction. It means that appropriately challenging content be included to promote access and attainment for all students.

For experienced educators, the National Board for Professional Teaching Standards (NBPTS) provides an assessment program to secure advanced professional certification in addition to their own state-level certification. The NBPTS developed five core propositions about teaching as well as sets of standards in 16 different subject areas. Proposition 1 (NBPTS, 2016) states that accomplished teachers are committed to their students and their learning. More specifically, this means that accomplished teachers believe that all children can learn, understand how children develop, respect cultural differences, and treat students equitably. Again, a deep understanding of and appreciation for culture appear to be at the core of effective teaching as defined by the NBPTS.

LEARNING OBJECTIVE 2.3 Describe Culture as the Core Element of Becoming a Multicultural Educator

Why Attend to Culture?

In reviewing the research about effective teachers and about multicultural educators, and in an analysis of the standards that support the professional development of educators, it is interesting to note a persistent theme throughout most of that work: the concept of culture. It appears time and time again that an effective teacher, a multicultural educator, and a teacher who meets the professional standards for teaching is a person who has a deep understanding of culture and is committed to using the culture of the students in the classroom to inform teaching and learning.

This is made clear through the seminal research on successful teachers of African American children conducted by Ladson-Billings (2009), who discovered four critical aspects of culturally relevant teaching. She found that successful teachers (a) reject the notion of "equity as sameness" (they see and value students' racial and ethnic differences), (b) encourage a community of learners, (c) hold a constructivist view about knowledge and the curriculum, and (d) focus on numeracy and literacy in meaningful ways.

Ladson-Billings (2009) and other education experts have found that the greater the gap between the child's culture and the school's culture, the greater the likelihood of failure or low student achievement. Conversely, the greater the overlap, the greater the likelihood of success or high student achievement.

This critical need for teachers to focus on students' culture is evident in the research and work of numerous professional organizations. For example, the Center for Research on Education, Diversity, and Excellence at the University of California–Berkeley Graduate School of Education developed *Five Standards of Effective Pedagogy* based on decades of research on diversity and education (Tharp, 2008). The standards represent generally accepted definitions of effective teaching among diverse student populations and include expectations that teachers will (1) work together with students, (2) develop language and literacy skills across the curriculum, (3) connect lessons to students' lives, (4) engage students in challenging lessons, and (5) emphasize learning through conversation as opposed to primarily lectures.

Effective educators know the important connections between a student's culture and their learning. Multicultural educators capitalize on cultural knowledge to enhance teaching and learning.

Ablestock.com/ablestock.com/Thinkstock

Demmert and Towner (2003) underscored the critical importance of teachers knowing and using the culture of their students to effect high levels of learning. In their research on Native American education, they found critical elements of "culturally based education." These elements include the understanding and use of Native languages, development of instructional strategies that use Native culture, development of curriculum that uses Native culture, and strong connections of the teachers to the Native community.

Roles and Responsibilities of Teachers in Using Culture

If the research appears compelling about the need for effective teachers to attend to culture, what are the specific roles and responsibilities of teachers regarding the use of culture? First, effective teachers make a commitment to learning about students' cultures—not only through holding celebrations of festivals and other special events but also through daily and ongoing conversations with students, reading, going into the community, and attending cultural events and courses. Effective multicultural educators also create an environment in which students believe that they can learn and want to engage in learning experiences that are meaningful and relevant (Gay, 2010; Ginsberg & Wlodkowski, 1995; Ladson-Billings, 2009; Sheets, 1995; Tharp & Gallimore, 1988). Effective multicultural educators create a culture of respect for students' cultures (Banks, 2009; Banks & Banks, 2015). Banks and Banks (2015) believe that teachers need to be very aware of how students see the teacher–student relationship and the extent to which students see teachers as caring about them.

Effective teachers also build bridges between content and students' prior understanding and knowledge (Ginsberg & Wlodkowski, 1995; Ladson-Billings, 2009). They do this through meaningful, culturally relevant activities and appropriate selection of instructional materials that link to students' culture and are bias free. Research indicates that when students' cultures are used, student academic achievement increases. Effective teachers seek out professional development that engages them in learning about culture and how to develop as culturally competent teachers.

Effective multicultural educators develop and use curriculum that reinforces and values the cultural knowledge of students. These educators know that a culturally responsive curriculum integrates cultural knowledge rather than adding it on in special lessons or units at special times of the academic year.

By being aware of their own cultural identities, teachers can encourage students to be knowledgeable about and proud of their cultural backgrounds. White teachers must understand how a life of privilege guides their teaching and that the lives of people of color are not the same (McIntosh, 1998). By having a deep understanding of our own lives, we are in a better position to appreciate the circumstances and lives of our students. Many monocultural teachers lack knowledge not only about their students' cultures but also about their own (Howard, 2006). With the proportion of people of color increasing in our nation to about 38% in 2025 and 47% in 2050, it is imperative that teachers be knowledgeable about issues of diversity (Irvine, 2003).

In addressing the critical importance of culture in being a multicultural educator, Geneva Gay (2010) described three key roles and responsibilities of teachers:

1. *Cultural organizers:* Teachers must recognize the role of cultural understanding in the classroom.

2. *Cultural mediators:* Teachers must create opportunities for students to be aware of and have a dialogue about cultural conflicts.

3. *Orchestrators of social contexts for learning:* Teachers must understand how culture affects learning.

Teachers who do not have a deep understanding of these critical roles and functions will miss important teaching opportunities in both racially monocultural and multicultural classrooms. Effectiveness will be diminished while shortchanging the learning potential of students. Furthermore, teachers will find that parents often need as much education as their children in that they do not see or ignore racist attitudes and behaviors (Van Ausdale & Feagin, 2001). Patricia Ramsey (2015) suggested developing a positive rapport around culture with parents by answering first, and then asking, questions such as these:

- Where are you from? How long have you lived in this community?

- How do you identify yourselves and your child?

- What groups do you as a family spend time with? Feel closest to?

- How are you teaching your child about his or her background?

- When you think about your racial, cultural, and class backgrounds, how have they influenced the values that you are teaching your child?

Information derived from these types of questions provides more insightful and useful information than the usual demographic questions asked in surveys. All students, regardless of their background and geographic location, must have a stronger knowledge of other cultures and peoples. In the twenty-first century, many of our business interactions are global in nature. To be competitive in the workplace, employees will be required to have a far greater knowledge of other countries and their habits and customs than they do now. A multicultural education is a commonsense idea in this new century, with new partners and new associations that are radically different from those of the past (Lisi & Howe, 1999).

LEARNING OBJECTIVE 2.4 Outline a Four-Step Model for the Professional Development of Multicultural Educators

To understand the application of theory, it often helps to view it in terms of conceptual models. Numerous models of multicultural education have been introduced in this book (Banks, 2009; Bennett, 2014; Grant & Sleeter, 2009). This section will attempt to paint a picture of what the various stages are that a person might go through to become a multicultural educator. This model has been developed based on an understanding of how teachers develop as professional educators, of the knowledge base and skills that are needed to be an effective teacher, and of the school improvement process.

It is first important to understand that although there may be a readily identifiable starting point for this journey, there may not be a clear end. In other words, to use a common expression in education, becoming a multicultural educator is a lifelong journey. The pursuit of knowledge and skills may never end. It might help to view this learning process as a continuous cycle as opposed to continuum with a beginning and ending.

Becoming a Multicultural Educator

Howe and Lisi (1995) developed a model for the professional growth of educators in multicultural education. The model indicates that to become an effective multicultural educator, teachers must move through four areas (Figure 2.1). The four stages are part of a cyclical process that includes knowledge, awareness, skills, and action.

First, educators must have a sound *knowledge* of other cultures and perspectives Second, educators must develop an *awareness* of the reality of the bias, prejudice, and discrimination faced by others and an acknowledgment of their own biases. Third is the need to develop the *skills* required to teach to diverse learning styles and cultures. And fourth is the need to develop a lifelong personal *action* plan to increase one's knowledge, skills, and dispositions around diversity and to work to develop an institutional action plan to support education that is multicultural.

Becoming a skilled teacher involves more than mastering subject matter. The process requires developing personal awareness, understanding of the influence of culture, and effective culturally relevant teaching strategies.

iStock/ECFutcher

- *Knowledge:* When confronted with questions about their knowledge of cultures or groups of people other than those with whom they identify, educators are often amazed to realize the limited exposure they have had to learning such information. To become resources for our students, we need to commit to expanding our knowledge base about people who are different from us. This includes knowledge of beliefs and values, communication and interaction patterns, histories, attitudes, and behaviors. This is a lifelong effort.

FIGURE 2.1   **A Model for Professional Development in Multicultural Education**

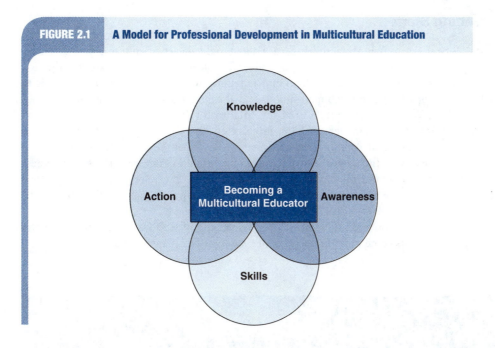

- *Awareness:* Education is value laden and embedded with conscious and unconscious values. Often, as educators, we are not fully aware of all the assumptions, beliefs, and values under which we operate. To be able to work with diverse students, we must first examine our own beliefs, biases, and prejudices and become aware of our own cultural essence. Then we can begin to become more aware of the value of the various dimensions of diversity in ourselves and others. Sensitivity, understanding, tolerance, and compassion about differences are key constructs.

- *Skills:* Working effectively with those who are different means learning new skills, including communication; lesson planning; integration of knowledge about motivation, diversity, and multiple intelligences; and so forth. We need to learn gender-neutral language that is inclusive and how to intercept statements and actions that are prejudicial. Teachers must also learn the various ways of infusing multiculturalism into the curriculum and pedagogical strategies. There are a variety of lesson plan formats that can guide teachers in developing lessons that offer multiple perspectives or focus on building positive regard for other dimensions of culture. There are different ways to teach that can offer a more responsive approach to educating students of different cultures. Learning the skills, including teaching strategies and communication styles, is important to becoming a culturally responsive educator.

- *Action:* Finally, teachers must learn how to develop individual and organizational action plans in order to implement education that is multicultural in their classroom and in the school. Teachers must first learn how they can get started with becoming more multicultural. They must also learn how to develop support networks and collaborations with other teachers. Strategies must be found also to ensure that institutional supports will arise.

With the new knowledge comes awareness. This leads to a change or acquisition of new skills. Ideally, an action plan is formed to complete the cycle.

Getting Started

It will be easier to help your students learn about and value their culture if you first delve deeply into your own heritage, beliefs, and values. People of color often remark that the day-to-day bias they encounter forces them into a lifelong awareness of their race and ethnicity. Caucasian or White people do not often have that experience of being reminded that they are White. White educators such as Peggy McIntosh (1998), Gary Howard (2006), and Carl Grant and Christine Sleeter (2009; also Sleeter, 2001) have addressed the importance of White teachers understanding the unearned privilege that they live with—that the color of their skin affords them benefits over people of color in a White-majority society. These educators talk about the importance of understanding what it is to be White. The task then is for White teachers to discover and understand not only their culture but also how the cultures of their students of color affect teaching and learning.

It is when we come to a full knowledge and valuing of who we are that we can better help our students come to that same level of awareness and pride in their heritage.

REFLECTING BACK

This chapter is written to introduce a model for becoming a multicultural educator. As you have read, multicultural educators possess significant and important knowledge and skills that will support diverse learners. At times, the process of becoming a multicultural educator may seem overwhelming. However, a starting point is to realize where you are. Then you can work to set meaningful goals for your own learning.

Questions

1. Did you have experiences in your schooling that made learning difficult? How did that make you feel? How did it affect your grades?

2. Imagine yourself as a persecuted racial, ethnic, or gender minority student trying to attain an education. How might your identity affect your ability to succeed?

3. Select 3 of the 10 InTASC standards, and write a brief reflection about how each of them is influencing your preparation as a multicultural educator. Also, write about why you chose these 3 standards. Reflect specifically on your capacity in InTASC Standard 2. How do you see that students differ in their approaches to learning?

How would you create instructional opportunities for these diverse learners?

4. What new aspects of your culture have you been able to discover?

5. What are your preferred modes of learning, based on your cultural upbringing?

6. What have you learned about specific teaching strategies that would respond to members of other cultures?

7. Investigate through an Internet search the concept of learning styles linked to culture. How might this information affect how you design learning experiences for diverse students?

8. Based on what you have read in this chapter, how would you rate yourself in your development toward becoming a multicultural educator?

9. Of the four components in the model for becoming a multicultural educator, in what stage(s) are you strongest and why? What contributed to your strengths in that area?

10. In which areas do you think you need to do the most work and why?

PROFILES IN MULTICULTURAL EDUCATION

CARL A. GRANT

© Mingfong Jan

Carl A. Grant is the Hoefs-Bascom Professor of Teacher Education in the Department of Curriculum and Instruction at the University of Wisconsin–Madison. He is a former classroom teacher and administrator and has spent time in England as a Fulbright Scholar.

In 1990, the Association of Teacher Educators selected Dr. Grant as one of 70 Leaders in Teacher Education. In 1997, he received the School of Education Distinguished Achievement Award from the University of Wisconsin–Madison. In 2001, he received the G. Pritchy Smith Multicultural Educator Award from the National Association for Multicultural Education (NAME) and the Angela Davis Race, Gender, and Class Award from the Race, Gender, and Class Project. His book *Global Constructions of Multicultural Education: Theories and Realities* (2001) received the Philip C. Chinn Multicultural Book Award from NAME.

In addition to his scholarly work, Dr. Grant is perhaps best known for being instrumental in his role as president of NAME from 1993 to 1999. During his tenure, he helped NAME establish itself as a national and international presence, opening an office in Washington, D.C., hiring its first executive director, developing a professional journal, and nurturing an annual conference on multicultural education, which was attended by top scholars and multicultural educators from around the world. Dr. Grant is well recognized for his work with numerous universities and several publishers of preK–12 books to help infuse multicultural education into their programs.

Among Dr. Grant's most important contributions to the field is that he has brought multicultural education to the forefront of modern education. He has mentored many in the field today and continues to contribute his time and talents in the interest of educational equity and social justice. Dr. Grant informs the teacher candidates, graduate students, second-generation multicultural education scholars, and teachers with whom he has worked about the "gifts"—commitment, knowledge, disposition, experiences, and so on—they bring to the field of multicultural education. He informs them about the challenges (and rewards) of being a multicultural educator—that it is very hard work and it is necessary for them to have a philosophical vision and a plan of action for making certain that social justice (i.e., distributive equality and equity and cultural recognition) is a real thing in their classrooms and schools. His most persuasive argument is to tell teacher candidates that they have—perhaps unknown or little known to them—a personal, almost selfish reason to want to be multicultural educators. Multicultural education will make their instruction much more intellectual and culturally engaging and academically enriching, and it will help them understand the real reason why learning is dynamic and why both students and teachers must be lifelong learners.

CASE STUDY
SCHOOL ISN'T LIKE IT USED TO BE

Key Issues to Be Explored in the Case

1. The critical need to use students' culture in the design of learning experiences

2. Attention to the research into and standards for effective teaching

3. Ways to enhance teacher understanding about culture and effective teaching

In my role inspecting inner-city schools, I was accustomed to seeing drab, impoverished schools, attended by the poorest students in the city, almost all of them children of color. Many of these inner-city schools lack libraries that are rich in resources and have little, if any, outdoor playground space. In several cases, students use outdated textbooks that may have been used by their parents. School supplies, teaching materials, and technology are limited. Teachers resort to using recycled paper, boxes, and other materials scrounged from their own homes or donated by corporations or local merchants.

Resources aside, however, if teachers have been well prepared to meet the learning needs of the diverse students in today's society, they would be knowledgeable about and capable of creating meaningful learning experiences for each student. Unfortunately, with few resources at their command, scant opportunities to work with colleagues to develop rich and meaningful learning experiences, and little professional training in how to address the learning needs of diverse students, teachers often resort to creating a teaching and learning environment similar to what they may have experienced themselves as learners. This type of learning environment was more often than not teacher directed, with students sitting in rows, ready to accept the information that was provided to them.

On that particular day, as I approached the entrance to one of the schools, the dark skies outside and the drizzling rain added to my sense of despair. Inside, I was led by the principal from one sparsely equipped classroom with mismatched desks and chairs to another. The enthusiasm of the teachers and the excited looks on the children's faces, however, told me that some good teaching and learning were happening there. Near the end of the tour, led by an anxious principal trying to show off her school in the best light, we entered the last classroom. It reminded me of the scene from the movie *The Wizard of Oz* when Dorothy and her trio of friends left the dark forest and entered a field of bright flowers basking in the brilliant sunshine. This classroom was awash in colors and almost cluttered with books, toys, crafts, board games, and other learning materials. The walls were adorned with art and posters depicting hopeful, multicultural faces. Signs everywhere proclaimed popular character-building sayings. Signs written in crayon showed off the good deeds or academic successes of each child. Two parent volunteers were in the room. Small groups of students working together were scattered throughout the classroom. The crowning sight was a mini computer lab—three computers surrounded by excited children, all engaged in the lessons on the screens.

Some children stood up to greet me. Others ran to hug the principal. The teacher waited until she was finished giving directions to a table of students and then walked over to me, offering a warm handshake and a huge smile. Prompted by the principal, who declined to accept credit for this marvelous classroom, the teacher quietly explained the purpose of each educational activity occurring in the classroom. She humbly accepted the effusive praise I gave her and the principal. Near the end of the visit, remembering the bureaucratic role that I was supposed to be playing, I started asking detailed questions about how the teacher had been able to create such an engaging learning environment. The teacher stood straight and calmly, simply replied, "I don't have a choice! This classroom is for each and every student here."

Discussion Questions

1. What evidence exists in this case that the teacher, in fact, is making use of students' culture?

2. What role does the principal appear to have played in this case? What else could the principal do to make sure that the teaching and learning in this classroom are culturally responsive?

3. Is it apparent that the teacher is adhering to teaching standards? Why or why not?

4. In what ways is this teacher demonstrating culturally responsive teaching? In what ways could the teaching be enhanced?

CHAPTER SUMMARY

2.1 Define the characteristics of an effective multicultural educator

There are distinct differences between an educator who is steeped in more traditional approaches to teaching and learning and a multicultural educator. These differences can be ascribed to differences in essential knowledge, skills, and dispositions. Specifically, a multicultural educator

- has a broad and deep understanding of different cultures and how culture affects teaching and learning;

- attends to standards about teaching, since many sets of standards guide the preparation of effective educators, as well as the work they do in the classroom;

- understands, appreciates, and uses students' cultural backgrounds;

- is aware of his or her personal cultural history and how it affects teaching;

- is aware of the cultural history of her or his students and how it affects their learning;

- is knowledgeable about and skilled in particular approaches to instruction, curriculum, and assessment;

- uses multiple teaching strategies to reach all students and support them in developing to their fullest potential;

- is knowledgeable about numerous useful models of a multicultural curriculum, because finding one that reflects the teacher's personal orientation while supporting the purposes of a multicultural education is important; and

- understands a model that can guide the development of a multicultural educator and includes knowledge, awareness, skills, and action. If an educator is committed to being the strongest multicultural educator in the interests of all children, that educator will probably continue to do work and develop in each of these components throughout his or her professional lifetime.

2.2 Identify professional teaching standards that will guide you in becoming a multicultural educator

Accomplished teachers believe that all children can learn, understand how children develop, respect cultural differences, and treat students equitably. A deep understanding of and appreciation for culture appear to be at the core of effective teaching as defined by the NBPTS.

An effective multicultural teacher "communicates verbally and nonverbally in ways that demonstrate respect for and responsiveness to the cultural backgrounds and differing perspectives learners bring to the learning environment" (InTASC, 2017).

2.3 Describe culture as the core element of becoming a multicultural educator

Effective multicultural educators know and use the culture of their students to effect high levels of learning. Effective multicultural educators also create an environment in which students believe that they can learn and want to engage in learning experiences that are meaningful and relevant. Effective multicultural educators develop and use curriculum that reinforces and values the cultural knowledge of students.

2.4 Outline a four-step model for the professional development of multicultural educators

First, educators must develop an *awareness* of the reality of bias, prejudice, and discrimination faced by others and an acknowledgment of their own biases. Second, educators must have a sound *knowledge* of other cultures and perspectives. Third is the need to develop the *skills* required to teach to diverse learning styles and cultures. And fourth is the need to develop a lifelong personal *action* plan to increase one's knowledge, skills, and dispositions around diversity and to work to develop an institutional action plan to support education that is multicultural.

KEY TERMS

behaviorist 41

curriculum standards 46

educational equity 45

ethnic 43

multiple perspectives 42

APPLICATION: ACTIVITIES AND EXERCISES

Individual

1. Create your own model for becoming a multicultural educator. What steps or components are important to your own development? Explain your rationale for creating the model you have developed. How does your model reflect the teacher standards you have read about? (Learning Objectives 2.2 and 2.4)

2. Select some of the qualities of several teachers with whom you are familiar who embody the best qualities of a multicultural educator. Develop a composite portrait of a multicultural educator, making use of those qualities. (Learning Objective 2.1)

3. Begin a personal family history project about your family's cultural background:

   • Construct a family tree.

   • Interview close and distant relatives about family history.

   • Read a book, view a movie, or watch a documentary about your culture.

   • Do all of the above with someone of another culture. (Learning Objective 2.3)

Group

1. As a group, come up with a common model of multicultural education. How have you improved on other models? Were there any strong agreements or strong disagreements on the components among your group? (Learning Objective 2.4)

2. In small groups, discuss each individual's strengths as well as weaknesses regarding the person's knowledge or expertise in cultural areas (e.g., race, ethnicity, religion, gender, sexual orientation, class, ability). Work as a team to develop goal statements about which areas of culture each person would like to deepen his or her knowledge in. (Learning Objectives 2.1, 2.2)

Self-Assessment

1. Fill in the right-hand column with your responses to the prompts in the left-hand column.

The areas of diversity that I am most comfortable with are . . . (e.g., race, gender)	
The areas of diversity that I am most uncomfortable with are . . . (e.g., race, gender)	
The cultures that I am most familiar with are . . .	
The cultures that I am most unfamiliar with are . . .	
My greatest strengths that I now have as a multicultural educator are . . .	
My greatest need areas that I now have as a multicultural educator are . . .	

ANNOTATED RESOURCES

BUENO Center for Multicultural Education

www.http://buenocenter.org

Since 1976, the BUENO Center for Multicultural Education has been an integral part of the School of Education at the University of Colorado–Boulder. Through a comprehensive range of research, training, and service projects, the center strongly promotes quality education with an emphasis on cultural pluralism. The center is deeply committed to facilitating equal educational opportunities for cultural and language minority students.

The Center for Multilingual, Multicultural Research

www.cmmr.usc.edu/

The Center for Multilingual, Multicultural Research is an organized research unit at the University of Southern California that facilitates the research collaboration, dissemination, and professional development activities of faculty, students, and others across the School of Education, university, and broader community. Faculty of the Rossier School of Education developed the center in the spring of 1983 as a result of deliberations of the Dean's Task Force for Bilingual Cross-Cultural Education. The center provides a base for those interested in multilingual education, English as a second language and foreign language instruction, and multicultural education and related areas, and the opportunity to come together for research and program collaboration.

Get the tools you need to sharpen your study skills. SAGE edge offers a robust online environment featuring an impressive array of free tools and resources. Access practice quizzes, eFlashcards, video, and multimedia at **edge.sagepub.com/howe3e**

Section I Assessment

Background

Major Assessment 1: Develop a Platform of Beliefs

The following major assessment involves integrating your knowledge and skills around defining multicultural education and being a multicultural educator.

You will write a platform of beliefs about teaching and learning. Your platform should be grounded in your growing understanding of teaching and learning, as well as the knowledge base about teaching and learning. You will also describe personal strengths and challenges as an educator in building an educational environment that reflects your beliefs.

In assessing your own strengths and challenge areas, include an analysis of the findings from the assessment instruments and exercises that are included in the previous chapter. You may also access additional assessment instruments.

Include in your platform the following sections:

1. Introduction

2. Your platform of beliefs about teaching and learning. Some essential questions that might be addressed in your platform are these:

   - What do you believe is the purpose of education?

   - What is the role of the teacher?

   - What should be taught (curriculum)?

   - How do people learn?

   - How do you view students as learners?

   - Who controls the curriculum in schools?

   - Whose knowledge is important to include?

   - Are state standards and tests desirable?

   - What is the impact of standardized testing on learning?

   - How do issues of race, class, and gender influence what you do?

   - What is your definition of effective teaching?

   - Who and what have influenced your beliefs (e.g., people, experiences, readings)?

   - What is the impact of your beliefs on teaching and learning for diverse students?

Make specific and clear connections between your platform and course readings and discussions.

3. Personal strengths and challenges in advancing a school vision of learning; promoting the success of all students; responding to diverse student interests and needs; understanding and responding to social, economic, legal, and cultural contexts

4. Personal goals (knowledge, skills, dispositions) that you will be working on in the future

5. Conclusions

SECTION II

KNOWLEDGE

3 Historical Perspectives on a Multicultural America

https://digitalcollections.nypl.org/items/
510d47da-d8d7-a3d9-e040-e00a18064a99

Immigrants seated on long benches, Main Hall, U.S. Immigration Station.

Learning Objectives

In this chapter, you will learn about the history of the United States and the civil rights events that shaped our nation, from a multicultural perspective. Much of what has been traditionally taught in schools minimizes or ignores totally the contributions and struggles of women, people of color, and other marginalized groups. You will learn, too, about the political struggles and legislative hurdles that needed to be overcome in order to achieve the equity that is in place today.

Through your study of and work on this chapter, you will be able to do the following:

3.1 Describe the founding and settling of this country

3.2 Explain the historical perspectives of peoples of the United States

3.3 Describe key events in the civil rights timeline

3.4 Summarize key legislation affecting education

America is perhaps the most multicultural of countries. People from around the world have found their way to our shores seeking a better life for themselves and for their children (Banks, 2009; Gollnick & Chinn, 2013). Unless you are a Native American, you are an immigrant or the descendant of **immigrants**. As Ronald Takaki (1993, 1998a, 1998b, 2001) wrote in his great works, the histories of our families often have much in common: escaping poverty and oppression, overcoming great obstacles to arrive here, and then living the often challenging experiences of strangers in a new land.

This chapter is a snapshot of key events and perspectives not commonly taught. Insights on major issues will be offered, along with suggestions for a focus in the classroom. This chapter will tell the stories of how this country was settled. These stories are not always pleasant. Racism, prejudice, discrimination, anti-immigrant sentiment, nativism, homophobia, sexism, anti-Semitism, and other hateful acts and attitudes have stained our history. This chapter will provide timelines of key demographic movements and the evolution of laws that protect us all. But most important, despite the struggles, we are a nation full of vibrant cultures. Our diversity is our strength.

Despite being one of the greatest countries in the world, America is haunted by the enduring shame of how it has treated its native peoples, people of color, immigrants, women, and other groups unfortunate enough to be targeted (Banks, 2009; Bigelow & Peterson, 2003; Deloria, 1979; Gollnick & Chinn, 2013; Loewen, 2008). As educators, we are obligated to ensure that our students learn the true history of our nation in order to stem the ongoing racism, sexism, homophobia, and other attitudes and acts of intolerance that linger (Au, 2014; Delpit, 2006; Derman-Sparks, 2000; Gollnick & Chinn, 2013; Howard, 1999). In this chapter, the stories of many groups of people will be shared, including the struggles and triumphs of these groups.

> Pit race against race, religion against religion, prejudice against prejudice. Divide and conquer! We must not let that happen here.
>
> —Eleanor Roosevelt, American politician, diplomat, and activist (1884–1962)

CASE STUDY
COMING TO AMERICA

Immigration patterns have changed dramatically. Refugees escaping war have been challenging the resolve and capacity of the United States and other countries. Afghanistan, Iraq, Syria, south-east Turkey, Yemen, Libya, Somalia, Sudan, Nigeria, and other countries have all experienced a mass exodus of people seeking safety in new lands. They bring with them their children who must adapt to a new culture and learn a new language, while attempting to deal with the trauma they have experienced in their former homelands.

The demands on the education system have also increased. Having transitioned from agricultural and assembly-line industries into a global, digital, and computer-driven economy, our society demands different skill sets of graduates. The advent of social media, inexpensive cell phones, and other electronic devices has changed our lives in so many ways.

The family structure has changed as well. With the need for two-income families, the prevalence of single-parent homes, and a high divorce rate have come additional problems for schools. Teachers are being asked for higher credentials, more degrees, and specialized training. And the No Child Left Behind legislation drastically changed the business of education. Therefore, various student experiences, cultures, languages, beliefs, and other differences face today's teachers. And facing the students is a rapidly changing, multicultural workplace.

Your Perspectives on the Case

1. How do you think that teaching has changed in the past 25 years? 50 years?

2. What skills must a teacher of today have that were not as critical during the middle of the past century.

3. What must teachers know about the cultures and backgrounds of their students?

THINKING AHEAD

There is an untold history of the United States—one that is not found prominently in textbooks. In this chapter, we will explore the history and settling of this country to see another reality—that belonging to non-European Americans. It will give us the background to understand better and serve all our students. Furthermore, we will review key civil rights milestones and the subsequent legislation that resulted. To prepare yourself for this journey, consider the following questions:

1. How much do you know of your own family's journey to this country?

2. How do you explain the numerous injustices against peoples that have occurred over the years? What events are most significant for you?

3. What legislation do you think has been most impactful?

LEARNING OBJECTIVE 3.1 Describe the Founding and Settling of This Country

When you stand in the Library of Congress in Washington, D.C., you are in the midst of a massive collection of books that represents the collective knowledge and culture of America. An alien coming from Mars and spending several years reading the books in the library would gain a perspective of what kind of country this is—our civilization, our values, and our beliefs. These books represent the kind of people we are.

Now ask yourself, "Who wrote most of these books, many dating back to the White settlement of the country?"

The correct answer is, "wealthy White men, mostly landowners." The reason is that for many years, women and people of color and people who were not affluent lacked the means, opportunity, or even the legal right to write and publish.

Now, if White men have written the majority of the books, this mythical person from Mars is reading stories primarily from the perspective of White men. Imagine if the majority of the books had been written by White women (or African American women or Native American women or . . .), would our culture and civilization be different? Many would argue, "Yes." If the majority of people in Congress were White women, instead of White men, would our country be run differently? Many would argue, "Yes."

Whoever has the opportunity to write the books has the ability to influence a culture. It is natural for anyone writing a book to offer his or her perspective—biased, impartial, or otherwise. Authors such as Ronald Takaki (1993, 1998a, 1998b, 2001), Howard Zinn (2003), James Loewen (2000, 2008), Helen Zia (2001), and James Banks (2009) have offered the untold narratives of the history of this country. They tell these stories from the perspectives of those who were not the mainstream authors or interpreters of historical events.

When Columbus arrived in (not discovered) the "New World" in 1492, there were already millions of inhabitants present. Taylor (2002) estimates that there were anywhere between 8.4 million and 112.5 million people living on the continent. This chapter will go on to discuss the various waves of immigration to this country. Each group of peoples brought with them the richness of their cultures to add to and strengthen a multicultural America. The founding of this country therefore took place over many years aided by the contributions of all peoples.

This section is not meant to be a comprehensive or an exhaustive history or social studies review but rather an opportunity to read a brief history from other perspectives. Teachers must educate students on the thoughts and beliefs of underrepresented people and encourage students to uncover the great injustices in our history. This leads to enhanced understanding and gives students insight into why others may see things differently.

Race as a Biological or Social Construct

Before we proceed further, it is important to discuss the concept of "race." A critical question is whether race is based on valid biological determinants or arbitrary social definitions (Banks, 2009; Gollnick & Chinn, 2013). Traditionally, one's race was said (by anthropologists and geneticists) to be determined by differences such as skin color, physical features, language, and nationality. For example, if a person had dark skin, a wide nose, kinky hair, and ancestors who came from Africa, he or she was most likely classified as being "Negro" or Black.

Unfortunately, categorizing people into races is not a precise science, and such classification may have done more harm than good because of stigmas against certain skin colors. Conservative Supreme Court justice Clarence Thomas and actor/activist Danny Glover are both "Black" men, yet they are miles apart in their political and social perspectives. Because of assaults by White slave owners, many African Americans in this country have European American blood. Attempts to ascribe social, psychological, and behavioral characteristics based on skin color are increasingly meaningless.

Defining people by their ethnicity is more accurate and useful and can be defined by indices such as the common language, customs, and characteristics of a group (Banks, 2009; Gollnick & Chinn, 2013; Nieto & Bode, 2018). A person may be European American as a racial category, while being Italian or Irish by ethnicity.

In this chapter, the categories established in the 1997 *Revisions to the Standards for the Classification of Federal Data on Race and Ethnicity* by the U.S. Office of Management and Budget (OMB) will be used for the sake of explaining how various groups of people arrived in this country and the contributions of such groups. The OMB has set categories of identities for people based on, among other things, race and ethnicity.

The OMB's definitions of several races are as follows:

- *American Indian or Alaska Native:* A person having origins in any of the original peoples of North and South America (including Central America) and who maintains tribal affiliation or community attachment

Wikimedia Commons/Jsalsman

"Leaving their homes and villages, they crossed the ocean only to endure confinement in these barracks. Conquering frontiers and barriers, they pioneered a new life by the Golden Gate." (Eddie Ngoot Ping Chin) Monument near U.S. Immigration Station at Angel Island.

- *Asian:* A person having origins in any of the original peoples of the Far East, Southeast Asia, or the Indian subcontinent, for example, Cambodia, China, India, Japan, Korea, Malaysia, Pakistan, the Philippine Islands, Thailand, and Vietnam

- *Black or African American:* A person having origins in any of the Black racial groups of Africa. Terms such as *Haitian* or *Negro* can be used in addition to *Black* or *African American.*

- *Native Hawaiian or Other Pacific Islander:* A person having origins in any of the original peoples of Hawaii, Guam, Samoa, or other Pacific Islands

- *White:* A person having origins in any of the original peoples of Europe, the Middle East, or North Africa

The OMB definition of one particular ethnic group is as follows:

- *Hispanic or Latino:* A person of Cuban, Mexican, Puerto Rican, South or Central American, or other Spanish culture or origin, regardless of race. The term *Spanish origin* can be used in addition to *Hispanic* or *Latino*

Why classify people at all based on how they look? Some of the reasoning comes from botanists or scientists who felt compelled to create such differentiations—some for valid research purposes, others to discredit certain races. The government uses categories to identify people based on race for legal and political reasons—to rectify past and prevent employment discrimination, for example. Although such purposes may be legitimate, the concept is under scrutiny.

With the past U.S. Census in 2010, the government attempted to be more accurate in defining race and to allow for more discrete classifications (U.S. Census Bureau, 2011). A growing issue is of biracial categories and the feeling that such classifications do more harm than good. Another issue is how ethnically Hispanic or Latino people identify themselves racially.

Population projections from the U.S. Census Bureau (2012c) indicate that the U.S. population will be much more racially and ethnically diverse by the year 2060. The non-Hispanic White population will reach a peak in 2024, at 199.6 million, but unlike other race or ethnic groups, its population will decrease by nearly 20.6 million from 2024 to 2060. The Hispanic population, in the meantime, will more than double to 128.8 million in 2060 when nearly one in three U.S. residents will be Hispanic. The Black population will increase to 61.8 million, going from 13.1% to 14.7% of the population. Asian Americans will more than double to 34.4 million, going from 5.1% to 8.2%. American Indians and Alaska Natives will increase by more than half to 6.3 million, going from 1.2% to 1.5%. Native Hawaiian and Other Pacific Islanders are expected to nearly double, from 706,000 to 1.4 million. People who identify themselves as being of two or more races are projected to more than triple, from 7.5 million to 26.7 million. By 2043, the United States is projected to become a majority–minority nation for the first time. The non-Hispanic White population will remain the largest single group, but no group will make up a majority.

Racial categorization brings with it issues that must be addressed in an educational setting. The most important issue is the false assumption that all people within a defined category act, think, and believe the same way. The increasing number of biracial people with a blend of cultures defies easy characterization, for example. In addition, income, education level, and social status often blur distinctions one might try to make on the basis of race.

LEARNING OBJECTIVE 3.2 Explain the Historical Perspectives of Peoples of the United States

Texts that provide a more complete coverage of the multicultural history of our country (e.g., Banks, 2009; Loewen, 2000, 2008; Takaki, 1993, 1998a, 1998b, 2001; Zinn, 2003) are rich resources. Often, they reveal stories untold by traditional history books and different perspectives from those found there. A multicultural educator can use these resources to better understand students, to incorporate their histories into the curriculum, to inform culturally responsive teaching strategies, and to prepare all students for life in a diverse world. The history, experiences, cultures, and perspectives of the various groups that make up this country are a rich source of information that need to be understood by all educators. Often untold, generally unknown, the challenges, as well as the triumphs, need to be included in the formal curriculum. What follows is a brief review of multicultural history.

Native Americans

Many theories abound about who were the first peoples to inhabit North America. The Vikings, the Spanish, and the Chinese have all been proposed as at least voyagers to the continent. People have been estimated to have inhabited this continent as long ago as 30,000 years (Parfit, 2000).

It can be reliably stated that the first populous indigenous peoples were the Native Americans or Indians (Parfit, 2000). The indigenous peoples of North and South America (Table 3.1) had rich histories, vibrant communities, and strong social structures and civilizations that existed long before Columbus arrived. Yet this history is relatively unknown (Bigelow & Peterson, 2003).

The history of the first Americans is one of both glory and tragedy, the latter a string of broken treaties, wholesale slaughter, and other conquering atrocities committed by invading Europeans. Few people need to be convinced that the treatment of Native Americans has been a great stain on this nation. At the time of the arrival of Columbus in 1492, the great Indian nations numbered up to 75 million and spread across both North and South America. Through war, disease, and starvation, that number of North Americans was reduced to, according to some estimates, 400,000 by 1900 (Thornton, 1987).

In any discussion of who discovered America, there is the debate about Christopher Columbus, whether he was a hero or a villain. While we now recognize the fallacy of the statement that "Columbus discovered the Americas," since other peoples had already "discovered" the Americas and had been living there for centuries, Columbus can be recognized for mapping and charting previously uncharted territories. However, the legacy of Columbus as a hero must be reexamined and explored in light of his role in the beginning of a national tragedy (Bigelow & Peterson, 2003). *Lies My Teacher Told Me* by James Loewen (2008) and *A People's History of the United States: 1492–Present* by Howard Zinn (2003) both give detailed and graphic accounts of the horrendous experiences of Native Americans at the hands of Columbus and other European settlers. The story of Columbus as a brave explorer must be balanced by a sharing of the atrocities committed by him: enslavement of native peoples; wholesale massacres of natives, including women and children; and the spreading of disease (Bigelow & Peterson, 2003).

In the decades and centuries following the explorations of Columbus and others, and as Europeans came to settle in the Americas in increasing numbers, more than 400 treaties and executive orders were eventually written to contain Native Americans and take their land.

Extended Explorations 3.1: Critique of Categorization Practices

Over the years, there has been an increasing blurring of the lines when it comes to determining a person's race. Hispanics are no longer considered a race, for example. Many individuals marry into other races. The number of individuals identifying themselves as biracial has increased. Is it time, perhaps, that we stop categorizing people by race? Develop a critique that describes the pros and cons of doing so.

TABLE 3.1   Native American Population: Largest American Indian and Alaska Native Tribes According to Number of Self-Identified Members, by Race and Tribal Group: 2000

Tribal Group	Total	American Indian/Alaska Native Alone	American Indian/Alaska Native in Combination With One or More Other Races
	4,119,301	2,475,956	1,643,345
American Indian tribes			
Cherokee	729,533	299,862	429,671
Navajo	298,197	275,991	22,206
Latin American Indian[a]	180,940	106,204	74,736
Choctaw	158,774	96,901	61,873
Sioux	153,360	113,066	40,294
Chippewa	149,669	108,637	41,032
Apache	96,833	64,977	31,856
Blackfeet	85,750	31,462	54,288
Iroquois[b]	80,822	47,530	33,292
Pueblo	74,085	63,060	11,025
Alaska Native tribes			
Eskimo	54,761	47,337	7,424
Tlingit-Haida	22,365	15,884	6,481
Alaska Athabascan	18,838	15,335	3,503
Aleut	16,978	12,773	4,205

Source: U.S. Census Bureau (2002).

Note: "Alone" refers to respondents who selected American Indian/Alaska Native and not any other race category. "In combination with one or more other races" refers to respondents who selected American Indian/Alaska Native and one or more other race categories. Both "alone" and "in combination" include persons of Hispanic ethnicity. Tribal groupings compiled by the Census Bureau do not necessarily correspond with federally recognized tribes. Self-identified membership does not necessarily correspond with official membership in a federally recognized tribe. Tribal populations do not sum to totals because totals include American Indian/Alaska Native populations from many additional tribes. In addition, the numbers by American Indian and Alaska Native tribal groupings do not sum to the total population because tribal groupings are tallies of the number of American Indian and Alaska Native responses rather than the number of American Indian and Alaska Native respondents. Respondents reporting several American Indian and Alaska Native tribes are counted several times. For example, a respondent reporting "Apache and Blackfeet" would be included in the Apache as well as in the Blackfeet numbers.

a. Latin American Indian refers to respondents listing any one of a number of Latin American tribes (e.g., the Maya or Yanomamo).

b. Iroquois is a language group that includes six federally recognized tribes in its confederacy.

One should be puzzled at how an explorer in 1492 can be said to "discover" what is now "America," a land already inhabited by millions of people.

Jack Hollingsworth/photodisc/
Thinkstock

And virtually every one of them was later broken by the government. The many treaties brokered with the U.S. government forced tribes to live on reservations while taking almost 1 billion acres of Indian land. Indian male heads of household, in return, were allocated approximately 160 acres of land and a promise of training on how to farm (Deloria, 1979). In addition, the promises of housing, schooling, employment, and health care never materialized. The struggle to maintain treaty-given rights and recognitions continues today.

Highlights From Native American History

1513. The explorer Juan Ponce de Leon arrives in Florida, beginning the Spanish connection with Native Americans. Although which explorers arrived here first may be debated, this date is significant because it is the date of first contact with the first peoples of this country—Native Americans. History and civilization did not begin with the arrival of Europeans.

1830. The U.S. Congress passes the Removal Act, forcibly moving Native Americans from the east to the west of the Mississippi. This is a shameful act in this country's history that must not be forgotten. This act and subsequent actions symbolized the policy of westward expansion, a belief that pioneers from the east had a God-given right to take lands from the people who had inhabited them for centuries.

1876. At Little Bighorn, in what is now Montana, Chief Sitting Bull leads Sioux tribes in a massacre of General Custer's 7th Cavalry. This seminal event is one that marks the beginning of the end of an era of Native life in this country.

1890. At Wounded Knee, South Dakota, 300 Sioux are killed in a battle with the U.S. 7th Cavalry Regiment. The book *Bury My Heart at Wounded Knee* (Brown, 2007) recalls the tragic history of conflict between the federal government and the various Indian nations. Historians generally cite this event as the end of the wars.

A Classroom Focus on Native Americans

Native Americans face myriad problems, including high unemployment, substance abuse, poverty, and poor education. Forced out of their ancestral homelands and the subsequent loss of their lifestyle, Native Americans have struggled to reclaim and rebuild their lives (Brown & Shevin, 2014; Deloria, 1979).

There are more than 500 recognized tribes operating as sovereign nations within the boundaries of the United States (Bureau of Indian Affairs, 2012). Native American culture is experiencing many positive developments. More tribes are becoming active and self-determining. There is progress toward economic self-sufficiency and a rebuilding of cultural ties. The opening of the National Museum of the American Indian on the last vacant land on the Washington Mall in September 2003 is symbolic of a strong will to survive and be recognized.

One of the curricular mistakes often made in schools is teaching about Native Americans as though they existed only in the past. Teachers tend to portray Native Americans as living in teepees and hunting buffalo. Today, Native Americans occupy all spheres of American life and live at all social and economic levels. The quaint image of the Indian must be balanced by the reality of modern life. The population is increasing, and the struggle for economic security and the right to reclaim lost land is ongoing.

> **Extended Explorations 3.2: Recognition of Native American Tribes**
>
> Many Indian tribes have attempted to receive federal recognition as bona fide Indian tribes. The potential results could be reclamation of lost lands through broken treaties and the creation of casinos or other gaming endeavors. Construct a plan for how we can, as a just society, repay Native Americans for their losses and bring them out of the widespread poverty that many live in. If you don't agree with this thought, develop your counterargument for why we shouldn't try to compensate Native Americans.

African Americans

The imagery and history of African Americans may forever be tied to perhaps the greatest stain on America's reputation—that is, 400 years of slavery and oppression.

Africans first arrived here as explorers and settlers. European explorers, including Columbus in 1502 and Balboa in 1513, had Africans on their journeys. In 1565, Africans were part of the establishment in Florida of St. Augustine, the oldest non-Indian settlement in the United

African Americans have had to struggle to overcome horrific obstacles in order to achieve equality in this country. Though many challenges are still present, African Americans are making great progress.

Library of Contress/Curtis, Edward S.

States (Banks, 2009). However, that soon changed with the Atlantic slave trade, which between the 14th and 19th centuries brought approximately 15 million slaves to the Americas. Altogether, the continent of Africa lost approximately 50 million people to death, and slavery perpetuated in the Americas and throughout the world (Zinn, 2003).

Jamestown, Virginia, is noted for being the first English settlement in America, founded in May 14, 1607. It was also the birthplace of American slavery when 20 African men were brought there in 1619 (Zinn, 2003). Eventually, up to 500,000 people were brought to the American colonies and the United States as slaves. At the beginning of the American Civil War, there were approximately 4 million slaves in the South. The Thirteenth Amendment officially abolished slavery in 1865, 246 years after the first captives had arrived in Jamestown. The economy of an emerging nation was built on the backs of enslaved men, women, and children.

Not until the Fourteenth Amendment was passed in 1868 were African Americans recognized as U.S. citizens.

Highlights From African American History

1619. First Africans arrive in Jamestown with White settlers. It is unclear whether they arrived as indentured servants or enslaved peoples, but they are the first African Americans in recorded history.

1863. During the Civil War, Abraham Lincoln signs the Emancipation Proclamation. It frees many, but not all, enslaved Americans.

1896. The U.S. Supreme Court rules in *Plessy v. Ferguson* that "separate but equal" facilities are legal. This notorious ruling makes segregated facilities legal under federal law.

1954. The U.S. Supreme Court rules that school segregation is unequal in *Brown v. Board of Education*, 347 U.S. 483. This supposedly ended the segregation of Black and White students. Kozol, in *The Shame of the Nation: The Restoration of Apartheid Schooling in America* (2005), reported that schools are still highly segregated, in some cases almost as segregated as before *Brown v. Board of Education*.

1955. Rosa Parks, a 43-year-old Black seamstress, is arrested in Montgomery, Alabama, for refusing to give up her bus seat to a White man. The yearlong Montgomery Bus Boycott begins. For more than a year, thousands of African Americans walk to work or share taxis and car rides. Finally, the Supreme Court rules that segregated buses are unconstitutional. The boycott is the start of the civil rights movement and the activism of Martin Luther King on the national stage.

1960. Sit-ins begin in Greensboro, North Carolina. Four college students dare to sit at a Whites-only lunch counter in Woolworth's department store. Their action spurs on other sit-ins. Six months later, the store chain desegregates all its stores.

1963. In March, in Washington, D.C., almost a quarter of a million people assemble in the nation's capital in the largest demonstration in history to that date. The civil rights demonstration features Dr. Martin Luther King and his now famous "I Have a Dream" speech.

1964. The Civil Rights Act of 1964 is passed. Initiated by John F. Kennedy, but passed thanks to the determination of Lyndon B. Johnson, the act makes illegal the **segregation** of public facilities.

1965–1968. Civil rights riots break out in many U.S. cities.

1968. Martin Luther King is assassinated.

2008. Barack Obama elected as America's first Black president.

A Classroom Focus on African Americans

The history of Africans in the Americas has led educators for many years to approach the education of African American children from what has been called the "deficit model." In this approach, the focus is on what these "poor" children have been missing out on and on what they don't have because of their race. Certainly, the prejudice, discrimination, poverty, crime, substance abuse, and poor education that are often associated with urban youth are very real problems and should not be ignored. However, students should not be seen primarily as victims or as people to be pitied and rescued. The approach to educating diverse students should not be from the perspective of a missionary but more from that of a cheerleader, mentor, or coach. Educators should consistently seek and expect high performance from all their students (Gay, 2010). Education should be self-affirming and foster positive self-images (Delpit, 2006).

Researchers, including Irvine (2003) and Nieto (2009), have cited research on African American students that shows higher graduation rates, fewer special education placements, more enrollments in gifted classes, and fewer disciplinary problems when there are larger numbers of African American teachers. Of course, White teachers can be very successful at educating minority children, just as teachers of color can be ineffective (Ladson-Billings, 2009). The successful education of minority youth requires an understanding and sensitivity to culture, background, and perspectives. Some suggestions for teaching African Americans also apply to other students. These include the following:

- Focus on each child's strengths and develop positive self-image.

- Involve parents, churches, and the community at large in your curriculum.

- Appreciate the very real problems of racism facing African Americans, among them higher incarceration rates, stiffer penalties for crimes, poor schools, persistent poverty, and fewer job opportunities. But don't allow these issues to be excuses for lower expectations.

- Adjust teaching and testing strategies to complement the culture of students.

> **Extended Explorations 3.3: Planning for Reparations**
>
> **Reparations** were paid to many Japanese American families who interned during World War II. The government has publicly apologized to various groups that have been wronged. Explain what the reparations movement means for you. Why do you believe or not believe that African Americans are owed money for the injustices done against them? Formulate an effective solution to address the injustices against African Americans.

Finally, make substantial use of the great strides, contributions, and changes made by members of the African American community. The Obama administration in Washington, D.C., for example, had more people of color, particularly African Americans, than any previous administration. A larger middle-class community of African Americans has become established. African Americans have achieved higher positions in education, government, and business. This speaks not only of a great resilience in the community but also of the impact of an effective education.

Asian Americans

Chinese Americans

The Chinese were the first Asian immigrants to arrive in the United States, coming in the mid-1800s. According to the Museum of Chinese in the Americas (Lee & Wong, 2001), the first record of any Chinese to arrive is of three sailors who landed in Baltimore in 1785. During the gold rush to California in 1848, 325 Chinese people arrived to join the quest for riches (Takaki, 1993). The U.S. Census of 1850 counted 450 Chinese immigrants in the United States (Banks, 2009). By 1870, that number had grown to 63,000, mostly in California (Takaki, 1993). Many worked to build the transcontinental railroad system.

White American workers quickly grew resentful of the Chinese, who were competing for jobs. Anti-Chinese riots occurred in San Francisco in 1877. A pattern of legislation to limit or ban immigration of Chinese people, considered to be inferior, was initiated with the Chinese Exclusion Act of 1882. These bans continued to 1943, when Chinese were finally permitted to become citizens (Louie & Omatsu, 2001; Min, 2006; Takaki; 1993; Zinn, 2003).

Japanese Americans

The Japanese started arriving as laborers in the late 1800s, settling in Hawaii and on the mainland. In 1870, there were 55 Japanese immigrants in the United States. This number had risen to 111,010 by 1920 (Lyman, 1970). After the Chinese Exclusion Act

Asian Americans, according to the 2010 U.S. Census are the fastest growing racial group in the United States (Hoeffel, Kim, & Shahid, 2012). Ironically, the model minority myth presents obstacles to student success.

iStock/monkey businessimages

was passed in 1882, Japanese immigrants began taking the places of Chinese American workers, taking jobs mainly in agriculture, farming, and gardening, and on the railroads and becoming self-employed businesspeople (Banks, 2009). However, the success of the Japanese triggered hostility from White Americans, leading to the internment of Japanese during World War II.

Filipino Americans

On October 18, 1587, the first Filipinos set foot in America in Morro Bay, California, as part of a Spanish exploration team. In 1763, Filipinos started the first Asian settlement on the U.S. mainland in Louisiana (Banks, 2009). Filipinos also participated in the 1848 gold rush in California. The Spanish–American War of 1898 resulted in Spain losing Cuba, Puerto Rico, the Philippines, Guam, and other islands. The Philippines became a U.S. protectorate after the United States bought it from Spain. In 1909, several hundred Filipino workers were recruited to Hawaii to labor on the plantations (Takaki, 1993). Perhaps the most significant arrival of Filipinos began in 1965 with the Immigration Reform Act, which allowed 32,000 Filipinos, mostly highly skilled professionals, to enter the country (Banks, 2009).

Highlights From Asian American History

1587. Filipinos land in Morro Bay, California.

1763. Filipinos start the first Asian settlement on the U.S. mainland in Louisiana.

1882. The Chinese Exclusion Act, a federal law banning the immigration of Chinese people, is passed. It will not be repealed until 1943.

1910. Angel Island in San Francisco opens up and becomes the major point of entry for Chinese immigrants.

1941. Japan attacks the Pearl Harbor Naval Base in Hawaii. The United States enters World War II.

1942. President Franklin D. Roosevelt signs Executive Order 9066, thereby forcing 110,000 Japanese Americans to be relocated to internment camps.

1943–1945. The 442nd Regimental Combat team (all *nisei* or second-generation Japanese Americans), serving in Italy and southern France, becomes the most highly decorated unit in U.S. military history.

1974. In *Lau v. Nichols*, 414 U.S. 563, Chinese American students in California sue, claiming that they are not getting equal education because of their inability to speak English. The U.S. Supreme Court rules in favor of the students. This results in English language learners (ELLs) nationally having the right to equal education.

1988. Congress passes legislation awarding reparations—formal payments—of $20,000 each to 60,000 surviving Japanese Americans who were imprisoned in internment camps.

While Asian Americans constitute a large segment of the country's population, many are unaware of the varied ethnic categories that exist. Table 3.2 illustrates the rich diversity that exists.

TABLE 3.2	The 20 Largest U.S. Asian Groups by Origin (Based on Self-Described Race or Ethnicity)

Total U.S. Asians: 17,320,856	
1. Chinese: 4,010,114	11. Laotian: 232,130
2. Filipino: 3,416,840	12. Bangladeshi: 147,300
3. Indian: 3,183,063	13. Burmese: 100,200
4. Vietnamese: 1,737,433	14. Indonesian: 95,270
5. Korean: 1,706,822	15. Nepalese: 59,490
6. Japanese: 1,304,286	16. Sri Lankan: 45,381
7. Pakistani: 409,163	17. Malaysian: 26,179
8. Cambodian: 276,667	18. Bhutanese: 19,439
9. Hmong: 260,073	19. Mongolian: 18,344
10. Thai: 237,583	20. Okinawan: 11,326

Source: U.S. Census Bureau (2012a).

A Classroom Focus on Asian Americans

Asian Americans face unique barriers to full participation in this country, a fact that clearly influences the education of Asian American children. To start with, Asian Americans make up the most diverse race in terms of ethnicities and national origins. Even within a race, there may be numerous ethnicities. For example, in China, there are 56 ethnic minorities and several languages. Many of these ethnic groups are represented in the United States. There are also pronounced cultural differences between first-generation and later-generation Asian Americans.

The 2010 U.S. Census listed 11 major Asian groups (Asian Indian, Chinese, Filipino, Japanese, Korean, Vietnamese, Hmong, Laotian, Thai, Pakistani, and Cambodian) in addition to a fill-in space for "Other Asian." Asians total 14.7 million or 4.8% of the population. Chinese Americans make up the largest proportion of Asians (U.S. Census Bureau, 2011).

With this significant diversity within one racial group, the needs of Asian American students are often not understood (Pang & Cheng, 1998). One of the most consistent roadblocks for Asian American students is the myth of the "model minority." Originally considered inferior, Asians are now touted as being hardworking, good in school, well mannered, and successful. Asians routinely score as high as or higher than White students on standardized tests.

Though normally these traits would be considered flattering, they often are a detriment. For one thing, this stereotype is often used in a racist fashion to criticize African American students for their failure to achieve at the same level. Furthermore, by emphasizing the success of Asian Americans, the very real problems of discrimination in housing and job promotion and

Extended Explorations 3.4: Cases of Wrongful Profiling

There have been several very high-profile legal actions taken against universities for profiling against Asian Americans in admissions because of their high test scores. Princeton University and Harvard University are just two examples of universities that have been charged with intentionally rejecting high-scoring Asian Americans in favor of other students with lower scores. Explain why this might be an example of reverse discrimination or **affirmative action** gone wrong. Identify at least two other cases of wrongful profiling against Asian Americans. Draft an admissions statement that might address this unfair process.

civil rights abuses, for example, are often minimized. Recent arrivals, particularly poor, non-English-speaking immigrants, suffer from failures and neglect in school similar to the experiences of their Hispanic and African American counterparts. Poverty, low-paying jobs, and poor housing are not uncommon. Like other ethnic groups, though, the Asian community has built a strong civil rights movement.

Asian Americans suffer, too, from the lack of understanding of the large number of different cultures and languages among Asian Americans. Some intercultural animosities go back centuries and can be as fierce as the conflicts between Northern and Southern Ireland or Palestine and Israel. Beliefs, values, and taboos vary widely among the many Asian cultures. Teachers are cautioned not to confuse one culture with another or assume similarities.

On the opening page of his book *A Different Mirror: A History of Multicultural America* (1993), Ronald Takaki recalled a painful, but familiar, conversation with a cab driver. He was asked, "How long have you been in this country?" As a *sansei*, a third-generation Japanese American, Takaki endured offering yet another clarification that he was American born. Perhaps no other ethnic minority faces the constant problem of having to assert its citizenship. An Asian face, for many people, still means *foreigner*.

Creatasimages/creates/Thinkstock

People of Hispanic origin are the nation's largest ethnic or race minority, pushing the importance of students and teachers to become proficient in speaking Spanish.

Hispanic Americans

Hispanic Americans include any person of Cuban, Mexican, Puerto Rican, South or Central American, or other Spanish culture or origin, regardless of race. According to the 2010 U.S. Census Bureau population estimate, there are roughly 50.5 million Hispanics living in the United States. This group represents 16% of the total U.S. population. In 2010, among Hispanic subgroups, Mexicans made up the largest group, followed by Central and South Americans, Puerto Ricans, and Cubans (Table 3.3).

TABLE 3.3   Subgroups of Hispanic Americans

Group	Percentage of the total Hispanic population in the United States
Mexican	63.0
Central and South American	13.0
Puerto Rican	9.2
Cuban	3.5
Other Hispanic	11.3

Source: U.S. Census Bureau (2010).

Much as with Asian Americans, there are wide cultural differences among the different Hispanic groups. The Spanish language is a common bond, but history and cultures vary, so distinctions are needed.

Mexican Americans

The centuries of Mexican American exploration and participation in the settlement of the United States is due more recognition. The Mexican American culture began with the Indians in the Americas. At the time of the arrival of Spanish explorers in 1517, there were 25 million Indians living in North, Central, and South America (Banks, 2009). Through direct wars with the natives and often with the support of various tribes who fought against other tribes, the Spanish were successful at conquering the peoples they encountered (Banks, 2009). The introduction of the Spanish culture, and then a blending with Anglo cultures, created the rich southwestern "Tex-Mex" culture that is now a vibrant part of American life.

A study of Mexican American history must include the Mexican American War of 1846–1848, in which the United States gained Mexican land, and the introduction of Mexican labor and the subsequent harsh treatment, racism, and discrimination suffered. Mexican Americans were welcomed and rejected many times as laborers. During the Great Depression, they were restricted from working and then brought back during World War II because of a shortage of workers. During the war, Mexican Americans fought bravely in large numbers in the U.S. Armed Forces.

Puerto Ricans

Columbus arrived in Puerto Rico on his second voyage in 1493 and immediately claimed it for Spain. At the time, as many as 60,000 Arawak or Taino Indians were living peacefully there. Columbus enslaved them by the thousands and killed those who resisted (Loewen, 2008). Juan Ponce de Leon became the island's governor in 1508. The island has a history of brutal slavery, poverty, and unemployment. The status of its statehood has been perennially in flux. Many Puerto Ricans have settled in large numbers on the mainland, mainly in New York and New Jersey, although large communities flourish in other states as well. Frequent travel back and forth to the islands is common. The Puerto Rican people pride themselves on the richness of their culture, their historical willingness and readiness to fight in wartime on behalf of the United States, and their many contributions to the political, sports, and entertainment culture of this country.

Cuban Americans

Like much of Latin America, Cuba was invaded and colonized by Spain (Phillips & Phillips, 1992). Unlike Puerto Rico, this island had a healthy economy based on commercial enterprises and agriculture. Revolts and upheavals against the Spanish were common and caused Cuba to be characterized as a country of revolutionaries. In recent history, the dictatorship of Fidel Castro and a strained relationship with the United States have been prominent. There are strong family ties between the two countries. As a leftover of the Cold War, Cuba remains a strategic military concern. Many people have left the island, both with and without the approval of the Cuban government, and have created a strong Cuban American culture.

Highlights From Hispanic American History

1513. Spanish explorer Juan Ponce de Leon lands in Florida.

1565. Founded by Spanish explorers, Saint Augustine, Florida, becomes the first European American settlement in North America.

1846. The United States invades Mexico and takes half the land area of Mexico, including Texas, California, most parts of Arizona, New Mexico, Colorado, Utah, and Nevada.

1954. The U.S. Supreme Court rules that Hispanics are a separate class of people.

1960s. The **Chicano** movement fights for civil rights.

1962–1965. Cesar Chavez leads the United Farm Workers in California in a successful strike and coordinates the first national boycott.

1965. More than 250,000 Cubans are airlifted to the United States before the program is halted by Fidel Castro in 1973.

1974. The Equal Educational Opportunity Act promotes equality in public schools by making bilingual education available to Hispanic youth.

1998. California voters pass Proposition 227, banning bilingual classroom education and English as a second language programs and replacing them with a 1-year intensive English immersion program.

2003. Hispanics are recognized as the nation's largest minority group at 37.1 million as of July 2001.

A Classroom Focus on Hispanic Americans

American history books highlight the arrival of the Pilgrims at Plymouth Rock in 1620 as the beginning of the country. Further emphasis is given to the formation of the colonies and westward expansion. What seems ignored or trivialized is who had explored and settled in the country before the arrival of the *Mayflower*. Much less is written about the long-standing Spanish settlements in the southwest that existed long before English settlers arrived. Mexican Americans, Puerto Ricans, and Cuban Americans have contributed greatly to the arts, sports, and politics of the country. Spanish is the second most common language spoken here after English. This rich history can be used effectively to engage students in a variety of disciplines.

In the United States, there continues to exist a wave of anti-immigrant sentiment, particularly toward undocumented immigrants. These attitudes create problems in educating children (Olsen & Jaramillo, 1999). Teachers should not be distracted by the immigration status of children in their schools but rather focus on effectively teaching every child who attends. The U.S. Supreme Court ruled in *Plyer v. Doe*, 457 U.S. 202 (1982) that children must be accepted into public schools regardless of immigration status (Gollnick & Chinn, 2013). The **English-only movement**, particularly the propositions in California and other states to make English the "official" language, and movements to eliminate bilingual education all speak of the xenophobia evident among those who do not, unfortunately, value or appreciate the contributions of Hispanic cultures.

Extended Explorations 3.5: Official Languages in the United States

In recognition of the diversity in the country, Canada has declared French and English as the official languages for all peoples there. Investigate five strong sources about whether or not the United States should pass a federal law that makes English and Spanish the official languages of the country. Then construct and justify your own argument for why or why not the United States should do this.

European Americans

The United States is a nation of immigrants, all bringing with them a rich culture. Such diversity is a strength in our society.

Thinkstock/Comstock/Thinkstock

European Americans are immigrants from countries such as England, Ireland, Scotland, Poland, Germany, and Australia. European Americans (White people) also include people from Bahrain, the Gaza Strip, Iran, Iraq, Israel, Jordan, Kuwait, Lebanon, Oman, Qatar, Saudi Arabia, Syria, the United Arab Emirates, the West Bank, and Yemen.

The Spanish were the first European Americans to arrive and settle here in 1565, followed by the English, French, Dutch, Germans, Scots, and Irish in large numbers (Banks, 2009). Many were poor and were seeking economic opportunities or were seeking relief from religious persecution, or both.

According to the U.S. Census Bureau (2012b), in 1900, approximately 90% of the people in the United States were identified as being European American. The rest were counted as being African American. Other races were not counted. As of the 2010 U.S. Census (2012a), European Americans are a minority in 48 of the largest 100 cities, up from 30 cities in 1990. In the 20 fastest growing cities, Hispanic (72%) and Asian (69%) populations grew much more rapidly than White (5%) and Black populations (23%). Whites are now a minority in California, Hawaii, and the District of Columbia and may soon be a minority in Texas and New Mexico.

Population projections call for the United States to grow to 403 million people by 2050 (U.S. Census Bureau, 2011). The leading origins of European American immigrants are the United Kingdom, Germany, Italy, Ireland, Sweden, and Norway.

Highlights From European American History

1513. Spanish Explorer Juan Ponce de Leon arrives in Florida.

1524. Italian explorer Giovanni da Verrazano arrives in what is now New York harbor.

1540. Spanish explorer Francisco Vasquez de Coronado explores the southwestern area of what will be the United States.

1565. Founded by Spanish explorers, Saint Augustine, Florida, becomes the first European American settlement in North America.

1607. The first English settlement in America is established in Jamestown, Virginia.

1620. Pilgrims arrive and establish a colony in Massachusetts.

1699. French settlers arrive in Mississippi and Louisiana.

1845–1849. Thousands of Irish arrive as a result of the Irish potato famine.

1900. In the first 10 years of the 20th century, almost 9 million immigrants arrive. Anti-immigrant sentiment increases greatly.

1921. The Johnson Act places quotas on European immigration.

1965. The Immigration Act of 1965 stops quotas on immigration and eases the way for more equitable entry into the country.

A Classroom Focus on European Americans

It is not uncommon for European American children to know very little about their cultural backgrounds and to be ignorant of the meaning of being White (Howard, 1999). Therefore, we must begin instilling in all children at a young age an awareness of and pride in their culture, along with an understanding of the privileges and obstacles that come with skin color (Derman-Sparks, 2000). A study of the oral histories of different cultures, exemplified in books such as *A Larger Memory: A History of Our Diversity, With Voices* (Takaki, 1998a) can help build the understanding that all Americans share much among our cultures.

An abundance of texts, videos, and popular literature treat the immigrant American experience. Students whose families have a long history in the United States will benefit from learning that they have a culture that is rich and meaningful. Italian American students, for example, who study their own culture will be better able to appreciate the culture of others. The classroom focus should also be on commonalties and shared experiences. Conflicts between cultural groups should be discussed at age-appropriate levels and should not be neglected. Educators themselves will find it much easier to promote cultural awareness among their students when they are first knowledgeable about their own background.

> **Extended Explorations 3.6: Enrollment Shifts in Schools and Teacher Preparation**
>
> In the fall of 2014, for the first time in history, White students enrolled in U.S. schools no longer were in the majority. Develop a statement that could be shared with local schools that describes the implications for the design of school curriculum. Identify the implications from this enrollment shift for the **preservice** and **in-service** preparation of teachers.

EXERCISE 3.1

SELF-ASSESSMENT ABOUT AMERICAN HISTORY

Evaluate each statement: Is it true or false? Correct responses are at the end of the chapter.

1. The Eighteenth Amendment gave women the right to vote.	True	False
2. Laws banning interracial marriage were not erased in every state throughout the country until 1967.	True	False
3. Only African Americans were lynched in this country.	True	False
4. Yale University refused to admit Japanese American students who lived in internment camps during World War II.	True	False
5. African American troops were among the first to liberate Nazi concentration camps.	True	False

Today's America

While discussion in this chapter has focused on only a few categories of racial and ethnic groups that constitute the American society, teachers are advised to look at their immediate community and state to determine additional ethnic groups, such as Bosnians, Albanians, and Iranians, who contribute to that particular community and about whom the teacher will want to be knowledgeable. The objective of a multicultural curriculum is not to feel compelled to teach about all ethnicities but to gain a foundational knowledge about and appreciation for different cultures. Within this framework, we must also include current societal issues such as the gay rights movement and its implications for schools (Casper & Schultz, 1999; Donahue, 2000). The role of religion in schools is also becoming an important debate (Nash, 1999).

LEARNING OBJECTIVE 3.3 Describe Key Events in the Civil Rights Timeline

This section provides a listing of key events in American history. Knowing about these events is critical for understanding how our society, its laws, and its customs have evolved. The timeline serves to frame the perspectives, feelings, attitudes, and actions of diverse peoples in the United States. The struggle for equality has been a common experience for too many (Southern Poverty Law Center, 2000).

Civil Rights Movement Timeline

Knowledge about the progress of civil rights in this country is a must for any educator. In addition to the key dates already listed, here are other important events.

Juan Ponce de Leon is credited in our history books with the title of Spanish explorer, discoverer of Florida in 1513. This raises again the debate of who was here first. The perspectives and experiences of the arrival of immigrants is an important part of our history.

State Archives of Florida, Florida Memory, "La Florida; su conquista y colonización por P. Menéndez de Avilés. [Illustrated.] 1893.

1857. In *Dred Scott v. Sanford*, 60 U.S. 393, the proslavery U.S. Supreme Court reinforces the legality of slavery. This decision is one of the key issues that will fuel the American Civil War.

1896. In *Plessy v Ferguson*, 163 U.S. 537, the Court declares that "separate" facilities for Blacks and Whites are constitutional as long as they are "equal." This leads to legal segregation in many areas of public life, including in restaurants, theaters, restrooms, and public schools.

1920. Women win the right to vote with the passing of the Nineteenth Amendment.

1948. President Truman integrates the Armed Forces.

1956. More than 100 southern members of Congress sign the Southern Manifesto, protesting desegregation. Only Lyndon Johnson, Estes Kefauver, and Albert Gore refuse to sign and be a part of the protest.

1957. A group of nine Black students attempting to enter all-White Central High in Little Rock, Arkansas, are barred from entering by the Arkansas National Guard. It takes President Eisenhower ordering more than 1,000 paratroopers to Little Rock before the students can enter and segregation is ended.

1961. In 1961, in what are known as the Freedom Rides, busloads of people across the country campaign to end the segregation of bus terminals.

1962. President John F. Kennedy orders 5,000 federal troops to escort James Meredith, the first Black student to enroll at the University of Mississippi, onto the campus. A riot breaks out, and two students are killed.

1962. Illinois becomes the first state in the United States to decriminalize homosexual acts between consenting adults in private.

1963. At the University of Alabama, Governor George Wallace stands in front of the schoolhouse door and promises segregation "today, tomorrow, and forever." President Kennedy forces Wallace to allow Blacks to enroll.

1963. Birmingham, Alabama, was one of the country's most segregated cities in the 1960s. Black men and women hold sit-ins at lunch counters where they have been refused service. "Kneel-ins" are held on the steps of churches they cannot enter. Hundreds of protesters are arrested and imprisoned. In 1963, Martin Luther King, Ralph Abernathy, and the Reverend Shuttlesworth hold a large protest march in Birmingham, where they are attacked by police officers and dogs. The three ministers are subsequently arrested and jailed.

1963. Medgar Evers, head of the Mississippi National Association for the Advancement of Colored People, is murdered outside his home.

1963. Four Black girls—Addie Mae Collins, Carol Denise McNair, Carole Robertson, and Cynthia Diane Wesley—are killed by a bomb planted in a Birmingham church.

1964. The Twenty-Fourth Amendment is passed, outlawing the practice of forcing Blacks to pay a poll tax in order to vote.

1964. The Civil Rights Act is passed, outlawing discrimination based on "race, color, religion, or national origin" in public establishments.

1964. Civil rights workers spend the summer working to register Blacks to vote. Michael Schwerner, Andrew Goodman, and James Chaney are killed.

1965. Martin Luther King leads a 54-mile march from Selma to Montgomery in support of voter registration.

1965. The Voting Rights Act is passed, encouraging more African Americans to vote and run for elected office.

1965. More than 100 riots occur in Watts, a suburb of Los Angeles.

1965. Malcolm X is assassinated.

1967. Race riots take place in Detroit, Michigan, and Newark, New Jersey.

1968. Martin Luther King is assassinated in Memphis, Tennessee, by James Earl Ray. Riots ensue throughout the United States.

1969. Patrons of a gay bar in New York's Greenwich Village, the Stonewall Inn, fight back during a police raid on June 27. The conflict turns into three days of riots. "Stonewall" becomes a major turning point for gay civil rights.

1973. The American Psychiatric Association removes homosexuality from its official list of mental disorders.

1974. The Equal Employment Opportunity Act passes, forbidding states from denying an education to students based on race, color, sex, or national origin.

1978. In *Bakke v. Regents of University of California*, 438 U.S. 265, the Supreme Court determines that fixed racial quotas are illegal.

1982. Wisconsin becomes the first state to outlaw discrimination on the basis of sexual orientation.

1982. In *Plyer v. Doe*, 457 U.S. 202, the Supreme Court rules that students, regardless of immigration status, have the right to attend public schools.

2000. Vermont becomes the first state in the country to legally recognize civil unions for gay and lesbian couples.

2003. The Supreme Court upholds the University of Michigan Law School's policy, ruling that race can be one of many factors considered by colleges when selecting their students because it furthers "a compelling interest in obtaining the educational benefits that flow from a diverse student body."

2004. Massachusetts legalizes same-sex marriages. Since then, same-sex marriage has become legal in a total of 37 states and the District of Columbia: Alabama, Alaska, Arizona, California, Colorado, Connecticut, Delaware, Florida, Hawaii, Idaho, Illinois, Indiana, Iowa, Kansas, Maine, Maryland, Massachusetts, Minnesota, Montana, Nevada, New Hampshire, New Jersey, New Mexico, New York, North Carolina, Oklahoma, Oregon, Pennsylvania, Rhode Island, South Carolina, Utah, Vermont, Virginia, Washington, West Virginia, Wisconsin, and Wyoming.

2009. The Matthew Shepard and James Byrd Jr. Hate Crimes Prevention Act expands federal hate crime laws to include crimes motivated by a victim's actual or perceived gender, sexual orientation, gender identity, or disability.

2015. On Friday, June 26, the U.S. Supreme Court ruled in a historic civil rights case (*Obergefell v. Hodges*, 576 U.S._) that the Constitution guarantees the right to same-sex marriage.

Patsy Mink was the first woman of color and the first Asian American woman elected to Congress. In recognition of her contributions toward equal rights in the country, Congress named the Title IX Amendment of the Higher Education Act the "Patsy T. Mink Equal Opportunity in Education Act."

Source: http://commons.wikimedia.org/wiki/File:Patsymink.jpg

LEARNING OBJECTIVE 3.4 Summarize Key Legislation Affecting Education

> **To live outside the law you must be honest.**
> —Lao Tse

It would be nice if we could live as a society without laws, but unfortunately, laws are needed to bring order and equity to society. The laws that have been passed that affect education were often not done so easily. They resulted from the suffering of peoples. In this section, we will review the major laws and court cases with which teachers should be familiar, as they affect teaching and learning.

Federal Civil Rights Laws

The U.S. Department of Education, Office for Civil Rights, is charged with enforcing five civil rights laws:

- Title VI of the Civil Rights Act of 1964, which prohibits discrimination on the basis of race, color, or national origin in all programs or activities that receive federal financial assistance

- Section 504 of the Rehabilitation Act of 1973, which prohibits discrimination on the basis of disability in all programs or activities that receive federal financial assistance

- Title IX of the Education Amendments of 1972, which prohibits discrimination on the basis of sex in all education programs or activities that receive federal financial assistance. This landmark legislation increased educational and athletic opportunities for girls and women and helped define sexual harassment as discriminatory.

- Age Discrimination Act of 1975, which generally prohibits discrimination on the basis of age in all programs or activities that receive federal financial assistance

- Title II of the Americans with Disabilities Act of 1990, which prohibits discrimination on the basis of disability by public entities. Students with disabilities, primarily physical disabilities, have benefited from better physical access to school facilities.

Other Education Laws

Education Law by Imber and Van Geel (2010) is a good resource on education law for nonlawyers.

- The Individuals with Disabilities Education Act Amendments of 1997 guarantee all children with disabilities access to free and appropriate public education.

- The Family Educational Rights and Privacy Act of 1974, also known as the Buckley Amendment, established federal guidelines regarding the privacy of student records. This act governs the confidentiality of student education records and who has access to them.

- Free Appropriate Public Education supports Section 504 of the Rehabilitation Act of 1973, providing that all disabled children are entitled to receive free appropriate public education, including special education and related services, at no cost to the child or to her or his parents.

- The Equal Access Act of 1984 permits noncurricular religious clubs to meet with the same rights and privileges as other noncurricular clubs in the school.

Free Speech Rights of Students

Several court cases have clarified the free speech rights of students. These have further strengthened the constitutional rights of students in schools. Some of the best-known court decisions are these:

- *Bethel School District No. 43 v. Fraser*, 478 U.S. 675 (1986), established that high school administrators have the right to punish student speech that has the effect of violating school rules and disrupting legitimate educational and disciplinary objectives.

- In *Hazelwood School District et al. v. Kuhlmeier et al.*, 484 U.S. 260 (1988), the Court cited *Bethel* in its decision to allow school administrators to censor a student-edited school paper that published writing on sensitive subjects such as student pregnancy or that could be considered an invasion of privacy.

- In *Papish v. Board of Curators of the University of Missouri et al.*, 410 U.S. 667 (1973), the Court ruled that the university violated a student's First Amendment rights when it expelled the student for distributing a controversial leaflet (including four-letter words and a cartoon showing the Statue of Liberty being raped) on campus.

- In *Tinker et al. v. Des Moines Independent Community School District et al.*, 393 U.S. 503 (1969), the Court ruled that the First Amendment protected the right of high school students to wear black armbands in a public high school as a form of protest against the Vietnam War. "Symbolic speech" can only be prohibited by school administrators if it causes a substantial disruption of the school's educational mission.

Perhaps the most well-known education law of recent times is the No Child Left Behind Act of 2001. A revised version of the Elementary and Secondary Education Act, it focuses on increasing student achievement for all students through a process of requiring comprehensive standardized testing and compliance with a set of standards. Among its provisions, which have created controversy, are the requirements for

1. a single, statewide set of accountability standards based on federal guidelines,

2. the adoption of measures of Annual Yearly Progress (AYP) targets for each public school district and individual schools,

3. penalties for schools that fail to make AYP targets,

4. schools to hire only "highly qualified teachers,"

5. state and local school report cards, and

6. the development of instruction, curriculum, materials, and staff based on "scientifically based research."

Protests have focused on various aspects of these requirements but mainly on the extensive testing required and the AYP, which many claim is demoralizing to both students and teachers. Supporters point out the positive aspects of holding schools accountable for the ongoing academic achievement of ELLs, special education students, and minority and handicapped students.

Finally, another federal law with important applications is Section 1983, which focuses on the deprivation of civil rights. It allows individuals an avenue of recourse against schools and educators for violation of their "federal, constitutional and statutory rights." Students and teachers have used it, for example, to seek monetary damages for violation of due process and free speech rights (Imber & Van Geel, 2010).

EXERCISE 3.2
WHICH LAW IS BEING VIOLATED HERE?

For each incident described, fill in which law is applicable. Correct responses are given at the end of the chapter.

Incident	Law
1. The school allows a local landscaping company to put up "help wanted" ads that ask for strong boys to apply.	
2. Class pictures are taken each year on a day when some students are absent to observe a Jewish holiday.	
3. On a field trip to a nuclear power plant, only the Middle Eastern students are stopped and searched.	
4. None of the town's three middle schools are handicapped accessible, forcing Mary several times a day to take her electric wheelchair out of the building and down the road to a rear entrance in order to get to class.	
5. Every chance Mark gets in school, he states his belief that homosexuality is a sin and that gay and lesbian students are not children of God. This angers many of the other students and has caused several students to seek out the social worker for counseling. Several fights have broken out because of his speech, and many students plan to walk out of school in protest.	

REFLECTING BACK

Questions

1. Easily available DNA testing kits have made tracing ancestry very popular. With smart phones able to record video and audio, it has become much easier to record oral histories. Numerous software applications are available to create family trees. How far back can you trace your roots? Who is still available now among family and friends who can provide insights to your cultural history?

2. Having read through the histories, and in particular the civil rights timeline, which events do you find most meaningful in terms of furthering social justice? Which ones do you find most troubling? And why?

3. Of all the laws that affect school life, which ones do you understand the best and which ones require further research? How effectively were these laws applied in your own schooling and in your current situation?

PROFILES IN MULTICULTURAL EDUCATION

RONALD TAKAKI (APRIL 12, 1939, TO MAY 26, 2009)

© Carol Takaki

Ronald Takaki was one of the most preeminent scholars of our nation's diversity. He was professor of ethnic studies at the University of California–Berkeley, where he taught more than 10,000 students over 32 years.

Born in 1939, Takaki was the grandson of immigrant Japanese plantation workers in Hawaii. He graduated from the College of Wooster, Ohio, in 1961. Six years later, after receiving his PhD in American history from University of California–Berkeley, Takaki went to the University of California–Los Angeles to teach its first Black history course. While there, he helped found its centers for African American, Asian American, Mexican American, and Native American studies.

In 1972, Takaki returned to Berkeley to teach in the newly instituted Department of Ethnic Studies. The Berkeley faculty honored Takaki with a Distinguished Teaching Award. In 1988, Takaki was awarded the Goldwin Smith University Lectureship at Cornell University, and in 1993, he was awarded Cornell's Distinguished Messenger Lectureship, the university's most prestigious lecturer appointment.

Professor Takaki was the author of 11 books, including *Strangers From a Different Shore: A History of Asian Americans* (1998b); *A Larger Memory: A History of Our Diversity, With Voices* (1998a); and *A Different Mirror: A History of Multicultural America* (1993). *Double Victory: A Multicultural History of America in World War II* (2001) is the only study of the "Greatest Generation" from the perspectives of our nation's diverse racial and ethnic minorities. This book challenges the memory of the war as a war fought only by White Americans, as reflected in the movie *Saving Private Ryan*.

In 1995, Takaki attended two seminars on race at Vice President Al Gore's home to advise him; in 1997, he attended a White House meeting with President Bill Clinton to help brainstorm ideas for his major speech, "One America in the 21st Century: The President's Initiative on Race." Significantly, Clinton took the dialogue on race beyond the Black–White binary and presented an inclusive view of Americans as a diverse people belonging to one nation. The *Los Angeles Times* has described Takaki as a "minority Everyman. He is a rare hybrid, a multicultural scholar" (Iwata, 1989).

Dr. Takaki's death in 2009 was a great loss to the field of multicultural education. His work lives on.

CASE STUDY
WORKING WITH IMMIGRANT AND REFUGEE STUDENTS

Key Issues to Be Explored in the Case

1. Need for teachers to understand specific challenges to culturally diverse student populations, including posttraumatic stress disorder

2. Importance of understanding the immigrant experience

3. Exploration of what teachers need to learn about educating ELLs

Tulon was new to the school, the small town of River Valley, and the country. He and his mother and father had just arrived as refugees a few months before. Their country had been engaged in a civil war for years, resulting in mass executions of innocent civilians. The family had lost everything. They endured 2 years in a refugee resettlement camp, waiting to be accepted by another country. During that time, his brother and sister both died of diseases.

Tulon was placed into Ms. Beeman's fifth-grade class because of his age, even though he spoke not one word of English. He had never been to any school and seemed terrified of his new surroundings. Ms. Beeman, a relatively new teacher, did her best to teach him reading and writing, but she didn't know how to start from the very beginning with a student. Some of Tulon's classmates made attempts to communicate but gave up quickly because of the huge language differences. Others began to tease him, which quickly turned to taunts from the bullies in the school. Once, when the D.A.R.E. officer came in to speak briefly to the class, Tulon ran and hid in the coat closet, frightened of a man in uniform. Loud noises and flashes of bright lights would cause him to begin sobbing uncontrollably. His classmates would either be frightened of him or be emboldened to bully him further. The name-calling increased; the hallways were an obstacle course where he endured kicks and punches; the bus ride from and to home was the most horrifying ordeal. Throughout it all, he could not understand why the other children hated him so much. And Ms. Beeman was oblivious to what he was enduring. Had he and his family not suffered enough in their homeland?

He sat alone at lunch and hid behind trees in the play yard at recess. Tulon was a lonely young boy who had seen enough horror to last a lifetime during the war in his home country. Now in a strange land, he faced new terrors.

Discussion Questions

1. What do you see as Tulon's needs?

2. What do you think his classmates and the rest of the school need?

3. If you were the teacher, where would you start?

4. How would you go about explaining the life that Tulon and other immigrants and refugees might face in a new country?

5. What civil rights violations might be occurring?

CHAPTER SUMMARY

3.1 Describe the founding and settling of this country

What are the major racial and ethnic groups that have populated this nation? When and how did they arrive?

How were they welcomed?

- What has been written in our history texts and what has been celebrated as our cultural heritage has been filtered through a male, European American lens. A singular perspective and reference point has marginalized the contributions and viewpoints of women and people of color. A more accurate accounting of the settling of this country would include the untold stories. Doing so is a revision or rewriting of history to the extent that it tells the whole story. Critics might claim that this is revisionist in that the reputation and accomplishments of "heroes" such as Columbus and Western settlers of our continent are diminished. As Loewen (2008) explained it, though, the "herofication" process has given far too much credit to some while ignoring the lives of others.

3.2 Explain the historical perspectives of peoples of the United States

What are some of the most important experiences, perspectives, and struggles experienced by members of diverse groups of people in this country? How have these diverse groups worked to overcome the barriers and obstacles? What experiences did groups have in common?

- As Takaki (1993, 1998a, 1998b, 2001) has so skillfully described in his works, our ancestors shared many similar experiences. Studying these stories can help us better understand the challenges of our newest arrivals. Learning and understanding the history can help develop empathy leading to better relationships between students.

3.3 Describe key events in the civil rights timeline

The rights, freedoms, and liberties that we enjoy were not always present for all. They were won through hard-fought battles. The horrors and injustices of the past—segregation, separate schools, sweatshops, lynchings, and outright discrimination under the authority of the law of the land—are the nightmares of this nation.

- Studying the tortured parts of our history, as well as the victories, may be a cornerstone of not reverting to the practices of a past era. Some would say that the nightmares have not ended.

3.4 Summarize key legislation affecting education

How have the laws that affect members of diverse groups changed? What critical laws affecting education have resulted?

- Understanding the law, holding on to our rights, and using all the legal avenues available to us are the rights we have as citizens. Indeed, it is the obligation of each and every one of us to uphold the constitution. As educators, one of our roles is to produce students who not only can read and write but also have a sense of civic responsibility instilled in them (Menkart, Murray, & View, 2004).

KEY TERMS

affirmative action 74

Chicano 77

English-only movement 77

immigrants 63

in-service 79

preservice 79

reparations 71

segregation 71

APPLICATION: ACTIVITIES AND EXERCISES

Individual

1. Many young people know very little about their ancestry. Conduct research into your family history using websites such as http://byub.org/ancestors.

2. What obstacles did your ancestors face in this country? Compare your findings with those of classmates and look for similarities and differences.

3. Do research in your town archives to find local history that might not be well known. Were there slaves and slave owners among your founding members? What incidents of unrest have taken place where you live?

Group

1. Visit cultural clubs or attend meetings and social events, as a group, that represent each of your cultures. Compare notes afterward as to similarities and differences.

2. Interview one another about your cultural past. Share what you have found with other members of your group. Again, compare similarities and differences.

3. Attend a local veteran's group meeting or interview residents of a Veteran's Administration hospital. Listen to the stories and reflect on them.

Self-Assessment

1. For each statement, mark whether it is true or not.

Federal Title IX requires that each school district have an identified Title IX coordinator. I know who that is in my town.	Yes	No
My college has made it known to me who the Title IX coordinator is.	Yes	No
I know what the school policies and procedures are for filing a civil rights complaint.	Yes	No
I can remember a time when my civil rights have been violated.	Yes	No
I know of incidents in which the school was in violation of federal civil rights laws.	Yes	No

ANSWERS TO EXERCISES

Exercise 3.1: Self-Assessment About American History

1. False—it was the Nineteenth Amendment.

2. True

3. False

4. True

5. True

Exercise 3.2: Which Law Is Being Violated Here?

1. Title IX—Sex Discrimination

2. Title VI of the Civil Rights Act

3. Title VI of the Civil Rights Act

4. Title II of the Americans with Disabilities Act

5. Several states have laws that prohibit discrimination in schools based on sexual orientation. Schools have authority to control situations that create a significant disruption to the educational environment.

ANNOTATED RESOURCES

Civilrights.org

https://civilrights.org/publications/

Civilrights.org is a collaboration of the Leadership Conference on Civil Rights and the Leadership Conference on Civil Rights Education Fund. Its mission is to serve as the site of record for relevant and up-to-the-minute civil rights news and information. Home to socially concerned, issue-oriented original audio, video, and written programming, Civilrights.org is committed not only to serve as the online nerve center for the struggle against discrimination in all its forms but also to build the public understanding that it is essential for our nation to continue its journey toward social and economic justice.

Greg D. Feldmeth's U.S. History Resources

http://faculty.polytechnic.org/gfeldmeth/USHistory.html

The purpose of this website is to assist students and teachers in U.S. history courses. One of the challenges that both students and teachers face in taking a survey history course is the overwhelming amount of material that must be covered. For some, understanding of the big picture gets lost in the sheer volume of facts, dates, people, and movements. So this site attempts to clarify, simplify, and synthesize the facts without making history simplistic.

Library of Congress

http://memory.loc.gov/learn/features/immig/timeline.html

This feature presentation link can make history come alive for students. The site provides an introduction to the study of immigration to the United States. It is far from the complete story and focuses only on the immigrant groups that arrived in greatest numbers during the 19th and early 20th centuries. The presentation was shaped by the primary sources available in the library's online collections.

Native Village

http://www.nativevillage.org

Native Village was created as an educational and current events resource for Native American youth, teens, families, educators, and friends. Weekly publications—*Native Village Youth and Education News* and *Native Village Opportunities and Websites*—are published on Wednesdays. Every issue shares Indian news and education across the Americas and is written in a condensed, easy-to-read format. Native Village libraries house links to quality learning opportunities and websites. The archives allow the browsing of past issues, and the site continually updates information in other areas to stay current with America's First Nations and Peoples.

Resources on Native Americans

The American Indian Education Foundation (http://www.aiefprograms.org) recommends these books, many by Indian authors, to those who want to know more about Indian issues from an Indian perspective.

Brave Bird, M., & Erdoes, R. (1990). *Lakota woman.* New York, NY: G. Weidenfeld.

Brave Bird, M., & Erdoes, R. (1993). *Ohitika woman.* New York, NY: Grove Press.

Brown, D. (2007). *Bury my heart at wounded knee.* New York, NY: Henry Holt.

Cash, J. H. (2004). *To be an Indian.* New York, NY: Holt, Rinehart & Winston.

Deloria, V., Jr. (1988). *Custer died for your sins: An Indian manifesto.* New York, NY: Macmillan.

Elk, B., & Neihardt, J. G. (1979). *Black Elk speaks: Being the life story of a holy man of the Oglala Sioux.* Lincoln: University of Nebraska Press.

Erdoes, R., & Ortiz, A. (1984). *American Indian myths and legends.* New York, NY: Pantheon Books.

Frazier, I. (2000). *On the Rez.* New York, NY: Farrar, Straus & Giroux.

Lame Deer, J., & Erdoes, R. (1994). *Lame deer, seeker of visions.* New York, NY: Washington Square Press.

Matthiessen, P. (1992). *In the spirit of crazy horse.* New York, NY: Penguin Books.

Nerburn, K. (2002). *Neither wolf nor dog: On forgotten roads with an Indian elder.* San Rafael, CA: New World Library.

Ross, A. C. (1998). *Mitakuye Oyasin: We are all related.* Denver, CO: Wiconi Waste.

Resources on African Americans

Hale-Benson, J. E. (1986). *Black children: Their roots, culture, and learning styles.* Baltimore, MD: Johns Hopkins University Press.

Ladson-Billings, G. (2009). *The dreamkeepers: Successful teachers of African American children.* San Francisco, CA: Jossey-Bass.

Lerner, G. (1992). *Black women in White America: A documentary history.* New York, NY: Vintage Books.

Massey, S. (2000). *Black cowboys of Texas.* College Station: Texas A & M University Press.

Powell Hopson, D., & Hopson, D. S. (1990). *Different and wonderful: Raising Black children in a race-conscious society.* New York, NY: Simon & Schuster.

Smitherman, G. (1986). *Talkin and testifyin: The language of Black America* (Rev. ed.). Detroit, MI: Wayne State University Press. (Originally published in Boston by Houghton Mifflin, 1977)

Tatum, B. (1997). *Why are all the Black kids sitting together in the cafeteria? And other conversations about race.* New York, NY: Basic Books.

Resources on Asian Americans

Chen, E., & Omatsu, G. (2006). *Teaching about Asian Pacific Americans: Effective activities, strategies, and assignments for classrooms and communities.* Lanham, MD: Rowman & Littlefield.

Louie, S. L., & Omatsu, G. K. (Eds.). (2001). *Asian Americans: The movement and the moment.* Los Angeles: University of California–Los Angeles Asian American Studies Press Center.

Pang, V., & Cheng, L. (1998). *Struggling to be heard: The unmet needs of Asian Pacific American children.* Albany: State University of New York Press.

Takaki, R. (1993). *A different mirror: A history of multicultural America.* London, England: Little, Brown.

Takaki, R. (1998a). *A larger memory: A history of our diversity, with voices.* Boston, MA: Little, Brown.

Takaki, R. (1998b). *Strangers from a different shore: A history of Asian Americans* (Rev. & updated ed.). Boston, MA: Little, Brown.

Takaki, R. (2001). *Double victory: A multicultural history of America in World War II.* Boston, MA: Little, Brown.

Zia, H. (2001). *Asian American dreams: The emergence of an American people.* New York, NY: Farrar, Straus & Giroux.

Resources on Hispanic Americans

Heyck, D. (Ed.). (1994). *Barrios and borderlands: Culture of Latinos and Latinas in the United States.* New York, NY: Routledge.

Kanellos, N. (1998). *Thirty million strong: Reclaiming the Hispanic image in American culture.* Golden, CO: Fulcrum.

Kanellos, K., & Perez, C. (Eds.). (1995). *Chronology of Hispanic–American history: From pre-Columbian times to the present.* New York, NY: Gale Research.

Meier, M., & Gutierrez, M. (2000). *Encyclopedia of the Mexican American civil rights movement.* Westport, CT: Greenwood Press.

Tenenbaum, B. (Ed.). (1996). *Encyclopedia of Latin American history and culture.* New York, NY: Scribner.

Visit the student study site at **study.sagepub .com/howe3e** for additional study tools including the following:

- eFlashcards
- Web quizzes
- SAGE journal articles
- Video links
- Web resources
- Assessments from the text
- Access to author's blog

Get the tools you need to sharpen your study skills. SAGE edge offers a robust online environment featuring an impressive array of free tools and resources. Access practice quizzes, eFlashcards, video, and multimedia at **edge.sagepub.com/howe3e**

4 Foundational Knowledge for Culturally Responsive Teaching

Stockbyte/stockbyte/Thinkstock

Learning Objectives

An understanding of current research and literature about multicultural education has led to the description of essential knowledge for multicultural educators. This essential knowledge is described in four learning objectives in this chapter. Through your study of and work on this chapter, you will be able to do the following:

4.1 Explain important knowledge about culture, diversity, and student assets

4.2 Identify the foundations of multicultural education and the achievement of equity

4.3 Summarize knowledge about academic achievement and diverse students

4.4 Describe important knowledge about teaching and learning

This chapter explores the fundamental knowledge that is required of educators who want to be culturally responsive and responsible. The need for educators to be knowledgeable about culture and culturally responsive teaching has been critically important for a long time. Fortunately, many scholars and experts have worked to define specific knowledge areas required of effective teachers.

The knowledge areas as presented can be both daunting and comforting. On the one hand, the sheer depth and breadth of the knowledge needed might seem overwhelming to an educator wondering how to learn what is described. The reality is that there is much to know to be an effective educator, and much of this pertains to culture. On the other hand, when the fundamental knowledge required of educators is grouped into categories, the process of goal setting for professional development becomes clearer and easier. Educators must remember that becoming a multicultural educator, or an effective educator for that matter, is a lifelong process.

There are several key reasons why educators must be lifelong learners as they become multicultural educators. First, culture influences in significant ways our thoughts, perceptions, and actions. Deep knowledge about various aspects of the diverse cultures in a classroom can be a distinct advantage when planning teaching and learning experiences. Deep understanding of culture can also aid in the development of positive and productive teacher–student and student–student relationships. As teachers build their own personal knowledge bases about diversity and multicultural education, they will be better equipped to be social justice educators who work to achieve equity and eliminate discrimination in schools. Learning about the various aspects of culture and their influence on teaching and learning is a worthwhile investment of the time and dedication needed.

> My first job after college was as a teacher in Cotulla, Texas, in a small Mexican-American school. Few of them could speak English, and I couldn't speak much Spanish. My students were poor and they often came to class without breakfast, hungry. . . . I often walked home late in the afternoon, after the classes were finished, wishing there was more that I could do. But all I knew was to teach them the little that I knew, hoping that it might help them against the hardships that lay ahead.
>
> —**President Lyndon Baines Johnson from his "We Shall Overcome" speech to Congress, March 15, 1965, asking for passage of the Voting Rights Act**

CASE STUDY

DO I REALLY NEED TO KNOW ABOUT STUDENT CULTURE IN ORDER TO BE AN EFFECTIVE TEACHER?

In our teaching courses consisting of graduate students in education and educational leadership, we try to use exercises and experiences to illustrate key concepts and to support students in having "aha" moments about themselves. One experience that we've used for many years is titled *Cultural Pursuit*. Cultural Pursuit is a very simple "board game." Students are given a worksheet that looks like a bingo card. Each of the 25 boxes on the worksheet contains one item of information about different cultural groups. The 25 items include foods (what is lumpia), pieces of history (who can name the lawyer who argued for the petitioners in *Brown v. Board of Education*), foreign words (what does *Nisei* mean), the significance of specific words (what is the significance of eagle feathers), and so on. Students are asked to circulate throughout the classroom and find a person who can answer or identify what the item is in a particular box. To finish the experience, a student must have found a colleague to initial 1 of each of the 25 boxes.

One winter day while teaching an introductory course in educational leadership, I engaged the students in this exercise, primarily as an opportunity for the

(Continued)

(Continued)

students to get to know one another a little more. The students, enjoying almost any chance to move around and interact with colleagues, started the exercise quickly and were experiencing some success in sharing the expertise about knowledge of cultures. These were, after all, graduate students entering a certification program in leadership. They were all practicing teachers with at least 3 years of teaching experience. They each believed they had had fairly strong educational preparation to serve as future educational leaders.

Invariably, as with most groups doing this experience, on this winter day, there was one item in one box that seemed to confound almost everyone. This item asked the participants to name the West Coast equivalent of Ellis Island. The entire group was completely stumped.

In debriefing the experience, the students discovered that they didn't know as much as they thought they knew about diverse peoples. And because some of the students had been raised in other parts of the country, they knew they couldn't blame their lack of awareness or knowledge about different people's histories on where in the country they grew up (the class was taught in a Connecticut university). This simple experience led to some really enlightening conversations about knowledge of cultures, how to acquire it, and the process of lifelong learning that is so critical for educators.

Your Perspectives on the Case

1. Do you know the West Coast equivalent of Ellis Island? Why or why not? If you don't know, do a little research to discover where it is and what it is.

2. An interesting saying has circulated in the educational community for many years, and that is, "A good teacher is a good teacher." What does the statement mean for you? What is the connection, in your view, between good teaching and culture?

3. How well would you do in an experience like "Cultural Pursuit"? Like most educators who engage in this experience, you might need to expand your knowledge about diverse cultural groups. How would you pursue and/ or enhance your own learning about cultures, differences, and teaching and learning with diverse students?

THINKING AHEAD
YOU AND CHAPTER 4 LEARNING OBJECTIVES

4.1 Explain Important Knowledge About Culture, Diversity, and Student Assets

Standards that guide the preparation and professional development of teachers today require teachers to make use of their knowledge of cultural diversity. Sometimes this requirement results in a somewhat superficial treatment of culture in the teaching and learning process. In fact, teachers must have a deep understanding of a wide variety of aspects of culture to be effective in educating all students.

Imagine visiting a school in a state with which you are unfamiliar. What would you like to know about the cultures of the students in that school so you could get a deep understanding of the teaching and learning processes in that school? Now describe a plan for what should be included in an effective teacher preparation program that supports you and others in learning deeply about culture and its impact on teaching and learning.

4.2 Identify the Foundations of Multicultural Education and the Achievement of Equity

A good starting place for becoming a multicultural educator is to develop a familiarity with key terms and definitions and to begin to consider essential questions to which you hope to find answers. Develop a list of at least 20 terms that you have heard that relate to multicultural education or culturally responsive teaching. Exchange your list with a colleague and try to define the terms on each other's lists. Discuss your definitions. Which terms appear to be particularly problematic? Work to find definitions of those terms.

4.3 Summarize Knowledge About Academic Achievement and Diverse Students

Every person has a preferred way to learn. As we discuss the connection between culture and learning, consider your own learning styles. After responding to the following prompts, reflect on the impact of your own cultural identities on your learning preferences. Predict what might happen in a classroom when a teacher's preferred learning style does not match the learning styles of students in the classroom.

I learn best by these methods:

These are my least favorite ways to learn:

My favorite teaching methods or strategies are . . .

My least favorite teaching methods or strategies are . . .

4.4 Describe Important Knowledge About Teaching and Learning

Most people understand that we are a product of how we were raised, including the influences of parents, church, friends, and community. Our family customs, habits, values, and ways of seeing and doing things are often passed on from generation to generation. Think of something you have learned very deeply. Describe in detail how you learned that knowledge. Describe how your own cultural identities (e.g., race, ethnicity, gender, religion, language) have affected how you prefer to learn. Explain ways that you might enhance your own understanding of and capacity in integrating knowledge of culture into the teaching and learning process

LEARNING OBJECTIVE 4.1 Explain Important Knowledge About Culture, Diversity, and Student Assets

The questions posed in the Thinking Ahead section above illustrate the critical importance of teachers knowing deeply about culture. Just as we believe that teachers in a different country could teach us more effectively if they knew about our histories, experiences, learning styles, communication styles, language, and so forth, so too do we believe that students in American classrooms will learn more effectively if teachers know deeply about many aspects of diverse cultures. Unfortunately, by the time they graduate from a teacher preparation program and assume a teaching position, many educators believe that they are educated well enough to teach students and that they do know about different cultures. To a degree, this is true.

Because of their own educational experiences and the communities in which they grew up, people who are entering the teaching profession now have probably had some experiences with people who are culturally diverse in terms of socioeconomic status (SES), gender, ethnicity, race, religion, sexual orientation, and ability. However, because of the nature of education, while students may have had experiences with diversity, in all likelihood, those experiences were not discussed in depth. And their experiences with diversity may have been at a relatively superficial level, sometimes referred to as the *tip of the iceberg*. This expression means that while people may have gained a small amount of information, perhaps knowledge about foods, the arts, celebrations, and some literature, they probably have not explored deeply the more important and substantial aspects of culture, such as traditions, beliefs, attitudes, preferences, patterns, and ways of communicating.

Educators have been reticent to engage students in discussions about diversity for a variety of reasons, including a lack of their own understanding about diverse cultures, a lack

Making connections with the cultural backgrounds of students helps teachers better understand how to best teach in ways that the students will understand. Learning about one another will enable students to reach out to one another and develop meaningful relationships.

iStock/bowdenimages

of skill in facilitating challenging conversations, maintenance of a belief that school time is for learning content, and a belief that because students in a school may be diverse and are in the same setting, they then know deeply about each other already. If we are committed to establishing learning environments that support all learners in achieving at high levels, then it is essential that educators develop a solid knowledge base about culture.

A major challenge in preparing culturally responsive and responsible teachers is to immerse them deeply in gaining a core knowledge base about teaching and learning as well as experiential knowledge. To acquire both types of knowledge, aspiring teachers must learn to reflect deeply about their experiences with diversity. Promising practices for engaging teachers in reflection about their own experiences around diversity include the journaling of anecdotal stories, personal narratives, and autobiographies. They need to consider their knowledge, perceptions, values, and understandings of diverse cultures.

Essential Elements of Culture

In learning about a culture, some people tend to believe they know the culture when they have eaten representative foods, heard representative music, or seen representative art or clothing. Unfortunately, exposure to a culture in only that manner, as stated earlier, is just the tip of the iceberg. Some schools, committed to being a "multicultural school," address diversity by having a multicultural festival or studying particular cultural groups for a relatively brief period. For example, teachers might provide students with opportunities in February, which has been declared to be Black History Month, to learn about important African Americans and some of the historical experiences of African Americans. Or students might learn about Hispanic Americans in May, around the time of Cinco de Mayo, or about women's involvement in American history in March, during Women's History Month. This is not bad, and in fact, if nothing else is being done to integrate multiculturalism into the mainstream curriculum, these celebrations are at least a minimal effort to address diversity. However, there is so much more to understanding and knowing deeply about a culture.

What are the essential elements of culture? Multicultural educators need to know about and be skilled in helping their students know about a culture's beliefs, values, customs, traditions, taboos, norms or ways of doing things, mores, and spiritual beliefs (Banks, 2009; Banks & Banks, 2015; Gollnick & Chinn, 2013, 2016; Grant & Sleeter, 2012; Huber-Warring, 2008; Nieto, 2010, 2017; Nieto & Bode, 2012, 2018; Smith, 1998). All students come to school with distinct cultural identities, grounded in these essential elements of culture. These identities and elements can usefully be viewed by educators as student assets. Nieto (2013) is clear about the critical need for educators to honor students' identities. If educators develop an understanding of students and their distinct assets, they are in a much better position to develop a learning environment that supports each student in deep and meaningful learning (Tomlinson, 2014). Unfortunately, some educators, believing perhaps that there is a right way of doing things and a right way of perceiving things, may see students as lacking, disadvantaged, or limited in their assets (Grant & Sleeter, 2012). Grant and Sleeter (2012) offered four recommendations to educators who want to use knowledge of student culture as an asset in building learning environments:

1. Put student interests and backgrounds at the core of teaching.

2. Use students' learning styles to plan instruction.

3. Use student language as a learning resource.

4. Connect with parents and the community.

Diller and Moule (2011) explored the elements of culture in a different way by describing the dimensions of culture. Their descriptions are based on the work of Brown and Landrum-Brown (1995). The dimensions described originally by Brown and Landrum-Brown include "psychobehavioral modalities, axiology (values), ethos (guiding beliefs), epistemology (how one knows), logic (reasoning process), ontology (nature of reality), concept of time, and concept of self" (cited in Diller & Moule, 2011, p. 69). Diller and Moule (2011) indicated that to support these dimensions, a culture develops cultural processes or traditions, rituals, and accepted ways of behaving. They believed that "what makes a culture unique, then, is the particular profile of where it stands on each dimension combined with the specific cultural forms it has evolved" (p. 69). An understanding of the existence of these dimensions and elements is critical for educators who aspire to be multicultural educators.

TABLE 4.1 Cultural Norms

1. Looking down while facing an elder at a family gathering may be interpreted as a sign of respect.	True	False
2. Looking down while facing a police officer who is questioning you may be interpreted as a sign of respect.	True	False
3. Shaking everyone's hands firmly when meeting a group of American businesspeople may be seen as a sign of self-confidence.	True	False
4. Holding up two fingers in a V to signify "victory" or "peace" is best not used in certain South American countries.	True	False
5. Smiling broadly is always a sign of agreement.	True	False
Answers: All true.		

Teachers are cautioned when evaluating minority students not to apply standards based on other cultural groups. Multicultural or at least bicultural skills help us bridge different worlds. Consider the scenarios described in Table 4.1. Whether or not the answer is true or false is clearly reflective of cultural norms.

Your consideration of the information in Exercise 4.1 will most likely cause you to realize that norms differ from culture to culture and are affected by factors such as politics, religion, and past practices. With this in mind, consider how students from diverse backgrounds and experiences might see life from other viewpoints. As an educator, this theme should be a constant in your lesson planning as you consider teaching and learning for all students.

EXERCISE 4.1
RELIGION AND EDUCATION

Identify a school with which you are familiar. Contact the principal or another leader in that school and arrange to conduct an interview about current practices related to religion in the school. Use the guidelines developed by the U.S. Department of Education (2003) as one basis for development of questions about religion and education in that school. Summarize your findings in a briefing, and then prepare to share your findings with class colleagues. When considering the data that all class colleagues have collected, are there common themes about religion and education practice? What factors might affect the findings (e.g., geographic location of the school)? How are you thinking differently about religion and education following your interview and collegial discussions? In what ways are you thinking differently about your role as a multicultural educator?

- Students may pray in school when they are not engaged in school activities. For example, they can read their Bibles, say grace at meals, and study religious materials during noninstructional time.
- Students can organize prayer groups and/or religious clubs. These groups must be provided with the same access to school facilities as any other noncurricular groups.
- School employees may not encourage or discourage student prayer. Teachers may not, in an official capacity, participate in these activities with students.
- Schools may allow students to go to off-campus religious instruction if they do not encourage or discourage participation in that instruction.
- Students may choose to show their beliefs about religion in classroom assignments. That work can be neither penalized nor given extra consideration due to its religious content.
- Student speakers at assemblies or extracurricular activities may neither be selected nor discounted based on religious beliefs of the student.
- School officials may not organize prayer at graduation.
- School officials may not organize religious ceremonies.

Socioeconomic Status and Education

Among the sources of diversity with which educators should become familiar is SES. Gollnick and Chinn (2013, 2016) described **socioeconomic status** as a way of measuring economic success in our society. In general, SES is determined through a combination of factors that include occupation, education, and income. SES can be further measured by looking at an individual's, or family's, wealth and power. Taken together, these five factors, according to Gollnick and Chinn (2013, 2016), affect how an individual lives. Often, a student's socioeconomic level can be determined by looking at that student's eligibility for free and/or reduced lunch.

For the most part, in terms of SES, people identify with one of four or five primary social classes: (1) the unemployed and the homeless, (2) the working class, (3) the middle class, (4) the upper-middle class, and (5) the upper class.

Developing a deep knowledge about SES, or class, is critical to educators because it affects, in particular, access. Education can play a critical role in helping students overcome economic inequalities. Students from low-income and working-class families, in particular, are susceptible to the challenges associated with attaining an equitable education. Education is a means for helping students improve their wealth and sense of power. Unfortunately, many elements related to SES are powerful barriers to what education can do for students. For example, lack of funds and resources can limit access to educational opportunities. Students from impoverished backgrounds may be misdiagnosed and inappropriately placed in special needs classrooms. Students without adequate funding support and without resources in the home may find themselves in lower tracks in schools and unable to move themselves out of those tracks. Students in lower-SES homes may not have advocates who argue effectively for them to receive equitable opportunities. Research demonstrates that teachers tend to have lower expectations of children from lower socioeconomic classes. And in the end, some students who are raised in homes in which parents are unemployed, homeless, and/or working poor may find themselves accepting their class status and believing that their lifestyles are not alterable. Research shows that students from lower socioeconomic classes have higher dropout rates, higher rates of placement in special needs classrooms, and a slower acquisition of academic skills than students from other socioeconomic classes.

What can an educator do to counteract the insidious effect of SES on a student's educational opportunities? First, educators must hold high expectations for each and every student in the classroom. Educators must also design curriculum that is relevant and accessible to each student. By relevant, we mean that all children should be able to see themselves reflected in the content of the curriculum. And finally, educators must continually strive for equitable funding support for education. This means that each child, no matter the community, should receive what he or she needs to be able to achieve at high levels.

Religion and Education

One type of **cultural identity** held dear by people the world over is religious identity. Centuries ago, legislators believed it important to guarantee for U.S. citizens the basic principle of separation of church and state, as well as a guarantee of religious freedom. The First Amendment of the U.S. Constitution, passed in 1791, reads,

Congress shall make no law respecting an establishment of religion, or prohibiting the free exercise thereof; or abridging the freedom of speech, or of the press; or the right of the people peaceably to assemble, and to petition the Government for a redress of grievances.

Because religion is so essential to human identity, there have been many challenges to the interpretation of this amendment. Issues have arisen related to prayer in school, appropriate dress, use of vouchers to obtain schooling, censorship of curriculum materials, and appropriate curriculum topic areas (e.g., creationism vs. evolution). Court cases have repeatedly been brought to try to influence the interpretation of the amendment.

In 1963, the U.S. Supreme Court found that religion may be taught in school as long as it is objective instruction about religion rather than indoctrination in a particular set of beliefs. In the early 1960s, the Supreme Court found school-sponsored prayer to be unconstitutional. At the same time, Supreme Court cases have protected individual rights to pray, wear religious dress, and express religious beliefs while in school. If these practices are disruptive or coercive to peers, however, they are considered unconstitutional. For example, school-led prayer and student-led prayer at graduation ceremonies and football games is considered unconstitutional because it is believed that students will be coerced into engaging in those prayers or that particular beliefs are being promoted. All of these cases apply to public school settings that receive public or federal funding. Because of these and other judicial decisions, public school officials must be neutral in their treatment of religion and neither favor nor demonstrate hostility against any religious beliefs. Public schools are forbidden to sponsor religious activity, while they are required to protect religious activity initiated by individuals.

While courts in the United States have worked repeatedly to define the parameters of the First Amendment, the legislative branch of the federal government has also worked to establish related policies. Section 9524 of the Elementary and Secondary Education Act of 1965, amended by the No Child Left Behind Act of 2001, requires that, as a condition of receiving federal funds, each school district or local educational agency must certify annually that it has no policy preventing or otherwise denying participation in constitutionally protected prayer in public schools (U.S. Department of Education, 2003). The U.S. Department of Education (2003) issued guidelines for addressing the separation of church and state in schools (see Exercise 4.1). For example, public schools may teach courses in religious history, comparative religions, and the role of religion in the history of the United States.

Apart from these guidelines, what else should educators know about religion? According to Gollnick and Chinn (2013), 90% of the population in the United States claims to have a religious preference or affiliation. Religion influences individuals (students as well as school employees, school board members, and community members) and the educational system. Gollnick and Chinn do an exceptional job of describing religious pluralism, or the capacity for a relatively wide variety of religions to coexist in relative peace, in the United States. While not in agreement, members of different religious groups and denominations do coexist in an atmosphere of respect and acceptance for one another. Gollnick and Chinn describe in detail the major types of religions, the effect of religion on education, and controversial issues related to religion and education. Resources provided at the end of this chapter will be helpful as you work to augment your understanding of the impact of religion on education.

Gender and Education

It has been well documented that girls and women have been shortchanged in their education (American Association of University Women [AAUW], 2004, 2010, 2016; Gollnick & Chinn, 2013, 2016; Sadker & Zittleman, 2016; Sadker, Zittleman, & Sadker, 2013).

Girls have not achieved equally, as compared with boys, in academic or professional realms. Interestingly, legislation was passed in 1972 to address gender discrimination and educational equity for boys and girls. According to information posted on the U.S. Department of Justice (2018) website (www.justice.gov),

> Title IX is a comprehensive federal law that prohibits discrimination on the basis of sex in any federally funded education program or activity. The principal objective of Title IX is to avoid the use of federal money to support sex discrimination in education programs and to provide individual citizens effective protection against those practices. Title IX applies, with a few specific exceptions, to all aspects of federally funded education programs or activities. In addition to traditional educational institutions such as colleges, universities, and elementary and secondary schools, Title IX also applies to any education or training program operated by a recipient of federal financial assistance.

The passage of Title IX was intended originally to address 10 specific areas. Currently, Title IX is designed to address six areas: (1) science, technology, engineering, and mathematics; (2) pregnant and parenting students; (3) sexual harassment and assault; (4) career and technical education; (5) athletics; and (6) single-sex education. Periodically, research has been conducted by a variety of organizations on progress in implementing Title IX (2018). Since 1991, the AAUW has pursued an extensive research agenda to highlight areas of need in achieving equity in education for girls and women. Its groundbreaking report *Shortchanging Girls, Shortchanging Women* (AAUW, 1991) looked at the impact of education on girls' self-esteem, participation in school, and career aspirations. Sharing of that research with schools and districts around the country was instrumental in redirecting the educational experiences of girls. Nevertheless, recent research supported by AAUW (2004), such as *Under the Microscope: A Decade of Gender Equity Projects in the Sciences*, indicates that educators must do more to support the participation of girls in the STEM (science, technology, engineering, and mathematics) areas.

Myra and David Sadker, two of the original national leaders of efforts to achieve equity for boys and girls, uncovered much of the bias in education through their research in the 1960s and 1970s (Sadker et al., 2013). Their findings especially highlighted the need for educators to pay attention to both blatant and subtle forms of bias in classrooms. The more subtle forms, such as the language used (using male pronouns more frequently than female pronouns) and the persons used as role models (the most prominent experts in a field of study), can be even more detrimental to the equitable education of boys and girls than the blatant forms. When girls don't hear about women who have achieved certain positions, they may wonder why they should believe they can do it themselves.

While much progress has been made since the passage of Title IX in 1972, gender discrimination, **gender bias**, and sexual harassment continue to be impediments to the education of girls and women. The AAUW has been at the forefront in supporting implementation of Title IX and monitoring the impact. In particular, the AAUW has investigated the actions of the Office for Civil Rights in promoting and ensuring equity and fairness in educational settings as well as in addressing violations of students' civil rights that can seriously undermine a student's access to education (AAUW, 2016). The AAUW has noted the important and critical work of the Office for Civil Rights in collecting data about schools and colleges in meeting the key gender equity indicators. For educators who are dedicated to equity in education, it will be important to be active in the promotion of equal opportunities to learn for all students.

Regarding specific areas of progress, in their 2008 report, *Title IX at 35: Beyond the Headlines*, the National Coalition for Women and Girls in Education (NCWGE) indicated that since the passage of Title IX in 1972 much has been achieved toward equity for girls and boys in the areas of athletics in schools, education in the so-called STEM subjects, career and technical education, employment in educational institutions, sexual harassment of students, and single-sex education.

In which areas does work remain to be done? Girls continue to experience discrimination in a variety of areas (NCWGE, 2008). For example, boys still disproportionately participate in courses that lead to high-skill, high-wage jobs. Women still pursue courses of study in college that lead the majority of them to participate in traditionally female occupations. And sexual harassment is present and is part of the school culture in many educational settings around the country. Finally, women continue to be underrepresented in the critical fields of STEM (AAUW, 2010).

The impact of inequitable educational opportunities and bias can be discerned when looking at the professional achievements of adult women. The gender pay gap continues to exist. The AAUW (2011) documented that, as of 2009, women earned 77 cents for every dollar earned by men for full-time year-round positions requiring equal education, skills, and training.

Given the challenges to achieving equity in education for girls and women, the NCWGE has provided a set of recommendations for educators at the local level to enhance the opportunities for girls in education and to promote the achievement of equity. For example, each school should appoint a Title IX coordinator who is charged with overseeing activities and efforts to comply with the law, respond to noncompliance complaints, and publicize information about Title IX. The coordinator should publicize information about Title IX protections and grievance procedures. The name and contact information of the

EXERCISE 4.2

GENDER AND EDUCATION

Locate and read one of the early groundbreaking studies about gender and education (e.g., one of the AAUW reports or one of the books authored by the Sadkers). Use specific information in the study to reflect on the progress made by schools in addressing gender equity since 1972 (the date of passage of Title IX). Specifically, describe areas of progress and areas that still need to be addressed, if any. Describe your own experiences in school, specifically in terms of access and gender. Organize a list of at least 10 ways that your gender influenced (positively or negatively) educational access for you:

1. Important terms related to the study of gender-inclusive education

2. The history of sexism in the United States

3. The theory and research on gender identity

4. The theory and research on sex discrimination in the education system (e.g., testing, teacher–student interactions, communication style preferences)

5. Principles of nonsexist culturally inclusive curriculum development

Title IX coordinator should be provided to all school community members. The Title IX coordinator should conduct an annual assessment of the school's compliance with Title IX regulations, as well as school actions in response to issues that arise under the regulations.

On a schoolwide basis, each school should develop ongoing professional development opportunities for educators and administrators to learn strategies for identifying and addressing sex stereotyping and sex discrimination. Educational institutions should also continue and expand programs to attract women into career fields relying on the STEM subjects at every level from career and technical education to higher education. Administrators and the Title IX coordinator should work with search committees and personnel departments to examine hiring practices. And all educators should work to ensure that the female and male students have equal opportunities to participate in athletics and other types of education programs.

In addition to knowing about how to support equitable education for girls and women, teachers should have an in-depth understanding of human sexuality, including sexual orientation. They should become familiar with lesbian, gay, bisexual, and **transgender** (LGBT) issues. The rights of LGBT students, in particular, need to be understood in light of the rampant homophobia in schools and society (Donahue, 2000). Considering the emotional cost of dealing with sometimes overwhelming discrimination while attempting to get an education, it is critical that educators understand the psychological and emotional needs of these students. Smith (1998) indicated that teachers who aspire to be culturally competent must understand sexual orientation identity development, have knowledge of the case law on gay and lesbian issues, and comprehend the unique psychological, emotional, and educational needs of LGBT students.

The leading advocacy organization for multicultural education, the National Association for Multicultural Education, has worked to require at least one foundational course in multicultural education for all school personnel. What does it mean to have a grounding in the foundations of multicultural education? As when a builder sets about constructing a new house, the first step is to lay a foundation on which the house can stand. The people who inhabit the house want to make sure that the foundation is solid, reliable, sturdy, and able to withstand the elements. A foundational course in multicultural education can be considered in the same way. When a person is "building" himself or herself as an effective educator, a strong foundation is critical. Understanding the foundations of multicultural education means learning the language of multicultural education, key terms used

TABLE 4.2   **Key Terms in Multicultural Education and Their Definitions**

Examples of Key Terms	Definitions
Multicultural education	Incorporation of diversity into daily teaching and learning
Global education	Study of peoples and their cultures in other countries
Assimilation	The process of people losing their cultural identity to become part of, or fit into, a new cultural group
Racism	Prejudice plus power
Diversity	Differences between people due to race, ethnicity, SES, gender, language, ability, sexual orientation, religion, and so forth
Social justice education	The achievement of equity in education through the process of teaching and learning; also, engaging students in learning problem-solving processes to confront social issues

by multicultural educators, important principles and practices, models for implementing multicultural education, and the research and theory in support of multicultural education. Foundational understanding also includes development of a grasp of the effects of race, class, gender, and other cultural influences on teaching and learning. Table 4.2 provides some of the key terms used by multicultural educators. In other chapters in this book, you will discover additional terms, models, theories, and supportive research and theory.

LEARNING OBJECTIVE 4.2 Identify the Foundations of Multicultural Education and the Achievement of Equity

An important aspect of having a strong foundation is an understanding that becoming an effective multicultural educator means continually working to expand one's awareness of differences and injustices and one's knowledge of culture, specific teaching strategies, and classroom applications (Howe & Lisi, 1995). In developing a foundation in multicultural education, teachers learn that young children also go through a process of becoming multicultural beings. A child learns and experiences first the culture of the family. Once the child grows older and meets other children and assumes some of the characteristics and actions of other cultures, that child becomes multicultural.

Understanding Racism

The history and impact of racism in this country, how prejudice is learned and unlearned, and the impact of racism on all peoples are critical areas of study (Smith, 1998). *Racism* is simply defined as "power plus privilege." This concept of privilege is of particular significance, particularly when considering **White privilege** and male privilege. The primary

There is much to learn about the backgrounds of our students. Time spent getting to know the experiences and perspectives of those we teach enables educators to better motivate and engage them as learners.

iStock/CEFutcher

point of this concept is that certain people, simply because of the cultural group to which they belong and through no effort on their own part, are imbued with a particular set of privileges that other people are not born with. This set of privileges stays with them for life, affecting all their interactions. Peggy McIntosh's study in this area is perhaps the best known. In a groundbreaking paper, *White Privilege and Male Privilege: A Personal Account of Coming to See Correspondences Through Work in Women's Studies*, McIntosh (1998) illustrated through simple statements the power of this privilege. Following are some examples:

1. If I should need to move, I can be pretty sure of renting or purchasing housing in an area that I can afford and in which I would want to live.

2. I can be reasonably sure that my neighbors in such a location will be neutral or pleasant to me.

3. I can go shopping alone most of the time, fairly well assured that I will not be followed or harassed by store detectives.

4. When I am told about our national heritage or about "civilization," I am shown that people of my color made it what it is.

5. I can be sure that my children will be given curricular materials that testify to the existence of their race.

Understanding power and privilege, as illustrated above, and who has it and who does not is important. It helps define better the lives that we, as well as our students, lead. It helps set an agenda in multicultural education of working toward justice in our society and ensuring an equal playing ground for all.

Understanding the Impact of Policy on the Learning Environment

This knowledge base addresses how policies and practices can sometimes have an adverse effect on students, particularly girls, students of color, recent immigrants, second-language learners, special education students, LGBT students, and students with disabilities. These policies and practices may not intend to create unfairness, but inequity can be the result when differential privilege is compounded by a lack of understanding of the different circumstances of students who are not White, male, and middle class.

For example, it is common for states to have a bilingual education policy that provides for 30 months (or 3 years) of bilingual instruction for new non-English-speaking students. Classes are formed in which all students speak the common foreign language. A teacher is provided who speaks both English and the native language of the speakers. Instruction is provided such that English is taught along with other academic subjects, but explanations are provided in the native language.

However, after 30 months, these students are mainstreamed into regular classes or go into an English as a second-language class. Here the teacher specializes in teaching nonnative speakers but does not speak or provide instruction in the native language. For students who have struggled to learn the English language, 3 years is often not enough, especially if they are not at their grade level academically even in their native language.

Can you see how policies and practices, even well-meaning ones, can be unfair to students? In the classroom, well-intended instructional practices can also have an adverse effect on diverse students. One of the most controversial practices—which research indicates has a significant negative impact on students—is the practice of grouping. Grouping students who are alike due to perceived academic achievement and placing them in separate classroom settings is sometimes referred to as *homogeneous grouping or tracking.* In most schools in this country, educators have come to believe that students will receive more effective instruction if they are grouped with other students like them. This belief is contrary to findings of the impact of tracking practices on students. Homogeneous grouping or tracking, in fact, does a tremendous disservice to students (Oakes, Lipton, Anderson, & Stillman, 2012).

Research conducted by Oakes and colleagues (2012) indicates that when the same content is taught to students who are in "leveled subjects" (e.g., basic, intermediate, advanced), several things happen. Students who are tracked in higher groups appear to receive particular advantages, including a curriculum that is concepts based, instructional strategies that approach students as thinking problem solvers, increased time in instruction, teachers who are more experienced, an enriched classroom setting, and access to computers as tools to enhance learning. Students who are tracked in lower groups are not expected to do well, are provided with a curriculum grounded in lower order thinking skills, are taught by teachers who are less skilled, and are engaged in a more didactic instructional approach and more passive learning activities. Many lower level classes are populated by students identified as special needs children or second-language learners—just the students who need the best teachers and the best instructional approaches the district has to offer! And when students are placed in a particular level or track, it is generally next to impossible for them to escape and move to a different level. Once they are "tracked," they are kept in that track for the duration of their educational careers.

Developing ways to support student achievement is key to the legislation. Efforts to increase achievement must focus more on "constructive reform strategies" and less on solely equating minority children with failure in school. To do this, teaching strategies must be adapted to be culturally responsive (Gay, 2010). How culture affects learning styles is an important consideration. Also of concern are communication styles, thinking styles, value systems, socialization processes, relational patterns, and performance styles (Smith, 1998).

LEARNING OBJECTIVE 4.3 Summarize Knowledge About Academic Achievement and Diverse Students

Learning Styles and the Achievement of Culturally Diverse Students

Teachers interested in knowing about how culture influences teaching and learning are indeed fortunate in that a large body of research exists and much has been written to describe the learning styles of culturally diverse groups of people, including, in particular, African Americans, Mexican Americans, and Native Americans (Smith, 1998). The term *cultural learning style* refers to the ways in which culture influences how people think, perceive, and process information. It also refers to how diverse peoples use their senses to take in information and the ways in which culture influences how people see themselves in relation to the learning process. While the extensive body of literature about culture, **cognition**, and learning has led to the development of cultural learning–style profiles, or descriptions of how different groups of people process information, teachers must be careful to use the information effectively and not overgeneralize, forcing children to fit exactly into a particular learning-style profile.

Smith (1998) indicated that knowledge of cultural learning styles is critical because that knowledge can help educators know how cultural groups pass on knowledge, values, learning structures, and ways of perceiving to group members. We can understand how culture influences learning styles by considering an example from China. In the United States, terms such as *teacher*, *instructor*, and *professor* are often used to describe the roles of educators. In the Chinese language, there is no equivalent term. In fact, the Chinese word for teacher is *laoshi*, which translates roughly in English to "prophet." In China, then, instead of referring to the teacher as Ms. Beeman, students would call her Laoshi Beeman. In accordance with this revered title is a commensurate degree of respect. Teachers, and parents, are held in high esteem in China. Culturally, one is taught not to criticize teachers or parents. Age is also highly respected. An older teacher, then, especially one with gray hair, commands much respect.

Given these facts, a teacher of Chinese American students, especially new arrivals, would use this knowledge of culture to adapt teaching strategies. Chinese American students, while learning that their culture is worthy of respect, must also be taught that to succeed in the American educational system, they need to learn to be critically reflective of what is being taught. The parents of the students would need to learn that offering suggestions and raising concerns is a legitimate and valued part of the parent–teacher communication process.

Data indicate that by 2020, 40% of schoolchildren nationally will be students of color, and in the 20 largest school districts, the percentage rises dramatically to 70% (Irvine & Armento, 2001). Our school community is rich with cultural influences. These influences help define who we are and what motivates us to act and think the way we do. For educators, tapping into this wealth of knowledge about how culture affects learning is like a miner uncovering nuggets of gold. Unfortunately, one of the weaknesses of studies on the achievement gap between African American students and their White counterparts is a lack of focus on the influences of culture (Irvine, 2003). It becomes evident that elevating the achievement of students of color will not be achieved until teachers are trained to place students and their cultures at the center of learning. In addition, teachers must first understand their own cultures before they can appreciate and use the culture of their students in effective instruction (Robins, Lindsey, Lindsey, & Terrell, 2012).

Jupiter images/bananastock/thinkstock

People learn in different ways. The one-style-fits-all approach of teaching benefits only certain students. Having a repertoire of teaching strategies expands the capability of reaching all students.

As educators consider how they might effectively support the achievement of diverse learners, they will want to make use of the research on learning styles (Willis & Hodson, 2013). Irvine and York (1995) defined **learning styles** as particular ways in which we receive and process information. *Learning style* preferences affect cognitive functioning, as well as affective functions, in all of us. And culture, to a large degree, affects ways in which people learn to receive and process information. So what do we need to know? Do we have to learn about every culture? How do we account for cultural difference and variations *within* each culture? For example, the cultural variations among Asian students are numerous. Likewise, the U.S. Census Bureau no longer classifies Hispanic Americans as one monolithic race but as a culture that crosses virtually all races.

The risk of focusing on specific cultural learning styles lies in stereotyping and generalizing. Nieto (2010, 2017) warned that some theories border on racist perceptions and have actually proven to be detrimental to minority students. Well-meaning teachers, relying on research on how students are supposed to learn best based on their culture, have forced students into one predominant learning style, minimizing opportunities to engage in variations on learning methods that might work better for them. At the same time, educators can benefit from knowing some of the research about learning styles associated with diverse groups of students.

Irvine and York (1995) summarized the research about how African American students, Hispanic American students, and Native American students tend to learn most effectively. Among their findings is the fact that African American learners tend to approximate space and numbers rather than adhere to exactness or accuracy and to be more proficient in nonverbal than verbal communication. Also, Hispanic learners tend to prefer group learning situations and prefer concrete representations to abstract ones. And Native American learners tend to prefer visual, spatial, and perceptual information to verbal information and use mental images, rather than word associations, to remember and understand words and concepts.

Knowledge About Communication Styles

This knowledge base covers how one learns a second language, verbal and nonverbal communication patterns linked to culture, and strategies for teaching English to second-language learners. Considering the increasing diversity of students in American classrooms for whom English is not the native language, deep knowledge and extensive skill in this knowledge base is critical.

An effective multicultural educator understands that learning how to communicate with ethnically diverse students and developing a set of culturally responsive instructional methods are worthy goals (Gay, 2010). The ongoing debate around Ebonics highlights the importance of understanding communication styles. **Ebonics** (or Black or nonstandard English) is a dialect or form of communication used by 80% to 90% of African Americans at some time or another. The "voice of Black America" evolved as an Africanized form of English created by American slaves as a way of retaining their culture (Smitherman, 1997). Its value today lies in supporting a strong cultural heritage. However, criticism is directed at those students who do not learn to use standard English in addition to Black English. Teachers should understand the great cultural value of Ebonics while pursuing the mastery of standard English with sensitivity.

Two misconceptions about English language learners are that they don't learn (or don't want to learn) English and that they hold on to their language

Extended Explorations 4.1: Knowledge About Academic Achievement and Diverse Students

Learning styles in students can be identified through observations of the students, interviews with students, and by using one of many available learning style inventories. Conduct research on the Internet about learning style inventories, and identify at least one that you might find useful in your teaching practice. If possible, take the inventory yourself, and administer it to at least two trusted colleagues. From the data, develop a brief statement about the implications for teaching in a classroom that includes you and your two colleagues.

from generation to generation to their detriment (Tse, 2001). The research according to Tse shows that immigrants are learning English and doing it quite well. In fact, there is concern that native languages are being lost, along with precious cultural heritage, through assimilation and that English language instruction itself needs improvement.

Nonverbal communication is also an important area of study (Samovar & Porter, 2012). What is not said can be just as important as what is verbalized. In addition to words, we communicate in significant ways through eye contact, body posture, gestures, and use of personal space. In fact, it is believed that most communication is nonverbal. Estimates of the range in the amount that we communicate nonverbally extends from approximately 75% to 90%. Think about this statement: The ways people make eye contact, dress, walk, cross their arms, lean forward or back, hold items, and use their hands all send messages about the person to the world. And these ways of "being" are learned within a cultural context. For example, the same hand gesture can mean different things to different cultural groups, and ways of making eye contact can mean different things to different cultural groups.

LEARNING OBJECTIVE 4.4 Describe Important Knowledge About Teaching and Learning

The Role of Culture in the Process of Learning

According to Oakes and colleagues (2012), cross-cultural studies of learning indicate that learning, intelligence, and culture are inseparable. Oakes and Lipton (2007) explained that

> different cultures teach different knowledge in different ways. Within our own society we have an abundance of ethnic, regional and neighborhood cultures in which common knowledge, customs, and how people express themselves are very different. . . . In diverse societies students can reach society's highest standards for knowledge and skills only when schools allow them to use all the knowledge (from all the cultures) they have experienced and when standards are not so narrow as to exclude the value of that knowledge and experience. (p. 84)

The implications of this theory about culture and learning are tremendous. When teachers demand that students learn in a particular way, they are denying those students the opportunity to use all of the "cultural tools" available to them (Spring, 2012, 2016). Teachers will support deep learning for all students when students are provided with opportunities to solve problems by making use of all the cultural tools at their fingertips. Being an effective teacher requires a willingness to understand students' perspectives and to cocreate with the learner a motivating experience. Motivationally effective teaching has to be culturally responsive teaching.

Developmental psychologist Jean Piaget (1970) pointed out the need to consider the role of culture in influencing how children learn and know. **Culture** provides a set of experiences of which children constantly are trying to make sense. According to Oakes and colleagues (2012), Piaget was perhaps most influential in helping educators understand that children think in significantly different ways than do adults. Furthermore, children's thinking develops as they acquire and understand additional experiences. A deep understanding of and use of the experiences children have as a result of their participation in cultural groups can serve teachers well in designing effective classroom learning experiences. For children to make meaning requires that they be engaged in learning broad concepts

Differences are not deficits. Having and recognizing the diversity among students is a rich resource in educating and preparing students for a world of diversity.

iStock/CEFutcher

and small bits of information, have experiences with the concepts, and engage emotionally (Oakes et al., 2012).

What are some examples of how culture influences how people think, perceive, and learn? We know that how we see the world depends on the lives that we have led. For instance, look at the image in Figure 4.1. Many people raised in the Western world will describe a flight of stairs going up. That is because we write and read from left to right. Many individuals in cultures in which reading and writing occur from right to left will describe a set of stairs going down. Those teachers who profess to be "color-blind" or to treat all students the same are doing a disservice. All students are not the same, just as all teachers teach based on past experiences and cultural influences.

Much has been written about how many Native Americans learn through visual means. They carefully watch skills being performed and observe facial expressions intently to gain insight (John, 1972). Learning occurs through careful imitation. Teachers who understand this cultural process can then capitalize on it to support learning. Performance areas such as verbal ability, reasoning, space conceptualization, and number ability may vary in degree based on student backgrounds (Hale-Benson & Hilliard, 1986).

In *Comprehensive Multicultural Education: Theory and Practice*, Bennett (2011, 2014) described five ways in which culture affects learning:

1. Children are socialized in the culture in which they are raised to adopt particular ways of perceiving the world, thinking, and learning. They also learn particular norms, values, and beliefs that are important to their cultures.

2. In some cultures, people stay closely connected to each other over an extended period of time. When individuals act, they know what to do immediately because of their close connections to others in their culture. This is known as sociocultural tightness.

FIGURE 4.1   Describe What You See in This Picture

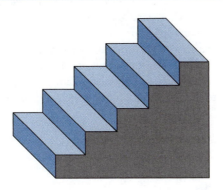

3. People learn to adapt and survive due to engagement with the ways of a particular culture. This is known as ecological adaptation.

4. The concept of biological effects focuses on the influences of nutrition, physical, and mental development, conveyed through participation in a culture, on learning.

5. Overt forms of language, such as pronunciation, vocabulary, and inflection, as well as the unstated aspects of communication, are important influences on how students learn.

Culturally Responsive Teaching and Curriculum Development

Two areas of responsibility for any teacher are to adapt the curriculum to be **culturally responsive** to all students and to prepare all students for a multicultural society. This involves using students' cultural backgrounds as strengths and supports to the curriculum and moving all students from monocultural to multicultural knowledge and skills. The cultures of diverse students are made a mainstream component of the curriculum along with the traditional European, middle-class perspective. This process is a key to ensuring that all students achieve at high levels (Zeichner, 1995).

One of the most interesting research studies in the field of multicultural education was conducted by Uri Treisman (Treisman & Asera, 1995). He examined the achievement levels of African American and Asian students taking first-year algebra at the University of California–Berkeley. African American students, although highly motivated and highly ranked academically, consistently failed to do as well as their Asian American counterparts. In trying to detect a reason for this disparity, Treisman noted a pattern of how each group studied that predicted varying levels of success.

The African American students tended to study intensively on their own, while Asian American students tended to study in mutually supportive groups. For the Asian students, eating meals and studying together were common. Noting this behavior and suspecting a correlation with better grades, Treisman arranged for the African American students to do the same. The results showed a significant increase in test scores for the African American students.

**Extended Explorations 4.2:
Culturally Responsive Teaching**

Arrange to conduct an interview with a local teacher about his or her approaches to teaching culturally diverse students and using students' cultural backgrounds in the teaching and learning process. Prior to the interview, develop a set of 10 powerful questions you might use to investigate how that teacher makes use of student culture in the design of curriculum and lesson plans. Summarize your findings and share them with colleagues in your class. Identify whether or not the teacher is an effective multicultural educator. Why or why not?

There are two important points here. One is the importance of understanding the culture of the students. For Asian American students, restaurants are focal points of community culture, much like local pubs in England and Ireland. Mutually supportive friendships, community development, political strategies, business deals, and romantic relationships are often developed in restaurants. This cultural practice can be applied appropriately to designing classroom learning opportunities. The second is that the research indicates that the effective strategies, such as group study, used to teach students of color can also be effective strategies for teaching middle-class, European American students (Smith, 1998). If you are interested in reflecting on this concept, consider responding to some of the prompts in Table 4.3.

TABLE 4.3   Integrating Diverse Cultural Traditions

European American Traditions	Including Materials and Examples From Diverse Cultural Traditions (Add Your Own)
Great American author (e.g., Mark Twain)	(e.g., W. E. B. DuBois, Sojourner Truth) 1. 2. 3.
Must-read book (e.g., Stephen Crane's *The Red Badge of Courage*)	(e.g., Toni Morrison's *The Bluest Eye*, Maxine Hong Kingston's *The Woman Warrior*) 1. 2. 3.
Classic American song (e.g., "My Old Kentucky Home" by Stephen Foster)	(e.g., "Buffalo Soldier" by Bob Marley, Otis Redding's "Respect" covered by Aretha Franklin, representing feminism; Billy Joel's "Allentown," representing working-class Americans) 1. 2. 3
Great contemporary Americans (e.g., John F. Kennedy)	(e.g., Delores Huerta) 1. 2. 3. Now name . . . 5 Native Americans 5 LGBT Americans 5 Jewish Americans 5 Americans from your ethnic background

REFLECTING BACK

You have just explored some of the growing research base about how people think, know, and perceive. The research indicates that, due to cultural and other factors, people process information, or learn, in different ways. Understanding these different ways of thinking can help educators better appreciate the thought processes of students as they develop curricula for and teach in the classroom.

4.1 Explain Important Knowledge About Culture, Diversity, and Student Assets

Reflect on the items listed below to gain an understanding of your culture and the cultures of others.

My Culture	Interview a Friend Who Represents a Culture Different From Your Own
1. A custom at the dinner table	1. A custom at the dinner table
2. A belief I hold dear	2. A belief my friend holds dear
3. One tradition in my family	3. A tradition in my friend's family
4. One thing that we do not do (a taboo)	4. One thing that is not done (a taboo) in my friend's culture

Now consider the influences on your responses to the questions in the table above. Did religion, SES, gender, or any other cultural identity affect your beliefs and actions and those of the friend whom you interviewed? Why or why not?

Hypothesize about how education might have been different for you if Title IX had not been passed.

4.2 Identify the Foundations of Multicultural Education and the Achievement of Equity

To understand the difficulties faced by second-language learners, read the vignette provided and answer the questions that follow. Reflect then on your capacity to address language differences.

Scenario: The United States erupts into a civil war. You, as a teenager, escape with your family by boat. After drifting at sea for days without food or water, you are rescued by a passing ship, which drops you off at the next port. Having arrived in this foreign country without proper travel documentation, your family is quarantined and placed in a camp with thousands of other American refugees. The years go by as you wait to be released to any nation that will accept you.

Finally, under a lottery, your family emigrates to a friendly Middle Eastern country. Although you are relieved to be finally free to start a new life, you cannot speak or read the native Arabic. You enroll at your new high school at the beginning of the year. Almost immediately, all students in your grade are required to take standardized tests. For days you sit helplessly, as you cannot even read the test questions. No one speaks English in your school.

1. How long do you think it would take to learn enough Arabic to graduate from high school?

2. You drop out of school to work in order to help feed the family. How long will it take to learn enough Arabic to get your GED (General Educational Development)?

3. How long do you think it would take your parents, one a doctor and the other a lawyer, to become proficient in Arabic in order to resume their previous careers?

4.3 Summarize Knowledge About Academic Achievement and Diverse Students

We have focused much on culture and its role in teaching and learning.

1. How might your own preferred modes of learning be affected by specific cultural influences?

2. Describe the cultural norms of the elementary or secondary school that you attended.

3. How closely matched was your school's culture to your own cultural influences?

4. If you agree that people possess different learning styles, do you agree or disagree that a one-size-fits-all approach works just fine?

4.4 Describe Important Knowledge About Teaching and Learning

You have just explored some of the growing research base about how people think, know, and perceive. The research

(Continued)

(Continued)

indicates that, due to cultural and other factors, people process information, or learn, in different ways. Understanding these different ways of thinking can help educators better appreciate the thought processes of students as they develop curricula for and teach in the classroom.

1. Consider the possibility that boys and girls might think and perceive information in different ways. Set up a chart for yourself. On one side of the chart, write "Boys" as a heading. On the other side of the chart, write "Girls" as a heading. Under these two headings, write "My experiences" and write, based on your own experiences, how you believe girls and boys learn in similar ways and in different ways. Now, explore research in the library or on the Internet about how boys and girls might think and perceive information in similar ways and in different ways. Log your findings on the chart under the new heading "Research."

2. As a teacher, how might you use your knowledge about thinking processes to ensure educational equity for boys and girls in the classroom?

PROFILES IN MULTICULTURAL EDUCATION

LINDA DARLING-HAMMOND

©Linda Darling-Hammond

Linda Darling-Hammond is the Charles E. Ducommun Professor of Education Emeritus at Stanford University, where she founded the Stanford Center for Opportunity Policy in Education and served as the faculty sponsor of the Stanford Teacher Education Program, which she helped redesign. She is currently the President and CEO of the Learning Policy Institute.

Darling-Hammond is past president of the American Educational Research Association and recipient of its awards for Distinguished Contributions to Research, Lifetime Achievement, and Research-to-Policy. She is also a member of the American Association of Arts and Sciences and of the National Academy of Education. From 1994 to 2001, she was executive director of the National Commission on Teaching and America's Future, whose 1996 report "What Matters Most: Teaching for America's Future" was named one of the most influential reports affecting U.S. education in that decade. In 2006, Darling-Hammond was named one of the nation's 10 most influential people affecting educational policy. In 2008, she served as the leader of President Barack Obama's education policy transition team.

Darling-Hammond began her career as a public school teacher and cofounded both a preschool and a public high school. She served as director of the RAND Corporation's education program and as an endowed professor at Columbia University, Teachers College. She has consulted widely with federal, state, and local officials and educators on strategies for improving education policies and practices. Among her more than 500 publications are a number of award-winning books, including *The Right to Learn*, *Teaching as the Learning Profession*, *Preparing Teachers for a Changing World*, and *The Flat World and Education*. She received an EdD from Temple University (with highest distinction) and a BA from Yale University (magna cum laude).

Among Darling-Hammond's primary contributions to the field of multicultural education has been her research and writing about the American promise of equal educational opportunity for all students. An important focus of her work has been on policy development, particularly investigating those policies that appear to hold promise for advancing equity. In a 2017 interview, Darling-Hammond explained that there are four primary ways in which the recently passed Every Student Succeeds Act (ESSA, 2015)

represents an opportunity for the federal government, states, districts and schools

to equitably design education systems to ensure that the students who have historically been underserved by these same education systems, receive an education that prepares them for the demands of the 21st century.

These ways are expectations that (1) states will design standards, curriculum, and assessments that develop and measure higher order thinking skills of all their children; (2) states use multiple measures to evaluate student and school progress; (3) ESSA directly addresses the resource gaps among our nation's public schools; and finally (4) ESSA emphasizes evidence-based practices for school improvement.

CASE STUDY
THE DREAM OF A LIFETIME

Key Issues to Be Explored in the Case

1. How helpful can it be for teachers to understand the cultural backgrounds of students in their classrooms?

2. How can the process of learning to become an effective teacher be supported in a collegial way in schools?

3. While teachers may secure an initial understanding about cultural diversity in their teacher preparation programs, what might they need to learn in ongoing, district-provided professional development?

It was the end of Martin's first week of teaching and while becoming a teacher was the achievement of a lifelong dream, he now felt exhausted, unsure, and unprepared. His first week of teaching had not gone well. In fact, things seemed to have steadily gotten worse as the week progressed. He spent his nights preparing

and revising lesson plans, rethinking how to share the content that he so dearly loved. And yet, each day, his presentations seemed to fall flat, and he appeared to be losing his students. To make matters worse, on Friday, Martin's supervisor, Maxine Grace, stopped in during a walk-through of the building while Martin was teaching a lesson on the American Revolution. When Ms. Grace left, she whispered to Martin that she wanted to make an appointment with him to talk about his first week.

Sitting in his living room at home on Saturday morning, Martin started looking back over the years. He knew that he had always felt teaching was a special calling for him. He had decided after college to pursue a career in the burgeoning computer industry, after being persuaded that it was a more lucrative profession. But after 20 years, he felt something was missing personally as well as professionally. After all, his true passion was history. He spent most of his spare time reading deeply about history and visiting museums and historic sites throughout the United States. Furthermore, he yearned to work

(Continued)

(Continued)

with young, eager minds, molding and shaping them and sharing his love of history. He had always enjoyed being a student and felt very comfortable in a classroom and a school setting. Although he was a success in his chosen career, he wanted something more fulfilling.

By juggling a full-time job and taking classes part-time, he secured his credential to teach high school. Even more exciting was that he found a job almost immediately, teaching in his beloved discipline of history in an urban school as a midyear replacement. His dream to become a teacher was becoming a reality. Since this was a midyear replacement situation, personnel at the school were busy with all the normal challenges of their jobs. Nevertheless, Martin did participate in a week's worth of orientation provided by Ms. Grace and the instructional leader and a team of teachers from the history department. Arriving early at the school for his first day of teaching, Martin went straight to the classroom. However, facing the classes of his dreams—several large groups of racially and ethnically diverse boys and girls—he panicked.

Particularly interesting to him were several Native American students. He had heard that several Native American families had moved to the area, but he had not stopped to consider that he might have some of the children in his classes. He struggled to remember what he had been taught about cultural learning styles. Did his training prepare him for teaching such diverse groups of students?

Discussion Questions

1. If you had ample preparation time, what steps would you have taken to prepare for this teaching assignment?

2. What resources might you seek out?

3. What theories do you have now on what you need to know and do?

4. How might your typical classroom day look in terms of your teaching methods?

CHAPTER SUMMARY

Several educational experts have worked to define, based on research and theories, the essential knowledge required for becoming a multicultural educator. Understanding these knowledge bases and their implications for teaching and learning is essential for any teacher working with any student.

Chapter 4 included four Learning Objectives.

4.1 Explain important knowledge about culture, diversity, and student assets

Research indicates several important aspects of culture with which teachers should be familiar. Clearly, educators should know about human development and connections to cultural background. Additionally, they must know essential knowledge bases related to particular forms of diversity, such as gender, SES, religion, and sexual orientation.

Multicultural educators must be aware of how students' cultural identities affect their preferred ways of learning. Those teachers must be able to use knowledge about students' cultures to develop effective curriculum and lesson plans that are relevant for all students. In particular, educators must pay attention to the impact of areas such as religion, gender, SES, and sexual orientation.

4.2 Identify the foundations of multicultural education and the achievement of equity

Educators must have essential foundational knowledge about multicultural education to be effective teachers of all children. It is essential that educators have a deep understanding of racism and other forms of discrimination. And they must know about the impact of educational policies on the learning environment.

Effective multicultural educators need to be knowledgeable about the foundations of multicultural education and ways in which to work toward the achievement of equity in schools. This includes a focus on understanding racism and how discrimination is subtly though strongly embedded in policies, procedures, curriculum, and instructional strategies.

4.3 Summarize knowledge about academic achievement and diverse students

Teachers should know about cultural learning styles and about the ways learning style affects opportunities for academic achievement. They should know about how culture influences communication styles of diverse students.

Multicultural educators must have a deep understanding in learning styles and communication styles as related to diverse students. Clearly, a teacher's attention to learning styles and communication styles will affect how strongly a student will engage in the teaching and learning process. At the same time, educators are cautioned about falling into the trap of using theories of cultural learning styles to stereotype students.

4.4 Describe important knowledge about teaching and learning

Educators must know about how people learn. They must understand the connection between how people learn and culture. Effective multicultural educators need to know how people learn. This includes a deep understanding of how children learn, as well as how adults learn. All learning is influenced by one's cultural background, histories, experiences, and belief systems.

KEY TERMS

cognition 106
cultural identity 99
culturally responsive 111
culture 109

Ebonics 108
gender bias 101
learning styles 108
socioeconomic status 99

transgender 103
White privilege 104

APPLICATION: ACTIVITIES AND EXERCISES

Individual

1. Write a brief statement about what you want educators to know about the aspects of culture that influenced, and continue to influence, you as a student. (Learning Objective 4.1)

2. Outline three sample lesson plans that support and/ or use this knowledge. (Learning Objectives 4.2, 4.3, and 4.4)

Group

1. Interview your own family, particularly your elders, to seek out information on patterns of learning and knowing. What were or are the cultural influences? Compare your findings with others in your group. What are the similarities and differences? (Learning Objectives 4.3 and 4.4)

2. Find on the Internet at least one example of a policy that has influenced the development of equity in education specifically in relation to gender, religion, or SES. As a team, prepare a presentation using current technology (e.g., PowerPoint) for colleagues in which you explain that policy and its long-range implications. In your summary, explain whether or not you believe the policy has made a difference in the lives of culturally diverse students. Why or why not? (Learning Objective 4.2)

3. Interview a veteran educator who has worked with diverse students. Seek out advice on teaching methods and theories about working with diverse students. Compare notes with others in your group. What are the similarities and differences? (Learning Objectives 4.1 and 4.4)

Self-Assessment

1. Write a story about the schooling experiences of your parents or other members of your family. Take note of specific cultural influences and insights on how the best teaching and learning took place.

2. Share this journal with as many family members as possible.

3. Create a summary of your findings. Share this, if possible, with members of your family, especially with young children.

ANNOTATED RESOURCES

Religion and Education

U.S. Department of Education

http://www2.ed.gov/policy/gen/guid/religionandschools/prayer_guidance.html

This site contains guidelines on the topics of religious expression in public schools and faith community support of children's learning.

The Pew Forum on Religion and Public Life

http://pewforum.org

Launched in 2001, this project of the Pew Research Center seeks to promote a deeper understanding of issues at the intersection of religion and public affairs. The Pew Forum conducts surveys, demographic analyses, and other social science research on important aspects of religion and public life in the United States and around the world. It also provides a neutral venue for discussions of timely issues through roundtables and briefings.

Gender Equity

American Association of University Women

https://www.aauw.org

AAUW has been empowering women as individuals and as a community since 1881. For more than 130 years, the AAUW has worked as a national grassroots organization to improve the lives of millions of women and their families. This website includes many excellent reports about gender equity and related issues in education and schools.

National Coalition for Women and Girls in Education

http://www.ncwge.org

NCWGE is a nonprofit organization established to educate the public about issues concerning equal rights for women and girls in education, monitor the enforcement and administration of current legislation, and conduct and publish research and analysis of issues concerning equity in education. This website provides reports and resources about equity for girls in education and about relevant activities and federal education legislation.

Title IX

National Women's Law Center on Title IX

http://www.nwlc.org

The center has worked for more than 40 years to protect and promote equality and opportunity for women and families. They champion policies and laws that help women and girls achieve their potential at every stage of their lives—at school, at work, at home, and in retirement. This website contains a wealth of information on the history and impacts of Title IX.

Title IX

http://www.titleix.info/Default.aspx

This useful website includes resources, information on the history of Title IX, information on how to identify your district's Title IX coordinator, and real-life stories of how Title IX has helped girls and women.

American Civil Liberties Union

https://www.aclu.org/know-your-rights/title-ix-and-sexual-assault

This website provides detailed information about the intent of Title IX and strategies for investigating Title IX violations, including harassment.

Section II Assessment

Knowledge

Major Assessment 2: The "Educated Person"

For educators to be effective in supporting diverse learners, they need to develop, possess, and continually refine their vision of the "educated person." In other words, they need to have a vision of their goals and outcomes for educating students.

Prepare a statement of your image of and beliefs and values about the educated person. Explain your beliefs about the role of the teacher in valuing and encouraging others to value the image of an educated person. Be certain to address the roles of cultural diversity in achieving a viable vision of the educated person.

Begin by reading the key documents discussed in the chapters in this section. Reference at least five additional current professional references to illustrate your position.

Organize your presentation by sections and use American Psychological Association style for citing references in the body of the text and for developing your reference list.

Include the following sections in your paper:

1. Introduction

2. Vision of learning and the educated person (critical knowledge, skills, dispositions)

3. Role of the teacher in providing an effective instructional program and applying best practices to student learning

4. Critical issues in promoting the success of all students and responding to diverse community needs

5. Capacity to translate the image of the educated person into educational aims and organizational goals and processes

6. Conclusion

7. References

SECTION III

AWARENESS

5 Understanding Cultural Identities and Their Influence on Teaching and Learning

Jupiter images/Comstock/Thinkstock

Learning Objectives

In this chapter, the topics and concepts presented will help you enhance your awareness of yourself as a cultural being. We will explore these topics and concepts through sharing of important information about cultural identity development as well as through a variety of exercises designed to help you reflect on your own cultural identities. Through your study of and work on this chapter, you will be able to do the following:

5.1 Describe the dimensions of cultural identity

5.2 Explain privileged cultural identities

5.3 Summarize the influence of personal cultural identities on teaching and learning

When students and teachers walk into any classroom, they walk in as cultural beings. As cultural beings, each and every person brings a unique blend of experiences, beliefs, and values to bear on the teaching and learning process. If educators are to have a hope of making a difference in the lives of diverse students, they must use regularly a process for enhancing their awareness of their own cultural identities and how those identities influence what happens in the classroom. Robins, Lindsey, Lindsey, and Terrell (2012) referred to this as an "inside-out perspective" on being a culturally proficient educator. Not only must educators know themselves as cultural beings and how their identification with different cultural groups influences everything they do in the classroom, but they must also be skilled in ways to become aware of and explore the cultural identities of students they teach. Both processes are equally critical.

For these purposes, Chapter 5 is devoted to helping teachers develop an awareness of themselves as cultural beings, and Chapter 6 is designed to help educators learn a process for understanding students as cultural beings. Specifically, through engagement in the learning and work of Chapter 5, teachers will develop working definitions of key concepts such as *cultural identity* and *privileged cultural identities*. They will also explore the impact of prevalent cultural and social norms on teaching and learning and analyze the impact of their own cultural identities, attitudes, and cultural backgrounds on student learning. Finally, they will be able to anticipate the consequences of their own behaviors in creating an optimal learning environment for their students and demonstrate effective methods for helping students explore their own cultural identities to enhance optimal learning environments.

> Our flag is red, white, and blue, but our nation is a rainbow—red, yellow, brown, black and white—and we're all precious in God's sight.
>
> —Jesse Jackson, Address before the Democratic National Convention (1984)

CASE STUDY
EXPERIMENT IN LEARNING ABOUT CULTURAL IDENTITIES

A psychology professor at a university in Chicago was curious to know how early in life individuals begin to develop a sense of cultural identity and what influences that development. She decided one day to take a class of psychology students to a nearby hospital for an experiment in the hospital's nursery. Prior to the experiment, she had talked with a nurse in the nursery, not explaining the experiment itself, but asking that when the students came into the hospital for the experiment the nurse have the babies all dressed in the same color.

On the day of the experiment, the students were lined up outside the nursery, looking through the glass panes at all the babies. One by one, the nurse held up each baby, and the students were asked to guess the gender of the infant. Remarkably, the students guessed correctly about 90% of the time! The reason? Without even knowing that she was doing so, when the nurse held up the male babies, she held them out in front of her, holding them under their arms to show them off. However, when she held up the female babies, she cradled them in a very gentle, nurturing baby-handling fashion.

The students were stunned. Certainly, the message in the experiment was that from the day we are born we receive distinct and different messages about who we are. However, the psychology students, for the most part, had never considered the type of subtle yet pervasive messages we receive throughout life. As they left the hospital, small groups of students chatted among themselves. One of the groups comprised seven female students, some of whom were Hispanic American, some Caucasian, and some Asian American. At first, they were giggling and chatting about their own experiences growing up and saying how now they understood why they had to do so much work in the kitchens in their homes! But after a while, they started talking more seriously about the implications of their gender and their race on their place in society.

Your Perspectives on the Case

1. Why do you think the psychology students were so surprised to learn about the results of the experiment?

2. Besides having been expected to adopt more gender-related roles in their families, what other implications do you think there were for these seven female students?

3. In what ways can you relate to the experiences shared in the opening case study? Describe three very specific ways that your gender has influenced choices in your life.

THINKING AHEAD
YOU AND CHAPTER 5 LEARNING OBJECTIVES

5.1 Describe the Dimensions of Cultural Identity

As an educator, the depth of awareness you possess about your cultural identities is very important. To begin thinking about your own cultural identities, reflect first about the ways in which you have learned about your cultural identity. With which primary cultural groups do you identify? Imagine that you were born into at least one different cultural group. For example, you have been born as a member of a different race or sex. Describe five very specific ways that you believe your life might have been different. Justify your reasons for why your life may have been different (e.g., based on your perceptions of members of that group).

5.2 Explain Privileged Cultural Identities

Unearned privilege or unacknowledged male privilege refers to the fact that European Americans (males) naturally benefit by virtue of their skin color and/or gender (McIntosh, 1988). They gain these benefits without effort. Women and people of color do not benefit from this phenomenon. Think about the unearned privileges you have because of your race, ethnicity, gender, religion, or other identity. Reflect also about what it means to be White.

5.3 Summarize the Influence of Personal Cultural Identities on Teaching and Learning

A classroom teacher, the person in charge of teaching and learning, holds a tremendous amount of power over what happens to children. With this in mind, it is important to consider the role of your cultural identities in the teaching and learning process. Describe five of the most important values you hold dear. How might your values influence how you interact with people from diverse cultural groups?

LEARNING OBJECTIVE 5.1 Describe the Dimensions of Cultural Identity

What Is Cultural Identity?

All individuals are guided in their behaviors by sets of values and beliefs. Do you ever wonder how you came to adhere to your particular set of beliefs and values? Certainly, growing up in the home that you did influenced the development of values, beliefs, ideas, and ways of behaving. More broadly speaking, each of us has been "trained" or conditioned, and thus, we have learned to respond, think, and act in certain ways due to our participation over a sustained period of time with groups of people with whom we identify. This process of learning to behave in a certain way in order to be accepted by members of groups with which we identify is called **socialization**. This process is about learning the requirements for acceptance into a cultural group (Cushner, 2014). Once an individual participates in the socialization process, what has been learned about accepted and acceptable behavior within a cultural group is so powerful that it's almost impossible for that individual to see any other ways of behaving acceptably. Ooka Pang (2005) expressed a strong vision of the influence of culture on individuals when she stated,

> Culture is like the air; it is always there but people who live in and follow its ways may have difficulty seeing it. . . . We are products of . . . a "cultural prison" because the culture that surrounds us teaches us how to look at and respond to our life experiences. (p. 5)

For better or worse, the influence of culture on each of us is very deep.

In general, individuals are socialized into a variety of cultural groups that influence their behaviors, values, and beliefs. A culture or cultural group may include those elements that are created by humans, such as musical forms, artwork, foods, rituals, celebrations, and so forth. These are the more overt elements that define a cultural group and constitute the tip of the iceberg. People who participate in a common culture have a tendency to dress in similar ways, prefer the same types of foods, celebrate important events with the same traditions, and appreciate the same types or forms of music and art. Sometimes, when we think we know about a cultural group, we actually just know the more overt and visible forms of that culture.

At a much deeper level, submerged beneath the water, are those elements of a culture that can't be seen or touched. The much larger and invisible core of a culture includes commonly held values, beliefs, histories, traditions, experiences, ways of behaving, attitudes, and feelings. To understand the essence of a culture is to know not only about its festivals, music and art forms, and important people but also about what is critically important—what is at the core—for that group of people. Cushner (2014) cautioned us that it is very difficult to get to know a culture at this level because it is in people's minds. However, Cushner also believed that if people are to be effective as multiculturalists they must understand both levels.

To apply this way of thinking, consider for a moment how you would like people to know the real you. On a surface level, people might describe you in terms of what you wear, what you eat, what types of music you listen to, and what holidays you celebrate. Is this enough for them to know the real you? Of course, this is not enough. You would probably want them to also know about your experiences with your family as you grew up, what you believe in, and some history about your family over a long period of time. These are the deeper, and probably more important, elements of culture.

Another way of looking at important elements of culture is for you to consider the dimensions of culture. Primary dimensions include race and ethnicity, gender, age, socioeconomic status, religion/spirituality, sexual orientation, ability, geographic location, and language. **Primary dimensions of culture** are those with which we are born and that are fairly challenging to change. Primary cultural identities are important contributors to the development of a person's self-concept. An example of primary dimensions of culture is an individual who may identify herself as of Italian heritage. Her grandparents may have emigrated from Italy many years ago. While she and her relatives today do not speak Italian at home, they may still enjoy a strong connection to Italy, value connections to extended family, and celebrate holidays with special Italian foods and music. During the holidays, this young woman may join the other members in the family in preparing elaborate Italian dishes for everyone to enjoy.

Obviously, an individual may identify with several primary dimensions of culture at the same time. Primary dimensions or identities, in general, form the core of how an individual defines himself or herself. At the same time, primary identities are generally more difficult to discuss than secondary dimensions or identities. And sometimes, characteristics of different primary dimensions or identities may

© istockphotos.com/Zurijeta

Teaching students to learn about and be proud of their culture first starts with learning about yourself as a cultural being. Knowledge about your identity and how it influences what you think and how you act are important steps in developing effective teaching skills.

cause internal conflict in an individual. For example, let's return to the example of the young Italian woman. She may have been trained as a lawyer and have a very busy practice. She is a professional woman and single. She may believe that her most important obligations at this point in time are to her profession. Sometimes she finds the expectation that she would spend significant amounts of time cooking special dishes to be unreasonable.

Secondary dimensions of culture are those over which we have some choice and those we can alter more easily than primary dimensions. Examples of secondary dimensions of culture are hobbies, work experiences, marital status, education, parental status, and participation in affinity groups. An example of the influence of secondary dimensions or identities is an individual who may be a member of a running club. As such, that individual may share with other members a belief in the importance and value of running to maintain good health, the ritual of stretching both before and after running, the experience of having run in road races, and the joyful histories of having competed in road races with other club members.

Both primary and secondary dimensions or identities have shared characteristics, including behaviors, beliefs, values, traditions, customs, habits, rituals, experiences, taboos, and histories. When viewed together, an individual's primary and secondary cultural identities contribute to forming a powerful set of beliefs, values, norms, perceptions, and experiences that affect his or her behavior throughout a lifetime. When describing oneself or another person, caution must be exercised not to describe a person in terms of only one cultural identity. Many characteristics from both primary and secondary dimensions of culture contribute to making each individual just that—a unique individual!

Why is it so important to learn about our cultural identities, both in terms of elements and dimensions? Some writers refer to culture as the "lens" we use to view and interpret behaviors, actions, words, and ideas of ourselves and of other people. Understanding culture and the influence of culture on our own development as individuals can provide important insights into who we are and why we do what we do. If we understand the essential core elements of, say, being female in America, then we can have greater insight into why we do what we do. So who are you as a cultural being?

Coming to a deep understanding of culture and cultural identities is not an easy process. In fact, the very nature of culture makes it a complex phenomenon. While we may find it useful to compress our thinking about culture into a few identities, Connerly and Pederson (2005) believed, "Culture's complexity is illustrated by the hundreds or perhaps even thousands of culturally learned identities, affiliations, and roles we each assume at one time or another" (p. 29). Ignoring culture and its influence on our behaviors can lead to significant problems in the teaching and learning process.

An excellent starting point for understanding the influence of culture is learning how you came to have the name you use. Ways in which members of a culture name their children can provide interesting insights into that culture's histories, beliefs, and traditions. For example, people in Iceland demonstrate the importance of family connections, and particularly the role of the father, in that culture by naming children according to a system of patronymics. In general, boys' names are derived by using the father's first name and adding the word for "son" (*son*). Girls' names are derived by using the father's first name and adding the word for "daughter" (*dottir*). Women always retain their given name when they marry. So in a family of four that includes a son and a daughter, all four members could have different last names! For example, the father could be named Einar Jonson (Jon being his father's first name). The mother, named after her father Mathias, could be Sigrud Mathiasdottir. Their son would be named Thorvald Einarsson. And their daughter would be named Hafdis Einarsdottir.

In this country, we can learn much about the history and culture of African Americans by considering naming traditions. During the time of slavery, when Africans were forcibly

TABLE 5.1	The Meaning of a Name

What is your full name?
What are the meaning and origin of your name?
Why were you given the name you have?
What do you particularly like about your name?
What do you find challenging about your name?
Do you have a nickname? If yes, what is it?
What do your names say about you?

brought to the United States, they were given new names, generally English names, that the slave owners could pronounce. Over time and generations, African Americans began to give their children English names when they were born. With this new tradition, many African Americans had no cultural connection to their Anglo names. Today, when asked what the meaning of their names are, many African Americans with Anglo names can't tell how they came to have the name they have. Unlike some Americans who can trace their ancestry to England, for African Americans their Anglo names may mean nothing. This lack of meaning connected to their names, and an interest in establishing connections for their children to Africa, has led many African American parents to name their children using African names, such as Jamal. This was particularly true during the Civil Rights era. Or they create names, such as Laquesha, to help develop a new identity apart from the slave names with which they don't identify. For many African Americans, this naming process provides a source of pride for their families. Not only did families begin to name their children using African names, but adults also began to adopt new names, indicating they had some ownership and pride in their cultural backgrounds. Examples of adults who changed their names include the great prizefighter Cassius Clay, who became Muhammad Ali, and activist Malcolm Little, who became Malcolm X. Basketball player Kareem Abdul-Jabar was, as a child, named Lew Alcindor. Take some time to reflect on the meaning of your name, and its relation to culture, by considering the items in Table 5.1.

Was it difficult to answer any of the questions? Why or why not? What does this tell you about your cultural identities?

Sources of Information About Our Identities

We learn information about our own cultural identities at a very young age (Derman-Sparks & Ramsey, 2011). Children learn messages or information about what they're supposed to be like and what they are expected to do from a variety of sources, including people, events, the environment, the language that surrounds them, and the media. According to Derman-Sparks and Ramsey (2011), children construct their identity and attitudes through the interaction of three factors: (1) experience with their bodies, (2) experience with their social environment, and (3) their cognitive developmental stage. Each of these three factors is powerful when considered alone.

First, experience with their bodies means children are constantly exploring through their senses. They explore responses to their physical actions and are in a constant state of discovering what they physically can do. Consider the youngster who discovers that hitting a pan with a spoon produces a ringing sound and then continues to hit that pan repeatedly until an adult, who has had enough noise, intervenes.

A child's experiences with the environment are also powerful. In the environment, certainly one of the most important sources of information about our identities is our parents. Other family members, other people, the media, and authority figures also convey information or messages about who we are. An example of reflective writing by students about the impact of the environment can be read in what have come to be known as "Where I'm From" poems (Exercise 5.1). In these poems, writers are able to reflect and connect deeply to the influences on the development of their identities. Examples of this type of work can be found on the Internet. For example, George Ella Lyon has written poems using "Where I'm From" as a jumping-off point (see http://www.georgeellalyon.com/where .html). Another website that may be useful is https://www.facinghistory.org/for-educators/ educator-resources/teaching-strategies.

Finally, in terms of cognitive developmental levels, children appear to be ready to inculcate concepts related to identity at an early age. Phyllis Katz (1982) indicated that children are able to see differences in terms of race and gender in themselves and others from an early age. Between the ages of 2 and 5, children start to observe racial cues, form basic concepts about race, differentiate among races, and make judgments about race. Derman-Sparks (1989) agreed that young children (between the ages of 2 and 3) notice gender

EXERCISE 5.1
WHERE I'M FROM

1. Find several examples of "Where I'm From" poems on the Internet. Discuss what these mean to you and what you have learned about the writers.

2. Now write your own "Where I'm From" poem, using as many of the following prompts as possible.

    a. Names of important people in your life
    b. Special places that have been important to you
    c. Special foods or meals
    d. Traditions that have been practiced regularly
    e. Favorite songs and stories
    f. Familiar phrases used by a parent or other family members
    g. Ordinary items in the place in which you grew up
    h. Important beliefs for the family members
    i. Significant events (happy and/or sad) that have happened in this place
    j. Sounds and smells that represent your youth

3. Share your poem with other class members.

4. Compare the similarities and differences between your poem and the poems of your classmates.

5. Discuss what you are discovering through this approach.

and race differences. Noticing differences in physical ability occurs perhaps a year later. By the age of 3, children begin to exhibit the willingness to make judgments that are influenced by social norms and based on gender, race, and physical ability. Between the ages of 3 and 5, children engage in a questioning and sorting process to determine their group identities. Between the ages of 4 and 5, children clearly engage in behaviors as defined by approved norms in the society in which they live.

Reflect again on the opening case study at the beginning of this chapter. The nurse did not know the purpose of the experiment by the psychology professor. She was just doing her work in the best way she knew how. She wasn't aware that by simply holding the boy and girl babies in the ways that she did, she was passing on messages from the day they were born about what was expected of them as people. She was passing on the cultural message that girls should be nurtured and cuddled and treated gently. She was also passing on the message that boys, from the moment they are born, are strong and don't require the nurturing and cuddling that girls do. Probably unconsciously, the nurse was participating in passing on cultural biases.

In another example of how early in life we learn about who we are in terms of our gender and racial identities, consider the true story of the little White girl in the South who was going off to her first week of school. She was assigned to a classroom in which the teacher was a kind and experienced Black woman. Her parents, well-intentioned and good people, believed that if they talked about racial differences with their little girl and highlighted the fact that she would have a Black teacher, she would somehow learn negative stereotypes about Black people. So they made a conscious decision not to discuss race with their daughter.

At the end of the first day of school, the little girl got off the bus, and her mother met her at the bus stop. Walking back to their house, the mother asked her daughter how the first day had gone. The child replied that things were just fine and she really enjoyed the day, and she went off to play. She didn't mention her teacher. Each day during that first week, the same scenario occurred: The mother met her daughter at the bus stop and asked about her day, and the girl presented a very positive picture of kindergarten but never mentioned her teacher. When Friday rolled around, however, the mother couldn't help herself. On the walk back home from the bus stop, the mother asked again about how school went. When the little girl replied that everything was just great, the mother finally asked her daughter how she liked her teacher. The little girl looked up at her mother with a quizzical expression and then replied, "I don't know about the teacher. So far, she's been sending her maid to school every day." Clearly by the time she entered school, the little girl had formed very specific ideas about race and cultural identity . . . for herself and others.

Challenges to Uncovering Our Cultural Identities

As described in the previous section, a major challenge to the development of our cultural identities is how we're socialized. We learn positive and negative messages about our identities and those of others. Other challenges to the development of our cultural identities are important to recognize as well. One challenge is that we are sometimes provided with limited or partial information about different cultural groups with which we might identify. Throughout our educational careers, we have learned information that

Extended Explorations 5.1: What Is Cultural Identity?

Locate on the Internet a true story (could be an article or a book) about the development of one person's cultural identities. A starting point might be the source *Choices in Little Rock* (Facing History and Ourselves, 2008). This organization (https://www.facinghistory.org) is an international education and professional development organization dedicated to engaging students of diverse backgrounds in an examination of racism, discrimination, and prejudice. There are many other resources available on the Internet (see the section on Annotated Resources at the end of this chapter for additional sources).

Read the book, chapter, or article carefully, noting the specific contributors to the development of cultural identities.

Now write your own cultural identity development "story." Identify a specific action or time when, now reflecting back, you solidified your notions and ideas of what it means to be you.

Share your story with colleagues. Identify the specific social norms that contributed to the development of your and others' cultural identities.

is presented to us, for better or worse. Interestingly, most Americans who have graduated from high school believe that they've had a pretty good education to that point. They've spent a significant amount of time in school and think they've been prepared with the knowledge and skills to become a productive member of society. However, for most Americans, what they've been presented with in school and, for that matter, what is presented through the media is sometimes limited to what is in textbooks. And textbooks don't always provide complete information. For example, most Americans can talk about the significance of Ellis Island. To them, it was the entry point for many immigrants into this country. This was an important topic in school. However, when asked the significance of Angel Island, very few people can tell you anything about it. This was not a topic covered in the majority of American schools, yet it is an important piece of Asian American history since it was the entry point, in San Francisco Bay, for thousands of Asians into this country. Certainly, this piece of information could be a point of pride for Asian Americans, and it is important information for all Americans to know as a component of our collective history.

The issue of politeness is another challenge to the identification of our cultural identities. In the United States, there is a pervasive valuing of politeness. Some people believe that there are just certain things we shouldn't talk about in polite company (e.g., politics, religion, money). Some people would add diversity and cultural differences to this list. People think that if we talk about differences, we are just going to exacerbate the "problems" that exist between groups of people. If we don't talk about differences, we won't have the problems, or so goes the thinking. However, it's not the discussion of differences that leads to problems. Rather it's lack of understanding of, valuing, and respect for differences that leads to problems. Without a clear understanding of the values, beliefs, traditions, norms, and ways of behaving of groups of people who are different from us, we continue to think that our way of doing things is the right way.

Another challenge to thinking about our own identities is the idea that if we focus on differences, we will just exacerbate the problems between and among groups and individuals. While it is absolutely important for us to understand and celebrate the characteristics and experiences and histories that we have in common with other people, it is not the commonalities that cause problems and conflict. Lack of understanding, recognition, and celebration of differences is what leads to conflict. Differences will always exist because individuals are unique. We need to understand and take pride in our own identities and then learn about and celebrate those of others. Differences are not deficits.

One way to explore our own identities in a reflective and deep way is by reflecting on the "messages" that we picked up about ourselves while we were growing up. Develop a deeper understanding and celebrate your own identities by writing about those "messages" in Exercise 5.2.

Sometimes the information that has been shared with us that leads to our development of sense of identity is positive, and sometimes it is not positive. We receive information about our cultural identities—both their primary and secondary dimensions—and internalize it in a variety of ways. Chappelle and Bigman (1998) summarized the impact that this internalization process can have on children. They cited an example of young blonde girls who might hear statements referring to them as "airheads" or brainless. After hearing these statements, whenever those girls made a mistake, they might feel stupid and as though they actually were brainless.

Extended Explorations 5.2: Uncovering Our Cultural Identities

At least three challenges exist to uncovering and understanding our cultural identities. These include (1) socialization, (2) an emphasis on politeness, and (3) a belief that discussion of differences in identity will lead to exacerbation of problems. These are just the major challenges. There are more.

Identify two specific instances when you were engaged in conversations about diversity but were impeded in deep and meaningful discussions due to one of these three challenges. Describe those two instances in detail. What were your feelings about the conversation? Critique why you responded the way you did.

Finally, construct a plan for how you could have moved through the discomfort and actually engaged in a productive dialogue.

EXERCISE 5.2
MESSAGES

Purpose

Understand the process of developing cultural identities.

Background

We have learned "messages" from the day we are born about others and ourselves. This process can lead to both positive and negative ideas about ourselves. If we have negative ideas about ourselves due to our identification with a cultural identity, or if we believe the stereotypes about a group with which we identify, we may be experiencing "internalized oppression." Even though we think we are rational, logical beings and basically good people, these negative messages can affect our actions, thoughts, and comments in profound ways.

Procedure

1. Locate the poem "The Average Child" by Mike Buscemi (1979) on the Internet (http://holyjoe.org/poetry/buscemi.htm). Read and discuss what that poem means to you. What "messages" had the writer received about himself?

2. Individually, write down some "messages" you have learned about groups with which you identify. Share these messages with the group as a whole.

Discussion

1. How did it feel to write the messages?

2. How did it feel to share your messages with others?

3. What occurred to you while you were reading other people's messages?

4. What do you think of the theories that support this exercise, including the following?

   a. No one is born prejudiced.
   b. Every person must first identify his or her own mistreatment before being capable of fully relating to the mistreatment of others.
   c. Permanent attitudinal and behavioral change is an ongoing process.
   d. People become empowered as attitudinal and behavioral changes occur.

(This exercise is adapted from one developed by Peggy McIntosh and Emily Styles of the SEED Project on Inclusive Curriculum, Wellesley College, http://www.wcwonline.org/Active-Projects/seed-project-on-inclusive-curriculum.)

Naming Groups With Which We Identify

Learning about who we are as individuals is both a complex and subtle act. We are constantly receiving information from a variety of sources that conveys to us values, beliefs, and norms about the groups with which we identify. Being able to name and describe the groups of people with whom we identify is challenging. A starting point for this process of naming groups is to reflect on various dimensions of culture. Working through the self-identity worksheet in Exercise 5.3 will help you move toward identifying your cultural identity.

Interestingly, while each of us probably believes that we have certain cultural identities, we've probably grown up acquiring those identities in subtle ways. According to Cushner (2014), people usually don't talk about their cultural identities, believing that most aspects of culture are shared. And yet, unless we make very conscious decisions to reflect deeply about our cultural identities, we will never be fully aware of the powerful influence those identities have on our lives. For educators, this is particularly critical. Grant and Sleeter (2011) underlined this critical importance:

EXERCISE 5.3
SELF-IDENTITY WORKSHEET

Purpose

Understand the various dimensions of diversity.

Procedure

1. Fill in each category on the self-identity worksheet.

2. Discuss your responses to the statements with a large group of colleagues.

    a. How easy or difficult was it to complete the worksheet? Explain your response.
    b. What do your answers tell you about your cultural identities?
    c. How do cultural stereotypes, or cues, affect your responses?
    d. How are your responses different from or the same as those of your colleagues?
    e. What have you learned about yourself by doing this exercise?

The cultural meaning of my name
My racial or ethnic identity
Places my grandparents were born
Sayings my mother taught me
My religion, faith, or belief system
Languages I speak
My preferred way of learning
My favorite song or music type
A person I greatly admire
Something in my lifetime I'd like to achieve

Source: Adapted from Jack Hasegawa (1998).

Teaching by its very nature is highly interpersonal. Teachers who know themselves well are in a much better position than teachers who do not know themselves well to treat students and their families with respect and fairness. If you know why you react to different people the way you do, you have some control over your reactions and can learn to modify them, question them, or grow beyond your present boundaries. If you do not know why you react as you do, interpersonal differences can lead to frustration and conflict. (p. 18)

Exercise 5.4 will give you an opportunity to explore the primary dimensions of your own cultural identity. This exercise also promotes an understanding of the primary and secondary dimensions of diversity.

EXERCISE 5.4
PERSONAL PIE CHART

Materials Needed

Blank sheets of paper (8½ inches × 11 inches)

Procedure

1. On a blank sheet of paper, draw a large circle. Divide the circle into sections representing your own cultural identities. The sizes of the sections should correspond to the degree of your identification with particular cultural identities. Fill in the sections with a descriptive word or set of words to show the different cultures with which you identify. Discuss why you drew the segments the size they are, reflecting on the fact that certain identities take on larger meanings at different times in life.

2. Discuss your pie charts with members of a small group.
   a. What identities did you select and why?
   b. What makes you particularly happy about or proud of those identities?
   c. What do you find challenging about membership in any of the groups with which you identify?

Debriefing

1. It's especially important to discuss Whiteness as a culture or group. What does being White mean for individuals in our society? Discuss the idea of privilege.

2. Gender is important to discuss. What does it mean to be female in our culture? In our schools? To be male in our culture and schools? Discuss the notion of privilege.

3. Discuss commonalities and differences—Why is it important to value differences?

4. Discuss the concept of labels. Some people are reticent to discuss labels for selves. However, everywhere we go, we take our identities, experiences, and so on with us. They affect everything we do and our choices and interactions. So we need to develop pride in our identities and respect the differences that others represent around us.

5. Develop one to three recommendations for how you can learn more about other people.

LEARNING OBJECTIVE 5.2 Explain Privileged Cultural Identities

The Challenge of Entitlement

A key challenge to thinking about diversity, either in terms of learning more deeply about one's own cultural identities or about the cultural backgrounds of children we teach, is that it requires an investment of time. Even before thinking about the cultural identities of children in our classrooms, we need to understand not only who we are as cultural beings but also how we think and feel about differences. Part of the awareness stage is to be completely open and honest about how we feel about people who are not like us.

McIntosh (1988) described two different kinds of privilege. One is "unearned entitlements," in which a person gains benefits, without effort, from simply belonging to a class of people. She wrote about White male privilege in this context. The other is what McIntosh referred to as "conferred dominance." In this case, one group controls another, as when men are naturally expected to dominate women in conversations. Another example is when law enforcement officers profile Black males driving expensive cars or suspect minority youths of shoplifting more than White youths. These are all assumptions based on culture.

The issue of privilege is challenging for some people to understand. Some people don't believe they have multiple cultural identities or haven't had to think much about how membership in certain cultural groups provides them with the privilege of not having to think about identity. They believe that they are "just American." Some White high school students, when asked about their cultural background, might not be able to answer knowledgeably or just claim to be a mixture of many cultures. Or they might respond that they are Irish, Italian, Polish, and so on but lack a deep understanding of the richness of their cultural history and an appreciation of the status in society that it accords. It is therefore important that students, and their teachers, understand the concept of privilege.

Oakes, Lipton, Anderson, and Stillman (2018) have discussed in detail the importance of educators learning about their own as well as others' cultural identities. Oakes and Lipton (2007) pointed out the critical problems associated with lack of educators attending to culture and its role in the teaching and learning process:

> McIntosh's provocative observations have caught the attention of many educators seeking to explain to themselves, colleagues, and students how, decades after the end of legalized segregation and racial discrimination, race plays such a powerful cultural role in enhancing or limiting access to school and life opportunities. (p. 61)

It is the responsibility of all educators to consider deeply who they are as cultural beings and how their participation and/or identification with diverse cultural groups influences their behaviors, both inside and

iStock/LifesizeImages

Who has power and privilege in our society are important discussions to have. Understanding the power inequities between men and women, between Caucasians and people of color, between rich and poor helps us understand how educational policies are made.

outside of the classroom. Mike Roberts wrote eloquently about his work as a White male educator in engaging students in meaningful conversations about race and discrimination. He stated,

> As teachers, who we are is as important as what we teach. . . . As a teacher, the person you are as well as your beliefs [are] important. . . . The person standing in front of that group (of students) and his or her background, beliefs, and understanding, are of utmost importance to the students. . . . A teacher with unspoken racist attitudes can perpetuate much hate in our world. Don't for a moment pretend that there aren't any out there. (Cited in Sleeter & Cornbleth, 2011, p. 54)

The inside/outside circles exercise (Exercise 5.5) is designed to support you in discussing issues of privilege with your colleagues. The exercise helps participants develop a climate of trust and support through personal contact with each other so that personal identities and issues of privilege can be explored.

EXERCISE 5.5
INSIDE/OUTSIDE CIRCLES

Activity

1. As a group, count off by twos. Ones should form an inner circle, facing out. Twos form a circle around the Ones, facing in. Each person will have a partner facing him or her.

2. Participants are provided with a series of questions or statements, one at a time. After each question, the partners will have approximately 1 minute each to respond to each other. The facilitator will keep time, telling partners when 1 minute and then 2 minutes are up.

3. After the two partners have responded to one statement, the outer circle moves one person to the right, so everyone has a new partner.

4. The facilitator uses any combination of the following questions. Allow approximately 15 to 20 minutes for this portion of the exercise.

   a. Share your name and what it means to you.
   b. Share what your favorite holiday is and why.
   c. Share one "message" you learned when you were growing up about what you were supposed to be like because of race, ethnicity, or gender.
   d. Share the first thoughts that come to you when you think of racism.
   e. Share one experience you had when you feel you were discriminated against.
   f. Share one feeling you have about dealing with racism.
   g. What is one thing you wish people would never again say, do, or think about a cultural group with which you identify.
   h. Share your strengths as an educator/trainer in facilitating dialogue and working toward valuing diversity.

(Continued)

(Continued)

    i.   Describe one time when you heard a prejudicial statement, joke, or slur and what your reaction was.

    j.   Share something about what you specifically want to work on as an educator/trainer to build your skills in teaching about valuing diversity.

Debriefing

After the questioning period, participants take their seats again and debrief the exercise. The facilitator uses questions such as the following to guide this discussion:

- What did you think about this exercise?

- What questions were you comfortable in answering? Uncomfortable? Why?

- What did you learn about yourself from this exercise?
  (Adapted from an exercise developed by Katz, 2003)

What Does It Mean to Be White?

The question "What does it mean to be White?" is more often than not a perplexing one for White people. While people of color generally recognize the existence of a White culture and know what that means, White people tend to think Whiteness is not a culture and do not think about and discuss the meaning of Whiteness. However, this in fact is a critical issue to be explored by all people and particularly by educators. If we acknowledge that our cultural identities influence how we see the world, then all of us, including those of us who are White, need to explore in a thoughtful way what it means to be White. Katz (2003) raised some additional interesting questions related to this issue: Why do White people see themselves as individuals rather than as part of a White culture? What privileges are assumed by Whites simply by virtue of being White in America? How do White people feel about their Whiteness?

Sleeter (2000) described multicultural education as, in one sense, a struggle against White racism rather than as a way to appreciate diversity. The benefits accorded Whites solely because of skin color and the subsequent study of what it means to be White is essential. White culture continues to dominate the education system (Howard & Banks, 2016), with the result that a system of education geared to White, middle-class culture and values does not necessarily support equitably the education of all children. Note what Julie Landsman (2009) wrote in *A White Teacher Talks About Race*:

> I was raised on Brooks Brothers and striped ties, Bass Weeguns and my father walking in the house in the evenings of my childhood with his leather briefcase and his London Fog thrown over his arm. But more than that, I was raised with *signals*, ways he frowned or turned his body slightly to the side in a subtle act of dismissal. . . .

> I knew, by the time I was in the summer of my fifteenth year, exactly how to speak to my boss, a neurologist who slept on the couch in his office some nights. I knew about *stance:* distance, silence, being discreet and off to the side. I learned these things because I was a white woman in a world where power was never spoken of but assumed. . . . I *absorbed* this culture without realizing it. (pp. 93–94)

Landsman (2009) went on to describe how her students of color, who lacked this upbringing, were at a disadvantage trying to gain an education and then employment in a culture foreign to many of them. The beliefs, values, and perspectives of White, middle-class America dominate our culture, while accurate, positive images and views of people of color are not necessarily portrayed (Cortes, 2000). While **privilege** has become a loaded word, ignoring its existence is a roadblock to improving race relations (Johnson, 2017). Use Exercise 5.6 to explore your own thoughts about White privilege.

While we have very few opportunities to discuss our cultural identities, we have even fewer opportunities to discuss the concept of privilege and how it has affected our lives. The practice of intergroup conversations—in other words, bringing diverse groups of students together for facilitated discussions about cultural differences—is a critically important instructional practice (Zuniga, Nagda, & Sevig, 2002). As a group, try participating in Exercise 5.7.

EXERCISE 5.6
WHITE PRIVILEGE

White Privilege, Male Privilege: Unpacking the Invisible Knapsack is a classic paper written by McIntosh (1988) of the Wellesley College Center for Research on Women. McIntosh illustrated how European Americans (males) have "unearned privileges." Answer yes or no to the following statements adapted from her work.

	Yes	No
1. If a police officer pulls me over, I can be pretty sure I haven't been singled out because of my race.		
2. I can go shopping alone most of the time, fairly well assured that I will not be followed or harassed by store detectives.		
3. I can be pretty sure that if I ask to talk to "the person in charge," I will face a person of my own race.		

How many yes answers did you get? Compare your answers to those of others—European Americans, women, and people of color. Discuss any differences in your answers.

White Privilege (Your Own Version)

Complete another five examples of your own to illustrate ways in which European Americans are privileged.

	Yes	No
1.		
2.		
3.		
4.		
5.		

(Continued)

(Continued)

Gender Privilege (Your Own Version)

Complete another five examples of your own to illustrate ways in which men in general have privilege over women.

	Yes	No
1.		
2.		
3.		
4.		
5.		

EXERCISE 5.7

PRIVILEGE WALK, OR THE HORATIO ALGER EXERCISE

There are many variations of this exercise in existence. The earliest source can be traced to Ellen Bettmann of the Anti-Defamation League from an activity developed by Martin Cano, Valerie Tulier, and Ruch Kacz of the "A World of Difference" program.

Materials (for facilitator only)

Copy of Horatio Alger questions

Space

A room large enough to accommodate the participants standing shoulder to shoulder in a single line

Directions

Participants form a line in the middle of the room and hold the hand of the person next to them. The facilitator reads a list. As a category is identified to which a participant belongs, he or she will either step forward or backward or stay stationary, as appropriate. Participants will keep holding hands until doing so is no longer possible. When people move too far away from each other, they will have to let go of each other's hands.

"All those who . . . "

1. have a parent or parents who completed college, take one step forward.

2. have a parent who never completed high school, take one step back.

3. went to a private school, take one step forward.

4. were raised in a community where the vast majority of police, politicians, and government workers were not of your ethnic or racial group, take one step back.

5. commonly see people of your race or ethnicity as heroes or heroines in television programs or movies, take one step forward.

6. commonly see people of your race or ethnicity on television or movies in roles you consider degrading, take one step back.

7. come from a racial or ethnic group that has ever been considered by scientists as "inferior," take one step back.

8. have ever been harassed by the police because of your ethnicity or race, take one step back.

9. have ancestors who were slaves in the United States, take one step back.

10. have ancestors who, because of their race, religion, or ethnicity, were denied voting rights or citizenship; had to drink from separate water fountains, ride in the back of the bus, or use separate entrances to buildings or separate restrooms; were denied access to clubs, jobs, or restaurants; or were precluded from buying property in certain neighborhoods, take one step back.

11. can walk into a store without having clerks assume by your appearance that you are going to steal something, take one step forward.

12. have parents who spoke English as a first language, take one step forward.

13. have never been told that someone hated you because of your race, ethnic group, religion, or sexual orientation, take one step forward.

14. have read about history of your ancestors in history books provided by your K–12 school, take one step forward.

15. have ever been denied a job because of your race, ethnic group, religion, or gender, take one step backward.

16. were raised in homes with libraries of children's books and some adult books, take one step forward.

17. were raised in homes where the newspaper was read daily, take one step forward.

18. have vacationed in a foreign country, take one step forward.

19. have been taken to art galleries or museums by your parents, take one step forward.

20. have an immediate family member who is a doctor or lawyer, take one step forward.

21. went to or currently attend a school where the majority of the teachers are of your same race or ethnicity, take one step forward.

Debrief

- What did you learn through this exercise?

- What is the point of this activity?

- Do we all start off equal in life?

- What does holding hands, then becoming so distant that you can't hold hands anymore, represent?

Privilege that is linked to identity has its grounding in the United States in the very beginnings of this country. We may want to think that every individual is created equal and if he or she just pulls his or her own weight, takes responsibility for his or her own destiny and in other words, "pulls himself or herself up by the bootstraps," things would be fine. In fact, diverse groups of people in this country, today, do not start on a level playing field.

Not all White people, of course, are unaware of the power they have, nor are they uninformed about their cultural backgrounds. Nor do all White people think in biased and act in discriminatory ways. It is, however, a struggle, and not an easy one, to develop a deep level of consciousness about privilege. For White people, learning what it means to be White can be a painful experience but one that is ultimately rewarding in that it opens up a much better multicultural life.

LEARNING OBJECTIVE 5.3 Summarize the Influence of Personal Cultural Identities on Teaching and Learning

Identification with cultural groups shapes our worldview (Cushner, 2014). Cushner believed that most individuals have participated in childhood experiences that have led explicitly to the development of certain values and perspectives.

McIntosh (1988) wrote the extensively cited and thought-provoking document *White Privilege and Male Privilege: A Personal Account of Coming to See Correspondences Through Work in Women's Studies* more than 25 years ago. You might want to locate the complete document and carefully read it a few times. In the intervening years since McIntosh penned this resource, some things have changed and some things have stayed the same. Take time to assess what you think has changed in terms of the concept of privilege, and what you believe has stayed the same. After reviewing your assessment, develop a rationale for your stance.

Another way of describing the phenomenon of White identity or White privilege is that individuals, as they grow, develop a picture of the world as they know it, and this mental image makes them feel secure. They acquire a set of values and beliefs about how the world operates. This is your worldview. Your worldview is the way you think the world should work. Your worldview is in operation every day.

Just because people come to a common purpose (e.g., learning in school, teaching, working on a common project) does not mean they have a common worldview. They may not possess the same values and beliefs and ways of behaving. Every difference in worldview is a potential point of conflict, and worldviews held by different groups of people may differ significantly. It follows that no one worldview is completely true; all are only partially accurate.

How does our worldview, based on cultural identity, positively and negatively affect teaching and learning? How we see things as an educator is grounded in our association with particular dimensions of culture or particular cultural groups. A young, White male raised in New England will "see" things much differently than an older, Black female raised in the Midwest. It may take quite a lot of effort to understand that our way of seeing events, behaviors, activities, and actions in the classroom is not necessarily the "right" way—it's just one way.

The Influence of Cultural Identity and Worldview on Approaches to Teaching and Learning

Culture affects what happens in classrooms on a daily basis (Gay, 2018; Sheets, 2005). Certainly children bring into the classroom diverse perspectives, histories, experiences, beliefs, and ways of behaving that are grounded in powerful identifications with cultural groups. We will explore in depth the impact of children's cultural identities on the teaching and learning experience in Chapter 6. Just as important to recognize, however, is the fact that educators also bring into the classroom diverse perspectives, histories, experiences, beliefs, and ways of behaving that are grounded in their identification with cultural groups. It is the lucky student whose cultural identities are a fairly close match to the teacher's. If there is no close match, then the teacher, who is the person in control of the classroom, could be the "winner" in the duel between conflicting cultural values. Sheets (2005) described the challenge well:

Creates/creates/thinkstock

It can be challenging to try gaining a better understanding of personal beliefs and values. Teachers should devote time to uncovering these elements of who they are and how it influences how they teach.

> In classrooms, some of the students' skills and competencies learned in their cultural group will differ from the behaviors and skills of their teachers who may be socialized in a different cultural group. Some teachers may not be aware of this cultural mismatch. Differences in teachers' and students' cultural strengths, norms, and values can be problematic in classrooms that operate with a single culture model. (p. 4)

In this type of classroom, students must assimilate into the classroom environment and adapt to the teacher's expectations of what are acceptable behaviors and acceptable approaches to learning. Otherwise, they risk falling behind quickly—that is, unless the teacher has worked hard to become culturally responsive and culturally responsible.

A culturally responsive and responsible teacher creates a classroom that is student centered as opposed to teacher centered. Ooka Pang (2005) cautioned,

> Teachers who are unaware of multicultural education and the powerful influence of culture on and in schools, have . . . never had the opportunity to examine how schools teach a strong mainstream culture and that many students must shift to new assumptions, beliefs, and values in order to do well in school. . . . . The most powerful reason why culture is ignored in schools is that most teachers cannot see the elements of culture in their own lives. Teachers may not understand that culture is always operating. Some cannot identify aspects of their culture. They don't see themselves as cultural beings. (pp. 30–31)

Grant and Gillette (2006) have summarized the work of several scholars and researchers by developing a list of characteristics of culturally responsive teachers. Such teachers have high expectations for all students, use their knowledge of students to design appropriate and relevant learning experiences, and make strong connections between the classroom and the community. However, of particular interest is the point Grant and Gillette make that culturally responsive teachers "are willing to be introspective and reflective about themselves and their teaching. They constantly monitor their beliefs and actions for bias and prejudice

Extended Explorations 5.3:
Impact of Identity on Teaching
and Learning

As stated in this section, the selection of curriculum materials, the design of lessons, and the selection and use of instructional strategies reflect our own worldview, perspectives, experiences, comfort levels, and belief systems. Given that fact, select a unit you teach (or at least are familiar with in terms of experiences) that includes multiple lesson plans. If you don't have something you've designed, locate a unit plan on the Internet that resonates with you. Conduct a critique of that unit plan and its associated lessons. Very specifically, how does it resonate with your own cultural identities? For example, who is represented in the lessons or textbook? Assess who is not represented in the same materials. Are the materials representative of a variety of cultures, perspectives, and backgrounds? Can a diverse group of children see themselves in the materials that have been selected to support learning?

Consolidate your findings in a written critique and share with colleagues. Draft a plan for how you might, as multicultural educators, work to make wider use of a greater diversity of cultural identities.

and will not tolerate manifestations of such from students" (p. 56). This summary statement underlines the critical importance of self-understanding. If teachers understand themselves in relation to culture, they will be in a better position to understand the impact of culture on the development of students' identities.

Unintentionally, educators tend to use the very powerful elements of the cultures with which they identify to influence teaching and learning in significant ways. Teachers decide daily about instructional materials, instructional strategies, curriculum, expectations of each student, how they need to communicate with each student, and how to assess learning. Each of these decisions is affected in significant ways by the worldview of the teacher and by his or her value system, which has developed as a result of identification with cultural groups. Two primary ways in which cultural beliefs can affect teaching and learning are in the selection of curriculum and teaching materials and in the selection of instructional strategies.

- *Selection of curriculum and teaching materials:* Educators often make selections because the materials and curriculum resonate with them. They've experienced it already. In fact, educators should be asking questions such as these: Are the

EXERCISE 5.8

WRITING A LIFE NARRATIVE

Take time to reflect and write about the following statements. Your responses should be a reflection of your own experiences, as well as your understanding of the knowledge base about culturally relevant teaching. Be prepared to share your responses with colleagues in class.

1. What beliefs do I hold dear?

2. Who are the people and what are the life experiences that have contributed to the development of my beliefs?

3. How might those beliefs affect how I work in schools?

4. How do I see the children and families and people with whom I work?

5. How do I see the curriculum?

6. How do I see best practices in terms of instruction?

7. What assumptions do I make about student motivation?

8. What are my prejudices?

9. How did I acquire them?

10. How might I address them?

materials representative of a variety of cultures, perspectives, and backgrounds? Can a diverse group of children see themselves in the materials that have been selected to support learning?

- *Selection of instructional strategies:* One saying that is well-known in education, and that appears to hold much truth, is that teachers generally teach the way they've been taught. Additionally, educators tend to teach in ways that are most comfortable for them. In fact, educators need to stretch beyond their comfort zones and teach in ways that recognize the diversity of experiences, cultures, learning styles, and ways of behaving that are defined by culture.

Not only do teachers need to know about themselves as cultural beings, but they need to be clear about why they have chosen to teach in the first place. Practice writing a life narrative as explained in Exercise 5.8.

REFLECTING BACK

In this chapter, we've explored the concepts of socialization, identity development, and dimensions of cultural identity. You've considered the fact that the journey to become culturally aware is a lifetime endeavor. You've read about the powerful ways in which our cultural identities can influence our work as educators. Who has power and privilege in our society is an important discussion to have, both in and out of the classroom. Understanding the power inequities between men and women, between Caucasians and people of color, between the rich and the poor helps us understand how educational policies are made.

Reflect on the following questions as you consider the influence of your own cultural identities on your work as an educator.

5.1 Describe the Dimensions of Cultural Identity

1. Give examples of the ways in which you've been socialized. Who contributed to your socialization?

2. Evaluate how the primary and secondary dimensions of your cultural identity have blended to make you the unique individual that you are.

3. Compare and contrast the influence of the primary and secondary dimensions of your cultural identity. Which are the more powerful dimensions for you at this point in your life? Are they the same as when you were growing up?

5.2 Explain Privileged Cultural Identities

1. What deeper awareness do you have now of your culture?

2. What awareness do you now have of the privileges you have or do not have?

5.3 Summarize the Influence of Personal Cultural Identities on Teaching and Learning

1. How can teachers minimize the negative effects of their own cultural identities on the teaching and learning process?

2. What are the implications of your own cultural identities for teaching?

3. What effect does or will your cultural background have on opportunities for children to learn in your classroom?

4. How do you think the students in the class relate or will be able to relate to your gender? Race/ethnicity? Age? Religion? Socioeconomic status?

PROFILES IN MULTICULTURAL EDUCATION

SONIA NIETO

© Sonia Nieto

Sonia Nieto is Professor Emerita of Language, Literacy and Culture at the School of Education, University of Massachusetts Amherst. A researcher, teacher, lecturer, and writer, Dr. Nieto taught students at all levels from elementary grades through graduate school. Her research focuses on multicultural education and on the education of Latinos, immigrants, and students of diverse cultural and linguistic backgrounds. Her books include *Affirming Diversity: The Sociopolitical Context of Multicultural Education* (with Patty Bode, 7th ed., 2018), *Language, Culture, and Teaching: Critical Perspectives* (3rd ed., 2018), *Why We Teach Now* (2014), *Brooklyn Dreams: My Life in Public Education* (2015), *Finding Joy in Teaching Students of Diverse Backgrounds: Culturally Responsive and Socially Just Practices in U.S. Classrooms* (2013), *The Light in Their Eyes: Creating Multicultural Learning Communities* (10th Anniversary ed., 2010), *Puerto Rican Students in U.S. Schools*, an edited volume (2000), and *What Keeps Teachers Going?* (2003). In addition, she has published dozens of book chapters and articles in journals such as *Educational Leadership*, *The Harvard Educational Review*, *Multicultural Education*, and *Theory Into Practice.* She serves on several national advisory boards that focus on educational equity and social justice, including Facing History and Ourselves and Educators for Social Responsibility, as well as on numerous editorial advisory boards for educational journals. Her many awards for scholarship, advocacy, and activism include the 1989 Human and Civil Rights Award from the Massachusetts Teachers Association, the 1996 Teacher of the Year Award from the Hispanic Educators of Massachusetts, the 1997 Multicultural Educator of the Year Award from the National Association for Multicultural Education, the Excellence in Education Award from Boricua College, and, most recently, the 2005 Outstanding Educator award from the National Council of Teachers of English. She was an Annenberg Institute Senior Fellow from 1998 to 2000, and she was awarded a month-long residency at the Bellagio Center in Italy in 2000. She is married to Angel Nieto, a former teacher and author of children's books, and they have 2 daughters and 12 grandchildren.

Dr. Nieto first took a multicultural education course more than 30 years ago. In that course, the work focused primarily on helping teachers celebrate diversity. However, Dr. Nieto believed, since taking that first course, that it would be essential to the achievement of equity that the educational community address the broader issues of structural inequality, as well as a lack of awareness of how institutional policies and practices influence educational outcomes. Dr. Nieto has been committed to making sure educators know that simply respecting differences and celebrating students' identities, while important, are not enough. Teachers also need to take into account the sociopolitical context of education, the sociocultural realities of their students' lives, and the structural inequalities that are embedded in our society and that can make academic achievement tremendously challenging for students of some social groups—through no fault of their own. Combining these elements with respect for differences can lead to a more sophisticated understanding of multicultural education and, in the long run, to a better chance for all students to be successful learners.

CASE STUDY
CULTURAL IDENTITY CONFUSION

Key Issues to Be Explored in the Case

1. The importance of educators having a deep awareness of their own racial and ethnic identities before they can support diverse students

2. Possibilities for conflict between an educator's cultural identity and cultural identities of students

3. The importance of educators understanding privilege due to majority group membership and how they can make significant and effective use of that privilege

Antonio Scarpaci was born in Bogota, Colombia, of immigrant parents. His father was born in mainland Italy, and his mother was originally from the Italian island Sicily. His parents met each other at a trade school, married, and decided to immigrate to Colombia, where they found positions at a local factory. They began taking Spanish classes at night right away. Antonio was born shortly after they arrived in Colombia and was educated in the Colombian education system. Nevertheless, his parents continued to speak Italian at home with him, and he grew to be fluent in both Spanish and Italian. The family celebrated both mainland Italian and Sicilian customs, ate traditional foods, celebrated the holidays they had celebrated in Italy, and taught Antonio their rich cultural heritage. The family also assimilated into the Colombian culture, learning the manners and ways of Colombians, and Antonio grew up with his friends and classmates as a fellow Colombian. Due to his facility in both languages, he excelled in school.

When Antonio was 10, the family moved to upstate New York, and he is now a student in your classroom, where you are his first American teacher. The town is a suburb, and there is relatively little racial, ethnic, and language diversity in the school. While he is fluent in Spanish and Italian, Antonio does not speak any English. He is reticent in class because of his lack of knowledge of English, but he is very alert and bright. Neither you nor anyone else in the school speaks Spanish or Italian.

Again, with his facility in language learning, Antonio applies himself right away to learning English. However, unable to speak much English in the beginning, he is regarded by the other students as something of an oddity. Although some of the students have tried to become friends with him, most children are not able to develop any kind of strong relationship with him.

Having been prepared in your teacher preparation program as a multicultural educator, you want to provide an environment that values diverse cultures. During your teacher preparation program, you were particularly intrigued by the notion that all individuals possess cultural identities. You, in fact, have spent a lot of time reflecting on who you are as a cultural being and the influence of your own cultural identities on teaching and learning. You were particularly influenced by the concept of cultural identity and privilege and are committed to using your understanding of your own identities to develop a multicultural classroom. Having Antonio in the classroom, however, is one of your first opportunities to use what you know about yourself to positively influence what happens for students.

Now watching Antonio on the playground, you are reflecting on what you have learned about yourself and Antonio. You realize that, for the first time, he is truly a "minority"—at least a linguistic minority—and you are part of the privileged majority. As you teach about various cultures, create lessons that will prepare your students for a multicultural world, and encourage students to understand and appreciate their own cultures, you realize that Antonio is in a unique situation. He seems confused about his cultural identity, and you struggle to help him define himself—and to use what you know about yourself—to improve teaching and learning for all students in the classroom.

Discussion Questions

1. Antonio does not know how to answer the questions on forms that ask him to identify his race. He asks you what you mean when you identify him as "Hispanic." His parents

(Continued)

(Continued)

are from Italy and Sicily. He grew up in Colombia. Is he Italian (or Sicilian), Spanish, or Colombian? What does it mean to be Hispanic, a new label and identity for him?

2. How important is it for Antonio to sort out his cultural identity? What would you tell him? How would you help him?

3. How do you explain to students the concepts of racial and ethnic identity, using yourself as a model?

4. What are the possibilities for conflict between your own cultural identity and that of Antonio? How might you use your own understanding of your own cultural identities to best support Antonio?

5. How might you use your standing as a privileged majority group member in a positive way in this situation?

CHAPTER SUMMARY

Chapter 5 explores the importance of self-awareness of cultural identity. This is particularly important for educators, since the values and beliefs that they have adopted as a result of socialization within different cultural identities will have a powerful impact on approaches to teaching and learning in the classroom. Multicultural educators must use regularly a process for enhancing their awareness of their own cultural identities and how those identities influence what happens in the classroom. Multicultural educators must know themselves as cultural beings and how their identification with different cultural groups influences everything they do in the classroom.

Chapter 5 included three Learning Objectives.

5.1 Describe the dimensions of your cultural identity

Each person is a cultural being with a distinct set of values, beliefs, histories, and experiences that influence how he or she reacts and behaves. Educators need to develop strategies for exploring important questions about their own cultural identity development such as these: How did they learn about the cultures with which they identify? With which cultural groups do they

identify? In what ways does culture contribute to one's self-identity? Coming to a deep understanding of culture and cultural identities is not an easy process. Ignoring the influence of culture on our behaviors can lead to significant problems in the teaching and learning process.

5.2 Explain privileged cultural identities

Knowledge of the benefits accorded Whites because of skin color and the subsequent study of what it means to be White is essential. A system of education geared toward White, middle-class culture and values does not necessarily support equitably the education of all children. Students of color who have not been able to participate in a White, middle-class culture are at a distinct disadvantage in a school that is grounded in traditional White, middle-class values and beliefs.

5.3 Summarize the influence of personal cultural identities on teaching and learning

The values and beliefs held by an educator due to cultural identification can influence not only the nature of relationships with students but also the selection of curriculum and instructional strategies. Educators bring into the classroom diverse perspectives, histories, experiences, beliefs, and ways of behaving that are grounded in their identification with cultural groups. It is the lucky student whose cultural identities are a fairly close match to the teacher's. If there is not a close match between the teacher's and the students' cultures, then the teacher, who is the person in control of the classroom, could be the "winner" in the duel between conflicting cultural values.

KEY TERMS

primary dimensions of culture 125   secondary dimensions of culture 126
privilege 137   socialization 124

APPLICATION: ACTIVITIES AND EXERCISES

Individual

1. Interview family members, particularly brothers or sisters or close cousins, to get insights into how they view the family's cultural identities. Develop a chart that compares and contrasts those perspectives with your own understanding of your cultural identities (Learning Objective 5.1).

2. Conduct a search of your family tree (Learning Objective 5.2). Use any of the search engines available on the Internet. Use the resources of a library or a local cultural club. Address the following in your search (based on Cushner, McClelland, & Safford, 2006):

   - What countries did your family come from originally?

   - Why and when did they leave those countries?

   - What challenges did they encounter when they arrived in the United States?

   - What languages did they speak? Does anyone in your family still speak those languages?

   - What traditions have been passed through the generations of your family that are still practiced today?

3. How do your cultural identities influence how and what you teach? What do these identities mean for your personal life and professional practice? (Learning Objective 5.3)

Group

1. Interview each other and compare and contrast your findings. Are there more elements and components that people have in common? Or are there more differences? What does this mean for you as an educator? (Learning Objective 5.1)

Self-Assessment

1. Think about how your life would be different if you had been born of the opposite gender. What insights could you identify? (Learning Objective 5.2)

2. Think about how your life would be different if you were born poor, a racial minority, or a religious minority. Or, if this is your circumstance now, how would your life have been if you were born a wealthy Anglo-Saxon? Think about how your perspectives as a human being and as a teacher might be different. (Learning Objective 5.2)

3. Write down five questions related to the influence of cultural identities on teaching and learning that you have after reading this chapter. Share those questions with classmates and use them for discussion. (Learning Objective 5.3)

ANNOTATED RESOURCES

Densho Project: The Japanese American Legacy Project

Densho's mission is to preserve the testimonies of Japanese Americans who were unjustly incarcerated during World War II before their memories are extinguished. It offers these irreplaceable firsthand accounts, coupled with historical images and teacher resources, to explore principles of democracy and to promote equal justice for all.

Watt, S. K. (2007). Difficult dialogues, privilege and social justice: Uses of the privileged identity exploration (PIE) model in student affairs practice. The College Student Affairs Journal, 26, 114–125.

This article will introduce the Privileged Identity Exploration (PIE) model. This model identifies eight defense modes associated with behaviors individuals display when engaged in difficult dialogues about social justice issues. Implications for the model and ways in which it can be used to assist facilitators as they engage participants in discussions about diversity are discussed.

Facing History and Ourselves

This organization is an international education and professional development organization dedicated to engaging students of diverse backgrounds in an examination of racism, discrimination, and prejudice. There are many other resources available on the Internet.

REACH (Respecting Ethnic and Cultural Heritage)

For more than 30 years, the REACH Center, a nationally recognized nonprofit organization, has positioned itself as one of the most respected establishments providing cultural diversity services to agencies throughout the United States, Canada, and Australia. The REACH Center is able to carry out its work through its cadre of nationally certified trainers. More than 250 nationally certified REACH trainers, located throughout the United States and Australia, have established records in public speaking, group facilitation, and program and curriculum development as well as having conducted research and training in the area of multicultural education and ethnic history.

The Schomburg Center for Research in Black Culture

The Schomburg Center for Research in Black Culture, a research unit of the New York Public Library, is generally recognized as one of the leading institutions of its kind in the world. For more than 80 years, the center has collected, preserved, and provided access to materials documenting Black life and promoted the study and interpretation of the history and culture of peoples of African descent.

Teaching Tolerance

Founded in 1991, Teaching Tolerance is dedicated to reducing prejudice, improving intergroup relations, and supporting equitable school experiences for children in the United States.

Wellesley Centers for Women

The Wellesley Centers for Women is one of the largest gender-focused research and action organizations in the world. Scholars there conduct social science research and evaluation, develop theory and publications, and implement training programs with women's lives and women's concerns at the center. The site offers an extensive set of resources and exercises that can be used to explore various components of self-identity.

Get the tools you need to sharpen your study skills. SAGE edge offers a robust online environment featuring an impressive array of free tools and resources. Access practice quizzes, eFlashcards, video, and multimedia at **edge.sagepub.com/howe3e**

6 Developing Awareness of All Humans as Cultural Beings

© iStockphotos.com/monkeybusinessimages

Learning Objectives

In this chapter, we will focus on how schools can work with diversity as a strength. Instructional leaders who link a positive focus on culture with the building of character are demonstrating that this linkage is a key component of a great school (Carter, 2011; Howard, 2010). We present experiences designed to help educators expand awareness about themselves as individuals who strongly influence the development of others, and we offer experiences that can be used with students to help them develop deep understandings of others as cultural beings. Four focus areas will be addressed.

Through your study of and work on this chapter, you will be able to do the following:

6.1 Explain seeing differences in human beings

6.2 Analyze responding to differences in human beings

6.3 Appraise ineffective responses to cultural differences in schools

6.4 Compose positive responses to cultural differences in schools

Each individual is a unique human being as a result of a distinctive set of experiences, cultural backgrounds, identities, beliefs, values, and histories. Whenever we interact with another human being, our interactions are deeply influenced by this unique blend of identities and cultural backgrounds. The ever-increasing diversity of our world, society, and schools can contribute to a richness of interactions never experienced before. Conversely, lack of understanding and appreciation of differences related to culture can lead to significant problems with interpersonal interactions (C. Bennett, 2014; M. Bennett, 1986).

To have awareness about culture in school settings, both educators and students must understand people as cultural beings who identify with a variety of cultural groups or categories. Culture can be viewed through the lenses of race, ethnicity, gender, age, language, socioeconomic status, religion, and sexual orientation, in addition to other categories. In developing awareness of others as cultural beings, we are trying to understand the influence of identification with any of these diverse categories. Important questions one might ask include these: "What does it mean to be Black?" "What does it mean to be White?" "What does it mean to be male, female, gay, Muslim, Jewish, biracial, adopted, or a person with a physical handicap in our society?" "How does age influence interactions with others?"

> There is always a place I can take someone's curiosity and land where they end up enlightened when we're done. That's my challenge as an educator. No one is dumb who is curious. The people who don't ask questions remain clueless throughout their lives.
>
> **—Neil deGrasse Tyson, American astrophysicist, cosmologist, author, and science communicator**

CASE STUDY
CLASS STRUGGLE

With this new school year, several new students of Asian descent appeared in class. Anxious to welcome them, the teacher made a concentrated effort to be even more energetic, cheerful, and upbeat with the entire class. Often, she would try to engage the students in activities designed to get them mingling with one another. The class overall enjoyed the lively interactive atmosphere, but the Asian students appeared withdrawn and hesitant. They seldom smiled, continually looked down when being addressed or answering questions, were soft-spoken, and seemed not to want to engage in activities with other students. They only talked when asked a question. They did not seem to understand the teacher's attempts at humor. When asked critical thinking questions that required them to challenge the teacher's opinion, they resisted. There was no hesitation when asked factual questions, however.

When assigned to small-group work, the Asian students appeared to take a lesser role, allowing other students to be in charge. They chose not to participate in vigorous debate. They seemed horrified at the aggressive tone of other students. Instead, their attempts to contribute in a more collegial manner resulted in them being ignored.

Academically, the students were doing well. They were studious and well behaved for the most part. They participated in some of the clubs. Their parents were very responsive but not always understanding of the teacher's concerns about their children fitting in. Some parents revealed that their children were needed to help after school hours and on the weekends in the family business. Some had to care for younger siblings as both parents worked long hours. The Asian students preferred to choose each other for company, notably in the lunchroom. Other students began ignoring them, and some of them teased the new students. The teacher was concerned that something was wrong but did not know how to go about correcting the situation. Knowing very little about the various Asian cultures, she was confused as to what approaches to take.

(Continued)

(Continued)

Your Perspectives on the Case

1. Can you explain the behavior of the Asian students?

2. What do you believe is happening in the classroom?

3. What recommendations might you give to the teacher?

4. What cultural knowledge would be most helpful to this teacher?

5. Where might the teacher go to acquire the knowledge?

Being an educator is never as simple as standing in front of a class and imparting wisdom to a group of eager, attentive students. The subtle nature of discrimination means that schools need to be very conscientious and proactive in dealing with matters of bias and bigotry that are embedded at all levels of schooling. Discrimination may not manifest in overt acts, but it almost certainly does show itself in the attitudes, language, and demeanor of students, parents, staff, and faculty. We need to recognize that we spend a lifetime accumulating our biases, values, and attitudes. Similarly, it will take the rest of our lifetimes to develop an ongoing awareness of our biases and prejudices and address them.

Expanding awareness of ourselves is a lifelong process and requires openness and commitment to exploring how we see other people and what might be standing in the way of our truly appreciating people who are different from us. Expanding awareness about oneself can be achieved through experiences designed to show us our own thinking processes and the influence of our own experiences. These facilitated experiences are best followed by a time for reflection and reaction to those experiences. Students will graduate from school with perceptions, attitudes, and behaviors that have prepared them well for a multicultural world—or handicapped them from being appropriately functional.

Understanding the beliefs, values, customs, and traditions that we hold, as well as those held by others, is a necessary process in learning how to live and work in a diverse world. Doing so broadens us intellectually and gives us important and useful awareness, knowledge, and dispositions. In this chapter, we will examine what we and our students need to know about people who are different from us so that we can more effectively engage them in the teaching and learning process.

LEARNING OBJECTIVE 6.1 Explain Seeing Differences in Human Beings

THINKING AHEAD

It is not uncommon for students to go through periods of questioning about who they are, especially with respect to the other students around them. This type of questioning may lead to feelings of insecurity, fear of social isolation or ostracism, and fear of people who are different. In turn, fear of people who are different and a lack of understanding of differences can lead to inappropriate interpersonal interactions.

Questions

1. What memories do you have of encountering people who were different from you?

2. Where did these perceptions come from? What influenced how you perceived students in those cultural groups?

3. How have your perceptions or relations changed?

4. Critique ways in which people of color are portrayed in the media. Think specifically about television and newspapers. Are the images, perceptions, and lives of non-White and nonstraight people portrayed accurately? If not, why not? Suggest at least three specific actions teachers can engage in to provide in their classrooms a more accurate image of diverse groups.

iStock/SimmiSimons

It is very common for children to go through stages in their lives where they question who they are and whether they "fit in." Insecurities about how they are perceived, their status, and being isolated do not end with childhood. A goal should be for all to develop a strong, healthy self-image that encourages seeking and developing bonds with people different from themselves.

Much more is being written for teachers about how people develop their own cultural identities (Brown, 2002; Darling-Hammond & Bransford, 2005; Gollnick & Chinn, 2016; King, Hollins, & Hayman, 1997). It is important for students and educators alike to understand how their own cultural identities develop, and it is just as important for them to understand how culturally different people see one another, how perceptions of others develop, how culturally different people interact with one another, and how to improve intercultural interactions. While we may declare that we see or would like to see people as essentially the same, in fact, no two people are exactly alike. We each possess unique identities based on gender, race, ethnicity, socioeconomic status, language, religious backgrounds, and other aspects of cultural identity. With this in mind, educators must be skilled in strategies to examine their own attitudes and beliefs about people who are different and understand how those beliefs and attitudes develop. Then they must also be able to help students to learn to recognize and value differences. We must also become knowledgeable about attribution and assessment across groups and conflict management. And this attention must be given to differences across groups as well as within groups (Cushner, McClelland, & Safford, 2009; Moule, 2011).

Factors That Influence Our Perceptions of Others

What influences how we see people across as well as within groups? Our understanding, attitudes, and beliefs about difference come from a wide variety of sources. Certainly, we derive a large percentage of our perceptions of others from personal interactions and encounters. When we have a positive or a negative interpersonal interaction with someone who is different from us, the quality of that interaction influences how we see other members of that cultural group. However, perceptions of people who are different from us also come from many other sources that surround us on a daily basis (Carter, 2011; Gallavan, 2011a, 2011b; Howard, 2010; Moule, 2011).

Perceptions of differences are strongly influenced by media exposure, through sources such as television, movies, music, newspapers, magazines, and the Internet. Two photos posted on the Internet by the Associated Press during Hurricane Katrina in 2005 caused a furor and international dialogue about media bias. The first showed a young, Black man wading in chest-deep water. The caption read,

> A young man walks through chest-deep flood water after *looting* [italics added] a grocery store in New Orleans on Tuesday, Aug. 30, 2005. Flood waters continue to rise in New Orleans after Hurricane Katrina did extensive damage when it made landfall on Monday.

A second photo showed a White couple, also wading through floodwater. The caption read,

> Two residents wade through chest-deep water after *finding* [italics added] bread and soda from a local grocery store after Hurricane Katrina came through the area in New Orleans, Louisiana.

Linda Christensen (2011) created a wonderful lesson plan on this incident, which was published in *Rethinking Schools*. The dialogue about why Black people were described as "looting" food while White people were described as just trying to survive by "finding" food highlighted how the media can be biased. In *The Children Are Watching: How the Media Teach About Diversity*, Cortés (2000) described how media "products—programs, papers and magazines—serve as textbooks on democracy."

We are also largely influenced by how people around us feel about diverse groups. People who contribute in critical ways to the development of our cultural attitudes, beliefs, and values, including our perceptions of differences, are family members and friends, caregivers, peers, teachers, coaches and counselors, heads of religious groups, leaders of extracurricular activities, and others. This development of cultural norms, values, and beliefs is often referred to as *socialization* (see Chapter 5 for additional information). According to Cushner et al. (2009), "The purpose of socialization is to teach the learner those habits of mind and action that will make him or her a loyal and functional member of a particular group" (p. 55). These habits of mind and action can include socially appropriate ways of seeing others and interacting with others, rightly or wrongly.

Socialization can have both positive and negative results. One particularly challenging result is ethnocentrism, or the belief that one's own view is the most appropriate view and the right view. Milton Bennett (1986) conceptualized responses to differences along a continuum, from those that are more ethnocentric to those that are more ethnorelative (see Figure 6.1).

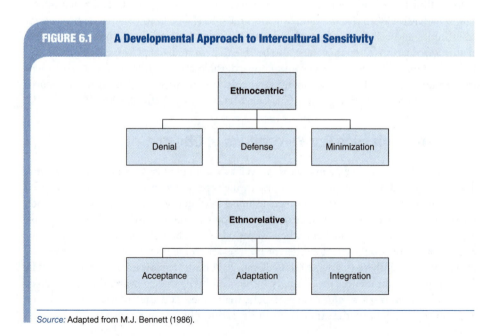

FIGURE 6.1   **A Developmental Approach to Intercultural Sensitivity**

Source: Adapted from M.J. Bennett (1986).

LEARNING OBJECTIVE 6.2 Analyze Responding to Differences in Human Beings

Self in Relation to Others as Cultural Beings

When you walk into a room of strangers for a meeting, or even to attend a party, do you look for people you don't know and walk up to them to introduce yourself? Or like most people, do you scan the room to find someone you know or who at least looks like you (e.g., same gender, same age) and head toward that person? There is absolutely nothing wrong with the latter behavior. In fact, it's quite normal for each of us to want to be with people with whom we feel comfortable because we appear to have something in common. Given the expanding diversity of our society, however, our challenge is to develop greater comfort levels with people who are significantly different from us. And it's critically important for educators to understand how people respond to differences. Just because educators or students are put together in schools does not mean they all get along. Perceptions of differences influence interactions. So what are some responses to differences?

Exercise 6.2 is an activity that teachers can use to help students understand beliefs and values. The Paseo or Circles of Identity is the result of collaborative work by Debbi Laidley (2001) of the University of California–Los Angeles School Management Program and Debbie Bambino, Debbie McIntyre, Stevi Quate, and Juli Quinn. It was created at the winter meeting of the National School Reform Faculty, December 2001, in Houston, Texas.

EXERCISE 6.2

MY PASEO

Procedure

1. Draw a diagram like the one in Figure 6.2. Write your name in the center circle. In the outer circles, write a word or a description that strongly identifies you, such as *female*, *Irish American*, *Southerner*, and so on. You should add as many circles as you wish, but each should be a strong identifier for you.

2. Now the class will count off by twos in Spanish, French, or any other language that one of them may know. Doing counting activities in a different language each time adds an element of culture to the activity. The ones will form a tight circle shoulder to shoulder, then turn and face outward. The twos will each pair up with a one so that the one and the two face each other.

3. Each person gets 2 minutes to pose questions to his or her partner. While one person is talking, the other must remain silent and concentrate on what is being said. Signal the end of 2 minutes by ringing a bell or making another sound. The partner now has 2 minutes to answer the same question. After each person has answered the question, the outside circle moves one person to the right so everyone has a new partner. Here are suggested questions:

   a. With which of the descriptors do you most strongly identify? Why?

   b. With which of the descriptors do others most strongly identify you? How do you feel about that?

(Continued)

(Continued)

   c. Talk about a time when one of the descriptors of your identity worked to your advantage, either in school or in other areas of your life.

   d. Talk about a time when one of the descriptors held you back, either in school or in other areas of your life.

Debrief

1. After this exercise is completed, debrief as a class. How was the activity for you? What did you learn about yourself or others?

FIGURE 6.2   **The Paseo or Circles of Identity**

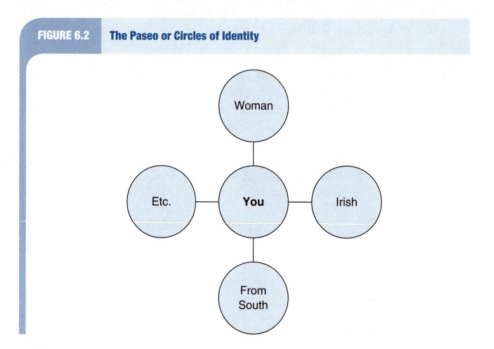

Responses to Differences: Stereotypes, Bias, Prejudice

In thinking about responses to differences, it is important to be familiar with related concepts. Important ideas to consider include stereotypes, bias, prejudice, discrimination, racism, and sexism. Teachers must learn about different cultures without dwelling inappropriately on stereotypes (Darling-Hammond & Bransford, 2005).

Stereotypes are the beliefs that all the individuals of a certain group will be the same and behave in the same way. Stereotypes pervade many, if not all, of our interactions. Throughout our lives, we "record" information and misinformation about people and what they and, for that matter, we are supposed to be like. This is akin to developing a personal internal recording about people. Then no matter how equitable we believe we are, the little bits of information and misinformation about different groups of people that we learn often result in the development of stereotypes about those people. When we are called to respond to someone, we don't take the time to mull over all of the information and misinformation we received. Instead, we resort quickly to stereotypes about people to direct our actions.

© iStockphoto.com/Kai Chiang

Many people struggle with how to maintain and be faithful to one identity while having to live, study, and work with a culture different from theirs. Learning to be multicultural enables us to understand that we can have multiple identities and be in harmony.

Given the power of stereotypes, awareness is the first step in the four-step model for personal development of multicultural educators, described in Chapter 2. But awareness of what? In this step, educators are encouraged to develop a heightened awareness of (1) themselves as individuals who influence the learning of others, (2) people's differing life experiences due to culture, (3) differing perceptions of diversity, and (4) multicultural education as a field of study and an educational practice.

It is perhaps human nature to assign beliefs about groups of people. Sometimes, they are positive. Often, they are not. Glasgow and Hicks (2003) provided an interesting way to describe how stereotypes can be seen as attributing traits to people.

1. Stereotypes imply internal, stable, controllable causes for controllable behaviors or states of affairs. *Examples:* Whites are bigoted. Certain girls are promiscuous. Mexicans are lazy.

2. Stereotypes suggest a trait, attribute, or behavior that is beyond the person's control. *Examples:* Jocks are dumb. Old people are senile. Women are weak. The Irish are lucky.

3. Stereotypes imply causes external to the individual being stereotyped, placing responsibility for behavior on factors outside the person's control. *Examples:* Some groups are underprivileged by a racist society. African Americans and Latinos as a group are not as successful as Whites because they are lazy or inept.

At least with stereotypes, people can be aware that they hold these beliefs. Sometimes, these attitudes and beliefs are hidden, however, so the individual is not even conscious of them. It is important, then, for people to try to uncover and articulate these biases. Paying attention to differences and being aware of their impact on our actions is important. While we may think that we are unbiased, in fact our biases, perceptions, and stereotyped beliefs influence our daily behaviors.

Another example of the impact of stereotypes on our actions is provided in Exercise 6.3. Supporting students in considering the impact of stereotypes and confronting their own biases and prejudices is confounded by the fact that our students are often in highly monocultural schools where they have little exposure to people who are different. Even K–12 teachers in public schools are highly segregated (Frankenberg, 2006). Developing knowledge and appreciation of other cultures and ethnicities becomes part of a healthy and fulfilling curriculum.

Another important concept is bias. Bias describes a mental leaning or inclination, or partiality. Bias can be directed in a positive way, such as a loving parent having a particular bias about a child's capacity, even if it is not warranted. Or it can be directed in a negative

EXERCISE 6.3

WOULD YOU TAKE MY PLACE?

Purpose

Identify stereotypes associated with different groups of people.

Materials

Enough sticky notes for each participant to have 10 each.

Procedure

1. Each participant thinks of all the cultural groups with which he or she identifies. The participants then write one group on each sticky note. The participants should think broadly when considering the groups (e.g., Native American, female, short, lesbian, athlete, nerd). Finally, the participants post all the notes on themselves.

2. Participants move silently throughout the room to view everyone else's identities.

3. After the initial viewing, participants are given 5 minutes to move among the groups again, but this time, they may negotiate "trades" (one of their notes for someone else's). Participants should be encouraged to trade at least once.

Debrief

- How did it feel to apply labels to yourself? How does this approximate reality?

- Were there any identities you were anxious to get rid of?

- Which identities did you want?

- How did it feel to read the other identities?

- Which identities did you not want? Why not?

- What are stereotypes? How did they affect your trading process?

- How do stereotypes affect our interactions with other people? What are the implications for teaching and learning?

- What are your key learnings today?

way, such as when a person has expectations, based on hearsay of another culturally different person that limit that person's access.

Closely related to bias is the concept of prejudice. Prejudice is an implied, preconceived, and unreasonable judgment or opinion, usually an unfavorable one marked by suspicion, fear, intolerance, or hatred. People are not born prejudiced. Prejudice is a learned behavior.

From the time we are born, due to a wide variety of influences, we learn to be biased about people. Among these influences are parents, the media, friends, schools, role models, and religious organizations. Sometimes, bias can be a positive factor. More often than not, bias and prejudice are negative factors in our interactions. The word *prejudice* actually means "prejudge." We use the little information we possess about a person to make a judgment about him or her. Oftentimes, this prejudgment is based on stereotypes. And oftentimes, this prejudgment is negative. The subtle nature of bias and prejudice is illustrated in the scenarios presented in Exercise 6.4.

EXERCISE 6.4
SCENARIOS ABOUT BIAS AND PREJUDICE

Scenario 1

Since I do most of the eating in my family, my wife is happy to let me do most of the grocery shopping too. Pushing the shopping cart down the meat aisle one day, I noticed a man in a wheelchair in my path. He was a Vietnam veteran, as evident by his beret, camouflage fatigues, little POW MIA (prisoner of war, missing in action) flag attached to his chair, and other regalia. He was also a double amputee from the midthighs down. I started to move my cart to go around him when I paused to let a young mother with her preschool-age boy walk by. The boy might have been 4 or 5 years old. It was then that he noticed the man in the wheelchair. As a father of two, I stopped to watch the little boy's reaction to seeing the veteran. As predicted, the boy pointed to the ex-soldier and said very loudly, "Look mom, a man with no legs!" Embarrassed, the mother clamped her hand over her son's mouth and hustled him quickly past the man in the wheelchair. I glanced at the vet, who looked hurt.

Questions

1. In that instant, what has the little boy learned?

2. Why did the boy say what he did?

3. Why did the veteran look hurt? Was it the boy's comment or the parent's reaction?

4. What would you have done if you had been the young parent?

5. What do you think would have been a proper response from the parent?

Scenario 2

A middle-aged, African American elementary school principal is taking his time walking home from the corner market. It's a glorious Saturday evening, and he has just spent the day working in the garden of his new home. Still in his gardening clothes, he is enjoying not having to wear his usual suit and tie but is looking forward to a hot shower to wash off the grime collected from his chores. Despite the waning light, in the distance he sees a young girl from his school walking down the residential street toward him with her father. Just as he raises his hand to wave hello, the father picks the girl up and rushes across the street to walk down the other side.

(Continued)

(Continued)

Questions

1. Why did the father of the young girl act the way he did?

2. Was it a reasonable action? Why or why not?

3. What has the young girl learned at that moment?

Scenario 3

I am chatting with a parent at an evening school reception. The young elementary school children have just completed a performance, and parents, teachers, students, and guests are enjoying some of the snacks provided. As the parent is talking to me, her youngster approaches and tugs on her skirt to get her attention. "Where is Jacob [a classmate]," he asks? The mother whispers to him to be quiet and not to interrupt. The boy persists and asks, "Where is Jacob?" After the third interruption, the parent leans down and in a stage whisper says to her son, "HE'S NOT HERE BECAUSE HE IS JEWISH." The boy looks confused. It occurs to me that the school has inadvertently scheduled the event on a Jewish holiday and that the Jewish students are away that day being observant.

Questions

1. What has the little boy learned at this moment?

2. How would you have handled this situation differently?

3. Is the mother a bigot? Why or why not?

In recent times, there has been an increase in the awareness of bias expressed in terms of explicit bias, implicit bias, and microaggressions. National media attention has been given to incidents such as two Black men arriving at a Starbucks coffee shop to meet a third person for a business meeting. One of the men asks to use the locked restroom but is told by the White manager that restrooms are only for paying customers. He sits down to wait for the third man to arrive in order to order coffee. Within 2 minutes of the men entering the coffee shop, the manager called the police and had them arrested. It became a public relations nightmare for Starbucks. In another incident, a Black, female graduate student at Yale University falls asleep while reading in the common room of her dormitory. A White dorm resident confronts her telling her that she should not be there. When the university police arrive and determine that the Black woman was indeed a Yale student who lived in the dorm, they declined to arrest her, while informing the White student not to make calls like that. This was followed shortly by an incident where four Black women were packing their car to leave the AirBnB (short-term rental home) they had rented. A White neighbor called the police reporting that the house was being robbed. In a California restaurant, a waiter refuses to serve four Latinas unless they could prove that they were in the country legally.

These and other almost daily incidents point to the need to understand some important concepts.

Explicit bias: occurs when people are consciously aware of their attitudes and beliefs about a person or a group. Much of the time, these biases and subsequent actions arise as a result of fear of that group. Examples include discrimination against the Irish in the early years of this country. Signs reading "Help Wanted—No Irish Need Apply" were common.

In more recent times, signs have appeared in restaurant windows reading "Service Is Denied to Queers." A school security guard stops all Latinx students asking for documentation that they are here legally.

Implicit bias: occurs when someone knowingly fights stereotypes and actively engages in antidiscrimination activities, while at the same time, unconsciously, has negative thoughts about people and situations. Examples include newspaper reports after Hurricane Katrina devastated New Orleans. People were without food or water. A photo caption showing a White couple "finding food," but another photo caption describing a Black couple as "looting" food. A Sports Illustrated magazine cover has a photo of tennis great Roger Federer dramatically returning a tennis serve. Another Sports Illustrated magazine cover displays tennis great Anna Kournikova, not in a tennis pose, but lying seductively on a pillow staring intently into the camera lens.

Microaggressions: Made more popular recently by Teachers College Professor, Dr. Derald Wing Sue (2010), in his book *Microaggressions in Everyday Life: Race, Gender, and Sexual Orientation.* According to Sue, microaggressions are the brief and everyday slights, insults, indignities, and denigrating messages sent to people of color by well-intentioned people who are unaware of the hidden messages being communicated. These messages may be sent verbally, nonverbally, and environmentally—symbols (Sue, 2010). Examples include when a White couple check their wallet and purse as a Black man approaches them on the street. The hidden message is that the Black man might be a thief. Another is when a third-generation Asian American is complimented on his or her command of the English language. The hidden message is that Asian Americans are often immediately perceived as foreigners. Other examples include the following:

- People surprised that a young, Black girl prefers country music.

- Asian American student being asked, "Where are you *really* from?"

- In a restaurant, when ordering a Coke, the server asks a girl whether she wants a Diet Coke. The boys are not asked the same question.

- Indian sports mascots portrayed as bloodthirsty savages.

These are examples of biases that occur daily in our schools and in public. Educators need to be not only personally aware of them but also build learning into the curriculum.

LEARNING OBJECTIVE 6.3 Appraise Ineffective Responses to Cultural Differences in Schools

Does Difference Make a Difference in Schools?

Responses to students' cultural differences vary. In developing and delivering the nationally renowned World of Difference program, the Anti-Defamation League (2003) portrayed the development of hatred in a pyramid to illustrate the compounding nature of negative responses to differences. On the pyramid base are acts of subtle bias; these may be activities that seem inconsequential, such as stereotyping, telling jokes, spreading rumors, and accepting negative information. However, left unchecked, acts of subtle bias can escalate into much more serious forms of hatred that include **harassment**, assault, and acts of extreme violence.

Another way to describe ineffective responses to differences is through the concepts of discrimination, racism, and sexism. Discrimination is defined as an act of exclusion

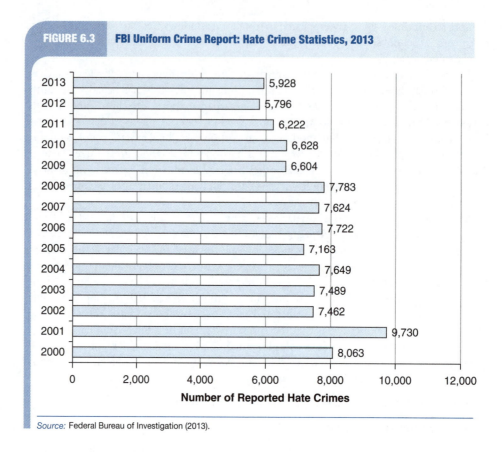

FIGURE 6.3   FBI Uniform Crime Report: Hate Crime Statistics, 2013

Number of Reported Hate Crimes

Source: Federal Bureau of Investigation (2013).

prompted by prejudice. Racism is a form of discrimination; it is unequal or discriminatory treatment of, or attitudes toward, individuals or groups based on race. Sexism is another form of discrimination; it is unequal or discriminatory treatment of, or attitudes toward, individuals or groups based on gender.

Hate Crimes, Bullying, and Harassment in Schools

The Federal Bureau of Investigation (FBI) reported 5,928 hate crimes involving 6,933 offenses against victims in the United States in 2013. About 65% of all reported hate crimes were against a person, while approximately 35% were property crimes. Victims are described as individuals, businesses, institutions, or society as a whole. Hate crimes, like many crimes, tend to be underreported, so the actual numbers could be much higher (U.S. Department of Education [USDOE], 1998). Figure 6.3 shows a somewhat sporadic history of reported hate crimes. The Southern Poverty Law Center (2005) disputed the FBI statistics, citing a Bureau of Justice Statistics report claiming that the actual number of hate crimes is 19 to 31 times higher than the official number reported by the FBI.

The USDOE, National Center for Education Statistics (2014) in its report *Indicators of School Crime and Safety* for 2013 revealed some significant data:

- Overall, the percentage of students who reported being bullied at school was highest for White students and lowest for Asian students in 2011.

- Specifically, 15% of Asian students of ages 12 to 18 years reported being bullied at school during the school year compared with 31% of White students, 27% of Black students, and 22% of Hispanic students.

- In 2011, about 37% of 6th graders reported being bullied at school compared with 30% of 7th graders, 31% of 8th graders, 26% of 9th graders, 28% of 10th graders, 24% of 11th graders, and 22% of 12th graders.

- By school sector, a higher percentage of public school students than of private school students reported being bullied and being subjects of selected **bullying** problems at school in 2011. Twenty-eight percent of public school students reported being bullied at school compared with 21% of private school students.

- In addition, there were differences by urbanicity: A lower percentage of students in urban areas (25%) reported being bullied at school than students in suburban and rural areas in 2011 (29% and 30%, respectively).

Clearly, schools, along with the home, must work harder to protect our students. The trauma of being bullied can last into adulthood. Schools are being held more accountable for the physical and emotional safety of students. Whether bullying will ever be totally eliminated and whether bullying is worse now than before are interesting debates. A key point to remember is that learning takes place best in a climate of respect.

The Gay, Lesbian and Straight Education Network reported in its 2014 National School Climate Survey that 74% of lesbian, gay, bisexual, and transgender (LGBT) students reported being verbally harassed, while 36% reported being physically harassed. Two out of every three LGBT students felt unsafe in school because of their sexual orientation (Gay, Lesbian and Straight Education Network, 2014).

There is less research in the United States on the problem of bullying than in other countries such as Britain, Norway, and Sweden (Sjostrom & Stein, 1996). Nonetheless, it is clear that there are problems with harassment in U.S. schools. Trying to understand the causes and the resulting effects that bullying has on students academically, physically, and emotionally is essential. The resulting fears and feelings are illustrated in Exercise 6.5.

How do we know if an action arises from bias or simply from a misunderstanding? Exercise 6.6, developed by Jack Hasegawa (1994) of the Connecticut State Department of Education, will help us understand the difference.

© istockphoto.com/Zhang bo

Children respond better to teachers when they feel they care for them as individuals and will act to protect them in all ways.

EXERCISE 6.5
HAND-SLAP

Purpose

Teach that bullying and harassment have negative impacts on learning.

Procedure

1. The facilitator will ask for a volunteer to help model the process. The volunteer will stand next to the facilitator, and the facilitator will ask the following questions:

   a. What is 2 plus 2?

   b. Minus 1?

   c. Times 6?

   d. What is the square root of 144?

2. The class forms pairs, and they ask one another simple math questions for 1 minute.

3. Then the facilitator asks for a volunteer to stand facing him or her with arms extended, bent at the elbows, palms down. The facilitator places his or her hands under the partner's, about an inch away, palms up. Then the facilitator quickly moves his or her hands and gently slaps the top of the other person's hands. This is an old childhood game, and the partner will quickly try to move his or her hands out of the way.

4. Step 3 is repeated three or four times.

5. Now the facilitator says that the volunteer cannot move his or her hands until he or she answers the question. Furthermore, the volunteer is told that if the volunteer moves his or her hands before he or she answers the question, or if the volunteer answers incorrectly, the volunteer must stand still to get a slap on the hands. The facilitator again asks the following questions:

   a. What is 2 plus 2?

   b. Minus 1?

   c. Times 6?

   d. What is the square root of 144?

6. Now the class again forms pairs and plays the game for about 3 to 4 minutes, until everyone has had a turn.

Debrief

Consider the following questions:

- What did you learn from doing this game?
- Which were you more concerned about—getting the correct answer or not getting your hands slapped?
- What metaphor could you create from this game that applies to school climate?
- Children cannot learn at their optimum if they do not feel safe, both physically and emotionally.

EXERCISE 6.6

YOU MAKE THE CALL: OVERSENSITIVITY, POOR PRACTICE, OR ACTUAL BIAS?

Read the paragraphs below. Each incident caused someone to say, "I am the victim of bias." Is the alleged victim expressing oversensitivity? Is the problem caused by poor administrative practice? Or is this a case of actual bias? Circle the response that expresses your judgment.

OS	PP	AB	A young mother goes into the school office to inquire about obtaining free lunches for her son. As the secretary is handing over the forms, she says, "You people should use the money you spend on fancy sneakers for your kids' lunches. You seem to have plenty of money for shoes!"
OS	PP	AB	Hector, on seeing his new Spanish teacher for the first time, says loudly, "What can a White lady teach us about Spanish?"
OS	PP	AB	Darrell is an African American Project Concern student who has been attending the same suburban district since first grade. In sixth grade, he is experiencing more difficulty than he had in previous years. He is tested for a learning disability, which is confirmed. One of his teachers comments, "I thought they were supposed to go back to Hartford if they're special ed."
OS	PP	AB	A school board member says, "Why should we pay for this ESL stuff? When people come to this country, they should learn English! Don't come to school unless you can speak our language."
OS	PP	AB	Billy came to the principal's office. He states that he is afraid of the gang kids from Hartford and the housing project, especially when they are all on the playground together. The principal probes a little but hears no evidence of any threats or violence. Billy is told to "stay away from them—just ignore them."
OS	PP	AB	Doris came to Connecticut from Puerto Rico when she was 8. She had always done well in school. In her first day in honors English, one of her classmates, noticing her pronounced Spanish accent, says, "You don't belong here. This is only for kids who are really good in English."
OS	PP	AB	A Jewish teacher becomes upset when she notices that the Connecticut Mastery tests are scheduled on a Jewish holy day. Even though her school allows Jewish teachers and students to take the day off, she feels that this places Jewish students at a disadvantage since they will miss 2 days of school: one for the holy day and one for the makeup exam.
OS	PP	AB	The junior high soccer coach is heard scolding two boys on the team: "You run like girls!" The coach of the girls' soccer team on the next field hears this and accuses her colleague of being sexist.
OS	PP	AB	Ms. Jones calls the school to complain about her son's placement in the average math group. She is referred to the director of mathematics and requests a higher placement. She concludes by saying, "I know that teachers often underestimate African American students, especially boys."

(Continued)

(Continued)

OS	PP	AB	The student council is meeting. Mari raises her hand, but other students and the faculty adviser keep jumping into the discussion. She finally manages to break into the discussion and complains about not being recognized earlier. The faculty adviser says, "You have to learn to just jump in. You can't wait for someone to call on you."
OS	PP	AB	Billy Saito, a third-generation Japanese American, is sitting in his new sixth-grade classroom on the first day of school. The teacher asked the students to introduce themselves by telling what they had done over the summer. When it was Billy's turn, the teacher comes to his desk and says, very slowly, "Do you understand what we are doing? Just do your best, and I will help you."
OS	PP	AB	An African American student new to the school charges that the assistant principal is hostile. The assistant principal says that the student has a real "urban" attitude and is hard to talk to because he slouches and speaks softly and in slang. The administrator feels that the student is making no attempt to fit into the small-town setting of the school.
OS	PP	AB	Ed and Betty, two teachers in a rural elementary school, are passing by the cafeteria. "Look at that kid. He's getting a free lunch and he's throwing most of it away," huffs Ed. "I drive by his house on my way home, and they've got a big boat. They don't really need a free lunch."

Note: OS = oversensitivity; PP = poor administrative practice; AB = actual bias; ESL = English as a second language.

Discussion

1. After each person has responded to the statements, form small discussion groups.

2. Appoint a reporter who will share your group's findings with the other groups. Make sure that you structure your time to allow your group to complete each of the following activities.

   a. Select three incidents and explore the reasons why people attached different meanings to the same incidents.

   b. Bias may be defined as "the negative recognition of diversity." Discrimination is unfair treatment based on some dimension of diversity. What were the triggers, actions, behaviors, or words in each of the incidents that caused someone to say, "I was the victim of discrimination"?

   c. Pick one or two vignettes. Assume that the person who complained of bias is a colleague of yours and answer these questions:

      • What could you have done if you were present when the incident occurred?

      • Is there anything you could have done (or should have done) if you heard about the incident afterward?

Source: Hasegawa (1997).

Dealing With Bullying and Harassment

For learning to occur at its optimum, students must experience a school climate where they are safe, both physically and emotionally. In her book *Creating Emotionally Safe Schools: A Guide for Educators and Parents*, Jane Bluestein (2001) provides a definition of "emotional safety." She describes this as a classroom or school environment that provides critical elements, such as when all students

- feel welcomed, valued, and that they belong;

- make mistakes but still feel respected;

- are free from harassment and intimidation;

- are free from prejudice and discrimination; and

- feel they can express their opinions, without judgment.

It is the creation of a safe and nurturing environment that will establish a culture where learning can truly occur. Recognizing that such an environment must exist as a priority for education is essential. Bazelon (2013) warns us of two risks in the efforts of schools to create such a climate. First, children must be allowed to learn and grow and to experience the natural struggles of growing up. Being overprotective can stifle growth. Second, the focus should not be on the desire to punish offenders swiftly and dramatically. A better focus is on prevention.

When might "bullying" be just "mean behavior"? A second grader repeatedly pushes a child out of line to get in front. Is this bullying? Another elementary schoolboy likes to kiss a particular girl on the cheek. Is that sexual harassment? Should examples such as these be investigated? What considerations might there be developmentally that need to be considered? Investigate the policies of a local school district around the topic of bullying. Investigate policies developed through your state's department of education. Include in your investigation the impact, if any, of school district policies or state department policies on incidences of bullying.

Wessler and Preble (2003) write about "respectful" schools. Educators must understand the powerful, negative impact on students who experience bias, prejudice, and harassment. Merely reading the newspaper on a regular basis will reveal numerous instances in schools where a negative climate has gone unchecked and where the pleas of victims and their parents have gone unheeded. Yet how to deal with bullying and harassment is often not a main component of teacher education. The matter is further confused by the cacophony coming from people claiming to be experts and helping schools rid themselves of bullying. No number of assemblies, special speakers, or videos will help unless schools fundamentally commit themselves to making it a priority to ensure that each and every member of the school community is protected from emotional and physical harm. Too often in our high-stakes testing environment, energies are placed toward increasing academic achievement while ignoring the fact that students cannot learn in an unhealthy environment. In a respectful school, teachers are trained formally in how to intervene, and student leaders are taught ideas of influence to foster a positive climate.

Numerous books focus on filling in the gaps for teachers who have not benefited from formal education in creating positive school climate. *The Little Book of Restorative Discipline for Schools* by Amstutz and Mullet (2005); *Reclaiming Youth at Risk* by Brendtro, Brokenleg, and Bockern (2009); *Defusing Disruptive Behavior in the Classroom* by Colvin (2010); and *The Classroom Management Book* by Wong, Wong, Jondahl, and Ferguson (2014) are examples of helpful resources.

The U.S. Department of Health & Human Services has established a website called StopBullying.Gov (http://www.stopbullying.gov) that contains a wealth of information for schools and parents.

LEARNING OBJECTIVE 6.4 Compose Positive Responses to Cultural Differences in Schools

The Need for a Safe School Climate

For every student to be able to learn and achieve at high levels, schools must first establish a safe climate. Students will not be able to learn in an environment in which they do not feel safe with other students and in which they feel that the adults are not fully protecting them. *Protecting Students From Harassment and Hate Crime: A Guide for Schools* is a comprehensive free manual published by USDOE, Office for Civil Rights (OCR), and the National Association of Attorneys General (1999). It is endorsed by the National School Boards Association. The manual outlines these fundamental steps in a comprehensive approach to eliminating harassment and hate crimes.

1. Develop written policies that prohibit unlawful harassment.

2. Identify and respond to all incidents of harassment and violence.

3. Provide formal complaint procedures.

4. Create a school climate that supports racial, cultural, and other forms of diversity.

5. Work with law enforcement agencies to address and prevent hate crimes and civil rights violations.

Schools that take aggressive steps to create positive school climates and institute steps such as those outlined above not only help protect students from harm but also foster a more productive learning environment.

Dialogue and conversation are critical in addressing bullying, harassment, and hate crimes. Without deep and meaningful conversations at all grade levels, it will be very difficult for educators and students alike to learn what is inappropriate and unacceptable and move to the point of valuing differences. Biases will continue unchecked and may escalate into hateful behaviors. These conversations are not easy to have, but they are essential. Some people refer to these as "dangerous dialogues" and "critical conversations."

Schooling isn't just about academics—it's about learning how to live and work with each other.

© iStockphotos.com/Catherine Yeulet

Understanding the Law and Education

Federal and state **civil rights** laws protect students, teachers, and staff in school settings. Virtually all public schools receive some form of federal funding, and because of this, they must adhere to federal civil rights laws. A typical school system may receive major federal funding from some 30-plus grants, which are often badly needed to operate. Some of this funding is well-known, such as the National School Lunch Program, special education, bilingual education, and Title 1 grants (compensatory education).

Schools should be particularly knowledgeable about USDOE, which oversees compliance with the major civil rights laws. The department maintains a thoroughly informative website that explains these laws at http://www2.ed.gov/about/offices/list/ocr/know.html

Title VI of the Civil Rights Act of 1964 (Title VI), 34 CFR Part 100, prohibits discrimination, including harassment, on the basis of race, color, and national origin. This law requires that any public funds must be used by schools without any bias based on race, color, or national origin. A school program cannot exclude students based on these protected categories. So if a school receives federal funds to run a tutoring program, for example, it must ensure that racial minority students can participate on an equal basis. Note that Title VI does not protect students based on sex. That is covered under another federal law, Title IX.

Title IX of the Education Amendments of 1972 (Title IX), 34 CFR Part 106, prohibits discrimination, including harassment, based on sex. Perhaps the most well-known of the laws pertaining to schools, Title IX actually covers any educational institution receiving any form of federal funding, including guaranteed student loans. These institutions include local school districts, colleges and universities, and charter and for-profit schools. Educational programs offered by noneducational institutions that receive federal funds, such as libraries, prisons, and museums, are also covered. Though most people know of Title IX because of the rules governing sports, Title IX also prohibits sexual harassment and enforces equity in vocational and career education.

Each school district must have at least one person designated as the Title IX coordinator to oversee compliance efforts and investigate any complaints of sex discrimination. All students and employees must be notified of the names, office address(es), and telephone number(s) of the designated coordinator(s) of Title IX. Grievance procedures and nondiscrimination policies must be made public. Each district must publish a nondiscrimination statement saying that it does not discriminate, based on sex, in any of its educational programs or its hiring practices. Furthermore, this statement must be published in any official document of the school district.

Section 504 of the Rehabilitation Act of 1973 (Section 504), 34 CFR Part 104, prohibits discrimination, including harassment, based on disability. Schools must ensure that disabled students have full and equal access to all school programs and activities.

Title II of the Americans with Disabilities Act of 1990 (ADA), 28 CFR Part 35, prohibits discrimination on the basis of disability by public entities. Students can be defined as disabled using a three-pronged approach to eligibility: students who (1) have a physical or mental impairment, (2) have a record of an impairment, or (3) are regarded as having an impairment. The ADA addresses issues such as architectural barriers and transportation, among other things.

Other federal laws include Title VII of the Civil Rights Act of 1964, which prohibits employment discrimination based on race, color, religion, sex, or national origin, and the

---

Extended Explorations 6.1: What Is Your Understanding of Freedom of Speech?

Should Holocaust deniers be permitted to address the student body to proclaim that the Holocaust never occurred? Should students be permitted to wear a T-shirt that says "Adam & Eve, not Adam & Steve"? Is it a violation of the U.S. Constitution to state in a public school setting that you believe that homosexuality is a sin? What do you think of Woody Allen's famous quote about the KKK [Ku-Klux-Klan]: "I think you should defend to the death their right to march, and then go down and meet them with baseball bats." Locate the exact wording of the First Amendment to the U.S. Constitution. What does it mean to you? Evaluate the implications of the First Amendment for schools.

Equal Pay Act of 1963 (EPA), which protects men and women who perform substantially equal work in the same establishment from sex-based wage discrimination.

The Individuals with Disabilities Education Act (formerly PL 94-142) governs the equal treatment and education of special education students.

Comprehensive high schools or middle schools that offer career and technical courses are also covered by the Vocational Education Programs Guidelines for Eliminating Discrimination and Denial of Services on the Basis of Race, Color, and National Origin, Sex and Handicap (Guidelines), 34 CFR Part 100, Appendix B. This legislation enforces civil rights compliance in all vocational programming in schools. It requires too that schools go through a periodic audit to ensure that the law is being followed.

EXERCISE 6.7

TEST YOUR UNDERSTANDING OF TITLE IX

Are these situations possibly a violation of Title IX? Check yes or no in response to each of the statements. These come from actual school complaints.

	Yes	No
1. To decrease the number of harassment complaints, a school has separate boys' and girls' recess areas.		
2. A teacher lines up students by alternating boy and girl.		
3. The girls' track team gets issued the same singlets that the boys wear. Since they are in boys' sizes, the armholes are too big, forcing girls to wear a T-shirt underneath or buy sports bras to avoid exposing themselves.		
4. Members of the winning football team each get a leather jacket and a school ring. Members of the winning girls' basketball team each receive a T-shirt.		
5. Virtually all the high school technical education classes have only boys enrolled.		
6. The high school guidance counselor routinely advises all the girls to enter into a nursing career.		
7. Physical education classes are segregated into boys' and girls' classes.		
8. Lewd jokes are routinely told in the teachers' lounge, despite the protests of a male teacher.		
9. When questioned, most students do not know who the Title IX coordinator is.		
10. A girls' basketball coach is fired because he files a Title IX complaint protesting inequities in the courts used by the boys versus the girls.		
Answers: All "yes"		

Source: Howe (2010).

State laws often mirror those of the federal government, but there are some differences. For example, there is no federal legislation on bullying, but 49 of 50 states have antibullying statutes, with Montana being the lone standout (Bully Police USA, 2018). Despite several attempts to enact it, there is no federal legislation on school bullying. In addition, 21 states, plus the District of Columbia, have hate crime laws that address crimes against sexual orientation (see American Civil Liberties Union, 2015, for a complete list of these states).

Try Exercise 6.7 to test your knowledge and understanding of Title IX.

A Look at School Discipline

Despite impressive civil rights laws, a look at data on school discipline indicates alarming concerns around how fairly all students are treated in our schools. Since 1968, USDOE OCR (2014) has collected data on school discipline. Each public school in the country has been asked to report data on discipline since 2000. This includes data from every public school in the nation (approximately 16,500 school districts, 97,000 schools, and 49 million students). You can find data on how well your school does by going to https://ocrdata.ed.gov/

Here are some of the highlights of a report published in March 2014 on School Discipline, Restraint, & Seclusion Highlights,.

Suspension of Preschool Children, by Race/Ethnicity and Gender

Black children represent 18% of preschool enrollment but 48% of preschool children receiving more than one out-of-school suspension.

In comparison, White students represent 43% of preschool enrollment but 26% of preschool children receiving more than one out-of-school suspension.

Boys represent 79% of preschool children suspended once and 82% of preschool children suspended multiple times, although boys represent 54% of preschool enrollment.

Disproportionately High Suspension/Expulsion Rates for Students of Color

Black students are suspended and expelled at three times the rate of White students. On average, 5% of White students are suspended compared with 16% of Black students.

American Indian and Native Alaskan students are also disproportionately suspended and expelled, representing less than 1% of the student population but 2% of out-of-school suspensions and 3% of expulsions.

Disproportionate Suspensions of Girls of Color

While boys receive more than two out of three suspensions, Black girls are suspended at higher rates (12%) than girls of any other race or ethnicity and most boys.

American Indian and Native Alaskan girls (7%) are suspended at higher rates than White boys (6%) or girls (2%).

Suspension of Students With Disabilities and English Learners

Students with disabilities are more than twice as likely to receive an out-of-school suspension (13%) than students without disabilities (6%).

In contrast, English learners do not receive out-of-school suspensions at disproportionately high rates (7% suspension rate, compared with 10% of student enrollment).

Suspension rates by race, sex, and disability status combined are as follows:

With the exception of Latino and Asian American students, more than one out of four boys of color with disabilities (served by Individuals with Disabilities Education Act)—and nearly one in five girls of color with disabilities—receives an out-of-school suspension.

The report goes on to provide numerous other indicators of disparities in how students are disciplined. Just as the collection of data is essential in planning effective instruction, schools must look at similar data on discipline to see where bias might play a factor.

Helping Students and Teachers Develop Positive Perspectives and Values

Having multiple perspectives is the capacity to see an event, an action, a topic, or an issue from another person's vantage point. This is not an easy thing to do. We may think that we are open-minded, yet in the end, we usually believe that our way is the right way or the only way of doing or seeing things. Developing the capacity to see things from multiple perspectives is difficult because each of us has learned deeply some set of values and beliefs. Developing the capacity to see things from multiple perspectives usually means respecting a different set of values.

The above concepts and priorities are not unfamiliar to teachers. But what is to be done when teachers, parents, and school board members share opposing beliefs and values?

REFLECTING BACK

This chapter has brought light to the more unpleasant side of school life. Most reasonable adults would agree that there is no room for bigotry and bias either in our schools or in our society.

Questions

1. What roles do teachers play in creating a safe school climate? Administrators? Parents?

2. Describe the steps you would take to establish a classroom where all children feel safe, both physically and emotionally.

3. What commitments might you have made to eliminate bias and hate while reading this chapter?

4. Should intolerant and bigoted individuals be permitted to teach? Is it possible for such an individual to separate out his or her biases from responsibilities as an educator? How might identification of an educator's biases and prejudices be uncovered through the teacher selection and hiring process? Should this be part of the hiring process?

There is a push me–pull me relationship between individual state education agencies and the federal agencies that provide services to educational entities. The USDOE has traditionally taken a role in overseeing and enforcing civil rights laws. Individual states sometimes take exception to education laws and policies. Current conflicts focus on issues such as Title IX and the rights of transgender students. Within states, conflicts can occur also, with some states having a wide range of authority over local school districts and others where individual districts hold ultimate authority. Issues such as teaching religion, evolution, and even climate changes can be very divisive.

The solutions to these conflicts may not be readily evident or attainable. What remains essential is protecting the rights of students provided under federal and state constitutions.

PROFILES IN MULTICULTURAL EExDUCATION

GLORIA LADSON-BILLINGS

© Gloria Ladson-Billings

Gloria Ladson-Billings is a retired Professor Emerita and Kellner Family Chair in Urban Education in the Department of Curriculum & Instruction at the University of Wisconsin–Madison. Additionally, Ladson-Billings was faculty affiliate in the Departments of Educational Policy Studies, Educational Leadership and Policy Analysis, and Afro American Studies. She is known for her groundbreaking work on "Culturally Relevant Pedagogy" that is chronicled in her critically acclaimed book, *The Dreamkeepers: Successful Teachers of African American Children* (2009). She followed *Dreamkeepers* with a book on preparing new teachers to engage in culturally relevant pedagogy titled, *Crossing Over to Canaan: The Journey of New Teachers in Diverse Classrooms* (2001). Ladson-Billings is also known (along with William F. Tate) for introducing critical race theory applications to education. Ladson-Billings has served as the President of the American Educational Research Association (2005–2006) and is currently the President of the National Academy of Education (a 4-year term that began November 2017). Ladson-Billings has dedicated her career to helping teachers work in more equitable ways by supporting student learning, developing cultural competence, and encouraging sociopolitical or critical consciousness. An active scholar, Ladson-Billings has written or edited nine volumes and more than 100 journal articles and book chapters. She is the recipient of national and international honors, including four honorary degrees (Umea University; Sweden University of Alicante, Spain; University of Massachusetts–Lowell; the Erickson Institute), the University of Wisconsin–Madison's Hilldale Award, the British Educational Research Association John S. Nisbet Award, and the American Educational Research Association Social Justice Award. In this phase of her career, Ladson-Billings's work focuses on incorporating and learning from adolescent culture, particularly Hip Hop Culture.

CASE STUDY
WORKING WITH ATTITUDES LEARNED AT HOME

Key Issues to Be Explored in the Case

1. What happens when the messages students learn at home conflict with what the school is trying to teach?

2. How can teachers, or should teachers, try to present more enlightened viewpoints without creating conflicts with the home?

It was a typical small high school in a sleepy suburban town, the kind of town where everyone seemed to know everyone else. It was also the kind of town where there seemed to be a church on virtually every corner. Most of the students had grown up with one another, but the town was growing with more families moving in, and many of them were families of color. The school prided itself on preparing students for a diverse workplace. Its curriculum focused highly on academic achievement and teaching students the value of celebrating diversity. Racial problems were virtually nonexistent. Teachers saw themselves as being progressive and passed those values on to students.

Students were encouraged to express themselves. Some students began coming out as lesbian, gay, bisexual, transitioning, or questioning (**LGBTQ**). For the most part, they were accepted by their peers and their teachers. But there were exceptions. Some students and, unfortunately, some teachers were less supportive and showed their displeasure. Tensions began to escalate. Pushing and name-calling elevated to fights and taunts. Punishment was meted out for unruly behavior. Teachers felt unsure and unprepared to deal with the issues. Students became confused as factions formed, pitting one group against another. Parents began complaining about the "disruptions caused by gay students."

Straight students, concerned about the safety of their friends, approached the principal, asking to form a club or group that would work to try to support their peers. Concerned about the increasing number of students being targeted by homophobic comments and actions, the school approved the creation of a gay–straight alliance (GSA). This organization became a safe haven for students both gay and straight. Teachers were relieved that there was now a program available to help educate teachers and staff and to take a stand against the bigotry.

Unfortunately, the father of a student in the school was a pastor of a very conservative church and preached vehemently from the pulpit against homosexuality, calling gay students sinners and condemning the school for not taking a stance against homosexuality and the newly created GSA. The student repeated the ideas from his father's sermons in school, creating a disruptive climate. The GSA brought in **Stonewall** speakers to give a talk during an assembly about LGBTQ issues. The enraged father believed that they were recruiters to the "gay lifestyle." He demanded equal time to address the student body in order to talk about the sins of homosexuality.

Discussion Questions

1. How would you address the homophobic statements being made by the students?

2. How would you deal with the pastor?

3. You have some very vocal, bigoted teachers who are creating tensions because of their comments. How should the school react?

CHAPTER SUMMARY

Children often learn biased attitudes from observing the words and actions of adults. Therefore, adults must be conscious of their influence and make targeted efforts to foster positive attitudes. Teachers must continually evaluate their own biases so as not to negatively influence their students. Parents and teachers must be vigilant about how the media play a powerful role in influencing attitudes and opinions. Schools can play a role in offsetting negative images that come from these influences. Of major concern are bullying and harassment as serious problems in schools. In some cases, these problems are unchecked. More effective steps must be taken to curb these threats to student security and safety. Understanding and helping enforce civil rights laws and other regulations are an important part of the teaching process.

Among the key ideas in this chapter are the following:

6.1 Explain seeing differences in human beings

How do we develop our attitudes about others? What experiences and actions influence how we view cultural differences?

- Just like many individuals grow up without ever having their parents sit down and have "the talk" with them, many parents are unwilling, unable, or uncomfortable talking to their children about racial, religious, or other issues. Learning to see differences or to understand and appreciate the lives that others lead is often accomplished in a proactive manner. With the guidance of teachers, children can learn to develop positive attitudes about others and to appreciate cultural differences. This begins with children learning about their own cultural identities.

6.2 Analyze responding to differences in human beings

What causes people to develop a wide range of personal responses to differences, from denial to tolerance to acceptance to valuing? Where are you on this continuum, and how can you move yourself and your students toward a greater valuing of difference?

- How is it possible that in one family a person can grow up to be positive and open-minded about differences while a sibling grows up to be intolerant? Unfortunately, it is often not until we are much older that we finally develop enough life experiences to help us develop a frame of reference for those who are different from us. Our journey must begin with learning about ourselves and valuing our cultures. From there, we can then learn from others and appreciate the differences. It is a social as well as an economic necessity.

6.3 Appraise ineffective responses to cultural differences in schools

What is happening in our schools as more students from diverse cultures are coming together? What are some responses to difference? How are bigotry and bias manifested in schools? What is the extent of the problem?

- Unfortunately, because of the rise of bullying and harassment in schools, teachers must become much more fully aware of the laws that govern us. We must be aware of the extent of the problems of bias by looking at the data. We must then incorporate, as part of our curriculum, strategies on how to teach our children to deal with differences in positive ways. It is important for teachers to understand the causes as well as the solutions in working with bias.

6.4 Compose positive responses to cultural differences in schools

What can teachers and the schools do to teach respect and healthy attitudes? What type of school climate will contribute to the development of positive responses to cultural differences?

- Fortunately, there is an abundance of resources on how to create positive school climate, and much of it is available at no cost. A fundamental task of all schools is to develop clear and transparent policies on appropriate school conduct. We cannot assume that students or parents will fully understand unless efforts are made to educate and communicate effectively. This chapter explains the most common education laws.

KEY TERMS

anti-Semite 156	discrimination 152	homophobe 156
bias 152	ethnocentric 155	implicit bias 163
bigotry 152	explicit bias 162	LGBTQ 176
bullying 165	gay–straight alliance (GSA) 176	microaggressions 163
chauvinist 156	harassment 163	prejudice 152
civil rights 171	hate crime 164	Stonewall 176

APPLICATION: ACTIVITIES AND EXERCISES

Individual

1. Conduct research on your hometown seeking any history of discrimination or bias among its peoples. Was there any oppressed group? What has been the legacy of tolerance or intolerance? How would you teach about that if you taught in that town?

2. Develop a set of questions about the development of prejudices and racist attitudes. Use your set of questions to interview several of your friends about their prejudices toward culturally different people and their ideas about how they learned those prejudices. Include questions that address how the interviewees learned prejudices about cultural groups with which they identify and how those prejudices have been integrated into their own self-images.

Group

1. Locate several instruments that are designed to measure attitudes toward diversity; analyze and critique the instruments as to their utility in school settings.

2. Locate a variety of antibias curricula; analyze and critique those curricula for applicability in school settings.

3. Together, watch television shows or videos and discuss biases that appear. Discuss positive role models (racial, ethnic, gender, etc.) that are provided in television programs and in movies.

Self-Assessment

1. If you could step into a machine and come out whoever or whatever you want to be, who would that person be and why?

2. What kind of person (race, ethnicity, sex) would you *not* want to be and why?

3. What challenges have you faced because of your race, religion, ethnicity, or any other type of diversity?

ANNOTATED RESOURCES

CultureGrams

http://www. culturegrams.com

Since its beginnings in 1974, CultureGrams has become one of the most trusted and widely used cultural reference products in the education, government, and nonprofit arenas. Its aim is to foster understanding and appreciation of the world's peoples by documenting the unique details of their customs, traditions, and daily life.

CultureGrams content is available in the CultureGrams Online Database and as PDF downloads of individual reports.

StopBullying.Gov

http://www. stopbullying.gov

A federal government website managed by the U.S. Department of Health & Human Services, this is a relatively new website created to stem the alarming increase in bullying. StopBullying.gov provides information from various government agencies on what bullying is, what cyberbullying is, who is at risk, and how you can prevent and respond to bullying.

U.S. Department of Education, Office for Civil Rights

http://www2.ed.gov/about/offices/list/ocr/know.html

OCR enforces several federal civil rights laws that prohibit discrimination in programs or activities that receive federal funds from the Department of Education. These laws prohibit discrimination on the basis of race, color, national origin, sex, disability, or age. These laws extend to all state education agencies, elementary and secondary school systems, colleges and universities, vocational schools, proprietary schools, state vocational rehabilitation agencies, libraries, and museums that receive USDOE funds. OCR also has responsibilities under Title II of the ADA (prohibiting disability discrimination by public entities, whether or not they receive federal financial assistance). In addition, as of January 8, 2002, OCR enforces the Boy Scouts of America Equal Access Act (Section 9525 of the Elementary and Secondary Education Act of 1965, as amended by the No Child Left Behind Act of 2001).

Visit the student study site at **study.sagepub.com/howe3e** for additional study tools including the following:

- eFlashcards
- Web quizzes
- SAGE journal articles
- Video links
- Web resources
- Assessments from the text
- Access to author's blog

$SAGE edge™

Get the tools you need to sharpen your study skills. SAGE edge offers a robust online environment featuring an impressive array of free tools and resources. Access practice quizzes, eFlashcards, video, and multimedia at **edge.sagepub.com/howe3e**

Section III Assessment

Awareness

International travel has the benefit of allowing one to immerse oneself in another culture. Yet this immersion experience can be done right here at home. Your assignment is to experience another culture in a meaningful way.

You will choose a cultural group (race, ethnicity, religion, sexual orientation, etc.) to explore. Choose a group that is as significantly different from your culture as possible. Plan to spend an extended period of time in that culture, perhaps over several hours over several days or weeks. Do *not* write about an experience you had prior to taking this course.

You will conduct research about this group using primary sources, such as written works about the history of this group written by members of this group. Films, poetry, music, art, and other expressions of culture are all appropriate to utilize in your study. In addition, speak to and interview people from this group, including students, parents, and particularly leaders in the community. Invest an extended period of time in attending religious services, festivals, club meetings, and other rich places of cultural immersion.

From this experience, you will develop a PowerPoint presentation and lecture for the class to last about 30 minutes, not including a question-and-answer period. You will provide a six- to eight-page handout about your cultural exploration and what you learned. Include a list of hard-copy and Internet resources.

SECTION IV

SKILLS

7 Curriculum Development and Lesson Planning

Learning Objectives

The National Association for Multicultural Education (NAME, n.d.) explains in a position paper that

> multicultural education advocates the belief that students and their life histories and experiences should be placed at the center of the teaching and learning process and that pedagogy should occur in a context that is familiar to students and that addresses multiple ways of thinking. In addition, teachers and students must critically analyze oppression and power relations in their communities, society and the world.

So if we are to be multicultural educators and prepare students for a global society, what should a multicultural curriculum look like? How does one know if the curriculum is multicultural? What steps need to be taken to create a multicultural curriculum? What are the essential elements of a curriculum that is multicultural, and how does one write multicultural lesson plans and units? This chapter will address these and other questions. It is important to keep in mind that whether or not a school district is composed of racially and ethnically diverse students, a multicultural curriculum benefits all students (Nieto & Bode, 2018). It prepares students for life by providing them with the awareness, knowledge, and skills necessary for a **global economy** (Howe & Lisi, 1995).

Through your study of and work on this chapter, you will be able to do the following:

7.1 Develop the school's curriculum

7.2 Develop a multicultural curriculum

7.3 Analyze texts and materials for cultural bias

7.4 Write multicultural lesson plans

iStock/PeopleImages

A fascinating phenomenon occurred in the beginning of the 2014–2015 school year in the United States. For the first time ever, White students were in the minority in public schools. Students of color (or minority students) made up the majority of students. Both the percentage and the number of White students are expected to drop slowly but steadily over the next several years, from 50% in 2013 to 45% in 2022 (Toppo & Overberg, 2014). Such a milestone calls for the education system to examine and reexamine what schools teach and how they teach it.

A core function of schools is the development of a curriculum of study (Arends, 1997, 2012, 2014; Kellough & Carjuzaa, 2013; Sadker & Zittleman, 2010, 2012). To teach children, educators must be clear about the content, or the "what," they are going to teach. However, the process of making decisions about content can be very challenging. Traditionally, the curriculum used in schools appeared to represent the perspectives, values, and experiences of a limited group of people in the United States—primarily White, middle-class males (Loewen, 2000, 2008; Takaki, 1993). When American schools were populated primarily by immigrants from European countries, this type of curriculum may have been fairly representative and appropriate. Students generally could relate to the examples and experiences of the people in the curriculum.

> Tell me, and I'll forget. Show me, and I may not remember. Involve me, and I'll understand.
>
> —Native American saying

CASE STUDY
SUMMER READING

Summer reading lists, issued by school districts to encourage students to read while on their vacations, are like archeological artifacts. They tell so much about the culture and values of a school system. In the mid-1990s, a large, urban school district composed of about 98% students of color issued its annual summer reading list. A copy made its way to one of us. On the list were the following books, recommended for an overwhelmingly African American and Hispanic student population: *Captains Courageous* by Rudyard Kipling (1897), *Old Yeller* by Fred Gipson (1956), and *A Tale of Two Cities* by Charles Dickens (1859). The rest of the books were in the same vein.

In another, more recent incident, a school board member from a very wealthy suburban district called me. The district was predominantly White but with a growing population of minority students. He asked me for my opinion on the summer reading list that the school board had approved the night before. He had voted to approve it based on the recommendation of the school superintendent, but the list made him "uneasy." The summer reading list had two sections. The first section was copied on white paper and was titled "Summer Reading List." The second section was copied on yellow paper and was titled "Summer Reading List for Diverse Students."

During our phone conversation, the school board member started to reflect on his own experiences with summer reading lists. He relayed that his summer reading list was more aligned with the one described in the first paragraph. He remembers having to read what were called "the classics," which included the books cited in the previous chapter. On further reflection, however, he started thinking out loud about how we have come to define *classic*. He started to raise such questions as "Who are the people who determine the list of classics? And what are the challenges to changing people's thinking about what constitutes classics?" He seemed to be headed in the direction of some important reflection.

(Continued)

(Continued)

Your Perspectives on the Case

1. There is some good news and some bad news in the opening case study. Can you identify each? Why do you identify parts of the case study positively and other parts negatively?

2. What books are on the summer reading list for a school and/or district with which you are familiar? What messages does that list send to the students?

3. How do you think a book is determined to be a classic? Who determines that classification?

4. Consider the classic reading selections with which you are familiar. From whose perspective, in terms of race and ethnicity, are these selections made?

5. What books would you include in a summer reading list for a diverse school district? Would your list be the same for a district that is not very diverse in terms of race and ethnicity? Why or why not?

However, in the current environment of rapidly expanding diversity, with children coming to our classrooms from all nations in the world, we now recognize that a traditional curriculum, while not necessarily presenting wrong information or knowledge, is limited in depth and breadth. Examples and experiences that are presented are not necessarily representative of the experiences of all or even of most Americans. And children in schools today may experience great difficulty in relating to and learning from a curriculum grounded in a singular set of experiences and histories (Aaronsohn, 2003; Banks, 2009; Banks & Banks, 2013; Bennett, 2014; Brown, 2002; Gay, 1994; Gollnick & Chinn, 2013; Grant & Sleeter, 2009; Nieto, 2013; Nieto & Bode, 2018).

If schools are to educate all children to achieve at high levels in a global society and to address social inequities, educators must know how to develop and implement curriculum that represents the diverse perspectives, experiences, and values of a changing world (Darling-Hammond & Bransford, 2005). A multicultural curriculum reflects the multicultural history of this country and the culture of the students served, and it broadens the perspectives of all students. It provides a fuller picture of the histories, the perspectives, and the achievements of a wide variety of people. Such a curriculum is culturally relevant since it engages all students through examples and experiences to which they can relate, and it prepares all students to address issues of social injustice.

The critical importance and value of a multicultural curriculum is evident at both preK–12 and college levels. A curriculum that forces assimilation is not the best way to assist students in attaining their educational goals. Research conducted on college campuses indicates that large numbers of respondents support a multicultural curriculum with multiple perspectives and that courses on ethnicity and women's studies have had positive effects on attitudes toward diversity (Mayo & Larke, 2012; Moses, 2002).

The responsibility for the development of curriculum has traditionally been placed, at the local level, in the hands of district administrators. Teacher responsibility for this work has been primarily in the area of lesson planning and curriculum implementation. However, trends have been identified that point more and more to teacher empowerment and ownership vis-à-vis the curriculum development process. And while curriculum development can be a daunting task, with a knowledge base and support in developing relevant skills, teachers can contribute to the development process in meaningful ways. In this chapter, you will learn what a curriculum is and the process for developing one. We will also discuss strategies for avoiding bias in the selection of teaching materials and explore how a multicultural lesson plan differs from a traditional lesson plan. Once again, you will be given opportunities to write short reflective pieces and try several exercises to help you understand the subject.

THINKING AHEAD

Most teachers receive relatively little training in curriculum development. This is evident as teachers attempt to rewrite a curriculum in order to make it multicultural. In this section, you will learn about the processes for developing a multicultural curriculum.

Questions

1. What do you believe are the key features of a multicultural curriculum?

2. What do you believe are the similarities and differences between a multicultural curriculum and a traditional curriculum?

3. Prioritize the components of what would go into a curriculum that is multicultural.

LEARNING OBJECTIVE 7.1 Develop the School's Curriculum

Defining Curriculum

The term *curriculum* derives from a Latin word meaning "racecourse." A school or a district curriculum traditionally consists of a list of courses that educators pursue throughout the year in their efforts to educate students. In actuality, it is so much more. It is a plan for learning and usually includes goals, specific objectives, and a timetable for implementation. A curriculum indicates the ways in which content is selected, organized, and presented. The curriculum may include a plan for assessment or evaluation of student learning. Some educators see the curriculum as a document. As a whole, curriculum can include what is taught in school, a set of subjects, the content, a program of studies, a set of materials, a sequence of courses, a set of performance objectives, a course of study, everything that goes on in a school, and a series of learner experiences (Kellough & Carjuzaa, 2013; Sadker & Zittleman, 2010, 2012).

If we agree that curriculum is the plan for what is taught in schools, important next questions are these: Who determines what is taught? Do teachers participate at all in the curriculum development and implementation process? Glatthorn and Jailall (2009) point out that a fiercely contested battle is being waged over control of the school curriculum among educators at a variety of levels.

- At the state level, departments of education are becoming deeply involved in establishing standards, **frameworks,** curriculum guidelines, high-stakes student assessments, and then sanctions to ensure that schools are addressing the standards.

- At the district level, educators develop curriculum policies or rules and criteria that guide the development and implementation of curriculum in the district's schools. Also at the district level, specialists work to align district and state curriculum goals, identify programs of study, develop curriculum guides, select instructional materials, develop scope and sequence plans, and provide resources and technical assistance.

- At the school level, educators develop a vision and their own program of studies that align with district curriculum goals. An example of a program of studies is the social studies curriculum at the elementary level in a district. Schools also design school improvement plans that focus on specific curricular areas to be addressed by everyone.

- Finally, at the classroom level, teachers develop units and lesson plans and evaluate their own implementation of the curriculum. Teachers work within the guidelines and frameworks established by the state and district to set specific learning goals and design unit and lesson plans that reflect the school's particular mission statement.

As illustrated above, teachers have been involved in curriculum development, for the most part, at the school or classroom levels. Primary and legal responsibility for curriculum rests with each state (Grant & Gillette, 2006). One way each state defines what is important in the curriculum is by developing standards. Standards are expectations of what students should know and be able to do as a result of their engagement in school. Standards can be developed through the state's department of education and with a focus on that state's children in particular. Standards have also been developed by national professional organizations, such as the National Council of Teachers of Mathematics and the International Reading Association. While Grant and Gillette (2009) point out that standards are not the curriculum, standards should inform the development of the curriculum in each district and school. States hold districts and schools accountable for aligning the development of curriculum with the standards by requiring public school participation in high-stakes, state-developed assessments that reflect the state standards. The topic of curriculum standards is one of the major by-products of this era of high-stakes testing (Benson, 2009).

Educators such as Ainsworth (2011) and Reeves (2008) have gained national influence in leading major reforms on how schools design curriculum and best practices for classroom instruction. Their work has been boosted by the Common Core State Standards. This state-led effort is coordinated by the National Governors Association Center for Best Practices and the Council of Chief State School Officers (2011). The Common Core State Standards attempt to clearly and uniformly define what preK–12 students need to know

The previously all-White Barnard Elementary School in Washington, D.C., acted quickly to integrate schools after the *Brown v. Board* of *Education* Supreme Court decision of 1954.

© Thomas J. O'Halloran. U.S. News & World Report Magazine Collection, Prints and Photographs Division

in certain subjects in order to be prepared for postsecondary work. The Common Core State Standards are expectations for what K–12 students need to know and be able to do in English language arts and mathematics. Beginning in 2012, the states began to review the standards and determine whether or not they would adopt the national standards. As of June 2014, 43 states; the Department of Defense Education Activity; Washington, D.C.; Guam; the Northern Mariana Islands; and the U.S. Virgin Islands have adopted the Common Core State Standards in English language arts/literacy and math and are in the process of implementing the standards at the local level. Implementation in schools has influenced important changes in teaching and learning. For example, the English language arts standards are designed to support students in learning to use critical thinking skills, cogent reasoning, and evidence collection skills. The standards could influence substantially the approaches teachers take to support diverse learners. What are the implications of an educator's orientation to, or beliefs about, the purpose of curriculum? In terms of being an educator who is culturally responsive and responsible, they are numerous. If an educator uses behavioral objectives, remains discipline based in the organization of curriculum, and expects students to memorize what he or she delivers, then this transmission orientation will probably result in maintenance of the status quo. In other words, it will support the maintenance of privilege for a select group of students. If, however, an educator develops a student-centered, problem-based approach to teaching and learning, asking students to use their own experiences and histories as the basis for learning, then this transformation orientation will result in the students addressing critical social challenges in significant ways.

The Curriculum Development Process

In light of a large body of research that indicates that education should be child centered and grounded in constructivism and cognitive science, what is a recommended process for developing curriculum to achieve those goals? Oakes, Lipton, Anderson, and Stillman (2012) advocated offering a curriculum and curriculum materials that support students in developing their capacity for higher order thinking and engage them in real-world problem solving. Such a curriculum builds on what students know, engages students in building knowledge in the context of solving problems, and provides multiple entry points for students to engage in learning.

While individual teachers certainly can develop units of study and multicultural lesson plans for their own classrooms, the recommended process (see Table 7.1) for building a multicultural curriculum at the school level starts with establishing a curriculum development team (Glatthorn, 2000). The team could and should be composed of representatives of a variety of stakeholder groups, including administrators, teachers, library information staff, special education teachers, and technology educators. The team should be provided with the time and resources to meet regularly. The curriculum improvement team provides leadership in developing a vision of a quality curriculum and the school's curriculum goals. The goals, and the eventual curriculum, must be aligned with learning standards—that is, expectations of what students should know and be able to do. The team needs to make decisions about whether to revise an existing curriculum or program of studies or create a new curriculum.

At this point, the team is charged with revising or creating a program of studies, which is "the total set of offerings provided for a group of learners at a particular level of schooling" (Glatthorn, 2000, p. 57). In developing the program of studies, the team may decide to use a variety of existing curriculum development models or adopt a new approach. Next, the team makes

---

Extended Explorations 7.1: Creating a New Curriculum

Imagine that you have the opportunity to create a new curriculum, one that has not been offered before in your school (e.g., a social justice course or a course creating apps for hand-held devices or composing songs). How would you go about it? What would be your objectives—multicultural and otherwise? How would the curriculum be tied to state or national standards? How would it contribute to increasing academic achievement? Go to the website for the Common Core State Standards (http://www.corestandards.org). Explore the standards for either English language arts or mathematics. Develop a one-page statement about your draft curriculum and the potential links to specific standards you have identified.

TABLE 7.1	The Curriculum Development Process
According to Glatthorn (2000), the recommended steps in the curriculum development process are as follows:	
Step 1	School leaders establish a curriculum development team.
Step 2	The team works to develop a vision of a quality curriculum and curriculum goals.
Step 3	The team conducts a needs assessment and decides whether to continue with what exists, revise an existing curriculum, or create a new curriculum.
Step 4	The team uses existing standards to determine what students should know and be able to do.
Step 5	The team determines appropriate assessments to gauge whether or not students have learned the expected concepts and skills.
Step 6	The team designs the program of studies, including structures or ways to convey the program of studies, and selects relevant materials.
Step 7	The team recommends instructional strategies that are relevant.
Step 8	The team develops a schedule for implementation, including monitoring and evaluation.

decisions about content and structures for addressing the goals. Traditionally, the curriculum is based on a set of topics to be learned. More recently, it has been strongly suggested that curriculum development be grounded in concepts or key, broader themes and ideas (Erickson & Lanning, 2013). Concepts are timeless and universal ways of organizing ideas and lend themselves easily to the integration of diverse content, whereas a topics approach keeps learning grounded simply in facts. Structures may include courses or units or other creative ways of encapsulating key concepts and themes. Finally, the team will need to identify potential instructional and assessment strategies and a suggested timetable for implementation of the curriculum.

This process results in multicultural curriculum development when significant consideration is given to addressing and incorporating the unique and diverse needs, backgrounds, and interests of learners. This applies to the selection of content, instructional strategies, and a variety of assessment strategies. Finally, the members of the curriculum development team need to be vigilant in recognizing how their own values, experiences, biases, and belief systems positively or negatively affect the whole process.

In the previous chapters, we explained the rationale for a multicultural curriculum: All students should receive an education of high quality that stresses academic achievement and attainment of skills that will enable them to thrive in a multicultural world (Banks, 2009; Bennett, 2014; Gollnick & Chinn, 2013; Grant & Sleeter, 2009; Nieto & Bode, 2018).

LEARNING OBJECTIVE 7.2 Develop a Multicultural Curriculum

Scott (1994) discusses research that reveals that students taught from an **inclusive curriculum** are more eager and engaged in the classroom. Faculty who integrate diversity into their curriculum report that their teaching is energized, students' evaluations of their teaching improve, and their overall satisfaction with teaching increases. Gorski and Swalwell (2015) emphasize that issues of equity should take precedence over culture in the curriculum, stressing the importance of incorporating social justice into the classroom. Lawrence-Brown and Sapon-Shevin (2014) follow the same theme, with directions to include issues of income disparity, language and religious rights, and gender identity and expression. Anderson and Davis (2012) write about "culturally considerate schools" where educators demonstrate "sincerity" in not only their words but also their actions, resulting in more equitable academic success.

Characteristics of a Multicultural Curriculum

Pritchy Smith (1998), in *Common Sense About Uncommon Knowledge*, provided an excellent conceptual overview of a multicultural curriculum. He described six broad principles of multicultural curriculum development. These address the multicultural aspects of curriculum that are often overlooked in favor of purely pedagogical approaches. According to Smith (1998), a well-designed multicultural curriculum includes the following:

1. Activities and teaching that help students navigate from the familiarity of their own culture to learning more about other cultures

2. Activities and teaching that promote positive ethnic identity

3. Activities and teaching that involve increasingly more frequent and positive relationships among students who are different from one another

4. Activities and teaching that build students' personal knowledge of their culture and the cultures of other people

5. Activities and teaching that help students see and understand issues, concepts, and events from the perspectives of other people

6. Activities and teaching that help students use their knowledge of other cultures to better understand and resolve social problems and, ultimately, lead lives as multicultural persons

The traditional curriculum does not reflect these principles. Culture is rarely addressed, except in reference to attempts to recognize and appreciate diversity on some level. One reason is that the traditional curriculum tends to be Eurocentric and does not incorporate the cultures of other students. Minimal attention is paid to issues of social justice, with exceptions being the civics requirements of many high school programs.

At the request of the National Council for the Social Studies, James Banks (1992) wrote a revised set of *Curriculum Guidelines for Multicultural Education*. These guidelines can be particularly useful in curriculum revision or development. Here is a summary of some of the key points:

- The entire school community should have a positive multicultural climate and continually strive for meaningful interactions and communications.

© Digital vision/digital vision/thinkstock

As with any career, much of what we need to know comes after graduation. It is through experience grounded in good training in theory that we are able to master our profession.

- The makeup of the faculty and staff should reflect the community and the country.

- The cultural learning styles of students should be incorporated into curriculum development.

- A student's education is not complete without learning about and understanding the history and experiences of the many different peoples who make up this country.

- A student's education should provide the cultural competency necessary to live and work in a diverse economy.

- The multicultural curriculum should include a strong component of actual experiences to help synthesize knowledge.

- The assessment process and methods should reflect the culture of student experiences.

Whether or not a school decides to revise an existing curriculum or create a new curriculum as described in Section 7.1, "Develop the School's Curriculum," these guidelines provide an excellent framework within which educators can work to ensure that the result is a multicultural curriculum. By establishing and using a multicultural curriculum, the potential exists for addressing critical problems in education, including the following:

- Closing the achievement gap, because students will more readily recognize themselves in the curriculum and thereby be more motivated to engage in learning

- Helping students increase their knowledge of, sensitivity to, and appreciation of other cultures, thereby preparing them to participate in a global economy

- Identifying bias, stereotypes, and inaccuracies in both the content and the process of education, thereby ensuring that the curriculum does not continue to convey negative messages about diverse cultures

- Acknowledging varied learning styles among students to better serve all students

Whether the curriculum is revised or newly created, to achieve a multicultural curriculum, three key factors need to be addressed (Scott, 1994). First, educators need to increase their own personal knowledge about multicultural issues and diverse cultures. This knowledge helps us understand how to integrate cultural knowledge and practices into the curriculum. Second, educators need to restructure existing course syllabi to add cultural content as a context for teaching and learning. And finally, methods need to be altered and varied to support different cultural learning styles and meet the learning needs and life experiences of a diverse student population while increasing the repertoire of knowledge and skills for all students.

LEARNING OBJECTIVE 7.3 Analyze Texts and Materials for Cultural Bias

Many states require that schools have textbook committees or other means for examining texts for cultural bias—racial, ethnic, gender, and so on. The first step in analyzing curriculum and materials for bias is to have a clear understanding of the potential forms of bias.

Seven Forms of Bias in Curriculum Materials

Bias in instructional materials occurs in many forms. According to Arends (2012), Banks and McGee Banks (2013), and Sadker and Zittleman (2010), bias can be categorized in the following ways:

1. *Invisibility or omission:* Women and people of color were virtually absent in text-books prior to the 1960s. It is important for students to see themselves and others portrayed in all walks of life and careers. Texts that routinely portray only people of one race do not reflect reality. One only needs to look at current programs on television, which tend to be devoid of people of color, to see that they do not mirror real life or support diverse lives. For example, popular television shows such as *Seinfeld* and *Friends* had people of color only in token roles.

2. *Stereotyping:* People in teaching resources should not be reduced to the stereotypes commonly assigned to them. Unfortunately, stereotyping is common, and it perpetuates prejudice. Domestic or custodial help should not be routinely seen as being provided by women and people of color. Nor should all White males be seen as ignorant racists. Girls need to be seen in strong, heroic roles. Boys should be occasionally seen in positions where they need the help of girls. Sometimes, the man needs to be shown tied on the railroad track and the woman riding up on her black horse to rescue him.

3. *Imbalance and selectivity:* The curriculum should not be one-sided but should give expression to other versions and perspectives. History should not be distorted to reveal only one point of view. The doctrine of manifest destiny claimed that it was the God-given right of settlers to move west in order to claim land for themselves, to tame the savages, and to bring them Christianity and civilization. How do you claim land where people have been living for centuries? Did the Native Americans feel that they needed a new religion and that they needed to be civilized? Why was that not taken into consideration?

4. *Unreality:* Texts have historically tended to ignore negative or unpleasant aspects of history or to trivialize them. During World War II, about 120,000 innocent Japanese Americans, many of them U.S. citizens who spoke only English and whose families had been in the country for generations, were rounded up, placed in internment camps, and accused of treason. As the war progressed and more fighting men were needed, the military appeared at these same internment camps and appealed to the imprisoned people to enlist and fight for their country—the United States. The Japanese Americans did fight for their country in large numbers. In fact, some of the all-Japanese American units liberated Jewish concentration camps in Europe. Meanwhile, their own families languished in prison camps in the United States. Other all–African American units also freed Jewish concentration camps, while their families still lived under the harsh rule of segregation.

5. *Fragmentation and isolation:* Instead of being included throughout the curriculum, women and people of color are often inserted as add-ons to the text. A typical example would be a short, highlighted section in a textbook called "Ten Great African American Scientists," while the rest of the text is devoid of any mention of people of color. This form of tokenism tends to minimize the contributions of diverse peoples instead of emphasizing them. This is often seen in the world of work when a company, wanting to prove its commitment to diversity, brings clerical staff to a meeting or a company event for all to see. The clerical staff are often primarily people of color, while the "professional staff" are all White.

The curriculum should not perpetuate bias. Heroes come in all sizes, shapes, colors, religions, genders, and abilities.

© Comstock/Thinkstock

6. *Linguistic bias:* Words are powerful. They can be used in pejorative ways to distort reality. Male pronouns, such as *policeman* and *fireman*, reinforce sexist assumptions that these jobs are for boys only. *Forefathers* ignores the contributions that women made in establishing this country. Ronald Reagan, as president, would often refer to "welfare queens" driving pink Cadillacs, reinforcing the stereotype of unmarried, Black women having numerous babies and living off welfare benefits instead of working. This coded language belied the reality that the majority of people on welfare are single White women.

7. *Cosmetic bias:* Textbooks and other teaching resources frequently showcase smiling images of diverse students on their covers. However, the insides of the books, where the content is, do not reflect the diversity on those covers. A picture of a diverse group of students on a college catalog cover was found to be deceptive when it was revealed that the sole Black student in the photo had not actually posed for the photograph. His image had been cut from another picture and inserted into a smiling group of White students to promote the college's assertion that it celebrated diversity.

Checking for Bias

Having a system by which to analyze teaching resources and understand the different forms of bias is essential (Banks, 2009; Gallavan, 2010a, 2010b). Systems adopted by schools can include the use of checklists and guidelines. Some of the more well-known guidelines are included in this focus area. For example, Table 7.2 presents a checklist that can be used to identify issues of bias in curriculum materials. An example of bias expressed as inappropriate language would be describing Jewish people as "cunning" or "miserly." As another example, sometimes Native Americans' lives are referred to as primitive or aboriginal, but English settlers are lauded for their brave spirit and heroics.

TABLE 7.2 **A Checklist for Examining Resources for Bias**

	Yes	No	Evidence
Bias: Material reveals a strong preference for one type of thinking.			
Discrimination: Material singles out or pictures a group in a particularly positive or negative way.			
Prejudice: Material reveals unfairly negative perceptions or viewpoints.			
Racism: Material reflects negative attitudes toward or treatment of people based solely on their race.			
Sexism: Material reflects negative attitudes toward or treatment of people based solely on gender.			
Stereotype: Material reinforces beliefs that all the members of one particular group think and behave in a certain way.			
Tokenism: Certain groups appear only as perfunctory additions, or their contributions appear in a limited way.			
Ethnocentrism: One cultural group is presented as the ideal.			
Exotica: Focus is on extreme examples of the culture, not on everyday life.			
Routine aspects of life: Focus is primarily on the Fs (foods, fashions, festivals).			
Inappropriate language: Material supports prejudice by using derogatory language.			
Authors: Authors and illustrators are not from the same cultural group as the people portrayed.			
Publication date: Materials, primarily textbooks, are dated.			

Source: Adapted from Beilke (1986), Harada (1995), Harris (1991), and Pang, Colvin, Tran, and Barba (1992).

The ERIC Clearinghouse on Reading English and Communication (Lu, 1998) outlined a set of *Guidelines for Evaluating and Selecting Multicultural Materials.* According to this document, multicultural literature should do the following:

- Avoid portraying people as stereotypes and, instead, give them positive, realistic personalities and behaviors

- Ensure that illustrations are authentic, not caricatures

- Include stories that portray diversity as a strength and an asset to the nation

- Provide historical as well as fictional stories that illustrate the ever-changing role and status of minority groups in society

- Be of high quality with engaging plot lines and strong cultural characterizations

- Be historically accurate

- Accurately reflect the cultural values of the characters

- Take place in settings in the United States that accurately portray the rich cultural diversity of this country and the legacy of various minority groups

Another often-quoted source for evaluating materials is from the Council on Interracial Books for Children (1980). Children can be taught to look for bias in books. The council provided the following "10 Quick Ways to Analyze Children's Books for Racism and Sexism."

1. *Check the illustrations:* Watch for people being portrayed in demeaning or stereotypical ways, either obvious or subtle. Images of people should look authentic in terms of coloration and features. People of color or ethnic minorities should not always be cast in stereotypically subservient roles but should occupy powerful positions as well. Girls, in particular, should be seen in capable, active, leadership roles.

2. *Check the story line.*

3. *Standard for success:* Does a person of color have to adopt White, middle-class behaviors in order to succeed? Do girls have to act like boys in order to be successful? Are people of color always seen as superior athletes (particularly African Americans) or extremely book smart (especially Asians)? Among diverse friends, are children of color most often the ones who have to be patient, understanding, and forgiving of their White peers?

4. *Resolution of problems:* If there are problems in the story, what are they and who has them—just girls and people of color? Is it clear that sometimes the problems faced are due to social injustices? Are people of color consistently "rescued or saved" by White people?

5. *Roles of women:* Are girls and women seen achieving independently by using their skills and intelligence, versus using their beauty and the help of boys? Are girls and women assigned to stereotypical gender roles?

6. *Look at the lifestyles:* Are people of color and their lifestyles portrayed negatively, as compared with White, middle-class people and their lives? Where do people live? Are suburbs filled with White, middle-class people while cities are characterized as ghettos full of unsavory, poor people of color? Do the lives of people of color seem genuine or stereotypical?

7. *Weigh the relationships between people:* Are White, middle-class people seen as heroic leaders, while others are depicted in helpless, supporting roles? In African American and Asian American families, are mothers seen as dominant, maybe even domineering? Are men absent?

8. *Note the heroes:* Are people of color described as quiet and harmless, or are they allowed to express themselves and their outrage at social injustices? When they are depicted as heroes, is it with the same level and type of adulation that is accorded White heroes and for the same qualities, such as bravery, selflessness, concern for others, and so on? Or are they heroes mainly because they have helped White people?

9. *Consider the effects on a child's self-image:* Is there a message that people must be of a certain hair and eye color, a certain weight or height, or a certain degree or type of attractiveness to be superior? How do children who do not measure up to this standard react to the images being portrayed as desirable, such as tall, thin females or White, muscular males? Do children see positive role models who look, think, and act like them?

10. *Consider the author or illustrator's background:* Check to see who are the authors and illustrators of books with multicultural themes. If they are not members of the cultural group that is being portrayed in the book, what in their background qualifies them to write or draw with authority on that culture?

11. *Check out the author's perspective:* Some bias is to be expected in any book. Most children's books have been written by White, middle-class authors, which has led to established notions of ethnicity biased in favor of White, middle-class people and, often, males. Examine the book for inconsistencies, inaccuracies, and vagueness in cultural interpretations. How do they affect the message of the book?

12. *Watch for loaded words:* Loaded words or "coded phrases" can be demeaning, inaccurate, racist, and sexist, among other faults. Watch for the use of descriptive words such as *cheap, savage, lazy, old wives' tale, inscrutable, treacherous,* and *conniving.* Sexist terms that promote males only, such as *forefathers* and *policemen,* are warning signs of possible bias.

13. *Look at the copyright date:* Books published prior to the 1960s were written mainly by White, middle-class men, lending them a certain ethnic and gender perspective. Caution, therefore, is advised when using materials from that era, especially those that claim to offer an ethnic or female viewpoint. This is not to say that all recently published books are bias-free.

    - In portrayals of people of color, there is always the risk of stereotyping. People should be seen as having many aspects to their character and to their lives.
    - The story should progress naturally, with cultural aspects included only when appropriate.
    - The language of the characters must be authentic. Terms, jargon, and colloquial expressions must be appropriate for the time period.

The guidelines above apply not just to textbooks but also to other literature and teacher resources used in class, such as videos, CDs, periodicals, computer software, and newspapers. Despite the best efforts of teachers, some biased material may enter the classroom. In these cases, acknowledge the bias, and use it to create a teachable moment. Discuss it in class, seeking comments from the students.

LEARNING OBJECTIVE 7.4 Write Multicultural Lesson Plans

Administrators and teachers will need to focus their attention on developing curriculum that is multicultural, as described in previous sections in this chapter. Tomlinson (2008) stressed that because of the increase of academically diverse schools, with a mixture of students having different learning needs, a practice of **differentiated instruction** becomes essential. However, individual teachers do not need to wait for a department, grade-level, or schoolwide curriculum development effort before they invest time and energy in transforming the content they teach in their own classrooms.

Interestingly, many teachers believe that to transform the units and lessons in their own classrooms, they need to start all over. Also, teachers who consider developing multicultural lesson plans tend to overthink the process. Some overemphasize the need to infuse race into their lessons. Others focus almost solely on augmenting the content of a lesson, when changing some instructional strategies and adding new activities might be just as powerful. Others infuse issues of diversity into the lesson in a clumsy fashion. A humorous example of this last point might be a science teacher exclaiming, during a lesson on clouds, "Clouds are classified as stratus, cumulus, and cirrus.... And oh, by the way, it was partly cloudy on the day Martin Luther King gave his 'I Have a Dream Speech.'"

© Irving Rusinow, Photographer. Department of Agriculture. Bureau of Agricultural Economics. Division of Economic Information

A good starting point for teachers who want to become multicultural educators is to create or transform lessons to be multicultural. The more involved a teacher is in this process, the more he or she will want to transform all lessons—and see the need to do so! In fact, all lessons should be multicultural; multiculturalism should not be reserved for special lessons included just for ethnic holidays. A teacher can begin to transform lessons by using the curriculum already designated by the school and/or district.

Planning Learning Experiences From a Multicultural Perspective

As described in Section 7.1, "Develop the School's Curriculum," most schools have established a program of studies and a curriculum for each subject area. That curriculum will address pertinent standards or expectations for student learning, broad goals, and recommended instructional strategies and assessments.

The next step is for teachers, or teams of teachers, to use the established curriculum to develop unit plans and daily learning experiences or lesson plans for students. A unit has been described as a chunk of content (from the established curriculum) and associated skills that are perceived as fitting together in a logical way. Normally, more than one lesson is required to accomplish a unit of instruction. The content for instructional units might come from chapters in books or from major sections of curriculum guides (Arends, 2009, p. 121).

Unit planning allows the teacher the opportunity to outline a primary theme or big idea (generally seen as the unit title), establish overall unit objectives, select the unit content and a series of learning experiences (lessons), identify pertinent materials, and select assessment mechanisms.

Within each unit, the format for those lesson plans may vary, depending on the instructional model or strategy that is used. For example, the lesson plan for a problem-based learning experience will be different from the lesson plan for a direct instruction learning experience. At the same time, lesson plans tend to follow a common format (Arends, 2012; Kellough & Carjuzaa, 2013). In this process, the teacher builds on an identified unit plan theme, goals, and content. Then for individual lesson plans, the teacher will do the following:

1. Identify the instructional objectives (including cognitive, affective, psychomotor, and other skill area objectives)

2. Outline and sequence the learning activities, providing for introduction of the lesson, a series of learning experiences, assignments, and closure

3. Select the materials and resources needed to teach the lesson

4. Determine how student learning will be evaluated

Teachers who are committed to becoming culturally responsible and to transforming lesson plans to be multicultural use a variation on the typical lesson-planning process described above. This variation engages teachers in a conscious effort to include multicultural principles and concepts in the preexisting curriculum. Instead of moving directly from unit goals to lesson objectives, multicultural lesson planning includes a step in which the teacher identifies one or two multicultural principles to be addressed. Addressing those will lead to the inclusion of important multicultural concepts in the development of instructional or learning plans. Also, an important variation on the more traditional lesson or unit plan process is the consideration given to assessment. More recently, an effective format for unit and lesson plans has been one in which the teacher actually plans for how student learning will be assessed before planning learning experiences and resources. It's important for students to know how they will be assessed prior to beginning work on new content. Learning experiences can then be designed with the objectives, key concepts, and assessments in mind. Figure 7.1 illustrates the differences between a traditional lesson plan and a multicultural lesson plan.

If a teacher works conscientiously in these areas, multicultural lesson and unit planning will look like this:

1. *Unit theme/title of unit:* The unit theme may already exist as part of a curriculum framework, the curriculum itself, or the textbook.

2. *Instructional goal:* One or two goals may be identified as the basis for this unit or lesson plan.

3. *Multicultural principle(s) or goals:* One of the six multicultural principles/goals may be applied in this lesson and/or unit as appropriate.

4. *Learning objectives:* Which instructional objectives are important and which are drawn from the cognitive, affective, and psychomotor and skill domains should be determined. Some of the objectives should be designed to address multicultural concepts.

FIGURE 7.1	Lesson Plan Formats
Traditional	**Multicultural**
1. Subject	1. Subject
2. Instructional Goals	2. Instructional Goals
3. Curriculum Objectives	3. Curriculum Objectives
	4. Multicultural Goals
4. Assessment/Evaluation	5. Assessment/Evaluation - multiple
5. Instruction/Delivery	6. Instruction/Delivery - multiple
6. Materials/Resources	7. Materials/Resources - varied

5. *Assessment/evaluation:* The assessment or evaluation methods to be used should be decided. By using a variety of assessment strategies to determine what students know and are able to do, you will be in a better position to meet the needs of diverse learners. Variations in assessment strategies are discussed in Chapter 10.

6. *Instructional delivery/student activities:* Ways to engage students in learning should be outlined, including the introduction of the lesson(s), learning activities, assignments to support continued learning, and provision for formative assessment. By making use of a variety of instructional strategies, such as cooperative learning, multiple intelligences–based learning, and problem-based learning, the teacher will be better able to meet the needs and interests of diverse students.

7. *Materials/resources:* A list of the materials and resources needed to teach the lesson and unit should be prepared. Care should be taken to use materials that are unbiased and to present content that represents the experiences and perspectives of diverse groups of people. The format for a lesson plan, or set of lesson plans, would look like what appears in Exhibit 7.1.

Exhibit 7.1   **Multicultural Unit and Lesson Plan Format**

Subject area: Grade level: Duration:

Teacher's name: Lesson focus:

1. **Instructional goal**

   Cite specific national Common Core State Standards or other standards that are the basis for teaching and learning in your state/setting.

2. **Curriculum objectives**

   Cite specific learning objectives. What are students expected to know and be able to do as a result of their engagement in this lesson or set of lessons? Use verbs that require students to participate at as high a level of critical thinking as possible.

3. **Multicultural goal(s) (Check one or more)**

   Place a checkmark in front of the specific multicultural goal(s) you will address in this lesson plan.

   ☐ Developing multiple historical perspectives
   ☐ Developing cultural consciousness
   ☐ Increasing intercultural competence
   ☐ Combating racism, prejudice, and discrimination
   ☐ Developing awareness of the state of the planet and global dynamics
   ☐ Developing social action skills (Describe pertinent multicultural concepts)

4. **Assessment options**

   What specific assessment strategies will you use? How will you determine if each student has achieved the learning objectives? Make sure to provide a variety of assessment strategies that address diverse learner needs.

5. **Instructional delivery/student experiences**

   Plan a variety of learning experiences that meet diverse learner needs, interests, learning styles, and cultural backgrounds.

6. **Materials/resources**

   Work to include culturally relevant materials.

Multicultural Principles

As indicated in the multicultural lesson plan format shown in Exhibit 7.1, one key feature that makes a lesson plan multicultural is the inclusion of one or two multicultural goals or principles. The principles used in this book are grounded in a set of goals for achieving multicultural perspectives in teaching and learning developed by Bennett (2014). Teachers are encouraged to use the multicultural principles explained below in their lesson planning:

Principle 1: Develops multiple perspectives: The traditional Eurocentric curriculum must be balanced with the perspectives and history of women and people of color. Multicultural lesson plans include concepts that help students see events and experiences from diverse perspectives.

Principle 2: Develops cultural consciousness: To become culturally competent requires developing the personal awareness that others in the world have different experiences, histories, values, viewpoints, and perspectives. Women, people of color, members of nonmajority ethnic groups, and citizens of other countries may see life differently than members of the dominant White, middle-class, English-speaking culture.

Principle 3: Increases intercultural competence: Intercultural competence is the ability to interact with people of different cultures.

Principle 4: Combats racism, sexism, prejudice, and discrimination: Lesson plans could be developed to help students become aware of racist and sexist behavior.

Principle 5: Develops awareness of the state of the planet and global dynamics: Lessons address the knowledge of prevailing world conditions, trends, and developments. It is also knowledge of the world as a highly interrelated ecosystem subject to surprise effects and dramatic ramifications of simple events.

Principle 6: Develops social action skills: Social action skills include the awareness, knowledge, skills, attitudes, and behaviors needed to work toward social justice.

After selecting one or two principles to address in a lesson plan, teachers will also want to select one or more key concepts and begin to include those concepts in their lesson objectives. These concepts can be incorporated into classroom learning experiences directly or indirectly.

Key Concepts for a Multicultural Curriculum

The multicultural curriculum should help students master higher levels of knowledge so that they can better understand race and ethnic relations and develop the skills and abilities needed to make reflective personal and public decisions. Sound multicultural lessons and units focus on higher level concepts and generalizations and use facts primarily to help students move from fundamental to more sophisticated concepts, thereby mastering higher forms of knowledge and decision making. Students must be able to make reflective decisions in order to take thoughtful personal, social, and civic action (Banks, 2009).

In addition to including one or more of the six multicultural principles in a lesson plan, teachers will want to select key multicultural concepts as described by Banks (2009). To support students in learning to consider multiple perspectives (Principle 1), any of the following concepts could be included in the lesson:

Communication: how behaviors and symbols are interpreted by others

Culture: the beliefs, values, and behaviors of a society

Diversity: cultural, ethnic, racial, religious, and language differences as well as differences in areas such as gender, sexual orientation, abilities, and others

Historical bias: the recognition that a historian's views of the past are influenced by his or her own social, cultural, and ethnic identities

Ethnic groups: groups in which members are descended from an ancestry that has a common language and religion, and common customs and behaviors

Perception: a viewpoint influenced by culture, experience, bias, cultural values, and other variables

To support students in learning to understand that culture is a part of our life (Principle 2), a teacher may elect to focus on concepts that include the following:

Acculturation: when members of the dominant cultural group adopt the cultural traits of a minority group

Assimilation: when a member of a minority group adopts the customs, behaviors, values, and lifestyle of the dominant culture

Community culture: the customs, habits, language, and lifestyles of an ethnic community

Self-concept: how individuals see themselves in terms of assumptions, knowledge, and feelings

To support students in learning to use and incorporate diverse perspectives in their daily lives (Principle 3), the teacher may choose to include the following concepts:

Intercultural communication: interpretations, misinterpretations, and ways in which miscommunication occurs because of culture differences

Culture: attitudes, beliefs, values, and behaviors shared by the members of a group

Values: cultural elements that are given high worth

Attitudes: biases and assumptions that influence how one views people or situations

Prejudice: negative feelings and attitudes toward other groups that are not grounded in facts

Discrimination: differential behavior toward a targeted group

Racism: negative beliefs that targeted groups possess certain mental, sociological, and cultural characteristics based on their biological makeup

Power: possessing influence, whether for good or bad; uses of power by one group over another

Ethnocentrism: a belief that one's own ethnic group is superior to that of others

Socialization: acquiring values, attitudes, and behaviors based on interactions with others

To help students understand that all people's success and problems are interdependent (Principle 5), the teacher may focus on the following:

Civic responsibility: the obligation to serve one's community through efforts to improve the conditions under which people live

Equity: fair and just accommodation of the needs of all

Interdependence: the mutual reliance of each group on the others

Justice: fair, ethical, and moral treatment of people

Respect: showing deference to and appreciation of others

Social action: seeking reform of elements of society in the pursuit of equity and justice

So far, we have established that a multicultural lesson plan serves the same purpose and follows the same format as a traditional lesson plan. The goals and objectives come from the approved textbook or curriculum. The difference is that multicultural principles and concepts are infused into the lesson.

Exhibits 7.2 and 7.3 show two sample lesson plans in history and social studies, respectively.

Exhibit 7.2   **Sample Multicultural Unit/Lesson Plans: Secondary History**

Developing Lesson Plans That are Multicultural

Subject area: History   Grade level: 10–12   Duration: Four block classes

Teacher's name: Eileen McKenzie   Lesson focus: African American history

1. Instructional goal(s)

   - Students will analyze the development of the identity of African Americans during the 1930s by examining works of art from the Harlem Renaissance.
   - Students will identify significant themes of the Harlem Renaissance by analyzing music, poetry, and artwork from the time period.

2. Curriculum objectives

(From the CT [Connecticut] Social Studies/History Framework)

Students will be able to do the following:

   a. Identify significant events and themes in U.S. history
   b. Interpret information from a variety of primary and secondary sources, including electronic media (maps, charts, graphs, images, artifacts, recordings, and text)

(From the National Common Core State Standards)

Students will be able to do the following:

   a. Cite specific textual evidence to support analysis of primary and secondary sources, connecting insights gained from specific details to an understanding of the text as a whole
   b. Integrate information from diverse sources, both primary and secondary, into a coherent understanding of an idea or event, noting the discrepancies among the sources

3. Multicultural goal(s)

   - Developing multiple historical perspectives
   - Developing cultural consciousness
   - Increasing intercultural competence
   - Combating racism, prejudice, and discrimination
   - Developing awareness of the state of the planet and global dynamics
   - Developing social action skills

(Continued)

Exhibit 7.2   (Continued)

4. Assessment/evaluation

   1. Students can choose one piece from the unit and create a coordinating piece (e.g., if a student chooses a piece of music or a poem, the student should create a coordinating piece of artwork to represent the lyrics/overall tone of the music; if a student chooses a piece of artwork, the student should create a poem or a piece of music to represent the artwork).

   2. Students should write a one-page response to describe how the two pieces of artwork go together and how they tie into the overall themes of the Harlem Renaissance (combating racism and discrimination against African Americans, establishing a new African American identity, etc.). Students will be evaluated according to the following:

      • Capacity of the writing response to cite specific textual evidence and include information from diverse sources
      • Quality of the connection made between the pieces of artwork
      • Connection of the individual's work to overall themes of the Harlem Renaissance

5. Instructional delivery/student activities

   1. *Introduction:* Discuss the causes of the Harlem Renaissance (e.g., the Great Migration and the response to discrimination/racism). Ask students if they were faced with discrimination, how would they combat it? Would they agitate, accommodate, or migrate? What would it take for them to leave their homes for a new life?

   2. Have students watch *Jazz*, a documentary by Ken Burns—Episodes 2 ("The Gift") and 3 ("Our Language"). Have students, working in groups, explain the evolution of jazz in the United States. They may develop a timeline about significant events.

   3. Have students participate in an "art auction," where they act as art retailers. Split them into groups, and give each group one piece of artwork from the Harlem Renaissance to "sell" to their peers in the class (see the resources list below). Their peers will be given fake money, which they will use to try to buy the piece of art.

   4. Compare and contrast the following:

      a. Pair students. Assign each pair to read one poem by Langston Hughes and then analyze the poem for themes.

      b. As a class, have students listen to "Take the 'A' Train" by Duke Ellington. First, have the students listen to the instrumental version of "Take the 'A' Train." The second time around, have them write a brief one- to two-sentence reflection. Then, have the students listen to "Take the 'A' Train" with lyrics. After the second time around, have them write another brief one- to two-sentence reflection.

      c. Have students compare and contrast the portrayal of Harlem between Ellington and Hughes.

   5. Have students create advertisements for an upcoming show at the Apollo Theatre.

6. Materials/resources

   Movie: Jazz by Ken Burns/PBS America
   Artwork: William H. Johnson: "Street Life, Harlem"; Aaron Douglass: "Play de Blues"; Palmer Hayden: "Jeunesse"; Malvin Gray Johnson: "Negro Soldier"; William H. Johnson: "Chain Gang"; Jacob Lawrence: "The Life of Toussaint L'Overture"
   Langston Hughes' poems: "The Weary Blues," "Jazzonia," "Red Silk Stockings," "Lenox Avenue: Midnight," "Dream Boogie," "Juke Box Love Song," "Trumpet Player," "Jam Session," "Harlem Night Club," "Midnight Dancer," "Saturday Night," "The Cat and the Saxophone (2 a.m.)"
   Music: "Take the 'A' Train" by Duke Eiiington

Exhibit 7.3   Sample Multicultural Lesson Plan: Secondary Social Studies

Developing Lesson Plans That Are Multicultural

Subject area: Social Studies   Grade level: 10   Duration: 2 weeks

Teacher's name: Jennifer Carr   Lesson focus: Westward expansion

1. Instructional goal
   - Students will understand key concepts, themes, and perspectives of the westward expansion movement by examining and analyzing maps, art, journals, film, and artifacts in a museum.

2. Curriculum objectives
   (From the CT State Social Studies Standards)
   Students will be able to do the following:
   Strand 1.1–2: Investigate the causes and effects of migration within the United States
   Strand 1.13–59: Demonstrate the importance of viewing a culture from diverse perspectives
   Strand 1.3–19: Assess how a civilization's/nation's art, architecture, music, and literature reflect its culture and history
   Strand 3.1–2: Evaluate the primary and secondary interpretations of a historical event
   (From the National Common Core Standards for History/Social Studies)
   Students will be able to do the following:
   Strand 7: Conduct short as well as more sustained research projects to answer or solve a problem; narrow or broaden the inquiry when appropriate; synthesize multiple sources on the subject, demonstrating an understanding of the subject under investigation

3. Multicultural goal(s)

   - Developing multiple historical perspectives
   - Developing cultural consciousness
   - Increasing intercultural competence
   - Combating racism, prejudice, and discrimination
   - Developing awareness of the state of the planet and global dynamics
   - Developing social action skills

4. Assessment

   Students will be informally assessed using class discussion, checks for understanding, think–pair–share, and teacher monitoring during group activities. Students will be formally assessed on the proposal they construct in groups during the simulation. These will be handed in and graded based on their content and participation in the simulation. The unit will culminate in a formal assessment in which students will be asked to write an editorial for a local newspaper supporting their opinion of whether westward expansion was beneficial or harmful to the future of the United States and why.

5. Instructional delivery/student activities

   1. Students will engage in a "think–pair–share" in which they consider the following questions: What do you already know about westward expansion? Do you think that it was beneficial or harmful to the future of the United States? Students will draw on their background knowledge and start to think critically about westward expansion before learning the content in greater depth.
   2. Students will be introduced to westward expansion through a PowerPoint presentation, which will introduce concepts such as manifest destiny, buffalo soldiers, the Louisiana Purchase, the Missouri Compromise, Andrew Jackson, the Trail of Tears, the Mexican–American War, and so on. As the presentation progresses, students will be asked critical questions and checks for understanding, such as "What drove the settlers and pioneers to move west?" "What implications do you see there being for westward expansion?" and "What would our country look like today had there not been westward expansion?"

(Continued)

Exhibit 7.3   (Continued)

3. Students will examine the painting *Manifest Destiny* in groups. Each group will be given a small section of the painting (one group will be assigned the train, one group will be assigned the Native Americans, one group will be assigned the western settlers, and one group will be assigned the angel). Each group will be asked to discuss and write a paragraph about the story being told in the section of the painting they were assigned, and then present their findings. The class will discuss how these stories contribute to the larger picture of westward expansion, analyzing how these stories compare and contrast and demonstrate multiple perspectives.

4. Students will take a field trip to the Pequot Museum in Mashantucket, Connecticut. Students will visit the following exhibits: "A Pequot Village," "Arrival of the Europeans," and "Mashantucket Pequots Today." Before visiting the museum, students will participate in an activity in which they list all the stereotypes, myths, prejudices, and background knowledge they have about Native American culture. After visiting the museum, students will discuss which of these were confirmed or disconfirmed by the museum.

5. Students will watch portions of the AMC series *Hell on Wheels* from Season 1, Episode 6 ("Pride, Pomp, and Circumstance"). Students will do a character-shadow in which they focus on the perspective of one particular character or group (e.g., Senator Crane, Hell on Wheels residents, Lily, Chief Many Horses, Cheyenne women).

6. The following class, students will participate in a poster potluck. During this activity, students will be given a colored marker correlated with their character shadow and will circulate around the classroom writing a brief response on each of the posters. The posters will ask questions such as "What are the views of your character on westward expansion?" and "What is the traditional role of your character during the time the series takes place?" Students will discuss their conclusions as a class, touching on the many perspectives and roles with respect to westward expansion.

7. Students will engage in a simulation in which they will be separated into groups that represent a range of groups involved in westward expansion. The groups will be given a map and an area of land that will potentially be transformed into part of the transcontinental railroad. The groups will work together to come up with a proposal that outlines their point of view on whether the railroad should be approved or not. They will use all materials, figures, maps, journals, and information that have been gathered throughout the unit to support their point of view. Eventually, the groups will present their proposals and come up with a fair compromise among the groups.

9. As a final assessment, students will write an editorial for a local newspaper of the late 1800s. In their editorial, they will argue whether they think westward expansion is/was beneficial or harmful to the future of the United States. Students must incorporate a variety of perspectives, arguments, and support in creating their editorials.

6. Materials/resources

U.S. history textbook, PowerPoint presentation, westward expansion music, *Manifest Destiny* painting, Mashantucket Pequot Museum, AMC series *Hell on Wheels* and television/DVD player, poster paper, markers, historical maps, historical journals, proposal outline, editorial outline

Exhibit 7.4 shows a sample multicultural lesson plan in elementary literacy.

Exhibit 7.4   Sample Multicultural Lesson Plan: Elementary Literacy

Developing Lesson Plans That Are Multicultural

Grade level: Second   Teacher's name: Kristen De Vizio

Subject area: Literacy   Duration: 60 minutes

Content Standard(s)

CCSS.ELA-Literacy.RL.2.2

Recount stories, including fables and folktales from diverse cultures, and determine their central message, lesson, or moral.

Multicultural Goals

Developing cultural consciousness

- Activities and teaching that help students see and understand issues, concepts, and events from the perspectives of other people

Student Learning Objectives

Second-grade students will be able to examine key details from the text to determine the central message.

Learner Background

- Students have determined the central idea/message from fictional text.
- Students have successfully worked in groups.
- Students have written short stories.
- Students have taken Likert-type scales.

Assessment

Pre-assessment: Likert-type scale (attached)

- Students will complete this scale before the lesson to determine where they stand.
- Students will retake this at the end of the lesson to see if/how their views have changed.

Observation: The teacher will observe students' interactions with one another during the whole group activity.

The teacher will assess students' short stories—the students are responsible for coming up with and writing down the central message/lesson of their story (they will write this down on another sheet of paper to keep it hidden from their classmates).

Materials/Resources

The Sneetches by Dr. Seuss

- Green construction paper
- Safety pins
- Pencils
- Paper
- Markers
- Colored pencils
- Crayons

Learning Activities

Initiation

- The teacher will initiate this lesson by activating students' prior knowledge on how to determine the central message of a fictional story.
- Teacher and students will review the anchor chart created the day before.

(Continued)

Exhibit 7.4   (Continued)

Modeling

- The teacher will read *The Sneetches* out loud to the students.

- Throughout the reading, the teacher will stop at previously determined points.

  o The teacher will model thinking out loud for students to hear the thinking process.

  o For example, "Hmmm . . . if I was a Star-Belly Sneetch I would feel really happy because I think I have more power than the Plain-Belly Sneetches!"

Guided Practice

- The teacher will ask students questions during the reading.

  o At the beginning, how were the Plain-Belly Sneetches treated?

  o How did this make them feel?

  o How did the Plain-Belly Sneetches feel when they got to put stars on their bellies?

  o How did the Star-Belly Sneetches feel when they saw that they were no longer unique?

- The teacher will ask students to determine the central lesson from this story.

  o Students will turn to talk with a partner in order to determine the central message.

  o The teacher will listen and interact with the students to determine their level of understanding of how to determine the central message of a story.

Independent Practice

Activities and teaching that help students see and understand issues, concepts, and events from the perspectives of other people

- This multicultural principle will manifest when students experience the pros/cons of being part of a certain group (as in *The Sneetches*).

- This will allow the students to gain the perspectives of other people and truly experience how other people feel.

- Using *The Sneetches* will allow the students to experience a much more realistic and age-appropriate example of racism that they are able to relate to.

Whole-group activity: The teacher will separate the class into two groups. These groups will be randomly assigned.

- One group will be given green cutout stars to pin to their shirts, and the other group will not have green stars.

- The teacher will create a predetermined list of privileges (lining up first, paper passer, extra center time, homework pass).

  o Those students with green stars will be allowed to choose from the list simply because they are wearing green stars.

  o The other students will not be allowed to choose anything from the list.

- Students will change their roles the following day—the students in the star group will give their star to a student who has not been a part of the star group yet.

- Allowing the students to experience both groups will allow them to experience the reality of how racism can affect their feelings.

○ Students will brainstorm and then create their own short story about the two groups—one group who were unique and had privileges because of their uniqueness and the other one not given privileges because they were not like the first group.

- The following day, the students will read one another's stories and try to figure out the central message/lesson of their stories.

Closure

- Students will gather in a circle on the meeting rug.

- Students will discuss the central message of *The Sneetches* again.

- The teacher will help the students connect between the central message and the underlying multicultural message of understanding and accepting others for who they are.

○ Students will turn and talk to two different partners to be exposed to multiple perspectives.

Teacher and students will review their Likert-type scales—discuss if their views have changed and why they think this may be.

Likert-Type Scale

We should treat people differently because of the way they look.

Awful   Not very good   Good   Really good   Brilliant

Some people are better than others.

Awful   Not very good   Good   Really good   Brilliant

People deserve to have more privileges because of how they look.

Awful   Not very good   Good   Really good   Brilliant

Exhibit 7.5 shows sample multicultural unit/lesson plans in secondary mathematics.

Exhibit 7.5	Sample Multicultural Unit/Lesson Plans: Secondary Mathematics

Subject area: Algebra

Grade level: 9

Duration: One class (80 minutes)

Teacher's name: Amy Langley, Metropolitan Business Academy, New Haven, Connecticut

Lesson focus: Ninth-grade algebra

1. Instructional goal: Students will be able to classify correlations from scatter plots and write an equation for the line of best fit.

2. Curriculum objectives

   Common Core State Standards
   CCSS.MATH.PRACTICE.MP1 Make sense of problems, and persevere in solving them.
   CCSS.MATH.CONTENT.HSS.ID.B.6.C Fit a linear function for a scatter plot that suggests a linear association.
   CCSS.MATH.CONTENT.HSS.ID.C.9 Distinguish between correlation and causation.

   21st-century competencies

   1. Problem solving and critical thinking
   2. Accessing and analyzing information
   3. Communication and collaboration

3. Multicultural goal(s)

   Increasing intercultural competence

4. Assessment options

   Students will be assessed on a rubric for their communication and collaboration during "Languages of the World."

   4. The teacher will observe interaction and cooperation occurring.
   5. Students will reflect on their experience working with their team.

   Students' knowledge of classifying correlation of data will be measured using an exit ticket with three questions.

5. Instructional delivery/student experiences

Time	Action
20 mins	Divide students into groups of four. Create heterogeneous groups by skill, ability, gender, race, and ethnicity. Consciously separate groups of friends to work on improving students' 21st-century skill of collaboration. *Lesson opener:* "Languages of the World" activity from *Get It Together: Math Problems for Groups Grades 4–12*. Students will work together to rank the top 10 languages spoken in 1990 from the options of Spanish, Russian, Portuguese, German, Arabic, Bengali, Chinese, Japanese, English, and Hindustani from the clues given out. Each student receives a unique piece of the problem. *Card 1:* "Although more people speak Chinese than any other language, very few non-Chinese speak it. About as many people speak Portuguese as Arabic or Bengali." *Card 2:* "Japanese and German are each spoken by less than 4% of the world's population. One percent of the world's population is roughly equal to 50 million people."

Card 3: "About as many people speak Hindustani as Spanish. About 200 million people speak Bengali. Your group's task is to rank the top 10 languages in the world in 1990."

Card 4: "Russian and Spanish, both spoken by about the same number of people, are very popular languages. Only two languages—English and Chinese—are spoken by more."

Extra clues, if modification or hint is needed, can be handed out during the activity.

Card 5: "We believe that the people of the world speak about 5,000 different languages. While English is the official language of India, Hindustani and Bengali are very common languages there. And more Indians speak Hindustani than Bengali.

Card 6: "Most of the world's roughly 200 million speakers of Portuguese live in Brazil. Attempts have been made to devise international languages—such as Esperanto—that are easy to learn and to speak, but they have not caught on."

Rules:

1. Only the student handed the card can read from it.

2. Students must ask all group members their question before asking the teacher.

3. Only one person can speak at a time.

4. Students must share their insight to solve the problem.

The teacher will monitor the room by walking around from group to group and answer any questions the whole group has. The teacher will note how students interacted with one another on the communication and collaboration rubric.

10 min	Discuss the process, any difficulties/successes in working together, and the top 10 languages. Questions to ask: "Do you think this list is still true today (2018)?" Students can look up the top 10 languages spoken today: "German is no longer in the top 10; what language has replaced it? Why?"
8 min	Students will reflect on their experience working together: "How did your group encourage or mentor one another?" "Can you describe in detail what it was like to work in your group?" "Explain your success or challenges in working with everyone." "Did your group use the time available in the best way possible?"
20 min	Teacher will present a mini whole-class lesson on how to classify the correlation (positive vs. negative, strong vs. weak) of a scatter plot. Notes and several examples will be given on identifying linear association and the differences between correlation and causation. *Note:* Make the connection that students must read the graph in order from the left like we do in English to determine if the data represent a positive (data are trending up) or negative (data are trending down) correlation. Discuss other languages that are read from left to right (Spanish, Latin, etc.) Pose the question "Do you know any languages that are read from right to left? (expect answers such as Arabic and Hebrew).
10 min	*Multicultural extension:* Watch this short video comparing the Spanish and Arabic languages: https://www.youtube.com/watch? v=AOe4mkzBdCs. Even though they are read/written in different directions, they share many similarities. Students can share experiences, thoughts, learnings, and so on. I have students who take Spanish and Arabic in school and are native speakers of both languages. If they are comfortable, they can teach our class how to greet people.

(Continued)

Exhibit 7.5   (Continued)

15 min	Students will practice their skills of identifying linear association of a scatter plot by determining the correlation of the data. They will also be asked to classify data as correlational or causational. Students can work independently or with their partner at their desks. The teacher will move around the classroom, answering questions and monitoring the room.
8 min	Exit ticket Students' knowledge of classifying correlation of data will be measured using an exit ticket with three questions.

6. Materials/resources

Get It Together: Math Problems for Groups Grades 4–12 book	Worksheet for practice
Photocopies of "Languages Around the World" problem (p. 154)	Exit ticket worksheet
	Calculator

Source: Erickson (1989).

EXERCISE 7.1
WRITING A MULTICULTURAL LESSON PLAN

1. Using the lesson plan format illustrated in Exhibit 7.3, create a totally new lesson plan. Do not use one that you have done before or one similar to the examples given.

2. Teach what you normally would teach.

3. Keep it simple.

4. Pick any subject or grade level.

REFLECTING BACK

Developing a curriculum of any sort is both challenging and fascinating in that one must cover important knowledge as well as inspire students to learn.

Questions

1. How much of your culture did you see reflected in the curriculum under which you were educated?

2. What key facts about your culture would you like to see reflected in the school curriculum?

3. What arguments have you heard against a multicultural curriculum, and how would you respond now given what you have learned?

4. Predict what might be the reaction of students to a curriculum that is more reflective of diverse cultures.

PROFILES IN MULTICULTURAL EDUCATION

CHRISTINE E. SLEETER

© Christine Sleeter

Christine E. Sleeter is an author, speaker, teacher, and activist who uses creative work to spark insight about respect for the diverse people who share space in classrooms, schools, and communities and to prompt action for equity and justice.

Her current memberships in various organizations reflect this blend: American Educational Research Association, National Association for Multicultural Education, the Monterey Peninsula branch of the National Association for the Advancement of Colored People, the Central Coast Writers branch of the California Writers Club, and International Association for Intercultural Education.

She is a past president of the National Association for Multicultural Education and previously served as vice president of Division K (Teaching and Teacher Education) of the American Educational Research Association. Her research focuses on antiracist multicultural education and teacher education, and she has developed a new area of study, critical family history.

Her experiences as a high school teacher in Seattle during the desegregation of the 1970s prompted her interest in urban youth and multicultural education and the beginnings of her awareness of social injustices. Since the early 1980s, as a university teacher-educator and scholar, she has published more than 140 articles and 20 books about racial and ethnic diversity, racism, and the intersections among race, class, gender, and disability in education. Much of her work focuses on teachers as they grapple with improving their ability to reach and teach their diverse students. Her recent books include *Teaching With Vision* (with Catherine Cornbleth, 2011), *Critical Multiculturalism: Theory and Praxis* (with Stephen May, 2010), and *Doing Multicultural Education for Achievement and Equity* (with Carl Grant, 2011).

Sleeter has developed several conceptual frameworks and tools to guide educators, such as the one in her best-selling book *Un-Standardizing Curriculum* for designing a multicultural curriculum. She has also produced research and research reviews that have helped in advocacy for racial justice in education, particularly ethnic studies. She came to California as a founding faculty member of California State University–Monterey Bay. There, she deepened the artistry of her teaching, which she conceives as a creative orchestration of students, ideas, and support that enables accomplishments beyond what students believe they can do.

Now retired from the university, she has published her first novel, *White Bread*, and is starting on a second one. *White Bread* plays with what she has learned about multicultural teaching, ethnic studies, and common reactions to these issues, exploring the journey of a White teacher in a school in which about half of the students are of Mexican descent, as she looks into her own identity using the tools of critical family history, which are developed in her blog at http://christinesleeter.org/.

CASE STUDY
THE HOLOCAUST

Key Issues to Be Explored in the Case

1. Understand the process of how to make changes in a school.

2. Learn how to infuse multicultural perspectives into different subjects.

3. Learn how to instill social justice concepts into teaching.

There comes a time in many teachers' careers when the Nazi Holocaust comes up in class, either as part of a formal, prescribed curriculum or in discussion around matters of discrimination. The Holocaust was one of the most horrific events of the 20th century. Thanks to popular books such as *Anne Frank: The Diary of a Young Girl* (Frank, 1947/1952) and movies such as *Schindler's List* (Spielberg, 1993), virtually every schoolchild learns about the rise of the Nazi Party in Germany, the creation of the death camps, and the extermination of 6 million Jewish people and others.

Tom Brunetti was the new curriculum director for a high school. He was aware that, as part of the state guidelines, the Nazi Holocaust needed to be included in the secondary curriculum. In the past, the objective was achieved in history and English classes with coverage of World War II and a reading of *The Diary of Anne Frank*. He was concerned about the rise in anti-Semitism and hate crimes against other groups in the community. He felt that a more concerted effort was needed among the faculty to speak out against bias and discrimination. He also felt that the burden of discussing these issues needed to be spread across the faculty and the curriculum.

With the support of the school administration and the curriculum committees, Brunetti spearheaded a curriculum policy change requiring that the Nazi Holocaust be covered to some extent in each course. He wanted it to be infused into each subject in a natural and meaningful way, rather than taught as an isolated event or mentioned briefly. The curriculum committee insisted that the topic support the curriculum frameworks for that subject. Brunetti began leading in-service work with department heads on how to do this.

As he got started, he began to wonder how he might best incorporate the teaching of the Nazi Holocaust in a variety of subject areas and what kind of advice and guidance he might offer. He came up with a set of brief recommendations for the faculty committees and decided to share them.

Art: (*Hint:* Avoid taking the easy way out by discussing artwork stolen by the Nazis. Think instead of asking students to create some form of artwork that illustrates the horror of the Holocaust.)

Health: (*Hint:* How many calories is the average man or woman supposed to consume in a day? How many calories are there in reducing diets? What was the caloric intake of those in the concentration camps?)

Mathematics: (*Hint:* Think about the math and geometry concepts you normally are required to teach, such as ratios and proportions, percentages, square footage, charting, and Venn diagrams. Use your textbook problems but change the contexts.)

Music: (*Hint:* Avoid taking the easy way out by discussing Hitler's favorite composer or the musicians forced to perform in the concentration camps. Think instead of asking students to bring in or create or perform music that expresses their feelings about the tragedies.)

Physical education: (*Hint:* Again, use the problems offered in the texts, but change the context. Repetitive motion?)

Science: (*Hint:* Teach what you normally teach as concepts in science. How can you change the context? Genealogy? Cloning?)

Discussion Questions

1. Critique Tom Brunetti's initial efforts to help faculty infuse the curriculum in each subject with understanding of the Holocaust.

2. For elementary teachers, what precautions would you take and changes might you make in your lessons in consideration

of age-level appropriateness and the sensitivities of the students?

3. Are some subjects more difficult to integrate than others? In the case of the Holocaust, is this a potentially difficult subject because of a

lack of familiarity with it or difficulty in infusing it across the curriculum?

4. Use the lesson plan format described in this chapter to write a lesson plan for any or all of the subjects listed in the case study.

CHAPTER SUMMARY

A curriculum is the master plan that teachers use to guide their teaching of students. A skillfully constructed curriculum will provide strong academic preparation that is culturally responsive. The following are the critical focus areas.

7.1 Develop the school's curriculum

What is a curriculum? What is the process for developing a curriculum? How does one choose an appropriate curriculum?

A curriculum is the master plan or blueprint listing the courses that a school district feels support state and national standards and the content of what the district feels an educated student should learn.

7.2 Develop a multicultural curriculum

How can educators create a culturally relevant and responsive curriculum? What should it look like?

The content of what is taught to American schoolchildren is a hotly debated topic, one about which there may never be total agreement. Several issues, though, must receive serious consideration. What is taught and how it is taught should reflect the children who are being taught. From a business viewpoint, you must do good market research to develop products that the consumer wants and needs. It is the same with schooling. The curriculum needs to reflect the diversity and the multiple perspectives that are in this country, not just the dominant culture.

7.3 Analyze texts and materials for cultural bias

How do educators select textbooks and other resources that will support students in meaningful and culturally relevant learning experiences? How does one screen for bias in these materials?

Closing the achievement gap will never be realized until we adapt our teaching methods to connect with the cultural backgrounds of our students. To end the generations of failure in school, we must address the many different strategies we can use to engage and excite all learners. Biases must be recognized in both what and how we teach to portray an accurate picture of this country, past and present. An examination of the books, videos, and other teaching materials that are used is needed to eliminate bias and to promote more positive and accurate portrayals of people's lives.

7.4 Write multicultural lesson plans

What are the components and characteristics of a multicultural lesson plan? How does it differ from a traditional lesson plan?

The traditional lesson plan format can easily be adapted to infuse multicultural perspectives, strategies, and materials. Key aspects include adding multicultural goals, multiple instructional strategies, and varied assessment methods. Particular attention is paid to incorporating the cultural backgrounds, experiences, and perspectives of students. Also essential are opportunities for students to interact with other students different from themselves. This will result in more culturally meaningful and enriching lessons that benefit all.

KEY TERMS

acculturation 200

assimilation 200

differentiated instruction 195

frameworks 185

global economy 182

inclusive curriculum 188

APPLICATION: ACTIVITIES AND EXERCISES

Individual

1. Interview someone of another race, ethnicity, or culture to gain insight into his or her experiences, perspectives, and cultures. Think how you would use your new information to adapt a lesson plan to be more culturally responsive.

2. Immerse yourself in another culture for as much time as you can—an evening, a day, a weekend, or longer. Choose one that you know very little about or feel uncomfortable about. You could choose a lesbian, gay, bisexual, and transgender organization or a church, temple, synagogue, or other religious place. Write about your experience. How would you teach about or to members of this group?

3. Using objectives from a textbook of any subject, write a multicultural lesson plan.

Group

1. In teams, select a school with which one member of your team is familiar. Use Banks's (1992) full list of 23 characteristics of a multicultural curriculum to analyze and critique the curriculum and curriculum development process in that school. Summarize your data, and share your findings with educators in that school.

2. Work with three others to create a multidisciplinary plan involving language arts, music, mathematics, and science.

3. Examine a school curriculum and textbooks to evaluate the level of multicultural infusion.

Self-Assessment

1. List aspects of different cultures with which you are possibly not as comfortable. Why do you feel less comfortable with these cultural characteristics?

2. Describe any elements in your school's hidden curriculum that militate against the success of particular students.

3. Design a curriculum model that represents your own philosophical, social, and psychological beliefs.

4. If you had your way, what major change would you make in the curriculum of your school?

ANNOTATED RESOURCES

ANNOTATED RESOURCES

Awesome Library

http://www.awesomelibrary.org

Awesome Library presents 32,000 carefully reviewed resources, including the top 5% in education, in an organized way.

Bill Howe on Multicultural Education

http://billhowe.org/MCE

This is a source for lesson plans, videos, poetry, articles, and more.

Common Core State Standards

http://www.corestandards.org

The Common Core Standards are a set of high-quality academic standards in mathematics and English language arts/literacy. These learning goals outline what a student should know and be able to do at the end of each grade. The standards were created to ensure that all students graduate from high school with the skills and knowledge necessary to succeed in college, career, and life, regardless of where they live. Forty-three states, the District of Columbia, four territories, and the Department of Defense Education Activity have voluntarily adopted and are moving forward with the Common Core Standards.

Instructional Consulting

http://www.indiana.edu/~icy/diversity.html

Indiana University–Bloomington's School of Education presents tips on teaching and diversity plus links to numerous other lesson-planning websites.

Multicultural Lesson Plans and Resources

http://www.eds-resources.com/edmulticult.htm

Use this page to find multicultural lesson plans and resources.

National Association for Multicultural Education

http://www.nameorg.org/resources.php

The website contains links to websites with multicultural lesson plans.

Get the tools you need to sharpen your study skills. SAGE edge offers a robust online environment featuring an impressive array of free tools and resources. Access practice quizzes, eFlashcards, video, and multimedia at **edge.sagepub.com/howe3e**

8 Instructional Approaches Needed by Multicultural Educators

Learning Objectives

Very few teachers finish their teacher preparation programs feeling fully prepared to teach. It takes time and practice to develop a style of instruction that is personally meaningful and effective for one's students. A teacher's instructional methods evolve and change over time as the educator becomes more experienced and learns to adapt to different students and their learning styles. Through your study of and work on this chapter, you will be able to do the following:

8.1 Describe how we teach and how we learn

8.2 Explain popular instructional practices and multicultural education

8.3 Define culturally responsive education

What makes a great teacher? How does one become proficient at teaching? What works and does not work in today's classrooms? In this chapter, we will try to answer these questions. We will review different theories and models of teaching and what we now know about best instructional practices. This will lead us to the theory and practice of culturally responsive education. Here you will learn how to capitalize on the fact that culture affects learning and how to incorporate that into your teaching.

Aaronsohn (2003) suggested that in the past "traditional teaching" had a much stronger focus on passing on content knowledge. Many teachers saw their role as being subject matter experts, while students were to watch and listen. Students spoke only when spoken to, and discussions about the subject with other students was generally limited. This bleak perspective historically has some validity, evident in well-known phrases such as "pouring from the big jug into the little mug," "chalk-talk," and the "sage on the stage." Fortunately, the teaching profession has progressed greatly beyond this era. Aaronsohn praised the more effective teaching strategies that do not interfere with **authentic learning**. Today, much exciting and effective work and research are going on in the teaching profession, and people young and old still seek to become part of the profession (Feden & Vogel, 2003; D. M. Sadker & Zittleman, 2012; M. P. Sadker & Sadker, 2005).

Understanding how students learn is a key step to developing effective teaching practices. Teaching in ways that lead to equitable outcomes for all students is what Nuri-Robins, Lindsey, Lindsey, and Terrell (2012) called *culturally proficient instruction*. The art of teaching requires that we know not only *how* but also *why* we do what we do in the classroom (Arends, 2009; Carjuzaa & Kellough, 2013). Grant and Gillette (2006) outlined three purposes of schooling: (1) preserving and transmitting cultural heritage, (2) selecting and preparing students for occupational status levels, and (3) preparing students for a better society. Nieto (2005), in *Why We Teach*, gathered the stories of 21 teachers who try to answer this question. What they share is a passion for teaching. Nieto goes on to summarize four critical ideas from their stories: (1) not all teachers are "born to be teachers," (2) teaching helps them make sense of the world, (3) helping students claim their place in the world is critical, and (4) becoming a teacher helps one become more human.

> I bring quadruple diversity to the Senate: I'm a woman; I'll be the first Asian woman ever to be elected to the U.S. Senate; I am an immigrant; I am a Buddhist. When I said this at one of my gatherings, they said, "Yes, but are you gay?" and I said, "Nobody's perfect."
>
> —Mazie Keiko Hirono, an American politician serving as the junior U.S. Senator from Hawaii

CASE STUDY
SMALL-TOWN TEACHER

Katy Joan Lee grew up in a small, blue-collar, suburban town in Maine. Her community was not particularly diverse, with just a scattering of people of color. The great majority of her classmates were just like her, descendants of immigrants from Europe long ago, staunch Catholics, and not well traveled outside the state. When it was time to go to college, she chose a school not far from her home. It was the first time she was encountering any significant diversity, and she enjoyed meeting people different from her.

Wanting to see more of the world and realizing how limited her experiences had been with people from other cultures, she accepted her first teaching position in a much larger town just outside Boston. It was going to be her first time living outside her home state. During her interview, she realized that the school district and town were going to be significantly diverse, with students from all over the world, speaking myriad languages. Katy worried about how she would cope with living in such a diverse area,

(Continued)

(Continued)

particularly whether she could make significant con-nections with her students despite her own lack of experience with diverse peoples. She worried that her teacher preparation left her ill prepared to teach students from different cultures. She was going to move and start a new job and life in a matter of mere months.

Your Perspectives on the Case

1. How would you advise Katy to prepare to teach in a vastly diverse school system?
2. What do you think her major challenges are going to be?
3. What specific curriculum, instruction, and assessment skills do you think she will need?

THINKING AHEAD

The history of how students have been taught follows the evolution of democratic progress and societal change in this country. Understanding where we came from will help us understand the practices we need now.

Questions

1. How has teaching changed since you were in grade school?

2. From your experience, what do you think have been effective and noneffective teaching strategies?

3. What effect do you think that civil rights, social changes, and demographic changes have had on the practice of teaching?

4. What conclusions can you draw about the current state of education in the United States?

LEARNING OBJECTIVE 8.1 Describe How We Teach and How We Learn

In *Learning to Teach* (Arends, 2012) and *Teachers, Schools, and Society* (D. M. Sadker & Zittleman, 2012), the respective authors provided brief histories of teaching in the United States that are well worth reading to gain new perspectives on education. To be a teacher in the early development of the country simply meant being literate and male. Education was provided mostly in the form of tutoring the children of the wealthy. Blacks and Native Americans were typically denied the opportunity to attend school. Girls' education prepared them to be wives and homemakers (M. P. Sadker & Sadker, 2005).

Public education began between 1825 and 1850 and consisted of the three R's—reading, writing, and arithmetic. This was in response to the skills needed to work in the jobs at the time. Comprehensive high schools began forming in the late 19th and

© Jupiterimages/Comstock/Thinkstock

Teaching is an honorable profession that requires great skill and knowledge. The evolution of the profession has required more intensive initial and ongoing training and a much more selective process for recruiting people to these careers.

early 20th centuries and included an expanded curriculum in response to a workplace that required more and different types of education. Remember that our economy has moved from primarily agricultural, to industrial and automated, to high-technology and service industries. Our education system must keep up with changes in economics and society.

Research in education has influenced changes in teaching methods and curriculum. Among the many critical issues raised in the landmark report *A Nation at Risk* (National Commission on Excellence in Education, 1983) was the realization that teaching had become a much more complex job. The era of computers plus an increasingly diverse student population called for more and different kinds of training for teachers. The nature of teaching has been rapidly adapting to keep up with changing demographics and social structures. Classrooms are more diverse. Schools realize that education requires more than basic academics; instead, it requires preparation for a global workplace.

Arends (2009) indicated that effective teaching requires at least

individuals who are academically able, who have a command of the subjects they are required to teach, and who care about the well-being of children and youth. It also requires individuals who can produce results, mainly those of student academic achievement and social learning. (p. 20)

The breadth of what students need to learn has expanded exponentially with each decade. Changes in our nation's society and increasing globalization have brought the need for more knowledge about and skills in multiculturalism. We can no longer afford to be insular but must prepare students for lives perhaps very different from the ones they lead. The teachers of today must have a very clear understanding of the purpose and content of education and their role in it (see Exercise 8.1).

EXERCISE 8.1
YOUR BELIEFS

Based on your years as a student or teacher, what are your beliefs about good and bad teaching and learning? Most people have some opinions about what is right or wrong about the education system.

Preparing to Write Your Personal Statement on Teaching and Learning

Consider the following:

1. What exactly is the purpose of education?

2. What is the role of students?

3. What preparation do you think students need in light of an increasingly diverse country and a global workplace?

4. What are your preferred instructional approaches?

5. What should be taught—the curriculum?

6. What is the role of assessment?

After you've written your personal statement about teaching and learning, write a brief statement about how your beliefs informed the kind of teacher you are or want to be and the kind of teacher you need to be.

The Purpose of Education

How do people learn? There are three main categories of learning theory: (1) behaviorism, (2) cognitivism, and (3) constructivism (Arends, 2012; Carjuzaa & Kellough, 2013; Feden & Vogel, 2003). **Behaviorism** focuses on the objectively observable aspects of learning—what you can see as a result of learning. The emphasis is on observable changes in behaviors, skills, and habits that generally happen as a result of some stimulus.

Cognitivism, instead of focusing on behavior as a response to a stimulus, is more interested in understanding brain-based learning and making use of research about how the brain works. Cognitive theorists are interested in changes in behavior but only in relationship to how a person thinks, remembers, and knows. Cognitivism emphasizes problem solving, critical thinking, and higher-order thinking skills.

Perhaps the newest and currently most popular theory is **constructivism**, which views learning as a process in which the learner actively constructs or builds new ideas or concepts. Constructivists are interested in how individuals make meaning of events and activities. Learning, therefore, is the construction of knowledge.

Each of these theories will now be examined in more detail in the context of their relevance to multicultural education principles. Do they support or contradict multicultural education?

Behaviorism

Contributors to the development of this theoretical model include Pavlov (1927) through his classical conditioning experiments, Thorndike (1913a, 1913b, 1913–1914) and his work on reward learning, and Watson (Watson, 1928; Watson & Rayner, 1920) and his research on human learning. B. F. Skinner's (1953) studies of **operant conditioning** have been perhaps the most influential in terms of applications to school settings.

Behaviorism is characterized by a focus on a consequences (reinforcement or punishment) control model. A stimulus is used to create a response. Program strategies such as token economies and behavior modification have been and continue in some form to be used in classrooms. Behaviors are shaped by rewarding desired behaviors for positive reinforcement and punishing undesired behaviors with negative consequences. Skills are often taught in small, sequential steps, such as in programmed instructional models and evident in reading, math, and science kits.

Behaviorism tends to be a teacher-centered approach. Goals and methods for learning are predetermined for students. The "stand and deliver" method of instruction, sometimes with timed schedules, is not uncommon. The lecture or presentation method, direct instruction, and concept teaching are all typical of this approach. Supporters indicate that learning does occur through the use of strategies based on this theory, although critics believe that it supports lower-level thinking skills and discourages students' independent thought and action.

In the behaviorist teaching model, the teacher sets clear and specific goals, gives clear and systematic praise, and recognizes genuine accomplishments readily. The mastery of learning is a key goal. Teachers attribute student success to effort and recognize positive behavior in ways that students value. Efforts are made to provide ample reinforcement when students tackle new materials. A variety of reinforcements are used. Behavioral approaches do shape behavior and work well for teaching small, discrete behaviors.

How students are educated varies among different countries. Teaching approaches vary based on tradition, culture, necessity, and other factors. In many Asian and European countries, for example, teaching has traditionally followed a more teacher-centered, didactic approach. Students from those countries will have more familiarity with that type of teaching. When attending classes in the United States, these students may need some adjustment to the unfamiliar teaching styles.

The behaviorist approach is an effective methodology for teaching at all levels of education when it is used in a carefully planned way. It can be very effective, for example, in educating English language learners; small, sequential steps are reinforced with much feedback, and acknowledgment of success is important. Students who struggle to learn concepts will benefit from clear, precise teaching in appropriate amounts.

Used too much, however, behaviorism reduces teaching to a more teacher-centered approach than is ideal. As mentioned in previous chapters, the overrepresentation of students of color in special education programs is a serious concern. Care must be taken to watch for bias when working with English language learners or students of color so that the overuse of a behaviorist approach does not limit the acquisition of higher-order thinking. The reduction of teaching by some schools to rote methods to achieve higher test scores is one of the tragedies of No Child Left Behind.

The challenge in a multicultural curriculum, then, is to use a variety of strategies that match and support a student's culture and also introduce new methods that advance learning to higher levels. Behaviorism, used selectively and with relevant cultural content, can be combined with challenging and enriching strategies to create a good stepping-stone tool.

Cognitivism

Cognitive theorists are interested in changes in behavior but only in relationship to how a person thinks, remembers, and knows. Cognitivism emphasizes problem solving, critical thinking, and higher-order thinking skills. Children are active agents of learning—making sense of, understanding, and creating knowledge rather than just receiving it. John Dewey (1916), Lev Vygotsky (1978), Jean Piaget (1954, 1972, 1990), and Jerome Bruner (1960, 1966, 1996) are some of the most influential theorists in this field.

Dewey believed that children's thinking is essentially problem solving. Learning is acquired when a student links new information to previous knowledge. Students learn best by being actively engaged in the learning process, instead of being passive recipients. In other words, children are encouraged to discover the learning themselves. Teachers help students focus on the most important information by learning skills such as underlining and taking notes. Teachers also help students organize information in meaningful units and provide students with opportunities to use verbal stories and visual images. They further provide for review and repetition of information and focus on meaning, not memorization.

Several aspects of cognitive learning theory have important connections to multicultural theory. Multicultural education challenges students to think about social justice issues, since the ultimate goal is to be a part of creating a better society. Issues such as racism, sexism, homophobia, and anti-Muslim sentiments are not ignored but are instead incorporated into the curriculum to help students develop awareness of their beliefs and values. Students are encouraged to engage in higher levels of thinking, leading to the development of a much clearer personal belief system.

We learn and understand new things by making connections to something we already know or understand. Sometimes this is done through the use of analogy and metaphor. In the early 1980s, when personal computers became popular and affordable, students new to the equipment saw what looked like a television and a typewriter. In explaining how computers worked, teachers would often describe the hard drive as being like a "file cabinet." Things typed on the keyboard would be saved as a "file" or document, and then these files would be stored in a "folder," just like a paper folder, in the hard drive (file cabinet). These analogies helped students understand the new concepts because they were linked to something they understood.

The key multicultural principle in cognitive theory, then, is the understanding that students of color often do not benefit from a Eurocentric curriculum because it does not relate to their experiences. The file folder and file cabinet example in the previous paragraph would not be relevant to a student from a culture where that office equipment is not used. Teachers must try to understand the cultures, experiences, and backgrounds of their students to help them link new knowledge to their past knowledge. Similar problems can occur even in monocultural European American classrooms when sports metaphors are used with students who do not understand or have knowledge of certain sports. A *hat trick* in hockey, a *free throw* in basketball, and a *mulligan* in golf are not universally understood.

The use of stories and images in cognitive learning is well suited to the understanding in multicultural education that culture influences learning and that learning styles and strengths may vary among cultures. African American students are known to have strengths in oral learning, mainly because of the strong tradition of oral history in the culture. If oral learning is not recognized or valued in the curriculum, these students will suffer.

Constructivism

Dewey (1916), Vygotsky (1978), Piaget (1954, 1972, 1990), and Bruner (1960, 1966, 1996) contributed to the **constructivist theory of education**. In constructivism, learning is an active process in which the learner links new information to prior knowledge. Students are involved in constructing information, not simply acquiring it. Prior knowledge is used to make associations with new learning or information (D. M. Sadker & Zittleman, 2010, 2012).

Students develop multiple strategies for acquiring and assessing information. Teachers create an environment that fosters critical thinking and problem solving, and they encourage student dialogue with the teacher and other students, as in cooperative learning and classroom discussions. In the multicultural classroom, social justice issues are often a focus of education. Teaching using a critically focused method "encourages a minority voice that challenges the status quo" (Cowhey, 2006, p. 13).

Teaching strategies are altered to use students' ideas and responses as the driving forces in the class. Constructivist, student-centered models of learning are more cognitive and require a higher level of thinking from the student. Learning is by doing. The emphasis is on teaching the whole child through activities-based education and cooperation, not competition:

> Classroom settings with students from different cultures, abilities, needs and interests provide rich learning opportunities, in part because they so clearly reflect one of the central tenets of constructivism: There is virtually an infinite variety of ways to know the world. (Marlowe & Page, 2005, p. 111)

EXHIBIT 8.1   **A Constructivist Lesson**

Chances are that as a student you have experienced constructivism or as a teacher you have incorporated constructivist strategies already. The following is a simplified illustration of the differences as seen in a lesson on government and countries.

Common Lesson Plan

1. The teacher lectures on the definition of a country.

2. The teacher describes the components of a country—its people, government, language, laws, constitution, and geography.

3. The teacher leads a class discussion on the components.

4. Students are assessed on their learning, primarily by paper-and-pencil tests.

In the preceding teacher-centered lesson, the teacher determines the method of learning and heavily guides the students.

Constructivist Lesson

1. The teacher initiates a discussion on what constitutes a country, asking for examples from students.

2. The teacher facilitates a group discussion on what students know about other countries—perhaps other countries they have lived in, have visited, or have relatives or friends from. The students are encouraged to discuss their personal knowledge and experiences.

3. The teacher divides the class into teams. Teams are assigned the task of creating a "model country." They are encouraged to include as many aspects of a country as they choose. They must then present what they have learned to the class, using any variety of media they wish.

Comments on This Lesson

From this assignment, students have the opportunity to learn about leadership and teamwork. They are free to engage in learning, using their own experiences and best methods of learning and expression. Imagine an artistic student designing a flag or a musically inclined student writing a national anthem. Imagine a discussion about what laws the country should have. Imagine students designing a model city as an art project, with houses, roads, trees, and so on.

In *Teaching to Change the World*, Oakes, Lipton, Anderson, and Stillman (2012) outlined guidelines for teachers to create classrooms in which "authentic learning" occurs through a curriculum with a focus on social justice: "Teachers and students are confident that everyone learns well; lessons are active, multidimensional, and social; assessment enhances learning; relationships are caring and interdependent; and talk and action are socially just" (p. 196). Teachers should also focus on providing broad and deep access to learning through a constructivist teaching approach and authentic assessment. A constructivist approach is one in which students are active creators and constructors of their own knowledge. Teachers are facilitators of knowledge. The classroom is student centered. Students are encouraged to work cooperatively. Instead of the teacher orchestrating all aspects of what and how students will learn, prompts and scenarios are given out, and students are given the opportunity to learn using a variety of self-determined methods (Exhibit 8.1).

How would you handle a decision by a group not to allow women to vote? How could teachers guide students toward a discussion of the culture, beliefs, values, and customs of this new country? Multicultural perspectives can be raised in this activity, which is enhanced by more active student engagement. The "develop a country model" can be used as a prompt for meaningful discussion. Constructivism helps free students to think on their own and draw on their own perspectives.

Constructivist teaching is one example of how today's classroom teacher is much more involved than teachers used to be with the lives of students, particularly with respect to how students learn. Constructivist teaching incorporates several principles of multicultural education. Teachers, to facilitate learning, need to allow students the freedom to utilize learning from their cultural strengths. Students should not be constrained from using personal knowledge, experiences, and skills to learn.

In summary, all three main categories of learning theory—behaviorism, cognitivism, and constructivism—are fundamental theories that can be used effectively by educators who consider the culture of students. Acknowledging that culture is a powerful influence on how we learn and how we teach is essential. Understanding different cultures and how best to incorporate that knowledge into theories of learning will benefit all students. But multicultural teaching is not just good pedagogy. It is a tool we can use to help students confront bias, bigotry, and discrimination, a critical skill to succeed in today's world. Application of learning theory must be combined with consideration of the diverse lives and perspectives of our students.

Models of Teaching

Now that we have an understanding of basic learning theory, we move on to how those theories are applied in teaching approaches or models. In *Models of Teaching*, Joyce, Weil, and Calhoun (2009) describe more than 20 styles, approaches, or models of teaching. Arends (2012) describe the classification of these approaches based on the instructional goals or learner outcomes, the syntax or process flow of the behaviors of teachers and students, and the nature of the learning environment. These 20 models are divided into four major "families" based on their orientations toward human beings and how students learn. Teachers are not expected to routinely use all 20 models but to develop a level of mastery in 4 or 5 models across the continuum, especially in working with diverse students (Arends, 2012; Joyce et al., 2009). Table 8.1 illustrates the grouping of these models of teaching into categories. As you study Table 8.1, think about how you would infuse ethnic or cultural content into these models.

Now that you have been exposed to an overview of the teaching models, consider the question asked previously about how you would infuse ethnic or cultural content into your

TABLE 8.1   Twenty Models of Teaching by Family

Behavioral systems: Focus on helping students learn basic information and attain skills. Use the concepts of observable skills and behaviors.	1. *Mastery learning:* Teach strategies in a linear fashion, starting from simple to complex, based on the student's individual pace of learning and using material appropriate for the student. 2. *Direct instruction:* Deliver information in controlled units while students respond accordingly. 3. *Learning self-control:* Teach students how their behaviors affect others as well as their own feelings. 4. *Training for skill and concept development:* Help students master new skills by modeling them and having the students engage in repeated practice and coaching. 5. *Assertive training:* Teach students how to express true inner feelings in ways that are not harmful to others.
Information processing: Help students learn how to use and process information and data.	6. *Concept attainment:* Teach students ways to organize data in order to learn more effectively. 7. *Inductive thinking:* Help students learn to find and organize information, give concepts a name, and test the relationships between different sets of information. 8. *Inquiry training:* Help students learn the art of asking questions to gain better understanding of the reasons behind issues. 9. *Advance organizers:* Teach students a method of organizing material derived from lectures, readings, and other media into a comprehensible format. 10. *Memorization:* Most music students know the meaning of "Every good boy deserves fudge." It is a way of remembering the names of the lines in music—EGBDF. The spaces are remembered via "FACE." "My very exciting magic carpet just sailed under nine palace elephants" is just one of the most recent mnemonics used to memorize the now 11 recognized planetary bodies in the solar system: Mercury, Venus, Earth, Mars, Ceres, Jupiter, Saturn, Uranus, Neptune, Pluto, and Eris. 11. *Developing the intellect:* Adapt classroom methods based on the stage or rate of intellectual development. 12. *Scientific inquiry:* Arrange for students to engage in activities in which they develop knowledge and understanding of scientific ideas.
Personal development: The focus is on developing a good self-image, positive self-esteem, a desire for continual self-improvement, and independence.	13. *Nondirective teaching:* Encourage students to become independent learners through your guidance. 14. *Synectics:* This form of brainstorming encourages students to challenge previously unexamined beliefs, shake up how and what they think, and develop new perspectives and understandings.
Personal development:	15. *Awareness training:* Teach students how to develop a better understanding of who they are, how they see themselves and how others see them, and the nature of interpersonal relationships. 16. *Classroom meeting:* Bring students together as a group to collectively develop understanding and consensus on how they will learn as a group and conduct themselves.

(Continued)

TABLE 8.1 (Continued)

Social interaction: The focus is on developing the concepts and skills needed to work in groups, both for social reasons and to learn with others.

17. *Group investigation:* Lead groups in working together to examine social and academic problems using the scientific method for research.
18. *Role-playing.* Students are assigned roles to play and then asked to act out parts.
19. *Jurisprudential inquiry:* Guide students in exploring societal issues. Problems are identified and then examined to understand policy formulation.
20. *Social science inquiry and laboratory training:* Organize students to learn content by working in teams to solve problems while learning more about themselves.

Source: Adapted from Joyce et al. (2009).

TABLE 8.2 Six Instructional Approaches

A. Traditional and Teacher Centered	B. Constructivist and Student Centered
1. *Lecture/presentation.* Three learner outcomes: a. Acquiring and assimilating new information. b. Expanding conceptual structures c. Developing habits of listening and thinking	4. *Cooperative learning.* Three learner outcomes: a. Academic achievement b. Tolerance and acceptance of diversity c. Social skills
2. *Direct instruction.* Two learner outcomes: a. Mastering well-structured academic content b. Acquiring all kinds of skills	5. *Problem-based learning.* Three learner outcomes: a. Inquiry and problem-solving skills b. Adult role behaviors c. Skills for independent living
3. *Concept teaching.* Four learner outcomes: a. Specific concepts b. Nature of concepts c. Logical reasoning and higher-level thinking d. Communication	6. *Classroom discussion.* Three learner outcomes: a. Conceptual understanding b. Involvement and engagement c. Communication skills and thinking processes

Source: Adapted from Arends (2012).

curriculum, keeping in mind that you are doing so to better engage students in learning and capitalize on their experiences and learning styles.

Arends (2012) focused on six models, which he believed to be a much more manageable number for beginning teachers. As illustrated in Table 8.2, Arends further divided these six models into two categories.

As you can see, teaching has become a more complicated process. The skills required of today's modern educator vary perhaps from when you were an elementary student. The skills required have changed because the makeup of our students is much more diversified with respect to race, ethnicity, economic status, language skills, abilities, and other differences. The family, too, has changed, with many of our students living in single-parent and blended-family households, and this affects students' experiences with school and learning. The development of a global economy and a diverse workplace also requires new skills of workers. The role of the educator has evolved from educated tutor of the humanities to highly skilled professional.

LEARNING OBJECTIVE 8.2 Explain Popular Instructional Practices and Multicultural Education

One of the benefits of the No Child Left Behind legislation has been an increased focus on examining how and what we teach, what theories are relevant, what strategies are effective, and what programs really work. This section will look at some of the more popular trends in education and their relationship to multicultural education.

In a study of the achievement test scores of more than 100,000 students, it was found that the single most significant factor in improving education was improving the effectiveness of teachers (Marzano, Pickering, & Pollock, 2001). Quality teaching combined with a quality curriculum is therefore essential for optimization of learning. The criteria for quality teaching have been drawn from the emerging body of literature on constructivist teaching and learning (Brooks & Brooks, 2001; Oakes et al., 2012), a powerful model that, as explained above, is based on current research on cognition and emphasizes meaning making and problem solving. The constructivist model seems to hold greater promise for achieving optimization of learning than does the earlier "behaviorist" or "teacher effectiveness" model, which was too teacher centered.

In *A Theory-Based Meta-Analysis of Research on Instruction*, Marzano (1998, pp. 134–135) described the following nine instructional techniques that should be used by teachers regardless of the instructional goals of a unit of instruction. After the description of each technique, consider its relationship to multicultural education.

1. When presenting new knowledge or processes to students, provide them with advanced ways of thinking about the new knowledge or processes prior to presenting them.

Multicultural connection: A popular classroom activity is the creation of a *Jeopardy* board game to introduce and test knowledge. It is based on the popular American TV game show

© Jupiterimages/bananastock/thinkstock

We know far more now than ever about how best to educate children. It is important to keep abreast of current practices. Learning is a lifelong endeavor for the professional educator.

that might not be familiar to newcomers, younger students, or those less exposed to television. Introducing the concept of the game first, where students must provide the question in response to being shown the answer, would be an important first step.

2. When presenting students with new knowledge or processes, help them identify what they already know about the topic.

Multicultural connection: Many people remember the "food pyramid," now known as the food plate (U.S. Department of Agriculture, 2015) that introduced the public to a proper diet based on U.S. foods. The new food plate is a graphic that breaks a healthy diet into four main sections: fruits, vegetables, grains, and proteins, with a small side of dairy. However, it suggests a mainstream American diet that might consist of bread and cereal for breakfast. Not all students have toast and cereal for breakfast. Have students create their own food plate based on what they eat at home or another culture. Have students compare the similarities and differences between their food plates and the newly prescribed U.S. Department of Agriculture food plate.

3. When students have been presented with new knowledge or processes, have them compare and contrast them with other knowledge and processes.

Multicultural connection: In the *Jeopardy* board game mentioned previously, a follow-up activity might be for students to create new categories of answers based on their own culture or another culture that they must research. This affirms students' cultures and perspectives, as well as creating new knowledge for all.

4. Help students represent new knowledge and processes in nonlinguistic ways as well as linguistic ways.

Multicultural connection: Other cultures have stronger oral or visual traditions than written traditions. Using this technique allows all students to benefit from their cultural learning strengths. For example, in studying slavery in the United States, in lieu of, or in addition to, a traditional written paper describing the tragic era, have students write a poem or song, draw a picture, create a sculpture, or perform a play.

5. Have students use what they have learned by engaging them in tasks that involve experimental inquiry, problem solving, and decision making and investigation.

Multicultural connection: Multicultural education is not only about content but also about process. Creating classroom learning experiences that encourage students to work with others who are different from them helps forge new relationships and cultural sensitivity. For example, have students form pairs or small groups and then immerse themselves in a cultural experience together that is foreign to them all. Students could attend religious services in different denominations, attend cultural events where English is not spoken, or join in a social event sponsored by a lesbian, gay, bisexual, and transgender group. From these experiences, they could prepare a PowerPoint presentation for the rest of the class.

6. Provide students with explicit instructional goals, and give them direct and precise feedback relative to how well those goals were met.

Multicultural connection: This is a fundamental technique for educating English language learners. Teach in small steps, checking for understanding at each step. Have students use a thumbs-up or thumbs-down to indicate understanding.

7. When students have met an instructional goal, praise and reward their accomplishments.

Multicultural connection: This is another fundamental technique for educating English language learners. Students must experience academic success to encourage meaningful engagement. Devise fun ways to acknowledge progress, such as learning how to give praise in multiple languages—good work, *buen trabajo, bon travail, gute Arbeit, buon lavoro, Bom trabalho, dobry praca, tot cong viec.* When students repeat these phrases, they not only learn a little of other languages but also receive validation for their own culture.

8. Have students identify their own instructional goals, develop strategies to reach their goals, and monitor their own progress and thinking relative to those goals.

Multicultural connection: This technique allows students to learn using examples and strategies more familiar to them, instead of always having to follow a Eurocentric curriculum and approach. As part of an economics class, each student must raise half of the cost of a field trip to Washington, D.C. Each student must devise his or her own strategies to meet those goals. This would be in lieu of all students being required to use one fundraising method.

9. When presenting new knowledge or processes, help students analyze the beliefs they have that will enhance or inhibit their chances of learning the new knowledge or processes.

Multicultural connection: Uncovering the biases, prejudices, perspectives, beliefs, values, and understandings of diverse fellow students is an important goal of a multicultural curriculum. There are numerous simulations and other activities listed in this text that would help facilitate this.

We can see that Marzano's theories are not only good pedagogy but also a strong ally to multicultural education when culture and cultural learning styles are taken into consideration. What follows are some of the more common programs in use today.

Differentiated Instruction

It is clear that teachers must focus on the needs of the learner and vary the methods that they use, an approach to teaching referred to as differentiated instruction. Differentiated instruction follows the motto "One size does not fit all" (Gregory, 2008). It is a culturally responsive model that meets learners where they are and addresses their individual needs (D. M. Sadker & Zittleman, 2010, 2012). "In a differentiated classroom, the teacher proactively plans and carries out varied approaches to content, process, and product in anticipation of and response to student differences in readiness, interest, and learning needs" (Tomlinson, 2005, p. 7). Differentiated instruction is linked to best practices and what we know about learners: Content must be personally meaningful, material should be challenging, power of choice is essential, construction of new knowledge is a main factor in learning, social interaction is a key part of the learning process, students need relevant learning strategies, and the creation of a positive emotional climate is central to teaching (Sprenger, 2008). Three key questions need to be addressed as you decide to differentiate:

1. What is the content to be learned?

2. Who will have a problem with it?

3. What do I need to do differently so that everyone can learn it?

Differentiated instruction redefines the role of the teacher to be that of a facilitator of time, space, and activities; an assessor of students; and a person who helps students learn to plan and to assess the effectiveness of their planning. The teacher uses a variety of instructional strategies to help fit instruction to student needs (Glasgow & Hicks, 2003). Students are assessed in multiple ways; assessment is ongoing and guides instruction. Tomlinson, Brimijoin, and Narvaez (2008) in *The Differentiated School* provide case illustrations of how schools can transform into settings using this method.

All students participate in work that is challenging, meaningful, interesting, and engaging. Students often have choices about the topics they wish to study, the ways they want to work, and how they want to demonstrate their learning. Students work in a variety of group configurations, as well as independently. Flexible grouping is evident. Students and teachers collaborate in setting class and individual goals, at the same time accepting and respecting similarities and differences. Assessment also is ongoing, varied, and observant of students in a natural setting, not just in a rigid, formal test situation (Smutny & Von Fremd, 2010).

Note that direct instruction is compatible with multicultural theory because it is important to use a variety of teaching strategies to match the needs of the learner, to use multiple forms of assessment so as to not penalize students based on their culture, to encourage students to use their experiences to make connections with new knowledge, and to foster an environment in which students learn to work with others. It would be an error to assume that direct instruction can be effective, however, without preparation for and education about cultural bias, prejudice, discrimination, equity, and cultural learning styles.

Multiple Intelligences

Howard Gardner's (1983, 1993, 2000) work on multiple intelligences offers a unique model for varying teaching strategies. His theories about the eight intelligences that humans possess provide a valuable approach to developing multiple teaching strategies that can support learning as well as encourage new learning processes in students. Since we all possess these eight intelligences innately, we are strengthened when we can learn using our dominant intelligence and can grow by developing those in which we are weaker.

The theory of multiple intelligences was developed in 1983 by Gardner. It suggests that the traditional notion of intelligence, based on intelligence quotient testing, is far too limited. Instead, Gardner proposed the eight intelligences (see Table 8.3) to account for a broad range of human potential in children and adults.

TABLE 8.3   Multiple Intelligences

Types of Intelligence	Commonly Known As
Linguistic intelligence	"word smart"
Logical–mathematical intelligence	"number/reasoning smart"
Spatial intelligence	"picture smart"
Bodily–kinesthetic intelligence	"body smart"
Musical intelligence	"music smart"
Interpersonal intelligence	"people smart"
Intrapersonal intelligence	"self-smart"
Naturalist intelligence	"nature smart"

EXERCISE 8.2

MY MULTIPLE-INTELLIGENCE TEACHING PROFILE

	Rarely	Sometimes	Often
1. *Linguistic intelligence:* I use the lecture method in teaching.			
2. *Logical–mathematical intelligence:* I teach incorporating mathematics.			
3. *Spatial intelligence:* I use art or visual images in teaching.			
4. *Bodily–kinesthetic intelligence:* I involve students in activities requiring physical movement.			
5. *Musical intelligence:* I incorporate music strategically in my lessons.			
6. *Interpersonal intelligence:* I create activities in which students work with one another.			
7. *Intrapersonal intelligence:* I incorporate self-reflective thinking in activities.			
8. *Naturalist intelligence:* I teach using the outdoors.			

Our comfort level with certain intelligences and not with others can also be seen translating into our teaching styles. We tend to focus on the areas in which we have more comfort. Exercise 8.2 will help you become more aware of where your preferences lie.

Imagine going to the weight room at the gym and doing curls using the dumbbells with just your right arm for 15 minutes. When the time is up, you leave. You come back the next day and then the next day for 6 months, each time just exercising your right arm with the dumbbells. What would you look like? Would your right arm be much more muscular than your other limbs?

Most of us know that in using resistance weights, it is important to achieve some degree of balance so that the body becomes uniformly developed. The same concept holds for exercising the eight intelligences. If we use only one or two of them, then the others will languish and not develop. We can also think of teaching skills in this way: If teachers only incorporate one or two intelligences into their methods, the others will remain dormant, and students who do better using the other intelligences will not benefit. Then everyone loses due to not uniformly developing overall. Table 8.4 illustrates how a teacher might develop lesson plans to systematically ensure that all eight intelligences are used. Complete the chart considering methods you would use.

TABLE 8.4   Diverse Teaching Strategies

	Strategy	1	2	3	4	5	6	7	8
1.	Write and deliver a speech about homophobia.	X							
2.	Interview Vietnam veterans about their experiences.	X							
3.	Create a graphic organizer explaining your family structure.	X							
4.	Chart the diversity in the class.		X						
5.	Create a crossword puzzle.		X						
6.	Develop a new card game based on numbers.		X						
7.	Draw, sculpt, or create other artwork on the Nazi Holocaust.			X					
8.	Create a photo montage of urban blight.			X					
9.	Illustrate a book cover for a novel.			X					
10.	Create a new country using modeling clay.				X				
11.	Collect samples of wasteful trash.				X				
12.	Build/invent a new device for people with disabilities.				X				
13.	Pick a popular tune/song to illustrate homelessness.					X			
14.	Use creative movement or dance to illustrate slavery.					X			
15.	Write a rap, blues, or country song about war.					X			
16.	Role-play male and/or female roles.						X		
17.	Draw political cartoons.						X		
18.	Create a documentary.						X		
19.	Tell your cultural story.							X	
20.	Keep a reflective journal.							X	
21.	Start a listserv.							X	
22.	Collect samples of trash for recycling.								X
23.	Count the stray animals in your community.								X
24.	Use a microscope to examine water samples.								X
25.									
26.									
27.									
28.									
29.									
30.									

Multiple intelligence theories are a natural support to multicultural education in that they acknowledge that we learn in different ways and that different cultures have certain ways of learning that are more dominant. It encourages focusing on learning strengths (understanding your own culture), as well as increasing skills in other ways of learning (learning about other cultures).

Response to Intervention

The Individuals with Disabilities Education Improvement Act, passed in 2004, included specific language that stipulated that schools assessing a student for a possible learning disability use scientific, research-based interventions. The National Association of State Directors of Special Education (NASDSE, 2005) defines Response to Intervention (RTI) as the practice of providing high-quality instruction and intervention matched to student needs, monitoring progress frequently to make decisions about possible changes in instruction or goals, and applying child response data to important educational decisions.

The RTI model emphasizes a three-tiered process of decision making and delivery of services. It flows from Tier I, which is the general good practices of educating any group of children; to Tier II, which calls for using benchmarks to track the progress of at-risk children; to Tier III, which is intensive intervention. RTI calls for a strategic process of evaluating and delivering services. Data-driven decision making therefore is an essential part of this model.

The effectiveness of the RTI model is bolstered when it includes consideration of cultural learning styles. Educational decisions should always take into account the influences of home, family, and culture to avoid focusing on strategies that may not fit with the best learning styles of that culture.

Responsive Classroom

Responsive Classroom has been in existence since 1981 (Northeast Foundation for Children, 2011). Developed by a group of teachers working with elementary school children, this model emphasizes that children learn best when encouraged to excel in both academic and social–emotional skills. There are seven core principles. Learning social skills is a major focus, and this goes hand in hand with the need to prepare students for a diverse, global workplace in which they must be able to work well with others. Process and content are both seen as critical elements, so that teaching effectively is as important as what we teach. From a multicultural perspective, then, a focus on culturally responsive teaching could be meaningfully paired with culturally relevant instructional materials. Understanding children as individuals and knowing and including families from a cultural perspective are Responsive Classroom tenets that match the principles of multicultural education.

Responsive Classroom is commonly used in schools, and the practices should be very familiar to anyone who has spent time visiting elementary schools.

Understanding by Design: Backward Design, also referred to as "backward planning" is a methodology for curriculum development created by Jay McTighe and Grant Wiggins (2005). The central concept is "teaching for understanding." The authors stress the importance of education in the development and deepening of student understanding. This is accomplished when students are provided with complex, authentic opportunities to (1) explain, (2) interpret, (3) apply, (4) shift perspective, (5) empathize, and (6) self-assess.

Extended Explorations 8.1: Difficult Conversations

Studying and fully understanding the impact of major historical events, particularly around social justice, is an essential component of a multicultural curriculum. However, subjects such as slavery, the Japanese American internment, the **Jim Crow** era, and the Holocaust can also elicit very powerful, emotional reactions from students. What safeguards would you put in place to ensure that students, as well as faculty, are protected in terms of their psychological and emotional safety? Develop a set of classroom guidelines for engaging students in challenging dialogues and activities. Be prepared to share your guidelines with colleagues and come to a group consensus about a universal set of guidelines.

Teachers can better assess student understanding when these six facets are applied to complex tasks.

In the three-stage process called "backward design," goals are clarified and assessments designed first. The planning of classroom activities comes next. This results in avoiding what the authors refer to as the common problems of trying to cover everything in the textbook and focusing heavily on teaching that is activity oriented where there is a lack of clear priorities and purposes.

Regular reviews of achievement data and student work, which inform changes in curriculum and instruction, lead to more targeted performance gains. Teachers actively seek feedback from students and their colleagues to adapt approaches to design and teaching.

Research-Based Instructional Strategies That Enhance Student Achievement

Based on an extensive study of the research on instructional strategies that have a high probability of enhancing student achievement for all students, Marzano et al. (2001) identified nine categories of instructional strategies that have a high probability of enhancing academic achievement of all students in all subject areas at all grade levels.

1. *Identifying similarities and differences:* Of the nine categories, this one has been shown to have the greatest potential impact on student achievement. Students are taught to take apart and analyze complex issues by dividing them into like and unlike components. Four specific forms of this instructional category appear to be highly effective in supporting student achievement: (1) comparing, (2) contrasting, (3) creating metaphors, and (4) creating analogies. For this category of instructional strategies to be used effectively, students need explicit instruction. A particularly promising approach to using this category is to engage students in portraying their work in graphic form by using, for example, Venn diagrams.

Multicultural example: Students compare a variety of aspects—demographic data, costs, roles of women, and people of color—of the Vietnam War with the war in Iraq.

2. *Summarizing and note taking:* Research indicates that verbatim note taking is the least effective means of taking notes in class. To counteract this problem, students can be taught new approaches to taking notes that help them analyze concepts and topics. For example, students can be taught to complete an analysis of a subject by determining key points and restating the subject in their own words. Students can be given "summary frames" or sets of questions to use to "frame" the topic.

Multicultural example: Requiring reparations from a country defeated in war is not uncommon. Germany made payments to the victims of World War II. Should African Americans receive compensation for slavery? State a summary of the issue, and provide arguments for and against.

3. *Reinforcing effort and providing recognition:* Teachers focus on helping students understand the importance of making good efforts and specifically show the connection between students' efforts and their achievement. This may necessitate the use of an effort rubric along with an achievement rubric.

Multicultural example: Have students work with a variety of partners, varying by sex, race, and religion.

4. *Homework and practice:* Teachers educate children, through a clear policy, on the value of homework. Homework should be meaningful assignments that are given to extend learning beyond the classroom. The purpose of homework is clearly articulated, and feedback is detailed and meaningful.

Multicultural example: Establish study buddies or homework partners, varying by sex, race, and religion.

5. *Nonlinguistic representations:* This category of strategies follows the theory that knowledge is captured in two forms—linguistic and visual. The more students experience both forms in the classroom, the more knowledge they will retain. Useful activities include creating graphic representations, making physical models, drawing pictures, and engaging in kinesthetic activity.

Multicultural example: Have students illustrate the evil of the Holocaust through an artistic representation in any form.

6. *Cooperative learning:* Students are placed into groups to work together in supportive ways. This enhances learning as well as develops social and communication skills. The key elements are positive interdependence, face-to-face interaction, individual and group accountability, interpersonal and small-group skills, and group processing.

Multicultural example: Create multicultural triads, and assign each person at different times to be the leader.

7. *Setting objectives and providing feedback:* Create a broad goal, and then work with students to identify specific objectives that are of interest to them. By narrowing down their objectives, students personalize teacher goals. Feedback should be corrective and specific to meeting the stated standards or expectations. A powerful feedback tool is a rubric.

Multicultural example: Create groupings that bring together students of different racial, religious, economic, and social backgrounds. Have them identify specific objectives that are of interest to them.

8. *Generating and testing hypotheses:* Teachers present a problem or situation to students based on a premise or hypothesis. Students, in turn, develop solutions or conclusions and justify them.

Multicultural example: The U.S. Congress consists mainly of wealthy European American men. Have students discuss the merits and drawbacks of this reality. Develop solutions or conclusions, and justify them.

9. *Cues, questions, and advance organizers:* Teachers use highly analytical cues, questions, and advance organizers with students to prepare them for new learning activities. Examples of advance organizers are telling stories, having the students skim a passage, using graphics, and describing new content.

Multicultural example: In a bilingual, English as a second language, or dual-immersion language class, present the lesson written or spoken in two languages. Require students to work in groups to decipher the lesson and complete it.

Schools will often adopt one instructional methodology to provide a consistent curriculum across grade levels and subject areas. External experts usually provide intensive professional development in preparation for implementation. Parents are usually informed of the program so that it has their support.

LEARNING OBJECTIVE 8.3 Define Culturally Responsive Education

Being technically proficient at teaching and being a subject matter expert are important but not sufficient unless teachers appreciate and understand how to incorporate the cultures, experiences, and needs of their students into their classrooms (Darling-Hammond & Bransford, 2005).

Geneva Gay (2018) stressed that culturally relevant pedagogy is imperative because it uses

> the cultural knowledge, prior experiences, frames of reference, and performance styles of ethnically diverse students to make learning more relevant to and effective for them. It teaches *to and through* strengths of these students. . . . It *is validating and affirming*. (p. 31)

Gay (2018) identified the power of caring as one of the most important components of culturally relevant pedagogy.

Culturally relevant education (CRE) was coined by Gloria Ladson-Billings (2009) to describe "a pedagogy that empowers students intellectually, socially, emotionally, and politically by using cultural referents to impart knowledge, skills, and attitudes" (p. 20).

A multicultural educator knows that culture influences learning. Years of research and practice tell us that the effective teacher uses a student's experiences to help make important connections to what needs to be learned and understood.

© Digital vision/digital vision/ thinkstock

Participating in culturally relevant teaching essentially means that teachers create a bridge between students' home and school lives, while still meeting the expectations of district and state curricular requirements. Culturally relevant teaching uses the backgrounds, knowledge, and experiences of students to inform the teacher's lessons and methodology.

According to Ladson-Billings (2009), CRE has three criteria:

1. *Students must experience academic success.* Teachers must believe that all students are capable of academic success.

2. *Students must develop and/or maintain cultural competence.* Teachers must focus on developing cultural competence while encouraging students to learn to maintain their "cultural integrity."

3. *Students must develop a critical consciousness through which they challenge the status quo of the current social order.* Students are taught to become active and show deep interest in societal matters.

CRE recognizes that all students are cultural beings, that is, that they reflect a variety of ways of being in the world. While culture does not define or determine individuals, it does influence how they view and participate in the world, including how they learn. This recognition has important implications for school and classroom practices and policies. For one, it means that curriculum should reflect the rich cultural heritage and history of all students without falling into simplistic or formulaic definitions of culture. It also implies that teachers must be aware of their students' histories and community strengths. Support for CRE means taking into account the various styles and strategies that students employ for learning, styles that are influenced by their individual personalities, cultural backgrounds, and life experiences. As a result, teachers employ multiple pedagogical strategies so that students of all backgrounds learn in ways that are most comfortable for them while also expanding their learning repertoires. Assessment, a key element of learning, builds on the prior knowledge, culture, and language of all students. Rather than neglecting these elements of students' lives as superfluous to the teaching and learning experience, CRE recognizes them as fundamental to learning. As a result, classroom and schoolwide traditions, values, and practices reflect respect for family and community assets, including students' native languages, cultural experiences, and family knowledge.

Culturally responsive schools exhibit the traits listed in Exhibit 8.2.

In preparation for today's global workplace, CRE better prepares students academically and socially by understanding their rich cultural backgrounds and using them in teaching and learning. CRE also instills in students a lifelong appreciation for understanding and valuing diverse cultures in all settings of life. In this way, schools can play a strong role in readying students for full participation in a democratic society.

In *Culturally Proficient Instruction*, Nuri-Robins et al. (2012) outlined five guiding principles of cultural proficiency (see Exercise 8.3):

1. *Culture is a predominant force:* Everyone has a culture. It forms our beliefs, values, and behaviors. It determines what kind of person we are and how we interact with others. Teachers must recognize this fact and that the cultures of diverse students may differ dramatically across the classroom and school.

Exhibit 8.2   Traits of Culturally Responsive Schools

- The curriculum content is inclusive, meaning it reflects the cultural, ethnic, and gender diversity of society and the world.

- Students are recognized and treated as intellectually capable, with particular attention paid to those whose futures are most tenuous.

- Instructional and assessment practices build on and legitimize students' prior knowledge, real-life experiences, cultures, and languages.

- Classroom practices stimulate students to construct knowledge, make meaning, and examine cultural biases and assumptions, drawing on the linguistic and experiential resources they bring.

- Within the classroom and school, students practice participating as citizens in a diverse and democratic society.

- Schoolwide beliefs and practices foster understanding and respect for cultural diversity and celebrate the contributions of diverse groups.

- School programs and instructional practices draw from and integrate community and family language and culture, and they help families and communities support students' academic success.

Source: Adapted from North Central Regional Educational Laboratory (1995).

2. *People are served in varying degrees by the dominant culture:* McIntosh (1988) outlined clearly the argument that White males have privileges and advantages over all others. To recognize that students of color do not lead the same lives or have the same status or experiences in life that White, male students enjoy is important for the classroom.

3. *People have personal identities and group identities:* In *Why Are All the Black Kids Sitting Together in the Cafeteria? And Other Conversations About Race,* Tatum (2003) discussed the importance of students' need to develop a cultural identity. Teachers must treat students as individuals while recognizing that identification with their cultural groups is often an evolving process.

4. *Diversity within cultures is vast and significant:* Not all stereotypes are entirely true, nor are they accurate for all people within that group. Vast differences can apply. Teachers must take care in making assumptions about students and their cultures. First, second, third, and more generations of Americans vary and evolve, while often still sharing common cultural traits and traditions.

5. *Each group has unique cultural needs:* The educational needs of students vary depending on their cultural backgrounds. For students of some cultures, linear, concrete teaching methods are preferred. Others understand better through random, abstract ideas. For others, a blend is needed. Respecting cultural educational needs is essential for the teacher.

Nuri-Robins et al. (2012) also described five essential elements of cultural proficiency: (1) assessing culture, (2) valuing diversity, (3) managing the dynamics of difference, (4) adapting to diversity, and (5) institutionalizing cultural knowledge.

EXERCISE 8.3
FIVE GUIDING PRINCIPLES OF CULTURAL PROFICIENCY

Using Nuri-Robins et al.'s (2012) five guiding principles, work with a partner to answer and share your answers to the following:

1. Culture is a predominant force. Everyone has a culture. Give examples of the beliefs, values, and behaviors of your culture. How do they match or differ from those of your partner?

2. People are served in varying degrees by the dominant culture. What experiences have you had that illustrate how some have privileges and advantages over all others?

3. People have personal identities and group identities. Where do you sit when you go to the cafeteria? Who do you sit with and why? Who do you not sit with and why? What other groups have you noticed?

4. Diversity within cultures is vast and significant. What stereotypes come with your culture?

5. Each group has unique cultural needs. Describe your educational needs in a cultural context. How do they differ from those of other people you know?

Ladson-Billings (2009) incorporated knowledge about multicultural education into six practices of culturally responsive teaching:

1. Teachers focus attention on students from traditionally **marginalized** backgrounds, who are also at the most risk of failing, so that they can become empowered intellectual leaders in the classroom.

2. Teachers involve students meaningfully and fully in the learning community instead of teaching them in isolated ways.

3. Teachers acknowledge and use students' true-life experiences as a legitimate part of the curriculum. This requires compassion for and understanding of the lives students lead.

4. Teachers view literacy as not only written words but also oral contributions.

5. Teachers and students work together to learn how to overcome the dominant social and political culture in order to succeed. Racism, classism, and other forms of bias and oppression continue to limit the success of many of our students.

6. Teachers realize that the education of students involves more than just the rote mechanics of passing on knowledge. Teachers are also part social worker, part therapist, and part advocate. The unjust lives that students may lead cannot be ignored in the continuum of education. Multicultural education, as emphasized in this text, is about educational equity *and* social justice.

REFLECTING BACK

This text focuses heavily on the importance of understanding students' cultures and incorporating that knowledge into teaching strategies.

Questions

1. What concerns might you have about your knowledge of cultures?

2. Are there cultures about which you feel very knowledgeable and that you are ready to begin integrating into your teaching?

3. What do you bring from your personal cultural background and experiences?

4. Predict the outcomes if the United States continues to educate students to be monocultural and monolingual. Consider implications at the local, national, and international levels.

PROFILES IN MULTICULTURAL EDUCATION

GENEVA GAY

© Geneva Gay

Dr. Geneva Gay is a professor of education at the University of Washington, Seattle, where she teaches multicultural education and general curriculum theory. She is the recipient of the Distinguished Scholar Award, presented by the Committee on the Role and Status of Minorities in Educational Research and Development of the American Educational Research Association; the first Multicultural Educator Award, presented by the National Association for Multicultural Education; the 2004 W. E. B. Du Bois Distinguished Lecturer Award, presented by the Special Interest Group on Research Focus on Black Education of the American Educational Research Association; and the 2006 Mary Anne Raywid Award for Distinguished Scholarship in the Field of Education, presented by the Society of Professors of Education.

Dr. Gay has written numerous articles and book chapters, including the monograph *A Synthesis of Scholarship in Multicultural Education*, and is the coeditor of *Expressively Black: The Cultural Basis of Ethnic Identity* (1987); the author of *At the Essence of Learning: Multicultural Education* (Kappa Delta Pi, 1994) and *Culturally Responsive Teaching: Theory, Research, and Practice* (3rd ed., 2018); and the editor of *Becoming Multicultural Educators: Personal Journey Toward Professional Agency* (2003). *Culturally Responsive Teaching* received the 2001 Outstanding Writing Award from the American Association of Colleges for Teacher

Education and is considered to be one of the classic texts in multicultural education. The book emphasizes that ethnically diverse students can improve academically in school through culturally responsive teaching and by equipping teachers in preservice education programs with the knowledge, attitudes, and skills needed to provide such teaching. She is also a member of the authorship team of the *Scott Foresman New Elementary Social Studies Series*. Her professional service includes membership on several national editorial review and advisory boards. International consultations on multicultural education have taken her to Canada, Brazil, Taiwan, Finland, Japan, England, Scotland, and Australia.

Dr. Gay began her teaching career as a high school social studies teacher in an urban school system in Akron, Ohio. When she decided to pursue a PhD, there were no programs in the country awarding a PhD in multicultural education. She had then gone back to graduate school to make sense of her relationships with her Black students. Because multicultural education was not offered, she took up cultural anthropology. Dr. Gay is now nationally and internationally known for her scholarship in multicultural education, particularly as it relates to curriculum design, staff development, classroom instruction, and intersections of culture, race, ethnicity, teaching, and learning.

CASE STUDY
CREATING YOUR DREAM SCHOOL

Key Issues to Be Explored in the Case

1. Understanding how students learn is important in using a student-centered approach versus a teacher-centered classroom.

2. With experience, teachers learn a variety of teaching theories and models, which they can adapt to the classroom based on the students and the subjects taught. Having skills and knowledge in many teaching methods is an asset in being able to adapt to the needs of students.

3. Teachers can be more effective in their teaching by learning about the cultures of

their students and using that information in developing lessons and enriching teaching strategies.

An immensely famous software genius and one of the richest men in the world has discovered your brilliance as an educator. He has given you and your fellow teachers a blank check to create the model school. You have been chosen as one of the lead teachers who will help create the curriculum for your new, ideal middle school.

Your school is in a renovated office building in the industrial part of a midsized New England town. The town is quickly changing from a blue-collar, factory economy to a more residential, small-business

(Continued)

(Continued)

community. Young, professional couples are moving into the town, along with immigrants and refugees attracted to the still somewhat affordable homes and the promise of work. The town is racially mixed and growing. As with many towns, a section is inhabited by more economically disadvantaged people, the majority of whom are people of color. Racial tension is subtle but palpable. There is an undercurrent of resentment in the established residents against the influx of more families of color and limited English ability.

Students will come from all schools within the system. Most have not had a diverse school experience. Most of the community is Protestant, with very little, if any, exposure to people of the Jewish or Muslim faiths. Your school model prides itself on accommodating students of all learning needs, so you expect a certain number of children with special needs. Your fellow teachers will be somewhat diverse and of all ages and levels of experience. Not all positions have been filled, and you have the opportunity to help select the balance of the faculty and staff.

Despite what might appear to be a bleak outlook for other schools, your school is imbued with optimism and a can-do philosophy. The school director and the school board have placed great faith in you and your promise to create a model, culturally responsive curriculum.

Where do you start?

Discussion Questions

1. Where would you look for professional development for yourself and the faculty?

2. What role would parents play in the development of the school? How would you use parents in the future?

3. What would you look for in a fellow teacher?

4. How would you prepare yourself and your students for cultural diversity?

5. What teaching skills do you have that you feel most secure about?

6. What teaching skills do you feel less secure about?

7. What theories of learning do you feel you would want to follow?

8. What model of teaching would you want the school to use?

9. What school policies and procedures would you insist on?

10. What would you do in class on Day 1? Week 1?

11. Write down your action plan, at least the first 10 things you would do in this position.

CHAPTER SUMMARY

In this chapter, we have discussed the instructional approaches needed by multicultural educators. We have addressed several key factors.

8.1 Describe how we teach and how we learn

What do we know from current research on how people learn that is useful for developing effective multicultural instructional strategies?

Not everyone learns the same way. Understanding students' cultures and learning styles is an important step in developing teaching strategies that are culturally responsive.

8.2 Explain popular instructional practices and multicultural education

What instructional strategies appear to hold promise for influencing the academic achievement of all students? What, if any, are the correlations to multicultural education?

There are many popular instructional practices in existence today. Becoming an effective multicultural educator may require choosing specific strategies or practices from a variety of theoretical perspectives. Educators will be successful when they are able to adapt strategies that match their orientation to teaching and learning. Strategies may also differ depending on the students that one teaches. There are numerous styles of teaching that give teachers flexibility in adapting to student needs.

8.3 Define culturally responsive education

How does one teach in ways that respect and capitalize on the cultural backgrounds and experiences of students?

Education goes beyond basic academics to the skills needed to flourish in a diverse, global world. A culturally responsive educator learns to match the culture and experiences of students to teaching strategies that are effective. Sometimes the skills and attitudes needed in the modern workforce may conflict with the beliefs and traditions of students and their families. The skillful teacher knows how to develop a relationship with students and their families so that they understand that their culture is not being disrespected and students are being taught skills that are necessary in the world of work.

KEY TERMS

authentic learning 217

behaviorism 220

cognitivism 220

constructivism 220

constructivist theory of
   education 222

Jim Crow 233

marginalized 239

operant conditioning 221

APPLICATION: ACTIVITIES AND EXERCISES

Individual

1. There are several lists of best teaching strategies in this chapter. Write down your top 10 strategies. Explain why you selected the ones you did.

2. Create a teaching model of your own. What would you call it? What would be the three main foundation statements of your model?

3. Observe several teachers at work. Give a name to the model or models of teaching that they are using.

Group

1. With a group of your colleagues, analyze the teaching that you have experienced in your teacher preparation, from a student perspective. Describe a composite of the teaching models. What name would you use to describe it? What are the strong points, and what are the areas that you would suggest changes in?

Self-Assessment

1. Imagine that you are interviewing for a teaching position. Answer the question "What kind of teacher are you?"

2. Describe what experiences you might have had in school that you could equate with those students whom this chapter has described as "marginalized." If you could go back in time, how would you advise your teachers?

3. How well did your elementary and secondary education prepare you for college and for life in general?

ANNOTATED RESOURCES

ASCD (formerly Association for Supervision and Curriculum Development)

http://www. ascd.org

The ASCD addresses all aspects of effective teaching and learning, such as professional development, educational leadership, and capacity building. It also offers broad, multiple perspectives—across all education professions—in reporting key policies and practices.

National Association for Multicultural Education

http://nameorg.org

The National Association for Multicultural Education is a nonprofit organization that advances and advocates for equity and social justice through multicultural education.

National Association of State Directors of Special Education

http://www.nasdse.org

The National Association of State Directors of Special Education offers strategies and tools to implement best practices through communities of practice, training on current issues, technical assistance, policy analysis, research, national initiatives, and partnerships to enhance problem solving at the local, state, and national levels. It works to engage students, families, communities, professionals, and policymakers as full partners. It engages in ongoing collaboration with the National Association of State Title I Directors.

National Center for Culturally Responsive Educational Systems

http://www. nccrest.org

The National Center for Culturally Responsive Educational Systems, a project funded by the U.S. Department of Education's Office of Special Education Programs, provides technical assistance and professional development to close the achievement gap between students from culturally and linguistically diverse backgrounds and their peers and reduce inappropriate referrals to special education. The project targets improvements in culturally responsive practices, early intervention, literacy, and positive behavioral supports.

Northeast Foundation for Children

http://www.responsiveclassroom.org

The nonprofit Northeast Foundation for Children was founded in 1981 by a group of public school educators who had a vision of bringing together social and academic learning throughout the school day. It is dedicated to helping those who want to learn about elementary teaching that emphasizes social, emotional, and academic growth in a strong and safe school community. It is the sole source provider of the Responsive Classroom approach.

Visit the student study site at **study.sagepub.com/howe3e** for additional study tools, including

- eFlashcards
- Web quizzes
- SAGE journal articles
- Video links
- Web resources
- Assessments from the text
- Access to the author's blog

9 Developing Skills in Teaching Language and Understanding Linguistic Diversity

© Jupiter Images/Brand X Pictures/Thinkstock

Learning Objectives

Being raised monocultural and monolingual places students at a disadvantage when competing for jobs in a global workplace. Failure to master English also creates roadblocks to furthering education and pursuing careers. It is essential that teachers understand the challenges of students whose first language is not English. All teachers need to develop a level of proficiency in working with English language learners.

Through your study of and work on this chapter, you will be able to do the following:

9.1 Describe language proficiency and student achievement

9.2 Explain the characteristics and needs of English language learners

9.3 Demonstrate teaching English language learners from a multicultural perspective

LEARNING OBJECTIVE 9.1 Describe Language Proficiency and Student Achievement

It is widely accepted among scholars and practitioners that teachers must have a solid knowledge of how students learn language (Arends, 2012; Darling-Hammond & Bransford, 2005; Feden & Vogel, 2003; Grant & Gillette, 2006; Kellough & Carjuzaa, 2012; Oakes & Lipton, 2012; Sadker, Zittleman, & Sadker, 2012). In a multicultural country inhabited by students speaking dozens of languages, teachers need to understand the interplay of culture and language and how to best educate second-language learners. This chapter will talk about best teaching strategies, as well as the controversies surrounding bilingual education. No discussion of education is complete without a study of language acquisition. Learning to read, write, and speak English is the cornerstone of a proper education in the United States. Teachers must be knowledgeable and skilled in the process of teaching and learning a language. In any discussion about the importance of educating **English language learners (ELLs)**, one must look at the changing demographics of this country. "In 2000–2001, states reported more than 460 languages spoken by **LEP [limited English proficient]** [emphasis added] students nationwide" (Kindler, 2002, p. 6).

One in five children in the United States is the child of immigrants, and it is projected that by 2040, this figure will rise to one in three children (Rong & Prissle, 1998). Almost 80% of new immigrants are people of color arriving from Latin America, Asia, and the Caribbean, with 75% being of Spanish-speaking origin (Rong & Prissle, 1998).

In U.S. homes, the number of school-age children (ages 5–17) who spoke a language other than English rose from 4.7 million in 1980 to 11.2 million in 2009. This was an increase from 10% to 21% of the students in this age-group. Students who spoke another

> When everyone at school is speaking one language, and a lot of your classmates' parents also speak it, and you go home and see that your community is different—there is a sense of shame attached to that. It really takes growing up to treasure the specialness of being different.
>
> —Sonia Marfa Sotomayor, Associate Justice of the Supreme Court of the United States

CASE STUDY
NEW BEGINNINGS

You have been awarded a grant to live and study for 2 years in Wakanda, a sub-Saharan country in Africa unknown to you. Being monocultural and monolingual, you are excited to experience living in a foreign country for the first time. After finding it on the map, you conduct an Internet search to learn more about it. As you read and learn more about Wakanda, you become increasingly anxious. They speak a language unknown to you. Their history, customs, values, beliefs, religion, and political and social structure are dramatically different from how you were raised—and very confusing to you. You will be living there on your own with no other people from your culture to support you.

Your Perspectives on the Case

1. What are the steps that you would take in preparation for living in Wakanda?

2. How would you go about learning the culture and background of the people?

3. If you have ever tried to learn a language, what were the challenges?

4. What do you think would be the social, emotional, economic, and political challenges of not being proficient in the Wakanda language?

THINKING AHEAD

The United States is an increasingly multilingual country, placing additional demands on schools and educators.

Questions

1. What are your thoughts about the importance of learning a second language?

2. Imagine what feelings and thoughts a student must have when going to a new school where both the culture and language are different.

3. Where might you expect some cultural conflicts, especially as they pertain to language acquisition?

4. What do you think are effective ways to educate students who do not speak English while teaching them the curriculum?

5. What is your opinion of our current policies and practices regarding the education of ELLs?

language at home and had difficulty speaking English at school went from 7% in 2000 down to 5% in 2009. When these students are disaggregated by race, the data reveal that in 2009, 16% of Hispanics and 16% of Asians spoke a non-English language at home and spoke English with difficulty. This compares with 6% of Pacific Islanders, 3% of American Indians/Alaska Natives, and 1% each of Whites, Blacks, and children of two or more races (National Center for Education Statistics, 2011, p. 30). Table 9.1 provides U.S. Census data outlining the most common languages spoken at home.

Note that after Spanish, Chinese is the most widely spoken non-English language in the country, with almost 2.9 million people ages 5 and older who speak Chinese at home. These data certainly have implications for teachers and schools. Our schools are changing

Mastering English as well as another language has become increasingly important in a multilingual country and workplace. The United States must keep up with other countries where learning a second and even a third language is commonplace.

© Jupiter images/Comstock/thinkstock

TABLE 9.1	Detailed Languages Spoken at Home and Ability to Speak English for the Population 5 Years and Over for United States: 2006–2008 and 2009–2013

Population and Language	Number of Speakers	
	2006–2008	2009–2013
Population ≥5 years	280,564,877	291,484,482
Spoke only English at home	225,488,799	231,122,808
Spoke a language other than English at home	55,076,078	60,361,574
Spanish	34,183,622	37,458,470
Chinese	2,455,583	2,896,766
Tagalog	1,444,324	1,613,346
French	1,304,758	1,253,560
Vietnamese	1,204,454	1,399,936
German	1,120,670	1,063,773
Korean	1,048,173	1,117,343
Russian	846,233	879,434
Italian	807,010	708,966
Portuguese	676,963	693,469
Polish	632,362	580,153
Hindi	531,313	643,337
Japanese	457,033	449,475
Persian	359,176	391,113
Greek	340,028	304,932
Urdu	335,213	397,502
Gujarati	301,658	373,253
Armenian	220,922	237,840

Source: U.S. Census Bureau (2012, 2015).

rapidly, and we must plan ahead and adapt. Much as businesses must think ahead, researching and planning to meet the changing needs of customers, schools must do the same. Like businesses, schools provide a service. The service will become outdated and obsolete if the school does not understand its consumers.

Not only is the United States rapidly changing, but also thanks to increased global travel and commerce, countries other than the United States are experiencing similar changes in demographic makeup. How U.S. schools meet these changing needs may well have a direct impact on the economic future and social system of our country.

Not everyone has welcomed our new residents or the way they are being educated. Not all people see the influx of people to this country as positive. Some fail to see the changes as enriching the country. Some lack empathy for those struggling to learn English while attempting to create better lives for themselves and their families. Anti-immigration sentiment has fostered a deep divide in this country. Attempts have been made, but defeated, to enact a federal English-only policy. Several states have passed statewide laws; more than half of the states have made English the official language. Some of the English-only movement is fueled by anti-immigrant sentiment, while others arise from a belief that learning and using one language is a good, sufficient practice. Such movements may serve to devalue a student's first language (Gollnick & Chinn, 2016).

The United States is one of the very few leading industrialized nations that is mostly monolingual. This puts us at a disadvantage as we try to compete in a global marketplace with countries where citizens grow up learning and using more than one official language, countries such as Canada, which has English and French as official national languages; Switzerland, which uses German, French, Italian, and Romansh; Belgium, which uses Dutch, French, and German; Singapore, which uses English, Chinese, Malay, and Tamil; and Spain, which uses Catalan/Valencian, Basque, Galician, and Aranese. Then there is South Africa, which has 11 official languages. And there are many other examples. Children in these countries grow up speaking multiple languages and have the knowledge about other cultures and the ability to adapt to different cultures. Some international citizens are much sought after not only for their language skills but also for their higher level of cultural competence. Americans, slowly overcoming their "ugly American" reputation, are trying hard to maintain equal footing with more cosmopolitan competitors in business.

By not routinely educating our students in a second language, we lose out on the great benefits of learning about other cultures. In school programs in which learning another language is the theme, such as Latino studies or Asian studies, students not only learn how to speak the language but also develop an understanding of the culture. In both Latino and Asian studies programs, students learn the essential beliefs and values of the culture, such as honoring elders and respecting parents and teachers. Traditions, customs, and ways of knowing and being are passed on through a full learning of the language. The failure of many U.S. schools to teach a foreign language places American students at a disadvantage.

By not mastering effective instructional strategies for ELLs, we fail to provide an equal and adequate education for all. Mastery of English is critical in so many ways. People in the United States are judged by their command of the English language. This affects not only job prospects but also social interactions. Teachers must be prepared to educate ELLs in respectful and meaningful ways.

Educating Second-Language Learners

Most educators are familiar with *Brown v. Board of Education*, 347 US 483 (1954), the historic civil rights case whereby the U.S. Supreme Court ruled that the segregation of students based on race was unconstitutional. Another important case dealing with language rights was *Lau v. Nichols*, 414 US 563 (1974), a Supreme Court case brought on behalf of Chinese American students living in San Francisco. The plaintiffs argued that ELLs were receiving an inferior education, thereby violating Title VI of the Civil Rights Act of 1964, which bans discrimination based on race, color, or national origin. The Supreme Court ruled in the students' favor, guaranteeing the rights of English language–learning students. In addition, the Equal Educational Opportunities Act of 1974 (20 USC 1701-1758) protects faculty, staff, and students from discrimination. It further bans racial segregation of students and requires school districts to ensure that ELLs have an equal and appropriate education.

Castaneda v. Pickard, 648 F.2d 989 (1981), outlined that school district programs for ELLs must meet three criteria:

1. The education programs used must be sound.

2. Programs must be implemented with adequate practices, resources, and staff.

3. If the program is determined to not be working, it must be stopped.

Another significant ruling was *Plyler v. Doe*, 457 U.S. 202 (1982), in which the Supreme Court ruled that school districts must educate students regardless of their immigration status. These laws have shaped the type and quality of services provided for ELLs.

The increase in the number of ELLs has brought with it several methods of language instruction, engendering some controversy. Which methods are most efficient and most effective? What kind of special training do teachers need? Making any of the following theories work depends on the preferences and perseverance of educators and school districts.

Students who do not have an understanding of English require **English as a second language (ESL)** services. The teacher does not necessarily speak the native language of the students, and the ESL classroom may have many students speaking numerous languages. ESL instruction can be provided in several different ways.

- *ESL pull-out programs:* ESL students learn in a regular classroom but leave for a short period each day or week to receive specialized ESL instruction or tutoring. They may go by themselves or with a small group of ESL students. Their ESL teacher may support what is being taught in class or teach special lessons. ESL pull-out programs are common in school districts with a small number of ESL students or with few specialized ESL teachers.

- *ESL as a class period:* This arrangement is common in schools where students rotate classes. ESL students attend an ESL class, which may be an elective class or serve as their language arts course.

- *Sheltered English (or content-based English instruction):* Much like bilingual education, subject matter teachers or grade-level teachers teach the standard class or curriculum, which is modified to accommodate ESL students. All the students in the class are ESL students. The teacher teaches all subjects in English according to the theory that while teaching a subject, the teacher also teaches English. Language is simplified, and there is much use of visual aids and hands-on activities.

- *Bilingual education:* In a bilingual program, ELLs all speak the same native language, and the teacher speaks both the native language and English. There are two types of **bilingual education**.

    - In **one-way developmental bilingual education**, students are assigned to classes based on their native language. The teacher teaches both in that native language and in English, with the intent of phasing out usage of the native language as students become more proficient in English.

    - In **two-way bilingual education**, the class is made up of 50% native English–speaking and 50% minority language–speaking students. In a Spanish/ English bilingual program, for instance, half of the students speak English and half Spanish. The teacher must be bilingual and teaches the entire course half in English and half in Spanish. Two-way bilingual education has proven to be very popular for three reasons: (1) ELLs learn English, (2) English speakers learn a second language, and (3) ELLs maintain their native language and culture (Grant & Gillette, 2006).

o   Determining which methods of instruction are used depends on the languages spoken, the number of students, the availability of qualified teachers, and the availability of classroom space. Bilingual education is a hot-button topic, with some claiming that forcing students to learn English while being taught only in English is the best solution. These opponents of bilingual instruction often favor an English-only country and further claim that the failure of ELLs to learn English is the result of bilingual education.

o   Krashen (1998) rebutted five myths about the failure of bilingual education:

Myth 1:   The high dropout rate among Hispanic students is *not* due to being in a bilingual education class.

Myth 2:   The belief that immigrants in the past did well without bilingual education is false. In fact, many came to this country already fluent to a degree in two languages. Also, the need for strong fluency was not as great as it is now.

Myth 3:   The United States is *not* the only country that uses bilingual education. In fact, many other countries have experienced success in its application.

Myth 4:   Bilingual education has *not* been a failure in California. Widespread poverty and lack of reading materials have contributed to students doing poorly.

Myth 5:   The belief that the general public is against bilingual education is based on surveys with biased language and is not supported in fact.

An excellent article, which can be read online, clearly spells out the criticisms of bilingual education and provides persuasive responses. "Bilingual Education: Talking Points" by J. David Ramirez (2012) can be found in English or Spanish on the Teaching for Change website. Ramirez lists numerous assertions versus facts that must be understood by teachers. These assertions are common beliefs raised by advocates of the English-only movement. Three of the most common are listed here in Table 9.2.

TABLE 9.2   Assertions Versus Facts by J. David Ramirez (2012) in "Bilingual Education: Talking Points"

English-Only Assertions	Facts
Bilingual education does not work.	Nationally almost all English learners or LEP (limited English proficient) students receive an English-only program.
The language of this land has always been English.	Not all of the colonists came from England. The early colonists also spoke and provided schooling in German, French, Dutch, and Spanish.
My grandparents were immigrants. They learned English without bilingual education, and they were successful.	It is a myth that all immigrant groups were successful. There were many low-skilled entry-level jobs that did not require advanced language skills.

Unfortunately, many ELL students do struggle to learn English. The success rate of mastering English at levels equal to those of students whose first language is English is not satisfactory. Deterrents such as poverty, social stigma against ELLs, and racism often hinder achievement. Forcing ELLs into immersion in English-only education has often proven to be very detrimental for students, leading to very poor results (Campbell, 2010).

Language Proficiency and Achievement

Thomas and Collier (1997), in a major study of 700,000 language-minority student records collected from 1982 to 1996, reported significant findings on how long it took non-English speakers to reach the proficiency level of native English speakers. Their study showed a consistent effect of how educated students were in their first language.

One study was of a group of Asian and Hispanic students from a wealthy suburban school district who received 1 to 3 hours daily of second-language support per day in an ESL program. These students, for the most part, were able to graduate from the ESL program in the first 2 years at or above grade level in native language literacy. Findings from this group included the following:

- Students aged 8 to 11 years with 2 to 3 years of native language education took 5 to 7 years to test at grade level in English language literacy.

- Those students with little or no formal schooling who arrived before age 8 years took 7 to 10 years to reach grade level in English language literacy.

- Students who were below grade level in native language literacy took 7 to 10 years to reach the 50th percentile, and many never reached grade-level norms.

- From these studies, one could conclude the following to be reasonable guidelines for educating ELLs:
  - Because learning English while learning the curriculum can be difficult, ensure that sufficient time is given to students to learn English. This is particularly important in the early grades but is also important in middle school.
  - Students should be encouraged not only to keep their first language but to continue to develop mastery in that language. Afterschool and weekend language classes are important not only for strengthening native language but also for building appreciation of culture.

Learning a second language can bring with it other benefits, such as employability in a global economy. In addition, research has shown that bilingualism can improve academic achievement. Bialystok and Martin (2004), who had children sort shapes on a computer, revealed that bilingual children were much more adept at the task. Kovács and Mehler (2009) conducted experiments with babies observing puppets on a screen. Some babies were presented with an audible sound and an image of a puppet on one side of the screen. Other babies were given the audible sound and the image of a puppet on the other half of the screen. In later experiments, those babies who were accustomed to seeing puppets on both sides of the screen looked automatically to the other side in anticipation after noticing the first puppet. Babies taught with just one puppet would only look at one side of the screen. The researchers concluded that babies taught with dual methods had a higher order of thinking.

Extended Explorations 9.1: English Only?

How do you account for the positions of those in the English-only movement? Are their positions valid? What do you believe are the driving motivations behind this movement? Should teachers care? What responsibilities do teachers have in this respect?

At the same time, command or mastery of English is a must. Without it, students will face challenges in other subjects. For example, math problems cannot be answered correctly if one cannot understand the written question. Science experiments will bewilder students who do not comprehend what they read. Furthermore, failure to learn to read at an early age leads to a greater likelihood that a student will drop out of school. Subsequently, a lack of a high school education increases the risk of a life working in poorly paying jobs.

One cannot claim, though, that lack of English mastery alone is a major reason for the low academic achievement of many ELLs. As stated previously, the circumstances that ELLs face often contribute to the obstacles holding them back. The sociopolitical context must be understood. Opponents of bilingual instruction and anti-immigrant advocates often make the assertions listed in Exercise 9.1.

Life in the United States when the first major waves of immigration occurred was simpler in many ways. People settled into enclaves surrounded by others from their homeland who spoke the same language and shared the same customs. People seldom moved from these neighborhoods. Jobs were heavily focused on the service industry, farming, and industrial work, and the need for mastery of English or even literacy was not as stringent. Those times changed with increased industrialization and increased ability to travel, which brought a demand for higher levels of literacy. Jobs are no longer plentiful in rote factory work or on farms. The advent of the computer and an international economy are just two drivers of an increased need for literacy. It is understood by all that mastery of English is a must. However, a message that discourages mastery and use of one's native language is clearly biased. Learning fluency in a primary language helps one develop higher skills in a second language (Nieto & Bode, 2018).

How teachers and society view ELLs has a significant impact on their ability and desire to learn and succeed. How well schools structure classrooms and foster an inclusive climate

EXERCISE 9.1

CRITICISM OF ENGLISH LANGUAGE LEARNERS AND LEARNING

Read the following criticisms of bilingual education and try to respond.

Critique	Your Response
1. My parents/grandparents/ancestors came to this country not speaking a word of English, and they did well.	
2. My parents/grandparents/ancestors came to this country and immediately became American by learning to speak English.	
3. When you come to this country, you should stop speaking your native language and just learn to speak English.	
4. Immigrants just don't want to learn to speak English.	
5. If we all just spoke English, there would be fewer problems.	

will foster the confidence of ELLs and create more positive relations with other students. ELLs who are educated primarily in separate parts of the school building, away from their peers, lose an important opportunity to improve their English and make social connections. In addition, other students lose the opportunity to learn more about other cultures. Teachers of ELLs must have knowledge about culture, the process of learning language, skills in adapting curriculum, and understanding of the sociopolitical effects on their students (Campbell, 2010).

LEARNING OBJECTIVE 9.2 Explain the Characteristics and Needs of English Language Learners

Experiences of English Language Learner Students

The popular image of the typical ELL student is of a refugee, immigrant, or other recent arrival who has survived revolution and war in some foreign country. He or she has overcome great obstacles and has arrived on our shores happy to be free in America. In reality, the majority are born in the United States of parents who are immigrants. Of these students, 70% to 80% are Spanish speaking, with the balance speakers of Asian languages (Gollnick & Chinn, 2016). It is not uncommon for these students to come from homes of low socioeconomic status and having parents of limited education. Because of these circumstances, graduation rates are often lower than average.

Schools are often the first place that immigrant children or ELLs get their first full exposure to American culture. This can be both an exciting and fearful experience. It is important therefore that schools are a warm, safe environment. Creating such an environment requires having a good understanding of the culture of students and their needs.

Understanding lives and the challenge as well as the strengths of English language learners can help teachers be more effective in the classroom.

© Creates images/creates/thinkstock

What must it be like to enter a school not knowing the language or the culture? For anyone who has ever tried to learn a new language or traveled to a foreign country and tried to be understood, the experience can be an anxious one. Typical behaviors include speaking very softly or hesitantly or not speaking at all. Feelings of embarrassment or frustration at not understanding what is happening are common. Fear of miscommunication or even panic also arises. These feelings are common in ELLs in school too.

Common reactions to or observations about the American education system and society in general from immigrant parents and students include the following:

- American children are disrespectful and unruly.

- Students do not sit quietly and obey teachers.

- Children lack deference and respect toward elders. In fact, in Mandarin the word for teacher—*laoshi*—translates roughly to "old teacher or prophet." Teachers command great respect, though low pay, in China.

- Parents may not be accustomed to being very involved in their children's education.

- School days are much shorter than they should be, and the school year is not long enough.

- Many students and parents from monocultural societies experience prejudice and discrimination because of race or religion for the first time.

- The Socratic method of teaching typical of American pedagogy, with its emphasis on critical thinking and debate, may be puzzling.

These and many more examples can fuel an anxious and even fearful response in children. The following unpublished exercise, developed by Dr. Chris Hasegawa (1998), Professor Emeritus at California State University, Monterey Bay, is an excellent simulation to help people understand this experience (Exercise 9.2). The authors have adapted it.

Being sensitive to the needs of students who do not fully comprehend English, much less understand European American culture, is an important aspect of teaching. Knowing

EXERCISE 9.2

SPEECKLE ENK

Purpose

To enable students to experience not understanding the language and being taught by a teacher insensitive to the needs of ELLs

Time Required

30 to 45 minutes, not including time for reflection and discussion

Materials Needed

String, plastic bags (grocery bags ideal), scissors, paper clips, pennies

Setup

There are two roles, "teacher" and "student." Students will form groups of one "teacher" for every four "students." Ideally, students who were or are ELL students or who are bilingual will be the "teachers." The students playing "teachers" along with their materials will go with the classroom teacher where the rest of the class cannot hear them.

Directions for the "Teachers"

When you go back into the classroom, I will assign you to be a teacher for a group of four students. You teach in a foreign country where no one speaks English. Your classmates will play students who are recent immigrants who only know English. You will teach them a science class, but you will use a made-up language that I will give you. Do not speak English to them. If they try to speak in English, you may reprimand them by saying "NO ENGLISH!" You will talk in a very loud voice because you think they will understand you better if you yell.

What you will be teaching the "students" to do is to pair up, take a pair of scissors, and cut two equal lengths of string. Then they will cut a square out of the plastic bag. Working in pairs, they will take one piece of string and tie one end to a corner of the plastic square. They will then tie the other end of the string to the opposite corner of the plastic.

Repeat this with the second string. Students will then attach a paper clip where the strings intersect. They will insert a penny into the paper clip. They have created a parachute and are done. Table 9.3 is your script.

Directions for the "Students"

Everyone in a "student" role is an immigrant who has arrived in this country where they speak a foreign language and no one knows English. You are now in a science class. Your "teachers" will explain what you are supposed to do.

Debrief

After the "teachers" have conducted the exercise, process the simulation with these questions.

Questions for the "students":

- How did you like this class?

- What was it like not being able to speak English?

- What did you think of your teachers?

- What recommendations do you have for your teachers?

Questions for the "teachers":

- What did you think of your teaching experience?

- What would you have done differently?

- What are the better approaches for teaching students who do not speak English?

how to help educate these students effectively is a must, not only for bilingual or ESL teachers but also for the teacher with just a few non-English speakers in class.

The number of children who speak a language other than English at home has grown to more than 20% (U.S. Census Bureau, 2009). In these homes, fluency in the native language and in English, as well as native literacy rates, ranges from poor to mastery. Many students

TABLE 9.3   Speeckle Enk

Made-Up Language	English Translation
Speeckle enk . . .	Count off . . .
Fant, feent . . .	One, two . . .
Proop glinkies!	To form pairs!
Fant, feent, fant, feent . . .	One, two, one, two . . .
Chootle fant koonmucs,	Cut one square,
Fant dag ug fant dag,	One unit by one unit,
Et bub gabs.	From the plastic bags.
Chootle feent burfs,	Measure and cut two strings,
Feent dags vin ap.	Two units long each.
Wexle ap burf pom numit queg zet bub koonmuc, pum ot zez.	Tie each string to opposite corners of the square, forming an X.
Serge ot pollywhopper pom bub zez.	Attach a paper clip to the X.
Serge ot quesflipper pom bub pollywhopper.	Attach a coin to the paper clip.
Ot float jobber!	A parachute!

and their parents require assistance. Virtually every school and most classrooms will have students who have greater literacy needs than do native English speakers. This translates into all teachers needing some level of expertise in second-language acquisition training, even when teachers are available with specialized skills and credentials.

All teachers therefore need to have the following:

- Awareness of how culture affects learning

- Knowledge of the cultural history of their students

- Understanding of how to teach English to second-language learners

- Knowledge of how to adapt curriculum for ELLs

- Knowledge of the role of parents in their children's education and how to best work with parents

- Understanding of what comprises a supportive classroom and school culture

Teachers must understand that mastering enough English to reach acceptable levels of academic achievement may take 4 to 7 years (Collier, 1989). Other issues are likewise important to understand. This chapter has focused on immigrant or refugee students, who are traditionally considered ELLs. There are also American-born students who have dialects that need to be addressed carefully and with understanding.

Code switching (moving from one language to another) is popular in many U.S. cultures. Many African American students use Black English or Ebonics, a popular dialect that is often mimicked by White students attempting to sound "hip." The roots of Black English come from African heritages. "Excellent" becomes *phat*. "Glittery, expensive jewelry" is *bling.* "That" becomes *dat,* as in "Dat's a cool car, yo," *yo* meaning "a good friend" in this sentence.

Latinos may use Spanglish, a combination of both English and Spanish in which English words are inserted in Spanish sentences, and vice versa. English words can also be adapted to Spanish versions. What is a *mercado* in Spanish and *market* in English becomes *marqueta. Almuerzo* or *lunch* becomes *lonche* (Smitherman, 1998).

Descendants of French and Spanish settlers in Louisiana often speak a Creole dialect. Such practices have roots in trying to preserve and honor the native language, but such adaptations also raise criticism and concern over the loss of a culture. Language, though, is a living concept. English and other languages evolve over time, influenced by a younger culture and multicultural contacts. Many U.S. students who have taken foreign language courses, such as French, travel to France where, to their dismay, the locals speak a different version of French. People from France visiting Quebec, Canada, a Francophone province, are often surprised to encounter a version of French that has both modernized components while vernacular similar to that spoken in France many years ago.

It is not uncommon for students to be able to code switch between standard English and a dialect. These colorful dialects add richness to American culture. Teachers need to be sensitive to teaching standard English while not denigrating the dialect or the first language. Overcorrection of the use of nonstandard English can cause students to rebel against teachers. There is a time and a place to correct a student using a dialect (Brown, 2002). In fact, strengthening both the first language and the second is a desired outcome.

Muriel Saville-Troike (1978) published an extremely practical summary of a framework to understand the home culture and the classroom. In *A Guide to Culture in the Classroom,* Saville-Troike poses questions for the classroom. Some of the questions she asks are in Exercise 9.3. For each question in the first column, write your response in the second column.

EXERCISE 9.3
A GUIDE TO CULTURE IN THE CLASSROOM

Questions to Ask About Culture	How Could This Information Influence Teaching and Learning?
Family: What is the hierarchy of authority in your family?	
Interpersonal relationships: How is deference shown?	
Communication: What are the characteristics of "speaking well," and how do these relate to age, sex, context, or other social factors? What are the criteria for "correctness"?	
Decorum and discipline: What behaviors are considered socially unacceptable for students of different age and sex?	

(Continued)

(Continued)

Food: What are the taboos or prescriptions associated with the handling, offering, or discarding of food?	
Dress and personal appearance: How does dress differ for age, sex, and social class?	
History and tradition: What individuals and events in history are a source of pride for the group?	
Holidays and celebrations: Do parents and students know and understand school holidays and behavior appropriate for them (including appropriate nonattendance)?	
Education: What methods for teaching and learning are used at home (e.g., modeling and imitation, didactic stories and proverbs, direct verbal instruction)?	

Now that you have completed this exercise, go back and answer the questions again, but using your own culture as the basis for the responses.

LEARNING OBJECTIVE 9.3 Demonstrate Teaching English Language Learners From a Multicultural Perspective

Prophet Muhammad has been quoted as saying "Don't tell me how educated you are, tell me how much you have traveled." Such words of wisdom are meant to inform us all that in our lifelong efforts to become self-actualized individuals, traversing another culture foreign to us is an immeasurably valuable experience. Teachers can help students experience what it must be like to be in a foreign country by using a number of simulation exercises in the classroom. Exercise 9.4 can be a fun way of teaching students how uncomfortable and confusing it can be in a culture that is truly "foreign" to you.

EXERCISE 9.4

THE UNITED NATIONS PARTY

Announce to the class that there is going to be a party at the United Nations and they are all invited. Divide the class into two groups called the "Hosts" and the "Guests." Each person will be given a named tag that identifies him or her as either a host or a guest. Instruct the hosts to stay in the room and discuss the ways they are going to make their guests feel welcomed when they come back to join the party. Take the guests into the hallway or another room and give them these instructions.

Instructions for the Guests

Tell these students, "You are new to this country and have a different culture. When you go back into the room, this is how you are going to behave." Give each student a sheet of paper in which you have written a new "culture" for them. Leave them to practice their new culture with each other while you go back into the classroom to work with the hosts.

Culture of the Guests

PLEASE STAY IN CHARACTER during the interactions. Introduce yourself to three or more people in the room and interact with them sticking to your "cultural code."

1. GREETING: Do NOT shake hands. Touch the person's arm, or hug when greeting people, before speaking.

2. Stand as close to the other person as possible.

3. Always address the person by his or her first name.

4. Pat the other person's arm or back frequently when talking. Laugh and smile frequently.

5. TRY TO FIND OUT about their family, health, children, or personal preferences such as their favorite food, movies, and so on.

6. Do NOT discuss politics, school, weather, world events, or other general topics.

Instructions for the Hosts

Tell these students, "You all have a new culture. When the guests come back into the room, this is how you are going to behave." Give each student a sheet of paper in which you have written a new "culture" for them. Leave them to practice their new culture with each other while you go back out of the classroom to work with the guests.

Culture of the Hosts

PLEASE STAY IN CHARACTER during the interactions. Introduce yourself to three or more people in the room and interact with them sticking to your "cultural code."

1. GREETING: Shake hands when first greeting a person. Other than that, you do not like to be touched. Do not make extended eye contact.

2. Maintain as much distance as possible between yourself and the other person. Keep your eyes mostly down.

3. Do NOT use their name, but address them with a title, as in sir/madam, Miss/Mr., Doctor, and so on, even if you are not sure which title is correct for them. NEVER use their first name.

4. TRY TO FIND OUT details about weather, sports, school, world politics. NEVER discuss a personal topic or your personal opinion. Also, do not ask or answer questions that have a NUMERICAL answer.

5. NEVER smile or laugh. Stay formal and serious. Use only minimal eye contact.

The Simulation

Bring the guests back into the room and encourage the two groups to mingle as they are in a party. After the students have enjoyed themselves "partying," stop the activity. Have the guests exchange the sheet of paper with their new culture on it with a host so that they now each have the opposite culture. Take the hosts out of the room so they can have some time practicing their new culture. Have the students remaining in the room, the guests, practice their new culture. After a while, bring the hosts back into the room and encourage both groups to mingle.

(Continued)

(Continued)

Close the activity by asking a host to pair up with a guest to share what they learned. Then, process the activity as a large group. Some of the prompt questions could be as follows:

1. How did you feel when you were studying your new cultures?

2. What was it like when you joined the party?

3. What did you learn from this exercise? About yourself? About culture?

Anyone who has traveled to a foreign country knows getting to know the language, customs, and history of the people is often just as enjoyable as seeing the attractions. Working with English language learners provides ample opportunities to take what we learn about the cultural background and use that effectively to connect with students.

iStock/Hadynyah

Mastering English involves more than just learning pronunciation, word formation, grammar, and vocabulary. ELLs must also learn to use multiple sentences, make and understand gestures and facial expressions, use verbal and nonverbal communication in context, and facilitate more advanced learning through the use of language (Arends, 2012). Language is not learned effectively in a vacuum. Anyone who has ever taken lessons to learn a foreign language will remember learning the language in contexts or scenarios.

In Spanish you might say, "*¿Como estas?*" (How are you?), but this language would be used with someone you know or with a child. In more formal situations, the correct phrase is "*¿Como esta?*"

As you can see, it would be impolite to use the first phrase in a formal setting or with an elder. Understanding the social context helps guide the language learner to use the proper words or phrases. In schools, the culture often guides the way language is used. For example, did students address teachers in your schools using first names? Did teachers ask parents to call them by their first name or their more formal last name—Ms. Smith or Mr. Jones? In some cultures and depending on how you were raised in the United States, you always address elders and people in authority formally. Students in Jamaica, raised in the traditional custom, are taught to always stand to ask a question or respond to the teacher, and they may be taught to always address the teacher formally. This may seem delightful to most U.S. teachers, but it can prompt teasing from American-born classmates.

People new to a culture may find it jarringly different from what they are used to in an experience known as "culture shock." The intensity of culture shock can vary. Newcomers from a mainly monocultural country, such as Japan, where the majority of people speak the same language and look alike, can take some time to adjust to the United States, where racial and ethnic diversity are very much in evidence and multiple languages are spoken. People in the United States often have the same experience when they move from one part of the country to another.

So in addition to culture shock, ELLs can experience what some call "language shock" on entering school. Unfortunately, these students often have to cope with the intricacies of learning a new language and a different culture while being confronted with prejudice and discrimination (Olsen, 2000). Great pressure to fit in to the school culture can result in developing shame about their own culture and a desire to abandon speaking their first language. Culture and language shock generate not only internal struggles over identity but clashes between child and parents.

Teachers need an understanding of how to navigate these obstacles and help students integrate into the school. Meyer (2000) defines four "loads" or barriers and what teachers can do to offer effective instruction.

1. *Cognitive load:* Teachers identify concepts and skills that students may lack and teach by trying to make connections to a student's past experiences. The "load" is the number of concepts contained in a lesson. Understanding students and being aware of the number of concepts that might be foreign to a student is the key theme. Managing a checking account is an example.

2. *Culture load:* As stated previously, learning a language means also learning the culture. Learning English may be complicated by not understanding the cultural meaning attached to the language. Our textbooks and curriculum are infused knowingly or unknowingly with cultural influences. Some of the language can be culturally insensitive (e.g., "too many chiefs and not enough Indians"). Frequent checking for comprehension is important. Understand that students may be reluctant to speak up or be unclear as to when it is appropriate to speak up. The role of the teacher is to develop a mutually respectful relationship with students and parents so they understand that the teacher has the best interests of the students in mind.

3. *Language load:* Anyone who has tried to learn another language is confronted immediately with vocabulary problems—too many words that are not understood. This problem is evident not only in the books students are required to read but also in the language teachers use. Teachers can provide simpler versions of the reading or explanations of the text. Complicated sentences can be broken down into more manageable parts. The vocabulary in a lesson can be reviewed before students begin the assignment. Teachers can be conscious of shifting their language from simpler to more sophisticated as students progress.

4. *Learning load:* Some classroom activities, especially games, are fast paced and heavily infused with language, with minimal verbal cues. This can be overwhelming to students, who struggle to keep up. Teachers should keep ELL students in mind as

they plan for these activities. Teachers can adapt the lesson for ELL students by giving them extra supports or reviewing vocabulary prior to the class.

This last section is illustrative of the fact that teaching requires caring, compassion, and foresight. The extra effort invested by teachers does not go unnoticed by students.

Language Diversity

People who have traveled throughout the United States or have met visitors from other parts of the country often marvel at the distinct variations on the way English is spoken, the terms used, and even the manner of speech. Visitors to this country must find it amusing and confusing at the same time. Exercise 9.5 allows you to explore this phenomenon.

EXERCISE 9.5
HEARING VOICES

Hear the sounds in your head as you recall the following:

- A slow southern drawl (think of comedian Jeff Foxworthy: "You might be a redneck if . . .").
- The Scandinavian-influenced speech of someone from North Dakota (think of the movie *Fargo*).
- A Brooklyn accent (think Bugs Bunny).
- Someone from Boston (think John F. Kennedy).

Now, how do people from these areas sound?

- New Orleans
- Atlanta
- Los Angeles
- Midwest

Of all the different aspects and elements of the classroom, language is the strongest cultural element (Villegas, 1991). It is important, then, to understand the relationship. In some cultures, girls are taught to defer to boys when it comes to communication. Children may be taught to be quiet in the presence of adults or taught not to question or challenge adults. These practices can create not only conflicts in the classroom but also personal conflict with the student. A teacher may challenge a student in a critical-thinking context, not understanding the cultural taboos against students speaking back. Children can become confused about their cultural identity and struggle to maintain a balance between family traditions and the culture of the American classroom. With these thoughts in mind, we must consider the interplay of language and culture.

Chinese is considered to be a very difficult language to learn. Both Mandarin and Cantonese rely on different tones. Mandarin uses four tones so that a word, such as *ma*, can mean mother, horse, rope, or a question depending on which tone is used. The written language is made up of pictures so that one reads by deciphering a picture. The Chinese word for *tree* looks like a tree with branches extending down. The word corresponding to *mountain* looks like mountain peaks. Many words are more complicated, incorporating two or more pictures. Mandarin speakers point to Cantonese as being difficult because it uses nine tones. To complicate matters more, a simplified Chinese script is used in mainland China, while in Hong Kong a traditional script is used. The difference is somewhat like that between Old English script and modern English.

Not to be outdone, English is also a very complicated language to learn. Americans tend to use slang more than speakers of other languages, complicating matters for students who have learned English from traditional texts. A language learner often translates words literally. This becomes a problem when slang expressions such as "Where is the action in this town?" or "We need to grab the bull by the horns" are used. Finally, there are regional and generational differences to take into account, as illustrated in Exercises 9.6 through 9.8.

EXERCISE 9.6
PRONUNCIATION AND CULTURE

Pronounce This Word	Compare With Colleagues or Classmates. How Did You Pronounce the Word? What Does It Say About Your Cultural Influence?
Aunt	
Wash	
Often	
Schedule	
Supper	
Butter	
Mischievous	
Birthday	

EXERCISE 9.7
REGIONAL DIFFERENCES

Compare With Colleagues or Classmates. What Do You Call the Picture? Why?

© Brand X pictures/Thinkstock

© PhotoObjects.net/Thinkstock

© istockphotos.com/marioloiselle

© istockphotos.com/pederk

What is this called in Rhode Island?

Traffic lights are called "robots" in South Africa. Elevators are "lifts" in England. Napkins are "serviettes" in Canada. Travelers throughout the United States often encounter amusing examples of how diverse American English is. A lunch bag or paper bag is a "sack" in some parts of the country. Exercise 9.7 points out other common differences in what we call things.

Idioms make language colorful, but they are the bane of English language learners and Americans are very fond of using them. In Exercise 9.8, how would you explain the idioms to an ELL?

EXERCISE 9.8
IDIOMS AND THEIR MEANING

Idiom	How Would You Explain These Common Idioms to an ELL?
A drop in the bucket	
A piece of cake	
An arm and a leg	
Bend over backward	
Close but no cigar	
Don't count your chickens before they hatch	
Get up on the wrong side of the bed	
Pig in a poke	
Rule of thumb	
Riding shotgun	
Smell a rat	
The ball is in your court	
To steal someone's thunder	
Water under the bridge	
You can't judge a book by its cover	

As you can see, depending on where they were raised and their cultural background, even Americans sometimes have difficulty understanding each other. A simple greeting such as "Hi, how are you?" that is tossed casually to a stranger can give an ELL pause. Teachers need to have some skill in practical steps to help students learn.

Farr and Quintanar-Sarellana (2005) outlined six helpful teaching principles for supporting language learners:

1. Incorporate students' past experiences, specifically what they have learned about the language and the context in which they learned it. For example, some students may have helped in a family business, so the extent and context of their knowledge of English may be from a business perspective. Greeting customers and negotiating prices may be their working knowledge of the language. Most children, once they feel safe, are very interested in talking about their lives.

2. Learning how to order in a restaurant, how to ask for directions, and how to make small talk are common, practical examples of real-life communication. Students will be more motivated to learn if the context of the learning has meaning and value. Role-modeling, visual displays, and gestures enhance learning.

3. Teach using clear, short segments, allowing time for absorption and feedback.

4. Create numerous opportunities to learn and practice language. Participating in small-group work, calling other students on the telephone while at home, and chatting in the lunchroom are all useful and informative ways to learn.

5. Make the learning fun and supportive. Be clear in your teaching and generous in your feedback. Allow ample time for discussion.

6. Help students learn not only how to speak, read, and write the language but also how they can best go about learning the language. Have students reflect on what has worked for them so they can understand how to help themselves learn better. Encourage students to think about how they think and learn.

A hands-on approach to teaching with frequent checks to ensure comprehension is effective. This, along with developing the basic knowledge in the first language through bilingual education and then ESL, is a proven successful teaching approach (Banks & Banks, 2013).

Schools and the Home

Ask friends and colleagues if they speak the native language of their parents. You might find that a common response is no, or that they might speak the language but cannot read or write it, or that they might understand but not speak it. A common phenomenon is for parents who are not native English speakers to speak to their children in their native language with the children responding in English. Parents speak to their children in their native language because they are more fluent in it. In this way, they help pass on their language and culture to some extent, and they have more parental control over children instead of being at the mercy of the language divide.

This setup has several possible outcomes. There may be tension between parents and children because the children are not sufficiently fluent in the parents' language. Not all parents, especially if they are less educated in their native language, are adept at teaching their children to speak the family language. Unless there are cultural language schools close by, opportunities to learn the language formally are limited. If not many other families in town speak the language, opportunities to practice are also limited.

Then there is the resistance of children to learn because they want to fit in with peers at school.

Teachers must be sensitive to these cultural conflicts and work with students and their families to provide the best possible support. In many cultures, there is a distinction between the role of teachers and the role of parents. Teachers are responsible for the formal education of children. Parents are responsible for caring and raising children and passing on culture and traditions. The two do not mix. Parents who are asked to be involved in school and to help with homework may be unfamiliar with this concept and confused by these demands. Schools, on the other hand, may feel that parents do not care when they do not attend parent–teacher meetings. Furthermore, many parents of ELLs both work, and sometimes a parent holds multiple jobs, making participation in school life difficult. Patience and understanding are required from both sides.

Misdiagnosis

Another area of concern is the overrepresentation of African Americans and Hispanic Americans in special education. Misunderstanding a student's culture can lead to believing that a child has some type of learning disability. When the student is an ELL, the data show that it is "notoriously" difficult to ascertain whether learning is affected by the efforts to learn the language or a true learning disability. This appears more among students who are weak in both their native language and English (Harry & Klinger, 2014).

An example of this difficulty is illustrated by the following test question:
STRAWBERRY: RED

A. peach: ripe

B. leather: brown

C. grass: green

D. orange: round

E. lemon: yellow

The answer seems straightforward unless you know that in Latin America, the fruit called *limon* is green. Hispanic students therefore are more likely to get this question wrong. Understanding a student's background and culture therefore is essential not only to teach but also to evaluate. Lack of understanding of culture is a contributing factor to African Americans and Hispanic Americans facing harsher discipline in schools and being diagnosed with behavioral and mental disorders at higher rates than other peers. Asian American students, because of the "model minority" stereotype, tend to be underdiagnosed for special education and mental health services.

For teachers, an understanding of the native language and culture is an important asset in proper and accurate assessment. In having this understanding, teachers will see their students as capable and not deficient (Valdés, Bunch, Snow, & Lee, 2005). Pang (2001) challenged teachers to view students as having rich sources of culture and knowledge that can be used to facilitate their learning.

Beyond Language: Preparation for a Diverse, Global Society

Beyond the acquisition of language proficiency comes the desire to also prepare students for living and working within a culture in which they may not be comfortable or familiar.

Learning language also requires teaching about the culture. ELLs, people of color, and women have the added burden of having to fit into the world of work that is heavily influenced by European American men. What is critical to remember is that people hire people they like and are comfortable with, in terms of both the work and social setting. In this last section, we will address seven critical social skills and seven essential cultural competence skills that must be included in educational preparation.

Seven Critical Social Skills

Look at the following picture. What do you see?

Have you ever had that experience yourself?

Some of you may know quite well what the issue is—being the only person who is different and receiving uncomfortable looks from others in the room. Women experience that when they enter a room filled with men only. People of color feel this when they walk into a room and suddenly the room falls quiet. For the person entering the room, they had several choices—turn around and leave, go into the room and disappear into a corner, or learn to work the room.

Of all the lessons that we can give to women and people of color, perhaps most important is to learn how to cope with this situation. It is critical, then, that we teach women and students of color seven key social skills that they will need to learn how to fit into the current world of work. For they will have to overcome the facts that people like to hire people that they like and that they are comfortable with, and unfortunately, there are many who do not have enough experience with women or people of color to have a comfort level. Therefore, we must teach these key skills valued in the American world of work since they are often the opposite of what is taught and valued in other cultures.

1. *Speaking up:* People who speak softly are often viewed in the American culture as being insecure and weak. This is, however, a cultural trait often taught to people

Those people who grew up in the 1950s and 1960s probably remember spending hours watching Westerns on television. A common scene is a noisy saloon filled with people. There are glasses clinking, loud arguments, a honky-tonk piano, and the occasional gunfire. Suddenly, a stranger comes to the saloon doors, and the place falls silent. People gaze in awe or contempt at the person entering.

iStock/Creatista

from other cultures as a demonstration of their modesty and humbleness. It is important to teach that although this skill is appropriate and valued in the culture, to succeed in the American workplace, we must learn to speak out in a louder voice.

2. *Small talk:* People are comfortable with people who are able to engage them in conversation. People who are good talkers or storytellers are able to make others feel at ease. This is a skill that must be learned by women and people of color to help others feel comfortable with them.

3. *Smiling:* Smiling is not culturally a common practice in other countries. Americans like people who smile because they look much more approachable. People who have great smiles not only look better but also look more friendly and sincere.

4. *Being assertive:* Assertive, not aggressive, is something that we should teach students. In the American workplace, assertiveness is valued. It is seen in other cultures as being impolite or rude.

5. *Handshaking:* We talk about shaking hands to close the deal. We shake hands to judge a person. A good firm handshake sends a message of confidence and sincerity. For those from other cultures where handshaking is not a common practice, it is important to teach this skill.

6. *Eye contact:* So often we hear about how quaint it is that Asians and Latinos look down to show deference to elders or their superiors. This is true. But it is not seen as a strength in the American world of work. Good eye contact must be taught.

7. *Self-promotion:* Most of us were probably raised being taught not to be a show-off or to brag. However, there is a time and a place when we must learn to sell ourselves. We must learn to state our skills and experiences without hesitation.

One may ask whether this is fair to ask students to fit into a culture that they obviously do not find comfortable. The reality is that the "minorities" have become the "majority" in our schools, and we must learn to adapt. The positive message that we must ensure is that we are not giving up our culture or denying our culture; we are learning how to be multicultural. We have learned how to survive and succeed in our home culture as well as the American world of work. This is a strength. Having a degree from a reputable college is often insufficient for women and people of color. They must learn the key social skills to get the job and to flourish in the organization. Once they rise to the top, they can begin changing the culture of the organization.

Another issue to consider is that students are frequently bullied and harassed because they are seen as different. By teaching students good social skills, they can better relate to all students. Relationship skills are key in forming alliances with others, both in school and in the workplace.

Seven Essential Cultural Competence Skills

Schools and families must help prepare students for a diverse world where cultural competence is becoming increasingly valuable. Cultural competence is the ability to think, feel, and act in ways that are respectful of cultural diversity. For ELLs, learning English is just part of the equation. The business world recognizes that strong academic preparation is inadequate without also teaching people how to adapt and get along well with others. The following are seven cultural competence skills valued in today's society:

Cultural Competence Skill 1: Demonstrates real empathy for the feelings, values, needs, and insights of other people.

Cultural Competence Skill 2: Demonstrates good will. In her or his interactions, is flexible, positive, pleasant, and sincere.

Cultural Competence Skill 3: Seeks out and learns more about other people, including their perceptions and expressions, and how he or she can learn from them.

Cultural Competence Skill 4: Able to deal with ambiguity. Holds off making judgments until essential facts are determined and possible outcomes are assessed. Understands the societal context in which decisions are made.

Cultural Competence Skill 5: Gives praise that is both acceptable and sincere.

Cultural Competence Skill 6: Invites trust by keeping confidences. Tries to avoid embarrassing himself or herself or others.

Cultural Competence Skill 7: Uses creative feedback from others and gives it as well. Uses caution if criticism is necessary.

Good social skills plus cultural competence skills are a must for all students. For ELLs, where home culture is sometimes in contradiction with mainstream American culture, these skills must be learned along with the language. Teachers are cautioned to ensure that students and their families understand that the home culture is not being disrespected, but in actuality, students are learning a second culture that will help them succeed in the world of work. Students therefore learn how to code switch, how to live with a foot planted firmly in two different cultures. That is the essence of being a multicultural individual, to be able to thrive with more than one identity.

REFLECTING BACK

It is clear that the demographics of the country are rapidly changing, with more people of color living here and more people arriving who speak different languages.

1. Name three skills teachers must have to work effectively with ELLs.

2. What understandings do teachers need of the lives of these students?

3. Suggest ways that schools can better serve ELLs. What have you learned are the weak areas? What successful initiatives have you seen or do you know about?

4. Predict what teaching will be like in the next decade or so. What conclusions can be drawn about the skills required of teachers in the future?

PROFILES IN MULTICULTURAL EDUCATION

PHILIP C. CHINN

© Philip C. Chinn

Philip C. Chinn began his professional education career as a special education teacher and then as a special education professor. In 1973, he was asked to make a presentation on Asian Americans at a national conference. Realizing that he knew little about the subject, despite being Chinese American, he began extensive reading on the subject. The effort awakened a realization of how little he understood his own cultural background and the variables that contributed to his own lack of understanding. This experience began his commitment to multicultural issues. He served as the special assistant to the Executive Director for Minority Concerns (now Diversity Affairs) at the Council for Exceptional Children from 1978 to 1984. He was the director of the California State University, Los Angeles Center for Multicultural Education until his retirement. Dr. Chinn served on the National Council for Accreditation of Teacher Education Board of Examiners and as a Commissioner on the California State Advisory Commission on Special Education.

He later served as a department head and division chair in special education at Texas A&M University–Commerce and California State University–Los Angeles, where he is currently Professor Emeritus. He is a senior adviser for the Monarch Center, a federally funded project providing technical assistance to special education faculty of historically Black colleges and universities and other minority institutions. In this capacity, he produced videos of noted educators such as Leonard Baca, Geneva Gay, Beth Harry, and Sonia Nieto, which was a joint effort between the Monarch Center and the National Association for Multicultural Education (NAME).

Chinn is the coauthor with Donna Gollnick of *Multicultural Education in a Pluralistic Society*, 10th edition (2016). He has also coauthored two texts in special education, and numerous textbook chapters. From 1997 to 2001, he served as coeditor of *Multicultural Perspectives*, the official journal of NAME, and also served as the vice president of NAME. In 2002, NAME honored him by naming its multicultural book award, the Philip C. Chinn Multicultural Book Award.

Perhaps Dr. Chinn's single most important contribution has been the writing and publication of the first edition of *Multicultural Education in a Pluralistic Society* in 1983 with Donna Gollnick. Until then, multicultural education was essentially the study of the four non-White racial/ethnic groups. While others had mentioned the importance of various microcultures as they related to multicultural education, their publication was the first to attempt to write a multicultural text devoting entire chapters to ethnicity and race, gender, class, language, religion, age, and exceptionality. By the time the second edition was completed, the field of multicultural education had begun to move in that direction.

CASE STUDY
A CHANCE TO WORK WITH NEW ARRIVALS

Key Issues to Be Explored in the Case

1. The cultural backgrounds of students play an important role in how well students learn English and in what ways.

2. Some of the major barriers to ELLs learning the language are the stigmas of being an ELL, having an accent, being of low socioeconomic status, and discrimination.

3. Using uncomplicated language, checking frequently for understanding, and reviewing vocabulary are just a few of the key strategies to use in teaching English.

After the Vietnam War ended in 1975, the United States took in many refugees from Vietnam, Cambodia, Laos, and other countries that were U.S. allies during the war. Other wars since then have followed that pattern, with families coming from Somalia, Bosnia, Albania, Iraq, Iran, Afghanistan, and more. Your school has received information from faith-based groups and relief agencies that the town where you teach will begin receiving dozens of families from one of these countries.

Among them will be many school-age children. Many will not have been in school for several years, if at all. The girls may be the least educated of the group due to traditions in their homeland. All will be suffering from some type of war trauma. They may have faced many personal family deaths. Some will have medical problems and mental health issues. Some may be orphans. Others may have been forced to fight during their country's conflicts. Others have been harmed physically as casualties of war. The adults, in addition to needing work, will need help learning the language and customs. Some were professionals in their homeland.

You are told that several of these students will be in your class starting in the fall. Your school, much less your town, does not have much diversity among its students or staff. There are no teachers trained to educate ELLs. You yourself have had no training and, other than basic high school French, are not conversant in another language.

You are hearing some townsfolk expressing resentment about "immigrants" moving into the neighborhood.

1. How will you as a teacher, your school, and your community prepare?

2. What resources and assistance will you need?

3. What are your major concerns and how do you think you will manage them?

4. Specifically, what needs to be done to create proper languages services for these students?

CHAPTER SUMMARY

It is clear that mastering English must be a priority in education. It is the cornerstone of a solid education. Along with language proficiency must also come cultural competence. Understanding the cultural backgrounds of our students will help facilitate their learning of language. Key factors to remember are as follows.

9.1 Describe language proficiency and student achievement

How important is learning a language? What debates exist around second-language acquisition? How does language proficiency affect student achievement?

The United States is rich in the number of languages spoken and the number of immigrants living here. Schools must take this wealth of multiculturalism into consideration. The world is getting smaller, generating an increased need for culturally competent and multilingual workers. Mastering language proficiency is a key step toward academic success.

9.2 Explain the characteristics and needs of English language learners

What are the needs and challenges of English language learners? What is the relationship between culture and the learning of language?

Barriers to ELL success are heavily influenced by poverty and a culture of bias. One of the great benefits of being bilingual or trilingual or more is the increased knowledge about other cultures that one obtains throughout the process of learning the language.

9.3 Demonstrate teaching English language learners from a multicultural perspective

What are effective strategies for teaching English language learners? How can culture be infused into the curriculum and teaching methods?

Schools must do a better job of educating ELLs and teaching all children a foreign language. There are multiple ways to teach ELL students, all of which require an understanding of the culture of students.

KEY TERMS

bilingual education 251
English as a second language
   (ESL) 251

English language learners
   (ELLs) 247
LEP (limited English proficient) 247

one-way developmental bilingual
   education 251
two-way bilingual education 251

APPLICATION: ACTIVITIES AND EXERCISES

Individual

1. Shop for your usual groceries at an ethnic grocery store that serves primarily non-English speakers. Write about your experiences afterward. How did the other customers treat you? Were you able to find all your usual groceries? Which of your usual foods did you come across? What was your checkout experience like?

2. Borrow a foreign language program and study it intensely for a month. Then practice using the language in public. How difficult was it to learn the language? Were you able to learn to read and write

as well as speak? How well did you develop conversational skills?

3. Interview someone, either a student or an adult, about his or her experiences coming to this country not speaking any English. What kind of stories does this person have to tell?

Group

1. Work in groups of two or three and interview each other's relatives or friends about their experiences coming to this country not speaking any English. Interview at least two individuals. Compare notes afterward about what you learned. What was different? What was similar?

2. Go as a group to an authentic ethnic restaurant, such as one featuring Ethiopian, Indian, or some less common cuisine. Make observations of how you are treated, any language issues, and the food and culture. If you are in a mixed group, are men and women treated the same?

3. Plan to attend an ethnic festival, such as Greek, Italian, and so on, where there will be vendors that speak another language. Learn 10 or more common phrases in that language. Practice using the language only at the event. Compare notes afterward.

Self-Assessment

1. Can you speak another language? What have been your experiences in doing so? What did you learn about the culture? What did you learn about yourself?

2. What have been your experiences working with or being taught by people whose first language was not English? Did any of them have thick accents? How did that affect you?

3. What is your opinion of English-only proponents and their agenda?

ANNOTATED RESOURCES

Center for Adult English Language Acquisition

http://www.cal.org/caela

The Center for Adult English Language Acquisition was created to help states build their capacity to promote ELLs and the academic achievement of adults learning English.

National Association for Bilingual Education

http://www.nabe.org

The National Association for Bilingual Education is the only national professional organization devoted to representing bilingual learners and bilingual education professionals.

U.S. Department of Education's Office of English Language Acquisition

http://www2.ed.gov/about/offices/list/oela/index.html

Visit the Office of English Language Acquisition for information about the administration of No Child Left Behind's Title III, which governs the education of LEP students.

National Clearinghouse for English Language Acquisition and Language Instruction Educational Programs

http://www.ncela.us

A project of OELA, the National Clearinghouse for English Language Acquisition collects, analyzes, and disseminates information to support high-quality education for ELLs.

Visit the student study site at **study.sagepub.com/howe3e** for additional study tools including

- eFlashcards
- Web Quizzes
- SAGE Journal Articles
- Video Links
- Web Resources
- Assessments from the text
- Access to Author's Blogs

10 Assessment That Is Culturally Responsive

© iStockphotos.com/andresr

Learning Objectives

Across the country, schools and teachers are increasingly held accountable for how well students perform on a variety of assessments, for developing sound assessment practices, and for using assessment data skillfully. In this chapter, these issues and more will be discussed, leading us to a better understanding of the assessment process. Through your work on topics in this chapter, you will be able to do the following:

10.1 Describe the purposes of classroom assessment

10.2 Explain the challenges to the development of quality classroom assessment

10.3 Determine appropriate classroom-based assessments to assess learning by diverse students

In the era of accountability, Race to the Top incentives, and teacher evaluation systems that are linked to student performance on standardized academic achievement tests, assessment of student learning is perhaps one of the most significant and most controversial topics. Assessing student learning is one critical point in the learning triad of curriculum, instruction, and assessment. All three points are integrally linked to each of the others. Student assessment provides critical feedback to students and teachers alike about what students are learning, as well as how teachers are teaching.

Assessment can provide evidence of what students know before they engage in learning a new unit or lesson (baseline information) and then provide information along the way about how they are doing. Done effectively, assessment can be a very useful practice that contributes to teaching and learning. Conversely, done ineffectively, assessment practices and outcomes can contribute to student and teacher frustration, inaccurate data, and extremely poor use of valuable instructional time. Effective assessment practices incorporate deep understanding of culture, of how diverse children learn, and of the role played by culture in the teaching and learning process (Grant & Gillette, 2006; Grant & Sleeter, 2011; Oakes, Lipton, Anderson, & Stillman, 2012, 2018; Sadker & Zittleman, 2012). Teacher capacity to use assessment data in order to enhance instruction is essential. Increasingly, school districts and state departments of education are developing systems for teacher evaluation that include student achievement data.

With this in mind, this chapter will describe the educational assessment process, provide a discussion of challenges to and issues in the development of effective assessments, and provide guidelines and strategies for developing and using assessment practices that support diverse learners.

> If there is no struggle, there is no progress. Those who profess to favor freedom, and yet deprecate agitation, are men who want crops without plowing up the ground. They want rain without thunder and lightning. They want the ocean without the awful roar of its many waters. This struggle may be a moral one; or it may be a physical one; or it may be both moral and physical; but it must be a struggle. Power concedes nothing without a demand. It never did, and it never will.
>
> —Frederick Douglass, letter to abolitionist associate (1853)

CASE STUDY
WHO ARE THE MOST IMPORTANT USERS OF ASSESSMENT INFORMATION?

One day, I was conducting observations in an inner-city elementary school with about 90% Latino students, many of whom were poor, recent immigrants, and second-language learners. The faculty was predominantly White and female. The district had just adopted a nationally well-known reading program that required all students to have a baseline assessment of reading levels.

I interviewed one faculty member, Martina, who had been given the assignment of testing all the students (about 1,000) personally. Martina was a young, energetic teacher who had taught for about 5 years. Near the end of the interview, I asked her how accurate she thought she was in assessing the predominantly Latino population. She volunteered that as an Italian American, English-only-speaking teacher, she might have had a disadvantage but that she had grown up in a neighborhood with many Spanish-speaking families. She indicated that having a basic understanding of Latino culture and knowing some conversational Spanish allowed her unique insights into the influence of culture on teaching and learning practices, including assessment. In the interview, she stated, "Having grown up around Latino families and having some understanding of the language and culture allowed me to be more confident that I can conduct a fair assessment." Without that background, she believed that she would have been less capable of testing the students fairly.

I also asked Martina how she was planning to use and share the assessment data that she had accumulated. Martina paused for only a moment before

(Continued)

(Continued)

stating that several actions would happen next. At the very least, that data would be used to create individual learning plans for each student. However, Martina indicated that she would need to work with the school's data team in order to coordinate additional professional development experiences for the school's teachers. I left very impressed by Martina—and wondered what type of professional development experiences would be needed.

Your Perspectives on the Case

1. Martina believes that it is very important for teachers to have a deep understanding of the relationship between classroom assessment and cultural identities. Describe how your own beliefs about the importance of this relationship are similar to or different from Martina's.

2. What types of professional development experiences do you think Martina is envisioning?

3. Based on the issues described in the case study, define five specific connections that exist between curriculum, instruction, and assessment.

THINKING AHEAD

When people hear the word *assessment*, their immediate reaction most often is one of fear, frustration, and trepidation. In general, the experiences of most people with school-based assessments have been negative. To progress in our discussion of effective practices for diverse learners, please reflect on your responses to the following questions.

Questions

1. What do you think are the most accurate ways of measuring what a student knows and is able to do?

2. How do you know when a student has truly learned something deeply?

3. What are your preferred assessment strategies? Why do or would you use these?

4. What do you believe are the primary purposes of assessments?

5. How can the use of assessment data be improved so that it is more useful in supporting high levels of achievement by all students?

LEARNING OBJECTIVE 10.1 Describe the Purposes of Classroom Assessment

Oakes et al. (2012, 2018) described assessment as a process within which educators gather or describe information about student performance. Student assessment should be designed to support student learning as well as improvements in teaching. If teachers can identify students' academic strengths and weaknesses, they can then enhance their instruction to better meet student needs. Huba and Freed (2000) defined assessment as

the process of gathering and discussing information from multiple and diverse sources in order to develop a deep understanding of what students know, understand, and can do with their knowledge as a result of their educational experiences; the process culminates when assessment results are used to improve subsequent learning. (p. 8)

© istockphotos.com/Christopher Futcher

Defining High-Quality Classroom Assessment

Few issues in education are as controversial and hotly debated as testing and assessment. The teachers of today must have a good understanding of the topic and know how to effectively incorporate it into teaching.

Stiggins and Cappuis (2012) indicated that quality assessment can be achieved when a variety of components are in place. These include, first, the identification of a clear purpose for the assessment. Teachers need to decide, for example, if the primary purpose is to give feedback to students or to provide data to administrative decision makers.

To address the second component, Stiggins and Cappuis (2012) underlined the importance of providing to students very clear ideas, or targets, of what they need to learn and/or achieve. Targets are expectations of what students should know and be able to do. They described five types of targets for students:

1. *Knowledge:* Students have mastery of substantive subject matter knowledge.

2. *Reasoning:* Students use information to solve problems through processes such as comparing and contrasting, classifying, constructing support, analyzing, judging, and deciding on action.

3. *Skill:* Students should be able to do behaviors and skills that demonstrate student use of procedural knowledge appropriately in performance.

4. *Product:* Students create quality products that present evidence that they have mastered foundational knowledge, requisite reasoning, problem-solving proficiencies, and production skills.

5. *Dispositions:* Students demonstrate appropriate attitudes, interests, and motivational intentions.

Quality assessments also call for sound design, which means that teachers understand the variety of assessment methods and choose the assessment method that appropriately matches the intended target. Sound design also means that teachers write assessment questions of all types well and attend to possible bias that can negatively influence assessments.

A fourth component of quality assessments, effective communication, means that teachers effectively communicate assessment results to students and a variety of other audiences, select the best reporting option for each learning target and set of users of assessment information, and use standardized test results correctly.

Finally, the fifth component of quality assessments is student involvement, which means that the teacher makes learning targets clear to students and involves students in tracking and setting their own learning goals. Using all five of these components will serve the learning needs of diverse learners well.

In recent years, educators have been making more effective use of assessment data by working in teams and using the data to make collaborative decisions about individual students. An important stimulus in this process is the fact that districts are increasingly required to provide student performance data that are disaggregated, or separated, according to a variety of categories. These categories may include gender, race and ethnicity, language, and socioeconomic status. In many instances across the country, there are major discrepancies between the performances of Caucasian students and students of color, and between boys and girls. These discrepancies are referred to as the achievement gap. As districts collect these data, a next step has been for educators to engage in conversations at the school and grade levels about the data and instructional strategies that need to be undertaken to close the achievement gaps. Close monitoring, through the use of additional assessments, of the impact of the strategies on student performance should result in the student's increased capacity or recommendations for additional supports.

An additional stimulus in the use of data to make collaborative decisions about student performance has been the development of a multitiered approach called Scientific Research-Based Instruction (SRBI) to identify and work with students with learning and behavioral needs. Effective implementation of SRBI includes high-quality, scientifically based classroom instruction, ongoing student assessment, tiered instruction, and parent involvement. In Connecticut, educators have adopted the process and use the term *Response to Intervention* (RTI) to describe how they apply the concepts of SRBI. Clearly, assessment plays a critical role.

From a description of the process by the RTI Action Network (n.d.) comes the following:

> The RTI process begins with high-quality instruction and universal screening of all children in the general education classroom. Struggling learners are provided with interventions at increasing levels of intensity to accelerate their rate of learning. These services may be provided by a variety of personnel, including general education teachers, special educators, and specialists. Progress is closely monitored to assess both the learning rate and the level of performance of individual students. Educational decisions about the intensity and duration of interventions are based on individual student response to instruction. RTI is designed for use when making decisions in both general education and special education, creating a well-integrated system of instruction and intervention guided by child outcome data.

Evolution of Assessments

A key outcome from the evolution of quality classroom assessments has been the establishment of data teams in many schools across the country. These teams can be established at the district, school, grade, or content-area levels. The key characteristic of data teams is that educators collect a variety of student data, discuss the data, and then collectively use the data to inform next steps around instructional support for students. Data teams meet regularly throughout the year. Connecticut has been a leader in the development of approaches to the use of data through SRBI. The Connecticut State Department of Education (2010) adopted SRBI in 2008 and described the process in *The Use of Data Teams in Connecticut's SRBI Process*. The SRBI process in Connecticut is grounded in the work of Douglas Reeves, Michael Schmoker, and Richard and Rebecca DuFour, and includes the following essential steps:

1. Universal screening and ongoing collection and charting of data

2. Analysis of data to determine strengths, challenges, and root causes

3. Establish, review, and revise SMART goals

4. Select scientific research–based interventions and instructional strategies

5. Monitor student learning

6. Begin the process again!

The good news for students, as well as educators, about this process is that the use of data by decision makers needs to be disaggregated. The disaggregated data are used to determine next steps for every individual child. This means that Connecticut and other states are working to close the achievement gap, making sure that diverse students are receiving what they need in terms of appropriate resources and support in order to achieve at high levels. Whether or not progress is being made is captured in reports generated at the national, state, and local levels. One of the national reports that captures disaggregated data regularly about student progress in a variety of content areas is the National Assessment of Educational Progress (NAEP), generated through the National Center for Education Statistics. NAEP administers assessments in 12 subject areas, including math, science, reading, writing, the arts, technology, and geography. NAEP then publishes reports about student progress. NAEP data are reported by grade level and by specific populations (e.g., gender and race).

A useful way to learn more about quality classroom assessment is to consider how assessments have evolved over time. For example, strategies such as the use of data-driven decision teams, RTI, and SRBI have been implemented since 2004 to address the challenges in supporting diverse learners. Locate one of the recent reports that shares and analyzes student data. An example is the NAEP. Review assessment trends in a particular content area over several years. Analyze the progress that is being made in this country and in your state in addressing diverse learner needs. What kind of grades would you give to educators on a progress report card nationwide in terms of addressing diverse learner needs? For your state? Explain your rationale.

Types of Assessments

Assessments can be viewed from a variety of perspectives. First, they can be placed into one of two categories that pertain to the developers of the assessments. These include standardized tests or classroom-based assessments (Oosterhof, 2009; Taylor & Nolen, 2007; Waugh & Gronlund, 2013). Large-scale or standardized tests, sometimes referred to as "high-stakes tests," are developed by experts and delivered to classrooms and schools across the country. Data accumulated through the use of **standardized assessments** are reported outside the classroom and are used to make decisions about student placement, college admissions, funding levels, identification for receipt of special services, and graduation.

Standardized tests are now also used as part of the SRBI progress monitoring or team data decision-making process discussed in the previous section. In this instance, standardized assessment results are used for making more immediate decisions about teaching and learning. SRBI experts believe that standardized assessments used for progress monitoring should be brief and easily administered by classroom teachers. In this case, and specific to Step 4 in the Connecticut SRBI process, examples of standardized assessments that are used for monitoring student progress may include the Test of Word Reading Efficiency, second edition (TOWRE 2; Torgesen, Wagner, & Rashotte, 2012) or the Woodcock-Johnson Achievement Battery (Schrank, Mather, & McGrew, 2014).

Standardized tests can be categorized as norm referenced or criterion referenced or both. Norm-referenced tests compare the results or scores of one student with those of a group of students who have taken the same test. Therefore, any student who takes the same test can be compared with the "norm," or mean or average, results of a larger group of students. Familiar examples include the California Achievement Test, the Iowa Test of Basic Skills, Tests of Academic Proficiency, and the Metropolitan Achievement Test.

In criterion-referenced tests, a student's scores are compared with a standard set by the test creators. In these cases, test designers determine pass rates or other levels of mastery. Typically in these types of tests, studies are done to determine where to set mastery levels. For example, a test creator might decide that getting 80% correct answers on a test shows a high level of mastery, while getting 60% might be midlevel mastery, and so on.

Teachers can develop classroom-based assessments. Such assessments can also accompany published curriculum and instructional materials. Classroom-based assessments can include observations and interactions (informal or using an observation checklist), written quizzes and tests, essays and research projects, and performances and exhibitions. The results of classroom-based assessments are summarized and used primarily by the teacher, teacher teams, and the school for the purpose of determining student progress over time in specific subject areas.

Assessments can also be categorized according to their purpose in making decisions. Again, some assessments are considered "high stakes" because they contribute to a teacher's making a judgment about a grade in a course. These assessments generally are given to students less frequently and are referred to as summative assessments. Examples include major end-of-unit projects or end-of-unit exams.

On the other hand, teachers should be assessing student progress regularly using a variety of assessment mechanisms for the purpose of providing regular feedback to students and to inform teachers of how they need to adjust instruction in order to meet student learning needs. This type of assessment is referred to as formative assessment. Faculty use the information to help students identify their own strengths and challenges and to adjust instruction. These assessments are generally "low stakes" because the data, for the most part, do not contribute to the student's grade. Examples of formative assessments include asking the students to develop a summary statement about their key learnings in a particular class or asking them to submit drafts of projects for feedback (see Exercise 10.1).

Whether on standardized tests or teacher-made tests, assessments tend to adhere to one of two particular formats: (1) traditional formats and (2) authentic or alternative formats

EXERCISE 10.1

SCHOOL PORTRAIT OF STUDENT ASSESSMENT

1. On a sheet of newsprint, create a portrait or pictorial diagram of the current status of student assessment in your school or a school with which you are familiar. In your portrait, try to address as many of the following questions as possible:

   a. How is student achievement assessed?

   b. Who are the primary "users" of assessment data?

   c. What is the process for the development of student assessments?

   d. What values, norms, and beliefs form the school culture around student assessment?

   e. What is the relationship between curriculum, instruction, and classroom assessment?

   f. How are decisions communicated to teachers and staff? To parents? To students?

   g. Illustrate ways in which teachers are supported in their professional growth around student assessment.

   h. Illustrate the capacity of classroom-based assessment to address the needs and learning styles of diverse learners.

   i. Illustrate the degree to which classroom-based assessments integrate knowledge of diverse cultures.

   j. Illustrate the capacity of the school to engage teams of teachers in data-driven decision making that is ongoing.

2. In small groups, explain your portrait to others.

   a. Describe three things you believe are positive about assessment practice in your setting in relation to addressing the learning needs of diverse students. Describe three things you believe that teachers in your setting need to address in order to make assessments culturally responsive and responsible.

(Oosterhof, 2009; Taylor & Nolen, 2007; Waugh & Gronlund, 2013). The most common traditional written assessment formats include multiple-choice, true/false, fill-in-the-blank, matching, and short-answer. Exhibit 10.1 provides examples of some of these formats. The design of these traditional formats, for the most part, means that they ask students to recall or recognize information that has been presented to them by the teacher. In other words, students use basic facts and skills and lower order thinking processes. The evaluation tool used in such assessments is typically the answer key. Such formats are limited in their capacity to assess whether or not students can apply the knowledge to solve problems or create new meaning.

Exhibit 10.1   Examples of Traditional Assessment Formats

I. Multiple-choice: Indicate the best answer from the choices.

In criterion-referenced tests, a student's scores are compared with

a. an average of all the test score results

b. the average IQ [intelligence quotient] of the entire class

c. a standard set by the test creators

II. True/False: Check the correct answer.

Real estate brokers often cite the high state-standardized test scores of school districts to entice families with school-age children to buy homes in those neighborhoods.

True_____   False_____

III. Matching of items: Draw a line from the item in the left column to the correct corresponding item in the right column.

1. Need to improve instruction	a. Neighborhood school has overall low state test scores
2. Distraught parent who wants daughter to go to medical school	b. Test reveals students have trouble multiplying by zero
3. Reduced property values	c. High school senior gets low test scores in science

IV. Fill in the blank:

Huba and Freed (2000) defined assessment as "the process of gathering and discussing _____ from multiple and diverse sources."

Correct Answers: I. c; II. True; III. a–3, b–1, c–2; IV. Information

Extended Explorations 10.1: Types of Assessments

Consider a unit of study that you have created. Outline the important knowledge and concepts for the unit. Now develop a plan for using a variety of assessments including traditional paper-and-pencil assessments, as well as performance- or projects-based assessments. Include in your plan a variety of formative as well as summative assessments. Once you've created your plan, evaluate it based on how it will address diverse learner needs.

While it may seem as though the use of traditional assessments is not in the best interests of student learning, there is a time and place for the more traditional paper-and-pencil tests (Oosterhof, 2009; Taylor & Nolen, 2007; Waugh & Gronlund, 2013). Paper-and-pencil assessments are particularly useful because they can assess certain types of knowledge in an expeditious manner. However, teachers need to recognize the significant problems and implications that can arise when teachers create their own assessments and rely primarily or fully on the more traditional formats.

Potential problems may arise with the student (e.g., lack of reading skill), with the assessment context, and with the assessment itself. With these concerns and resulting changes in curriculum and instruction, teachers are coming to understand that improvements in assessment are going to be critically important. Examples of changes in curriculum include greater integration of culture, as well as requirements that assessment be resonant with teaching and learning standards. Significant changes include greater use of the research on cognitive science and constructivism so that teachers provide students with greater choice, relevancy, and engagement in authentic problem solving and recognize the role of culture in the teaching and learning processes (Chapman & King, 2011; Feden & Vogel, 2002; Reeves, 2007).

Research about the evolution of assessment practices indicates that significant changes are taking place in American schools in how assessment is being conducted (Oakes et al., 2012, 2018). Those shifts are outlined in Exhibit 10.2. Teachers are moving away from a

Exhibit 10.2	Major Changes in Assessment Practice

Increased . . .

Assessment of students' full understanding within a content area

Comparison of students' performance with established criteria or standards

Opportunities for students to demonstrate their learning

Collaborative work among teaching colleagues to develop a shared vision of teaching and learning and specifically of assessment

Viewing students as active participants in the assessment process

Focus on connecting assessment with curriculum and instruction in meaningful ways

steady reliance on traditional forms of assessment to use a greater variety of assessment practices that make use of authentic or alternative forms of assessment. These forms of assessment are seen as more fair to the country's diverse students and as better determining what they know and are able to do than are traditional forms of assessment.

Alternative assessments are designed to assess the application of knowledge and may include formats such as performance, extended response (e.g., exhibitions and oral defenses), and extended tasks in which students might be engaged in decision making, investigating, experimenting, problem solving, and researching. Alternative assessments best measure conceptual learning and higher order thinking. The evaluation tools that are used most often to measure learning are **rubrics** or assessment lists.

If teachers are working to become multicultural educators who are committed to teaching and learning practices that integrate knowledge of culture, they are well advised to make use of a variety of assessment approaches. Using a combination of traditional and authentic assessment strategies and developing a deep understanding of ways to develop assessments that are responsive to and respectful of student cultures will serve all students well.

LEARNING OBJECTIVE 10.2 Explain the Challenges to the Development of Quality Classroom Assessment

While assessment is a critical and necessary component of the teaching and learning process, educators still continue to struggle with it. Among other things, educators are challenged by the demand to learn effective means of assessing student learning; the stress of the current high-stakes testing movement; and the ever-present political battles around high-stakes testing that produce anxiety and incur the wrath of students, parents, and the community in general. Sometimes lost in the conflict is the fact that assessment is a valued tool in determining how well learning is occurring and how instruction can be adjusted to be more effective.

Numerous barriers to quality assessment continue to influence the process. Stiggins (1999) explained that these barriers can include emotions about evaluation (e.g., fear); community beliefs (e.g., that all educators are competent masters of assessment); lack of time to assess well, particularly in light of the fact that the most-recommended assessment methods are perhaps the most labor-intensive; and lack of assessment expertise (educators are not prepared adequately in assessment). Specific to classroom-based assessment, according to Grant and Sleeter (2011), are other considerations:

> From a multicultural point of view, at least two considerations are important. First, is the assessment designed to capture what all of the students know and can do? For instance, are students given adequate time to take the test, and are they familiar with the vocabulary that is used in it? Second, does the assessment reflect multicultural content that . . . should guide curriculum design? (p. 195).

In addition, educators need to address other major barriers or challenges with assessment.

High-Stakes Testing

No Child Left Behind Act (NCLB) brought with it a heightened awareness of controversies in education around the emphasis on standardized tests. Clearly, the usefulness of standardized tests is limited. Results from standardized tests provide only a glimpse into the total picture of what students know and are able to do. Unfortunately, as discussed briefly in the previous section, these assessments are referred to as "high-stakes" because so many critical decisions depend on the results. For example, results are often used to determine instructional and program effectiveness and student capacity, as well as possibilities for funding. More recently, decisions have been made in states across the country to develop teacher evaluation systems in which teacher performance is linked in part to student outcomes on standardized achievement tests. Because of the high-stakes nature of standardized tests, schools and educators often find themselves "teaching to the test," as opposed to using test results to improve teaching and learning and spending

How do we know if students are learning what we teach them? What are the benefits as well as the challenges of tests?

© Thinkstock/Comstock/Thinkstock

appropriate/limited amounts of time in preparing students to take the tests. Also, the ways in which standardized tests are currently constructed do not necessarily measure real-life application of skills and knowledge.

The era of high-stakes testing can be viewed from a different, perhaps more positive perspective. NCLB and its attendant focus on high-stakes tests has highlighted the long-standing achievement gap, also described briefly in the previous section, between White students and students of color and between students from a variety of socioeconomic classes and language groups. It is well-known and well documented that White students overall do better on standardized tests than students of color. Interestingly, since the advent of NCLB and the intense scrutiny on test scores, schools and districts are now learning to disaggregate data more effectively and determining which student populations and individual students require different instructional strategies. This is clearly a matter of equity, and the question of how to provide what each individual student needs to achieve at high levels is now being addressed at the local level. NCLB forces the education system to be accountable for rectifying these long-standing problems.

In this era of high-stakes testing, several new assessment systems are being implemented for purposes of assessing student knowledge as well as teacher capacity. In terms of teacher assessments and evaluations, edTPA—an assessment system for new educators—is emerging as an important assessment of teacher capacity. According to its website (www .edtpa.com), edTPA is an assessment process that focuses on the level of preparedness of future and new teachers. The assessment looks at a teacher candidate's authentic teaching materials as a means for documenting the candidate's ability to teach his or her subject matter to all students. edTPA is comparable with entry-level licensing exams for other professions, such as medical licensing exams and the bar exam in law.

However, edTPA is not without controversy. The National Association for Multicultural Education (NAME) has published a position paper raising concerns around corporate involvement in education.

> NAME calls on educators and community members to investigate how the edTPA undermines critical multicultural education, and demands an end to the standardization and outsourcing of teacher candidate assessment required by this test. In taking this stance, NAME takes its lead from student teachers and faculty at the University of Massachusetts Amherst who have spoken out against the standardization and corporatization of teacher education occurring through the marketing and imposition of the Teacher Performance Assessment (edTPA). (NAME, 2015)

NAME raises concerns about the validity of the test and whether it actually is able to measure what it claims. The NAME Position Statement on the edTPA goes on to outline areas where such efforts to "commodify" teachers and students can actually reinforce systemic racism and bias. As educators who are working toward becoming culturally proficient, it will be important for you to be well informed about these initiatives and determine what is in the best interests of the students.

In terms of assessment systems for practicing teachers, individual states are working to develop systems that make use of a variety of data sets, including numerous teacher observations, and linking teacher performance to student outcomes. For example, the State of Connecticut developed the System for Educator Evaluation and Development (SEED; Connecticut State Department of Education, 2017, 2018), one model evaluation system that links student test scores, teacher observations, parent and/or student surveys, and the whole school academic performance to the evaluation of teachers and school and district leaders. SEED, a value-added evaluation tool, is controversial because of the link between teaching and student performance. A number of researchers have criticized the model because of the belief that other factors influence student learning, such as parental involvement and family socioeconomic status. All local and regional boards of education are required to submit their educator evaluation and support plans to the Connecticut State Department of Education annually for review and approval. The approved plans must be consistent with the CT Guidelines for Educator Evaluation, which ensures that all teachers within their respective districts will be evaluated annually.

Standardized assessments of students have also moved in significantly new directions in recent years. With this in mind, educators must learn to balance a focus on learning standards with appropriate assessments (Reeves, 2014). The primary stated goal of the Smarter Balanced Assessment Consortium (SBAC) is to make sure that all students leave high school prepared for postsecondary success. According to its website (www.smarterbal anced.org), the Smarter Balanced Assessment system is aligned with the Common Core State Standards (CCSS) and provides mechanisms for helping educators improve teaching and learning. In particular, the Smarter Balanced system strives to provide information and tools for teachers and schools to improve instruction and help all students succeed— regardless of disability, language, or subgroup. In actuality, the development of the CCSS and SBAC has raised concerns among educators. Not all states have adopted the CCSS, seeing them as overly prescriptive. In terms of SBAC, many educators believe that they are driving schools toward an accountability system, rather than one that is focused on students. People who are pro–standardized achievement testing believe that it will help educators to uncover areas that contribute to the achievement gap. Those who do not adhere to this stance believe that the intense focus on standardized testing and data pushes schools to become data driven, rather than student driven.

The assessment systems designed for teachers and students have tremendous implications for influencing the preparation of teachers for working effectively with the diversity of students in our nation's classrooms. At the same time, the development of these systems has been quite controversial in that it appears that teachers will be held accountable for student outcomes in new ways. In the end, systems are being developed that link expectations of what students should know and be able to do, powerful strategies for curriculum development and student performance data for individual students. If schools are able to implement these systems, the potential impact on diverse students could be strong.

Bias in Assessment

Another barrier to quality assessment is the fact that testing and assessment are fraught with bias. The types of tests used and how they are interpreted create unfair results for poor, minority students in particular. Standardized tests have improved greatly in terms of identifying and eliminating cultural bias. Nevertheless, significant concerns exist about bias in classroom-based assessments created by teachers. Unlike standardized tests and tests associated with published curricula, whose publishers can conduct extensive reviews for bias, teachers frequently work alone in developing tests. Even the best efforts to create bias-free tests can fail without knowledge and skill in creating quality assessments that meet the needs of diverse learners.

You might be able to understand challenges to quality classroom assessment, including the existence of bias, by reflecting on courses you took in high school or college. Analyze the primary assessments that were used for you in one of your high school or college courses in terms of strengths and weaknesses. Would you judge them as quality assessments? What are your criteria for judging quality? To what extent did they address diverse learner needs? What types of bias do you believe may have been embedded in the assessments?

In its *Tool Kit for Professional Developers*, the Northwest Regional Educational Laboratory (1998a, 1998b) explained how bias in testing can occur in a variety of ways.

1. An aspect of the assessment could prevent students from being able to demonstrate what they know and are able to do. This bias is called extraneous interference and may involve the student's capacity to read or write or a physical limitation.

2. Fairness means that students of both genders and all backgrounds should be given the opportunity and support to do equally well. Everyone must have an equal opportunity to demonstrate what he or she knows and is able to do relative to what is being assessed.

3. Bias in a task occurs when particular groups of students know less about what is being tested because of cultural identities. For example, if students are expected to solve a problem that is grounded in the context of sewing, students who have a cultural knowledge of sewing will probably have an advantage on the task, and the context becomes a biasing factor.

4. Fair tasks are also as free as possible of stereotypes based on culture, gender, and sexual orientation.

To summarize the statements above, bias problems can arise from a variety of sources. These include challenges from within the

1. **student** (e.g., lack of reading skill, language barriers, lack of testwiseness, lack of personal confidence leading to evaluation anxiety),

2. **testing context** (e.g., lack of rapport with the assessor/teacher, cultural insensitivity in the assessment, unclear directions, lack of time for the teacher to score the assessment effectively), and

3. **specific type of assessment** (e.g., essay-type tests that require some writing skill, teacher's lack of skill in developing scoring mechanisms).

Standardized tests without cultural bias are difficult to develop. To illustrate this issue, consider the Dove Test. The Dove Counterbalance General Intelligence Test was developed in 1968 by Adrian Dove, an African American sociologist, who wanted to show that dialect alone can create cultural bias (Neill, 2004). Using humor to illustrate his point, Dove created a set of "test" questions that are skewed toward African Americans. Exhibit 10.3 has some samples. As you may see, those who would know the answers are those who grew up in the culture (and era) in which such knowledge was familiar. Dialect, socioeconomic class, and culture influence our responses in assessments.

Exhibit 10.3   The "Chitling" Test

I.   A "gas head" is a person who has (a) a fast-moving car, (b) a stable of "lace," (c) "process hair," (d) a habit of stealing cars, (e) a long jail record for arson.

II. "Hully Gully" came from (a) East Oakland, (b) Fillmore, (c) Watts, (d) Harlem, (e) Motor City.

III. T-Bone Walker got famous for playing the (a) trombone, (b) piano, (c) "T-flute," (d) guitar, (e) "hambone."

Answers: I. c; II. c; III. d

LEARNING OBJECTIVE 10.3 Determine Appropriate Classroom-Based Assessments to Assess Learning by Diverse Students

Principles of High-Quality Assessment Systems

If educators are to improve their assessment practice in the interests of their students, they need to be provided with principles and guidelines as a framework for improvement. In 1995, the National Forum on Assessment developed a set of seven principles of high-quality assessment systems (see below). The principles were drafted by a coalition of education and civil rights organizations to guide reform of assessment practices at all levels, from the classroom to large-scale accountability exams.

Each of the seven principles includes a list of detailed "indicators" to evaluate assessment systems. The seven principles are valuable for educators working to develop assessments that are fair to and useful for the diverse students in our nation's schools (Exercise 10.2). Educators should do the following:

1. Make certain that the guiding purpose of assessment is to improve student learning.

2. Ground important decisions about teaching in multiple assessments.

3. Design assessment systems to be fair for all students, providing multiple methods and opportunities for students to demonstrate their knowledge.

4. Collaborate with colleagues to design and implement powerful assessment systems.

5. Engage the broader community in the assessment process.

6. Share assessment results and information frequently with students, parents, and other educators.

7. Continually evaluate and enhance the quality of the assessment system.

What does the research tell us about the most effective ways to assess learning? How do we use what we find out?

iStock/ranplett

EXERCISE 10.2

USING THE PRINCIPLES AND INDICATORS FOR STUDENT ASSESSMENT SYSTEMS

1. Arrange to interview a curriculum and instruction specialist or supervisor in your district or at a school with which you are familiar.

2. Develop a set of interview questions grounded in the principles developed by the National Forum on Assessment that address the methods and processes used by educators in that school and/or district to develop and improve assessment processes.

3. If possible, ask for representative samples of assessments that might be typically used in assessing student learning in that setting.

4. Review the data from the interview and the document review and analyze them in light of the seven principles developed by the National Forum on Assessment.

5. Develop a presentation using the data from your interview and review of assessments.

6. Share your presentation with colleagues. Initiate a discussion of improvements that could be made to meet the learning needs of diverse populations.

EXERCISE 10.3

NEASC ACCREDITATION STANDARDS

Use the 10 points from the NEASC accreditation standards on assessment as a checklist to evaluate your own school's approach to assessing student performance (https://cpss.neasc.org/standards/ 2011-standards). Write a brief summary of your findings, describing specific strengths and challenge areas. Then make three specific recommendations for improving assessment practice at your site.

More principles of high-quality assessment systems can be found in school accreditation criteria. The New England Association of Schools and Colleges (NEASC) in Bedford, Massachusetts, is the nation's oldest regional accrediting association. One of its seven standards for accreditation addresses assessment. NEASC (2011) accreditation standards (Exercise 10.3) describe the importance of assessment as follows:

Assessment informs students and stakeholders of progress and growth toward meeting the school's 21st century learning expectations. Assessment results are shared and discussed on a regular basis to improve student learning. Assessment results inform teachers about student achievement in order to adjust curriculum and instruction.

Guidelines for Development of Classroom-Based Culturally Responsive Assessments

It is important for schools to examine their assessment systems. In addition, classroom-based educators must examine their own assessment strategies to ensure equity for all learners. For educators to engage in effective assessment practice that is culturally responsive, it is useful to have guidelines. The guidelines offered in Exhibit 10.4 can be used as a checklist in the development of classroom-based culturally responsive assessments.

Authentic Assessments

Authentic assessment. Performance assessment. Alternative assessment. These and related terms represent a significant change in our nation's schools regarding how we determine what students should know and be able to do. This move toward what is called **authentic assessment**

Exhibit 10.4   A Checklist for the Development of Culturally Responsive Assessments

Assessments that are designed to meet the needs of individual diverse learners should do the following:

1. *Reflect student experiences:* Consider cultural factors in the earliest stages of assessment instrument development. Develop assessments that reflect student experiences in and out of the classroom.

2. *Attend to student learning styles:* Use your understanding of culture and learning styles to construct assessment tasks/items that suit students' known ways of thinking and demonstrate their learning.

3. *Convey expectations clearly to students:* Be sure that students understand what they are expected to do on an assessment. Consider the language that is used in the assessment. Consider defining terms, rephrasing, translating, or using examples.

4. *Provide ample time:* Allow students ample time to complete an assessment.

5. *Provide multiple ways for students to demonstrate their learning:* Always use a variety of assessments to evaluate student learning. Don't rely on a single assessment to make a major decision.

6. *Provide clear standards for good performance:* Let students know before the assessment if they are being assessed on knowledge, skills, reasoning, or the development of products. Provide examples of what "excellence" looks like.

7. *Tap into higher order thinking:* In particular, provide opportunities for learners to apply their knowledge and skills through assessments that call for solving multilayered problems. Emphasize what the learners both know and can do.

8. *Balance formative and summative assessments:* Educators should provide formative assessments that are not high stakes and provide clear, immediate, and useful feedback to students about their progress.

9. *Connect evaluation to instruction:* Use the results of the assessments to reflect on the instruction, noting how you can enhance instructional design to enhance student performance for every learner.

10. *Provide choice in assessments:* Give students choices whenever possible to demonstrate their learning. Provide learner control over the process (e.g., students can maintain a portfolio of assessed work over time).

11. *Develop assessments collaboratively in teacher teams:* Work with colleagues in ongoing professional development to ensure proficiency in interpreting and scoring alternative assessments.

12. *Provide for disaggregation of data:* When looking at data summaries, teachers should disaggregate by specific groups that may be of interest or concern. For example, as a teacher, do you think that boys and girls may perform differently on a specific assessment? The assessment report will show gaps, as well as specific areas in which students of diversity perform well.

13. *Report instructional strategies that appear to work:* Assessment data should include information not only about student performance but also about the instructional strategies that are and are not working well for diverse students. For example, how much time was spent on direct instruction of higher order cognitive processes? What specific culturally responsive instructional techniques were used? What types of resources were different groups of students able to access?

14. *Share the results with interested people:* Teachers need to share assessment data frequently with students, parents, and the community. Sharing should occur not only at the end of the term but also weekly.

focuses the attention of educators and students more on the application of skills and knowledge rather than simply the knowledge itself. While authentic assessment is certainly very promising as a research-based educational practice, no one would advocate the sole use of it in the classroom. Particularly when considering the needs of diverse learners, teachers must remember the importance of using a variety of assessments.

What is authentic assessment? Grant Wiggins (1991) has generally been credited with much of the early thinking about and development of what is called *authentic assessment.* According to Einbender and Wood (1995), researchers for the Four Seasons Project of the National Center for Restructuring Education, Schools, and Teaching, the term *authentic* provides an important differentiation between the contrived, artificial kinds of tasks that appear on standardized tests and the more meaningful problems that are connected to the world outside the classroom. Authentic assessments involve the application of skills to a task that requires students to go beyond the instructional context.

Although authentic assessment can assume a variety of formats, there appear to be some common characteristics among all approaches. A primary characteristic is that authentic assessment happens on a daily basis, often through observations of student engagement and progress in learning. Another common characteristic of all approaches is the involvement of students in self-assessment. Perhaps most important, authentic assessment is grounded in content and learning standards rather than in standardization being imposed (Exercise 10.4).

What happens in schools that commit to shifting toward a use of **performance assessment?** Teachers report a need to make concurrent shifts in curricular and instructional practices (Oakes et al., 2012, 2018; Reeves, 2007, 2014; Sadker & Zittleman, 2012, 2015; Tomlinson, Moon, & Imbeau, 2015). Rather than covering extensive amounts of material in a given amount of time, teachers and students explore topics and issues in depth. Instructional practices shift from the teacher as "teller" to the teacher as coach—someone who provides quality feedback. And the resulting student outcomes appear to be enhanced abilities in problem solving and higher order thinking skills (Lockwood, 1992).

Schools that integrate performance assessment are characterized by a culture of high expectations of students and staff. Students assume more of the responsibility for their learning, participate in assessing their own work, and regularly revisit past performances and products to ascertain changes over time (Hibbard, 1994). Students are engaged in demanding tasks and may demonstrate their skills and abilities through a variety of formats, including portfolios and exhibitions (Wolf, LeMahieu, & Eresh, 1992).

Why should educators seriously consider performance assessment? One reason is that if they are committed to the preparation of students for real-world work, performance assessment appears to provide a more complete picture of students' abilities (O'Neill, 1992). According to Richard Stiggins, director of the Center for Classroom Assessment at the Northwest Regional Educational Laboratory,

the achievement targets we have are more complex than ever before. We now realize that without performance assessment methodology, it's not possible to create a complete portrait of student achievement. You can't evaluate writing without asking students to write, and you can't evaluate whether a student has learned a foreign language without asking that student to speak. (as cited in O'Neill, 1992)

Extended Explorations 10.2: Enhancing Student Assessments

All educators need to be knowledgeable about and be able to compare, contrast, explain, and critique the state, national, and international assessments and the results of these assessments. Educators need to understand the value of various assessments and the links to student learning.

In this activity, imagine that you are a teacher leader who will work with a team of teachers to investigate, learn about, and present information on a specific assessment. Each team will investigate a different type of assessment. Imagine that you will be making a presentation at a school staff meeting; the audience will be other teachers. Work in teams to accomplish this activity. Your task as the instructional team is to present

1. background information about the assessment (What is the purpose of the assessment? Why was it designed? What are the costs? How well does the test assess critical thinking? What types of scores are reported?),

2. a summary of the pros and cons of the students taking the assessment (Who takes the assessment? What are the accommodations? Is the test biased toward any underrepresented groups?), and

3. a description of the usefulness of the assessment for student learning (What are the most recent scores? How might the scores be used to inform student learning?).

Teams

Smarter Balanced http://www.smarterbalanced.org; Trends in International Mathematics and Science Study (TIMSS) http://timss.bc.edu; Program for International Student Assessment (PISA) http://nces.ed.gov/surveys/pisa

EXERCISE 10.4

ASSESSMENT TRANSFORMATION

1. Select a paper-and-pencil test you have developed or borrow one from a teacher you know.

2. Use the National Forum on Assessment's set of seven principles of high-quality assessment systems provided in this text to transform that assessment into one that is culturally responsive.

3. Exchange projects with a peer. Check each other's "before" and "after" assessments, using the guidelines in this chapter as a set of criteria. Provide and discuss a friendly written critique of the transformed assessment.

The next section in this chapter presents a portrait of one school's efforts to integrate authentic assessments into the daily work of the school.

Portrait of a School in an Assessment Transition

No two schools approach the use of authentic assessment in the same way. The description in this section illustrates one school's efforts to integrate authentic assessment into teaching and learning in an effort to meet the needs of diverse learners.

Introduction

It is 9:15 a.m. by the time I have driven to the district's high school on an early June day. A few other visitors and I quietly enter the front doors. As we enter, we're greeted by several young students who are anxious to register each person at the sign-in table, provide a brief orientation, show people to the hospitality room, and then escort them to the presentation they came to view. The students, on questioning, are sixth graders in the building's middle school. Although the limelight is on the building's high school seniors, these sixth graders are aware of the special event that is taking place over the next few days, and they share in the excitement that evidently and distinctly pervades the school. They know that they, too, will one day be responsible for completing a senior project.

As one of the visitors, I am escorted to the auditorium to hear a senior project presentation on the "History of Basketball." According to the school's teachers, this presentation is the result of at least a year's worth of research and work by a graduating senior. Starting on time, the student begins by sharing his research on the history of basketball. Early in the presentation, the student explains that he selected the topic for his senior project because, in his words, "When I grow up, I want to be a physical education teacher and coach, and I thought this would be a neat thing to do." As it evolves, the presentation, in fact, is a combination of historical information and a narrative of the student's experiences running a basketball clinic for middle school students. By the end of the 45-minute period, it is apparent that he has skillfully mixed research, his experience in communicating with many others, knowing something so well that he can teach it, giving something of himself to younger students, and organizing the results of all his efforts into a coherent presentation.

An adult stands to thank the others in the audience for their attendance at this important event and announces that the student's advisory committee will be convening to discuss the student's presentation with him. As an outsider, I wonder how well he did in the minds of those responsible for his education. Who makes the decision about whether or not he did well enough to pass the requisite graduation requirement? And what does he think of his own effort? More broadly, what processes within the school have led to today's student presentations? Does authentic assessment lead to enhanced learning by students? Do changes required of students in the learning process due to new assessment approaches call for concurrent changes in teaching approaches?

The School and Community: A Social Context for Change

The current principal began his tenure with the school in 1998. By most accounts from the school's faculty, his greatest strength is in the area of curriculum. He is regarded as a highly energetic and dynamic leader and a role model, and he is linked to national school reform efforts. Many faculty agree with one colleague's statement, "The educational leadership here is phenomenal. The push is constant—always new ideas for enhancing and improving what we do. There is immense faculty growth with this approach." Linking the school to the community is viewed as a critical component of the educational process.

Evolution of Senior Projects

When asked why he is so supportive of the senior projects, the principal stated,

> I wonder what it would be like to meet these students (who are graduating) in 25 years and ask them what they remember they learned in school. Will it be something related to a test they took, or something like the senior project? I'm concerned about preparing students with life skills. I'm concerned about the long-term impact of what we're doing with them.

Shortly after his arrival at the school, the principal held a series of meetings with teachers to talk about what the school should be like. A key question posed during the meetings was, "What should each student know and be able to do by the time he or she finishes high school?" The outcome of those discussions was the creation of the student competencies, a set of nine "qualities of mind, character and behavior that permit an individual to fulfill the civic, vocational, ethical, and interpersonal roles of a mature modern-day adult."

The following areas of competency are required of all graduating seniors:

1. Self-educating, autonomous, lifelong learner

2. Interpersonal skills

3. Ethical values

4. Adaptability

5. Global awareness and stewardship

6. Creative problem solving

7. Self-worth (confidence)

8. Commitment

9. Effective communication

The discussion group evolved into the Senior Project Steering Committee. The Steering Committee and other faculty members developed a common sense of this new approach to teaching and learning that would manifest itself most notably in the senior projects. Following development of the competencies, the next task for the Steering Committee was to examine the curriculum and develop ways for integrating, measuring, and evaluating the nine student competencies. It was decided that, among a variety of suggested authentic assessment options, a "senior project" would be an appropriate way of addressing the competencies at the school.

Soon the Senior Project Team had emerged, composed of five teachers and the principal. The team met weekly at school and for several daylong retreats. The team, which is the driving force behind the senior projects, is collaborative in nature.

Beyond the student competencies, the senior project took on additional life through the establishment of project goals. These were to promote intellectual curiosity; put classroom knowledge into use; allow authentic, genuine, creative work; promote competencies; measure competencies; force commitment; push students into action/work; provide fair facsimiles of real-world tasks; build confidence; and build student credentials. Additionally, a major goal for the school became the integration of the competencies into existing curricula.

Assessment of student progress was a regular topic of discussion within the Senior Project Team. The teachers were concerned with how to convey to students the high-stakes nature of this project. In addition, they were interested in supporting student self-assessment of progress. Thus, the Senior Project Team added a requirement that all students must complete a set of four quarterly reports about their progress. Collectively, the Senior Project Team discussed individual students, and committee members decided how to work with particular students. Teachers were anxious to have students take more responsibility for their learning.

The Senior Project Year

The Senior Project Team outlined four stages for the senior project (Table 10.1). Even before Stage 1 begins in the senior year, an orientation is held in the prior spring to familiarize juniors with the project and its requirements.

Project faculty seemed to spend a fair amount of time counseling students about how they might select a topic. Early on, many students declared that they couldn't select a topic because they didn't have any outside interests or hobbies to explore in depth. Eventually, these students either conceptualized their own project or were encouraged toward a particular topic. Examples of topics that were selected included Writing and Producing a Screenplay, Composition and Recording of Classical Music, Design Logos for Cars and Trucks, Construction of a Cross-Country Course, Construction From Scratch of an Electric Guitar, Eating Disorders—A Self-Study, Illustrated Book of Edible Plants, and Rock Climbing—The Environmental Impact.

Each student composed an Advisory Team, which included a teacher project coordinator, an administrator, and a technical adviser. Together, the Advisory Team members provided support for the student. The team approved the student's project at four "milestone" points throughout the year. The responsibilities of the technical adviser were to provide technical assistance to the project in the form of identification of resources; suggest ideas and direction for research, field study, and lab production; offer advice on format; check on motivation and time commitment; and contact the project teacher if there were problems or concerns.

How was time managed in the senior project process? Throughout the senior year, and beginning with the graduating class for which senior projects were mandatory, each student

TABLE 10.1	Senior Project Timeline			
Stage	**Stage 1**	**Stage 2**	**Stage 3**	**Stage 4**
Dates	September–October	October–January	February–March	April–June
Goal	Proposal and committee development	Problem solving	Preparation for public presentation	Project public presentation
Tasks	Student identifies thesis topic, issue, or problem; determines essential questions; designs methods of investigation or research; describes final form of project; and begins a work journal. Technical adviser is assigned.	Student clarifies problem, issue, or thesis; brainstorms and creates divergent approaches; gathers information through field study, laboratory work, or telecommunications research; analyzes results of information gathering; and maintains a work journal.	Student organizes findings; determines effective modes/media of communication; produces tapes, spreadsheets, photographs, artwork, choreography, and written synopsis; and practices presentation.	Student communicates project findings or results to a public committee; answers questions from committee and audience; prepares written synopsis for the audience.
Milestones	Milestone 1: Presentation of proposal to project committee (comprising of senior project adviser, technical adviser, and an administrator)	Milestone 2: Presentation of progress to project committee	Milestone 3: Committee review of progress with presentation	Milestone 4: Review and evaluation by senior project committee

had one period each day in his or her schedule that was devoted to the senior project. After conferring with the period's project adviser teacher, the students were free to conduct individual research in the library or write in their journals.

Although the primary result of the new focus on student competencies has been the senior project, progress continues to be made in terms of systemic change within the school. The teachers reported that the competencies help focus the entire school. Students reported that the teachers had been giving them "real-life problems" to solve.

Issues

The Changing Role of the Teacher

An interesting outcome of the implementation of authentic assessment approaches to teaching and learning is that the role of the teacher appears to change gradually. In a traditional approach to education, the teacher is the transmitter of knowledge and information and then the judge and evaluator. There is a routine to the process that is commonly accepted by students and teachers alike.

The focus in the performance assessment classroom moves from being teacher centered to being student centered. According to senior project faculty participants, their involvement in the project has had a major impact on their teaching. Stated one, "Yes, my involvement leads to my emphasizing more real-world applications in my other classes." Another stated, "The competencies are forcing me and my colleagues to reevaluate both content and methods." Several faculty have pursued curriculum mapping—developing goals that reflect the competencies and mapping out the content, lessons, and activities for individuals and for classes. The impact on teaching is also noticeable in faculty discussions about expectations of students and the mandatory nature of the projects.

Changing Student Orientations to Learning

All seniors were required to complete successfully a senior project as a graduation requirement. Considering the high-stakes nature of this performance assessment approach, and despite isolated cases of resistance, student reaction to the project was very positive. Although there certainly were times when they didn't know how to attack the next phase of their projects, the students were proud of their accomplishments. Students reported that the strengths of the project were the focus on real-world work, the requirement to learn the competencies, and developing commitment.

Nevertheless, in interviews, the students were very clear about having had to learn a new "system" for demonstrating their knowledge and skill. Assessment through performance was not something to which they were accustomed. Several expressed frustration about the requirement that they maintain a journal throughout the year, saying, "It's tough to document your thought processes." When asked under which "system" they learned more—traditional testing or the performance approach—their reaction was mixed. One student stated, "I think I'm learning more through doing the senior project and through performance-based assessment. But I think I prefer tests because they're quick, easier to take, and you get a grade immediately."

Although the faculty were anxious to give as much responsibility for the learning process as possible to the students, they realized that some students need some additional supports. At one point, one very caring and well-intentioned teacher explained, "They're just kids—adolescents—we have to tell them what to do." In reply, another stated, "But we come back to the purpose of our project—for them to accept responsibility. They have to show us they're worthy of graduation—not us doing it for them." Teachers who were accustomed to using grades as a motivator were now grappling with other ways to keep students on track.

Linking Curriculum, Instruction, and Assessment

All parties involved in senior projects—the principal, teachers, and students—agree that the competencies and authentic assessment approaches need to be incorporated throughout the students' school experiences. They realize that they cannot wait until the senior year to "spring" this type of assessment on the students. In the words of one faculty member,

> The way we're currently working with performance assessment is akin to children in a swimming pool. They've been swimming doggy-paddle in the shallow end for a long time, and all of a sudden we throw them in the deep end and expect them to swim. More teachers have to get their feet wet in this process and make it an integral part of the entire educational process.

Many students are not accustomed to self-assisted, let alone self-directed, learning. For the most part, they are accustomed to didactic instruction in the classroom. With senior projects, they have to complete their work while "learning a new way of learning." Some students find this painful, some find it challenging, and some find it exciting. Most, in the end, find it highly rewarding.

As the school attempts to match instruction with the new approaches to assessment, a primary challenge will be to move the use of the competencies and performance assessment into earlier grades. A conscious effort has been initiated to do just that. Faculty and administrators are working on systemic change to link curriculum, assessment, and instruction.

The Changing Role of the School in Preparing Students for Life Work

The senior projects process reflects and conveys messages about what are emerging as important considerations in preparing students for life work. Going out into the world of work doesn't mean just taking your place in the work hierarchy. Individuals are increasingly being held responsible for their own work/products and for their own assessment of quality. It is no longer enough to enter the workplace with content knowledge or cognitive skills. People must make use of a different set of skills. The competencies established as a basis for the senior projects are designed with this different set of skills in mind.

In Closing

On the presentation days of the senior projects in June, each visitor received an orientation packet containing documents about the projects. One particular document was indicative of the uniqueness of the project and the process. A statement read,

> The Senior Project is part of a bigger idea. It is the culmination of learning activities in the high school years during which the students are rigorously challenged to investigate their choice of real-world problems and issues. They are involved in authentic tasks. They must develop a commitment to work. They must develop further their skills in problem solving and their skills in working and in communicating with people. They all are involved in the creative process. They are all involved in developing their credentials beyond the levels of most public high school students.

An interesting question that was raised through the project was, "What influence, if any, will this project have on the futures of these students?" "Will they be more motivated, more skilled, more ready for higher levels of work in our society?" Already, at least one student from a previous graduating class has returned and explained to a Steering Committee member that the one thing that prepared him well for college work was his participation in the senior project. It appears that the project's outcome is not as important as the process. It would be interesting to see where these students are in 10 to 15 years and to know their impressions at that time of the senior project experience. The principal has wondered about the same thing.

REFLECTING BACK

John Goodlad (1984/2004) believed that teachers' most important work in support of student motivation to learn is to make subject matter relevant to students and use instructional strategies that use all the senses. Above all, teachers must create opportunities for students to connect the knowledge to their own experiences. Following your work on the objectives in Chapter 10, take time to reflect on your responses to the following statements.

1. Write a brief reflection in which you compare and contrast criterion-referenced tests and norm-referenced tests. In particular, compare the fairness and utility of each type of test, especially in consideration of diverse groups of students in today's schools.

2. Based on your knowledge acquired in this chapter, what thoughts might you have about your future work in assessment, lesson planning, and teaching strategies?

3. Describe specific ways in which the Portrait of a School in an Assessment Transition described in Learning Objective 10.3 exemplifies culturally responsive and responsible practice in linking curriculum, instruction, and assessment.

PROFILES IN MULTICULTURAL EDUCATION

JACQUELINE JORDAN IRVINE

© Jacqueline Jordan Irvine

Jacqueline Jordan Irvine is the Charles Howard Candler Professor Emeritus at Emory University and Visiting Professor at the University of Maryland. Dr. Irvine's specialization is in multicultural education and urban teacher education, particularly the education of African Americans. Her books include *Black Students and School Failure* (1991), *Growing Up African American in Catholic Schools* (1996), *Critical Knowledge for Diverse Students, Culturally Responsive Lesson Planning for Elementary and Middle Grades, In Search of Wholeness: African American Teachers and Their Culturally Specific Pedagogy*, and *Seeing With the Cultural Eye*. In addition to these books, she has published numerous articles and book chapters and presented hundreds of papers to professional education and community organizations. Some of her awards and recognitions include the American Educational Research Association (AERA)'s Outstanding Achievement Award—Research Focus on Black Education (RFBE) Special Interest Group; Distinguished Career Award from Committee on the Role and Status of Minorities; Dewitt-Wallace/AERA Lecture Award; President's Distinguished Service Award from the Special Interest Group: Research Focus on Black Education; AERA Social Justice Award; and Division G's award for Outstanding Service in the Preparation of the Next Generation. The American Association of Colleges of Teacher Education has recognized her work with the Outstanding Writing Award, Hunt Lecture, and Lindsay Award for Distinguished Research in Teacher Education. Emory University noted Dr. Irvine's accomplishments with the Distinguished Emory University Faculty Lecture and Award; Thomas Jefferson Award, an award given at commencement to a faculty member for contributions in research and service; and Crystal Apple Award for Excellence in Teaching Graduate Education. Dr. Irvine was elected to the National Academy of Education in 2007.

Among Dr. Irvine's most important contributions to the field of multicultural education is her work in the area of culturally responsive pedagogy. Dr. Irvine believes that culturally responsive teachers understand that all students, regardless of race or ethnicity, bring their culturally influenced cognition, behavior, and dispositions to school. For example, they understand how semantics, accents, dialect, and discussion modes affect classroom interactions. These teachers know how to adapt and employ multiple representations of subject matter knowledge using students' everyday lived experiences. They learn from families and community organizations and use this knowledge to inform their teaching and help students' families support their children's education. Culturally responsive teachers treat cultural differences as assets on which to build rather than as deficits to overcome.

Dr. Irvine believes that *preservice teachers must work* to be multicultural educators in order to meet the needs of all students, regardless of their cultural and linguistic background, social class status, or immigrant status. Schools are becoming increasingly diverse. In the largest school districts, half or more of the students are students of color, and by 2023, the majority of students will be non-White. These demographic data imply that all educators should be able to master effective multicultural approaches. There is also growing empirical evidence that multicultural teaching approaches, like culturally responsive teaching practices, have been associated with improved student learning. Most important, multicultural educational approaches resonate with our democratic ideals and values, such as liberty, justice, and equality, and honor the unique experiences of students of color.

CASE STUDY

JASON HATHAWAY: A TEACHER MAKING CHANGES IN ASSESSMENT OF STUDENT LEARNING

Key Issues to Be Explored in the Case

1. When teachers learn to differentiate their instruction in order to meet diverse learner needs, they also need to adjust their assessment strategies.

2. Expectations that teachers ground student learning objectives in standards convey stress to teachers who believe that, in the end, they don't have the time to develop diverse assessment strategies.

3. Teachers need to work collaboratively in order to develop strong assessment mechanisms that many can use.

Jason Hathaway has been a social studies teacher for 15 years. The teacher preparation program through which he received his credentials taught him about behavioral approaches to teaching and learning, as well as more constructivist approaches. Jason has always believed that he was well prepared to enter a classroom and use these cutting-edge instructional strategies.

Interestingly, while Jason is recognized for the variety of instructional strategies that he uses to support student engagement and motivation, he has always struggled with assessing what students know and are able to do. In reality, he did not have any coursework devoted to the development of authentic assessments. And with the numbers of students for whom he is responsible, he quite frankly has not been able to make the time to support students in authentic assessments. Truth be told, Jason has always believed that if he had to figure out how to deal with paper-and-pencil tests, his students should do so as well. It's just a skill that needs to be learned. So while he has engaged students in constructivist learning, he has generally used paper-and-pencil tests, as well as essays and research papers, to assess student learning.

Halfway into the fall semester, Jason is now quite aware that several of his students, particularly the girls, are struggling with these traditional assessments. These girls appear to be engaged in class discussions. However, their chapter test scores have progressively gotten worse and worse. Through recent professional development workshops, Jason is aware that philosophies about student assessment have changed significantly since his teacher preparation years, due primarily to important research about how children learn. Jason has worked hard to be the best teacher he can be. He believes sincerely that he needs to prepare students for the type of assessments they'll encounter when they take the state's standardized exams and that means preparing them in fairly traditional paper-and-pencil testing formats. In the process, Jason has become adept at writing sound selected-response exams that require his students to spend significant amounts of time on memorization. At the same time, he is increasingly concerned that this group of female students is not showing what they are really capable of. He just doesn't quite know what to do. And he is feeling as though he may not be alone.

A new principal was hired during the past year. The principal, Mary Weathers, is a visionary and is intent on enhancing teaching and learning in the school. Strongly committed to equity in education, she believes firmly in the need for teachers to be adept in using a variety of instructional strategies as well as diverse approaches to classroom assessment and in supporting individual students in deep and meaningful learning experiences.

You have been hired to serve as assessment and evaluation adviser to the school. Your first task is to work with Jason Hathaway on improving his approach to student assessment.

Discussion Questions

Develop a plan that addresses the following:

1. How would you convince Jason of the importance of this work? Develop a set of

(Continued)

(Continued)

talking points for a consultation with him. Address the value of quality assessment, equity in education, and meeting diverse learner needs.

2. How would you use your understanding of data teams?

3. How would you use your knowledge about the capacity of teacher collaboration?

4. Plan for how you would coach Jason. Develop a model assessment plan that integrates best practices around assessment and multicultural education. Focus on a specific unit of instruction (e.g., volcanoes).

CHAPTER SUMMARY

In this chapter, key issues and strategies to develop culturally responsive assessments are discussed. This chapter focused on three critical areas.

10.1 Describe the purposes of classroom assessment

The purpose of student assessment is to support learning and teaching by identifying students' academic strengths and weaknesses, informing instruction and the provision of supplemental intervention and support, and tracking students' learning over time. Teachers need to be able to use a variety of approaches for effectively assessing what each individual student knows and is able to do. These approaches need to be grounded in an understanding of the cultural identities of the student.

10.2 Explain the challenges to the development of quality classroom assessment

Key challenges and issues in creating and using assessments as required in today's schools include the presence of bias in assessments, the emphasis on tradition in creating and using assessment information, and the presence of high-stakes testing in the teaching and learning process. Educators must be very focused to try to counteract these key challenges.

10.3 Determine appropriate classroom-based assessments to assess learning by diverse students

Common traditional written assessment formats include multiple-choice, true/false, fill-in-the-blank, matching, and short-answer. These are best for measuring student capacity for simple recall of information. Such formats are limited in their capacity to assess whether or not students can apply the knowledge to solve problems or create new meaning. Alternative assessments, on the other hand, are designed to assess application of knowledge and may include formats such as performances, extended responses (e.g., exhibitions and oral defenses), and extended tasks in which students might be engaged in decision making, investigation, experimentation, problem solving, and research. Alternative assessments best measure conceptual learning and higher order thinking. The evaluation tools that are used most often to measure learning are rubrics and assessment lists.

KEY TERMS

alternative assessment 287

authentic assessment 294

performance assessment 295

rubric 287

standardized assessments 283

APPLICATION: ACTIVITIES AND EXERCISES

Individual

1. If you were forced to select only one method for assessing each of the five kinds of achievement targets, which method would you choose and why? Develop a matrix and use it to write a detailed plan.

2. If our objective was to assess your teaching proficiency, what assessment method should we use and why? Develop a plan to share with your supervisor that reflects good assessment practice. How could the plan be adapted to meet the needs of diverse teachers?

3. Write a personal history of your assessment experiences in school. What were your most memorable experiences? How did they influence your schooling experience? What emotions do they trigger? What inferences would you draw about quality assessment in your classroom or school? What was the impact on diverse learners?

4. Interview three teachers in a school in which you work. Before the interview, develop a set of appropriate questions to ask about their classroom assessment practices. Specifically address the use of authentic assessments. Summarize your data from your interviews. Develop a set of recommendations for how to support teachers in developing assessments that meet diverse learner needs.

Group Assessment Planning Project

This project is intended to help you become assessment literate. In small work teams, you will develop an assessment plan for a unit of study that addresses the learning needs of diverse learners. Parts 1 through 3 should be developed collaboratively as a team. Part 4 should be written individually.

Part 1: Identify Achievement Targets

Select a unit of instruction that is important to a member of your team. This should be a unit that has goals, objectives, instructional materials, and instructional interventions. You may create a new unit or use one that is already well developed by a team member. Remember, this is for practice! The unit should include at least several days or even weeks of instruction. The unit may be one you teach or plan to teach.

Your first task is to identify the unit's important achievement targets. What important knowledge are students to understand? What patterns of reasoning might you expect your students to acquire? What might be some of your problem-solving targets? Identify any skill or product development targets. What do you want your students to be able to do or create? Finally, what dispositions do you hope your students will acquire?

Part 2: Devise an Assessment Plan

Devise a general assessment plan for your unit. What do you plan to assess? When? How? Reflect on the targets you've established. How would you sequence appropriate assessments? What assessment methods might work best in this plan? How will you work to integrate content from your students' cultural backgrounds? How will you address the challenges of working with learners with specific aspects of diversity (e.g., language)?

Part 3: Design a Performance Assessment Related to Your Identified Targets

Identify one or more achievement targets. Go through the step-by-step process of designing an authentic assessment. Devise appropriate exercises or tasks, rubrics, and a plan for scoring and recording. Finally, write a brief outline of the steps you might use to involve your students in developing and using these assessments as part of the teaching and learning process.

Part 4: Reflect

When you have finished, evaluate your team's plan in terms of the attributes of sound assessment for multicultural education. What makes this plan appropriate for use with diverse learners?

Self-Assessment

1. What are your concerns about standardized and classroom-based assessments? Develop a T-sheet to compare and contrast your responses. What potential benefits do you see for both types of assessments?

2. Imagine that you are a high school principal. The assistant superintendent wants the schools in the district to investigate the feasibility and advisability of using performance assessment approaches to meet diverse learner needs. She asks you to initiate the effort. What do you do?

3. Historically, assessment and evaluation during school years have carried a distinctly negative connotation. Most adults would not return to those experiences. Yet some contend that this is the way school is supposed to be—it's a rite of passage. They made it through, and others should be forced to deal with it too. Do you agree? How do your perspectives address the issue of equity in education?

ANNOTATED RESOURCES

Center for Research on Education, Diversity, and Excellence (CREDE)

http://manoa.hawaii.edu/coe/crede/

The CREDE Hawai'i Project promotes educators' use of research-based strategies of effective practice for culturally and linguistically diverse students. These strategies are derived from Vygotsky's theory and over 30 years of research from the national CREDE project, now at University of Hawai'i at Mānoa. These standards were recognized by the national What Works Clearinghouse.

Center for Research on Evaluation, Standards, and Student Testing

http://cresst.org

Code of Fair Testing Practices in Education

https://www.apa.org/science/programs/testing/fair-testing.pdf

Published in 2002 by the Association for Assessment in Counseling and Education.

edTPA

https://www.edtpa.com/

Stanford University faculty and staff at the Stanford Center for Assessment, Learning, and Equity developed edTPA. They received substantive advice and feedback from teachers and teacher educators and drew from experience gained from over 25 years of developing performance-based assessments of teaching (including the National Board for Professional Teaching Standards, the Interstate Teacher Assessment and Support Consortium Standards portfolio, and the Performance Assessment for California Teachers.

National Center for Education Statistics

http://nces.ed.gov/nationsreportcard/ltt

The National Center for Education Statistics (NCES) is the primary federal entity for collecting and analyzing data related to education in the United States and other nations. NCES is located within the U.S. Department of Education and the Institute of Education Sciences. NCES fulfills a Congressional mandate to collect, collate, analyze, and report complete statistics on the condition of American education; conduct and publish reports; and review and report on educational activities internationally. NCES oversees the NAEP tests. NAEP is the largest nationally representative and continuing assessment of what America's students know and can do in various subject areas. Assessments are conducted periodically in mathematics, reading, science, writing, the arts, civics, economics, geography, U.S. history, and Technology and Engineering Literacy.

National Center for Fair and Open Testing

http://www.fairtest.org

The National Center for Fair and Open Testing works to end the misuses and flaws of standardized testing and to ensure that evaluation of students, teachers, and schools is fair, open, valid, and educationally beneficial.

Program for International Student Assessment

www.oecd.org/pisa/

PISA is an international assessment that measures 15-year-old students' reading, mathematics, and science literacy every 3 years. First conducted in 2000, the major domain of study rotates between mathematics, science, and reading in each cycle.

RTI Action Network

http://www.rtinetwork.org/learn/what/whatisrti

The RTI Action Network is dedicated to the effective implementation of RTI in school districts nationwide. Its goal is to guide educators and families in the large-scale implementation of RTI so that each child has access to quality instruction and that struggling students—including those with learning and attention issues—are identified early and receive the necessary supports to be successful.

System for Educator Evaluation and Development

http://www.connecticutseed.org

Connecticut's SEED is a model evaluation and support system that is aligned with the Connecticut Guidelines for Educator Evaluation. The evaluation process has the potential to help move teachers along the path to exemplary practice and to raise student achievement by clearly defining excellent practice and results; giving accurate, useful information about teachers' strengths and areas for development; and providing opportunities for growth and recognition.

Smarter Balanced Assessment Consortium

http://www.smarterbalanced.org

Smarter Balanced is a state-led consortium developing assessments aligned with the CCSS in English language arts/literacy and mathematics. The goal is to prepare all students to graduate from high school or college and to become career ready.

Trends in International Mathematics and Science Study

http://timss.bc.edu

The TIMSS provides reliable and timely data on the mathematics and science achievement of U.S. students compared with that of students in other countries. TIMSS data have been collected from students in Grades 4 and 8 since 1995 every 4 years, generally.

Get the tools you need to sharpen your study skills. SAGE edge offers a robust online environment featuring an impressive array of free tools and resources. Access practice quizzes, eFlashcards, video, and multimedia at **edge.sagepub.com/howe3e**

Section IV Assessment

Skills

Most educators agree that major influences on the achievement of students are the activities and support materials; environment; and types of expectations, interactions, and behaviors to which they are exposed. Therefore, an understanding of bias and skill in discerning subtle and/or overt bias in curriculum, instruction, and assessment are extremely important.

Conduct a cultural bias investigation to examine a particular textbook with which you are familiar. Your investigation will focus on identifying instructional and assessment practices that reflect cultural bias and inhibit learning. The investigation will include reflection on the impact of these practices on student learning.

Procedure

1. Make sure that you are familiar with the key authors and experts described in the chapters in this section.

    Review at least five research-based sources that clarify the research to expand your understanding of the influence of culture on teaching and learning and the presence of bias in curriculum, instruction, and assessment.

2. Select and analyze a textbook with which you are familiar. Use the Sadkers's (Sadker & Zittleman, 2012) list of the seven prevalent forms of bias in the curriculum to conduct a critical analysis of the textbook.

    Look at aspects such as pictures, names of people, the relative marginalization or integration of groups of people throughout the text, examples used, and so on. Summarize and present your data in displays (charts, tables, etc.).

3. Include in a written report the following:

    - Introduction (text selected, rationale for selection, description of the text, and the context in which it is used)

    - Review of the research on the influence of culture in teaching and learning and bias in the curriculum

    - Summary of your findings (data tables and appropriate narratives)

    - Discussion of the findings, including the following:
        - resonance with the research on bias
        - your understanding of bias and the challenges it poses to teaching and learning
        - the implications of your findings for teaching and learning

    - Relate your discussion of the findings to class discussions and readings of the philosophy of education and purposes of the curriculum.

    - Be sure to adhere to APA guidelines in writing the final paper.

    - Use the following tables to display your data.

TABLE 1   Textbook Profile

Edition	
Number of pages	
Number of chapters	
Glossary and appendices	
Index	
References	
Total number of text pages	

TABLE 2   Analysis of Four Chapters for Frequency of Mention of Each Search Category

- Whites/Caucasians (male/female)
- African Americans (male/female)
- Hispanics/Latinos/Latinas (male/female)
- Native Americans (male/female)
- Asian Americans (male/female)
- Disability and deaf culture
- Gay, lesbian, bisexual, and transgendered persons (male/female)
- Religious groups
- Other

EXAMPLE TABLE 2 FORMAT   Textbook Chapter Analysis

Search Category	1 # Mentions/ # Pages	2 # Mentions/ # Pages	3 # Mentions/ # Pages	4 # Mentions/ # Pages	Total # Mentions/ # Pages
White males					
White females					
African Americans					
Hispanics/Latinos/Latinas					

TABLE 3   Analysis of Each Chapter for Portrayal of Group Members

Use the description of each type of bias to determine its existence in the selected textbook chapters.

EXAMPLE TABLE 3 FORMAT   Textbook Chapter Analysis

Search Category	1 Evidence by Group	2 Evidence by Group	3 Evidence by Group	4 Evidence by Group	Summary
Invisibility					
Stereotyping					
Imbalance and selectivity					
Unreality					
Fragmentation and isolation					
Linguistic bias					
Cosmetic bias					

In addition, you may optionally include other tables that summarize data obtained from the use of additional instruments.

SECTION V

ACTION

11 Creating the Multicultural Classroom

Learning Objectives

As explained in earlier chapters, becoming a multicultural educator requires an investment of time and energy devoted to (1) expanding awareness, (2) building a knowledge base, (3) developing and enhancing skills, and (4) action planning. We will address the fourth stage—action planning—in this section (see Figure 11.1). Since action planning takes place on individual and schoolwide levels, we will focus specifically on creating the effective multicultural classroom in Chapter 11 and the effective multicultural school in Chapter 12. Through your exploration of concepts and topics in Chapter 11, you will enhance your capacity in the following key learning objectives for taking action toward an effective multicultural classroom. Having completed work on this chapter, you will be able to do the following:

11.1 Enunciate a clear vision, beliefs, and set of goals about what you want to accomplish as an effective teacher for all learners

11.2 Explain ways to design learning experiences that put students first

11.3 Establish effective strategies to collaborate with like-minded individuals who have made the same commitment to becoming a multicultural educator

11.4 Critique the value of using data to examine your own instructional practices to make changes that will affect learning for all students

11.5 Develop a plan for your own ongoing professional development as a multicultural educator

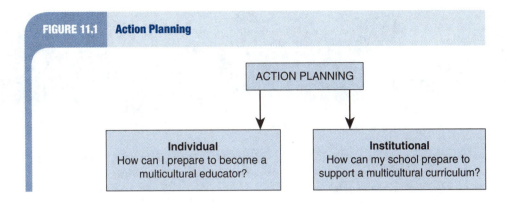

FIGURE 11.1   **Action Planning**

ssume that an educator understands the importance of self-awareness as a cultural being, is working to enhance his or her knowledge base about multicultural education, and is developing skills to teach all children well. Is that enough to ensure becoming an effective multicultural educator?

While these areas are certainly important, we believe that they are not enough to ensure the implementation of new ways of teaching. In addition to work in knowledge, awareness, and skills, you will want to bridge these components by establishing and following an action plan. Action planning is an important component of the literature on effective teaching (Arends, 2015; Boykin & Noguera, 2011; Oakes, Lipton, Anderson, & Stillman, 2018; Robbins, Lindsey, Lindsey, & Terrell, 2011). Action planning on an individual level is particularly critical given the variety of challenges, strategies, traditions, and other demands that compete for one's time.

A strong Individual Multicultural Educator Action Plan is a collection of documents, sometimes in the form of a portfolio that can be amended, adapted over time, and referred to regularly. It provides you with a sense of direction as well as a summary of progress in the process of becoming a multicultural educator. Exhibit 11.1 offers a suggested list of components in an Individual Multicultural Educator Action Plan. You may wish to augment this set with other items.

> All of us in the academy and in the culture as a whole are called to renew our minds if we are to transform educational institutions—and society—so that the way we live, teach, and work can reflect our joy in cultural diversity, our passion for justice, and our love of freedom.
>
> —bell hooks (2006), American author, feminist, and social activist

Exhibit 11.1   **Sample Components of an Individual Multicultural Educator Action Plan**

1. A platform of your beliefs about education that supports deep learning for all students

2. Personal vision statement of multicultural education and goals (what do you want to achieve, and where you are headed)

3. Samples of curriculum units, lesson plans, learning experiences, and assessments that work well with diverse groups of students

4. A list or network of colleagues with whom you are working in your process of becoming an effective multicultural educator

5. Samples of data used to gauge your progress as a multicultural educator

6. Outline of your professional development activities that will support or are supporting your growth as a multicultural educator, including a tentative time frame for growth activities

7. Journal in which you record periodically your reflections on your growth

CASE STUDY
TEACHERS LEARNING TOGETHER

A group of experienced teachers studying to be leaders gathered on a snowy winter evening as part of an inquiry group on teaching and learning. For this evening, they had been reading Gloria Ladson-Billings's book *The Dreamkeepers* (2009). In preparation for that evening, they had divided into groups, each group being assigned a particular chapter on which they needed to become experts. One after the other, the groups shared what they believed to be the essence of each chapter and its implications for leadership, teaching, and learning. As the groups responded to each other's comments, it became clear that everyone understood the importance of culturally relevant teaching. After chapter summaries were presented, the professor asked for comments in response to two essential questions: (1) Did they truly *believe* that culturally relevant teaching was critical? (2) Where were the students themselves on a continuum of becoming culturally responsible?

One teacher said, "This is nice, but isn't this going to be expensive to implement?"

Said another, "I just thought all teachers are doing this. If they're not doing this in my school, we just get rid of them."

Said a third, "This book makes me understand that we are engaged in a battle for kids."

Your Perspectives on the Case

1. Do you believe that culturally relevant teaching is critical?

2. In every school, there are teachers who are not knowledgeable and skilled in culturally responsive education. How would you work to support your colleagues in moving in that direction?

3. What is your response to the question of funding for this type of professional development work? Is developing multicultural education just a nice thing to do when time and resources permit?

4. Reflect on the potential of participation in a book study with colleagues. If you could participate in such a group, identify a book you would like to read and discuss. What is your rationale for your selection?

THINKING AHEAD
REFLECTING ON THE CHAPTER 11 LEARNING OBJECTIVES

As you consider putting into practice the knowledge and skills you have learned, you may be wondering where to start. Like the teachers described in this chapter's opening case study, you may think that multicultural education sounds great in theory but is pretty challenging to initiate and implement regularly. Take time to reflect on becoming a multicultural educator by responding to the following prompts.

1. List three to five specific goals you have for yourself in becoming a multicultural educator.

2. Where would you place yourself on a continuum of "centeredness"? At one end of the continuum is an entirely teacher-centered classroom, and at the other end is an entirely **student-centered classroom**. Why did you place yourself where you did? How might you move more in the direction of being student-centered?

3. Which school groups and local and national professional organizations might serve as a resource for you to find allies and critical

friends with whom to collaborate in becoming a multicultural educator?

4. Educators are increasingly discovering the power of collecting, summarizing, and analyzing data to make decisions about teaching and learning. You may already have learned specific strategies for collecting and examining data in the classroom.

What do you think are some effective ways of collecting data to examine your own practice? Why?

5. What learning strategies do you prefer to use in order to enhance your capacity as an educator? How might you apply those strategies to a plan for expanding your understanding and skill as a multicultural educator?

LEARNING OBJECTIVE 11.1 Enunciate a Clear Vision, Beliefs, and Set of Goals About What You Want to Accomplish as an Effective Teacher for All Learners

A Starting Point: Developing a Multicultural Education Platform of Beliefs

Someone once said, "If you don't know where you are going, it's going to be difficult to get there." Traditionally, educational leaders were expected to have and convey a sense of vision, whereas teachers were just supposed to fall into line behind the omnipotent leader. More recently, however, the literature on organizational change indicates that a vision will have a greater chance of being achieved if it is developed collaboratively (Blankstein, 2013; Fullan & Hargreaves, 1996; Sergiovanni & Starratt, 2007). This means that teachers need to be engaged in developing a vision of what the school and their classrooms could and should be. Also, teachers are now expected to become teacher-leaders—in other words, to be engaged in decision making and significant school improvement efforts.

Early in your journey toward becoming an effective multicultural educator, you'll want to examine and clarify your own perceptions, assumptions, and beliefs about the teaching and learning process. These beliefs could be encapsulated in a platform of beliefs about teaching and learning. You can be assured that the statements in your platform will change with your own **professional development**. The important action to take now is to put your beliefs in writing. Exhibit 11.2 provides a sample set of beliefs developed by one school district in its efforts to support multicultural education.

There may be other areas you wish to consider in developing your platform. Use the questions in Exercise 11.1 to write a **Multicultural Education Platform of Beliefs**. In writing your

Exhibit 11.2 Sample Set of Beliefs About Teaching and Learning for All Students

I believe that . . .

1. learning must take place within a social context in which students are learning from and with one another, making connections, and constructing meaning.
2. when students make connections during learning, they are more likely to understand larger concepts and to apply learning.
3. inquiry-based teaching and learning can lead students to organize information, solve problems, and formulate problems.
4. to be "educated" means developing competency in a variety of content areas and being able to use those competencies to address critical and essential questions.
5. students learn more deeply when they are engaged in a variety of instructional and assessment experiences.
6. an "educated" citizen today and in the future will value and work effectively with diverse people.

EXERCISE 11.1

MULTICULTURAL EDUCATION PLATFORM OF BELIEFS

Take stock of your beliefs by asking yourself the following questions:

1. How do I define effective teaching?

2. What are my five most important goals as a teacher?

3. What is the purpose of teaching?

4. What do I expect of students? Do I expect different levels of achievement of different types of students? Why?

5. In what ways do I believe that cultural differences affect the teaching and learning process?

6. How do I select instructional strategies to ensure that all students are learning to be culturally proficient?

7. What important knowledge, skills, and dispositions do effective teachers of culturally diverse students possess?

platform, be honest about yourself and the kind of teacher that you are and your attitude toward and perception of students. Be clear about your commitment to the principles of educational equity and social justice. Be prepared to not only defend your beliefs but also find kindred spirits. Keep returning to your platform and share it with your supervisor and other colleagues.

Visioning

A vision for a classroom or a school is a picture—sometimes graphically portrayed, sometimes explored linguistically—of what a teacher or the members of that school community hope to achieve. It represents the values and beliefs of that person or community. What are the components of a vision? As you develop your vision for the classroom and/or school, you might consider including any or all of the following components:

- People who are present in the vision
- People who are in positions of power (including children)
- Decision-making processes in the classroom and/or school
- Communication mechanisms and processes
- A philosophy of how children learn
- Physical orientation of furniture and materials

Remember that visions can change. As you develop your vision, consider what supports are in place to help you achieve your vision and what barriers might hinder its achievement. Table 11.1 offers some examples of barriers and supports you may encounter.

© istockphotos.com/Steve Debenport

Much like preparing for a race, we have trained, planned, and strategized. It is time to put into action what you have learned.

TABLE 11.1	Sample Supports and Barriers to Achieving a Vision of Multicultural Education	

Supports	Barriers
1. Like-minded colleagues who are interested in achieving equity in schools	1. Feelings of insecurity about tackling controversial issues
2. Access to resources such as local teacher education programs and service centers that support this work	2. Anxiety about the extent to which the school leaders, other teachers, and parents will support this type of work
3. Time set aside by the school leader for this work	3. Feelings of being in this work by yourself
4. Disaggregated data from standardized and other achievement tests	4. Belief that you are not a change agent and not wanting to take the risk of stretching into this area
5. A variety of ongoing professional development activities focused on helping teachers support individual students in their learning	

Goal Setting as a Multicultural Educator

An Individual Multicultural Educator Action Plan is your own layout of what you plan to do and when you plan to do it. It is also your "track record" of what you have done as you enhance your knowledge and skills as a multicultural educator and your assessment of how well you are doing in meeting your own goals. The Individual Multicultural Educator Action Plan is particularly useful as a reference about your own growth. Once you have explored your beliefs and started to develop a vision of yourself and your classroom, you will want to establish goals or targets for your work as a multicultural educator.

Goal setting can be a challenging process. People sometimes become frustrated because they don't believe that their goals can really be achieved. A widely popularized acronym of guidelines for goal setting indicates that they should be SMART! In other words, they should be *specific, measurable, attainable, realistic,* and *timely.* The more *specific* your goals are, the more likely you will achieve them. Set goals so that you can *measure* your progress through data collection. Set goals that you believe you can *attain* in a specified period of time. *Realistic* goals are set with an awareness of available resources and supports. And finally, *timely* goals are those for which you have set a manageable time frame for achievement.

How might you select your goals? Think back to your vision. What do you want to do? Now what will you need to learn more deeply to achieve this? You might select and organize your goals according to areas covered in previous chapters that you believe are particularly critical. For example, you may specify the goal of exploring yourself as a cultural being in more depth. You may want to spend time learning more about specific cultural groups so that you can be more responsive to their needs and styles as learners. Or you may want to explore and experiment with specific promising practices in curriculum designs, instructional strategies, or assessment approaches.

Another way to select and organize goals is according to teaching standards. Teacher preparation programs are designed to prepare future teachers according to sets of standards or expectations, which describe what teachers should know and be able to do. One approach to organizing standards is according to three broad areas: knowledge, skills, and dispositions. If you are using this umbrella approach to goal setting, you might organize your individual goals (targets) according to the following three areas:

1. Goals for expanding knowledge and understanding (about self, content, cultures)

2. Goals for enhancing skills (with teaching, learning, curriculum development, assessment, and so forth)

3. Goals for addressing beliefs and attitudes (capacity for reflection, disposition, understanding of values and beliefs)

To select your goals, you might also turn to a source list, such as the "13 Knowledge Bases" developed by G. Pritchy Smith (1998). The knowledge bases explicate specifically what teachers who are culturally responsible and responsive need to know, and they are an excellent treatment of the knowledge needed. Smith wrote his groundbreaking book titled *Common Sense About Uncommon Knowledge: The Knowledge Bases for Diversity* (1998) in which he identified 13 areas of knowledge for culturally competent educators. If you were to write an article today about critical knowledge bases for culturally competent educators, what would you include and why? You might make time to develop your own list of critical knowledge bases. Then locate Smith's knowledge bases and compare the two sets. How do they differ? How are they alike? What has changed since 1998, if anything?

Finally, you might describe your goals more specifically by clarifying whether or not they are short-term or long-term goals. Short-term goals are relatively easy to achieve and can be addressed within a few days or weeks. Long-term goals are more challenging to accomplish, are larger in scope, and can be addressed in a few months to a few years. Examples of short-term, or proximal, goals related to becoming a multicultural educator include subscribing to a journal that might help inform your thinking (e.g., *Rethinking Schools*). You might also consider designing some introductory experiences for students to get to know one another through their cultural identities at the beginning of the school year.

Examples of long-term, or distal, goals related to becoming a multicultural educator are learning to speak a language other than your native language, learning more about a particular cultural group that is represented in your student population, conducting a cultural bias investigation of the curriculum materials you use or will be using, or designing unit and lesson plans according to the theory of multiple intelligences.

LEARNING OBJECTIVE 11.2 Explain Ways to Design Learning Experiences That Put Students First

Learn About Your Students

A traditional way to approach the teaching and learning process is for teachers to start with the content and then organize activities. This is no longer believed to be beneficial for students. The starting point, in fact, should be the students and the outcomes we expect from them. If teachers are to design learning experiences that are appropriate for individual learners, scaffold learning effectively, and build on what students know and are able to do, the starting point must be a clear understanding and knowledge of the students. The process of learning about your students is particularly important at the start of the school year, but it must also continue throughout the year.

Before the start of the school year, learn about your students, their families, and the communities in which they live. How might you do this? At the least, you will want to access and review student records that are maintained by the school administration. However, these sources present limited insights into student ability, beliefs, values, and understandings. You can extend your learning about students by examining student portfolios of work passed on from previous grades. To get a sense of the cultural backgrounds and experiences of the students you will teach, you will also invest time in exploring the local community.

At the school level, schools and districts in some states are required to develop a strategic school profile (SSP). The SSP is useful for schools as they collect data and work to use those

iStock/CEFutcher

Understanding where students "are coming from" can help teachers design lessons that can help students prepare "for where they are going."

data about students and about the school to make decisions about teaching and learning. For example, in recent years, categories of information that have been addressed in the Connecticut SSPs include gender, race, age, number of students who go on to college, number of dropouts, and number of students in special education.

Individual teachers will be aided in making decisions about teaching and learning on a classroom level by developing a **classroom demographic profile** (Davidman & Davidman, 2001). The classroom demographic profile is a fairly straightforward tool for identifying the diversity that exists in any classroom setting. Once a profile is established, it can be used to inform instruction for individual students. Teachers may list students under the following categories: those who are linguistically different, those who have an Individual Education Plan, those who have a suspected learning disability, those who are immigrant students, those receiving medication, those who are gifted and talented, and those who are from an ethnic minority background. Davidman and Davidman (2001) stressed that teachers include in this last category students who are Hispanic, African American, Native American, Asian American, and so forth only if their cultural background may have instructional implications. You may wish to add other categories, such as gender. As you progress through the year and learn more about your students, you can add to the list areas such as preferred learning styles, preferred intelligence, and so forth. Exhibit 11.3 provides a sample classroom demographic profile.

Maintain High Expectations for Student Outcomes

Some educators decry the development of a classroom demographic profile, stating that they treat all students equally. Other educators indicate that developing a classroom demographic profile itself could lead to stereotyping and labeling, as well as lowering expectations for certain groups of students. Interestingly, it is the very rare educator who manages to treat all students equally. The range of influences—including personal experiences, deep-seated and subconscious stereotypes, traditions, cultural learning, and the process of socialization, to name a few—on how we interact with people is just too extensive.

Certainly, educators need to be cautious about succumbing to stereotypes. However, the research on educational expectations indicates that even the most well-intentioned educators have differing expectations of different students. And in every classroom, *all students are different* for one reason or another. Differences are expressed in attitudes, experiences, and understandings as well as cultural backgrounds.

Furthermore, teachers tend to see students in one of two primary ways. First, teachers may profess that they don't look at differences—particularly cultural—that students bring to the classroom (the "culture-blind" phenomenon). When differences do surface, they often are viewed as problems, and the teacher doesn't know how to respond to them. On the other hand, as a result of socialization processes, learning prejudices, and developing preconceptions, teachers may have differing expectations of different groups of students, often based on cultural characteristics or identities. Myra and David Sadker (as cited in Sadker & Zittleman, 2012) conducted extensive research on differing expectations of boys and girls in the classroom and found that teachers overwhelmingly had lower expectations of girls than of boys. Teacher expectations are conveyed through assignments, the amount and type of feedback to student responses, wait time, seating assignments, and posting of student work on classroom walls. As a result of differing teacher expectations, some students learn not to have high expectations of their own achievements, and their confidence in their own ability to achieve is eroded.

A very clear representation of this phenomenon emerged in the blue-eye/brown-eye experiment conducted by Jane Elliot in the 1960s. Elliot, a third-grade teacher in Riceville, Iowa, wanted to find out how early in life students learn to discriminate based on a physical

EXHIBIT 11.3 Sample Classroom Demographic Profile

Teacher's name: Date:

Grade: School: District:

Types of students; instructionally relevant information about specific students

Linguistically different

1.

2.

Individual Education Plan

1.

2.

Suspected learning disability

1.

2.

Ethnic minority background

1.

2.

Immigrant students

1.

2.

Receiving special medication

1.

2.

Gifted and talented

1.

2.

Other categories

1.

2.

Source: Adapted from Davidman and Davidman (2001).

feature. She divided the class into two groups: the blue-eyed group and the brown-eyed group. On the first day of the experiment, she clearly told one group that they were not as smart as the other group. On the next day, she switched the students' "identities." On both days and in both groups, the students lived up—or down—to her conveyed expectations.

How might we work to "construct" the competence of low-status children? Oakes et al. (2018) indicated that the accomplished multicultural educator *expects* differences, begins with the presumption that there is "no normal" way of being or learning, understands that the classroom is a richer learning environment because of differences, and believes that

Extended Explorations 11.1: Teacher Expectations

Decades of research has indicated a link between teacher expectations of students and actual student achievement. Locate an article on teacher expectations and the impact on students. Some of the more well-known authors on teacher expectations include Jere Brophy, Claude Goldenberg, Jackie Jordan Irvine, and Jeannie Oakes. Following your reading of the article or resource, reflect on specific teacher behaviors that might influence the achievement of diverse students in a positive or negative way. Develop a one-page reflective statement about your beliefs, and prepare to share your reflection with course colleagues.

every student is smart. The teacher's role, then, is to develop an environment that builds *confidence* and assigns genuine and merited *competence* to every student. Clearly, we need to have very specific information about our students and their backgrounds so that we can design appropriate and challenging learning experiences for each one and construct the learning environment in such a way as to make sure that each individual achieves at high levels. We simply cannot do this without knowing about our students' cultural and experiential backgrounds.

Work to Integrate Multiple Perspectives

One of the great benefits of classrooms today is that teachers can make use of the diverse perspectives students bring into the classroom. Learning to value multiple perspectives should be a daily experience. Valuing and respecting diversity must be a conscious effort, not an add-on. Just because diverse students are in the same setting does not mean that they will value one another's opinions, experiences, values, beliefs, and culture-specific knowledge.

Diverse perspectives of all students can be integrated into both the teaching and the learning process. Engaging students in opportunities to practice diverse perspectives is important for two primary reasons. First, students need opportunities to take pride in the cultures with which they identify. Teachers should look for opportunities for students to share information about their own cultures and other cultures with which they have some experience. Second, students need opportunities that allow them to step into "someone else's shoes."

To this end, teachers should design learning experiences that engage students in grappling with important concepts and themes about people, communication, justice, interpersonal relationships, and so forth. Students should be engaged in thinking critically about those concepts; they should have opportunities to offer their thoughts and debate the merits and value of diverse perspectives. These kinds of debates should be facilitated so that students "try on" another person's perspective—try seeing events from another point of view. Clearly, this will demand skill in team building, facilitating debates and dialogues, resolving conflict, and communicating. For the teacher as well as the student, these are important skills. Below are some guidelines for establishing multiple perspectives in the classroom.

1. Start small. Begin by selecting one or two American ethnicities, preferably those that hold special meaning for your students, the community, and yourself.

2. Become informed about the perspectives of the members of these groups regarding current events and the subject areas you teach.

3. Become acquainted with community resources.

4. Examine your texts and supplementary materials for bias (see frameworks).

5. Develop a resource file of primary source materials and teaching strategies that will help you present the selected groups' perspectives to your students.

6. Select one or more areas of your course in which the groups' contributions and viewpoints have been overlooked. Create and teach a lesson that provides more accurate knowledge by including the groups' perspectives.

LEARNING OBJECTIVE 11.3 Establish Effective Strategies to Collaborate With Like-Minded Individuals Who Have Made the Same Commitment to Becoming a Multicultural Educator

About Collaboration

One proven strategy for supporting teachers in learning more and more is through teacher collaboration. Unfortunately, a particularly problematic issue facing teachers today is isolation. Professional isolation is one of the greatest impediments to learning to teach! Experienced teachers are often isolated from one another, and exemplary role models are not accessible to those teachers who could use peer coaches. Some outcomes of teachers working in isolation are feelings of inadequacy, insecurity, and lack of recognition.

Collaboration is a means for overcoming the isolation that so often pervades many schools. Collaboration provides teachers with a sense of connectedness and community. Teachers need to feel that they are part of a community for their own intellectual and professional development (Kruse, 1999). Collaboration calls for the development of strong relationships that transcend the traditional boundaries of departments and grade levels. According to Kruse (1999), teachers in collaborative school environments "engage in mutual decision making to resolve their problems of practice" (p. 15).

Participation in inquiry or study groups is a type of job-embedded learning, or learning that occurs while teachers engage in their daily work (Wood & McQuarrie, 1999). Study or inquiry group members can engage in exploring and discussing together the literature on a particular topic (e.g., multiple intelligences, culturally responsive teaching, and constructivism). For example, a group of teachers might visit a model program and then discuss how that particular approach might be applied in their own setting.

The research about learning, for both adults and children, indicates that deep and meaningful learning occurs when people work in collaborative learning environments, in which they have opportunities to learn from and with one another. Therefore, it is essential that schools encourage and support collaboration and value diverse perspectives. The work that emerges through collaboration and reflective dialogue with other professionals will result in inquiry and innovation. Collaborative environments, with well-developed networks of communicative relationships, will accelerate the dissemination of new knowledge throughout the system so that it can benefit students as quickly as possible.

In his book *Failure Is Not an Option*, Alan Blankstein (2013) cites collaborative teaming that is focused on teaching for learning as one of six key principles for advancing student achievement. Blankstein describes four types of school cultures that include individualistic, balkanized (taking sides), contrived collegiality, and collaborative. Blankstein recommends that areas of collaboration might include professional practice forums, peer classroom observation, teachers working together in planning curriculum, vertical teams, professional study groups, grade-level or subject-area teams, interdisciplinary teams, professional interest teams, and leadership teams. If your school is not operating yet as a collaborative culture, the biggest challenge will be to find like-minded teachers who want to work together and can find the time to do so. Below are some suggestions for finding time for collaboration.

1. Common preparation time

2. State allocation of staff development days

3. Early release 1 day a week

Extended Explorations 11.2: School Culture

Take time to reflect about a school culture with which you are familiar. Which of Blankstein's four types of culture most closely characterizes your school? Provide your rationale for your statement. How is team effectiveness measured in your school? How frequently and in what ways do staff members in your school work together to solve problems? Discuss the ways in which each of these areas might be improved.

4. Use of specialists

5. Administrators stepping in to teach

6. Large-group instruction

7. Independent study

8. Volunteers

9. Student teachers

10. Team teaching

The process and practice of becoming an effective multicultural educator will be challenging. It will not be accomplished in a period of just a few months or a few years. However, the process is enhanced immensely when educators find like-minded colleagues with whom to collaborate and when they know where to turn for support. These people will become your partners, allies, and/or critical friends.

A partner is a person who has identified the same or similar goals as you have. A partner is someone who is headed in the same direction as you are, operating within a similar belief system. In the case of education, partners are often teachers. The word *partner* connotes two people working together. However, the concept of partnership can also be applied to small groups of people working as a team (e.g., a grade-level team). Partners generally work collaboratively to accomplish some mutual goal(s). An example of a mutual goal accomplished collaboratively might be the development of a new curriculum unit.

An ally is someone who operates under the same or a similar belief system as you do, but the two of you may be moving side by side, or in parallel tracks rather than in the same

Working collaboratively with other teachers and staff can help generate richer ideas for planning of instruction. Finding allies and supports in the school community are important steps in establishing yourself as a teacher.

© Banana stock/banana stock/ thinkstock

track, in accomplishing the work of multicultural education. Allies can provide support to each other in the achievement of different goals. For example, one ally may be working on developing a new curriculum unit, and another may be working on learning to use a multiple intelligences approach to instruction. Allies may be teachers but could also be staff members, administrators, community members, and/or parents.

A colleague may also be a critical friend supporting your development as a multicultural educator. The primary role of a critical friend is to offer support, encouragement, and friendly critique. A critical friend is someone whose opinion you trust and whom you know to be knowledgeable about multicultural education. He or she can be someone in your own institution (e.g., someone in a different department in your school) or from a different institution altogether. For example, you might identify someone at a regional service center, university, or state department of education who is knowledgeable about multicultural education (perhaps someone who has facilitated a workshop or taught a course on multicultural education) and who can provide some feedback as you move forward.

In your work to become a multicultural educator, it is helpful to identify people in each of the three categories identified above. They each play a different role in your development.

Functioning as a Partner

A partnership is a special relationship that merits some advanced thought and planning. Once you have clarified your own belief system and goals, then through collegial conversations, you will be able to identify people with whom you might want to partner. Consider the scope of your partnership work. Does it make sense, in light of your goals and the educators in your setting, for you to partner with one other person or several people? If you believe that several people might work well together, make sure to keep the team size manageable. A team that expands beyond three to four people might be challenged to find mutually agreed-on time to work, as well as common goals and approaches to doing the work. With your partner(s), establish parameters for your partnership work. A key parameter is when you will meet. Finding and making time to do this work is often the biggest challenge and can become a barrier to progress.

What Can You Do as Partners Toward Multicultural Education?

What might you do as partners? The primary reason to work in a partnership is to solve problems! Imagine you and your partner(s) have identified a goal or something that needs to be accomplished, to be changed, or to be initiated. In addressing the problem or goal, you might start by engaging in mutual study. In fact, you may have identified your partner by having attended the same workshop, course, or other professional development activity on some aspect of multicultural education. So you may already be on the road of collaborative study, investigation, and enhancing your knowledge base in multicultural education.

Another area of work for partners is practice. Through their study, partners may identify a promising practice, instructional strategy, or skill they want to develop. Partners may practice this skill together and share their outcomes with each other, giving and receiving feedback in the process. Educators need to practice a skill many times in order to become comfortable in applying it. Ideally, partners will engage in practice immediately following learning a new skill so the newly acquired knowledge doesn't dissipate.

An example of what you might do with your partners, allies, and critical friends is the development of a portion of a curriculum that is multicultural. The outcomes of your collaborative work might be included in your Individual Multicultural Educator Action Plan portfolio. To work collaboratively and productively, you might do the following:

1. Identify a specific area of focus related to developing a curriculum that is multicultural.

2. Identify your specific goal(s) for the curriculum project.

3. Identify the resources you will need to do this work.

4. Specify the steps needed to reach your goal(s).

5. Identify the supports your team has and the ways in which you can increase that support.

6. Identify the resistance you might encounter and the ways in which you can decrease it.

7. Identify types of data you will collect to indicate that this work is making a difference.

Partners may also choose to observe and coach each other's work in order to learn from each other. As you both practice implementing new instructional strategies or a new curriculum to meet diverse learner needs, make time to go into each other's classrooms to see what you can learn from each other and how you might encourage each other along the way. Joyce and Showers (2002) defined this type of relationship as "coaching," with the person who is demonstrating or teaching called the "coach." The person observing is looking for new approaches to inform his or her own practice.

Partners might also develop new curriculum materials together. You might start small by developing a new lesson or set of lessons that integrates multicultural concepts or you might revise a curriculum unit to make sure that it is integrating diverse perspectives. If you divide the work, you will each have double the return on your efforts.

As you and your partner integrate new instructional practices and new curriculum materials, you will want to investigate how this is affecting the teaching and learning process. Are your new instructional practices, in fact, helping individual students learn more effectively and deeply? This is a critical component of improving teaching and learning. For this purpose, you and your partner can engage in collaborative analysis of planning for appropriate use of the innovation and the teaching that uses it. When you design a study of a particular innovation or intervention in your own classroom to determine its impact, you are engaging in **action research** (Mertler, 2016). Action research is a study that is designed and carried out by an individual or a group of teachers to investigate a question of interest. These individuals collect data in manageable ways, such as by examining student work or conducting surveys of students. Teachers then summarize the data and discuss them with their partners. This should lead teachers to making some decisions about that innovation, thus fine-tuning their teaching practice.

LEARNING OBJECTIVE 11.4 Critique the Value of Using Data to Examine Your Own Instructional Practices to Make Changes That Will Affect Learning for All Students

Instructional Practice

As you work to integrate new instructional practices and curriculum materials designed to meet diverse learner needs, you will want to plan for regular assessment of your progress and the impact of these new practices on student learning. Collecting evidence of progress will be useful in your own reflections, in your own development as an educator, and in sharing with others (e.g., partners, colleagues, and supervisors).

How might you easily and effectively collect data? The most helpful data will be the kinds that inform you of your own progress as a teacher. Certainly, as a teacher you will be collecting much evidence about student progress in your classroom. Self-assessment can take many forms, including the following

- Inventories
- Journals and anecdotal logs
- Assessment instruments
- Action research projects

iStock/monkeybusinessimages

A teacher needs to know their students well in order to more accurately assess their needs as well as measure what they are learning.

Inventories

You can think of an inventory as being a catalog of items that might exist. It is often a listing of items accompanied by a space to check, usually with a simple "yes" or "no," the presence or absence of particular items. In the case of self-assessment, an inventory might be a tool that provides "benchmark" information about skills, knowledge, approaches, and strategies that a developing multicultural educator does or does not possess.

You might also want to check yourself periodically on your progress in enhancing curriculum, instruction, and assessment. Exercise 11.2 is a checklist approach to self-assessment in these three areas. Check *yes* or *no* depending on your self-assessment.

EXERCISE 11.2
MY MULTICULTURAL CLASSROOM

Curriculum

☐ YES ☐ NO	1. I am consciously aware of incorporating models of multicultural education into the curriculum.
☐ YES ☐ NO	2. My curriculum is connected to local, state, and national standards.
☐ YES ☐ NO	3. My classroom visually recognizes and supports diversity focusing on how we are both similar and different.
☐ YES ☐ NO	4. The curriculum that I use represents diverse perspectives.
☐ YES ☐ NO	5. A range of cultural groups, girls and boys, and lesbian, gay, bisexual, transgender, and questioning students are represented equitably in the curriculum.
☐ YES ☐ NO	6. Texts and other teaching materials are multicultural.
☐ YES ☐ NO	7. Students can quickly and easily identify with positive role models from the curriculum that reflect their culture from a historic and a modern perspective.
☐ YES ☐ NO	8. In addition to texts, I use literature, historical records, archival material, and other authentic resources.
☐ YES ☐ NO	9. The services and support of the library or media center are a strong component of my curriculum.

Instruction

☐ YES ☐ NO	10. I have high expectations for all students.
☐ YES ☐ NO	11. I use multiple teaching strategies.
☐ YES ☐ NO	12. I am aware of the various learning styles among my students.
☐ YES ☐ NO	13. I use culturally appropriate teaching strategies.

☐ YES	☐ NO	14. I incorporate students' experiences in my lessons.
☐ YES	☐ NO	15. I incorporate examples, experiences, and perspectives from a variety of cultures.
☐ YES	☐ NO	16. I use cooperative learning.
☐ YES	☐ NO	17. I encourage critical thinking.
☐ YES	☐ NO	18. I have incorporated technology into the classroom.
☐ YES	☐ NO	19. Teacher's aides are treated respectfully as teaching partners.
☐ YES	☐ NO	20. I use the help of parents and community members in my class.
☐ YES	☐ NO	21. I show respect for students' first language.
☐ YES	☐ NO	22. Expectations for student behavior and consequences of misbehavior are equitable.
☐ YES	☐ NO	23. I encourage positive interactions among students and ensure that they all have opportunities to work with one another.
☐ YES	☐ NO	24. I model support for and respect of diversity.
☐ YES	☐ NO	25. I have a zero tolerance policy toward discrimination based on race, ethnicity, national origin, sexual orientation, and other protected classes.

Assessment

☐ YES	☐ NO	26. I use multiple forms of unbiased assessment.
☐ YES	☐ NO	27. In testing, I take into consideration the learning styles of my students.
☐ YES	☐ NO	28. I make sure that my students understand what is expected of them in assessment.
☐ YES	☐ NO	29. Students are involved in their own self-assessment.
☐ YES	☐ NO	30. I have reviewed tests that I use to ensure that they are free of bias.
☐ YES	☐ NO	31. The tests that I use take into consideration multiple perspectives.
☐ YES	☐ NO	32. For new English learners, whenever possible, I test in their native language.

Journaling and Anecdotal Logs

While educators do, in fact, reflect many times throughout the day as they go about their work and think about their activities, this type of reflection can be fragmented. If you truly want to improve your teaching and become an effective multicultural educator, you should commit to putting your reflections into writing. Primary reasons for committing your reflections to writing are that (1) you can go back through your writing and look for patterns or themes in your comments, (2) the discipline of writing will push you to consider your strengths and areas of weakness, and (3) writing will help you consider more deeply the areas you want to address. Killion (1999) believed that journals are a powerful professional development design and can "become a place for learners to record observations, toy with various perspectives, analyze their own practice, interpret their understandings of topics, keep records, make comments, or reconstruct experiences" (p. 36).

The most common form of reflective writing is in a journal or a logbook. More and more, teachers are writing their reflections on their computers, having set up a simple framework or matrix with a variety of columns (e.g., date, activity, children who were intended to benefit from the activity, outcomes, and reflections on teaching and learning). Teachers who find this technique most useful are those who write fairly frequently, at least a few times per week. It is usually easier to record shorter reflections more often than to write longer reflections infrequently. If you don't develop the habit of writing reflections frequently, important details about the teaching and learning experience seem to disappear.

Assessment Instruments

An assessment instrument is similar to an inventory in purpose but is a way of fine-tuning self-evaluation. With an assessment instrument, you can assess yourself on the quality or the degree of the presence or use of a skill, action, approach, or strategy. Often, this means assigning a rating on a scale. You may also want to assess yourself on your acquisition of specific areas of knowledge in education that is multicultural.

Action Research

Action research is carried out by practitioners with a view to improving their professional practice and understanding it better. Action research is a systematic way of evaluating the consequences of educational decisions and adjusting practice. It can be used to select and evaluate educational alternatives (Mertler, 2016). *The purpose of action research is to maximize learning for children.* Action research can be a particularly useful way for educators to discern which strategies are more effective for different learners. Data collection and analysis as a part of the action research process lead educators to make data-based decisions about teaching and learning.

Action Research Is Usually Composed of Five Phases

Phase 1: Focus. A teacher determines an area of teaching and learning on which to focus. In the case of becoming a more effective multicultural educator, the study could focus on a curricular approach or an instructional strategy that the teacher has been using. The teacher may be wondering about the impact of that approach or strategy on diverse learners. Examples of focus areas might be the use of multiple intelligences or the use of performance-based assessments with diverse learners. During the focus phase, the teacher poses a specific question related to the focus area. This question will ground the study.

Phase 2: Plan. The teacher plans to collect data in a variety of ways (methods) and from a variety of sources (e.g., students, other teachers, staff, parents, and community members). The teacher will want to collect data about the *impact* of the instructional approach or curricular strategy over a period of time. The teacher will also want to collect information or data about the *implementation* of the approach or strategy (commonly called the *intervention*). Data collection methods could include examining examples of student work over time, interviews, surveys or questionnaires, focus group sessions, test scores, school records (e.g., behavioral referrals, suspensions, attendance), and other sources of information. During this planning phase, the teacher will collect data from a variety of subjects. If the teacher is wondering, for example, how well a particular intervention works with diverse student groups, he or she will want to "sample" students from a variety of groups.

Phase 3: Implement. The teacher implements the action research plan.

Phase 4: Organize and analyze the data. At this point, the teacher-researcher makes sense of the data. This phase involves developing frequencies of responses and perhaps performing some simple statistical procedures such as determining the mean, median, and mode of response sets.

Phase 5: Report, decide, and take action. The teacher might share the results of the study with colleagues or supervisors. One of the most important activities in this phase, however, is to make some decisions about the instructional strategy or curricular approach. Based on the data, is the strategy or approach having the desired effect on diverse student learners? If not, what might the teacher want to do in order to adjust his or her practice? And then, with that decision made, the teacher will want to take action in some direction. From there, the action research cycle begins again.

LEARNING OBJECTIVE 11.5 Develop a Plan for Your Own Ongoing Professional Development as a Multicultural Educator

Professional Development Options

Teachers continue their learning for two primary reasons: (1) to have a variety of skills and strategies for working effectively with diverse learners and (2) to be able to modify their approaches in order to address the changing needs of learners (Robbins et al., 2011). In the past, with a more homogeneous student population, it may have been acceptable to have a limited number of curriculum development and instructional strategies. However, learner needs in our current and future environment differ widely. Educators must be skilled and knowledgeable in a variety of strategies. Clearly, to address these changing needs and to support high levels of achievement of all learners, instructors will need to engage continuously in their own professional development.

Fortunately, a tremendous amount of information is available about what constitutes useful professional development (DuFour, 2004; Fullan & Hargreaves, 1996; Hord, 2004; Hord, Roussin, & Sommers, 2009; Joyce & Showers, 2002; Killion, 1999; Kruse, 1999; Reagan, Case, & Brubacher, 2000; Schon, 1983; Wahlstrom, Seashore Louis, Leithwood, & Anderson, 2010). The good news is that effective professional development can take a variety of forms that move well beyond the traditional workshop and training formats. What forms can professional development assume that will be particularly beneficial to multicultural educators? The most powerful professional development happens when learning opportunities are job embedded and ongoing.

A particularly powerful form of professional learning is teacher engagement in professional learning communities (PLCs). PLCs are opportunities for teachers to come together in a formalized way in order to learn from and with one another. Building on the work of numerous respected researchers and writers (DuFour, 2004; Hoy & Miskel, 2012; King, Artiles, & Kozleski, 2009; Kruse, Seashore Louis, & Bryk, 1994; Senge, 1990), Shirley Hord established the term *professional learning community* in 1997 and delineated five primary characteristics of a PLC. Specifically, members of a PLC (1) engage in supportive and shared leadership, (2) share values and a vision, (3) engage in collective learning and application, (4) share personal practice, and (5) are provided with supportive conditions (Hord, 2004).

Workshops are perhaps the most commonly recognized form of professional development. They can be useful as a professional development tool if there is support for follow-up and practice to put into action what was learned. Stronger workshop designs certainly provide knowledge, demonstrations, and opportunities for practice. However, transfer of that knowledge into practice will be more likely if teachers are engaged in **peer consultation** with one another (Joyce & Showers, 2002).

Peer consultation happens when two or more colleagues come together regularly to give and receive feedback on an area of mutual interest. Peer consultation might lead to teachers developing curriculum together. Or they might observe one another and give feedback on those observations. For example, two colleagues might work together over a year to develop multicultural lesson plans around a big idea or concept such as assimilation. Peers might also come together to learn how to examine student work.

Finally, you might consider ways to further your own professional development through other avenues, including participation in professional organizations that have a multicultural education agenda or strand. Similarly, you might consider joining a network of educators who are committed to the same topic (e.g., multicultural education, gender and

Teachers never stop learning themselves. Knowing what they need to learn, how to best acquire those knowledge and skills to be personally meaningful, and then effectively turning learning into effective teaching practices is a vital process.

© George Doyle/stockbyte/thinkstock

education, multiple intelligences in teaching and learning) and have a shared sense of purpose. In any of these cases, you will want to look for opportunities for meaningful activity that will translate directly into your own practice. A powerful professional organization we recommend that you join is the National Association for Multicultural Education (NAME). NAME was established in 1990 for the purposes of achieving equity in education. Membership in NAME provides you with opportunities to network with like-minded educators through online resources, publications, and the annual conference.

Enhancing Your Skills as a Reflective Practitioner

Once you have made the decision and commitment to become a multicultural educator, there is work to be done. Whether you are a new or an experienced teacher, the process requires reflection on your values and beliefs, your knowledge and understandings, and your skills and behaviors. Developing habits as a reflective multicultural educator means setting aside time regularly to consider strengths and weaknesses and to set short- and long-term goals for yourself. Becoming a multicultural educator means learning and engaging in the process of reflection.

What is **reflective practice**? John Dewey (as cited in Simpson, Jackson, & Aycock, 2005) described the importance of reflective thinking many decades ago. He believed that it involves (1) a state of perplexity or mental difficulty in which thinking originates and (2) the act of seeking material to address and dispose of the perplexity. Reflective practice is a systematic approach to solving problems and to self-assessment. It entails taking time to think deeply about what one does as an educator, why one does those things, and what are one's professional strengths, areas of weaknesses, and goals for self-improvement.

Taggart and Wilson (1998) indicated that reflective thinking occurs on three levels. The first and most basic level—the technical level—occurs as educators simply describe events and activities without much thought as to reasons or rationale. The second level—the contextual level—is a deeper type of reflection during which the educator tries to explain the use of particular approaches, why certain decisions were made, or how contextual aspects (e.g., student needs or available resources) influenced outcomes. The third and the deepest level of reflective practice—the dialectical level—is where an educator reflects on moral and ethical issues that are involved in his or her own teaching and considers the implications of decisions made.

Why is reflective practice particularly critical to the multicultural educator? As you discover new information about yourself through the process of expanding self-awareness, you also discover important and sizable differences between yourself and your students. You do not need to know all about all cultures deeply in order to be culturally proficient. However, you do need to know how to learn from the learners—to learn about the students and about their cultural backgrounds. Reagan et al. (2000) stated that to justify the selection of particular instructional strategies,

> the teacher cannot rely solely on instinct alone or on prepackaged sets of techniques . . . In other words, the teacher must engage in reflection about his or her own practice. . . . Good teaching . . . requires reflective, rational, and conscious decision making. (p. 20)

It has been estimated that during a typical workday, a teacher makes hundreds of decisions related to the teaching and learning process. With that many decisions being made, teachers will often state that they don't have the time to reflect or examine in depth their own belief systems. And yet, teachers make these many decisions based on a particular set of beliefs, values, expectations, experiences, and life histories, and their decisions may ignore, contradict, or conflict with the beliefs, values, and life histories of students. In this light, reflective practice becomes essential.

What kinds of activities are involved in reflective practice? Taggart and Wilson (1998) explained that reflective thinking or practice can be accomplished through a variety of activities (action research, case studies, and observations). The most common and widely used activity is journaling. Kouzes and Posner (2017) supported the development of a dialogue journal in which one writes about events and activities and receives regular written feedback from or participates in a discussion with a mentor or an interested colleague. Kouzes and Posner explained that a dialogue journal can include things such as details about an event (date, who was involved, explanation of what happened) as well as an analysis of the event (in light of the context and with an explanation of what the writer learned). Educators moving toward becoming multicultural educators might also want to check periodically how they are doing in their action plans. The Inventory of Progress in Implementing an Individual Multicultural Educator Action Plan in Exercise 11.3 may be useful for this purpose.

EXERCISE 11.3

INVENTORY OF PROGRESS IN IMPLEMENTING AN INDIVIDUAL MULTICULTURAL EDUCATOR ACTION PLAN

☐ YES ☐ NO   1. I have a plan for how I am going to learn more about cultures other than my own.

☐ YES ☐ NO   2. I have a good idea of what the common barriers are to multicultural education and how to resolve them.

☐ YES ☐ NO   3. I have a good idea of some areas where I might find resistance but also where I can find support for multicultural education.

☐ YES ☐ NO   4. I have a plan for how my multicultural classroom will look.

☐ YES ☐ NO   5. I know the areas or knowledge bases of diversity in which I need more education.

☐ YES ☐ NO   6. I have developed a plan for engaging in regular reflection about my practice as a multicultural educator.

☐ YES ☐ NO   7. I have set goals for myself for the coming year for my journey toward becoming a multicultural educator.

☐ YES ☐ NO   8. I have identified professional development needs and strategies.

☐ YES ☐ NO   9. I have a plan for obtaining and using student data.

☐ YES ☐ NO   10. I know with whom I will collaborate around this work.

PROFILES IN MULTICULTURAL EDUCATION

JEANNIE OAKES

© Jeannie Oaks

Jeannie Oakes is Presidential Professor Emeritus in Educational Equity at University of California–Los Angeles (UCLA), where she founded UCLA's Institute for Democracy, Education, and Access; the University of California's All Campus Consortium on Research for Diversity; and Center X, UCLA's urban teacher preparation program. In 2014, she completed a 6-year term at the Ford Foundation as Director of Educational Opportunity and Scholarship programs worldwide.

Oakes's scholarship examines the effect of social policies on the education of low-income students of color, and it investigates equity-minded reform. Among Oakes's numerous books, articles, and chapters, *Keeping Track: How Schools Structure Inequality* was named one of the 20th century's "most influential" education books; and *Becoming Good American Schools: The Struggle for Civic Virtue in Education* Reform won the American Educational Research Association's (AERA) Outstanding Book Award. She has received the 2013 Social Justice in Education Research Award from AERA, and she holds the Multicultural Research Award from the National Association for Multicultural Education, the Distinguished Achievement Award from the Educational Press Association of America, and the Southern Christian Leadership Conference's Ralph David Abernathy Award for Public Service.

Oakes served as president of AERA from 2015 to 2016. Formerly a senior social scientist at RAND, Oakes received her PhD in education from UCLA in 1980 after a 7-year career as a public school English teacher. Since 1993, Oakes has served as an expert witness in three federal school desegregation cases in Rockford, Illinois; San Jose, California; and Wilmington, Delaware. In these cases, she testified to the contribution of tracking and ability grouping to within-school segregation and the impact of these practices on students' opportunities to learn (e.g., curricular content, teaching resources and strategies, and classroom processes) and students' achievement.

In terms of the most significant contributions to the field, Dr. Oakes has spent her career studying how seemingly "race-neutral" or "culture-neutral" education policies have actually diminished the schooling and life chances of students of color, particularly those who are also poor. She has helped educators and policymakers understand that deeply held, but also deeply flawed, beliefs about learning ability and the way in which we enact those beliefs in schools are bound up tightly with race and culture. As a consequence, practices such as ability grouping and tracking negatively affect the expectations, learning opportunities, and outcomes of students from disparaged groups and, ultimately, their social and economic circumstances. Oakes states,

> The fact that we consistently find African Americans, Latinos, and other groups of young people whom our cultural tools (such as tests) disparage as "less able" concentrated in classrooms where they are offered less and learn less cannot be understood or tolerated as reflecting either truth or fairness.

REFLECTING BACK

1. Take time to practice setting specific goals for your development as a multicultural educator. The more specific your goals are, the greater the chance you have of achieving them. List three to five specific goals in response to the question, "What do you want to do in order to enhance your knowledge, skills, and dispositions as a multicultural educator?" Rank order the importance of these goals in your professional life (with one being most important). Rank order the goals a second time by how difficult it will be to achieve them. Rank order the goals a third time by the amount of time you may need to realize them.

2. Select a concept that you want to teach your students. Design several learning experiences to make use of multiple perspectives in addressing the concept. Reflect on your strengths and challenges in designing these experiences. What does this tell you that you need to do in terms of your own professional development? Identify at least three specific areas of knowledge or skills that you wish to address in your own growth.

3. Identify at least one person who can serve as a partner and a critical friend as you work to do the following:

   - Enhance your awareness of yourself as a cultural being.

   - Build a knowledge base as a multicultural educator.

   - Enhance your skills as a multicultural educator.

   - Develop and implement an action plan.

   Explain your rationale for selection of the people in this experience.

4. Think of a particular curriculum or instructional strategy you have been working with for a while and whose results in terms of student learning you are curious about. Identify three school-based data sources that would inform you about the impact of the curriculum or strategy on learning by diverse students.

5. Write about three specific areas that are related to multicultural education in which you wish to extend your knowledge and skill. Then reflect on how you will go about your own professional growth in those areas.

CASE STUDY

WHERE ON EARTH TO START: MOVING FROM A TEACHER FOCUS TO A STUDENT FOCUS

Key Issues to Be Explored in the Case

1. The importance of having a clear vision and set of goals about what you want to accomplish as an effective teacher for all learners

2. How teachers might design learning experiences that put students first

3. The importance of data in helping teachers reflect on their capacity as multicultural educators

4. How teachers might develop a plan for ongoing professional development as multicultural educators

As he drove home from school on a snowy December evening, Andy found himself suddenly considering leaving his high school teaching position. This was a particularly painful moment for him because he absolutely loved his subject area—history—and had always dreamed of passing on that enjoyment of the subject to young people. And he was thrilled to have landed the teaching position he had. Brookfield High School was a midsized school in a large suburb adjacent to a major metropolitan area. In recent years, the community population had been becoming more and more diverse. While other teachers talked about the demographic changes, Andy's philosophy was that students are students and he was there to teach history.

While his first year or so in the classroom had been difficult, Andy was now well into his second year, and he thought that he was making progress in getting through to students. He worked especially hard to know the textbooks, design student exams that measured important knowledge, and prepare lectures that incorporated the important facts. Many students applied themselves and did well on the tests, and the rest . . . well, he just figured that they weren't working hard enough and they needed to get serious. If he were to admit it, he also believed that maybe they wouldn't ever perform too well.

In his first year of teaching, Andy had been observed several times by the principal, Mr. Snyder. Mr. Snyder had been encouraging with Andy and not too intrusive. After all, he was about to retire and believed that Andy just needed some time to get his feet firmly planted on the ground. Now in his second year, Andy was facing a second set of performance observations conducted by the new principal, Dr. Switzer. Dr. Switzer had previously been a principal of a multicultural magnet school that was lauded for its focus on individual students and integration of cultural knowledge into subject areas. Andy prepared extensively for the first observation, developing what he believed to be some of his strongest lectures ever. In his second observation with Dr. Switzer, he prepared strong lectures again and this time made sure to call on some of the best and brightest students in the class to illustrate particular points. At the end of that observation, Dr. Switzer set a time for the two of them to meet to discuss Andy's performance.

Andy went into the postobservation conference with great optimism and was caught completely off guard when Dr. Switzer presented a summary of the data she had been collecting during the observations. According to the data, Andy appeared to use primarily one type of instructional strategy (lecture), called on White males most of the time, and didn't appear to use strategies for making the material relevant to the students' lives. Dr. Switzer summarized the observation by saying that Andy's classroom appeared to be much more teacher centered than student centered. She was particularly concerned about the limited number of instructional strategies in use, Andy's apparent inability to make the content meaningful and relevant for his students, and his apparent lack of high expectations for all students. Andy was devastated. Dr. Switzer finished the postobservation discussion by saying that she wanted him to develop a plan for how he was going to learn to be more student centered and how he was going to work to become a multicultural educator.

After Dr. Switzer left, Andy pulled his materials together, turned out the lights, and walked out to his car. On the drive home, he reflected on the conference and thought that, perhaps, he wasn't really doing all he could for his students. Now remembering some college courses on multicultural education, Andy tried to think about how he might develop and implement a plan for becoming a multicultural educator. Andy drove on, wondering what his next steps should be.

Discussion Questions

1. What are the primary issues in the case?

2. If you were providing peer consultation with Andy, what are the most important next steps you would coach Andy to take?

3. In the long term, what should Andy include in his action plan for becoming a multicultural educator in this particular setting?

4. In addition to you as a peer consultant, who else should Andy turn to for assistance in addressing his particular problems? Why?

5. How does a school leader play a critical role in the professional development of multicultural educators?

CHAPTER SUMMARY

In this chapter, the key issues and strategies for taking action toward becoming a multicultural educator are discussed. This chapter explores the process of preparing an Individual Multicultural Educator Action Plan and portfolio. The portfolio will be a record of your development and action in becoming a multicultural educator. Over time, as you grow and develop as a multicultural educator, the components in your portfolio will change. You will want to make additions and deletions. The important point is to have a record of your progress and process. The components of your portfolio might be the following:

- Platform of beliefs (beliefs inventory)

- Personal vision of multicultural education and goal statements of what you want to accomplish in the short term and long term as a multicultural educator

- Enumeration of a network of colleagues with whom you are working in your process of becoming an effective multicultural educator

- Samples of data used to gauge your progress as a multicultural educator. These might include a classroom demographic profile, assessment tools as described in this chapter, or an action research project in which you implement a promising practice that supports individual learners.

This chapter focused on five learning objectives.

11.1 Enunciate a clear vision, beliefs, and set of goals about what you want to accomplish as an effective teacher for all learners

Multicultural educators have a clear vision and set of goals about what they want to accomplish as effective teachers for all learners.

- Teachers are expected to engage in school improvement work in order to support high levels of academic achievement for every student. This means that teachers need to be engaged in developing a vision of what the school and their classrooms could and should be. Teachers are expected to become teacher-leaders and engage in decision making and significant school improvement efforts. Given these expectations, teachers will need to have a clear set of goals for improving their own practice. You might consider aligning your goals with important teaching standards. One approach to organizing standards is according to three broad areas: knowledge, skills, and dispositions.

11.2 Explain ways to design learning experiences that put students first

Multicultural educators start with the students and put them first in their action plans.

- Accomplished multicultural educators *expect* differences and begin with the presumption that there is "no normal" way of being or learning. The teacher's role is to develop an environment that builds *confidence* and assigns genuine and merited *competence* to every student. We need to have very specific information about our students and their backgrounds so that we can design appropriate and challenging learning experiences for each one and construct the learning environment in such a way as to make sure that each individual achieves at high levels. We simply cannot do this without knowing about our students' cultural and experiential backgrounds.

11.3 Establish effective strategies to collaborate with like-minded individuals who have made the same commitment to becoming a multicultural educator

Multicultural educators partner with like-minded individuals or join networks of people who have made the same commitment as they have to becoming multicultural educators.

- Collaboration is a means for overcoming the isolation that so often pervades many schools. Collaboration provides teachers with a sense of connectedness and community. Teachers need to feel that they are part of a community for their own intellectual and professional development. Collaboration calls for the development of strong relationships that transcend the traditional boundaries of departments and grade levels. Partners generally work collaboratively to accomplish some mutual goal(s). An example of a mutual goal accomplished collaboratively might be the development of a new curriculum unit that includes multicultural concepts.

- Partners may also choose to observe and coach each other's work to learn from each other.

11.4 Critique the value of using data to examine your own instructional practices to make changes that will affect learning for all students

Multicultural educators know strategies for using data to examine their own instructional practices. They use that information to make changes that will affect learning for all students.

- As you work to integrate new instructional practices and curriculum materials designed to meet diverse learner needs, you will want to plan for regular assessment of your progress and the impact of these new practices on student learning. Collecting evidence of progress will be useful in your own reflections, in your own development as an educator, and in sharing with others (e.g., partners, colleagues, and supervisors).

- How might you easily and effectively collect data? The most helpful data will be the kinds

that inform you of your own progress as a teacher.

11.5 Develop a plan for your own ongoing professional development as a multicultural educator

Multicultural educators develop a plan for their own ongoing professional development.

- A particularly powerful form of professional learning is teacher engagement in PLCs. PLCs are opportunities for teachers to come together in a formalized way in order to learn from and with one another. Hord established the term *professional learning community* in 1997 and delineated five primary characteristics of a PLC. Specifically, members of a PLC (1) engage in supportive and shared leadership, (2) share values and a vision, (3) engage in collective learning and application, (4) share personal practice, and (5) are provided with supportive conditions (Hord, 2004).

- Workshops are perhaps the most commonly recognized form of professional development. They can be useful as a professional development tool if there is support for follow-up and practice to put into action what was learned. Stronger workshop designs certainly provide knowledge, demonstrations, and opportunities for practice. However, transfer of that knowledge into practice will be more likely if teachers are engaged in peer consultation with one another.

KEY TERMS

action research 326
classroom demographic profile 320
collaboration 323

Multicultural Education Platform of Beliefs 315
peer consultation 332
professional development 315

reflective practice 333
student-centered classroom 314

APPLICATION: ACTIVITIES AND EXERCISES

Individual

1. Develop an Individual Multicultural Educator Action Plan portfolio. Include sections in your portfolio that address the five learning objectives covered in this chapter. Begin work in at least two areas.

   a. Which of the components have you already started to address in your professional development as an educator?

   b. Which of the components do you believe will be particularly valuable and why?

   c. What other components would you add to your action plan? What is your rationale for the additional items?

Group

1. Develop a proposal for an action research project that investigates an aspect of the application of multicultural education in your own practice.

2. Form an inquiry study group with at least three other interested individuals. Engage in a discussion of an aspect of multicultural education that you all find particularly intriguing. Use the inquiry group format to investigate further the selected aspect. Summarize your deliberations and present them to a group of colleagues or classmates.

3. Plan to interview a teacher in your district or region who is noted for being a multicultural educator who is culturally responsive and responsible. Prepare questions in advance. Summarize and present your findings to your colleagues.

Self-Assessment

In your journal, reflect on and respond to the following:

1. How would you systematically learn important information about each of your students? What types of information would you want to include?

2. Select a content area and reflect on how you would integrate the student information into your teaching in that content area.

3. Do you agree or disagree with the need for teaching to become student focused? Why or why not? Why is the degree to which a classroom is teacher or student focused particularly important in light of the diversity of today's students?

ANNOTATED RESOURCES

The following websites may be particularly useful in supporting your professional development as a culturally responsive educator.

AllThingsPLC

http://www.allthingsplc.info

This site was created to serve as a collaborative, objective resource for educators and administrators who are committed to enhancing student achievement. Teaching professionals are invited to share knowledge, ask questions, and get expert insight into the issues teachers face each day in the classroom.

Annenberg Institute for School Reform

http://annenberginstitute.org

The Annenberg Institute for School Reform at Brown University engages in intensive work with urban school systems across the country that are pursuing systemwide efforts to improve educational experiences and opportunities, particularly for English language learners and students from low-income backgrounds. The institute supports and encourages the use of PLCs as a central element of effective professional development as part of a comprehensive reform initiative.

ASCD (formerly the Association for Supervision and Curriculum Development)

http://www. ascd.org

Founded in 1943, ASCD is an educational leadership organization dedicated to advancing best practices and policies for the success of each learner.

EdChange

http://www.edchange.org

EdChange is a team of passionate, experienced, established educators dedicated to equity, diversity, multiculturalism, and social justice. The educators have joined to collaborate in order to develop resources, workshops, and projects that contribute to progressive change in ourselves, our schools, and our society. They offer a variety of projects and resources, workshops and consulting services, and scholarship grounded in equity and social justice in schools and communities.

Learning Forward (formerly the National Staff Development Council)

http://www.learningforward.org

Learning Forward is an international membership association of learning educators focused on increasing student achievement through more effective professional learning. Learning Forward's purpose is to ensure that every educator engages in effective professional learning every day so that every student achieves.

National Association for Multicultural Education

www.nameorg.org

NAME is a nonprofit organization that advances and advocates for equity and social justice through multicultural education. The organization's objectives are to provide opportunities for learning in order to advance multicultural education, equity, and social justice; to proactively reframe public debate and affect current and emerging policies in ways that advance social, political, economic, and educational equity through advocacy, position papers, policy statements, and other strategies; and to provide the preeminent digital clearinghouse of resources about educational equity and social justice.

Get the tools you need to sharpen your study skills. SAGE edge offers a robust online environment featuring an impressive array of free tools and resources. Access practice quizzes, eFlashcards, video, and multimedia at **edge.sagepub.com/howe3e**

12 Creating the Multicultural School

© Hemera Technologies/ablestock.com/ thinkstock

Learning Objectives

In this chapter, we will focus on four learning objectives for teachers as they help schools transition toward multicultural education. As you read about and investigate this area, think of your role as a teacher-leader, either now or in the not-too-distant future. The well-being of diverse students is in your hands! Through your work on concepts, strategies, and ideas in this chapter, and as you work to become a multicultural educator, you will be able to do the following:

12.1 Develop a schoolwide plan for the implementation of multicultural education

12.2 Explain the components of a school culture that supports teaching and learning for all students

12.3 Establish a school improvement process that uses data to support all children

12.4 Identify strategies that support teacher professional development for multicultural education

As illustrated in Figure 12.1, action planning to implement multicultural education needs to take place on both an individual level and a schoolwide level. We discussed action planning on an individual level in Chapter 11. In this chapter, we focus on teacher participation in schoolwide action planning. When educators are working on both levels, they can make a difference in teaching and learning that benefits all children. Of particular concern when thinking about action planning on a schoolwide level are components such as the **school culture** and climate, the ways in which school improvement occurs, and how teachers can be supported in their growth as multicultural educators.

Based on her synthesis of research in multicultural education, Geneva Gay (1994) believed that the implementation of multicultural education must include four features. Effective multicultural education must be (1) a total school reform effort; (2) present for all students in all grade levels and all subjects; (3) an opportunity for students to acquire knowledge about diverse groups of people, develop social action skills necessary for cultural pluralism, and examine dispositions; and (4) an opportunity for the recognition and celebration of diversity as a basic fact of human life. Given Gay's stipulations, it is apparent that the implementation of multicultural education is not just a nice thing to be done by a few interested teachers. It must be viewed as a school reform effort and engaged in by everyone.

> Everything now, we must assume, is in our hands;
>
> we have no right to assume otherwise.
>
> If we do not falter in our duty now,
>
> we may be able, handful that we are,
>
> to end the racial nightmare,
>
> and achieve our country,
>
> and change the history of the world.
>
> —James Baldwin (1963)

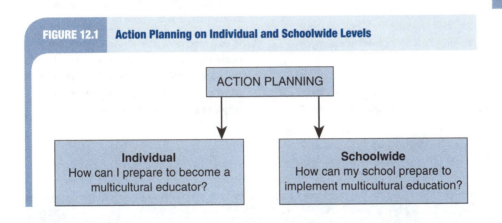

FIGURE 12.1   **Action Planning on Individual and Schoolwide Levels**

ACTION PLANNING

Individual
How can I prepare to become a multicultural educator?

Schoolwide
How can my school prepare to implement multicultural education?

CASE STUDY
A TALE OF TWO CITIES

Jean had been a teacher for more than 10 years in a virtually all-White, wealthy suburban school. This was her first teaching position, and she loved the school system and the town. Jean had grown up in a similar kind of community. Still she felt that something was missing in both her personal life and her career as an educator. Her students had the best advantages of life—good homes, the latest clothes, computers, summer camps, vacation trips to island paradises, and promising college opportunities. But she knew that there were teachers and students in other schools who were not living the American dream.

Mary taught eighth-grade science in a poor inner-city school with virtually all African American and Latino

(Continued)

(Continued)

students. Each day in class was a struggle. The science texts she was using were the same she had been given to teach from 8 years earlier when she started. They were now 20 years old. Although she taught four sections of eighth-grade science, there were barely enough books for one class. She was forced to have her students leave the texts behind when they rotated so the next class could use them; because of the scarcity of books, students were not permitted to take them home to study. And because of the perennial budget crisis, she had no budget for science kits. What few instructional materials she had were hand-me-downs from suburban schools, crafted out of cheap everyday goods, given to her by the parents who could ill afford the expense, donated by charitable organizations, or paid for out of her own pocket. Because of this, students, although eager to learn, received an inferior education, lessening their chances of college opportunities and good careers. Life for her students was much different.

Jean and Mary met one day at a workshop that they were both fortunate enough to be able to attend. They began sharing their stories about their respective careers and their schools. From this, they learned the stark contrast between their two situations. One of the primary concerns was racial isolation. With or without funding, they vowed to do something about it. They embarked on a one-on-one teacher exchange. But they couldn't help but wonder why this type of important activity was being left to individual teachers, working in isolation, to address. A major question in both of their minds was, "What might be accomplished if entire schools were engaged in becoming multicultural schools?"

Your Perspectives on the Case

1. What does the case illustrate about the culture in each school?

2. Is funding, or lack thereof, the only or the primary issue in this case?

3. If, as a teacher-leader who is knowledgeable about multicultural education, you were to initiate a school improvement effort to move either school forward, what specific steps might you urge the school to take?

THINKING AHEAD
YOU AND CHAPTER 12 LEARNING OBJECTIVES

As an individual, you can make significant changes on the classroom level toward becoming a multicultural educator. However, action toward achieving education that is multicultural must occur also at the school level. Consider your role as a teacher-leader in your school. In this role, you can provide critical and important leadership for moving your school toward becoming a multicultural school. Think about the important skills needed to take school-wide action by responding to the following prompts.

1. What do you think might be the most important steps a school must take to become a multicultural school?

2. Think of an educational setting in which you have spent a significant period of time. Describe at least five student behaviors that were considered acceptable or normal and desirable. What does your list illustrate about the school's culture? Which students do not seem to "fit in"?

3. Your school is committed to multicultural education. Identify a specific area in your school that you believe needs attention and is related to curriculum, instruction, or assessment. As the school works to address that area, how will you know that this work is making a difference in the academic performance of all students? What data will you collect?

4. Imagine that you have been asked to participate on a school committee charged with designing professional development for teachers as they work to learn about and implement multicultural education. What are the most promising strategies for supporting teacher learning in the identified curriculum, instruction, or assessment practice?

LEARNING OBJECTIVE 12.1 Develop a Schoolwide Plan for the Implementation of Multicultural Education

Fortunately, in recent years a growing body of research and work on school improvement has emerged that can be applied to the implementation of multicultural education (Blankstein, 2013; Blankstein & Houston, 2011; Fullan, 2007; Fullan & Quinn, 2017; Wagner, 2014). Schmoker (2006) believed that effective school improvement efforts are results driven. Educators must have a clear idea of what they need to do, select appropriate interventions, and then examine the impact of interventions on student achievement and adjust accordingly. A results-driven, schoolwide action plan to support diverse learners means setting specific goals for student achievement, using multicultural curriculum and diverse instructional and assessment strategies to meet those goals, measuring the impact of the strategies, and then adjusting as needed.

According to Schmoker (2006), the following are among the approaches that appear to affect the success of school improvement efforts:

1. Use teamwork as a strategy to promote improvement.

2. Set measurable goals for improvement.

3. Collect and use performance data to determine progress.

These three actions can be applied to implementing multicultural education as a school improvement initiative. Educators working in teams will be a critical element in implementing multicultural education. Teams might be set by grade level or discipline or be interdisciplinary. In teams, educators together determine the learning needs to be addressed for particular students. In many cases, teachers may come together in a powerful professional learning opportunity called professional learning communities, or PLCs (discussed in Chapter 11). PLCs bring teachers together to dialogue about data, to set goals for improvement, and to develop and oversee implementation of teaching and learning strategies that will raise levels of student achievement.

In this book, we offer an action plan process that incorporates important components from the literature on multicultural education and school improvement planning. The process that we offer is illustrated in Table 12.1. Steps 1, 2, and 3 pertain primarily to assessing school culture and readiness for change toward multicultural education. Steps 4 through 9 resonate with steps that have been identified as important to continuous school improvement planning. Each step is essential to creating and implementing a schoolwide action plan, and each will be discussed further in the next sections of this chapter.

Working with others as a team on planning can be an exciting and rewarding strategy. Diversity in people and ideas creates a richer outcome.

iStock/asiseeit

TABLE 12.1	Components of a Schoolwide Multicultural Education Action Plan
Assessing culture and readiness for change	1. Clarify important school values and beliefs.
	2. Create a shared vision of a school that is culturally responsive and responsible.
	3. Establish a culture of collaboration, teamwork, and shared decision making.
School improvement work	4. Collect, analyze, and discuss baseline data, identifying needs.
	5. Establish measurable goals.
	6. Identify and implement promising research-based practices or specific interventions.
	7. Implement and monitor the impact of the interventions on student performance.
	8. Adjust the plan as required.
Supporting teacher growth	9. Provide and engage in ongoing job-embedded professional development.

LEARNING OBJECTIVE 12.2 Explain the Components of a School Culture That Supports Teaching and Learning for All Students

School Culture as a Shared Set of Values and Beliefs

Human culture is the set of values, ideals, beliefs, experiences, styles of community, forms of linguistic expression, histories, and standards of behavior that guide the actions of individuals who share an identity. School cultures possess many of the same elements as human cultures, including commonly held beliefs, values, norms, experiences, and histories. School culture provides the social context for learning—the understandings and expectations that teachers and students use to make sense of each other's behavior. Organizational or school culture is the shared set of beliefs, norms, values, expectations of behavior, habits, attitudes, and customs that define an organization. These beliefs and values may be formalized in some type of publication, but more often than not, they are not written but rather are understood. **Enculturation** is the passing on of values and patterns of behaviors promoted by a culture—in this case, within a school.

Glickman, Gordon, and Ross-Gordon (2017) underscored the critical importance of attending to school culture. They believed that if we understand the values and beliefs that undergird our schools, we can work effectively to transform the organization. Most important is to bring all members of the organization into the belief system that schools are for students and that all students can learn.

School culture includes a shared view of, among other things, learning, teaching, the purpose of education, differences, and even leadership.

An understanding of school culture is important to moving a school toward multicultural education in three primary ways. First, students whose cultural identities do not match those of other students or teachers representing the general norm often feel alienated and devalued as they go through the educational system. Students bring diverse cultural backgrounds into a school, as discussed in previous chapters. Do these students sense that their differences are understood and valued and incorporated into the teaching and learning process? An important belief that guides a movement toward multicultural education is that there is often no one right way of doing things—just different ways. For example, there is no right way to teach all students. Everyone must see value in differences.

Second, teachers may have different ideas about diversity and school improvement. Some may believe that culture does not affect the teaching and learning process. Others may attempt to "change the system" and be viewed with suspicion. A culture that values diversity and the positive integration of multicultural education into teaching and learning must be nurtured.

Finally, an understanding of the values, norms, and beliefs inherent to a school's culture is

© istockphotos.com/Thomas Perkins

Creating a strong school culture where diversity is encouraged, valued, and strengthened should be seen as a key strategy in building great minds and lasting friendships

important to supporting new initiatives, such as multicultural education. Does the school's culture value collaboration and teamwork as a means for supporting student achievement, or do community members tend to work in isolation? Is there a sense of collegiality, and is risk taking celebrated and recognized? Do members of the community value shared decision making and **data-based decision making**, or are important decisions made by one administrator?

Lezotte and Jacoby (1990) outlined nine correlates of effective schools that are considered applicable and useful today. Effective schools are those that have (1) a productive school climate and culture reflecting shared values, (2) a focus on student acquisition of central learning skills, (3) appropriate monitoring of student progress, (4) practice-oriented staff development at the school site, (5) outstanding leadership, (6) salient parent involvement, (7) effective instructional and organizational arrangements, (8) high operationalized expectations and requirements for all students, and (9) multicultural instruction and sensitivity. **Effective schools research** has tremendous implications for schoolwide action planning for multicultural education.

As you consider your role as a teacher-leader in the effort to develop schools that support all students, you might take time to develop your own vision. Imagine that you are a teacher-leader in a school 5 years from now after a significant school improvement effort to implement multicultural education. Write a story about your school that illustrates the important changes that have taken place, especially in terms of the culture of the school. Address the beliefs, norms, and values of the school community. Who is involved in making decisions? How are data used?

Assessing School Culture

An assessment or audit of characteristics of the school culture will reveal whether or not the school is ready to implement multicultural education as a total school improvement effort. Such an audit will reveal community members' strongly held beliefs and values. The audit will help answer questions about how group members view the following:

1. Cultural differences (e.g., are linguistic differences viewed positively or negatively?)

2. The appropriateness and feasibility of various instructional strategies (e.g., students do learn differently, but is there enough time to differentiate instruction?)

3. The role of culture in the teaching and learning process (e.g., while a focus on learning about cultures may be appropriate during particular months or holidays, is it necessary to maintain throughout the school year?)

4. Roles of students, teachers, and administrators in the teaching and learning process (e.g., if the role of teachers has traditionally been to teach and lecture and the role of students has been to let teachers know that they know the content, how do we move toward a more student-centered approach?)

5. Change and expectations (e.g., changes that are mandated today are largely assessment driven, so how do we empower teachers to take charge?)

DuFour, DuFour, Eaker, Many, and Mattos (2016) and DuFour (2004) have written about the utility of using a cultural audit, or assessment, to help identify values, beliefs, and norms of an education organization. Models of their work have been enhanced to include considerations of beliefs around diversity and equity, and which serve as the basis for Exercise 12.1.

EXERCISE 12.1

A CULTURAL AUDIT OF VALUES, BELIEFS, AND NORMS FOR MULTICULTURAL EDUCATION

1. Bring together all participants in the school improvement process. Present a brief introduction to the nature of school culture, which includes a focus on values, beliefs, and traditions. Then as a group, brainstorm a list of one-word descriptors of school cultures. The descriptors may be positive or negative. For example, descriptors may include the following: *collaboration*, *communication*, *bias*, *children*, *learning*, *multicultural education*, *prejudice*, *tension*, *accountability*, and *survival*. Keep working with the group until you have generated a list of at least 60 descriptors. Place these on a worksheet, and make enough copies for all participants.

2. Ask each participant, working individually, to circle six words on the list that he or she believes best describe the current school culture.

3. Tally the responses of all participants. This can be done in small groups, which then report out all responses for their group members.

4. As a full group, identify the six most frequently identified words.

5. Facilitate a discussion about why and how these six words describe the current culture of the school. During the discussion, important questions may include the following:

    a. What are the implications of the collective responses for building a school that values diversity and is working to achieve equity?

    b. Why focus on multicultural education?

    c. Do all community members (teachers, leaders, staff, parents) believe that multicultural education is important?

    d. Are educators willing to engage deeply in the school improvement process, making changes in teaching practices with the belief that this is the right thing to do for all children?

    e. What do they believe is the ultimate purpose of education?

    f. Does the school have a culture of collaboration and teamwork that will support school improvement efforts for multicultural education?

Since school culture is such a powerful force in guiding behavior, it is critically important to get a sense of the "inner reality" of the school before starting down the road to school improvement (Blankstein, Noguera, & Kelly, 2016; Deal & Peterson, 2016). Examining the culture of a school may illuminate certain areas (beliefs, values, norms) that need to be addressed before setting out on a school improvement effort that focuses on implementing multicultural education. How else can an existing school culture be examined? Terrell and Lindsey (2009) suggested looking at the following:

- *Rituals and ceremonies:* These are activities and other manifestations of culture that reinforce a school's values, norms, and beliefs through predictable patterns of behavior.

- *Communication and language:* These involve groups of people who share information and the ways in which they collaborate, including vocabulary used, reflect cultural norms, values, and beliefs.

- *"Heroes:"* These are the people in the school who are held up for recognition, particularly during annual award ceremonies.

- *Signs, symbols, and spaces:* Values and beliefs are conveyed by the use of physical space in the school. This may include locations of particular offices in the school that service diverse students and student groups and special places for the heroes of the school. What is considered an attractive space? Who decides who works and studies where?

- *Politics and participation in activities:* Which students and teachers take part in different kinds of activities? Who has power in the school? How is it conveyed?

Additionally, an examination of artifacts includes a review of school documents, which may reveal the values, norms, and beliefs to which a school community adheres and specifically how diversity, equity, and multicultural education are addressed. Documents could include student and teacher handbooks; curriculum guides; the school newspaper and yearbook; minutes of faculty meetings, parent–teacher association meetings, and school board meetings; and reports for accrediting agencies and state departments of education.

A review of school policies and procedures will reveal beliefs and values about multicultural education. Have antibias policies been written for the school? A review of the budget might focus on how resources are allocated in the school. A review of hiring protocols would show how teacher and administrator candidates are screened for their levels of understanding of multicultural education. A review of the textbook selection process would uncover the level of understanding and valuing of multicultural education on the part of the teachers and administrators: Are textbooks and instructional materials selected only after a thorough review for bias? And what about school policies and practices around tracking? What are the criteria for selection into gifted programs?

Developing a Shared Vision

Having a clear idea of the current school culture and whether or not it includes norms, values, and beliefs conducive to multicultural education is one important component of this work. Another important component is the development of a **shared vision** of what teaching and learning will look like if school community members embed multicultural education in their practices. Vision building should result in a shared sense of purpose. Therefore, developing a vision must be done by individuals and groups who demonstrate the capacity and commitment to enter into partnerships. Developing a shared vision of multicultural education requires all constituent groups (teachers, students, administrators, other staff, parents, community members) to have a clear idea of what multicultural education means for their school. Developing a shared vision takes time (Senge, Cambron-McCage, Lucas, Smith, & Dutton, 2012; Senge, Kleiner, Roberts, Ross, & Smith, 1994; Williams, 2003). But investing time in reflection and dialogue about what really matters to individuals within the school will contribute to the development of a deep, strongly shared, and meaningful vision of multicultural education.

Developing a vision is a never-ending process. A vision is a picture of what can be. And as school constituent members continue to learn more about multicultural education, about research-based best practices, and about students, they will want to enhance and update their vision of what the school can be. School constituent group members should be engaged regularly in reflecting on their values and beliefs, the school's deep purpose, and whether or not current practice resonates with the school's shared vision.

What are some strategies for developing a shared vision of multicultural education? Senge et al. (1994) believed that building a shared vision is all about coming to a shared understanding of what is important in the school and why. The primary strategy for getting to this point is engaging constituent group members in dialogue about their personal views of the school's purpose, specifically asking members to share their views. The more people have an opportunity to discuss their views about the deep purpose of the school, the more a shared vision, or picture, of what that school can be will emerge. And the more detailed the picture is of where everyone wants the school to go, the more useful it will be in providing direction for future work.

Blankstein (2013) believes that a school's vision is a statement about where it wants to be going. The vision should guide the collective action of the stakeholders. When a school does not have a clear and shared vision, decisions are made that are not necessarily aligned to that vision. Blankstein believes that powerful vision statements are clear and realistic, secure broad-based ownership, describe the changes that are envisioned, and guide a school's actions.

Development of a shared vision of multicultural education and the school should be grounded in deep and meaningful discussions (Blankstein et al., 2016). Among the topics of those discussions might be the following:

1. How does your school look? How are classrooms set up?

2. Which students' successes are celebrated, and how are they celebrated?

3. What is on the walls and in the hallways?

4. How does teaching look when you attend to the distinct learning styles of all learners?

5. How does curriculum look when you use content that respects culture?

6. How does assessment look when you respect diverse learners?

7. How are you measuring successes?

8. If you want to establish a culture for deep learning, what does that look like?

As a meaningful shared vision evolves, and as constituent group members become more deeply committed to it, the next steps in the process are to make use of school data to discover the current reality and then determine the goals, objectives, and actions that will achieve the vision.

Developing a Culture of Collaboration and Teamwork

Many writers (Darling-Hammond, 1996; DuFour et al., 2016; Fullan, 2007; Fullan & Quinn, 2017; Hord, Roussin, & Sommers, 2009; Joyce & Showers, 2002; Katzenbach & Smith, 1993; Loucks-Horsley et al., 1987; Oakes, Lipton, Anderson, & Stillman, 2012; Schmoker, 2006; Senge et al., 1994; Senge et al., 2012) firmly believe that an important contributor to lasting and significant school improvement is collaboration or teamwork. The concept of collaboration was introduced in Chapter 11. Unfortunately, the traditional approach to work in schools is one of isolation. Teachers are just not accustomed to consulting with one another about how they design the curriculum, analyze student work, or select appropriate instruction and assessment strategies. However, deep learning appears to take place when individuals have regular opportunities to engage in collaborative activity and reflect on that activity.

Both individual learning and **team learning** are critical foundations for learning communities (Senge et al., 1994). For both individuals and organizations, important learning occurs when time is provided for public reflection on their actions. Such time and commitment to public reflection establish a social context for learning in which shared meanings are uncovered. When teachers work in isolation and have limited time for professional growth activities, and when principals are the primary decision makers, change initiatives reach a choke point.

Establishing teams through learning communities can be particularly useful in creating and implementing a schoolwide multicultural education action plan. Senge et al. (1994) identified five key factors in the development of an effective learning community:

1. Enhance personal mastery (e.g., grow the capacity to create results desired for all students in all settings)

2. Address mental models (e.g., reflect on our internal pictures of the world in terms of diversity and see how they shape our actions and decisions with respect to all types of learners)

3. Develop shared vision (e.g., build a group sense of commitment to multicultural education)

4. Engage in team learning (e.g., in groups, develop intelligence and ability about multicultural education that is greater than the sum of individual members' talents)

5. Engage in systems thinking (e.g., understand how all the systems in the school must be addressed to make the school truly multicultural).

In terms of the connection between school culture and multicultural education, writers have indicated a positive connection between school culture and high levels of academic achievement by diverse students (Blankstein & Houston, 2011; Gay, 1994; Sadker & Zittleman, 2016; Williams, 2003). Critically important to establishing a school culture that supports academic achievement by all students are long-term caring relationships, a rich curriculum that is open to all students, and teachers working collaboratively toward school improvement (Oakes et al., 2012). Banks (2009) indicates the following:

An important dimension of multicultural education is a school culture and organization that promote gender, racial, and social-class equity. The culture and organization of the school must be examined by all members of the school staff. They all must also participate in restructuring it. (p. 22)

Implementing multicultural education truly must be a systemic and organized process!

Extended Explorations 12.1: Cultures of Collaboration

School culture has been the focus of much research and writing over the past several years. Based on your readings, reflect on the following questions:

1. Define organizational culture.
2. Describe your school's culture in terms of norms, values, and beliefs.
3. What are some norms and core values of effective schools?
4. Compare them with your current setting.
5. How are norms and values conveyed?
6. How would you approach changing the school culture to be responsive to diverse learner needs?

Now, locate at least two articles that discuss school culture, preferably related to multicultural education. How do your responses mirror what you have read in the articles? Develop a two-column matrix (title the left-hand column "similarities" and the right-hand column "differences"). Make six rows for your matrix, one for each question above. Log your responses and prepare to share with colleagues.

LEARNING OBJECTIVE 12.3 Establish a School Improvement Process That Uses Data to Support All Children

Acting on your vision to move from a school that doesn't value, or has only tinkered with, the implementation of multicultural education to one that embeds it in every aspect of teaching and learning is a major effort. For some, the process of getting from reality to a vision is insurmountable because they lack the knowledge and skills necessary to make school improvement happen.

Implementing multicultural education in a school can be viewed usefully as a significant school improvement effort. When looked at in this light, the process always holds student learning at its core, and there is a consistent focus on curriculum, instruction, and assessment, since these are the essence of educators' contributions to student learning. School improvement for multicultural education, similar to any other school improvement effort, includes the following components:

1. Collection and analysis of student and other data

    a. Which students are of most concern to you and the school? Why? What data or evidence speaks to this concern?

    b. What school policies, practices, and materials are of concern when providing an equitable education to all students?

2. Goal setting for student learning

    a. At what level do you expect students to be achieving?

    b. Are the goals set for student achievement measurable?

© Jack Hollingsworth/Digital Vision/Thinkstock

A vision of a world for our students where people have finally learned to live in harmony starts right here in our classrooms. Schools have the power to influence the future.

3. Identification and selection of research-based promising practices

    a. Is there a need to analyze the curriculum for bias?
    b. What teaching models and instructional strategies have been proven to be effective with diverse students across subject areas?
    c. What assessment practices are being used in the school, and which ones are most useful in supporting students in demonstrating what they know and are able to do?

4. Ongoing evaluation and reflection (formative evaluation)

    a. How will you monitor on a regular basis how well students are responding to the use of the identified promising practices?
    b. What other supports do teachers need to implement successfully the identified promising practices?
    c. What opportunities are being made available for teachers to talk about the interventions and their impact?

5. Adjustment of plan as required

Collection and Analysis of Student and Other Data

Making decisions that affect students must be grounded in more than whim. Decisions about interventions to support deep and meaningful learning must be grounded in data. Bernhardt (2017) indicated that essentially four types of data can inform decisions about teaching and learning. These can be applied to making decisions about multicultural education.

1. *Demographics:* include enrollment, attendance, and dropout rates, all disaggregated by ethnicity, gender, socioeconomic status, and language proficiency

2. *Perceptions:* include attitudes, beliefs, and observations made by students, teachers, and parents

3. *Evidence of student learning:* gathered from standardized test results, teacher-made tests, teacher observations, and authentic assessments

4. *School processes:* include descriptions of instructional programs and strategies, as well as other school programs

Where might you find some of this information? Much data to aid in the decision-making process are already on record or in files with your state's department of education or in the school district's office. Examining strategic school profiles provides important information. Data about school practices, policies, and procedures also can be collected and analyzed using a variety of existing assessment instruments or tools. Banks (2009) has developed a well-known checklist for assessing school progress in multicultural education. We add here (Table 12.2) an adaptation of an assessment instrument that is used by the Connecticut State Department of Education.

Goal Setting and Multicultural Education

In preparing to set goals, educators are urged to make sure that goals are measurable (Schmoker, 2006). Schmoker (2006) believed that a failure to set goals is a primary reason for failure to

TABLE 12.2   **Schoolwide Action Planning Self-Assessment**

Use the Following Questions to Guide Progress in Developing and Implementing a Schoolwide Action Plan for Multicultural Education

1. Staff composition	• Has the school established and enforced policies for recruiting and maintaining a staff made up of individuals from various racial and ethnic groups? • Are procedures and opportunities in place for examining the attitudes, perceptions, beliefs, and behaviors of the staff to be certain that they are ethnically and racially sensitive?

2. Formalized curriculum	• Is the curriculum rigorous for all students?
	
	• Is the curriculum designed to help students learn how to function effectively in various cultural environments and learn more than one cognitive style?
	
	• Is the curriculum designed to help students develop greater self-understanding in light of their ethnic and cultural heritages?
	
	   a. Does the curriculum reflect ethnic and cultural diversity?
	
	      o Does the curriculum include the study of the societal problems that some ethnic and cultural group members experience, such as racism, prejudice, discrimination, and exploitation?
	
	      o Does the curriculum include the study of historical experiences, cultural patterns, and social problems of various ethnic and cultural groups?
	
	      o Does the curriculum examine the total experiences of groups instead of focusing exclusively on "heroes"?
	
	      o Does the curriculum present diversity as a vital societal force that encompasses both potential strength and potential conflict?
	
	   b. Does the curriculum help students develop the decision-making abilities, social participation skills, and sense of political efficacy necessary for effective citizenship?
	
	      o Does the curriculum help students develop the ability to distinguish facts from interpretations and opinions?
	
	      o Does the curriculum help students develop skills in finding and processing information?
	
	      o Does the curriculum provide opportunities for students to take action on social problems affecting racial, ethnic, and cultural groups?
	
	      o Does the curriculum help students develop a sense of efficacy?
	
	   c. Does the curriculum help students develop the skills necessary for effective interpersonal and intercultural group interactions?
	
	      o Does the curriculum help students understand ethnic and cultural reference points that influence communication?
	
	      o Does the curriculum help students participate in cross-ethnic and cross-cultural experiences and reflect on them?
	
	   d. Is the multicultural curriculum comprehensive in scope and sequence, presenting holistic views of ethnic and cultural groups, and is it an integral part of the total school curriculum?
	
	      o Does the curriculum include the role of ethnicity and culture in the local community as well as in the nation?

(Continued)

TABLE 12.2   (Continued)

	o Does content related to ethnic and cultural groups extend beyond special units, courses, occasions, and holidays?
	
	o Does the curriculum provide for development of progressively more complex concepts, abilities, and values?
	
	e. Does the program provide opportunities for students to participate in the aesthetic experiences of various ethnic and cultural groups?
	
	   o Are multiethnic literature and art used to promote empathy and understanding of people from various ethnic and cultural groups and to promote self-examination and self-understanding?
	
	   o Do students read and hear the poetry, short stories, novels, folklore, plays, essays, and autobiographies of a variety of ethnic and cultural groups?
	
	   o Do students examine the music, art, literature, architecture, and dance of a variety of ethnic and cultural groups?

3. Professional development	• Do staff development programs provide opportunities to gain knowledge and understanding about various racial, ethnic, and cultural groups? • Do staff development programs include a variety of experiences (e.g., lectures, field experiences, and curriculum projects)? • Do staff development programs provide opportunities for participants to explore their attitudes and feelings about their own ethnicity and that of others? • Do staff development programs provide opportunities to learn how to create and select multiethnic instructional materials and how to incorporate multicultural content into curriculum materials?
4. Parent/community involvement	• Does the program involve parents from diverse ethnic and cultural groups in program activities and planning? • Are members of the local ethnic and cultural communities regularly used as program resources? • Are field trips to various local ethnic and cultural communities provided for students?
5. Teaching strategies and learning styles	• Does the teacher have high expectations of students from all ethnic and racial groups? • Does the teacher create a classroom atmosphere that reflects acceptance of and respect for ethnic and cultural differences? • Are interdisciplinary and multidisciplinary perspectives used in the study of ethnic and cultural groups and related issues? • Are perspectives of various ethnic and cultural groups represented in the instructional program? • Are students taught why different ethnic and cultural groups often perceive the same historical event or contemporary situation differently? • Are students taught to communicate (speaking, reading, and writing) in a second language?
6. Materials and resources	• Are instructional materials examined for ethnic, cultural, and gender bias? • Do instructional materials treat racial and ethnic differences and groups honestly, realistically, and sensitively? • Do school libraries and resource centers offer a variety of materials on the histories, experiences, and cultures of many racial, ethnic, and cultural groups?

7. Student assessment	• Do teachers use a variety of assessment procedures that reflect the ethnic and cultural diversity of students?
	• Do teachers' day-to-day assessment techniques take into account the ethnic and cultural diversity of their students?
	• Do teachers understand and take into consideration the diversity of student learning styles as they consider assessment design?
8. Policy and practices	• Do policies and practices foster positive interactions among students and educators of various racial, ethnic, and cultural groups?
	• Do policies and practices accommodate the behavioral patterns, learning styles, and orientations of students of various racial, ethnic, and cultural groups?
9. Program evaluation	• Does the school conduct ongoing, systematic evaluations of the goals, methods, and instructional materials used in teaching about ethnicity and culture?
	• Is the effectiveness of curricular programs, both academic and nonacademic, evaluated regularly?

Source: Questions adapted from a questionnaire developed by the Connecticut State Department of Education (2005), in turn adapted from a 1993 instrument developed by the Northeast Consortium for Multicultural Education.

raise student achievement and to improve schools. Goals should reflect the baseline data your school teams have discussed. Following are examples of broad goals that might guide school improvement for multicultural education:

- Develop a positive school climate that reflects the diversity of the students.

- Assess curriculum and instruction for multicultural infusion.

- Develop multicultural curriculum.

- Implement instructional strategies that are responsive to diverse learning styles.

- Develop and use a variety of assessment strategies that allow each student to demonstrate fully what he or she knows and is able to do.

- Ensure representation of diverse student groups in school activities.

- Reduce racial and ethnic isolation, for example, in terms of tracking.

Blankstein (2013) believes that goals help educators stay focused and should provide an indicator of what success will look like. Many educators set goals that use the SMART acronym. They set goals that are specific, measurable, attainable, results-oriented, and time-bound. Examples of SMART goals include these:

- By 2020, 90% of Grades 3 through 8 teachers will demonstrate proficiency in using differentiated instruction to meet diverse learner needs as measured through peer observations.

- By 2020, student achievement in mathematics in Grades 3 through 8 will increase by 15% as measured on the state assessment.

> **Extended Explorations 12.2: Data and Multicultural Education**
>
> In a school with which you are familiar, what data besides test scores have guided recent decisions and planning? You may want to interview school educators and/or review publicly available documents. What other data sources might provide you, as a school decision maker, with helpful information to make better, more informed decisions? Summarize your beliefs in a one-page briefing. Prepare to share with colleagues.

Identification and Selection of Promising Practices

Once measurable goals are set, a planning team should investigate research-based approaches to meet these goals. The previous chapters on curriculum, instruction, and assessment provide many research-based approaches from which to choose, and through its own research, the planning team will uncover other research-based strategies that may meet the needs raised.

Implementation and Monitoring

Throughout the work of implementing multicultural education, the planning team will collect data regularly and summarize those data for discussion with all participants. This process is referred to as *formative evaluation*. These discussions, or "data dialogues," will afford opportunities for making important, though perhaps slight, changes in the application of interventions.

The planning team will also want to collect data at the end of the academic year (*summative evaluation*) to inform decisions about whether or not the intervention is having an impact on student achievement. On the basis of the data, the team will decide whether to maintain the program or go with something else.

LEARNING OBJECTIVE 12.4 Identify Strategies That Support Teacher Professional Development for Multicultural Education

Professional development is the process of improving staff knowledge, skills, and competencies to achieve high-level educational results for students. A schoolwide action plan for implementing multicultural education must include numerous and continual opportunities for educators to acquire knowledge and to develop new skills that will help them meet the needs of diverse learners. Fortunately, a large body of literature describes effective approaches to supporting educator growth, and this body of work is aptly applied to designing professional development for multicultural education.

Joyce and Showers (2002) described characteristics of schools that are progressing in the implementation of school improvement projects. Offering extensive opportunities for staff development that is related to the school improvement focus area is high on the list of priorities. Other priorities include time allocated for faculty collaboration, data collection, a focus on curriculum and instruction, a clear decision-making process, and sharing of the goals by the entire faculty. Joyce and Showers further explain that effective staff development must be school based and embedded in teacher work, be collaborative, focus on student learning, include regular collection and use of data, include targeted measurable goals, include structural variety to respond to diverse educators' needs and desires, include time for collaborative inquiry and learning, and be standards based.

Joyce and Showers (2002) believed that schools that progress in the implementation of school improvement projects provide more time for faculty collaboration, include data collection in their process, provide extensive staff development related to the school improvement area of focus, have a clear decision-making process, ensure that the entire faculty shares the goals, have high expectations for student learning, relate the school improvement project to curriculum and instruction (what's happening in the classroom), and reach out to parents. As you think as a teacher-leader about how you can enhance professional development in your setting, you might reflect on your own experiences with professional development. For example, think about what your most memorable experiences were. What inferences would you draw about quality professional development for multicultural education?

© istockphotos.com/Kai Chiang

New and veteran teachers have much to learn from each other. A teacher's skills and effectiveness are honed through ongoing professional growth.

TABLE 12.3	Learning Forward's Standards for Staff Development

Professional Learning That Increases Educator Effectiveness and Results for All Students	
Learning communities	Occurs within learning communities committed to continuous improvement, collective responsibility, and goal alignment
Leadership	Requires skillful leaders who develop capacity, advocate, and create support systems for professional learning
Resources	Requires prioritizing, monitoring, and coordinating resources for educator learning
Data	Uses a variety of sources and types of student, educator, and system data to plan, assess, and evaluate professional learning
Learning designs	Integrates theories, research, and models of human learning to achieve its intended outcomes
Implementation	Applies research on change and sustains support for implementation of professional learning for long-term change
Outcomes	Aligns its outcomes with educator performance and student curriculum standards

Source: Learning Forward (2011).

Learning Forward (2011) has developed standards for professional development that provide useful benchmarks in analyzing school staff development programs. The standards provide important guidance to schools as they develop professional development for teachers to support multicultural education. As you can read in Table 12.3, standards exist that specifically address supporting teachers in developing the capacity to achieve equity. In Exercise 12.2, use Learning Forward's standards to analyze professional development standards in a setting with which you are familiar.

EXERCISE 12.2
EVALUATING PROFESSIONAL DEVELOPMENT

Critique professional development practices in your own setting using the Learning Forward standards.

Context Standards	Strength (Evidence)	Emerging (Evidence)	Not Evident
Professional learning that increases educator effectiveness and results for all students			
Learning communities: Occurs within learning communities committed to continuous improvement, collective responsibility, and goal alignment.			
Leadership: Requires skillful leaders who develop capacity, advocate, and create support systems for professional learning.			
Resources: Requires prioritizing, monitoring, and coordinating resources for educator learning.			
Data: Uses a variety of sources and types of student, educator, and system data to plan, assess, and evaluate professional learning.			
Learning designs: Integrates theories, research, and models of human learning to achieve its intended outcomes.			
Implementation: Applies research on change and sustains support for implementation of professional learning for long-term change.			
Outcomes: Aligns its outcomes with educator performance and student curriculum standards.			

Source: Learning Forward (2011).

Strategies to Support Teacher Learning

Traditional approaches to professional development for teachers involve a few workshops facilitated by well-intentioned people from outside the school or district. Teachers are not given choices and often find the workshops inapplicable to their daily lives in the classroom. They sit and listen to the presenters, possibly see a demonstration of the intervention, and then probably have a brief opportunity to practice the new intervention.

New approaches to professional development do not start with the content but instead have educators identify learning gaps experienced by their students. Teachers then learn and develop specific interventions to close those gaps. And while they are learning and developing those strategies and interventions, they are being coached regularly along the way, receiving specific feedback on how well they are doing. An illustration of how all the pieces might be put together in developing and implementing a schoolwide action plan for multicultural education is provided in the next section.

If educators are intent on improving schools for multicultural education, they need to engage in ongoing and varied professional development that is proven to raise student achievement. Fortunately, educators are becoming more aware of the many alternatives that exist to augment or replace the traditional and mostly unproductive workshop scenario (Darling-Hammond, 1996; Easton, 2004; Glickman et al., 2017; Joyce & Showers, 2002; Sergiovanni, Starratt, & Cho, 2013; Terrell & Lindsey, 2009). Alternatives include teacher as researcher, clinical supervision, peer coaching, advising teachers, mentoring beginning teachers, teachers' centers, networks, partnerships, individually guided professional development, and portfolios. Above all, teachers need to be given ample opportunities for dialogue with colleagues about multicultural education.

Bringing many of these components together, a PLC can be a powerful professional learning experience (DuFour, 2004; Hord et al., 2009). According to DuFour (2004), "Educators who are building a professional learning community recognize that they must work together to achieve their collective purpose of learning for all. Therefore, they create structures to promote a collaborative culture" (p. 8). Teachers working together in PLCs are able to overcome the traditional environment of teacher isolation in schools by working together to discuss data, develop curriculum, implement research-based instructional strategies, and develop and implement common assessments. For teachers working to become culturally responsive, participation in a PLC provides critical support. The next section presents an illustration of a school that engaged teachers in collaborative learning opportunities in support of diverse students.

The Diversity Project: An Illustration of Schoolwide Action Planning to Implement Multicultural Education

Many educators agree that implementing multicultural education should be approached as a school improvement effort. As with other school improvement efforts, a primary purpose is to enhance student achievement. And, as with any school improvement effort, professional development is a critical component. Unfortunately, teachers are often left to do this work on their own. The Diversity Project is one example of the implementation of a schoolwide action plan for multicultural education that supports both students and teachers in deep learning. This model is unique in that it links research-based approaches to education that is multicultural, knowledge of effective professional development practice, and school improvement–planning processes on individual and systemic levels.

Needs Assessment

Elmfield Middle School was a beautiful, large, new school that appeared to be organized and successful in promoting students, most of whom went on to college. As with most towns in the Northeast, Elmfield was attracting an increasingly culturally diverse population. It was evident to the assistant principal, Ms. Meythaller, that teachers were challenged by more and more students being "unavailable" for deep and meaningful learning.

Extended Explorations 12.3: Professional Development for Multicultural Education

As stated in this chapter, professional development is traditionally thought to mean a series of workshops, with the expectation that teachers will then be able to implement new learning on their own. Go to the websites for organizations that provide resources on professional development (e.g., Learning Forward, ASCD). Read several resources about promising professional development practices. Imagine that you are developing a yearlong plan to support the professional development of yourself and several colleagues, either in your department or at your grade level, in the area of becoming culturally proficient educators. Draft a plan that includes the following:

1. Describe the purpose of the professional learning plan. Identify two student goals and two teacher goals. Use SMART goal formatting if possible.
2. Describe the learning plan for participants.
3. Briefly describe what participants will be learning over the course of the year (e.g., how to differentiate instruction, how to develop unit and lesson plans that are culturally responsive).
4. Select at least five powerful professional development strategies to support teacher growth. Describe how each of the strategies will be implemented. Who will be responsible for implementation? How long will it take to implement? What specific resources will be needed?
5. Describe the ways in which this plan specifically addresses the needs of diverse learners.
6. Describe your rationale for the development of your plan. How does your plan address each of the Learning Forward staff development standards?
7. Prepare to share your plan with colleagues for feedback.

Scores on standardized tests, as well as reviews of student grades, clearly illustrated academic problems in a variety of content areas, including science, language arts, social studies, world languages, and physical education. Some students predictably performed very well, and others just fell by the wayside. In addition, a review of behavioral and attendance records indicated that a cross-section of students just didn't seem to care about school or about one another. Ms. Meythaller determined to do something about this problem.

She had been reading about the impact of experiential learning activities through adventure-type activities on student learning. Coincidentally, Dr. Brigham, the district director of curriculum and instruction, had been learning more about the importance of multicultural education. The two administrators often met to discuss their dreams of improving teaching and learning in the district. One summer, they began to blend their excitement about experiential learning through adventure activities and multicultural education.

Assessment of Current School Culture

The initiative to engage students in experiential education activities as a means of enhancing learning skills came from the principal and the district director of curriculum. However, they knew that for the teachers to buy in to the work that would need to be done, a representative planning team had to be established in order to provide direction for the project. The planning team that emerged included teachers, school leaders, university and experiential learning organization representatives, and district staff. Early in the development of the project, the members of the planning team discovered differences in how they envisioned this work and its impact on teaching and learning. They determined that, to ensure project success, they needed to discuss at length individually held beliefs on the way toward establishing a set of commonly held beliefs in order to guide the project.

The team met throughout the first summer of the project to engage in meaningful conversations. Based on these discussions, the team drafted a statement of their combined beliefs about teaching and learning. Through open and honest conversation, the team began to understand that their overarching purpose was to ensure students' success as active and productive citizens in a diverse, democratic nation, founded on the principles of justice and equality. The team articulated core values regarding student learning patterns and instructional theory. Among these core values and beliefs were the following.

About Students and Learning

- Students need learning to be set within a large conceptual and social context so that students can make connections and construct meaning.
- When students make connections during their learning experiences, they are more likely to understand larger concepts and to apply learning. Experiential learning solidifies student understanding, drives connections to larger concepts, and increases the probability of application in real life.

- Through inquiry-based teaching and learning, students generate and organize information not only to solve but also to formulate problems collaboratively in order to prepare themselves as productive citizens.

- Students learn more comprehensively in environments that offer a variety of instructional and evaluative experiences within the classroom and beyond the classroom, the school, and the immediate community.

- Learning demands social interaction. Socialization within the classroom and connectivity beyond the classroom are key instructional goals, processes, and outcomes.

About Curriculum and Instruction for Diverse Student Populations

- Learning in a dynamic, creative, and exploratory environment demands an extensive repertoire of teaching strategies.

- Curricula constructed for such a dynamic, creative, and exploratory learning environment need to be culturally responsive.

About Adult Learning and Becoming Multicultural Educators

- The adults who build these curricular experiences to lead students to success in a pluralistic society must first examine their own belief systems and interruptions for biases.

- The adults who work with children need continuous support to ensure quality interaction for optimum learning. Support includes formal/traditional professional development and peer coaching/reflective feedback experiences.

- Teachers will work more productively and effectively in environments that value collaboration among students, staff, parents, and community members.

About Education and Equity

- Daily educational practices must affirm pluralism and reject discrimination.

- An educated citizen in the 21st century will value and work effectively with diverse people.

While the planning team was elated that they had developed collaboratively a strong set of beliefs, they knew that a critical next step was to share and discuss the set of beliefs with the entire school staff. That set of conversations took place in the following fall. Again, the conversations drew out some differing opinions. Nevertheless, staff members felt as though their opinions mattered and that finally, for the first time, the whole school was moving in the direction of operating from the same set of values.

The staff then had opportunities to discuss summaries of disaggregated student performance data from recent years. They agreed with the planning team: Students were "falling through the cracks," and the curriculum they had been using for years, while beloved, was not multicultural and, in the way in which it was constructed, not as useful as it could be in addressing student needs.

A Culture of Collaboration and Teamwork

One particularly useful outcome of the exploration of commonly held beliefs was the value placed on a team approach to doing this work. Leadership for the project was provided collaboratively by the planning team (a team grounded in many of the same components and concepts as a PLC), which included representatives from the area university, a nonprofit adventure-programming organization, community youth service agencies, and administrators and teachers in the affected school. The planning team met regularly to discuss possible interventions to address the challenges in the school as illustrated by the baseline data. As specific student needs became more apparent, the planning team began to investigate the literature around multicultural curriculum.

The planning team decided to use multicultural curriculum development in order to address the delineated student needs. Teams of teachers were trained in experiential activities in the classroom and in multicultural curriculum development. These teams worked throughout the year in PLCs to develop and implement curriculum that was multicultural. The peer consultation training, coaching, and implementation was designed to engage teachers collegially in reflection and feedback.

Goal Setting

Three student outcome goals emerged to guide the Diversity Project: (1) building self-esteem, confidence, and trust; (2) developing positive relationships; and (3) improving student achievement, attendance, and communication. Knowing that goals need to be specific and measurable, the planning team also established mechanisms early on for how to measure achievement of the goals. The mechanisms were varied, including observations of student interactions, attitudinal surveys, document reviews (e.g., attendance records, behavioral records, lesson plans), and review of student work as illustrated in standardized achievement tests and collections of performance assessments. Baseline data would be collected at the initiation of the project, formative assessment data would be collected during the project, and then a summative evaluation would be conducted annually.

Identification of Research-Based Interventions

The program that was eventually designed focused on multicultural curriculum development as the primary intervention. A core component of the program was the use of experiential learning to help students acquire skills essential to the learning process. As students acquire these essential skills, they become more available for meaningful learning in content areas, especially those in which curriculum and instruction have been transformed to be multicultural.

Rather than relegate diversity study to February and March, educators learned to thread multiple perspectives throughout units and throughout the year. Some units focused entirely on topics such as immigration or international America. Through the Diversity Project, a new crop of interdisciplinary units emerged. The "Invention Convention" unit in the sixth grade was one example. Traditionally, students became inventors and recorded their experiences throughout the process. The unit expanded to ask critical questions, one of which was about minority inventors and the obstacles they must overcome. In an eighth-grade unit, "Race to the Sea," through the study of loggerhead turtles, students learned ways in which to minimize factors that contribute to the extinction of endangered species. They became "turtles," guiding one another in "trust walks" toward their "nesting ground among newly built condos." The unit's critical questions expanded to include "What are the implications of this for human dynamics in a multicultural society?"

Classroom activities improved cooperative learning, listening, contracting, reasonable risk taking, goal setting, and problem solving. A high degree of teamwork was essential for each group to accomplish initiatives.

Support for Teacher Growth

In developing new approaches to teaching and learning that integrate multicultural curriculum development, teachers are as much learners as are their students. From the beginning, it was apparent that professional development support for teachers needed to be extensive, ongoing, and collaborative and provide opportunities for experimentation. In the professional development sequence that emerged, teachers were engaged in cooperative learning, listening, reasonable risk taking, goal setting, and problem solving. Participants expanded their capacity to trust one another and to strategize, communicate, and solve problems together. Through numerous workshops, networking sessions with members of the planning team, and participation in PLCs, teachers learned the important tenets of education that is multicultural.

Monitoring of Impact

Formative and summative evaluations were conducted throughout the project to assess the impact of the Diversity Project on teaching and learning. Following each workshop, teacher perceptions about the utility of the workshop were assessed through questionnaires. More important, the impact on teaching and learning was assessed using a variety of data collection methods. These eventually included engagement of teachers and administrators in focus group interviews and requests for responses to several iterations of a questionnaire about perceived impact. Samples of unit and lesson plans developed throughout the project were collected and analyzed. Additionally, student performance as ascertained through authentic assessments, teacher-developed assessments, and standardized tests was summarized and analyzed.

New Approaches to Teaching and Learning Pay Off

The project appeared to have had a positive impact on teacher beliefs and classroom practice in Elmfield Middle School. Almost all respondents agreed that they were now able to define more clearly education that is multicultural and engage students more frequently in activities to build social action skills. The Diversity Project resulted in respondents believing that they were better able to use resources to address multiple perspectives, use cooperative learning and team activities to foster positive classroom interactions, and incorporate multicultural perspectives, experiences, content, concepts, and adventure programming into the classroom.

A review of the lesson plans developed as a result of the project revealed that numerous units had been developed. Those units that were considered to be strongly representative of multicultural curriculum supported students in seeing events, issues, and problems from multiple cultural perspectives. Key concepts were clear, and student understanding was supported through activities.

Summary

The Diversity Project appeared to affect the teaching and learning processes because it was a long-term endeavor. In terms of continued school improvement, the planning team realized that all educators need to be supported in their examination of their own levels of awareness about differences, as well as stereotypes and biases they may hold on to that affect teaching and learning. More time had to be allocated for teachers to come together in order to provide and receive feedback on curriculum development and discuss data they are collecting.

PROFILES IN MULTICULTURAL EDUCATION

DONNA M. GOLLNICK

© Donna Gollnick

Donna M. Gollnick is an international consultant for accreditation. She served as senior consultant for the transition of the National Council for the Accreditation of Teacher Education (NCATE) to a new accrediting organization, the Council for the Accreditation of Educator Preparation, after being the senior vice president for NCATE for 25 years. She is past president of the National Association for Multicultural Education and is a recognized authority in multicultural education.

She is coauthor with Philip C. Chinn of *Multicultural Education in a Pluralistic Society*, 10th edition (2016), which she first coauthored with Dr. Chinn in 1982. It was one of the first textbooks for potential teachers that expanded the definition of multicultural education beyond race and ethnicity. Dr. Gollnick and Dr. Chinn included groups based on socioeconomic status, gender, sexual orientation, language, religion, age, and geography in their definition and expanded their coverage of those groups in every edition. The book remains one of the most popular textbooks in this field. With James A. Johnson, Diann Musial, and Gene Hall, she is a coauthor of one of the leading educational foundations textbooks: *Foundations of American Education: Becoming Effective Teachers in Challenging Times*, 17th edition (2018). She has written about multicultural education for more than 35 years.

When Dr. Gollnick was asked to reflect on her most important contribution to the field, she stated, "Being involved in the maintenance of the concepts of multicultural education in the standards of NCATE has been my major contribution to the field of multicultural education." In the mid-1970s, Dr. Gollnick staffed the committee at the American Association of Colleges for Teacher Education that first wrote a standard on multicultural education for inclusion in the NCATE standards that all accredited institutions were required to address. NCATE's Unit Accreditation Board continued to refine how the standards incorporated multicultural concepts in five revisions, with diversity now being one of the six standards that institutions must meet to be accredited.

Throughout her career, Dr. Gollnick has always believed that the ultimate goal of teaching is to ensure that students learn the content being taught. In the process, students should learn how to work together and respect one another. To ensure these outcomes, teachers must have an understanding of the different cultural groups represented in the school and community. They must know how to bring the students' cultures into the learning process, drawing on real examples from their lives. They must believe that all students can learn at high levels and work toward ensuring that students with the most obstacles (e.g., homelessness, an illness, a disability, or social discrimination) are academically successful.

REFLECTING BACK

1. Consider the components essential to a schoolwide multicultural education action plan illustrated in Table 12.1. Analyze the order of the steps. Would you place each of the steps in the order in which they are listed? Why or why not?

2. Reflect on a school culture with which you are familiar. Think about whether or not that school is ready to engage in school improvement around multicultural education. Take a sheet of paper and make a T-chart. As the heading for the left-hand side of the T, write the word *barriers*. On the right side of the T, write the word *supports*. Now develop a list under each heading of barriers and supports, respectively, that exist in that school culture regarding achievement of a vision of the school as having implemented multicultural education.

3. Think of a school that you know. How does the school improvement process described in teaching and learning in this book take place in that setting? How do you think the process described in this chapter might improve education in that setting?

4. Consider your own experiences with professional development. How do your experiences resonate with the processes and strategies described in this chapter? In reflecting on what you've learned about professional development, how would you support yourself and some department colleagues in learning to implement multiple intelligences as an instructional strategy?

CASE STUDY
CHANGING THE SCHOOL CULTURE

Key Issues to Be Explored in the Case

1. The need for a comprehensive plan for the integration of multicultural education

2. The critical importance of ongoing professional learning opportunities for teachers

3. Leadership that is empowering

Janet Maxwell, director of curriculum and instruction for the Crystal City Public School District, was ecstatic when she learned in late May that the district had been awarded a federal grant to support a 3-year project to develop and implement multicultural curriculum in the district. She had worked with two high school teachers, Alex Patton and Stephanie Powell, in developing the proposal. Alex and Stephanie had attended a national curriculum development conference during which they attended a daylong workshop on multicultural education. They returned to Crystal High School very enthusiastic about the potential for multicultural education and shared their enthusiasm with Janet. While the district was becoming more diverse in terms of race and ethnicity, the two teachers were concerned that not all the schools were as responsive to all students as needed. Working together, the three educators wrote a very strong proposal and obtained the full endorsement

(Continued)

(Continued)

of the district's superintendent and each of the school principals. For the first 2 years, the primary efforts would be aimed at the high school level. Work at the middle and elementary school levels would be phased in next.

The project's primary goals included development of a multicultural curriculum, increasing the cultural competency of staff, and a review of programs, policy, and procedures to ensure that they reflected and responded to the cultural needs of the students. Janet was anxious to get started, and the three of them spent most of the summer on the project. Their primary summer activities included the development of a 3-day model training institute for the district's educators in developing a curriculum that is multicultural and purchase of multicultural education materials for a Multicultural Education Center to be established at the high school. Janet kept the school and district administrators fully apprised of her activities.

In the fall, primarily through Janet's efforts, the Multicultural Education Center was established in the high school to serve as a resource center housing the leading texts and curricula in the field of multicultural education, serve as a focal point for training the district's teachers, and assist educators in curriculum development. Also in the fall, all teachers in the district were trained in multicultural curriculum development through the 3-day institute. Among the training topics were self-reflection, knowledge of diverse cultures, learning styles, multicultural curriculum development models, organizational development for multicultural education, prejudice, and racism. Training approaches included the sharing of knowledge, demonstrations, and opportunities to practice new skills. Once they were trained, teachers were expected to begin to develop a multicultural curriculum. Janet believed that they had the necessary supports for doing this work, and she believed that, during the training institute sessions, most teachers had shown tremendous enthusiasm for the topics.

They appeared to be committed to diving into the work that needed to be done. Alex and Stephanie were to make themselves available through the Multicultural Education Center as questions arose.

The fall proved to very busy for Janet, and she assumed that Stephanie and Alex were monitoring the multicultural education project for the school. However, by mid-December, just before the winter break, Alex and Stephanie made an appointment to meet with Janet. When they sat down together to debrief the fall activities on the project, Alex and Stephanie only shared their growing sense of frustration. Despite their best intentions, Alex and Stephanie found that they couldn't manage this project alone. Also, despite the immediate enthusiasm following the 3-day training institutes, only two teachers had approached them with any questions about the process. Janet began to have a sinking feeling that, despite the teachers' good intentions, not much curriculum development work was being done. Alex and Stephanie ended the conversation by saying that they, too, had too much work to do and wouldn't be able to continue in their monitoring roles in the spring semester.

Discussion Questions

1. What do you recommend that Janet do at this point?

2. What might be done to engage the teacher-leaders once again in the project?

3. What critical components of the **school improvement cycle** were missing from Janet's project?

4. To ensure teacher participation in this work, how might Janet, Alex, and Stephanie have designed the professional development support for all teachers?

5. How do the approaches to supporting school improvement and professional development of teachers in this case mirror or run contrary to your own experiences?

CHAPTER SUMMARY

In this chapter, we addressed knowledge and skills that will be important for you as a teacher-leader supporting school improvement efforts for multicultural education. Chapter 12 included four learning objectives.

12.1 Develop a schoolwide plan for the implementation of multicultural education

The implementation of multicultural education in the school must be more than an initiative of interested individual teachers. It will be most effective and useful when the implementation of multicultural education is supported as a whole-school reform effort.

- A results-driven, schoolwide action plan to support diverse learners means setting specific goals for student achievement, using multicultural curriculum and diverse instructional and assessment strategies to meet those goals, measuring the impact of the strategies, and then adjusting as needed. Educators working in teams will be a critical element in implementing multicultural education as a school improvement process.

12.2 Explain the components of a school culture that supports teaching and learning for all students

The beliefs, values, and norms in the school guide teaching and learning practices. With that in mind, the beliefs, values, and norms that constitute the school's culture must address the needs of all learners. Above all, there must be a pervasive ethos in the school that teaching and learning practices must be culturally responsive and responsible.

- When beginning significant efforts to implement multicultural education in schools, the community must focus in particular on the readiness of the school for change. Assessing school culture is a critical starting point. This means looking at values, beliefs, and norms that are held about diversity, learning, the purpose of school, and roles of teachers and learners. It is important to get a sense of the "inner reality" of the school before starting down the road to school improvement. Examining the culture of a school may illuminate certain areas (beliefs, values, norms) that need to be addressed before setting out on a school improvement effort that focuses on implementing multicultural education.

12.3 Establish a school improvement process that uses data to support all children

The school should have an established process for identifying school improvement needs and working to improve teaching and learning for all children. The school community should identify, through the use of data, those student populations that raise the most concerns.

- Achieving education that is multicultural is a school improvement process. As such, the implementation of multicultural education should adhere to research-based strategies and processes for school improvement. These include a focus on data, keeping student learning at the core, teamwork as a means for achieving results beyond what individuals can do, and frequent monitoring of progress. Professional development is a critical component. In preparing to set goals, educators are urged to make sure that goals are specific, measurable, attainable, realistic, and time bound.

12.4 Identify strategies that support teacher professional development for multicultural education

Members of the school community must be given ongoing, job-embedded professional development so they can enhance their instructional practice to meet the needs of all students.

- A schoolwide action plan for implementing multicultural education must include numerous and continual opportunities for educators to acquire knowledge and develop new skills that will help them meet the needs of diverse learners. Alternatives to traditional professional development workshops include teacher as researcher, clinical supervision, peer coaching, advising teachers, mentoring beginning teachers, teachers' centers, networks, partnerships, individually guided professional development, and portfolios. Above all, teachers need to be given ample opportunities for dialogue with colleagues about multicultural education.

KEY TERMS

data-based decision making 348

effective schools research 348

enculturation 347

school culture 343

school improvement cycle 368

shared vision 350

team learning 352

APPLICATION: ACTIVITIES AND EXERCISES

Individual

1. Arrange to interview the director of curriculum and instruction for a local district about the implementation of multicultural education in that district. How does that process resonate with the processes described in this chapter? (Learning Objective 12.1)

School Culture

1. With a particular school in mind, make a list of 10 policy, curricular, resource, or other changes you believe would improve the school culture and markedly improve student achievement. You may want to interview some school educators and/or review some pertinent school documents that are available to the public. How are the changes you recommend attuned to culturally responsive teaching and learning? Summarize your beliefs and statements in a one-page briefing. Prepare to share your briefing with colleagues. (Learning Objectives 12.2 and 12.3)

2. Identify, using data, a professional need related to multicultural education that is responsive to diverse student needs. Choose a professional development model, and develop a professional development plan for implementation within a department or grade level of teacher colleagues to address the need. (Learning Objectives 12.3 and 12.4)

Groups

1. In small groups, practice developing a shared vision of multicultural education in a specific school. What does the vision mean to you? Then, proceed to develop collaboratively, using the steps identified in this chapter, a draft schoolwide action plan for multicultural education. (Learning Objective 12.1)

2. In small groups, come to an agreement about a school with which most of you are familiar and whose culture you want to explore. Find the strategic school profile or a set of data about that school (look on the Internet or request it from the school). Individually, analyze the information on the profile from the point of view of multicultural education. Who are the students of most concern? What can you gather about the culture (values, beliefs, norms) of the school, if anything? Come together to discuss your findings. Debrief your group process. What were you able to learn as a group that you didn't see as an individual? As a group, develop a list of additional information you need in order to develop a sense about the school's culture and the students in the school. (Learning Objectives 12.1, 12.2, and 12.3)

3. In groups of four, imagine that you will need to collect data about a particular school with which you are familiar. Each of you should take one of Bernhardt's four components of data collection for school improvement and develop specific data collection strategies in that area. For example, you might want to explore teacher perceptions about second-language learners in your school. Develop a questionnaire that collects those perceptions. When all four of you have developed your strategies, discuss the process as a group and the implications for school improvement for multicultural education. Then, work as a team to develop a professional development plan that addresses an area of need related to teachers of second-language learners. (Learning Objectives 12.3 and 12.4)

Self-Assessment

Answer the following questions either yes or no. Then write about your rationale for your responses.

1. I can use one of the assessment instruments or strategies discussed in this chapter to collect data about a particular school setting. I can summarize and analyze the data to convey what it says about the school as it implements multicultural education.

2. As a teacher-leader, I know strategies and processes to address some of the resistance or apathy that might emerge as a school plans to implement multicultural education.

3. I can apply school improvement–planning processes to the implementation of multicultural education.

4. I believe that I am developing the knowledge and skills to participate on a school action planning team for the implementation of multicultural education.

ANNOTATED RESOURCES

ASCD

http://www.ascd.org

ASCD is dedicated to excellence in learning, teaching, and leading so that every child is healthy, safe, engaged, supported, and challenged. Comprising 115,000 members—superintendents, principals, teachers, and advocates from more than 128 countries—the ASCD community also includes 51 affiliate organizations.

EducationWorld

http://www.educationworld.com

Founded in 1996, EducationWorld's goal is to create a home for educators on the Internet, a place where teachers can gather and share ideas. This resource includes lesson plans, practical information for educators, information on how to integrate technology into the classroom, articles written by education experts, website reviews, special features and columns, and employment listings.

Learning Forward

https://learningforward.org

Learning Forward is an international membership association of learning educators focused on increasing student achievement through more effective professional learning. Learning Forward's purpose is to ensure that every educator engages in effective professional learning every day so that every student achieves.

National Association of Secondary School Principals

http://www.nassp.org

The National Association of Secondary School Principals (NASSP) is a national organization of, and voice for, middle level and high school principals, assistant principals, and aspiring school leaders from across the United States and more than 45 countries around the world. The organization provides a wide variety of resources for school leaders. NASSP aims to provide leaders of diverse schools with professional resources as part of their diversity initiative.

National Association of Elementary School Principals

www.naesp.org

The National Association of Elementary School Principals, founded in 1921, is a professional organization serving elementary and middle school principals and other education leaders throughout the United States, Canada, and overseas. The association believes that the progress and well-being of the individual child must be at the forefront of all elementary and middle-school planning and operations. Furthermore, this association supports elementary and middle-level principals as the primary catalyst for creating a lasting foundation for learning, driving school and student performance, and shaping the long-term impact of school improvement efforts.

National School Reform Faculty

https://www.nsrfharmony.org

The National School Reform Faculty is an organization that empowers educators to create meaningful learning experiences for all by collaborating effectively in reflective democratic communities that foster educational equity and social justice.

Visit the student study site at **study.sagepub.com/howe3e** for additional study tools including the following:

- eFlashcards

- Web quizzes

- SAGE journal articles

- Video links

- Web resources

- Assessments from the text

- Access to author's blog

Get the tools you need to sharpen your study skills. SAGE edge offers a robust online environment featuring an impressive array of free tools and resources. Access practice quizzes, eFlashcards, video, and multimedia at **edge.sagepub.com/howe3e**

Section V Assessment

Action

Major Assessment 5: Collegial Briefing

Educators must be deeply immersed in a variety of research-based strategies to support teaching and learning. They must be able to work collaboratively with other teachers to support them in their growth and development in order to meet the needs of diverse learners.

As a means of expanding your capacity to develop school environments that support diverse learners, you will first outline a plan for analysis and development of a school environment that supports deep and meaningful learning by all students. Second, select one promising research-based strategy for supporting all students in deep and meaningful learning. Finally, conduct a collegial briefing with course colleagues.

Part 1: Plan for Development of a School Environment

1. Locate the website of a school with which you are familiar. Read and reflect on the school's mission and statement of values. What philosophy appears to be most in evidence? What leads you to think this?

2. Locate the curriculum links for an elementary school, a middle school, or a high school (select one). Look at the curriculum descriptions in the area you've selected.

   - What is the role of standards?

   - How are standards and benchmarks reflected in the curriculum?

3. Based on your analysis, what appears to be the primary purpose of curriculum (transmission, transaction, transformation)? What leads you to think this?

4. What appears to be the prevalent curriculum orientation (learner centered, needs of society, academic subjects)? What leads you to think this?

5. Is there resonance between the mission/values and the curriculum as provided?

6. If you were a member of the curriculum development committee at the school, what steps would you want to make sure are included in future curriculum work?

7. If you were a member of the professional development committee at the school, what steps would you want to make sure are included in future professional development work?

Part 2: Collegial Briefing

Investigate the research and literature about one specific strategy or element related to achieving education that is multicultural. Prepare a one-page (typed double-spaced) briefing statement. In your written briefing statement, please (1) describe the strategy or practice and (2) include useful and current resources. Plan to engage colleagues in a discussion about the strategy for approximately 30 to 40 minutes. Engage your colleagues in a discussion of teacher-leader implications (e.g., explore how and when you would support teachers in using these strategies). The purpose of each briefing is for individual students to engage colleagues in a collegial discussion on the role of teachers in meeting diverse learner needs.

You may choose from the topics below or select a different topic.

1. Differentiated instruction

2. Response to intervention

3. Understanding by design

4. Partnership for 21st century learning skills

5. Common formative assessments

6. Constructivist teaching

7. Teaching for social justice and equity

8. Cooperative learning

9. Teacher evaluation/professional development

10. Promising practices in professional development

Appendix

The Vital Multicultural Classroom

Resources, Organizations, and Associations

About This Appendix

The great thing about the information age is that there are countless sources of information in print, on video, and on the Internet. However, one of the worst things about the information age is that there are countless sources in print, on video, and on the Internet. Too much information and endless lists of resources often confuse teachers. This appendix will offer carefully vetted sources that may be of use to classroom teachers in planning a multicultural curriculum. Many more resources are available but are not listed here. By keeping a tight focus on free resources for multicultural curriculum, we hope that users will not be overwhelmed by information overload.

The following criteria were used for inclusion of resources here:

- *Affordability:* We recognize the financial limitations of new as well as veteran teachers. The main driver of selection of sources to list here has been that they be freely available through the Internet. While we know these sites exist as this book goes to press, readers should keep in mind the fact that it is not unusual for websites to become obsolete or stop functioning.

- *A focus on multicultural curriculum development:* Much of what could arguably have been included was omitted if it did not directly support development of a multicultural curriculum, specifically designing curriculum and implementing it through classroom instruction.

- *The existence of a website:* Museums and historical sites are not included unless they have websites that offer curricular information.

- *Utility:* Publications were chosen if they demonstrated usefulness and wide application. Several types of resources are included in this chapter. In each section, there may be useful websites; videos, films, and CDs; LISTSERVs; and publications. Videos on multicultural education as a field are somewhat rare. On the other hand, numerous videos are available on racism, gender, sexual orientation, and commonly disenfranchised groups. A LISTSERV is an email discussion group. Once you subscribe, you may submit email messages to create or join on a discussion. Most of the annotations that describe websites are presented as they appear on those websites. The references at the end of each chapter in this book are the best sources of information on books to use as resources.

Organizations With Facebook Sites

Facebook, the social media site, is a great resource for current and interactive resources on teaching. Below, we list several organizations of interest that have Facebook sites. Each organization's standard website is listed as well. Many other organizations listed in this appendix may have Facebook sites, but we have found these organizations' Facebook sites to be particularly helpful.

Colorlines.com

Facebook site: https://www.facebook.com/colorlines *Website:* http://colorlines.com

Colorlines.com is a daily news site offering award-winning reporting, commentary, and solutions to today's racial justice issues.

Colorlines.com is produced by a multiracial team of writers whose daily reporting and analysis serves as a leading voice on a broad range of issues, including politics, immigration reform, the economy, and jobs. Colorlines.com offers readers the opportunity to take action on these issues through its Action channel.

FairTest: The National Center for Fair and Open Testing

Facebook site: https://www.facebook.com/FairTest *Website:* http://www.fairtest.org

FairTest works to end the misuses and flaws of standardized testing and to ensure that evaluation of students, teachers, and schools is fair, open, valid, and educationally beneficial.

National Association for Multicultural Education

Facebook site: https://www.facebook.com/groups/25246622051 *Website:* http://www.nameorg.org

The National Association for Multicultural Education (NAME) was founded in 1990 to bring together individuals from all academic levels and disciplines, from diverse educational institutions, and from other organizations, occupations, and communities—all of whom had an interest in multicultural education. NAME is committed to a philosophy of inclusion that embraces the basic tenets of democracy and cultural pluralism.

NAME celebrates cultural and ethnic diversity as a national strength that enriches a society and rejects the view that diversity threatens the fabric of a society. NAME believes that multicultural education promotes equity for all, regardless of culture, ethnicity, race, language, age, gender, sexual orientation, belief system, or exceptionality. NAME believes that multicultural education enables the individual to believe in his or her own intrinsic worth and culture, transcend monoculturalism, and, ultimately, become multicultural. This developmental process is at the center of the individual's quest to define his or her relationship and responsibility to our global society. NAME recognizes that individuals have not always been and perhaps never will be in complete agreement regarding the definitions and goals of multicultural education and believes that continuing debate is healthy.

Race Forward: The Center for Racial Justice Innovation

Facebook site: https://www.facebook.com/RaceForward

Race Forward advances racial justice through research, media, and practice. Founded in 1981, Race Forward brings systemic analysis and an innovative approach to complex race issues to help people take effective action toward racial equity. Race Forward publishes the daily news site Colorlines and presents Facing Race, the country's largest multiracial conference on racial justice.

Rethinking Schools

Facebook site: https://www.facebook.com/rethinkingschools *Website:* http://www.rethinkingschools.org

Rethinking Schools remains firmly committed to equity and to the vision that public education is central to the creation of a humane, caring, and multiracial democracy. Rethinking Schools emphasizes problems facing schools, particularly racism.

Rethinking Schools is a nonprofit magazine and publishing house that focuses on teaching for social justice, antiracist education, and issues of equity and equality in public education policy and practice today.

Southern Poverty Law Center

Facebook site: https://www.facebook.com/SPLCenter *Website:* http://www.splcenter.org

The Southern Poverty Law Center (SPLC) is dedicated to fighting hatred and bigotry and to seeking justice for the most vulnerable members of our society. Using litigation, education, and other forms of advocacy, the SPLC works toward the day when the ideals of social justice and equal opportunity will become a reality. The SPLC is a nonprofit civil rights organization that combats hate and intolerance and fights for the rights of the most vulnerable in our society. It has won numerous landmark legal victories on behalf of the exploited, the powerless, and the forgotten. SPLC's lawsuits have toppled institutional racism in the South, crippled some of the nation's most violent White supremacist groups, and won justice for exploited workers, disabled children, and other victims of discrimination. (See also a discussion of SPLC's main website under "Advocacy, Civil Rights, and Social Justice Organizations" below.)

Teaching for Change

Facebook site: https://www.facebook.com/TeachingforChange *Website:* http://www.teachingforchange.org

Teaching for Change provides teachers and parents with the tools to create schools where students learn to read, write, and change the world.

Voices of a People's History of the United States

Facebook site: https://www.facebook.com/VoicesofaPeoplesHistory *Website:* http://www.peopleshistory.us

Howard Zinn's Voices of a People's History brings history to life in communities and classrooms worldwide. By giving public expression to rebels, dissenters, and visionaries from our past and present, Voices of a People's History seeks to educate and inspire a new generation working for social justice. Founded by historian Howard Zinn in 2007, Voices of a People's History of the United States brings to life the extraordinary history of ordinary people who built the movements ending slavery and Jim Crow, protesting war and the genocide of Native Americans, creating unions and the 8-hour workday, advancing women's rights and gay liberation, and struggling to right the wrongs of the day.

Zinn Education Project

Facebook Site: https://www.facebook.com/ZinnEducationProject *Website:* http://www.zinnedproject.org

The Zinn Education Project promotes and supports the use of Howard Zinn's best-selling book *A People's History of the United States* and other materials for teaching *A People's History* in middle school and high school classrooms across the country. The Zinn Education Project is coordinated by two nonprofit organizations, Rethinking Schools (www.rethinkingschools.org) and Teaching for Change (www.teachingforchange.org).

The goal of the Zinn Education Project is to introduce students to a more accurate, complex, and engaging understanding of U.S. history than is found in traditional textbooks and curricula. The empowering potential of studying U.S. history is often lost in a textbook-driven, trivial pursuit of names and dates. Zinn's *A Peoples History of the United States* emphasizes the roles of working people, women, people of color, and organized social movements in shaping history. Students learn that history is made not by a few heroic individuals but, instead, by people's choices and actions and that, therefore, students' own choices and actions also matter.

We believe that through taking a more engaging and more honest look at the past, we can help equip students with the analytical tools to make sense of—and improve—the world today.

Advocacy, Civil Rights, and Social Justice Organizations (General)

American Civil Liberties Union

Website: http://www.aclu.org

The American Civil Liberties Union (ACLU) is our nation's guardian of liberty, working daily in courts, legislatures, and communities to defend and preserve the individual rights and liberties guaranteed to all people in this country by the Constitution and laws of the United States.

Anti-Defamation League

Website: http://adl.org

The immediate objective of the Anti-Defamation League (ADL) is to stop, by appeals to reason and conscience and, if necessary, by appeals to law, the defamation of the Jewish people. Its ultimate purpose is to secure justice and fair treatment for all citizens and to put an end forever to unjust and unfair discrimination against and ridicule of any sect or body of citizens. In addition to offering diversity training workshops throughout the nation, ADL provides resources on how to address anti-Semitism, racism, and prejudice. The League's website includes teaching resources on these subjects as well as links to Holocaust studies resources. Here one can find books, newsletters, online bibliographies, lesson plans at all grade levels from elementary to college level in a variety of areas, and coverage of topical events.

National Conference for Community and Justice

Website: http://www.nccj.org

The National Conference for Community and Justice (NCCJ) is the only national human relations organization that focuses on a broad range of "isms," the multiple manifestations of discrimination and oppression that are based on one's religion, race, gender, or sexual orientation. From bias crimes to racial profiling, the challenges ahead are real. To confront and overcome them, NCCJ maintains an abiding commitment to work with decision makers and leaders to support their work to build an inclusive society.

Southern Poverty Law Center

Website: http://www.splcenter.org

The Southern Poverty Law Center (SPLC) was founded in 1971 as a small civil rights law firm. Today, SPLC is internationally known for its tolerance education programs, its legal victories against White supremacists, and its tracking of hate groups. SPLC is a nonprofit organization that combats hate, intolerance, and discrimination through education and litigation. The website includes details on their KlanWatch and militia task force. The main website leads to specific education resources (see also the discussion of SPLC's Facebook page under "Organizations With Facebook Sites" above).

U.S. Department of Education, Office for Civil Rights

Website: http://www.ed.gov/about/offices/list/ocr/index.html

The mission of the Office for Civil Rights is to ensure equal access to education and to promote educational excellence throughout the nation through vigorous enforcement of civil rights.

Discussion Forums

MCP (formerly MCPavilion)

MCP is the Multicultural Pavilion's email discussion forum. Its purpose is to engage an international group of educators and activists in an ongoing dialogue about equity, social justice, and multicultural education. The discussion ranges from current issues (e.g., standardization and high-stakes testing) to equity issues (e.g., homophobia and sexism in schools) to the sharing of resources.

Join a group of more than 600 educators from around the world dedicated to multicultural education at all levels of schooling.

National Association for Multicultural Education

Website: http://nameorg.org

The National Association for Multicultural Education (NAME) hosts a LISTSERV, also known as an email discussion group. The LISTSERV, named NAME-MCE, provides a forum to discuss multicultural education, share resources, post job openings, announce conferences or other events, and ask questions of almost 1,000 educators and activists around the world.

African American Resources

The African American Mosaic: A Library of Congress Resource Guide for the Study of Black History and Culture

Website: https://www.loc.gov/exhibits/african/
Provided by the Library of Congress, this website hosts a collection of rare books, photographs, and historical information on the African American experience.

Association for the Study of African American Life and History

Website: http://www.asalh.org
The mission of the Association for the Study of African American Life and History (ASALH) is to promote, research, preserve, interpret, and disseminate information about Black life, history, and culture to the global community.

Association of African American Museums

Website: http://www.blackmuseums.org
The Association of African American Museums (AAAM) is a nonprofit membership organization established to support the African- and African American–focused museums nationally and internationally, as well as the professionals who protect, preserve, and interpret African and African American art, history, and culture. Established as the single representative and principal voice of the African American museum movement, the association seeks to strengthen and advocate for the interests of institutions and individuals committed to the preservation of African-derived cultures. The services provided by AAAM enhance the ability of those museums to serve the needs and interests of persons of African ancestry and those who wish to know more about the art, history, and culture of African-derived cultures.

Digital Schomburg African American Women Writers of the 19th Century

Website: http://digital.nypl.org/schomburg/writers_aa19
This is an online collection of writings by African American women.

Internet Public Library

Website: http://www.ipl.org/IPLBrowse/GetSubject?vid=13&cid=1&tid=7166&parent=7165
Here is an extensive guide to African American resources on the Internet.

Museum of African American History, Boston and Nantucket

Website: http://www.afroammuseum.org
The website of the Museum of African American History includes information on African Americans in the 19th century and links to other museums of comparable focus.

National Association for the Advancement of Colored People

Website: http://www.naacp.org
Founded in 1909 in New York City by a group of Black and White citizens committed to social justice, the National Association for the Advancement of Colored People (NAACP) is the nation's largest and strongest civil rights organization.

National Urban League

Website: http://www.nul.org

Established in 1910, the National Urban League is the nation's oldest and largest community-based movement devoted to empowering African Americans to enter the economic and social mainstream. Today, the National Urban League, headquartered in New York City, spearheads the nonpartisan efforts of its local affiliates. There are over 100 local affiliates of the National Urban League located in 35 states and the District of Columbia, providing direct services to more than 2 million people nationwide through programs, advocacy, and research. The mission of the Urban League movement is to enable African Americans to secure economic self-reliance, parity, power, and civil rights.

African American Publications

African Voices Magazine

Website: http://www.africanvoices.com

African Voices magazine is dedicated to highlighting the rich artistic heritage of people of color. The magazine offers an exciting mix of short stories, poetry, book and music reviews, historical profiles, and features on contemporary artists and musicians such as playwright August Wilson and jazz great Max Roach.

Diverse: Issues in Higher Education

Website: http://www.diverseeducation.com

Since 1984, Diverse: Issues In Higher Education (originally founded as Black Issues in Higher Education) has been America's premier news source for information concerning diversity in American higher education. The magazine received the 2002 Folio Award as the best education publication in America; this attests to how well Diverse has carried out its mission of being the most reliable source for those who understand the importance of issues of diversity in higher education.

Arab American and Muslim American Resources

American-Arab Anti-Discrimination Committee

Website: http://www.adc.org

The American-Arab Anti-Discrimination Committee (ADC) is a civil rights organization committed to defending the rights of people of Arab descent and promoting their rich cultural heritage. The organization's website provides educational resources, such as a bibliography of Arab American children's books, to foster awareness of the Arab American community.

America-Mideast Educational and Training Services

Website: http://www.amideast.org

The America-Mideast Educational and Training Service (AMIDEAST) is a leading American nonprofit organization engaged in international education, training, and development activities in the Middle East and North Africa. The organization's website provides books, articles, and online educational materials on Arabs and Muslims.

Resources for Understanding Islam and the Arab World

Website: http://www.friendsofmorocco.org/who.html

Friends of Morocco is an organization of Americans, mostly returned Peace Corps volunteers, with experience in Morocco and Moroccans in America united with an interest in promoting educational, cultural, charitable, social, literary, and scientific exchange between Morocco and the United States of America.

Council on American-Islamic Relations

Website: http://www.cair.com

The Council on American-Islamic Relations (CAIR) is a grassroots civil rights and advocacy group. CAIR is America's largest Islamic civil liberties group, with regional offices around the United States and in Canada. The national headquarters is located on Capitol Hill in Washington, D.C.

Since its establishment in 1994, CAIR has worked to promote a positive image of Islam and Muslims in America. Through media relations, government relations, education, and advocacy, CAIR puts forth an Islamic perspective to ensure that the Muslim voice is represented. In offering this perspective, CAIR seeks to empower the American Muslim community and encourage Muslims' participation in political and social activism.

Institute on Religion and Civic Values

Website: http://www.ircv.org

The Institute on Religion and Civic Values (IRCV) is a nonprofit organization that supports freedom of conscience for people of all faiths and none. A nonadvocacy organization, it plays a neutral, scholarly role in advancing knowledge about world religions and cultures in various arenas to increase understanding, mutual respect, and cooperation. It assists companies, government agencies, civic organizations, and religious institutions in the areas of history—social studies curriculum, religion in the public square, interreligious education, and media coverage of religion news. The website provides lesson plans, assessments, and other resources for teachers.

Middle East Outreach Council

Website: http://www.meoc.us

Established in 1981, the Middle East Outreach Council (MEOC) is a national, nonprofit organization working to increase public knowledge about the peoples, places, and cultures of the Middle East, including the Arab world, Israel, Iran, Turkey, and Afghanistan.

MEOC is a national network of educators dedicated to disseminating apolitical and nonpartisan information, resources, and activities furthering understanding about the Middle East. MEOC's target audience is nonspecialists at the K–12 and college levels, although its services are also relevant to broader community needs. MEOC has members around the country, and its services include a semiannual newsletter, member LISTSERV, an annual book award, and a website.

TeachMideast

Website: http://www.teachmideast.org

TeachMideast is a resource designed primarily to give middle and high school teachers the tools they need to teach about three critical, complex, and intriguing subjects: the Middle East, Islam, and Muslims. Elementary- and college-level teachers will also find much of use here for both their classrooms and their personal edification. This website is the core project of the Middle East Policy Council's educational program and underpins MEPC's free teacher institutes.

Asian American Resources

AsianWeek

AsianWeek, the only English-language, national newsweekly for Asian Pacific Americans, has become a place for American-born Asians to better understand their community. It has become a bridge for Asian immigrants to mainstream American culture. Likewise, it is the primary vehicle for mainstream America to learn of the concerns and aspirations of one of the country's fastest-growing communities.

Asian American Net

Website: http://www.asianamerican.net

Asian American Net's mission is to serve all Asian American communities and to promote and strengthen cultural, educational, and commercial ties between Asia and North America. It is a unique website in the sense that it endeavors to highlight and promote all the different Asian cultures and peoples as well as the Asian Americans originally from all these countries. This site encourages high school, college, and university students and teachers to learn more about Asia, and it reminds Asian Americans of their national and cultural origins, of which they can be proud.

Asian American Resources

Website: http://www.dartmouth.edu/~hist32/Books/Topic.htm

This website includes a comprehensive bibliography from Dartmouth College.

Asian-Nation

Website: https://www.facebook.com/pg/Asian-Nation-The-Landscape-of-Asian-America-99634358822/about/?ref=page_internal

Asian-Nation is an information resource on the historical, demographic, political, and cultural issues that bear on today's diverse Asian American community. You can think of Asian-Nation as an online version of "Asian Americans 101."

Japanese American Citizenship League

Website: http://www.jacl.org

The Japanese American Citizens League (JACL) is a membership organization whose mission is to secure and maintain the human and civil rights of Americans of Japanese ancestry and others victimized by injustice.

Organization of Chinese Americans

Website: http://www.ocanational.org

Founded in 1973 as the Organization of Chinese Americans (OCA), this organization aims to embrace the hopes and aspirations of Asian Pacific Americans in the United States. OCA is engaged in organizing its more than 80 chapters and affiliates across the nation to develop both leadership and community involvement. OCA chapters and their affiliates are establishing strong local programs in all parts of the country. OCA's headquarters in Washington, D.C., gives the OCA National Center an effective vantage point for monitoring legislation and policy issues affecting Asian Pacific Americans. In addition, OCA is able to build national support and to work in coalition with other national groups around issues affecting Asian Pacific Americans. OCA takes no collective position on the politics of any foreign country but instead focuses on the welfare and civil rights of Asian Pacific Americans.

University of California–Irvine Asian American Studies

Website: http://libguides.lib.uci.edu/asian_american

It provides links to assortment of Asian American resources.

University of California–Santa Barbara Asian American Studies

Website: http://guides.library.ucsb.edu/asianamerican

It provides links to numerous websites, journals, archives, and other resources on Asian Americans.

Civil Rights Educational Resources

The Civil Rights Project/Proyecto Derechos Civiles, University of California–Los Angeles

Website: http://civilrightsproject.ucla.edu

The Civil Rights Project (CRP) is a leading organization devoted to civil rights research. It has found eager collaborators among researchers nationwide and wide open doors among advocacy organizations, policymakers, and journalists. Focusing initially on education reform, it has convened dozens of national conferences and roundtables; commissioned more than 300 new research and policy studies; produced major reports on desegregation, student diversity, school discipline, special education, dropouts, and Title I programs; and published seven books. CRP has initiated joint projects across disciplinary and institutional lines at universities, advocacy organizations, and think tanks throughout the country. CRP directors and staff testify and provide technical assistance on Capitol Hill and in state capitals. Its research has been incorporated into federal legislation, cited in litigation, and used to spur Congressional hearings.

Cultural Identities Resources

Center for Migration Studies

Website: http://cmsny.org

The Center for Migration Studies of New York (CMS) is a nonprofit organization that was founded in 1964. Its primary goal is to support and undertake research and to provide a forum for debate on international migration. It publishes International Migration Review, a leading peer-reviewed scholarly journal specialized in this subject. It also publishes books and monographs and undertakes original research. It organizes conferences and forums on international migration, including the Annual National Legal Conference on Immigration and Refugee Policy.

Mixed Heritage Center

Website: http://www.mixedheritagecenter.org

The Mixed Heritage Center (MHC) is a clearinghouse of information and resources relevant to the lives of people who are multiracial, multiethnic, transracially adopted, or otherwise affected by the intersections of race and culture. It is an organic resource that will grow and change with the contributions of users.

Voice of the Shuttle: Minority Studies Page

Website: http://vos.ucsb.edu/browse.asp?id=2721

This web page from the University of California–Santa Barbara has links to African American, American Indian, Asian American/ Pacific, and U.S. Latino (mostly Chicano) Internet resources plus refugee/immigrant population resources, Jewish resources, and European minorities resources.

Disability Resources

American Foundation for the Blind

Website: http://www.afb.org

The American Foundation for the Blind (AFB) is a national nonprofit that expands possibilities for people with vision loss. AFB's priorities include broadening access to technology, elevating the quality of information and tools for the professionals who serve people with vision loss, and promoting independent and healthy living for people with vision loss by providing them and their families with relevant and timely resources.

The Autism Society

Website: http://www.autism-society.org

This website offers a wealth of information for parents and service providers, including information packages on topics such as educational rights, medical insurance, residential options, employment, and much more.

Disability Resource Network, Inc.

Website: http://disability-resource.org/

Disability Resource Network, Inc., is a consumer-driven, community-based resource organization providing an array of supportive services to adults and students with disabilities. We are dedicated to giving individuals with disabilities a better understanding of living independently and helping them become positive, productive members of their community.

Gallaudet University's Technology Access Program

Website: http://tap.gallaudet.edu

Gallaudet University's Technology Access Program (TAP) is a research group focusing on technologies and services that eliminate communication barriers traditionally faced by people who are deaf and hard of hearing.

KidSource Online, Inc.

Website: http://www.kidsource.com/#sthash.wTleh8pc.dpbs

Welcome to KidSource OnLine! We are a group of parents who want to make a positive and lasting difference in the lives of parents and children. We've created an online community that shares our values and goals in raising, educating, and providing for our children. We believe that parents and caregivers want to take greater responsibility for their children's health and education, but don't always have the right information, resources, or advice to do so. Our goal is to provide that knowledge and advice to help you better raise and educate your children.

LD Online

Website: http://www.ldonline.org

This useful website on learning disabilities is geared toward parents, students, and teachers. Contents include newsletters, a discussion forum, and access to resources.

National Center for Learning Disabilities

Website: http://www.ncld.org

The National Center for Learning Disabilities (NCLD) provides essential information to parents, professionals, and individuals with learning disabilities; promotes research and programs to foster effective learning; and advocates for policies to protect and strengthen educational rights and opportunities.

National Dissemination Center for Children with Disabilities (NICHCY)

Website: http://www.nichcy.org

The National Dissemination Center for Children with Disabilities (NICHCY) is a central source of information on disabilities in infants, toddlers, children, and youth; IDEA, the law authorizing special education; No Child Left Behind, as it relates to children with disabilities; and research-based information on effective educational practices.

National Library of Medicine: Learning Disorders Website

Website: http://www.nlm.nih.gov/medlineplus/learningdisorders.html
Provided by the National Library of Medicine, this website provides extensive resources on learning disabilities.

National Youth Network

Website: http://www.nationalyouth.com
The mission of National Youth Network is to educate parents of troubled teens on child behavior, including attention-deficit disorder (ADD), attention-deficit/hyperactivity disorder (ADHD), drug abuse, teen depression, and behavior modification or intervention programs such as wilderness programs, boarding schools, residential treatment, weight loss camps, and other adolescent programs.

SchwabLearning

Website: http://www.schwablearning.org
This website is devoted to helping parents of children with learning disabilities.

Educational Policy Resources

Equity Assistance Centers Directors (2016–2021)

Website: https://www2.ed.gov/programs/equitycenters/contacts.html
The four Equity Assistance Centers are funded by the U.S. Department of Education under Title IV of the 1964 Civil Rights Act. They provide assistance in the areas of race, gender, national origin, and religion to public school districts to promote equal educational opportunities.

U.S. Department of Education

Website: http://www.ed.gov
The U.S. Department of Education is the agency of the federal government that establishes policy for, administers, and coordinates most federal assistance to education.

European American Resources

Center for the Study of White American Culture

Website: http://www.euroamerican.org
Not an organization for White supremacists, as some people might infer, this is instead a multiracial organization that looks at Whiteness and White American culture.

Gender Resources

American Association of University Women

Website: http://www.aauw.org
American Association of University Women (AAUW) promotes equity for all women and girls, lifelong education, and positive societal change. Since 1881, AAUW has been the nation's leading voice promoting education and equity for women and girls.

Discovering American Women's History Online

Website: http://digital.mtsu.edu/cdm/landingpage/collection/women

This site from Middle Tennessee State University provides access to digital collections of primary sources (photos, letters, diaries, artifacts, etc.) that document the history of women in the United States. These diverse collections range from Ancestral Pueblo pottery to interviews with women engineers from the 1970s.

Feminist Majority Foundation

Website: http://www.feminist.org

The Feminist Majority Foundation works for social, political, and economic equality for women by using research and education to improve women's lives. The Feminist Majority Foundation Online features daily feminist news with "take action" ideas, domestic violence and sexual assault hotlines, a feminist career center, information on feminism (including women and girls in sports), and more feminist research resources.

National Organization for Women

Website: http://www.now.org

The National Organization for Women (NOW) is the largest organization of feminist activists in the United States. NOW has 500,000 contributing members and 550 chapters in all 50 states and the District of Columbia.

National Women's History Museum

Website: http://www.nmwh.org

Founded in 1996, the National Women's History Museum is dedicated to revealing, presenting, and celebrating the rich and diverse history of women's contributions that have shaped American culture and society. The Museum will be established in Washington, D.C., where the world's most prominent museums and monuments are located. The National Women's History Museum affirms the importance of an accurate and complete understanding of the past. The Museum will fill in the missing part of history—women's history.

The National Women's History Project

Website: http://www.nwhm.org

The National Women's History Project is an educational nonprofit organization whose mission is to recognize and celebrate the diverse and historic accomplishments of women by providing information and educational materials and programs.

National Women's Law Center

Website: http://www.nwlc.org

The National Women's Law Center has worked since its inception in 1972 to protect and advance the progress of women and girls at work, in school, and in virtually every other aspect of their lives.

Jewish American Resources

Aish HaTorah

Website: http://www.aish.com

This website provides information on contemporary issues affecting the Jewish community. Aish HaTorah has become one of the world's largest organizations dedicated to answering the vital question "Why be Jewish?"

The American Jewish Historical Society

Website: http://www.ajhs.org
The American Jewish Historical Society provides access to more than 25 million documents and 50,000 books, photographs, works of art, and artifacts that reflect the history of the Jewish presence in the United States from 1654 to the present. The organization's website provides exhibits, online archives, publications, and links.

Jewish History Resource Center

Website: http://jewishhistory.huji.ac.il
The Jewish History Resource Center provides a collection of links pertaining to the Holocaust as well as other aspects of Jewish history.

United States Holocaust Memorial Museum

Website: http://www.ushmm.org
The United States Holocaust Memorial Museum is America's national institution for the documentation, study, and interpretation of Holocaust history, and it serves as this country's memorial to the millions of people murdered during the Holocaust.

Latino/Hispanic American Resources

Mexican American Legal Defense and Educational Fund

Website: http://www.maldef.org
The Mexican American Legal Defense and Educational Fund (MALDEF) is an advocacy organization that seeks to protect the rights of Hispanics and to support the education of a limited number of Hispanic law students. MALDEF has been responsible for the majority of civil rights class-action litigation affecting Hispanics.

National Latino Children's Institute

Website: http://www.nlci.org
The National Latino Children's Institute's (NLCI) mission is to focus the nation's attention on Latino children and empower communities for the full and healthy development of young Latinos in a culturally relevant environment. Started in 1994, the institute continues to promote and implement the National Latino Children's Agenda, a comprehensive statement of principles created by 48 national organizations and endorsed by hundreds of individuals and organizations since then. NLCI is the only Latino organization with young Latinos as its primary emphasis.

Smithsonian Latino Center

Website: http://latino.si.edu
Created in 1997, the Smithsonian Latino Center works paninstitutionally with the entire network of Smithsonian museums, research centers, programs, and almost 200 affiliates nationwide to ensure that Latino culture, achievement, and contributions are celebrated and recognized.
The Smithsonian Latino Center ensures that Latino contributions to the arts, sciences, and humanities are highlighted, understood, and advanced through the development and support of public programs, research, museum collections, and educational opportunities at the Smithsonian Institution.

Multicultural Education Theory and Practice Resources

These sites offer excellent summaries and explanations of multicultural education theory.

Diversity Within Unity: Essential Principles for Teaching and Learning in a Multicultural Society

Website: http://www.cwu.edu/teaching-learning/sites/cts.cwu.edu.teaching-learning/files/documents/diversityunity.pdf

A consensus panel of interdisciplinary scholars worked over a 4-year period to determine what we know from research and experience about education and diversity. The panel was cosponsored by the Center for Multicultural Education at the University of Washington and the Common Destiny Alliance at the University of Maryland. The panel was supported by a grant from the Carnegie Corporation of New York and chaired by James A. Banks. The 12 major findings of the panel, which are called essential principles, constitute this publication. They are presented in this Executive Summary. This publication also contains a checklist designed to be used by educational practitioners to determine the extent to which their institutions and environments are consistent with the essential principles.

On Educating for Diversity: A Conversation With James A. Banks

Website: http://www.ascd.org/publications/educational-leadership/may94/vol51/num08/On-Educating-for-Diversity@-A-Conversation-with-James-A.-Banks.aspx

Through a conversation with James A. Banks, sponsored by the Nation Education Association, readers learn how to "transform the mainstream" so that all students function better in their home communities as well as in the larger world.

15 Misconceptions About Multicultural Education

Website: http://billhowe.org/MCE/?p=146

This is an article by Jerry Aldridge and Charles Calhoun, originally published in 2000 in *Focus on Elementary*, *12*(3).

The movement toward multicultural education has gained momentum over the past 20 years. Guidelines from professional organizations have been in place for some time. While many elementary educators support multicultural development and genuinely try to incorporate diverse cultural issues into the curriculum, some widespread misconceptions about what multicultural education is and how it should be implemented hinder the process.

A Synthesis of Scholarship in Multicultural Education

Website: http://www.ncrel.org/sdrs/areas/issues/educatrs/leadrshp/le0gay.htm

This monograph is a brilliant and concise explanation of multicultural education. Written by Geneva Gay, PhD, professor of education and faculty associate of the Center for Multicultural Education at the University of Washington–Seattle, it was originally published in 1994 by NCREL's Urban Education Program as part of its Urban Education Monograph Series.

Multicultural Teaching and Learning Resources

Awesome Library

Website: http://www.awesomelibrary.org

This website organizes the Web by presenting links to 30,000 carefully reviewed resources, including the top 5% in education.

Educational Resources and Lesson Plans

Website: http://www.cloudnet.com/~edrbsass/edres.htm
   This website includes thousands of links to lesson plans and other potentially useful information for current and future teachers. It also includes lesson plans and other resources unique to this site.

Educator's Desk Reference

Website: http://www.eduref.org
   This website builds on over a quarter century of experience providing high-quality resources and services to the education community. From the Information Institute of Syracuse, the people who created AskERIC, the Gateway to Educational Materials, and the Virtual Reference Desk, the Educator's Reference Desk brings you more than 2,000 lesson plans, more than 3,000 links to online education information, and more than 200 question archive responses.

Effective Lesson Planning for English Language Learners

Website: http://www.moramodules.com
   Created by Jill Kerper Mora, EdD, at San Diego State University, this site contains basic instructional strategies as well as lesson plans.

Houghton Mifflin Harcourt Education Place

Website: http://www.eduplace.com/activity/
   This website is produced by Houghton Mifflin School Division, which publishes a variety of educational materials, including textbooks and resource materials for preK teachers and students. Launched in January 1996, Education Place is the longest-running website of any educational publisher. With more than 50,000 pages of engaging content to explore, visitors to the award-winning Education Place can delve further into the subjects they most enjoy to find helpful teaching resources, textbook support, educational games, and more.

Lesson Plans for Teachers

Website: http://www.lessonplans4teachers.com
   This website offers a complete guide to online lesson plans for K–12 teachers.

Multicultural Pavilion

Website: http://www.edchange.org/multicultural
   This website includes multicultural education resources for educators, students, and activists.

New Horizons for Learning

Website: http://education.jhu.edu/PD/newhorizons
   Under the direction of the editorial team at Johns Hopkins University School of Education, this nonprofit, international network of educators focuses on identifying, communicating, and implementing the most effective teaching and learning strategies for all ages and abilities. There is information here on neuroscience, creativity, counseling, technology, data-driven decision making, museum education, arts integration, special education, early education, cultural literacy, action research, Universal Design, international exchange programs, higher education, and teacher preparation.

Teaching for Change

Website: http://www.teachingforchange.org

This website provides professional development workshops, publications, a parent-empowerment program, and a catalog of innovative K–12 resources.

Bilingual Books for Kids

Website: http://www.bilingualbooks.com

Written with Spanish and English appearing side by side, these books introduce bilingual skills, increase language and learning abilities, and positively heighten awareness of many cultures. We have carefully selected these books, musical- and language-learning tapes, and games for their educational value, engaging prose, and delightful illustrations and for depicting multicultural images in an affirmative manner.

Diversities (formerly International Journal on Multicultural Societies)

Website: http://www.unesco.org/new/en/social-and-human-sciences/resources/periodicals/diversities

Diversities is a scholarly and professional journal published by UNESCO. It provides a platform for international, interdisciplinary, and policy-related social discipline research in the fields of migration, multiculturalism, and minority rights. Established by UNESCO's social sciences research and policy division in 1998, *Diversities* aims at improving the linkages between academic communities in various regions and across different social science disciplines. One of *Diversities*'s particular goals is to promote the policy relevance of social science research. Each issue is devoted to a coherent thematic debate on a key issue in the field of migration and multiculturalism.

International Journal of Multicultural Education

Website: http://ijme-journal.org/index.php/ijme/index

International Journal of Multicultural Education is a peer-reviewed open-access journal for scholars, practitioners, and students of multicultural education. Committed to promoting educational equity for diverse students, cross-cultural understanding, and global justice for marginalized people in all levels of education.

Lee & Low Books

Website: http://www.leeandlow.com

Lee & Low Books is an independent children's book publisher specializing in multicultural themes. The company's goal is to meet the need for stories that children of color can identify with and that all children can enjoy. Lee & Low makes a special effort to work with artists of color and takes pride in nurturing many authors and illustrators who are new to the world of children's book publishing.

Multicultural Education Magazine

Website: http://caddogap.com/periodicals.shtml

Of interest to classroom teachers and other educators, Multicultural Education magazine offers practical suggestions and information on current resources in multicultural education and important articles about current research and issues in the field.

Multicultural Perspectives

Website: https://www.nameorg.org/mcp_journal.php

This publication promotes the philosophy of social justice, equity, and inclusion. It celebrates cultural and ethnic diversity as a national strength that enriches the fabric of society. The journal encourages a range of material from academic to personal perspectives, poetry and art, articles of an academic nature illuminating the discussion of cultural pluralism and inclusion, articles and position papers reflecting a variety of disciplines, and reviews of film, art, and music that address or embody multicultural forms. *Multicultural Perspectives* is published four times a year by the National Association for Multicultural Education.

New America Media

Website: http://newamericamedia.org

New America Media (NAM) is the country's first and largest national collaboration of ethnic news organizations. Founded by the nonprofit Pacific News Service in 1996, NAM is headquartered in California, where ethnic media are the primary source of news and information for over half of the state's new ethnic majority. NAM's goal is to promote the editorial visibility and economic viability of this critical sector of American journalism as a way to build inclusive public discourse in our increasingly diverse, global society. NAM produces and aggregates editorial content from and for the ethnic media sector and develops pioneering marketing services on behalf of corporations, foundations, and nonprofits that are targeting ethnic media and ethnic communities.

Rethinking Schools

Website: http://www.rethinkingschools.org

Rethinking Schools began as a local effort to address problems such as basal readers, standardized testing, and textbook-dominated curriculum. Since its founding in 1986, Rethinking Schools has grown into a nationally prominent publisher of educational materials, with subscribers in all 50 states, all 10 Canadian provinces, and many other countries.

Teaching Tolerance

Website: http://www.tolerance.org

Teaching Tolerance's educational kits and subscriptions to its magazine are free to classroom teachers, school librarians, school counselors, school administrators, professors of education, leaders of home school networks, youth directors at houses of worship, and employees of youth-serving nonprofit organizations.

Culture, Difference, and Power (Interactive Video CD)

Website: http://store.tcpress.com/0807745243.shtml

Featuring Dr. Christine Sleeter, this CD-ROM text on multicultural education is designed for use in teacher preparation programs.

Native American Resources

American Indians in Children's Literature

Website: http://americanindiansinchildrensliterature.blogspot.com

Established in 2006, American Indians in Children's Literature (AICL) provides critical perspectives and analysis of indigenous peoples in children's and young adult books, the school curriculum, popular culture, and society. Scroll down for links to book reviews, Native media, and more.

American Indian Higher Education Consortium

Website: http://www.aihec.org

American Indian Higher Education Consortium (AIHEC) represents 34 colleges in the United States and one Canadian institution. Its mission is to support the work of these colleges and the national movement for tribal self-determination. AIHEC has four objectives: Maintain commonly held standards of quality in American Indian education, support the development of new tribally controlled colleges, promote and assist the development of legislation to support American Indian higher education, and encourage greater participation by American Indians in the development of higher education policy.

American Indian Library Association

Website: https://www.ailanet.org

The American Indian Library Association (AILA) is a membership action group that addresses the library-related needs of American Indians and Alaska Natives. AILA is committed to disseminating information about American Indian cultures, languages, values, and information needs to the library community.

American Indian Movement

Website: http://www.aimovement.org

AIM is pledged to fight Whites' injustice to Indians—their oppression, persecution, discrimination, and malfeasance in the handling of Indian affairs. No area in North America is too remote when trouble impends for Indians. AIM shall be there to help the Native People regain human rights and achieve restitution and restoration.

National Museum of the American Indian

Website: https://nmai.si.edu/explore/collections/archive/

The National Museum of the American Indian (NMAI) Archive Center actively acquires and serves as a repository for the records of contemporary Native American artists, writers, activists, and organizations. In addition, the Archive Center holds the records of the NMAI's predecessor institution, the Museum of the American Indian (MAI), Heye Foundation.

Association for the Study of American Indian Literatures

Website: http://people.uwm.edu/asail/

The purpose of Association for the Study of American Indian Literatures (ASAIL) is to promote study, criticism, and research on the oral traditions and written literatures of Native Americans, to promote the teaching of such traditions and literatures, and to support and encourage contemporary Native American writers and the continuity of Native oral traditions.

Bureau of Indian Affairs

Website: http://www.bia.gov

The Bureau of Indian Affairs's (BIA) responsibility is the administration and management of 55.7 million acres of land held in trust by the United States for American Indians, Indian tribes, and Alaska Natives. There are 562 federally recognized tribal governments in the United States. Developing forestlands, leasing assets on these lands, directing agricultural programs, protecting water and land rights, developing and maintaining infrastructure, and promoting economic development are all agency responsibilities. In addition, the BIA provides education services to approximately 48,000 Indian students.

The Cradleboard Teaching Project

Website: http://www.cradleboard.org

Backed by lesson plans and an excellent curriculum, the Cradleboard Teaching Project is also live and interactive. Children learn with and through their long-distance peers, using new technology alongside standard tools with the help of several American Indian colleges. Cradleboard reaches both Indian and non-Indian children with positive realities.

Indian Country Today

Website: https://newsmaven.io/indiancountrytoday/

Indian Country Today is a daily digital news platform that covers the Indigenous world, including American Indians and Alaska Natives. Indian Country Today is the largest news site that covers tribes and Native people throughout the Americas. Our primary focus is delivering news to a national audience via a mobile phone or the Web.

Labriola National American Indian Data Center

Website: http://lib.asu.edu/labriola

The Labriola National American Indian Data Center is a research collection, international in scope, that brings together in one location current and historic information on government, culture, religion and worldview, social life and customs, and tribal history of individuals from the United States; Canada; and Sonora and Chihuahua, Mexico. It disseminates this information through the use of the Internet, computer databases, and CD-ROM.

National Congress of American Indians

Website: http://www.ncai.org

The National Congress of American Indians (NCAI) serves to protect the rights of Indian nations and Native governments; to enhance the quality of life of Indian and Native people; and to promote a better understanding among the general public about Indian and Native governments, people, and rights.

Native Village

Website: http://www.nativevillage.org

Native Village was created as an educational and current events resource for Native youth, teens, families, educators, and friends. Weekly publications—Native Village Youth and Education News and Native Village Opportunities and Websites—are published on Wednesdays. Every issue shares Indian news and education across the Americas and is written in a condensed, easy-to-read format. Native Village libraries house links to quality learning opportunities and websites. The archives allow browsing of past issues, and we continually update information in other areas to stay current with the Americas' First Nations and Peoples.

NativeWeb

Website: http://nativeweb.org

NativeWeb is an international, nonprofit, educational organization dedicated to using telecommunications, including computer technology and the Internet; to disseminate information from and about indigenous nations, peoples, and organizations around the world; to foster communication between Native and non-Native peoples; to conduct research involving indigenous peoples' usage of technology and the Internet; and to provide resources, mentoring, and services to facilitate indigenous peoples' use of this technology.

Mashantucket Pequot Museum and Research Center

Website: http://www.pequotmuseum.org

The world's largest and most comprehensive Native American museum and research center offers an array of engaging experiences for young and old, from life-sized walk-through dioramas that transport visitors into the past to changing exhibits and live performances of contemporary arts and cultures. Four full acres of permanent exhibits depict 18,000 years of Native and natural history in thoroughly researched detail, while two libraries, including one for children, offer a diverse selection of materials on the histories and cultures of all Native peoples of the United States and Canada.

American Indian Culture and Research Journal

Website: http://www.books.aisc.ucla.edu/

The foremost refereed research journal of American Indian studies is released quarterly by the University of California–Los Angeles American Indian Studies Center Publications Unit. Each issue is packed with timely, well-researched articles; haunting, lyrical literature; and the latest reviews of the academic literature available—in short, a vista on the world of American Indian studies.

Tribal College Journal of American Indian Higher Education

Website: http://www.tribalcollegejournal.org

On behalf of the American Indian Higher Education Consortium's member tribal colleges and universities, this culture-based publication addresses subjects important to the future of American Indian and Alaska Native communities. *Tribal College Journal* features both journalistic and scholarly articles.

American Indian Quarterly

Website: http://www.nebraskapress.unl.edu/product/American-Indian-Quarterly,673174.aspx

The complexity and excitement of the burgeoning field of Native American studies are captured in *American Indian Quarterly (AIQ)*, a peer-reviewed, interdisciplinary journal of the histories, anthropologies, literatures, religions, and arts of Native America. Wide-ranging in its coverage of issues and topics, *AIQ* is devoted to charting and inciting debate about the latest developments in method and theory. It publishes original articles, shorter contributions, review articles, and book reviews.

Sexual Orientation and Gender Identity Resources

Gender Spectrum

Website: https://www.genderspectrum.org

Gender Spectrum provides an array of services to help youth, families, organizations, and institutions understand and address concepts of gender identity and gender expression, including how societal, cultural, organizational, and community definitions of gender can be detrimental to any young person that does not fit neatly into these categories.

The Gay & Lesbian Alliance Against Defamation

Website: http://www.glaad.org

The Gay & Lesbian Alliance Against Defamation (GLAAD) is dedicated to promoting and ensuring fair, accurate, and inclusive representation of people and events in the media as a means of eliminating homophobia and discrimination based on gender identity and sexual orientation.

The Gay, Lesbian & Straight Education Network

Website: http://www.glsen.org

The Gay, Lesbian & Straight Education Network (GLSEN) is working to ensure safe and effective schools for all students.

Lesbian/Gay/Bisexual/Transgender Issues

Website: http://litmed.med.nyu.edu/Keyword?action=listann&id=100

Created by New York University's School of Medicine, this site contains an annotated bibliography of films, books, and artwork pertaining to lesbian, gay, bisexual, and transgender (LGBT) issues.

Parents, Families and Friends of Lesbians and Gays

Website: http://www.pflag.org

Parents, Families and Friends of Lesbians and Gays (PFLAG) promotes the health and well-being of gay, lesbian, bisexual, and transgendered persons and their families and friends by providing support to cope with a biased society, education to enlighten an ill-informed public, and advocacy to end discrimination and to secure equal civil rights. PFLAG provides opportunities for dialogue about sexual orientation and gender identity and acts to create a society that is healthy and respectful of human diversity.

Queer Resources Directory

Website: http://www.qrd.org/qrd

The Queer Resources Directory (QRD) is an electronic research library specifically dedicated to sexual minorities—groups that have traditionally been labeled as "queer" and systematically discriminated against.

It's Elementary

GroundSpark
Website: http://groundspark.org/our-films-and-campaigns/elementary

This documentary for educators shows how acknowledging gay and lesbian people in schools prevents prejudice and violence. *It's Elementary* is the first film of its kind to address antigay prejudice by providing adults with practical lessons on how to talk with kids about gay people. Hailed as "a model of intelligent directing," *It's Elementary* shows that children are eager and able to wrestle with stereotypes and absorb new facts about what it means to be gay or lesbian.

That's a Family!

GroundSpark
Website: http://groundspark.org/our-films-and-campaigns/thatfamily

Helping kids understand about all kinds of family structures, *That's a Family!* is an entertaining documentary that breaks new ground in helping children in Grades K–8 understand the different shapes families take today. With courage and humor, the children in *That's a Family!* take viewers on a tour through their lives as they speak candidly about what it's like to grow up in a family with parents of different races or religions, divorced parents, a single parent, gay or lesbian parents, adoptive parents, or grandparents as guardians. This award-winning film will stretch your mind and touch your heart no matter what your age.

Social Justice Educational Resources

Justice Matters

Website: http://www.justicematters.org

Justice Matters is dedicated to ensuring that education policy is rooted in community vision. As a racial justice movement–building organization, we are actively engaged in powerfully amplifying the voices, visions, and values of communities of color. This site gives us yet another platform to do our work.

Teaching Tolerance

Website: http://www.splcenter.org/what-we-do/teaching-tolerance

The Teaching Tolerance program is working to foster school environments that are inclusive and nurturing—classrooms where equality and justice are not just taught, but lived. The program points to the future, helping teachers prepare a new generation to live in a diverse world.

As one of the nation's leading providers of antibias education resources, the Teaching Tolerance program reaches hundreds of thousands of educators and millions of students annually through the award-winning Teaching Tolerance magazine, multimedia teaching kits, online curricula, professional development resources such as Teaching Diverse Students Initiative, and special projects such as Mix It Up at Lunch Day. These materials are provided to educators at no cost.

Tolerance.org

Website: http://tolerance.org

Tolerance.org is a principal online destination for people interested in dismantling bigotry and creating, instead, communities that value diversity.

A Class Divided

PBS/WGBH

Website: http://www.pbs.org/wgbh/pages/frontline/shows/divided/etc/view.html

The story in The Eye of the Storm is also told by Frontline in its award-winning 1985 program A Class Divided. The 46-minute runtime is divided into five video chapters and includes follow-up with the now-adult students. It comes with a teacher's guide.

The Color of Fear

Stirfry Seminars & Consulting

Website: http://www.stirfryseminars.com

This is an insightful, groundbreaking film about the state of race relations in America as seen through the eyes of eight North American men of Asian, European, Latino, and African descent. In a series of intelligent, emotional, and dramatic confrontations, the men reveal the pain and scars that racism has caused them. What emerges is a deeper sense of understanding and trust. This is the dialogue most of us fear but hope will happen sometime in our lifetime. (Running time: 90 minutes)

The Eye of the Storm

ABC News

Website: http://janeelliott.com

This best-selling program, produced by ABC News, was the first video to document Jane Elliott's courageous undertaking to help her third-grade class understand the meaning of prejudice. Following the assassination of Martin Luther King Jr., her all-White, all-Christian third-grade class hungered to understand the significance of Dr. King's mission. Living in the homogeneous farming community of Riceville, Iowa, many of Ms. Elliott's students harbored subtle and not-so-subtle prejudices, despite the fact that many of them had never even seen a Black person before. So where did these prejudices come from? And, more important, how could she make them understand how arbitrary and unfair those prejudices were? This Emmy Award–winning video chronicles her now-famous exercise in which she divided her class based on the color of their eyes and bestowed on one group privileges and on the other group impediments. Dividing them by eye color and discriminating against first the blue eyes and then the brown eyes, she proved how quickly they could be made to live down to expectations. This video remains a classic in its field and is the most requested Jane Elliott title.

Let's Get Real

GroundSpark

Website: http://groundspark.org/our-films-and-campaigns/lets-get-real

In this powerful documentary, kids speak up about bullying. Name-calling and bullying are at epidemic proportions among youth across the country and are often the root causes of violence in schools. *Let's Get Real* gives young people the chance to tell their stories in their own words—and the results are heartbreaking, shocking, inspiring, and poignant. Unlike the vast majority of videos made for schools about this issue, *Let's Get Real* doesn't sugarcoat the truth or feature adults lecturing kids about what to do when "bad" kids pick on them.

Not in Our Town

Website: https://www.niot.org/history

Not in Our Town and Not in Our School are both projects of The Working Group, an Oakland-based nonprofit founded in 1988. Not in Our Town was launched in 1995 with our landmark PBS film that documented the heroic efforts of Billings, Montana citizens who stood up for their neighbors after a series of hate crimes. They inspired hundreds of communities in the United States and around the world to take action against hate.

Skin Deep

Iris Films
Website: http://www.irisfilms.org/films/skin-deep

This film tells a tale of the complexities of race relations in America today, as experienced by a diverse but strikingly candid group of college students. Academy Award–nominated producer Frances Reid chronicles these young adults' attitudes and feelings about race through interviews, scenes from campus and family life, and a weekend retreat of interracial dialogue. This 53-minute film was produced in response to the growing wave of racial hatred and violence in this country. It was made out of the belief that talking about racial issues, both in interracial dialogue and in homogeneous groups, is a necessary first step toward taking action to undoing the racial inequalities that permeate our institutions and communities and affect us all deeply as individuals. *Skin Deep* takes the viewer on a journey of dialogue with a group of contemporary college students.

True Colors

ABC News
Website: http://www.understandingprejudice.org/teach/activity/rdiscrim.htm

In this startling expose, ABC News Prime Time Live anchor Diane Sawyer explores skin color prejudice in America with the help of two friends who are virtually identical in all respects but one—John is White, and Glen is Black. Together, they take part in a series of hidden-camera experiments exploring people's reactions to each in a variety of situations. Acting within the scenario of moving to a new town, Prime Time Live follows John and Glen separately as they each try to rent an apartment, respond to job listings, purchase a car, and conduct everyday activities such as shopping. The responses in the White and racially mixed communities are shocking and consistent. In every instance, John is welcomed into the community while Glen is discouraged by high prices, long waits, and unfriendly salespeople. Diane Sawyer concludes *True Colors* with a discussion with John and Glen about the outcome of these experiments and their experiences with discrimination in daily life.

Videos: Free Online Videos

Acting White Part 1

Website: http://abavtooldev.pearsoncmg.com/myeducationlab/singleplay.php?projectID=foundations2008ABC&clipID=Actng_White.flv (Length: 8:09)

Acting White Part 2

Website: http://abavtooldev.pearsoncmg.com/myeducationlab/singleplay.php?projectID=foundations2008ABC&clipID=Acting_White_2.flv (Length: 5:52)

In this ABC News video, the interviewer talks about Black students at East High School in Madison, Wisconsin, and rapper John Forte about the concept of "acting White." As discussed in this video, *acting White* is a derogatory term used by Black students against other Black students they perceive as being racially disloyal—those they perceive as having "sold out" by adopting the social expectations of the White society. Using standard English, studying hard, and answering questions in class are behaviors that can be construed as acting White. Being accused of acting White can be so hurtful that many Black students will consciously underperform and hold back to avoid the charge. Sociologists and psychologists in the video suggest that this deliberate underachieving may be a contributing factor in the achievement gap between White and Black students on assessments such as the NAEP (National Assessment of Educational Progress).

A Girl Like Me Featurette

Website: https://www.youtube.com/watch?v=PAOZhuRb_Q8 (Length: 13:02)

Caroline Casey: Looking Past Limits

Website: http://www.ted.com/talks/caroline_casey_looking_past_limits (Length: 19:17)
   Activist Caroline Casey tells the story of her extraordinary life, starting with a revelation (no spoilers). In a talk that challenges perceptions, Casey asks us all to move beyond the limits we may think we have.

Columbus: The Hidden History

Website: http://vimeo.com/24976074 (Length: 10:00)
   This was a documentary submitted to the National History Day competition. It explores several individuals' inaccurate educations about Christopher Columbus and the truth about his arrival in the Americas. National History Day allows participants to sample photos, music, and videos so long as credit is given to the original creators.

The Danger of a Single Story: Chimamanda Ngozi Adichie

Website: http://www.ted.com/talks/chimamanda_adichie_the_danger_of_a_single_story?language=en (Length: 18:49)
   Our lives, our cultures, are composed of many overlapping stories. Novelist Chimamanda Adichie tells the story of how she found her authentic cultural voice and warns that if we hear only a single story about another person or country, we risk a critical misunderstanding. Inspired by Nigerian history and tragedies all but forgotten by recent generations of Westerners, Chimamanda Ngozi Adichie's novels and stories are jewels in the crown of diasporan literature.

Hari Kondabolu Where Are You From?

Website: https://www.youtube.com/watch?v=PAZTWRqaAwA (Length: 2:13)
   Hari Kondabolu hates being asked "Where are you from? "because "New York City" is apparently not a sufficient answer. This is the original version of this joke. It was filmed at the Comedy Underground in Seattle on June 12, 2007.

I Am a Muslim Woman

Website: https://www.youtube.com/watchivTh9VF6jRsHtg (Length: 2:44)
   Talking about some misconceptions!

Family Matters Racist Scene

Website: https://youtu.be/n7jPuQfkE9w (Length: 00:53)
   Racist scene from the 1990s show Family Matters. It is useful for discussion on actions students and teachers should take.

TEDxSIT: Lee Mun Wah "But . . . I am an American"

Website: https://www.youtube.com/watch?v=7DWl5KXvCGA

Lee Mun Wah is an internationally renowned Chinese American documentary filmmaker, author, poet, Asian folkteller, educator, community therapist, and master diversity trainer. For more than 25 years, he was a resource specialist and counselor in the San Francisco Unified School District. He later became a consultant to private schools, working with students who had severe learning and behavioral issues. Lee Mun Wah is now the Executive Director of Stirfry Seminars & Consulting, a diversity training company that provides educational tools and workshops on issues pertaining to cross-cultural communication and awareness, mindful facilitation, and conflict mediation.

Listening to Latinas: Lucy Flores

Website: https://www.youtube.com/watch?v=s171IgapxMc (Length: 3:18)

To help keep girls in school and on track for success, the National Womens Law Center and the Mexican American Legal Defense and Education Fund went straight to the source: Latina students and the adults who work with them every day. *Listening to Latinas: Barriers to High School Graduation* explores the causes of the dropout crisis for Latinas and identifies the actions needed to improve their graduation rates and get them ready for college.

Welcoming Schools Film: *What Do You Know?*

Website: http://www.welcomingschools.org/what-do-you-know-the-film (Length: 13:00)

What Do You Know? Six to Twelve Year-Olds Talk About Gays and Lesbians is an award-winning, 13-minute film produced by the Human Rights Campaign Foundation's Welcoming Schools Project. The film features students from Alabama and Massachusetts discussing what they hear about LGBTQ topics at school and how they'd like teachers to address hurtful name-calling and harassment.

Title IX

Title IX is a federal law that was passed in 1972 to ensure that male and female students and employees in educational settings are treated equally and fairly. It protects against discrimination based on gender. The preamble states,

> No person in the United States shall, on the basis of sex, be excluded from participation in, or denied the benefits of, or be subjected to discrimination under any educational program or activity receiving federal assistance.

Title IX of the Education Amendments of 1972 to the Civil Rights Act of 1964.

Association of Title IX Administrators

Website: https://atixa.org

Association of Title IX Administrators (ATIXA) provides a professional association for school and college Title IX coordinators and administrators who are interested in serving their districts and campuses more effectively. Since 1972, Title IX has proved to be an increasingly powerful leveling tool, helping to advance gender equity in schools and colleges. Title IX's benefits can be found in promoting equity in academic and athletics programs, preventing hostile environments on the basis of sex, prohibiting sexual harassment and sexual violence, protecting from retaliation and remedying the effects of other gender-based forms of discrimination. Every school district and college in the United States is required to have a Title IX coordinator, who oversees implementation, training, and compliance with Title IX. ATIXA brings campus and district Title IX coordinators and administrators into professional collaboration to explore best practices, share resources, and advance the worthy goal of gender equity in education.

Bill Howe on Title IX

Unofficial Information on Title IX
Website: http://billhowe.org/TitleIX/
    This is an unofficial website devoted to Title IX for Connecticut schools. The target audience is Title IX Coordinators. It is not endorsed by any government agency. Information contained here should not be construed as legal advice.

Stop Sexual Assault in Schools

Website: http://stopsexualassaultinschools.org/
    Stop Sexual Assault in Schools (SSAIS) tells parents,

> what Title IX requires and how to file federal civil rights complaints if they see violations. They say they want to save other families the heartache and upheaval that they endured as they tried to help their daughter recover—and go back to school—after her rape. . . . [They] believe that addressing the problem will take a massive movement of students and families who know what their Title IX rights are and demand that schools meet them.

—The Washington Post

Title IX and Sex Discrimination

Website: http://www2.ed.gov/about/offices/list/ocr/docs/tix_dis.html
    The U.S. Department of Education's Office for Civil Rights (OCR) enforces, among other statutes, Title IX of the Education Amendments of 1972. Title IX protects people from discrimination based on sex in education programs or activities that receive federal financial assistance.

Title IX Blog

Website: http://title-ix.blogspot.com
    It is an informative blog on Title IX legal news and is founded by Erin Buzuvis, professor of law, Western New England University and Kristine Newhall, PhD, Women's Studies.

Title IX Info

Website: http://www.titleix.info
    This website explains the regulations in easy-to-understand language and uses real case studies as examples. In addition, it provides ways to find out about Title IX in your local community, links to many governmental and educational organizations for more detailed information, and an easy-to-use email system, whereby you can contact the secretary of education in Washington, D.C., about Title IX.

Know Your IX

Website: http://knowyourix.org/title-ix
    Founded in 2013, Know Your IX is a national survivor-run, student-driven campaign to end campus sexual violence. Running on grassroots energy, we educate students across the country about their civil right to education free from sexual violence and harassment while also pushing policy and legislative change on the national level for better federal enforcement of that same right. Know Your IX fills the gap between the law on the books and survivors on the ground: We work to educate our fellow students about their rights and empower them to take action for safety and equality on campus; and bring students' voices, experiences, and concerns to policymakers writing the next chapter in Title IX's history.

Glossary

Acculturation: The results of different cultures interacting over time, thereby absorbing one another's cultural identities.

Achievement gap: In many instances across the country, there are major discrepancies between the performances of Caucasian students and students of color, and between boys and girls. These discrepancies are referred to as the achievement gap.

Action research: The process by which individuals or teams of educators systematically collect data to answer a question that is related to their instructional practice. An example is the investigation of the impact of the use of multiple intelligences as an instructional strategy on the academic performance of diverse students.

Affirmative action: Proactive steps in employment to ensure equal representation based on sex and race.

Alternative assessment: Measurements that require students to demonstrate what they know and are able to do in ways other than traditional paper-and-pencil tests.

Anti-Semite: One who has an intense dislike of people of the Jewish faith.

Assimilation: The process of members of a cultural group adapting to and becoming part of another cultural group. *See* persistence of ethnicity.

Authentic assessment: Assessment activities that resemble real life and are connected to instruction.

Authentic learning: Real-world education, as opposed to contrived examples.

Behaviorism: A learning theory that focuses on objectively observable aspects of learning—changes in behaviors, skills, and habits—usually in response to a stimulus.

Behaviorist: One who focuses on changing behavior by manipulating stimulus and response.

Bias: Having a prejudice or preference for a point of view or a people.

Bigotry: The practice of prejudice and intolerance; a *bigot* is someone who is ignorant or intolerant of other people, their lives, and their viewpoints.

Bilingual education: A classroom model in which students are taught in their native language as well as in English. They transition eventually, usually after about 3 years, to an English as a second-language class with limited, if any, instruction in their native language; generally, the teacher speaks both the native language and English and teaches using both.

Brown v. Board of Education: This landmark civil rights case decided by the U.S. Supreme Court in 1954 determined that racially segregated schools are unconstitutional.

Bullying: The repeated use of force, threats, or coercion to abuse, intimidate, or aggressively control others.

Chauvinist: Someone who believes in his or her own superiority.

Chicano: A term created and used as a political statement for Americans of Mexican descent.

Civil rights: Those rights generally held as pertaining to all people, especially those guaranteed by the U.S. Constitution, including the Due Process and Equal Protection clauses.

Civil Rights Act of 1964: Landmark federal legislation that banned racial segregation.

Classism: The bestowal of privileges and benefits based on economic wealth; the belief that wealthier economic groups are superior to those with less wealth.

Classroom demographic profile: A tool for identifying the diversity that exists in any classroom setting. Once a profile is established, the information can be used to inform instruction for individual students.

Cognition: The process of being aware, thinking, or knowing.

Cognitivism: Learning theory interested in how the brain works, particularly in problem solving and critical thinking. Changes in behavior are interesting only in relationship to how a person thinks, remembers, and knows.

Collaboration: Collaboration is a means for overcoming the isolation that so often pervades many schools. Collaboration provides teachers with a sense of connectedness and community. Collaboration calls for the development of strong relationships that transcend the traditional boundaries of departments and grade levels.

Common Core State Standards: State education chiefs and governors in 48 states came together to develop the Common Core, a set of clear college- and career-ready standards for kindergarten through 12th grade in English language arts/literacy and mathematics.

Constructivism: Learning theory that posits that a learner actively constructs or builds new ideas or concepts, making meaning of events and activities.

Constructivist theory of education: A model of education in which students see personal meaning in the teaching strategies and content and make connections between past and new learning. When students recognize language, examples, and illustrations from their own cultures, they are more motivated to learn.

Cultural competence: The ability to think, act, and feel in ways that are respectful of diversity.

Cultural identity: This term refers to the shared characteristics, including behaviors, beliefs, values, traditions, customs, habits, rituals, experiences, taboos, and histories among a group of people. This is the "lens" we use to view and interpret behaviors, actions, words, and ideas about ourselves and about other people.

Culturally responsive: Being sensitive to or respectful of shared beliefs, values, and customs of a group or society.

Culture: Shared beliefs, values, and customs of a group or society.

Curriculum standards: These are expectations of what students should know and be able to do.

Data-based decision making: The process of collecting data, summarizing it, and using it to make decisions about which instructional strategies, curriculum, and assessment approaches will be most appropriate to improve student achievement.

Deficit model of education: Focuses on what students cannot do versus what they can do.

Developmental disabilities: A more appropriate and modern term to describe the condition of individuals who lag behind most others in mental and physical abilities.

Differentiated instruction: A pedagogical approach that uses different teaching strategies to help students of all abilities and intelligences achieve at high levels.

Discrimination: Unfair treatment of others.

Ebonics: A slang dialect used by some members of the African American community.

Educational equity: A condition in which students have comparable environments, opportunities, and achievement levels; students are provided what they need individually to attain at high levels.

Effective schools research: Research that has identified the characteristics of schools that are considered effective in educating students at high levels of achievement.

Enculturation: The passing on of the values and patterns of behaviors promoted by a culture.

English as a second language (ESL): A classroom model in which the teacher does not speak the native language of the students but has specialized training in educating English language learners.

English language learners (ELLs): People whose native language is not English but who are in the process of learning English.

English-only movement: A belief that bilingual education is a failed practice and that students will learn English faster if taught only in English; a belief that only one language should be spoken in the United States. Critics claim that the English-only movement is tainted with racist and anti-immigrant sentiments and that it does not acknowledge the great difficulty of developing deep proficiency in English.

Ethnic: Relating to the common characteristics of a group of people based on a common language, racial, or national origin.

Ethnocentric: Viewing the world mainly through one's own perspectives or cultural lenses.

Eurocentric: Curriculum that focuses primarily on the history and perspectives of peoples of European descent.

Explicit bias: Occurs when people are consciously aware of their attitudes and beliefs about a person or a group. Much of the time, these biases and subsequent actions arise as a result of fear of that group.

Frameworks: The design, structure, or blueprint of how education is imparted.

Gay–straight alliance (GSA): A constitutionally sanctioned club in a school, often joined by allies, to support gay students.

Gender bias: Belief that persons of one gender are superior or inferior to those of another in some respect. *See* sexism.

Gender identity or expression: As opposed to one's biological sex, gender identity refers to "one's sense of oneself as male, female, or transgender" (American Psychological Association,

2006). Gender expression is how one chooses to act to communicate gender within a given culture; for example, in terms of clothing, communication patterns, and interests.

Global economy: The interplay and interdependence of international commerce.

Goth: A youth subculture that entails a lifestyle with dark themes, clothing, makeup, music, and art.

Graphic organizer: Visual charts and tools used to represent and organize a student's knowledge or ideas.

Harassment: Stated simply, bullying based on protective classes such as race, religion, and sex.

Hate crime: Offense against another person or people because they belong to a protected class, such as a racial, religious, national origin, or sexual orientation group.

High-stakes testing: Refers to a curriculum with an inordinately strong focus on obtaining high test scores on standardized tests versus a focus on teaching and learning.

Homophobe: One who has irrational fear and hatred of lesbian, gay, bisexual, and transgender (LGBT) people.

Homophobia: An irrational fear of LGBT people.

Ideology: Formalized collection of ideas and theories.

Immigrants: People who voluntarily move from one country to another.

Inclusive curriculum: A curriculum that includes the interests, strengths, and needs of all students.

In-service: Professional development provided to practicing teachers.

Implicit bias: Occurs when someone knowingly fights stereotypes and actively engages in antidiscrimination activities, while at the same time, unconsciously, has negative thoughts about people and situations.

Jim Crow: Named after the era following Reconstruction up until 1965, when there were local and state laws in force that segregated people by race.

Lau v. Nichols: A major civil rights case brought by Chinese American students living in California in which the Supreme Court ruled, in 1974, that schools had failed to adequately teach limited-English students.

Learning styles: Preferred modes of learning.

LEP (limited English proficient): Students unable to communicate effectively in English.

LGBTQ: Lesbian, gay, bisexual, transgender, questioning people.

Marginalized: In reference to students, describes those who have had less power and fewer advantages and influence than students in the dominant culture.

Melting pot: A metaphor for a society reflecting an outdated theory that as immigrants come to this country, they give up their ethnicity to blend or "melt" into an amorphous "American culture." *See* salad bowl.

Microcultures: A small group of people within a larger organization or grouping of people, such as a school.

Microaggressions: Brief and everyday slights, insults, indignities, and denigrating messages sent to people of color by well-intentioned people who are unaware of the hidden messages being communicated.

Multicultural Education Platform of Beliefs: A written statement of an educator's core perceptions, assumptions, and beliefs about learners, the purpose of education, and teaching and learning.

Multiple intelligences: A theory that people have a variety of types of intelligence and that individuals possess more than one kind of intelligence.

Multiple perspectives: Viewing and understanding events from the point of view of people who are culturally different. Learning to value multiple perspectives should be a daily experience for students, since just having diverse students in the same setting does not mean they will value one another's differing opinions, experiences, values, beliefs, and culture-specific knowledge.

No Child Left Behind Act of 2001: Legislation that stipulates schools achieve, on a rigorous timeline, increased student performance as measured on standardized tests or suffer punitive sanctions. Passed in response to concerns over U.S. students' performance relative to that of students in other countries and the persistent achievement gap between students of different races.

One-way developmental bilingual education: Students are assigned to classes based on their native language. The teacher teaches both in that language and in English, and phases out the native language as students become more proficient in English.

Operant conditioning: In psychology, increasing or decreasing the likelihood of the occurrence of a specific behavior by the introduction of a reward or punishment.

Oppression: The use of authority or power in an abusive or unfair manner.

Pedagogy: The art and science of teaching.

Peer consultation: The regular engagement of two or more colleagues to give and receive feedback on curriculum or instructional development.

Performance assessment: Assessment that provides students with an opportunity to demonstrate knowledge, skills, and reasoning through activities.

Persistence of ethnicity: The maintenance of distinct cultural identities. *See* assimilation.

Prejudice: Unfounded negative beliefs about another or negative actions taken against another based on unfounded negative beliefs.

Preservice: Professional development provided to teachers-in-training.

Primary dimensions of culture: Dimensions of culture that provide people with their most important identities. These include race and ethnicity, gender, age, socioeconomic status, religion/spirituality, sexual orientation, ability, geographic location, and language. Primary dimensions of culture are those that people can't change. *See* secondary dimensions of culture.

Privilege: A set of "unearned entitlements" from which a person gains benefits without effort but simply by belonging to a class of people.

Professional development: A systematic approach to continuing one's professional growth beyond graduation from a teacher certification program; the process of improving staff knowledge, skills, and competencies to achieve high-level educational results for students. Professional development is essential for multicultural educators who are committed to addressing changing needs in American schools and to supporting high levels of achievement for all learners.

Racism: Hatred of people based on skin color; the belief and practice that one race is superior to another and that those races deemed inferior are deficient in physical, intellectual, social, and other characteristics.

Reflective practice: A systematic approach to problem solving and self-assessment, accomplished through taking time to think deeply about what one does as an educator, why one does those things, and one's professional strengths, areas of weaknesses, and goals for self-improvement. This is most often accomplished through writing about events and analyzing those events over time.

Refugees: People who flee a country due to civil unrest, war, poverty; they are often seeking protection.

Reparations: A political position that African Americans who have suffered from the results of slavery among their ancestors should be compensated.

Rubric: List of criteria that describes or defines differing levels of performance on a variety of key components of a project or performance.

Salad bowl: Metaphor for a society in which individual members retain their unique cultures while assuming common customs and habits. *See* melting pot.

School culture: School culture includes a shared view of, among other things, learning, teaching, the purpose of education, differences, and even leadership. School culture is the set of values, beliefs, attitudes, histories, and norms of behavior that pervades the school environment. School culture provides the social context for learning and can be positive or negative.

School improvement cycle: A process with clearly delineated steps for improving teaching and learning in schools.

Secondary dimensions of culture: Dimensions of culture over which we have some choice and that we can alter. Examples are hobbies, work experiences, marital status, education, parental status, and participation in affinity groups. *See* primary dimensions of culture.

Segregation: Legally endorsed separation of the races in virtually all aspects of life (e.g., restaurants, schools, public transportation, and hospitals).

Sexism: Belief that one sex is inferior; prejudice and/or discrimination based on gender. *See* gender bias.

Shared vision: A group commitment to multicultural education.

Social justice: Righting the wrongs of society or achieving a state in which members enjoy equality and fairness; the pursuit of fair treatment for all in society.

Socialization: "Training" or conditioning that individuals experience as they grow up and learn ways to respond, think, and act due to participation over a sustained period with groups of people with whom they identify.

Socioeconomic status: Class to which an individual or family may belong due to earning power or wealth.

Standardized assessments: Large-scale or standardized tests, sometimes referred to as "high-stakes tests," are developed by experts and delivered to classrooms and schools across the country. Data accumulated through the use of standardized assessments are reported outside the classroom and used to make decisions about student placement, college admissions, funding levels, identification for receipt of special services, and graduation.

Stonewall: A series of violent demonstrations in 1969 sparked by a hate crime at the Stonewall Inn in New York City. Stonewall was the start of the gay rights movement. Stonewall speakers are volunteers who speak to audiences explaining homosexuality.

Straight-edge: A youth subculture that pledges to a lifestyle of no alcohol, no drugs, and no sex without love.

Student-centered classroom: A classroom model in which knowledge and understanding of student needs and background are the basis for designing teaching and learning events.

Team learning: Developing intelligence and ability about a topic in a group.

Transgender: A term used to describe a broad range of gender role definitions that are neither clearly male nor clearly female.

Two-way bilingual education: Students are taught in their own language and in English, leading to a level of mastery.

Voting Rights Act of 1965: Federal legislation banning discriminatory practices that interfered with the voting rights of people of color.

White privilege: Advantages enjoyed by European Americans based on the color of their skin to the disadvantage of people of color.

References

CHAPTER 1

American Psychological Association. (2006). *Answers to your questions about individuals with intersex conditions.* Washington, DC: Author. Retrieved from http://www.apa.org/topics/sexuality/intersex.pdf

Anti-Defamation League. (2010). *Audit of anti-Semitic incidents* [Press release]. Retrieved from https://www.jewishvirtuallibrary.org/2010-adl-audit-of-anti-semitic-incidents-in-u-s

Banks, J. A. (1970). *Teaching the Black experience: Methods and materials.* Belmont, CA: Fearon.

Banks, J. (1993). Approaches to multicultural curriculum reform. In J. Banks & C. Banks (Eds.), *Multicultural education: Issues and perspectives.* Boston, MA: Allyn & Bacon.

Banks, J. A. (1996). *Multicultural education, transformative knowledge, and action: Historical and contemporary perspectives.* New York, NY: Teachers College Press.

Banks, J. A. (1999). *An introduction to multicultural education* (2nd ed.). Boston, MA: Allyn & Bacon.

Banks, J. A. (Ed.). (2004). *Diversity and citizenship education: Global perspectives.* Hoboken, NJ: Wiley.

Banks, J. A. (2005). *Cultural diversity and education: Foundations, curriculum, and teaching* (5th ed.). New York, NY: Pearson.

Banks, J. A. (2006). *Race, culture, and education: The selected works of James A. Banks.* New York, NY: Routledge.

Banks, J. A. (2007). *Educating citizens in a multicultural society* (2nd ed.). New York, NY: Teachers College Press.

Banks, J. A. (2009). *Teaching strategies for ethnic studies* (8th ed.). Boston, MA: Allyn & Bacon.

Banks, J. A. (Ed.). (2012). *Encyclopedia of diversity in education.* Thousand Oaks, CA: Sage.

Banks, J. A. (2014). *An introduction to multicultural education* (5th ed.). Boston, MA: Allyn & Bacon.

Banks, J. A., & Banks, C. A. M. (Eds.). (2004). *Handbook of research on multicultural education* (2nd ed.). San Francisco, CA: Jossey-Bass. (Original work published 1995)

Banks, J. A., & Banks, C. A. M. (2010). *Multicultural education: Issues and perspectives* (7th ed.). Hoboken, NJ: Wiley.

Bennett, C. I. (2014). *Comprehensive multicultural education: Theory and practice* (8th ed.). Boston, MA: Pearson.

Coates, R., Ferber, A., & Brunsma, D. (2018). *The matrix of race: Social construction, intersectionality, and inequality.* Thousand Oaks, CA: Sage.

Darling-Hammond, L., & Bransford, J. (2005). *Preparing teachers for a changing world.* San Francisco, CA: Jossey-Bass.

Frankenberg, E., Lee, C., & Orfield, G. (2003). *A multiracial society with segregated schools: Are we losing the dream?* Cambridge, MA: Civil Rights Project, Harvard University. Retrieved from http://pages.pomona.edu/~vis04747/h21/readings/AreWeLosingtheDream.pdf

Gardner, H. (1985). *Frames of mind: The theory of multiple intelligences.* New York, NY: HarperCollins.

Gollnick, D. M., & Chinn, P. C. (1998). *Multicultural education in a pluralistic society* (5th ed.). Upper Saddle River, NJ: Merrill.

Gollnick, D. M., & Chinn, P. C. (2013). *Multicultural education in a pluralistic society* (9th ed.). New York, NY: Pearson.

Gorski, P. (2013). *Reaching and teaching students in poverty: Strategies for erasing the opportunity gap.* New York, NY: Teachers College Press.

Grant, C., & Sleeter, C. E. (2008). *Turning on learning: Five approaches for multicultural teaching plans for race, gender, and disability* (5th ed.). Columbus, OH: Merrill.

Gurwitch, R. H., Silovsky, J. F., Schultz, S., Kees, M., & Burlingame, S. (2002). Reactions and guidelines for children following trauma/disaster. *Communications Disorders Quarterly, 23*(2), 93–99.

Howard, T. (2010). *Why race and culture matter in schools: Closing the achievement gap in America's classrooms.* New York, NY: Teachers College Press.

Howe, W. A., Lisi, P. L. (2013). *Becoming a multicultural educator: Developing awareness, gaining skills, and taking action* (2nd ed.). Thousand Oaks, CA: Sage.

Jiang, Y., Ekono, M., & Skinner, C. (2014). *Basic facts about low-income children: Children aged 6 through 11 years, 2012.* Retrieved from http://nccp.org/publications/pub_1090.html

Lewellen, D. (2009). *Hate crimes based on sexual orientation.* Phoenix: Equality Arizona.

Millions of Mouths. (n.d.). *Millions of mouths to feed: Information.* Retrieved from http://millionsofmouths.com/info.html

National Association for Multicultural Education. (n.d.). *Definitions of multicultural education.* Retrieved from http://www.nameorg.org/definitions_of_multicultural_e.php

National Center for Education Statistics. (2012). *Indicators of school crime and safety: 2011* (NCES 2012-002). Washington, DC: U.S. Department of Education. Retrieved from https://nces.ed.gov/pubs2012/2012002rev.pdf

Neuman, S. (2009). *Changing the odds for children at risk: Seven essential principles of educational programs that break the cycle of poverty.* New York, NY: Teachers College Press.

Nieto, S., & Bode, P. (2018). *Affirming diversity: The sociopolitical context of multicultural education* (7th ed.). Boston, MA: Pearson.

Nuri-Robins, K. J. N., Lindsey, D. B., Lindsey, R. B., & Terrell, R. D. (2012). *Culturally proficient instruction: A guide for people who teach* (3rd ed.). Thousand Oaks, CA: Corwin Press.

Oakes, J., Lipton, M., Anderson, L., & Stillman, J. (2012). *Teaching to change the world* (4th Rev. ed.). Boston, MA: McGraw-Hill.

Reyes, P., Scribner, J. D., & Scribner, A. P. (Eds.). (1999). *Lessons from high-performance Hispanic schools: Creating learning communities.* New York, NY: Teachers College Press.

Richie, B. E. (2000). *Exploring the link between violence against women and women's involvement in illegal activity. Research on women and girls in the justice system: Plenary papers of the 1999 Conference on Criminal Justice Research and Evaluation—Enhancing Policy and Practice Through Research* (Vol. 3, NCJ No. 180973). Washington, DC: U.S. Department of Justice, Office of Justice Programs. Retrieved from http://www.nij.gov/pubs-sum/180973.htm

Ruiz, N. G., Passel, J. S., & Cohn, V. (2017). *Higher share of students than tourists, business travelers overstayed deadlines to leave U.S. in 2016.* Retrieved from http://www.pewresearch.org/fact-tank/2017/06/06/higher-share-of-students-than-tourists-business-travelers-overstayed-deadlines-to-leave-u-s-in-2016/

Sadker, M., & Sadker, D. (1987). *The intellectual exchange: Excellence and equity in college teaching.* Kansas City, MO: Mid-Continent Regional Educational Laboratory.

Sadker, M., & Sadker, D. (1994). *Failing at fairness: How America's schools cheat girls.* New York, NY: Macmillan.

Shor, I., & Freire, P. (1987). *A pedagogy for liberation: Dialogues on transforming education.* South Hadley, MA: Bergin & Garvey.

Sleeter, C. E., & Grant, C. (2009). *Making choices for multicultural education* (6th ed.). Hoboken, NJ: Wiley.

Takaki, R. (1998). *Strangers from a different shore: A history of Asian Americans.* Boston, MA: Little, Brown.

U.S. Census Bureau. (2010). *Race.* Retrieved from https://www.infoplease.com/us/population/us-population-race

U.S. Census Bureau. (2013). *How the Census Bureau measures poverty: 2013.* Retrieved from https://www.rosemonteis.us/files/references/045732.pdf

U.S. Department of Housing and Urban Development. (2009). *The 2008 annual homeless assessment report to Congress.* Retrieved from https://www.huduser.gov/portal/publications/4thHomelessAssessmentReport.pdf

U.S. Department of Justice. (2010). *National crime victimization survey, 2006–2010.* Retrieved from http://www.bjs.gov/index.cfm?ty=pbdetail&iid=2224

Zeichner, K. M. (1995). Educating teachers to close the achievement gap: Issues of pedagogy, knowledge, and teacher preparation. In B. Williams (Ed.), *Closing the achievement gap: A vision to guide changes in beliefs and practice* (pp. 39–52). Philadelphia, PA: Research for Better Schools.

Zong, J. & Batalova, J. (2017, June 7). *Refugees and asylees in the United States.* Retrieved from https://www.migrationpolicy.org/article/refugees-and-asylees-united-states

CHAPTER 2

Adams, M., & Bell L. E. (2016). *Teaching for diversity and social justice* (3rd ed.). New York, NY: Routledge.

Arends, R. L. (2015). *Learning to teach* (10th ed.). New York, NY: McGraw-Hill.

Banks, J. A. (2009). *Teaching strategies for ethnic studies* (8th ed.). Boston, MA: Allyn & Bacon.

Banks, J. A., & Banks, C. M. (2015). *Multicultural education: Issues and perspectives* (9th ed.). New York, NY: Wiley.

Bennett, C. I. (2011). *Comprehensive multicultural education: Theory and practice* (7th ed.). Boston, MA: Allyn & Bacon.

Bennett, C. I. (2014). *Comprehensive multicultural education: Theory and practice* (8th ed.). Boston, MA: Pearson.

Bryk, A. S., & Schneider, B. (2002). *Trust in schools: A core resource for improvement.* New York, NY: Russell Sage Foundation.

Cummins, J. (2000). *Language, power, and pedagogy*. Clevedon, England: Multilingual Matters.

Demmert, W. G., Jr., & Towner, J. C. (2003*). A review of the research literature on the influences of culturally based education on the academic performance of Native American students*. Portland, OR: Northwest Regional Educational Laboratory. Retrieved from http://educationnorthwest.org/sites/default/files/cbe.pdf

Gardner, H. (2000). *Intelligence reframed: Multiple intelligences for the 21st century*. New York, NY: Basic Books.

Gardner, H. (2006). *Multiple intelligences: New horizons in theory and practice*. New York, NY: Basic Books.

Gardner, H. (2011). *Frames of mind: The theory of multiple intelligences* (3rd ed.). New York, NY: Basic Books.

Gay, G. (2010). *Culturally responsive teaching: Theory, research and practice* (2nd ed.). New York, NY: Teachers College Press.

Ginsberg, M. B., & Wlodkowski, R. J. (1995). *Diversity and motivation: Culturally responsive teaching*. San Francisco, CA: Jossey-Bass.

Gollnick, D. M., & Chinn, P. C. (2016). *Multicultural education in a pluralistic society* (9th ed.). New York, NY: Pearson.

Grant, C. A., & Gillette, M. (2006). *Learning to teach everyone's children: Equity, empowerment, and education that is multicultural*. Belmont, CA: Wadsworth, Cengage Learning.

Grant, C. A., & Sleeter, C. E. (2009). *Turning on learning: Five approaches for multicultural teaching plans for race, class, gender and disability* (5th ed.). New York, NY: Wiley.

Graziano, C. (2005, February–March). School's out. *Edutopia*, pp. 38–44. (ERIC Document Reproduction Service No. ED491742)

Gregg, J. (1995). Discipline, control, and the school mathematics tradition. *Teaching and Teacher Education, 11*(6), 579–593.

Herzog, M. (2010). Using the NCSS national curriculum standards for social studies: A framework for teaching, learning, and assessment to meet state social studies standards. *Social Education, 74*(4), 217–222.

Howard, G. (2006). *We can't teach what we don't know: White teachers, multiracial schools* (2nd ed.). New York, NY: Teachers College Press.

Howe, W. A., & Lisi, P. L. (1995). Focusing on diversity: Strategies for adult educators. *Adult Learning, 6*(5), 19–21, 31.

Huber-Warring, T. (Ed.). (2008). *Growing a soul for social change: Building the knowledge base for social justice*. Charlotte, NC: Information Age.

Interstate New Teacher Assessment and Support Consortium. (2017). *InTASC model core teaching standards and learning progressions for teachers 1.0*. Washington, DC: Council of Chief State School Officers. Retrieved from https://www.ccsso.org/resource-library/intasc-model-core-teaching-standards-and-learning-progressions-teachers-10

Irvine, J. J. (2003). *Educating teachers for diversity: Seeing with a cultural eye*. New York, NY: Teachers College Press.

Ladson-Billings, G. (2009). *The dream keepers: Successful teachers of African American children*. San Francisco, CA: Jossey-Bass.

Lisi, P. L., & Howe, W. A. (1999). Supporting teachers in becoming multicultural educators: A model staff development program. *MultiCultural Review, 8*(3), 30–40.

Mankiller, W. (2001). In J. L. Selig (Ed.), *What now? A little book of graduation wisdom*. Kansas City, MO: Andrews McMeel. (Original work published 1992)

McIntosh, P. (1998). *White privilege and male privilege: A personal account of coming to see correspondences through work in women's studies*. Wellesley, MA: Wellesley College Center for Research on Women.

Moule, J. (2011). *Cultural competence: A primer for educators* (2nd ed.). Belmont, CA: Wadsworth, Cengage Learning.

National Board for Professional Teaching Standards. (2016). *What teachers should know and be able to do*. Retrieved from http://www.nbpts.org/standards-five-core-propositions/

National Council for the Social Studies. (2010). *National curriculum standards for the social studies: A framework for teaching, learning, and assessment*. Waldorf, MD: Author.

National Council for the Teaching of Mathematics. (2000). *Principles and standards for school mathematics*. Reston, VA: Author.

Noddings, N. (2005). *The challenge to care in schools: An alternative approach to education* (2nd ed.). New York, NY: Teachers College Press.

Oakes, J., Lipton, M., Anderson, L., & Stillman, J. (2012). *Teaching to change the world* (4th Rev. ed.). Boston, MA: McGraw-Hill.

Ramsey, P. G. (2015). *Teaching and learning in a diverse world: Multicultural education for young children* (4th ed.). New York, NY: Teachers College Press.

Robins, K. N., Lindsey, R. B., Lindsey, D. B., & Terrell, R. D. (2012). *Culturally proficient instruction: A guide for people who teach* (3rd ed.). Thousand Oaks, CA: Corwin Press.

Schneidewind, N., & Davidson, E. (2014). *Open minds to equality: A sourcebook of learning activities to affirm diversity and promote equality* (4th ed.). Milwaukee, WI: Rethinking Schools.

Sheets, R. H. (1995). From remedial to gifted: Effects of culturally centered pedagogy. *Theory Into Practice, 34*(3), 186–193.

Sleeter, C. E. (2001). Preparing teachers for culturally diverse schools: Research and the overwhelming presence of Whiteness. *Journal of Teacher Education, 52*(2), 94–106.

Sleeter, C. E. (2011). Are standards and multicultural education compatible? *ASCDExpress, 6*(15). Retrieved from www.ascd.org/ascdexpress

Sleeter, C. E., & Cornbleth, C. (Eds.). (2011). *Teaching with vision: Culturally responsive teaching in standards-based classrooms.* New York, NY: Teachers College Press.

Smith, G. P. (1998). *Common sense about uncommon knowledge: The knowledge bases for diversity.* Washington, DC: American Association of Colleges for Teacher Education.

Tharp, R. (2008). *Effective teaching: How the standards come to be.* Berkeley, CA: Center for Research on Education, Diversity, and Excellence.

Tharp, R. G., & Gallimore, R. (1988). *Rousing minds to life: Teaching, learning, and schooling in social context.* New York, NY: Cambridge University Press.

Thompson, F. (2009). The development and validation of the Multicultural Dispositions Index. *Multicultural Perspectives, 11*(2), 94–100.

U.S. Bureau of Labor Statistics. (2014). Kindergarten and elementary school teachers. In *Occupational outlook handbook.* Washington, DC: Author. Retrieved from http://www.bls.gov/ooh/education-training-and-library/kindergarten-and-elementary-school-teachers.htm

Van Ausdale, D., & Feagin, J. R. (2001). *The first R: How children learn race and racism.* Lanham, MD: Rowman & Littlefield.

Viloria, D. (2016). Teaching for a living. *Career Outlook.* Retrieved from https://www.bls.gov/careeroutlook/2016/article/education-jobs-teaching-for-a-living.htm?view_full

Ward, D. (2017). *4 key components of effective teaching, now and for the future.* Retrieved from http://cteblog.ku.edu/4-key-components-of-effective-teaching-now-and-for-the-future/

CHAPTER 3

Au, W. (2014). *Rethinking multicultural education: Teaching for racial and cultural justice.* Milwaukee, WI: Rethinking Schools.

Banks, J. A. (2009). *Teaching strategies for ethnic studies* (8th ed.). Boston, MA: Allyn & Bacon.

Bigelow, B., & Peterson, B. (Eds.). (2003). *Rethinking Columbus: The next 500 years.* Milwaukee, WI: Rethinking Schools.

Brown, D. (2007). *Bury my heart at wounded knee.* New York, NY: Holt, Rinehart & Winston.

Brown, D., & Shevin, M. (2014). *Condition critical: Key principles for equitable and inclusive education.* New York, NY: Teachers College Press.

Bureau of Indian Affairs. (2012, August 10). Indian entities recognized and eligible to receive services from the Bureau of Indian Affairs. *Federal Register, 77*(155), 47868–47873.

Casper, V., & Schultz, S. B. (1999). *Gay parents, straight schools: Building communication and trust.* New York, NY: Teachers College Press.

Chen, E., & Omatsu, G. (2006). *Teaching about Asian Pacific Americans: Effective activities, strategies, and assignments for classrooms and communities.* Lanham, MD: Rowman & Littlefield.

Deloria, V. (1979). *A brief history of the federal responsibility for the American Indian.* Washington, DC: U.S. Department of Health, Education and Welfare, Office of Education.

Delpit, L. (2006). *Other people's children: Cultural conflict in the classroom.* New York, NY: New Press.

Derman-Sparks, L. (2000). *Anti-bias curriculum: Tools for empowering young children.* Washington, DC: National Association for the Education of Young Children.

Donahue, D. M. (2000). *Lesbian, gay, bisexual and transgender rights: A human rights perspective.* Minneapolis: University of Minnesota, Human Rights Center.

Gay, G. (2010). *Culturally responsive teaching: Theory, practice, and research* (2nd ed.). New York, NY: Teachers College Press.

Gollnick, D. M., & Chinn, P. C. (2013). *Multicultural education in a pluralistic society* (9th ed.). Boston, MA: Allyn & Bacon.

Hoeffel, S. R., Kim, M. O., & Shahid, H. (2012). *The Asian population: 2010.* Retrieved from http://www.census.gov/prod/cen2010/briefs/c2010br-11.pdf

Howard, G. (1999). *We can't teach what we don't know.* New York, NY: Teachers College Press.

Imber, M., & Van Geel, T. (2010). *Education law* (4th ed.). New York, NY: Routledge.

Irvine, J. J. (2003). *Educating teachers for diversity: Seeing with a cultural eye.* New York, NY: Teachers College Press.

Iwata, E. (1989, August 15). A new history of Asians in U.S. *Los Angeles Times*. Retrieved from http://articles.latimes .com/1989-08-15/news/vw-538_1_asian-americans

Kozol, J. (2005). *The shame of the nation: The restoration of apartheid schooling in America*. New York, NY: Three Rivers Press.

Ladson-Billings, G. (2009). *The dream keepers: Successful teachers of African American children*. San Francisco, CA: Jossey-Bass.

Lee, C., & Wong, M. (Eds.). (2001). *Timeline: 400 years of history of Chinese in the Americas*. New York, NY: Museum of Chinese in the Americas.

Loewen, J. W. (2000). *Lies across America: What our historic sites get wrong*. New York, NY: Touchstone.

Loewen, J. W. (2008). *Lies my teacher told me: Everything your American history textbook got wrong* (Rev. & updated ed.). New York, NY: New Press.

Louie, S. L., & Omatsu, G. K. (Eds.). (2001). *Asian Americans: The movement and the moment*. Los Angeles: University of California–Los Angeles Asian American Studies Press Center.

Lyman, S. (1970). *The Asian in the West*. Reno, NV: Desert Research Institute.

Menkart, D., Murray, A. D., & View, J. (2004). *Putting the movement back into civil rights teaching: A resource guide for K–12 classrooms*. Washington, DC: Teaching for Change.

Min, P. (2006). *Asian Americans: Contemporary trends and issues*. Thousand Oaks, CA: Pine Forge Press.

Nash, R. J. (1999). *Faith, hype and clarity: Teaching about religion in American schools and colleges*. New York, NY: Teachers College Press.

Nieto, S. (2009). *The light in their eyes: Creating multicultural learning communities*. New York, NY: Teachers College Press.

Nieto, S., & Bode, P. (2018). *Affirming diversity: The sociopolitical context of multicultural education* (7th ed.). Boston, MA: Pearson.

Olsen, L., & Jaramillo, A. (1999). *Turning the tides of exclusion: A guide for educators and advocates for immigrant children*. Oakland: California Tomorrow.

Pang, V., & Cheng, L. (1998). *Struggling to be heard: The unmet needs of Asian Pacific American children*. Albany: State University of New York Press.

Parfit, M. (2000, December). Dawn of humans: Hunt for the first Americans. *National Geographic, 198*(6), 40–67.

Phillips, W. D, Jr., & Phillips, C. R. (1992). *The worlds of Christopher Columbus*. Cambridge, England: Cambridge University Press.

Southern Poverty Law Center. (2000). *A place at the table*. Montgomery, AL: Author.

Takaki, R. (1993). *A different mirror: A history of multicultural America*. London, England: Little, Brown.

Takaki, R. (1998a). *A larger memory: A history of our diversity, with voices*. Boston, MA: Little, Brown.

Takaki, R. (1998b). *Strangers from a different shore: A history of Asian Americans* (Rev. & updated ed.). Boston, MA: Little, Brown.

Takaki, R. (2001). *Double victory: A multicultural history of America in World War II*. Boston, MA: Little, Brown.

Taylor, A. (2002). *American colonies: Vol. 1. The Penguin history of the United States, History of the United States Series*. New York, NY: Penguin Books.

Thornton, R. (1987). *American Indian holocaust and survival: A population history since 1492*. Norman: University of Oklahoma Press.

U.S. Census Bureau. (2002). *The American Indian and Alaska Native population, 2000: Census 2000 brief*. Washington, DC: U.S. Department of Commerce.

U.S. Census Bureau. (2010). *The Hispanic population: 2010* (2010 Census Briefs). Retrieved from https://www.census .gov/prod/cen2010/briefs/c2010br-04.pdf

U.S. Census Bureau. (2011). *Annual estimates of the population by sex, race and Hispanic or Latino origin for the United States: April 1, 2000, to July 1, 2005* (NC-EST2005-03). Retrieved from https:// www2.census.gov/programs-surveys/popest/technical-documentation/methodology/2000-2005/v2005-nat-char-meth.pdf

U.S. Census Bureau. (2012a, March). *The Asian population: 2010*. Retrieved from https://www.census.gov/prod/cen2010/ briefs/c2010br-11.pdf

U.S. Census Bureau. (2012b). *Most children younger than age 1 are minorities* (Census Bureau reports). Retrieved from http:// www.census.gov/newsroom/releases/archives/population/ cb12-90.html

U.S. Census Bureau. (2012c). *U.S. Census Bureau projections show a slower growing, older, more diverse nation a half century from now*. Retrieved from http://www.census.gov/newsroom/ releases/archives/population/cb12-243.html

U.S. Office of Management and Budget. (1997). *Revisions to the standards for the classification of federal data on race and ethnicity*. Retrieved from https://obamawhitehouse.archives.gov/omb/fedreg_1997standards

Zia, H. (2001). *Asian American dreams: The emergence of an American people*. New York, NY: Farrar, Straus & Giroux.

Zinn, H. (2003). *A people's history of the United States, 1942–present*. New York, NY: Perennial Classics.

CHAPTER 4

American Association of University Women. (1991). *Shortchanging girls, shortchanging women*. Washington, DC: Author.

American Association of University Women. (2004). *Under the microscope: A decade of gender equity projects in the sciences*. Washington, DC: Author.

American Association of University Women. (2010). *Why so few? Women science, technology, engineering, and mathematics*. Washington, DC: Author.

American Association of University Women. (2011). *The simple truth about the gender pay gap*. Washington, DC: Author.

American Association of University Women. (2016). *Making Title IX history at the Office of Civil Rights*. Washington, DC: Author.

Banks, J. A. (2009). *Teaching strategies for ethnic studies* (8th ed.). Boston, MA: Allyn & Bacon.

Banks, J. A., & Banks, C. A. M. (2015). *Multicultural education: Issues and perspectives* (9th ed.). Hoboken, NJ: Wiley.

Bennett, C. I. (2011). *Comprehensive multicultural education: Theory and practice* (7th ed.). Boston, MA: Allyn & Bacon.

Bennett, C. I. (2014). *Comprehensive multicultural education: Theory and practice* (8th ed.). Boston, MA: Pearson.

Brown, M. T., & Landrum-Brown, J. (1995). Counselor supervision: Cross-cultural perspectives. In J. G. Ponterotto, J. M. Casas, L. A. Suzuki, & C. M. Alexander (Eds.), *Handbook of multicultural counseling* (pp. 263–286). Thousand Oaks, CA: Sage.

Diller, J. V., & Moule, J. (2011). *Cultural competence: A primer for educators* (2nd ed.). Belmont, CA: Wadsworth, Cengage Learning.

Donahue, D. (2000). *Lesbian, gay, bisexual, and transgender rights: A human rights perspective*. Minneapolis: University of Minnesota Human Rights Resource Center.

Gay, G. (2010). *Culturally responsive teaching: Theory, research, and practice* (2nd ed.). New York, NY: Teachers College Press.

Gollnick, D., & Chinn, P. C. (2013). *Multicultural education in a pluralistic society* (9th ed.). Upper Saddle River, NJ: Merrill.

Gollnick, D. M., & Chinn, P. C. (2016). *Multicultural education in a pluralistic society* (9th ed.). Boston, MA: Pearson

Grant, C. A., & Sleeter, C. E. (2012). *Doing multicultural education for achievement and equity* (2nd ed.). New York, NY: Routledge.

Hale-Benson, J. E., & Hilliard, A. G., III. (1986). *Black children: Their roots, culture, and learning styles* (Rev. ed.). Baltimore, MD: Johns Hopkins University Press.

Howe, W., & Lisi, P. (1995). Beyond diversity awareness: Action strategies for adult education. *Adult Learning, 6*(5), 19–21, 31.

Huber-Warring, T. (Ed.). (2008). *Growing a soul for social change: Building the knowledge base for social justice*. Charlotte, NC: Information Age.

Irvine, J. J. (2003). *Educating teachers for diversity: Seeing with a cultural eye*. New York, NY: Teachers College Press.

Irvine, J. J., & Armento, B. J. (2001). *Culturally responsive teaching: Lesson planning for elementary and middle grades*. New York, NY: McGraw-Hill.

Irvine, J. J., & York, D. E. (1995). Learning styles and culturally diverse students: A literature review. In J. A. Banks & C. A. M. Banks (Eds.), *Handbook of research in multicultural education* (pp. 484–497). New York, NY: Simon & Schuster.

John, V. P. (1972). Styles of learning—styles of teaching: Reflections on the education of Navajo children. In C. Cazden, D. Hymes, & V. P. John (Eds.), *Functions of language in the classroom* (pp. 331–343). New York, NY: Teachers College Press.

McIntosh, P. (1998). *White privilege and male privilege: A personal account of coming to see correspondences through work in women's studies*. Wellesley, MA: Wellesley College Center for Research on Women.

National Coalition of Women and Girls in Education. (2008). *Title IX at 35: Beyond the headlines*. Washington, DC: Author.

Nieto, S. (2010). *Language, culture, and teaching: Critical perspectives* (2nd ed.). New York, NY: Routledge.

Nieto, S. (2013). *Finding joy in teaching students of diverse backgrounds: Culturally responsive and socially just practices in US classrooms*. Portsmouth, NH: Heinemann.

Nieto, S. (2017). *Language, culture, and teaching: Critical perspectives* (3rd ed.). New York, NY: Routledge.

Nieto, S., & Bode, P. (2012). *Affirming diversity: The sociopolitical context of multicultural education* (6th ed.). Boston, MA: Pearson.

Nieto, S., & Bode, P. (2018). *Affirming diversity: The sociopolitical context of multicultural education* (7th ed.). Boston, MA: Pearson.

Oakes, J., & Lipton, M. (2007). *Teaching to change the world* (3rd ed.). New York, NY: McGraw-Hill.

Oakes, J., Lipton, M., Anderson, L., & Stillman, J. (2012). *Teaching to change the world* (4th Rev. ed.). Boston, MA: McGraw-Hill.

Piaget, J. (1970). *The science of education and the psychology of the child*. New York, NY: Orion Press.

Robins, K. N., Lindsey, R. B., Lindsey, D. B., & Terrell, R. D. (2012). *Culturally proficient instruction: A guide for people who teach* (3rd ed.). Thousand Oaks, CA: Corwin Press.

Sadker, D. M., & Zittleman, K. (2016). *Teachers, schools and society: A brief introduction to education* (4th ed.). New York, NY: McGraw-Hill.

Sadker, D. M., Zittleman, K., & Sadker, M. (2013). *Teachers, schools, and society* (10th ed.). New York, NY: McGraw-Hill.

Samovar, L. A., & Porter, L. E. (2012). *Communication between cultures*. Boston, MA: Wadsworth, Cengage Learning.

Smith, G. P. (1998). *Common sense about uncommon knowledge: The knowledge bases for diversity*. Washington, DC: American Association of Colleges for Teacher Education.

Smitherman, G. (1997). *Talking and testifying: The language of Black America*. Detroit, MI: Wayne State University Press.

Spring, J. (2012). *Deculturalization and the struggle for equality: A brief history of the education of dominated cultures in the United States* (7th ed.). New York, NY: McGraw-Hill.

Spring, J. (2016). *Deculturalization and the struggle for equality: A brief history of the education of dominated cultures in the United States* (8th ed.). New York, NY: McGraw-Hill.

Tomlinson, C. A. (2014). *Differentiated classroom: Responding to the needs of all learners* (2nd ed.). Alexandria, VA: Association for Supervision and Curriculum Development.

Treisman, U., & Asera, R. (1995). Routes to mathematics for African-American, Latino and Native American students in the 1990s: The educational trajectories of summer mathematics institute participants. In N. D. Fisher, H. B. Keynes, & P. D. Wagreich (Eds.), *Issues in mathematics education: Vol. 5. Changing the culture: Mathematics in the research community* (pp. 127–152). Providence, RI: American Mathematical Society.

Tse, L. (2001). *"Why don't they learn English?" Separating fact from fallacy in the US language debate*. New York, NY: Teachers College Press.

U.S. Department of Education. (2003). *Guidance on constitutionally protected prayer in public elementary and secondary schools*. Retrieved from http://www2.ed.gov/policy/gen/guid/religionandschools/prayer_guidance.html

U.S. Department of Justice. (2018). *Overview of Title IX of the Education Amendments of 1972*, 20 U.S.C. AS 1681 ET.SEQ. Retrieved from https://www.justice.gov/crt/overview-title-ix-education-amendments-1972-20-usc-1681-et-seq

Willis, M., & Hodson, V. K. (2013). *Discover your child's learning style*. Roseville, CA: Infinity.

Zeichner, K. M. (1995). Educating teachers to close the achievement gap: Issues of pedagogy, knowledge and teacher preparation. In B. Williams (Ed.), *Closing the achievement gap: A vision to guide changes in beliefs and practice* (pp. 39–52). Philadelphia, PA: Research for Better Schools.

CHAPTER 5

Buscemi, M. (1979). *The average child*. Retrieved from http://holyjoe.org/poetry/buscemi.htm

Chappelle, S., & Bigman, L. (with Hillyer, F.). (1998). *Diversity in action: Using adventure activities to explore issues of diversity with middle school and high school age youth*. Hamilton, MA: Project Adventure.

Connerly, M. L., & Pederson, P. B. (2005). *Leadership in a diverse and multicultural environment: Developing awareness, knowledge, and skills*. Thousand Oaks, CA: Sage.

Cortes, C. E. (2000). *The children are watching: How the media teach about diversity*. New York, NY: Teachers College Press.

Cushner, K. (2014). *Human diversity in education: An intercultural approach* (8th ed.). Boston, MA: McGraw-Hill.

Cushner, K., McClelland, A., & Safford, P. (2006). *Human diversity in education: An integrative approach* (5th ed.). New York, NY: McGraw-Hill.

Derman-Sparks, L. (1989). *Anti-bias curriculum: Tools for empowering young children*. Washington, DC: National Association for the Education of Young Children.

Derman-Sparks, L., & Ramsey, P. G. (with Edwards, J. O.). (2011). *What if all the kids are White? Anti-bias multicultural education with young children and families* (2nd ed.). New York, NY: Teachers College Press.

Facing History and Ourselves. (2008). *Choices in Little Rock*. Retrieved from https://www.facinghistory.org/for-educators/educator-resources/resources/choices-little-rock

Gay, G. (2018). *Culturally responsive teaching: Theory, research and practice* (3rd ed.). New York, NY: Teachers College Press.

Grant, C. A., & Gillette, M. (2006). *Learning to teach everyone's children: Equity, empowerment, and education that is multicultural*. Belmont, CA: Wadsworth, Cengage Learning.

Grant, C. A., & Sleeter, C. E. (2011). *Doing multicultural education for achievement and equity* (2nd ed.). New York, NY: Routledge.

Hasegawa, J. (1998). *Self-identity exercise*. Unpublished manuscript. Hartford: Connecticut State Department of Education.

Howard, G., & Banks, J. A. (2016). *We can't teach what we don't know: White teachers, multiracial schools* (3rd ed.). New York, NY: Teachers College Press.

Johnson, A. G. (2017). *Privilege, power, and difference* (3rd ed.). Boston, MA: McGraw-Hill.

Katz, J. (2003). *White awareness: A handbook for anti-racism training* (2nd ed.). Norman: University of Oklahoma Press.

Katz, P. (1982). Development of children's racial awareness and intergroup attitudes. In L. G. Katz (Ed.), *Current topics in early childhood education* (Vol. 4, pp. 17–54). Norwood, NJ: Ablex.

Landsman, J. (2009). *A White teacher talks about race* (Classroom ed.). Lanham, MD: Rowman & Littlefield.

McIntosh, P. (1988). *White privilege: Unpacking the invisible knapsack*. Wellesley, MA: Wellesley College Center for Research on Women. Retrieved from https://www.csusm.edu/sjs/documents/unpackingtheknapsack.pdf

Nieto, S. (Ed.). (2000). *Puerto Rican students in U.S. schools*. Mahwah, NJ: Lawrence Erlbaum.

Nieto, S. (2003). *What keeps teachers going?* New York, NY: Teachers College Press.

Nieto, S. (2010). *The light in their eyes: Creating multicultural learning communities* (10th anniversary ed.). New York, NY: Teachers College Press.

Nieto, S. (2013). *Finding joy in teaching students of diverse backgrounds: Culturally responsive and socially just practices in U.S. classrooms*. Portsmouth, NH: Heinemann.

Nieto, S. (2014). *Why we teach now*. New York, NY: Teachers College Press.

Nieto, S. (2015). *Brooklyn dreams: My life in public education*. Harvard, MA: Cambridge Education Press.

Nieto, S. (2018). *Language, culture, and teaching: Critical perspectives* (3rd ed.). New York, NY: Routledge.

Nieto, S., & Bode, P. (2018). *Affirming diversity: The sociopolitical context of multicultural education* (7th ed.). Boston, MA: Pearson.

Oakes, J., & Lipton, M. (2007). *Teaching to change the world* (3rd ed.). Boston, MA: McGraw-Hill.

Oakes, J., Lipton, M., Anderson, L., & Stillman, J. (2018). *Teaching to change the world* (5th ed.). Boston, MA: McGraw-Hill.

Ooka Pang, V. (2005). *Multicultural education: A caring-centered, reflective approach* (2nd ed.). Boston, MA: McGraw-Hill.

Robins, K. N., Lindsey, R. B., Lindsey, D. B., & Terrell, R. D. (2012). *Culturally proficient instruction: A guide for people who teach* (3rd ed.). Thousand Oaks, CA: Corwin Press.

Sheets, R. H. (2005). *Diversity pedagogy: Examining the role of culture in the teaching learning process*. Boston, MA: Pearson.

Sleeter, C. E. (2000). Diversity vs. White privilege [Interview by B. Miner & B. Peterson]. *Rethinking Schools, 15*(2).

Sleeter, C. E., & Cornbleth, C. (2011). *Teaching with vision: Culturally responsive teaching in standards-based classrooms*. New York, NY: Teachers College Press.

Zuniga, X., Nagda, B. A., & Sevig, T. D. (2002). Intergroup dialogues: An educational model for cultivating engagement across differences. *Equity & Excellence in Education, 35*, 7–17.

CHAPTER 6

American Civil Liberties Union. (2015). *Non-discrimination laws: State by state information—map*. Retrieved from https://www.aclu.org/map/non-discrimination-laws-state-state-information-map

Amstutz, L., & Mullet, J. (2005). *The little book of restorative discipline for schools: Teaching responsibility, creating caring climates*. Intercourse, PA: Good Books.

Anti-Defamation League and Survivors of the Shoah Visual History Foundation. (2003). *The pyramid of hate*. Retrieved from http://www.adl.org/education/courttv/pyramid_of_hate.pdf

Bazelon, E. (2013). *Sticks and stones: Defeating the culture of bullying and rediscovering the power of character and empathy*. New York, NY: Random House.

Bennett, C. I. (2014). *Comprehensive multicultural education: Theory and practice* (8th ed.). Boston, MA: Pearson.

Bennett, M. J. (1986). Towards ethnorelativism: A developmental model of intercultural sensitivity. In R. M. Paige (Ed.),

Cross-cultural orientation: New conceptualizations and applications (pp. 27–69). Lanham, MD: University Press of America.

Bluestein, J. (2001). *Creating emotionally safe schools: A guide for educators and parents*. Deerfield Beach, FL: Health Communications.

Brendtro, L., Brokenleg, M., & Bockern, S. (2009). *Reclaiming youth at risk: Our hope for the future*. Bloomington, IN: National Educational Service.

Brown, D. F. (2002). *Becoming a successful urban teacher*. Portsmouth, CT: Heinemann.

Bully Police USA. (2018). Retrieved from http://www .bullypolice.org

Carter, S. C. (2011). *On purpose: How great school cultures form strong character*. Thousand Oaks, CA: Corwin Press.

Christensen, L. (2011). *Hurricane Katrina: Reading injustice, celebrating solidarity. Rethinking Schools, 21*(1). Retrieved from http://www.rethinkingschools.org/index.shtml

Colvin, G. (2010). *Defusing disruptive behavior in the classroom*. Thousand Oaks, CA: Corwin Press.

Cortés, C. E. (2000). *The children are watching: How the media teach about diversity*. New York, NY: Teachers College Press.

Cross, W. E., Jr. (2001). Shades of black: Diversity in African-American identity. In V. Ooka Pang (Ed.), *Multicultural education: A caring-centered reflective approach*. Boston, MA: McGraw-Hill.

Cushner, K., McClelland, A., & Safford, P. L. (2009). *Human diversity in education: An integrative approach* (6th ed.). New York, NY: McGraw-Hill.

Darling-Hammond, L., & Bransford, J. (2005). *Preparing teachers for a changing world: What teachers should learn and be able to do*. San Francisco, CA: Jossey-Bass.

Derman-Sparks, L., Gutierrez, M., & Phillips, C. (1989). *Teaching young children to resist bias: What parents can do*. Washington, DC: National Association for the Education of Young Children.

Federal Bureau of Investigation. (2013). *Hate crime statistics report*. Retrieved from: http://www.fbi.gov/about-us/cjis/ucr/hate-crime/2013

Frankenberg, E. (2006). *The segregation of American teachers*. Cambridge, MA: Harvard University, Civil Rights Project. Retrieved from http://campaignforethnicstudies.pbworks.com/f/segregation_american_teachers12-06.pdf

Gallavan, N. P. (2011a). *Navigating cultural competence in Grades K–5: A compass for teachers*. Thousand Oaks, CA: Sage.

Gallavan, N. P. (2011b). *Navigating cultural competence in Grades 6–12: A compass for teachers*. Thousand Oaks, CA: Sage.

Gay, Lesbian and Straight Education Network. (2014, October 22). *GLSEN releases new national school climate survey on America's middle and high schools* [Press release]. Retrieved from https://www.glsen.org/article/glsen-releases-new-national-school-climate-survey

Glasgow, N. A., & Hicks, C. D. (2003). *What successful teachers do: 91 Research-based classroom strategies for new and veteran teachers*. Thousand Oaks, CA: Corwin Press.

Gollnick, D. M., & Chinn, P. C. (2016). *Multicultural education in a pluralistic society* (10th ed.). Boston, MA: Pearson.

Hasegawa, J. (1994). *You make the call: Oversensitivity, poor practice, or actual bias?* Hartford: Connecticut State Department of Education.

Hasegawa, J. K. (1997). Unpublished manuscript. Hartford: Connecticut State Department of Education.

Howard, T. C. (2010). *Why race and culture matter in schools: Closing the achievement gap in America's classrooms*. New York, NY: Teachers College Press.

Howe, W. A. (2010). *You make the call: Oversensitivity, poor practice, or actual bias*. Unpublished manuscript. Hartford: Connecticut State Department of Education.

King, J. E., Hollins, E. R., & Hayman, W. C. (1997). *Preparing teachers for cultural diversity*. New York, NY: Teachers College Press.

Laidley, D. (with Bambino, D., McIntyre, D., Quate, S., & Quinn, J.). (2001). *The paseo or circles of identity*. Retrieved from http://schoolreforminitiative.org/doc/paseo.pdf

Moule, J. (2011). *Cultural competence: A primer for educators* (2nd ed.). Belmont, CA: Wadsworth, Cengage Learning.

Sjostrom, L., & Stein, N. (1996). *Bully proof: A teacher's guide on teasing and bullying for use with fourth- and fifth-grade students*. Wellesley, MA: Wellesley Centers for Women.

Southern Poverty Law Center. (2005, Winter). Report: FBI hate crime statistics vastly understate problem. *Intelligence Report*. Retrieved from http://www.splcenter.org/get-informed/intelligence-report/browse-all-issues/2005/winter

Sue, D. (2010). *Microaggressions in everyday life: Race, gender, and sexual orientation*. Hoboken, NJ: Wiley.

U.S. Department of Education, National Center for Education Statistics. (2014). *Indicators of school crime and safety: 2013* (NCES 2014-042). Retrieved from https://nces.ed.gov/pubsearch/pubsinfo.asp?pubid=2014042

U.S. Department of Education, Office for Civil Rights. (2014, March 21). *Civil Rights data collection: Data snapshot (School Discipline)*. Retrieved from https://www2.ed.gov/about/offices/list/ocr/docs/crdc-discipline-snapshot.pdf

U.S. Department of Education, Office for Civil Rights, & the National Association of Attorneys General. (1999). *Protecting students from harassment and hate crime: A guide for schools*. Retrieved from http://www.ed.gov/offices/OCR/archives/Harassment/harassment.pdf

U.S. Department of Education, Safe and Drug-Free Schools Program. (1998). *Preventing youth hate crime: A manual for schools and communities* (ERIC Document Reproduction Service No. ED423491). Retrieved from http://www.ed.gov/pubs/HateCrime/start.html

Wessler, S., & Preble, W. (2003). *The respectful school how educators and students can conquer hate and harassment*. Alexandria, VA: Association for Supervision and Curriculum Development.

Wong, H., Wong, R., Jondahl, S., & Ferguson, O. (2014). *The classroom management book*. Mountain View, CA: Harry K. Wong.

CHAPTER 7

Aaronsohn, E. (2003). *The exceptional teacher: Transforming traditional teaching through thoughtful practice*. San Francisco, CA: Jossey-Bass.

Ainsworth, L. (2011). *Rigorous curriculum design: How to create curricular units of study that align standards, instruction, and assessment*. Englewood, CO: Lead & Learn Press.

Anderson, K. L., & Davis, B. M. (2012). *Creating culturally considerate schools: Educating without bias*. Thousand Oaks, CA: Corwin Press.

Arends, R. I. (1997). *Classroom instruction and management*. New York, NY: McGraw-Hill.

Arends, R. I. (2009). *Learning to teach* (8th ed.). New York, NY: McGraw-Hill.

Arends, R. I. (2012). *Learning to teach* (9th ed.). New York, NY: McGraw-Hill.

Arends, R. (2014). *Learning to teach* (10th ed.). Dubuque, IA: McGraw-Hill.

Banks, J. A. (1992). *Curriculum guidelines for multicultural education* (Rev. ed.). Silver Spring, MD: National Council for the Social Studies.

Banks, J. A. (2009). *Teaching strategies for ethnic studies* (8th ed.). Boston, MA: Allyn & Bacon.

Banks, J. A., & Banks, C. A. M. (2013). *Multicultural education: Issues and perspectives* (8th ed.). Toronto, Ontario, Canada: Wiley.

Beilke, P. (1986). *Selecting materials for and about Hispanic and East Asian children and young people*. Hamden, CT: Library Professional.

Bennett, C. I. (2014). *Comprehensive multicultural education: Theory and practice* (8th ed.). Boston, MA: Pearson.

Benson, B. (2009). *How to meet standards, motivate students, and still enjoy teaching! Four practices that improve student learning* (2nd ed.). Thousand Oaks, CA: Corwin Press.

Brown, D. (2002). *Becoming a successful urban teacher*. Portsmouth, NH: Heinemann.

Council on Interracial Books for Children. (1980). *Guidelines for selecting bias-free textbooks and storybooks*. New York, NY: Author.

Darling-Hammond, L., & Bransford, J. (2005). *Preparing teachers for a changing world: What teachers should learn and be able to do*. San Francisco, CA: Jossey-Bass.

Erickson, H. L., & Lanning, L. (2013). *Transitioning to concept-based curriculum and instruction: How to bring content and process together*. Thousand Oaks, CA: Corwin Press.

Erickson, T. (1989). *Get it together: Math problems for groups, Grades 4–12*. Berkeley, CA: Equals.

Frank, O. H. (Ed.). (1952). *Anne Frank: The diary of a young girl*. Garden City, NY: Doubleday. (Original work published 1947 in Amsterdam, The Netherlands, as *Het Achterhuis. Dagboekbrieven 14 juni 1942 – 1 augustus 1944*)

Gallavan, N. (2010a). *Navigating cultural competence in Grades K–5: A compass for teachers*. Thousand Oaks, CA: Sage.

Gallavan, N. (2010b). *Navigating cultural competence in Grades 6–12: A compass for teachers*. Thousand Oaks, CA: Sage.

Gay, G. (1994). *A synthesis of scholarship in multicultural education* (Urban Monograph Series No. 94). Oak Brook, IL: North Central Regional Educational Lab. (ERIC Document Reproduction Service No. ED378287)

Glatthorn, A. (2000). *The principal as curriculum leader: Shaping what is taught and tested* (2nd ed.). Thousand Oaks, CA: Corwin Press.

Glatthorn, A. A., & Jailall, J. M. (2009). *The principal as curriculum leader: Shaping what is taught and tested* (3rd ed.). Thousand Oaks, CA: Corwin Press.

Gollnick, D. M., & Chinn, P. C. (2013). *Multicultural education in a pluralistic society* (9th ed.). New York, NY: Pearson Merrill.

Gorski, P., & Swalwell, K. (2015). Equity literacy for all. *Educational Leadership, 72*(6), 34–40.

Grant, C. A., & Gillette, M. (2006). *Learning to teach everyone's children: Equity, empowerment, and education that is multicultural.* Belmont, CA: Wadsworth, Cengage Learning.

Grant, C. A., & Sleeter, C. E. (2009). *Turning on learning: Five approaches for multicultural teaching plans for race, class, gender, and disability* (5th ed.) Columbus, OH: Merrill.

Grant, C. A., & Sleeter, C. E. (2011). *Doing multicultural education for achievement and equity* (2nd ed.). New York, NY: Routledge.

Harada, V. H. (1995). Issues of ethnicity, authenticity, and quality in Asian-American picture books, 1983–1993. *Journal of Youth Services in Libraries, 8*(2), 135–149.

Harris, V. J. (1991). Multicultural curriculum: African American children's literature. *Young Children, 46*(2), 37–44.

Howe, W., & Lisi, P. (1995). Focusing on diversity: Strategies for adult educators. *Adult Learning, 6*(5), 19–21, 31.

Kellough, R. D., & Carjuzaa, J. A. (2013). *Teaching in the middle and high schools* (10th ed.). Upper Saddle River, NJ: Pearson.

Lawrence-Brown, D., & Sapon-Shevin, M. (2014). *Condition critical: Key principles for equitable and inclusive education.* New York, NY: Teachers College Press.

Loewen, J. (2000). *Lies across America: What our historic sites get wrong.* New York, NY: Touchstone.

Loewen, J. (2008). *Lies my teacher told me: Everything your American history textbook got wrong* (Rev. ed.). New York, NY: Touchstone.

Lu, M.-Y. (1998). *Multicultural children's literature in the elementary classroom.* Bloomington, IN: ERIC Clearinghouse on Reading English and Communication. (ERIC Document Reproduction Service No. ED423552)

May, S., & Sleeter, C. E. (Eds.). (2010). *Critical multiculturalism: Theory and praxis.* New York, NY: Routledge.

Mayo, S., & Larke, P. (2012). *Integrating multiculturalism into the curriculum: From the liberal arts to the sciences.* New York, NY: Peter Lang.

Moses, M. S. (2002). *Embracing race: Why we need race-conscious education policy.* New York, NY: Teachers College Press.

National Association for Multicultural Education. (n.d.). *Definitions for multicultural education.* Retrieved from https://www.nameorg.org/definitions_of_multicultural_e.php

National Governors Association Center for Best Practices & Council of Chief State School Officers. (2011). *Common Core State Standards initiative: About the standards.* Retrieved from http://www.corestandards.org/about-the-standards

Nieto, S. (2013). *Finding joy in teaching students of diverse backgrounds: Culturally responsive and socially just practices in US classrooms.* Portsmouth, NH: Heinemann.

Nieto, S., & Bode, P. (2018). *Affirming diversity: The sociopolitical context of multicultural education* (7th ed.). Boston, MA: Pearson.

Oakes, J., Lipton, M., Anderson, L., & Stillman, J. (2012). *Teaching to change the world* (4th Rev. ed.). Boston, MA: McGraw-Hill.

Pang, V. O., Colvin, C., Tran, M., & Barba, R. H. (1992). Beyond chopsticks and dragons: Selecting Asian-American literature for children. *The Reading Teacher, 46*(3), 216–224.

Reeves, D. B. (2008). *Making standards work: How to implement standards-based assessment in the classroom, school, and district* (3rd ed.). Englewood, CO: Lead & Learn Press.

Sadker, D. M., & Zittleman, K. (2010). *Teachers, schools, and society: A brief introduction to education* (9th ed.). New York, NY: McGraw-Hill.

Sadker, D. M., & Zittleman, K. (2012). *Teachers, schools and society* (10th ed.). Boston, MA: McGraw-Hill.

Scott, B. M. (1994). Integrating race, class, gender, and sexual orientation into the college curriculum. In J. Q. Adams & J. R. Welsch (Eds.), *A multicultural prism: Voices from the field* (Vol. 1, pp. 61–72). Macomb: Illinois Staff and Curriculum Developers Association.

Sleeter, C. E., & Cornbleth, C. (Eds.). (2011). *Teaching with vision: Culturally responsive teaching in standards-based classrooms.* New York, NY: Teachers College Press.

Smith, G. P. (1998). *Common sense about uncommon knowledge: The knowledge bases for diversity.* Washington, DC: American Association of Colleges for Teacher Education.

Spielberg, S. (Director). (1993). *Schindler's list* [Motion picture]. United States: Universal.

Takaki, R. (1993). *A different mirror: A history of multicultural America.* Boston, MA: Little, Brown.

Tomlinson, C. A. (2008). *The differentiated school: Making revolutionary changes in teaching and learning.* Alexandria, VA: Association for Supervision and Curriculum Development.

Toppo, G., & Overberg, P. (2014, November 25). Diversity in the classroom. *USA Today.* Retrieved from www.usatoday.com/story/news/nation/2014/11/25/minnesota-school-race-diversity/18919391

CHAPTER 8

Aaronsohn, E. (2003). *The exceptional teacher.* San Francisco, CA: Jossey-Bass.

Arends, R. (2009). *Learning to teach* (8th ed.). New York, NY: McGraw-Hill.

Arends, R. (2012). *Learning to teach* (9th ed.). New York, NY: McGraw-Hill.

Brooks, J. G., & Brooks, M. G. (2001). *In search of understanding: The case for constructivist classrooms* (2nd ed.). Alexandria, VA: Association for Supervision and Curriculum Development.

Bruner, J. (1960). *The process of education.* Cambridge, MA: Harvard University Press.

Bruner, J. (1966). *Toward a theory of instruction.* Cambridge, MA: Harvard University Press.

Bruner, J. (1996). *The culture of education.* Cambridge, MA: Harvard University Press.

Carjuzaa, J. A., & Kellough, R. D. (2013). *Teaching in the middle and high schools* (10th ed.). Upper Saddle River, NJ: Pearson.

Cowhey, M. (2006). *Black ants and Buddhists.* Portland, ME: Stenhouse.

Darling-Hammond, L., & Bransford, J. (Eds.). (2005). *Preparing teachers for a changing world: What teachers should learn and be able to do.* San Francisco, CA: Jossey-Bass.

Dewey, J. (1916). *Democracy and education: An introduction to the philosophy of education.* New York, NY: Macmillan.

Feden, P. D., & Vogel, R. M. (2003). *Methods of teaching: Applying cognitive science to promote student learning.* Boston, MA: McGraw-Hill.

Gardner, H. (1983). *Frames of mind: The theory of multiple intelligences.* New York, NY: Basic Books.

Gardner, H. (1993). *Multiple intelligences: The theory in practice.* New York, NY: Basic Books.

Gardner, H. (2000). *Intelligence reframed: Multiple intelligences for the 21st century.* New York, NY: Basic Books.

Gay, G. (2018). *Culturally responsive teaching: Theory, research, and practice.* New York, NY: Teachers College Press.

Glasgow, N. A., & Hicks, C. D. (2003). *What successful teachers do: 91 Research-based classroom strategies for new and veteran teachers.* Thousand Oaks, CA: Corwin Press.

Grant, C. A., & Gillette, M. (2006). *Learning to teach everyone's children: Equity, empowerment, and education that is multicultural.* Belmont, CA: Wadsworth, Cengage Learning.

Gregory, G. (2008). *Differentiated instructional strategies in practice: Training, implementation, and supervision* (2nd ed.). Thousand Oaks, CA: Corwin Press.

Joyce, B., Weil, M., & Calhoun, E. (2009). *Models of teaching* (8th ed.). Boston, MA: Allyn & Bacon.

Ladson-Billings, G. (2009). *The dream keepers: Successful teachers of African American children* (2nd ed.). San Francisco, CA: Jossey-Bass.

Marlowe, B. A., & Page, M. L. (2005). *Creating and sustaining the constructivist classroom* (2nd ed.). Thousand Oaks, CA: Corwin Press.

Marzano, R. J. (1998). *A theory-based meta-analysis of research on instruction.* Aurora, CO: Mid-Continent Regional Educational Laboratory.

Marzano, R. J., Pickering, D. J., & Pollock, J. E. (2001). *Classroom instruction that works: Research-based strategies for increasing student achievement.* Alexandria, VA: Association for Supervision and Curriculum Development.

McIntosh, P. (1988). *White privilege and male privilege: A personal account of coming to see correspondences through work in women's studies* (Working Paper No. 189). Wellesley, MA: Wellesley College Center for Research on Women.

National Association of State Directors of Special Education. (2005). *Response to intervention: Policy considerations and implementation.* Alexandria, VA: Author.

National Commission on Excellence in Education. (1983). *A nation at risk: The imperative for educational reform.* Washington, DC: U.S. Department of Education.

Nieto, S. (2005). *Why we teach.* New York, NY: Teachers College Press.

North Central Regional Educational Laboratory. (1995). *Strategic teaching and reading project: Comprehension resource handbook* (Rev. ed.). Oak Brook, IL: Author.

Northeast Foundation for Children. (2011). *Responsive classroom.* Turners Falls, MA: Author.

Nuri-Robins, K. J., Lindsey, R. B., Lindsey, D. B., & Terrell, R. D. (2012). *Culturally proficient instruction: A guide for people who teach* (3rd ed.). Thousand Oaks, CA: Corwin Press.

Oakes, J., Lipton, M., Anderson, L., & Stillman, J. (2012). *Teaching to change the world* (4th Rev. ed.). Boston, MA: McGraw-Hill.

Pavlov, I. P. (1927). *Conditioned reflexes: An investigation of the physiological activity of the cerebral cortex* (G. V. Anrep, Trans. & Ed.). London, England: Oxford University Press.

Piaget, J. (1954). *The construction of reality in the child.* New York, NY: Basic Books.

Piaget, J. (1972). *The psychology of the child.* New York, NY: Basic Books.

Piaget, J. (1990). *The child's conception of the world.* New York, NY: Littlefield Adams.

Sadker, D. M., & Zittleman, K. R. (2010). *Teachers, schools, and society* (9th ed.). New York, NY: McGraw-Hill.

Sadker, D. M., & Zittleman, K. R. (2012). *Teachers, schools, and society* (10th ed.). New York, NY: McGraw-Hill.

Sadker, M. P., & Sadker, D. M. (2005). *Teachers, schools, and society* (7th ed.). New York, NY: McGraw-Hill.

Skinner, B. F. (1953). *Science and human behavior.* New York, NY: Macmillan.

Smutny, J. F., & Von Fremd, S. E. (2010). *Differentiating for the young child: Teaching strategies across the content areas, preK–3* (2nd ed.). Thousand Oaks, CA: Corwin Press.

Sprenger, M. (2008). *Differentiation through learning styles and memory* (2nd ed.). Thousand Oaks, CA: Corwin Press.

Tatum, B. D. (2003). *Why are all the Black kids sitting together in the cafeteria? And other conversations about race.* New York, NY: Basic Books.

Thorndike, E. L. (1913a). *Educational administration: Quantitative studies.* New York, NY: Macmillan.

Thorndike, E. L. (1913b). *An introduction to the theory of mental and social measurements* (2nd ed.). New York, NY: Teachers College Press. (Original work published 1904)

Thorndike, E. L. (1913–1914). *Educational Psychology* (Vols. 1–3). New York, NY: Teachers College Press.

Tomlinson, C. A. (2005). *How to differentiate instruction in mixed-ability classrooms* (2nd ed.). Alexandria, VA: Association for Supervision and Curriculum Development.

Tomlinson, C., Brimijoin, K., & Narvaez, L. (2008). *The differentiated school making revolutionary changes in teaching and learning.* Alexandria, VA: Association for Supervision and Curriculum Development.

U.S. Department of Agriculture. (n.d.). *Choose my plate.* Retrieved from http://www.choosemyplate.gov

Vygotsky, L. S. (1978). *Mind in society.* Cambridge, MA: Harvard University Press.

Watson, J. B. (1928). *The ways of behaviorism.* New York, NY: Harper.

Watson, J. B., & Rayner, R. (1920). Conditioned emotional reactions. *Journal of Experimental Psychology, 3*(1), 1–14.

Wiggins, G. P., & McTighe, J. (2005). *Understanding by design.* Alexandria, VA: Association for Supervision and Curriculum Development.

CHAPTER 9

Arends, R. (2012). *Learning to teach* (12th ed.). New York, NY: McGraw-Hill.

Banks, J., & Banks, C. A. M. (2013). *Multicultural education: Issues and perspectives* (8th ed.). Hoboken, NJ: Wiley.

Bialystok, E., & Martin, M. M. (2004). Attention and inhibition in bilingual children: Evidence from the dimensional change card sort task. *Developmental Science, 7*(3), 325–339.

Brown, D. F. (2002). *Becoming a successful urban teacher.* Portsmouth, NH: Heinemann.

Campbell, D. (2010). *Choosing democracy: A practical guide to multicultural education* (4th ed.). Boston, MA: Allyn & Bacon.

Collier, V. P. (1989). How long: A synthesis of research on academic achievement in a second language. *TESOL Quarterly, 23*(3), 509–531.

Darling-Hammond, L., & Bransford, J. (Eds.). (2005). *Preparing teachers for a changing world: What teachers should learn and be able to do.* San Francisco, CA: Jossey-Bass.

Farr, B., & Quintanar-Sarellana, R. (2005). Effective strategies for students learning a second language or with other language differences. In E. Trumbull & B. Farr (Eds.), *Language and learning: What teachers need to know* (pp. 113–158). Norwood, MA: Christopher Gordon.

Feden, P. D., & Vogel, R. M. (2003). *Methods of teaching: Applying cognitive science to promote student learning.* Boston, MA: McGraw-Hill.

Gollnick, D. M., & Chinn, P. C. (2016). *Multicultural education in a pluralistic society* (10th ed.). Boston, MA: Pearson.

Grant, C. A., & Gillette, M. (2006). *Learning to teach everyone's children: Equity, empowerment, and education that is multicultural.* Belmont, CA: Wadsworth, Cengage Learning.

Harry, B., & Klinger, J. (2014). *Why are so many minority students in special education? Understanding race and disability in schools* (2nd ed.). New York, NY: Teachers College Press.

Hasegawa, C. (1998). *Speeckle enk.* Unpublished manuscript.

Kellough, R., & Carjuzaa, J. (2012). *Teaching in the middle and secondary schools* (10th ed.). Boston, MA: Allyn & Bacon.

Kindler, A. L. (2002). *Survey of the states' limited English proficient students and available educational programs and services: 2000–2001.* Washington, DC: National Clearinghouse for English Language Acquisition & Language Instruction Educational Programs. Retrieved from https://ncela.ed.gov/rcd/bibliography/BE021853

Kovács, Á. M., & Mehler, J. (2009). Flexible learning of multiple speech structures in bilingual infants. *Science, 325,* 611–612.

Krashen, S. (1998). *Condemned without a trial: Bogus arguments against bilingual education.* Portsmouth, NH: Heinemann.

Meyer, L. (2000). Barriers to meaningful instruction for English learners. *Theory Into Practice, 39*(4), 228–236.

National Center for Education Statistics. (2011). *The condition of education 2011* (NCES 2011-033). Alexandria, VA: U.S. Department of Education. Retrieved from http://nces.ed.gov/pubs2011/2011033.pdf

Nieto, S., & Bode, P. (2018). *Affirming diversity: The sociopolitical context of multicultural education* (7th ed.). Boston, MA: Pearson.

Oakes, J., & Lipton, M. (2012). *Teaching to change the world* (4th ed.). Boston, MA: McGraw-Hill.

Olsen, L. (2000). Learning English and learning America: Immigrants in the center of a storm. *Theory Into Practice, 39*(4), 196–202.

Pang, V. (2001). *Multicultural education: A caring-centered, reflective approach.* Boston, MA: McGraw-Hill.

Ramirez, J. D. (2012). *Bilingual education: Talking points.* Retrieved from http://www.teachingforchange.org/wp-content/uploads/2012/08/ec_bilingualed_talkingpoints_english.pdf

Rong, X. L., & Prissle, J. (1998). *Educating immigrant students: What we need to know to meet the challenge.* Thousand Oaks, CA: Corwin Press.

Sadker, D. M., Zittleman, K., & Sadker, M. P. (2012). *Teachers, schools, and society.* Boston, MA: McGraw-Hill.

Saville-Troike, M. (1978). *A guide to culture in the classroom.* Rosslyn, VA: National Clearinghouse for Bilingual Education.

Smitherman, G. (1998). Black English/Ebonics: What it be like? In T. Perry & L. Delpit (Eds.), *The real Ebonics debate: Power, language, and the education of African American children* (pp. 29–37). Boston, MA: Beacon Press.

Thomas, W. P., & Collier, V. P. (1997, December). *School effectiveness for language minority students* (National Clearinghouse for English Language Acquisition [NCELA] Resource Collection Series, No. 9). Retrieved from http://www.thomasandcollier.com/assets/1997_thomas-collier97-1.pdf

U.S. Census Bureau. (2009). *Population Reference Bureau, analysis of data from the U.S. Census Bureau, Census 2000 Supplementary Survey, 2001 Supplementary Survey, 2002 through 2016 American Community Survey* (American Fact Finder table C16007). Retrieved from https://factfinder2.census.gov/

U.S. Census Bureau. (2012). *American Community Survey (B16003: Age by language spoken at home for the population 5 years and over in linguistically isolated households; C16004: Age by language spoken at home by ability to speak English for the population 5 years and over).* Retrieved from http://factfinder.census.gov

U.S. Census Bureau. (2015). *American Community Survey: Detailed languages spoken at home and ability to speak English for the population 5 years and over for United States: 2009–2013.* Retrieved from http://factfinder.census.gov

Valdés, G., Bunch, G., Snow, C., & Lee, C. (with Matos, L.). (2005). Enhancing the development of students' languages. In L. Darling-Hammond & J. Bransford (Eds.), *Preparing teachers for a changing world: What teachers should learn and be able to do* (pp. 126–168). San Francisco, CA: Jossey-Bass.

Villegas, A. M. (1991). *Culturally responsive pedagogy for the 1990s and beyond* (Trends and Issues Paper No. 6). Washington, DC: ERIC Clearinghouse on Teacher Education. (ERIC Document Reproduction Service No. ED339698)

CHAPTER 10

Chapman, C. M., & King, R. S. (2011). *Differentiated assessment strategies: One size doesn't fit all* (2nd ed.). Thousand Oaks, CA: Corwin Press.

Connecticut State Department of Education. (2010). *Connecticut's framework for response to intervention: The use of data teams in Connecticut's SRBI process.* Hartford, CT: Author.

Connecticut State Department of Education. (2017). *SEED handbook: Connecticut's System for Educator Evaluation and Development.* Hartford, CT: Author.

Connecticut State Department of Education. (2018). *SEED model.* Hartford, CT: Author.

Einbender, L., & Wood, D. (1995). *An authentic journey: Teachers' emergent understandings about authentic assessment and practice.* New York, NY: Columbia University, Teachers College. (ERIC Document Reproduction Service No. ED384585)

Feden, P. D., & Vogel, R. M. (2002). *Methods of teaching: Applying cognitive science to promote student learning.* Boston, MA: McGraw-Hill.

Goodlad, J. (2004). *A place called school: Twentieth anniversary edition* (2nd ed.). Boston, MA: McGraw-Hill. (First edition published 1984)

Grant, C. A., & Gillette, M. (2006). *Learning to teach everyone's children: Equity, empowerment, and education that is multicultural.* Belmont, CA: Wadsworth, Cengage Learning.

Grant, C. A., & Sleeter, C. E. (2011). *Doing multicultural education for achievement and equity* (2nd ed.). New York, NY: Routledge.

Hibbard, M. K. (1994). *Performance assessment: A+ user-friendly system for teaching and learning.* Unpublished manuscript.

Huba, M. E., & Freed, J. E. (2000). *Learner-centered assessment on college campuses: Shifting the focus from teaching to learning.* Boston, MA: Allyn & Bacon.

Irvine, J. J. (1991). *Black students and school failure: Policies, practices, and prescriptions.* Santa Barbara, CA: Praeger.

Irvine, J. J. (1996). *Growing up African American in Catholic schools.* New York, NY: Teachers College Press.

Lockwood, A. T. (1992). A leap of faith. *Focus in Change, 3*(1), 9–13.

National Association for Multicultural Education. (2015). *NAME Position Statement on the edTPA.* Retrieved from http://www.nameorg.org/docs/Statement-rr-edTPA-1-21-14.pdf

Neill, J. (2004). *Cultural bias in intelligence testing.* Retrieved from http://wilderdom.com/personality/intelligenceCulturalBias.html

New England Association of Schools and Colleges. (2011). *Teaching and learning standards.* Retrieved from https://cpss.neasc.org/standards/2011-standards

Northwest Regional Educational Laboratory. (1998a). *Improving classroom assessment: A toolkit for professional developers* (Toolkit 98). Portland, OR: Author.

Northwest Regional Educational Laboratory. (1998b). *Improving science and mathematics education: A toolkit for professional developers; alternative assessment.* Portland, OR: Author. (ERIC Document Reproduction Service No. ED381360)

Oakes, J., Lipton, M., Anderson, L., & Stillman, J. (2012). *Teaching to change the world* (4th Rev. ed.). Boston, MA: McGraw-Hill.

Oakes, J., Lipton, M., Anderson, L., & Stillman, J. (2018). *Teaching to change the world* (5th ed.). New York, NY: Routledge.

O'Neill, J. (1992, May). Putting performance assessment to the test. *Educational Leadership, 49*(8), 14–19.

Oosterhof, A. (2009). *Developing and using classroom assessments* (4th ed.). Upper Saddle River, NJ: Merrill.

Reeves, D. B. (2007). *Ahead of the curve: The power of assessment to transform teaching and learning.* Bloomington, IN: Solution Tree.

Reeves, D. B. (2014). *Standards, assessment, and accountability.* Boston, MA: Houghton Mifflin.

RTI Action Network. (n.d.). *What is RTI?* Retrieved from http://www.rtinetwork.org/learn/what/whatisrti

Sadker, D. M., & Zittleman, K. (2012). *Teachers, schools and society* (10th ed.). Boston, MA: McGraw-Hill.

Sadker, D. M., & Zittleman, K. (2015). *Teachers, schools and society: A brief introduction to education* (4th ed.). Boston, MA: McGraw-Hill.

Schrank, F. A., Mather, N., & McGrew, K. S. (2014). *Woodcock–Johnson IV Tests of Cognitive Abilities examiner's manual, Standard and Extended Batteries.* Itasca, IL: Riverside.

Stiggins, R. J. (1999). Evaluating classroom assessment training in teacher education programs. *Educational Measurement: Issues and Practice, 18*(1), 23–27.

Stiggins, R. J., & Cappuis, J. (2012). *Introduction to student-involved assessment for learning* (6th ed.). Boston, MA: Allyn & Bacon.

Taylor, C. S., & Nolen, S. B. (2007). *Classroom assessment: Supporting teaching and learning in real classrooms* (2nd ed.). Upper Saddle River, NJ: Pearson.

Tomlinson, C. A., Moon, T., & Imbeau, M. B. (2015). *Assessment and student success in a differentiated classroom.* Alexandria, VA: Association for Supervision and Curriculum Development.

Torgesen, J. K., Wagner, R. K., & Rashotte, C. A. (2012). *Test of Word Reading Efficiency* (TOWRE-2) (2nd ed.). Retrieved from http://www.wpspublish.com/store/p/3061/test-of-word-reading-efficiency-second-edition-towre-2#sthash.s5JUkz3A.dpuf

Waugh, C. K., & Gronlund, N. E. (2013). *Assessment of student achievement* (10th ed.). Boston, MA: Addison Wesley.

Wiggins, G. (1991). Standards, not standardization: Evoking quality student work. *Educational Leadership, 48*(5), 18–25.

Wolf, D. P., LeMahieu, P. G., & Eresh, J. (1992). Good measure: Assessment as a tool for education reform. *Educational Leadership, 49*(8), 8–13.

CHAPTER 11

Arends, R. (2015). *Learning to teach* (10th ed.). New York, NY: McGraw-Hill.

Blankstein, A. (2013). *Failure is not an option: Six principles that guide student achievement in high-performing schools* (3rd ed.). Thousand Oaks, CA: Corwin Press.

Boykin, A. W., & Noguera, P. (2011). *Creating the opportunity to learn: Moving from research to practice to close the achievement gap.* Alexandria, VA: ASCD.

Davidman, L., & Davidman, P. T. (2001). *Teaching with a multicultural perspective: A practical guide* (3rd ed.). New York, NY: Allyn & Bacon.

DuFour, R. (2004). What is a "professional learning community"? *Educational Leadership, 61*(8), 6–11.

Fullan, M., & Hargreaves, A. (1996). *What's worth fighting for in your school? Working together for your school.* New York, NY: Teachers College Press.

Hord, S. M. (2004). *Learning together, leading together: Changing schools through professional learning communities.* New York, NY: Teachers College Press.

Hord, S. M., Roussin, J. L., & Sommers, W. A. (2009). *Professional learning communities: Guiding professional learning communities, inspiration, challenge, surprise, and meaning.* Thousand Oaks, CA: Corwin Press.

Hoy, W. K., & Miskel, C. G. (2012). *Educational administration: Theory, research, and practice* (9th ed.). Boston, MA: McGraw-Hill.

Joyce, B. R., & Showers, B. (2002). *Student achievement through staff development: Fundamentals of school renewal* (3rd ed.). Alexandria, VA: Association for Supervision and Curriculum Development.

Killion, J. (1999). Journaling. *Journal of Staff Development, 20*(3), 36–37.

King, K., Artiles, A., & Kozleski, E. (2009). *Professional learning for culturally responsive teaching.* Tempe: Equity Alliance at Arizona State University.

Kouzes, J. M., & Posner, B. Z. (2017). *The leadership challenge* (6th ed.). San Francisco, CA: Jossey-Bass.

Kruse, S. D. (1999). Collaborate. *Journal of Staff Development, 20*(3), 14–16.

Kruse, S. D., Seashore Louis, K., & Bryk, A. S. (1994). *Building professional community in schools.* Madison, WI: Center on Organization and Restructuring of Schools.

Ladson-Billings, G. (2009). *The dreamkeepers: Successful teachers of African American children* (2nd ed.). San Francisco, CA: Jossey-Bass.

Mertler, C. A. (2016). *Action research: Improving schools and empowering educators* (5th ed.). Thousand Oaks, CA: Sage.

Oakes, J., Lipton, M., Anderson, L., & Stillman, J. (2018). *Teaching to change the world* (5th ed.). New York, NY: Routledge.

Reagan, T. G., Case, C. W., & Brubacher, J. W. (2000). *Becoming a reflective educator: How to build a culture of inquiry in the schools* (2nd ed.). Thousand Oaks, CA: Corwin Press.

Robbins, K. N., Lindsey, R. B., Lindsey, D. B., & Terrell, R. D. (2011). *Culturally proficient instruction: A guide for people who teach* (3rd ed.). Thousand Oaks, CA: Sage.

Sadker, D. M., & Zittleman, K. (2012). *Teachers, schools and society* (10th ed.). New York, NY: McGraw-Hill.

Schon, D. A. (1983). *The reflective practitioner: How professionals think in action.* New York, NY: Basic Books.

Senge, P. (1990). *The fifth discipline: The art and practice of the learning organization.* New York, NY: Doubleday/Currency.

Sergiovanni, T., & Starratt, R. (2007). *Supervision: A redefinition* (8th ed.). Boston, MA: McGraw-Hill.

Simpson, D. J., Jackson, M. J. B., & Aycock, J. C. (2005). *John Dewey and the art of teaching: Toward reflective and imaginative practice.* Thousand Oaks, CA: Sage.

Smith, G. P. (1998). *Common sense about uncommon knowledge: The knowledge bases for diversity.* Washington, DC: American Association of Colleges for Teacher Education.

Taggart, G. L., & Wilson, A. P. (1998). *Promoting reflective thinking in teachers: 44 Action strategies.* Thousand Oaks, CA: Corwin Press.

Wahlstrom, K. L., Seashore Louis, K., Leithwood, K., & Anderson, S. E. (2010). *Investigating the links to improved student learning: Executive summary of research findings. Executive Summary.* New York, NY: The Wallace Foundation. http://www.wallacefoundation.org/knowledge-center/school-leadership/key-research/Pages/Investigating-the-Links-to-Improved-Student-Learning.aspx

Wood, F. H., & McQuarrie, F., Jr. (1999). On-the-job learning. *Journal of Staff Development, 20*(3), 20–22.

CHAPTER 12

Baldwin, J. (1963). *The fire next time.* New York, NY: Dial Press.

Banks, J. A. (2009). *Teaching strategies for ethnic studies* (8th ed.). Boston, MA: Allyn & Bacon.

Bernhardt, V. L. (2017). *Data analysis for continuous school improvement* (4th ed.). New York, NY: Routledge.

Blankstein, A. (2013). *Failure is not an option: Six principles that guide student achievement in high-performing schools* (3rd ed.). Thousand Oaks, CA: Corwin Press.

Blankstein, A., & Houston, P. (2011). *Leadership for social justice and democracy in our schools.* Thousand Oaks, CA: Corwin Press.

Blankstein, A., Noguera, P., & Kelly, L. (2016). *Excellence through equity: Five principles of courageous leadership to guide achievement for every student.* Alexandria, VA: Association for Supervision and Curriculum Development.

Darling-Hammond, L. (1996). The quiet revolution: Rethinking teacher development. *Educational Leadership, 53*(6), 4–10.

Deal, T. E., & Peterson, K. D. (2016). *Shaping school culture* (3rd ed.). San Francisco, CA: Jossey-Bass.

DuFour, R. (2004). What is a professional learning community? *Educational Leadership, 61*(8), 6–11.

DuFour, R., DuFour, R., Eaker, R., Many, T. W., & Mattos, M. (2016). *Learning by doing: A handbook for professional learning communities at work* (3rd ed.). Bloomington, IN: Solution Tree.

Easton, L. (2004). *Powerful designs for professional learning.* Oxford, OH: National Staff Development Council.

Fullan, M. (2007). *Leading in a culture of change* (Rev. ed.). San Francisco, CA: Jossey-Bass.

Fullan, M., & Quinn, J. (2017). *Deep learning: Engage the world change the world.* Thousand Oaks, CA: Corwin Press.

Gay, G. (1994). *A synthesis of scholarship in multicultural education.* Retrieved from https://eric.ed.gov/?id=ED378287

Glickman, C. D., Gordon, S. P., & Ross-Gordon, J. M. (2017). *SuperVision and instructional leadership: A developmental approach* (10th ed.). Boston, MA: Allyn & Bacon.

Gollnick, D. M., & Chinn, P. C. (2016). *Multicultural education in a pluralistic society* (10th ed.). Boston, MA: Pearson.

Hord, S. M., Roussin, J. L., & Sommers, W. A. (2009). *Professional learning communities: Guiding professional learning communities, inspiration, challenge, surprise, and meaning.* Thousand Oaks, CA: Corwin Press.

Johnson, J. A., Musial, D. L., Hall, G. E., & Gollnick, D. M. (2018). *Foundations of American education: Becoming effective teachers in challenging times* (17th ed.). New York, NY: Pearson.

Joyce, B. R., & Showers, B. (2002). *Student achievement through staff development: Fundamentals of school renewal* (3rd ed.). Alexandria, VA: Association for Supervision and Curriculum Development.

Katzenbach, J. R., & Smith, D. K. (1993). *The wisdom of teams: Creating the high-performance organization.* New York, NY: Harper Business.

Learning Forward. (2011). *Standards for professional learning: Quick Reference Guide* (3rd ed.). Oxford, OH: Author. Retrieved from http://www.learningforward.org/standards-for-professional-learning

Lezotte, L. W., & Jacoby, B. C. (1990). *A guide to the school improvement process based on effective schools research.* Okemos, MI: Effective Schools.

Loucks-Horsley, S., Harding, C. K., Arbuckle, M. A., Murray, L. B., Dubea, C., & Williams, M. K. (1987). *Continuing to learn: A guidebook for teacher development.* Providence, RI: Regional Laboratory for Educational Improvement of the Northeast and Islands.

Northeast Consortium for Multicultural Education. (1993). *Multicultural education: Moving from theory to practice.* Unpublished report of the proceedings.

Oakes, J., Lipton, M., Anderson, L., & Stillman, J. (2012). *Teaching to change the world* (4th Rev. ed.). Boston, MA: McGraw-Hill.

Sadker, D. M., & Zittleman, K. (2016). *Teachers, schools and society: A brief introduction to education* (4th ed.). New York, NY: McGraw-Hill.

Schmoker, M. J. (2006). *Results now: How we can achieve unprecedented improvements in teaching and learning.* Alexandria, VA: Association for Supervision and Curriculum Development.

Senge, P. M., Cambron-McCage, N., Lucas, T., Smith, B., & Dutton, J. (2012). *Schools that learn (Updated and Rev.): A fifth discipline fieldbook for educators, parents, and everyone who cares about education.* New York, NY: Crown Business.

Senge, P. M., Kleiner, A., Roberts, C., Ross, R. B., & Smith, B. J. (1994). *The fifth discipline fieldbook: Strategies and tools for building a learning organization.* New York, NY: Doubleday.

Sergiovanni, T., Starratt, R., & Cho, V. (2013). *Supervision: A redefinition* (9th ed.). Boston, MA: McGraw-Hill.

Terrell, R. D., & Lindsey, R. B. (2009). *Culturally proficient leadership: The journey begins within.* Thousand Oaks, CA: Corwin Press.

Wagner, T. (2014). *The global achievement gap: Why even our best schools don't teach the new survival skills our children need—and what we can do about it.* New York, NY: Basic Books.

Williams, B. (2003). *Closing the achievement gap: A vision for changing beliefs and practice* (2nd ed.). Alexandria, VA: Association for Supervision and Curriculum Development.

Index